Lecture Notes in Computer Science 3326

Commenced Publication in 1973
Founding and Former Series Editors:
Gerhard Goos, Juris Hartmanis, and Jan van Leeuwen

Editorial Board

David Hutchison
  Lancaster University, UK

Takeo Kanade
  Carnegie Mellon University, Pittsburgh, PA, USA

Josef Kittler
  University of Surrey, Guildford, UK

Jon M. Kleinberg
  Cornell University, Ithaca, NY, USA

Friedemann Mattern
  ETH Zurich, Switzerland

John C. Mitchell
  Stanford University, CA, USA

Moni Naor
  Weizmann Institute of Science, Rehovot, Israel

Oscar Nierstrasz
  University of Bern, Switzerland

C. Pandu Rangan
  Indian Institute of Technology, Madras, India

Bernhard Steffen
  University of Dortmund, Germany

Madhu Sudan
  Massachusetts Institute of Technology, MA, USA

Demetri Terzopoulos
  New York University, NY, USA

Doug Tygar
  University of California, Berkeley, CA, USA

Moshe Y. Vardi
  Rice University, Houston, TX, USA

Gerhard Weikum
  Max-Planck Institute of Computer Science, Saarbruecken, Germany

Nabanita Das   Arunabha Sen
Sajal K. Das   Bhabani P. Sinha (Eds.)

Distributed Computing – IWDC 2004

6th International Workshop
Kolkata, India, December 27-30, 2004
Proceedings

Springer

Volume Editors

Nabanita Das
Bhabani P. Sinha
Indian Statistical Institute, Advanced Computing and Microelectronics Unit
203, B.T. Road, Kolkata 700 108, India
E-mail: {ndas, bhabani}@isical.ac.in

Arunabha Sen
Arizona State University, Dept. of Computer Science and Engineering
Tempe, AZ, USA
E-mail: asen@asu.edu

Sajal K. Das
University of Texas at Arlington, Dept. of Computer Science and Engineering
Arlington, TX 76019-0015, USA
E-mail: das@cse.uta.edu

Library of Congress Control Number: 2004116725

CR Subject Classification (1998): C.2, D.1.3, D.2.12, D.4, F.2, F.1, H.4

ISSN 0302-9743
ISBN 3-540-24076-4 Springer Berlin Heidelberg New York

This work is subject to copyright. All rights are reserved, whether the whole or part of the material is concerned, specifically the rights of translation, reprinting, re-use of illustrations, recitation, broadcasting, reproduction on microfilms or in any other way, and storage in data banks. Duplication of this publication or parts thereof is permitted only under the provisions of the German Copyright Law of September 9, 1965, in its current version, and permission for use must always be obtained from Springer. Violations are liable to prosecution under the German Copyright Law.

Springer is a part of Springer Science+Business Media

springeronline.com

© Springer-Verlag Berlin Heidelberg 2004
Printed in Germany

Typesetting: Camera-ready by author, data conversion by Scientific Publishing Services, Chennai, India
Printed on acid-free paper   SPIN: 11366812   06/3142   5 4 3 2 1 0

General Chairs' Message

It was our great pleasure to extend a cordial welcome to all the attendees of the 6th International Workshop on Distributed Computing (IWDC 2004) held at the Indian Statistical Institute, Kolkata (formerly Calcutta) on December 27–30, 2004. In the previous five years, this meeting was held in Jadavpur University, University of Calcutta and at the Indian Institute of Management, Calcutta. We hope that IWDC 2004 continued the tradition of providing a forum for fruitful interactions among the participants from academia, government organizations and industry, coming from 12 different countries around the world.

We express our sincerest thanks to the keynote speakers, Guru Parulkar and Michel Raynal, who kindly agreed to speak on frontier topics in networking and distributed computing. Our thanks are also due to Amar Mukherjee, for delivering the Prof. A.K. Choudhury Memorial Lecture, and to N. Vittal for delivering the banquet speech.

We are immensely grateful to both Nabanita Das and Arunabha Sen for performing an outstanding job as the technical program chairs. With the help of an excellent committee of international experts, they followed very stringent criteria for selecting only the very best technical papers out of a large number of submissions in order to maintain the high quality of the workshop.

We would also like to thank Somprakash Bandyopadhyay for arranging four tutorials on exciting topics by eminent researchers – Biswanath Mukherjee, Archan Misra, Jiannong Cao and Mohan Kumar. We believe that the participants, particularly young researchers and students, highly benefited through these tutorials. Thanks are also due to Bishnu Pradhan for arranging a very interesting panel discussion on the role of distributed computing and networking in food distribution. We are also thankful to all the panelists for their participation.

Our sincere thanks are due to K.B. Sinha, Director of the Indian Statistical Institute, for co-sponsoring this workshop as well as providing both financial and infrastructural supports. We gratefully acknowledge the support of the Department of Science and Technology, Ministry of Communication and Information Technologies, All India Council of Technical Education, DRDO, BSNL, Reserve Bank of India, Council of Scientific and Industrial Research, Hewlett-Packard, Tata Consultancy Services, Cognizant Technology Solutions, Interra Systems, and Interra Information Technologies in sponsoring this event, without which the workshop could not have been organized on this scale.

We are grateful to all the members of the local organizing committee, consisting of Krishnendu Mukhopadhyaya (chair), Bhargab B. Bhattacharya, Jayasree Dattagupta, Susmita Sur-Kolay, Subhas C. Nandy, Chandan Mazumdar, Swapan Bhattacharya, Ujjwal Moulik, Buddhadeb Sau, Nabendu Chaki, Debasish Saha and Partha Bhowmik. Special thanks are also due to Sandip Das (finance chair), Srabani Mukhopadhyaya (publication chair), and the publicity team comprising Mandar Mitra (chair), Mainak Chatterjee and Jiannong Cao, for providing their excellent service to make this workshop a grand success.

Last, but not least, thanks to all the participants and authors. We hope that they enjoyed the workshop as much as the wonderful and culturally vibrant city of Kolkata!

Bhabani P. Sinha
Indian Statistical Institute, Kolkata, India
December 2004

Sajal K. Das
University of Texas, Arlington, USA
December 2004

Program Chairs' Message

On behalf of the Technical Program Committee of the 6th International Workshop on Distributed Computing, IWDC 2004, it was our great pleasure to welcome the attendees to Kolkata, India.

Over the last few years, IWDC has emerged as an internationally renowned forum for interaction among researchers from academia and industries around the world. A clear indicator of this fact is the large number of high-quality submissions of technical papers received by the workshop this year.

The workshop program consisted of 12 technical sessions with 54 contributed papers, two keynote addresses, four tutorials, a panel, a poster session and the Prof. A.K. Choudhury Memorial Lecture. The IWDC Program Committee, comprising 38 distinguished members, worked hard to organize the technical program. Following a rigorous review process, out of 157 submissions only 54 papers were accepted for presentation in the technical sessions; 27 of the accepted papers were classified as regular papers and the remaining 27 as short papers. Another 11 papers were accepted for presentation in the poster session, each with a one-page abstract appearing in the proceedings.

It is needless to mention that behind the success of any such event, there lies the considerable time, effort and devotion of many individuals. We would like to thank all of them, their contributions nurtured this workshop from its very inception. Firstly, we wish to thank the entire program committee for the excellent job it did in organizing the technical sessions. Special thanks are due to all the reviewers for their commitment in reviewing the papers within a very short time. The names of the reviewers who were not program committee members are listed later in the organization pages of this proceedings. Please accept our apologies for any errors or omissions in the list.

We are indebted to Sukumar Ghosh for arranging two exciting keynote speeches and the Prof. A.K. Choudhury Memorial Lecture. We would like to thank Somprakash Bandyopadhyay for organizing four excellent tutorials on cutting-edge technologies. Thanks are due to Bishnu Pradhan for organizing the panel on a topic of immense national importance.

We wish to acknowledge the continuous help and tremendous support provided by the research fellows of the Advanced Computing and Microelectronics Unit of the Indian Statistical Institute. Without their collective efforts this workshop would not have taken place. Special thanks go to the publication chair, Srabani Mukhopadhyay, for her superb job in compiling the proceedings.

Last, but not least, we would like to thank the general chairs of the workshop, Sajal K. Das and Bhabani P. Sinha, for giving us immense support and encouragement throughout this period.

Once again, we hope all delegates enjoyed the historic and eclectic city of Kolkata. We hope the reader will see that the Technical Program of IWDC 2004 was an enjoyable and invigorating one.

Arunabha Sen
Arizona State University, Tempe, USA
December 2004

Nabanita Das
Indian Statistical Institute, Kolkata, India
December 2004

Executive Committee

General Chairs
Bhabani P. Sinha, Indian Statistical Inst., Kolkata, India
Sajal K. Das, Univ. of Texas, Arlington, USA

Program Chairs
Nabanita Das, Indian Statistical Inst., Kolkata, India
Arunabha Sen, Arizona State Univ., USA

Keynote Chair
Sukumar Ghosh, Univ. of Iowa, USA

Panel Chair
Bishnu Pradhan, Indian Inst. of Technology, Bombay, India

Tutorial Chair
Somprakash Bandyopadhyay, Indian Inst. of Management, Kolkata, India

Organizing Chair
Krishnendu Mukhopadhyaya, Indian Statistical Inst., Kolkata, India

Finance Chair
Sandip Das, Indian Statistical Inst., Kolkata, India

Publicity Chairs
Mandar Mitra, Indian Statistical Inst., Kolkata, India
Mainak Chatterjee, Univ. of Central Florida, Orlando, USA

Publication Chair
Srabani Mukhopadhyaya, Indian Statistical Inst., Kolkata, India

Asia-Pacific Co-ordination Chairs
Tetsuro Ueda, ATR, Japan
Jiannong Cao, Hong Kong Polytechnic Univ., Hong Kong

Steering Committee Chair
Sukumar Ghosh, Univ. of Iowa, USA

Advisory Committee Chair
Kalyan B. Sinha, Indian Statistical Inst., Kolkata, India

Program Committee

Chairs

Arunabha Sen	Arizona State Univ., Tempe, USA
Nabanita Das	Indian Statistical Inst., Kolkata, India

Members

Ajay D. Kshemkalyani	Univ. of Illinois, Chicago, USA
Ajit Pal	Indian Inst. of Technology, Kharagpur, India
Ajoy K. Datta	Univ. of Nevada, Las Vegas, USA
Amitava Bagchi	Indian Inst. of Management, Kolkata, India
Amiya Bhattacharya	New Mexico State Univ., USA
Anand Tripathi	Univ. of Minnesota, USA
Anwitaman Datta	École Polytechnique Fédérale de Lausanne, Switzerland
Archan Misra	IBM T.J. Watson Research Center, USA
Arobinda Gupta	Indian Inst. of Technology, Kharagpur, India
Asim Pal	Indian Inst. of Management, Kolkata, India
Biswanath Mukherjee	Univ. of California, Davis, USA
Bobby Bhattacharya	Univ. of Maryland, USA
Chita R. Das	Penn. State Univ., USA
Goutam Chakrabarty	Iwate Prefectural Univ., Japan
Kalyan Basu	Univ. of Texas, Arlington, USA
Mohan Kumar	Univ. of Texas, Arlington, USA
Nabendu Chaki	Calcutta Univ., Kolkata, India
Nitin Vaidya	Univ. of Illinois, Urbana-Champaign, USA
Partha Dasgupta	Arizona State Univ., Tempe, USA
Pradip K. Das	Jadavpur Univ., Kolkata, India
Prasant Mahapatra	Univ. of California, Davis, USA
Prasanta K. Jana	Indian School of Mines, Dhanbad, India
Priya Narasimham	Carnegie Mellon Univ., USA
Rajeev Shorey	IBM India Research Lab, India
Rajkumar Buyya	Univ. of Melbourne, Australia
Ratan K. Ghosh	Indian Inst. of Technology, Kanpur, India
Rushikesh K. Joshi	Indian Inst. of Technology, Bombay, India
Samir R. Das	State Univ. of New York, Stony Brook, USA
Samrat Ganguly	NEC Labs, USA
Sandip Sen	Univ. of Tulsa, USA
Shikharesh Majumdar	Carleton Univ., Canada
Subhankar Dhar	San Jose State Univ., USA
Stefan Olariu	Old Dominion Univ., USA
Subir Bandyopadhyaya	Univ. of Windsor, Canada
Suranjan Ghose	Jadavpur Univ., Kolkata, India
Swapan Bhattacharya	Jadavpur Univ., Kolkata, India
Ted Herman	Univ. of Iowa, USA
Y. Chee Tseng	National Chiao Tung Univ., Taiwan

External Reviewers

The following reviewers external to the program committee participated in the review process. We greatly appreciate their contributions.

Aditya Bagchi
Adriaan de Groot
Amar Mukherjee
Amitava Mukherjee
Anish Shrutanjay Jayavant
Anurag Dasgupta
Amlan Bhattacharya
Arijit Bishnu
Bhargab B. Bhattacharya
Bimal Roy
Biplab Sikdar
Buddhadeb Sau
C.A. Murthy
C.K. Maiti
C.T. Bhunia
Chandan Majumdar
Debashis Saha
Dabesh Das
David Levin
Dhruba Bhattacharya
Dilip Saikia
Dipankar Sarkar
Dongkook Park
Eric Parsons
Frank Stomp
Hansa Jain
Imran Ahmad
Indranil Sen Gupta
Istabrak Abdul-Fatah
Iti Saha Misra
Ivan Osipkov
Jaideep Sarkar
Jayesh Vinod Kataria
Jiannong Cao
K.M. Rajesh
Krishnendu Mukhopadhyaya
Mainak Chatterjee
Mandar Mitra
Michael Marsh

Mike Rieck
Mikhail Nesterenko
Nikhil R. Pal
Pradip K. Srimani
Partha P. Chakrabarty
Palash Sarkar
Pallab Dasgupta
Partha Dasgupta
Philippe Rapin Parvdy
Rajat De
Rajib K. Das
Rana Barua
Robert Sherwood
Ruggero Morselli
Subhas C. Nandy
Sabyasachi Saha
Samiran Chattopadhyaya
Sandip Das
Sanjeev K. Aggarwal
Santi Maity
Sarmistha Neogy
Sasthi C. Ghosh
Sebastien Tixeuil
Sengjoon Lee
Shamik Sengupta
Shamik Sural
Shubhomay Moitra
Sompraksh Bandyopadhyaya
Srabani Mukhopadhyaya
Sriram Pemmaraju
Stephane Airiau
Subhashis Bhattacharya
Sudeb P. Pal
Sugata Sanyal
Sungwon Yi
Sunho Lim
Susmita Mitra
Susmita Sur-Kolay
Swarup Mondal

Teena Idnani   Umesh Deshpande
Tetsuro Ueda   Vinayak Naik
Umar Farooq

Table of Contents

Session II A: Distributed Systems

Session II B: Wireless Networks

A. K. Choudhury Memorial Lecture

Session III A: Information Security

Session III B: Network Protocols

Keynote Talk II

Session IV A: Reliability and Testing

Session IV B: Networks: Topology and Routing

Session V: Mobile Computing I

Session VI: Ad Hoc Networks

Session VII: Mobile Computing II

Session VIII: Sensor Networks

Poster Presentations

The Next Chapter in Networking Research: Evolutionary or Revolutionary?

Guru Parulkar

Division of Computer and Network Systems
National Science Foundation (NSF), USA
gparulka@nsf.gov

Abstract. Starting with the invention of packet switching in 1960s, the networking research community has made tremendous contributions towards creation of the Internet and its continued growth on various fronts. Clearly the Internet has emerged to be a very critical infrastructure for all aspects of our modern society. However, the Internet also suffers from serious limitations for its expanding role in the society.

Success of the Internet and its continued limitations have been a double edged sword for the research community: it has led to numerous new research opportunities and challenges, and at the same time, the success has severely limited research community's ability to influence Internet evolution during the past several years.

NSF and members of the research community have been inventing ways to continue the pace of network innovation to ensure continued evolution of Internet as well as to develop disruptive new networking technologies and solutions that would take us beyond Internet and serve the society for the next several decades.

In this talk, firstly a context for networking research will be provided and then several key NSF programs are outlined, that are aimed at keeping the pace of networking innovation high and enrich the next generation networking infrastructure.

A. Sen et al. (Eds.): IWDC 2004, LNCS 3326, p. 1, 2004.
© Springer-Verlag Berlin Heidelberg 2004

Performance of Fair Distributed Mutual Exclusion Algorithms

Kandarp Jani and Ajay D. Kshemkalyani

Computer Science Department, Univ. of Illinois at Chicago, Chicago, IL 60607, USA
{kjani,ajayk}@cs.uic.edu

Abstract. The classical Ricart-Agrawala algorithm (RA) has long been considered the most efficient *fair* mutual exclusion algorithm in distributed message-passing systems. The algorithm requires $2(N-1)$ messages per critical section access, where N is the number of processes in the system. Recently, Lodha-Kshemkalyani proposed an improved *fair* algorithm (LK) that requires between N and $2(N-1)$ messages per critical section access, and without any extra overhead. The exact number of messages depends on the concurrency of requests, and is difficult to prove or analyze theoretically. This paper shows the superior performance of LK over RA using extensive simulations under a wide range of critical section access patterns and network loads.

1 Introduction

Mutual exclusion is a fundamental paradigm in computing. Over the past two decades, several algorithms have been proposed to achieve mutual exclusion in asynchronous distributed message-passing systems [2, 8]. Designing such algorithms becomes difficult when the the requirement for *"fair"* synchronization needs to be satisfied. The commonly accepted definition of fairness is that requests for access to the critical section (CS) are satisfied in the order of their logical timestamps [4]. If two requests have the same timestamp, the process identifier is used as a tie-breaker. Lamport's logical clock [4] is used to assign timestamps to messages to order the requests. The algorithm to update the clocks and to timestamp requests keeps all logical clocks closely sychronized. A fair mutual exclusion algorithm needs to guarantee that requests are accessed in increasing order of the timestamps. Of the many distributed mutual exclusion algorithms, the only algorithms that are fair in the above context are Lamport [4], Ricart-Agrawala (RA) [7], and Lodha-Kshemkalyani (LK) [5].

The performance metrics for mutual exclusion algorithms are the following: the *number of messages*, the *synchronization delay*, the *response time*, and the *waiting time*. Others such as the *throughput* can be expressed in terms of the above metrics and inherent characteristics of the programs – such as the CS execution time, and the time spent executing non-CS code. For a system consisting of N processes, let d denote the time for a message hop and css, the time

A. Sen et al. (Eds.): IWDC 2004, LNCS 3326, pp. 2–15, 2004.
© Springer-Verlag Berlin Heidelberg 2004

spent executing the CS. The lower bounds on the *waiting time T*, the *response time* (which is $T + css$), and the *synchronization delay* are $2d$, $2d + css$, and d, respectively, for both the Lamport [4] and the RA [7] algorithms. The message complexity of Lamport is $3(N - 1)$ messages per CS access. The message complexity of RA is $2(N - 1)$ messages per CS access. The RA algorithm has been considered a classic in mutual exclusion algorithms, since 1983. It has been presented in many textbooks on distributed algorithms and distributed systems.

Recently, Lodha and Kshemkalyani proposed an improved algorithm (LK) [5], over the RA algorithm. This algorithm uses the same model as RA, but has a message complexity between N and $2(N-1)$ messages per CS access. All other metrics measure the same as or better than those of RA. The exact number of messages per CS access depends on the concurrency of the requests being made.

The improvement achieved by LK is difficult to determine theoretically or analytically. In this paper, we show via simulations that the performance of LK is better than that of RA. We consider two performance measures – the number of messages and the waiting time, to access the CS. As the response time can be derived from the waiting time, we view the waiting time as a more fundamental measure than the response time. The simulations study the performance of the algorithms under a wide range of requesting patterns (high load and low load), and under a wide range of program behaviors (time spent executing the CS). The study also accounts for a wide range of network dimensions and loads.

2   Overview of RA and LK Algorithms

The system model assumes there are N processes in the error-free asynchronous message-passing system. Message transit times may vary. Channels are FIFO. It is assumed that a single process runs on each site. So a site is synonymous with a process. A process requests a CS by sending REQUEST messages and waits for appropriate REPLY messages from the other processes. While a process is waiting to enter the CS, it cannot make another request to enter CS. Each process executes the following loop forever: execute the noncritical section, request to enter the CS, wait to get permission, execute the CS. In each iteration, the three durations are denoted NCSS, Waiting, and CSS. The time relations among the durations, and λ, the mean inter-request time, are shown in Fig. 1.

2.1   Ricart-Agrawala's Algorithm [7]

1. When a process P_i wants to enter the CS, it sends a timestamped REQUEST message to the other processes.
2. When a process P_j receives a REQUEST from P_i, it sends a REPLY to P_i if (i) P_j is not requesting nor executing the CS, or (ii) P_j is requesting with lower priority. Otherwise, P_j defers P_i's request.
3. P_i can enter the CS after it receives a REPLY from all other processes.
4. When P_i exits its CS, it sends as REPLY to all the processes whose requests it had deferred (step 2).

Thus, there are exactly $2(N - 1)$ messages exchanged per CS access.

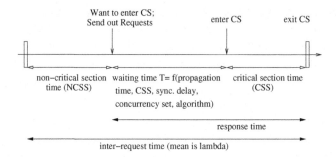

Fig. 1. The relationships among CSS, NCSS, λ, and Waiting time at a process

2.2   Lodha-Kshemkalyani Algorithm [5]

The LK algorithm assumes the same system model as that of RA but reduces the number of messages required per CS access. To realize this objective, LK uses three types of messages and a queue, the Local Request Queue (LRQ), which contains "concurrent requests".

Concurrent Requests: Consider two requests R_i initiated by process P_i and R_j initiated by process P_j. R_i and R_j are concurrent iff P_i's REQUEST is received by P_j after P_j has made its REQUEST and vice versa.

Concurrency Set: The concurrency set of request R_i^k, the kth request made by P_i, is defined as: $CSet_i(R_i^k) = \{R_j | R_i \text{ is concurrent with } R_j\} \bigcup \{R_i\}$. As a single request by P_i can be outstanding at a time, we simply use $CSet_i$ to denote its concurrency set.

Three types of messages are used by the LK algorithm: REQUEST, REPLY, and FLUSH. The REQUEST message contains the timestamp of the request. The REPLY and FLUSH messages contain the timestamp of the last completed CS access by the sender of that REPLY or FLUSH message. The REQUEST and REPLY messages hold a different significance from that in the RA algorithm, and have substantially enhanced semantics! FLUSH is the extra type used by the LK algorithm to achieve the savings in the messages. We emphasize that the size of messages used by LK is the same as that used by RA. The savings in the number of messages is not at the cost of any other parameter. The following observations indicate how the savings are achieved.

Observations

1. All requests are totally ordered by priority, similar to the RA algorithm.
2. A process receiving a REQUEST message can immediately determine whether the requesting process or itself should be allowed to enter the CS first.
3. Multiple uses of the REPLY message:
   - It acts a reply from a process that is not requesting.
   - It acts a collective reply from processes with higher priority requests.

The $REPLY(R_j)$ message from P_j indicates that R_j is the latest REQUEST for which P_j executed the CS. This indicates that all requests that have priority greater than that of R_j have finished CS and are no longer in contention. When a process P_i receives $REPLY(R_j)$, it can remove those REQUESTs whose priority $\geq$ priority of R_j, from its local request queue (LRQ_i). Thus, $REPLY(R_j)$ is a logical reply that denotes a collective reply from all processes that had made higher priority requests than or equal to R_j.

4. Multiple uses of FLUSH message: A FLUSH message is sent by a process after executing the CS, to the concurrently requesting process with the next highest priority (if it exists.) When entering the CS, a process can determine the state of all other processes in some consistent state with itself. Any other process is either requesting CS access and its (lower) priority is known, or it is not requesting. After executing CS, P_i sends a $FLUSH(R_i)$ message to P_j which is the concurrently requesting process with the next highest priority. $FLUSH(R_i)$ is a logical reply that denotes a collective reply from all processes that had made higher priority requests than or equal to R_i.

5. Multiple uses of REQUEST message: A process P_i that wants to invoke CS sends a REQUEST message to all other processes. On receipt of a REQUEST message, a process P_j that is not requesting sends a REPLY message immediately. If process P_j is requesting concurrently, it does not send a REPLY message. If P_j's REQUEST has a higher priority, the received REQUEST from P_i serves a reply to P_j. P_j will eventually execute CS (before P_i) and then through a chain of FLUSH/REPLY messages, P_i will eventually receive a logical reply to its REQUEST. If P_j's REQUEST has a lower priority than P_i's REQUEST, P_j likewise awaits P_i's logical permission via a chain of FLUSH/REPLY messages.

RA-Type Messages: The REPLY messages sent by concurrently requesting processes in RA, but not in LK (where LRQ prioritizes concurrent requests).

3 Objectives of Simulation

The total number of messages used for a particular CS access is $2N - |Cset|$, where $Cset$ is the concurrency set of that CS access request [5]. This is because there are $N - 1$ REQUEST messages, $(N - 1) - |Cset|$ REPLY messages, and 1 FLUSH message. The number of concurrent requests potentially depends on: the number of processes, inter-request time, time spent in the CS, and the propagation delay. The actual number of messages in a real system is difficult to analyze theoretically. The objectives of the simulation are as follows.

- To measure the message overhead of LK, per CS access, under a wide range of requesting conditions and network conditions. The message overhead of RA is always $2(N - 1)$ messages per CS access.
- To compare the waiting time of RA and LK under varying requesting and network conditions.

3.1   Simulation Parameters

Input Parameters

1. **Number of Processes** (N)**:** As N increases, and assuming that the mean inter-request time is not changed, there are more requests for the CS. This affects the concurrency set and waiting time also increases. Hence N is an important parameter. By varying N, we also study scalability. On the Intel Pentium 3 with 128 MB RAM used for the simulation, up to 45 processes could be simulated. Note that the earlier comprehensive performance study of distributed mutual exclusion algorithms assumed only 21 processes, and did not test for sensitivity to N [2].

2. **Inter-request Time** (λ)**:** Inter-request time is the time between generating two requests by a process. This parameter is exponentially distributed with λ as the mean. As processes begin requesting more furiously (λ decreases), there will be more requests, the probability of concurrent requests is higher, and hence a reduction in the number of messages per CS access. λ directly affects the concurrency set. Also, the inter-request time is related to the waiting time, propagation delay and CSS (see Section 3.2), and is therefore of interest. The typical values of the mean λ used in the simulations range from 10^{-4}s to 10s.

3. **Critical Section Sitting Time** (CSS)**:** The critical section sitting time is the amount of time a process executes in the critical section. It is modeled as an exponential distribution with a mean of CSS. It is difficult to analyze how the concurrency set is affected by CSS. However, CSS impacts the waiting time (see Section 3.2). Also, a process cannot request when executing the CS. This puts a bound on how frequently a process can request the CS. The values of the mean CSS used in the simulations range from 10^{-7}s to 10^{-3}s.

4. **Propagation Delay** (D)**:** The link propagation delay is the time elapsed while propagating a message from one process to another over the network. Realistic systems inherently exhibit this delay, and the waiting time at a process depends on this delay. The network is a complex entity to model [3]. As we would like to consider a single parameter to characterize (i) physical network size and/or distances, (ii) speed for all the links, and (iii) congestion, we model transmission time as an exponential distribution about the mean, D, as representative of all links. This distribution can also approximate TCP delays [1]. While simulating the mutual exclusion algorithms, we only implicitly model this parameter D because, (i) it follows the same distribution as CSS, and (ii) the occurrence of this delay D is tightly coupled with the CSS (see Section 3.2). Rather, we assume that CSS implicitly includes D. Note that the earlier comprehensive performance study of distributed mutual exclusion algorithms did not model this delay [2].

Output Parameters

1. **Normalized Message Complexity** (M_{norm})**:** The normalized message complexity is ((total number of messages exchanged per CS access) / N).

2. **Waiting Time** (T): The waiting time is the time a process has to wait to enter the CS after requesting the CS. The LK algorithm uses LRQ to track the concurrent requests at each process. By having to wait for fewer replies, LK's waiting time decreases with respect to RA but enqueuing and dequeuing may add some time overhead.

3.2 Inter-relation Amongst CSS, λ, T, and D

- The mean inter-request time λ equals the mean critical section sitting time (CSS), the mean waiting time (T), and the mean noncritical section time ($NCSS$), as seen from Fig. 1. Further, T is a function of the CSS, D, the concurrency set, and the mutual exclusion algorithm used. Thus,
$$\lambda = CSS + NCSS + T = CSS + NCSS + f(CSS, D, Cset, ME. \ algorithm)$$
λ, CSS, and D are assumed to be the means of exponential distributions. Hence, propagation time can be viewed as being incorporated in CSS.
- $\lambda > CSS$ because a process cannot request when executing the critical section and the rate of CS executions cannot exceed the rate of request generation. If we allow the processes to request while executing the critical section, those requests will be lost. As a result, the input distribution of CS requests will no longer remain exponential.
- The total waiting time of the system is directly proportional to CSS and D. As CSS increases, system-wide waiting time also increases. The average-case waiting time $T_{avg} = (|CSet|/2)(CSS + D)$. This equation also justifies why the propagation delay D can be viewed as being incorporated within CSS.

The above points explain how the value of λ is constrained by CSS, D, and T.

4 Simulation Results

4.1 Experimental Setup

The LK and RA algorithms were implemented in C using the simulation framework of OPNET [6]. We report three experiments, in which we test the performance for various combinations of the input parameters N, CSS, λ.

1. The number of messages exchanged in the system was measured for multiple settings of the tuple (N, CSS), as the mean inter-request time (λ) is varied.
2. The number of messages exchanged in the system was measured for multiple settings of the tuple (CSS, λ), as the number of processes (N) increased.
3. The average waiting time (T) in the system was measured for both the LK and RA algorithms, for different settings of the tuple (CSS, λ), as the number of processes (N) was varied.

The machine used for simulation is an Intel Pentium 3 with 128 MB of RAM. For each simulation run, statistics were collected for 1000 CS requests per process, which amounted to a minimum of 10,000 requests and a maximum of 45,000 requests. For each simulation run, the statistics collected for the initial 10% requests were discarded to eliminate the effects of startup. Each statistic reported in the results is an average of the statistics of ten simulation runs with different seeds. Propagation delay (D) was implicitly accounted for (Section 3).

The ranges and distributions of the three input parameters were discussed in Section 3.1. Based on the observations (Section 3.2), the range of λ is adjusted based on the value of CSS (and D).

To present the results on message overhead, following statistics are collected.

1. Total number of requests messages in the system after steady state. (M_{req})
2. Total number of messages in the system after steady state. (M_{tot})

For each experiment, the normalized message complexity is reported as $M_{norm} = M_{tot}/M_{req}$. For RA, $M_{norm} = 2$. M_{norm} for KS will vary from 1 to 2.

4.2 Expt. 1: Impact of Inter-request Time (λ) on Message Overhead

The worst-case message complexity of the LK algorithm is the same as that of RA. However, on an average, LK performs better than RA. Here, the goal is to study LK's message overhead M_{norm} as the processes request more furiously. The simulations were performed for 20 settings of the tuple (N, CSS) while varying λ from 10^{-4} to 10^{1}. The settings were formed by taking all combinations of the values of N: 10, 20, 30, and 40, and the 4 values of CSS: 10^{-7}, 10^{-6}, 10^{-4}, and 10^{-3}. The results are plotted in Figs. 2, 3, 4, and 5.

Fig. 2: $SP_{11}(10, 10^{-7})$, $SP_{12}(10, 10^{-6})$, $SP_{13}(10, 10^{-4})$, $SP_{14}(10, 10^{-3})$
Fig. 3: $SP_{21}(20, 10^{-7})$, $SP_{22}(20, 10^{-6})$, $SP_{23}(20, 10^{-4})$, $SP_{24}(20, 10^{-3})$
Fig. 4: $SP_{31}(30, 10^{-7})$, $SP_{32}(30, 10^{-6})$, $SP_{33}(30, 10^{-4})$, $SP_{34}(30, 10^{-3})$
Fig. 5: $SP_{41}(40, 10^{-7})$, $SP_{42}(40, 10^{-6})$, $SP_{43}(40, 10^{-4})$, $SP_{44}(40, 10^{-3})$

The mean inter-request time (λ) is varied as per the constraint imposed (see Section 3.2). As seen from the plots for sets $SP_{x3}(N, 10^{-4})$ and $SP_{x4}(N, 10^{-3})$, there are no data points for $\lambda < 7 \times 10^{-4}$ and $\lambda < 7 \times 10^{-3}$ respectively.

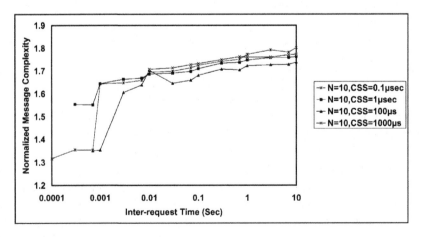

Fig. 2. Normalized message complexity vs. inter-request time ($SP._x$)

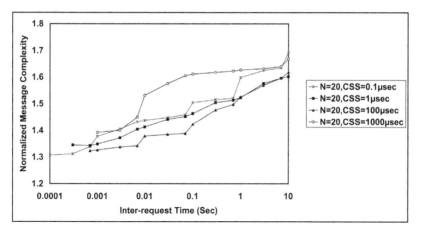

Fig. 3. Normalized message complexity vs. inter-request time $(SP._x)$

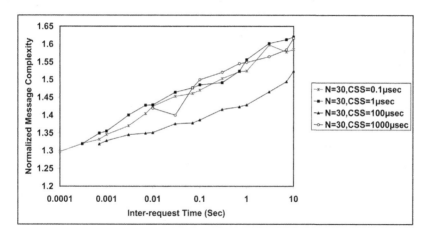

Fig. 4. Normalized message complexity vs. inter-request time $(SP._x)$

Observations

- As the value of λ increases, the value of M_{norm} increases but is still lower than the value for RA, which is 2. With an increase in the value of λ, the concurrency set grows sparse. This results in more number of messages of RA-type being exchanged. Thus, LK performs much better when the load on the system is heavier, conforming to the expression, $2N - |Cset|$, for the message overhead.
- For lower values of N (Fig. 2), as λ increases, there is a jump in the value of M_{norm} which later saturates, and tends towards a value of 1.8. But for higher N (Figs. 3, 4, 5), M_{norm} is lower and follows a smoother curve. The effect of N on M_{norm} is studied in Section 4.3.
- No definite relationship can be readily inferred between CSS and M_{norm}.

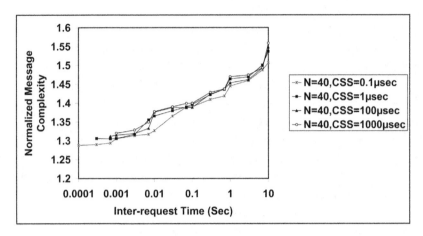

Fig. 5. Normalized message complexity vs. inter-request time $(SP._x)$

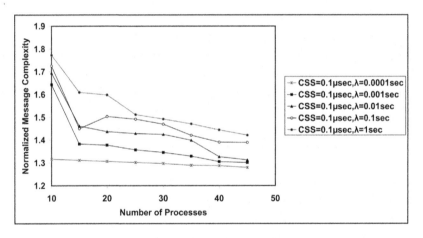

Fig. 6. Normalized message complexity vs. number of processes $(SC._x)$

Thus, we experimentally see how the LK algorithm outperforms RA under heavy CS request load. Even under light load, LK shows some improvement over RA.

4.3   Expt. 2: Scalability with Increasing Number of Processes

This experiment studies the message overhead of the LK algorithm as the number of processes in the system is increased. This also measures scalability. The simulations were performed for 20 settings of the tuple (CSS, λ) while varying N from 10 to 45. The settings were formed by taking all combinations of the 4 values of CSS: 10^{-7}, 10^{-6}, 10^{-4}, and 10^{-3}, and the 5 values of λ: 10^{-4}, 10^{-3}, 10^{-2}, 10^{-1} and 10^{1}. The results are plotted in Figs. 6, 7, 8, and 9.

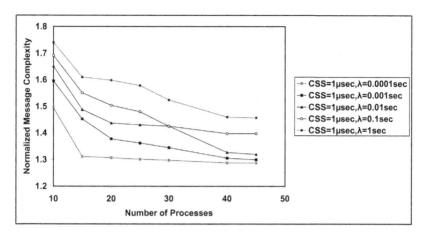

Fig. 7. Normalized message complexity vs. number of processes $(SC._x)$

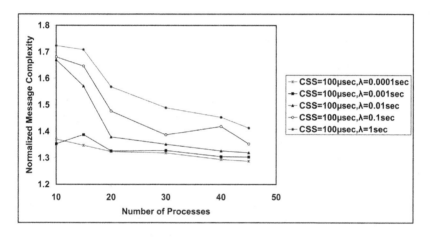

Fig. 8. Normalized message complexity vs. number of processes $(SC._x)$

Fig. 6: $SC_{11}(10^{-7}, 10^{-4})$, $SC_{12}(10^{-7}, 10^{-3})$, $SC_{13}(10^{-7}, 10^{-2})$, $SC_{14}(10^{-7}, -10^{-1})$, $SC_{15}(10^{-7}, 1)$

Fig. 7: $SC_{21}(10^{-6}, 10^{-4})$, $SC_{22}(10^{-6}, 10^{-3})$, $SC_{23}(10^{-6}, 10^{-2})$, $SC_{24}(10^{-6}, -10^{-1})$, $SC_{25}(10^{-6}, 1)$

Fig. 8: $SC_{31}(10^{-4}, 7 \times 10^{-4})$, $SC_{32}(10^{-4}, 10^{-3})$, $SC_{33}(10^{-4}, 10^{-2})$, $SC_{34}(10^{-4}, -10^{-1})$, $SC_{35}(10^{-4}, 1)$

Fig. 9: $SC_{41}(10^{-3}, 7 \times 10^{-3})$, $SC_{42}(10^{-3}, 10^{-2})$, $SC_{43}(10^{-3}, 10^{-1})$, $SC_{44}(10^{-3}, 1)$

Note from Fig. 9 that SC_{4x} consists of four data sets instead of five as $\lambda > CSS$.

Observations

– As N increases, M_{norm} decreases first but then levels off. This shows the scalability of LK. With an increase in N and at a fixed λ, the number of

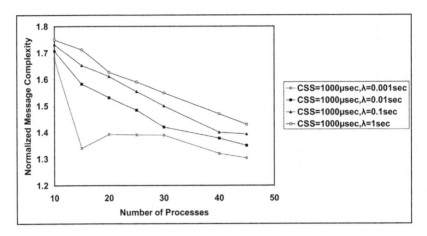

Fig. 9. Normalized message complexity vs. number of processes $(SC._x)$

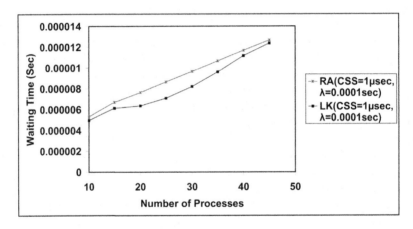

Fig. 10. Waiting time vs. number of processes $(WT.)$

concurrent requests increases (load increases), and hence the waiting time increases. Waiting times will tend to overlap more, as also the non-CSS reduces. This potentially affects the probability of two processes making concurrent requests. The exact impact observed on M_{norm} is difficult to explain by theory.

- For low values of N, as N increases, the dip in M_{norm} is quite noticable. However, the curves tend to saturate for $N > 30$. This suggests that M_{norm} will tend to a steady value as the number of processes increases.
- Another observation which complements the results of Section 4.2 is that, for lower values of λ, the curves are also lower. Lesser the inter-request time, the probability that there will be more number of concurrent requests increases. Consequently the message overhead reduces. As the value of λ increases, so does the normalized message complexity.

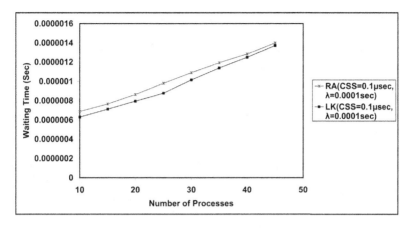

Fig. 11. Waiting time vs. number of processes (*WT.*)

Recall from Section 4.2 the propagation delay D is treated as being a part of CSS. Modeling D independently is beyond the scope of this simulation.

4.4   Expt. 3: Improvement in Waiting Time

This experiment compares the waiting times in the RA and LK algorithms. Theoretically, it can be predicted that the waiting time of LK is at least as good as that of RA. This is because the "RA-type" messages are absent in LK, and hence, a requesting process need not wait to receive REPLY messages from all the concurrently requesting processes. Specifically, LK has two cases.

- A high-priority process does not have to wait for a REPLY message from a lower priority process. Under low load, this savings may not be large because there are not many processes requesting concurrently; thus, there may not be many lower priority concurrent requests. Under high load, this savings may not be large because there are many concurrently requesting processes, and a process may need to wait anyway because there are several higher priority processes that need to execute their CS before this process can enter its CS. Hence, not having to wait for the REPLY messages from lower priority processes may not reduce the waiting time substantially.
- A low-priority process does not have to wait for a REPLY message from all the higher priority processes. It suffices if the FLUSH/REPLY message with the *immediately* higher priority than that of the requesting process, reaches the requesting process; the LRQ queue would get purged of all higher priority requests than that on the received REPLY/FLUSH. Here, the reduction in waiting time may not be high, as also seen from the following scenario. Assume that P_j's request has a higher priority than P_k's request which has a higher priority than P_i's request. Statistically, the probability of a REPLY/FLUSH sent later by P_k arriving at P_i earlier than the REPLY of P_j (which would be sent in RA) is low.

It is difficult to theoretically analyze the improvement in waiting time of LK over RA. Hence, we simulate both algorithms. The curves in Figs. 10 and 11 are plotted for the following settings of (CSS, λ), with N varying from 10 to 45.

Fig. 10: $WT_1(10^{-6}, 10^{-4})$
Fig. 11: $WT_2(10^{-7}, 10^{-4})$

In the graphs, the RA curve is clearly above the LK curve. Thus, LK gives a better waiting time than RA. The following observations can also be made.

Observations

- Initially, with a low N, the concurrency set is small. The LK curve follows the RA curve but is below it because of having to wait for fewer messages.
- As the value of N increases, contention for CS increases. The rate of increase of waiting time for RA curve remains the same. However, the same decreases for the LK curve. This behavior can be attributed to the increase in the size of the concurrency set with increasing N. A larger concurrency set implies not having to wait for more number of RA-type replies (that will never get sent in the LK algorithm). Consequently, there is a relative reduction in the waiting time for LK.
- As N is increased further, however, the two curves start getting closer. The LK curve runs much more closer to the RA curve for $N > 30$. This may be attributed to the fact that there are now more higher-priority processes that need to execute their CS first. Therefore, not having to wait for the REPLY messages from lower priority processes as well as (earlier) higher priority processes is not as effective in reducing the waiting time. Another reason is that, along with increase in the size of the concurrency set, the number of enqueue and dequeue operations (for LRQ) at each process also increases. and their overhead becomes nontrivial.

The simulations show that the waiting time in the LK algorithm is somewhat lower than in the RA algorithm under all conditions tested.

5   Conclusions

The RA algorithm was the most efficient *fair* algorithm for distributed mutual exclusion for about two decades. This paper experimentally studied the performance of the recently proposed LK algorithm, and showed that it outperforms the RA algorithm in both message complexity and waiting time, without compromising on *fairness* or any other metrics.

Acknowledgements

This work was supported by US NSF grant CCR-9875617. We thank Shashank Khanvilkar for his help with OPNET.

References

1. P. Chandra, P. Gambhire, A. D. Kshemkalyani, Performance of the Optimal Causal Multicast Algorithm: A Statistical Analysis, IEEE Transactions on Parallel and Distributed Systems, 15(1):40-52, January 2004.
2. Y.-I. Chang, A Simulation Study on Distributed Mutual Exclusion, J. Parallel and Distributed Computing, Vol. 33(2): 107-121, 1996.
3. S. Floyd, V. Paxson, Difficulties in Simulating the Internet, IEEE/ACM Transactions on Networking, Vol. 9(4): 392-403, August 2001.
4. L. Lamport, Time, Clocks and the Ordering of Events in Distributed Systems, Comm. ACM, Vol. 21(7): 558 - 565, Jan 1978.
5. S. Lodha, A. Kshemkalyani, A Fair Distributed Mutual Exclusion Algorithm, IEEE Trans. on Parallel and Distributed Systems, 11(6): 537-549, June 2000.
6. OPNET, Available at: ⟨http://www.opnet.com/products/modeler/home.html⟩
7. G. Ricart, A. K. Agrawala, An Optimal Algorithm for Mutual Exclusion in Computer Networks, Comm. ACM, 24(1):9-17, Jan. 1981.
8. M. Singhal, A Taxonomy of Distributed Mutual Exclusion, J. Parallel and Distributed Computing, 18(1):94-101, May 1993.

A Framework for Automatic Identification of the Best Checkpoint and Recovery Protocol

Himadri S. Paul[1,*], Arobinda Gupta[1], and Amit Sharma[2]

* Department of Computer Science and Engineering,
Indian Institute of Technology, Kharagpur, India 721302
{hpaul, agupta}@cse.iitkgp.ernet.in
* Department of Computer Science,
University of Illinois at Urbana-Champaign, Illinois, USA
sharma6@uiuc.edu

Abstract. Fault tolerance is important for a distributed system to increase its reliability and throughput. Checkpoint and recovery protocols have been proposed as fault tolerance for non-critical applications. The performance of checkpoint and recovery protocols plays an important role in the overall performance of a distributed system. The performance of these protocols depends on system characteristics as well as an application characteristics. In this paper, we propose a novel technique to automatically identify the checkpoint and recovery protocol which is likely to perform the best for a given system and an application the system is currently running. We present experimental results to show that the scheme can efficiently determine a suitable checkpoint and recovery protocol for many applications.

1   Introduction

Fault tolerance techniques are employed in distributed systems to enhance system reliability and performance [1]. Fault tolerance through backward error recovery is popular in non-critical distributed systems. However, all checkpoint and recovery protocols have their own overheads in the form of time and space needed for checkpointing, time to recover in case of a fault, and the amount of loss of computation due to rollback during recovery. These overheads differ for different protocols. A checkpoint and recovery protocol is expected to impose low checkpointing overhead in terms of time and space, low recovery overhead, and yet save most of the useful computation by the application processes. The throughput of a distributed system depends upon the performance of its checkpoint and recovery protocol.

However, the overheads incurred by a checkpoint and recovery protocol are dependent on many system and application characteristics, and judicious choice of parameters of the protocol. The set of parameters which affect the overheads

---

* Supported by a graduate fellowship from Infosys Technologies Ltd., Bangalore, INDIA.

A. Sen et al. (Eds.): IWDC 2004, LNCS 3326, pp. 16–27, 2004.
© Springer-Verlag Berlin Heidelberg 2004

of a checkpoint and recovery protocol can be divided into three broad categories [6]: (i) system parameters, which include link characteristics like bandwidth, message drop rate etc stable storage latency, and fault frequency, (ii) application parameters, which include process count, checkpoint size, application message size, and communication pattern, and (iii) protocol parameters which include the exact checkpoint and recovery protocol used and checkpointing frequency. However these overheads are interrelated in the sense that trying to reduce one may increase the other. For example, if the fault frequency of a system is low, it makes sense to take checkpoints less frequently to reduce the checkpointing overhead, as most of the checkpoints will not be used anyway if faults do not occur for a large period of time. However, choosing a low checkpointing frequency may result in a large loss of computation in case a fault does happen.

Present day distributed systems which use backward error recovery employ a pre-selected checkpoint and recovery protocol, which remains static throughout the life of the system. To improve the throughput and utilization of system resources, it is important to choose a checkpoint and recovery protocol which performs the best for a given distributed system as well as for the application it is running. Since a distributed system may execute different distributed applications at different times, a statically configured checkpoint and recovery protocol cannot give the best performance for all the applications that it may run. The system should automatically identify a checkpoint and recovery protocol and its parameters which are likely to produce the best performance with the changes in application characteristics and then dynamically employ it. In this paper, we present a scheme to automatically determine the best checkpoint and recovery protocol for a given application by matching its characteristics with a database of pre-simulated application scenarios. The crucial part of the scheme is a novel technique to match the communication patterns of two distributed applications. At the heart of this technique is a new graph similarity problem. We present some results of extensive experiments to show that the correct checkpoint and recovery protocol can be chosen dynamically by this method for a variety of applications.

The rest of the paper is organized as follows. Section 2 discusses a system architecture required for identification of a checkpoint and recovery protocol suitable for the running distributed application. Section 3, presents a technique for matching two communication patterns. The results of the experiments are discussed in Section 4. Finally, Section 5 presents some concluding remarks.

2   System Architecture

A *decision system* attached to the distributed system enables it to automatically identify the best checkpoint and recovery protocol and its parameters for the application currently running, from a pool of protocols available to the system. The decision system 'observes' the application and decides/suggests a checkpoint and recovery protocol. The decision system has at its disposal a *CR performance database*. The attributes for the database are (1) link bandwidth, (2) fault frequency, (3) stable storage latency, (4) process count, (5) checkpoint size, (6) application message size, (7) communication pattern, (8) checkpoint protocol, (9) checkpoint frequency, (10) checkpoint protocol overhead (C), (11) recovery protocol overhead (R), and (12) average computation waste (W). The CR performance database can be a publicly available database which contains performance data for a wide variety of system, application, and checkpoint and recovery protocol parameters. The database can be built up by simulating different checkpoint and recovery protocols on a wide range of applications and under different system characteristics by a simulator like dPSIM[6].

The system characteristics are predefined or can be estimated for a given distributed system, and therefore are statically configured into the decision system. The application characteristics can be estimated at runtime. For example, the communication pattern can be captured at runtime by capturing the messages at the communication layer. The decision system then searches the CR performance database for records having system and application characteristics (the first seven attributes) which match closely with those of the application currently running in the system. The checkpoint and recovery protocol and checkpointing interval (the 8th and 9th attributes respectively) of the record with the *lowest* overhead are suggested. The definition of the *lowest* overhead may depend upon user preference. For example, a user may prefer to reduce the checkpointing overhead only.

Finding close matches for all the system and application parameters except the communication pattern is simple and straightforward since they are all integer/real values. A communication pattern is the log of all send and receive activities by the distributed application and there is no straightforward, trivial way to compare two such patterns. In Section 3, we present a scheme to match two communication patterns that produces a positive integer value between 0 and 1, where a value closer to 1 indicates a closer match. Given this scheme, we can define the following notion of similarity between two distributed applications:

Definition 1. *A pair of distributed applications is said to be* (ϕ, ψ)-*similar to each other if,*

1. *For each of the features link bandwidth, fault frequency, stable storage latency, process count, checkpoint size, and application message size, if f_1 is the value of the feature in the first application and f_2 is the value in the second, then* $|f_1 - f_2| \leq \phi \times f_1$ $(0 \leq \phi \leq 1)$
2. *The communication patterns of the two applications match with value ψ or higher* $(0 \leq \psi \leq 1)$.

The values of ϕ and ψ can be configured for the system based on the level of accuracy needed. Note that with $\phi = 0$ and $\psi = 1$, two applications will match only if they match exactly in all the attributes.

3   Communication Pattern Matching

A communication pattern of a distributed system consisting of n processes, is an ordered set of events logged with respect to their time-stamps. In a message passing distributed system we consider two events logged in the communication pattern - send and receive events. We assume the communication pattern is logged with respect to a tightly synchronized clock.

There are several issues related to the problem of communication pattern matching. Consider the case when an *application communication pattern* is to be matched with some *reference communication pattern*. Even though the basic application that generated both the reference and the application communication patterns may be the same, but in one case, say for the generation of the application pattern, the processes in the system may have been slow. Therefore, the application communication pattern will be stretched out in time. Differences in delays can also cause two patterns, generated from the same application, to appear different. The complexity of the problem is further compounded by the fact that the nature of the communication pattern of a distributed application drastically varies with the number of processes it uses. Therefore, a communication pattern matching technique should identify *similar* patterns, and not only *same* patterns.

We first assume that the number of processes is n in both the reference and the application communication patterns. We shall later discuss how this assumption can be relaxed. To match a reference communication pattern and an application one, we can model each pattern as a weighted directed graph with n nodes, where each node represents one process. An edge indicates communication from the source node to the sink node and the edge weight represents the number of messages sent from the source node to the sink node in the entire pattern. We can then measure the similarity between the two graphs. Thus, some measure of similarity between two weighted directed graphs have to be defined, and algorithms to find the similarity measure between the two graphs need to be developed. This is first addressed in Section 3.1.

3.1   The Weighted Directed Graph Similarity Problem

A weighted directed graph G can be defined as $G = \{V_G, E_G, W\}$, where V_G is the set nodes of G, E_G is the set of edges, and W is an weight function such that $W : E_G \rightarrow \Re$. The *graph similarity problem* can be stated as follows. Given two weighted directed graphs, we need to find a node-map between the graphs under which the *difference* between them is minimum among all possible node maps between the two graphs. To quantify the difference between two graphs, we introduce a similarity measure for a pair of weighted directed graphs,

Definition 2. *Given two weighted directed graphs G and H and a node map Π between them, the ϵ-edge similarity measure, $\mathcal{R}_{\Pi}^{\epsilon}(v_i, v_j)$, for a pair of nodes, v_i, v_j of G, where $0 \leq \epsilon \leq 1$, is defined as follows:*

$$
\begin{aligned}
\mathcal{R}_{\Pi}^{\epsilon}(v_i, v_j) = \quad & 0 \ \ if \ (v_i, v_j) \notin E_G \ \wedge \ (\Pi(v_i), \Pi(v_j)) \notin E_H \\
= & +1 \ \ if \ (v_i, v_j) \in E_G \ \wedge \ (\Pi(v_i), \Pi(v_j)) \in E_H \\
& \wedge \ |W(v_i, v_j) - W(\Pi(v_i), \Pi(v_j))| \ \leq \epsilon W(v_i, v_j) \\
= & -1 \ \ otherwise.
\end{aligned}
$$

The ϵ factor in the ϵ-edge similarity measure implies a relative closeness measure between the corresponding edges. Let e_G be an edge in G and e_H be the corresponding edge (under some node map Π) in H. If $(1 - \epsilon)W(e_G) \leq W(e_H) \leq (1 + \epsilon)W(e_G)$, then we say that the edge matches and we assign a reward of 1. Otherwise, we consider the edge to mismatch and impose a penalty. By varying ϵ, we can make the match tight or slack.

Definition 3. *Given two weighted directed graphs G and H and a node map Π between them, the mapped ϵ-similarity measure, $\mathcal{I}_\Pi^\epsilon$, between two weighted directed graphs G and H, under the given node map Π, is defined as follows:*

$$\mathcal{I}_\Pi^\epsilon = \frac{1}{2}\left(1 + \frac{\sum_{\substack{i \neq j}}^{v_i,v_j \in V_G} \mathcal{R}_\Pi^\epsilon(v_i, v_j)}{\sum_{\substack{i \neq j}}^{v_i,v_j \in V_G} |\mathcal{R}_\Pi^\epsilon(v_i, v_j)|}\right)$$

It can be easily shown that $0 \leq \mathcal{I}_\Pi^\epsilon \leq 1$.

Definition 4. *Given two weighted directed graphs G and H the ϵ-similarity measure, $\mathcal{I}^\epsilon$, is defined as the maximum of $\mathcal{I}_\Pi^\epsilon$ over all possible node maps Π.*

Note that the well known graph isomorphism problem can be easily reduced to this weighted directed graph similarity problem by replacing each undirected edge by two directed edges of weight 1 in opposite directions and choosing $\epsilon = 0$. The undirected graph is isomorphic if and only if the similarity measure between the corresponding weighted directed graphs is 1. Intuitively the graph similarity problem is harder than the graph isomorphism problem. Below we present two heuristics for computing graph similarity between a pair of weighted directed graphs. Since we are only interested in discovering similar patterns, we try to design heuristics which should be able to distinguish between similar and dissimilar graphs, and should return a high similarity value for similar graphs. We are not interested in finding an accurate similarity measure for graph pairs which are too much different anyway and we expect a very low value for them (which may be lower than the actual similarity measure).

3.2   Heuristics for the Graph Similarity Problem

The heuristics developed for graph similarity are primarily based upon the node invariant and the node neighborhood heuristics [2, 7]. A node invariant is a value $i(v)$ of a node v such that if there is an isomorphism which maps v to u, then $i(v) = i(u)$. However, the converse is not true. We use a four tuple as the node invariant property which includes indegree, outdegree, the total weight of the in-coming edges, and the total weight of the out-going edges.

Neighborhood Based Heuristic: The neighborhood based heuristic is designed on the assumption that for a pair of similar graphs G and H and a node-map Π which produces the highest similarity value between them, the neighborhood set of a node v in G and that of $\Pi(v)$ in H are similar. The nodes with the highest outdegree, amongst the highest indegree nodes, are put into one cluster, called the *seed cluster*. A pair of nodes is chosen, one from each of the seed clusters corresponding to the two graphs. We call this node pair *seed nodes*. Minimum spanning trees are constructed with the seed nodes as roots. Nodes at distance of 1 hop from the seed node are placed in a cluster called the level-1 cluster, nodes at distance of 2 hops from the root are placed in level-2 cluster, and so on. In general, nodes at distance of d hops are put into level-d cluster. Now different permutations of node-maps are tried within the clusters at the same level. The whole procedure is iterated for all possible permutations of the seed node-pairs from the seed clusters. In order to reduce the number of permutations, we also apply some heuristic to exclude the computation of node-maps which match nodes with very different node invariant values.

Edge Match Based Heuristic: Unlike the previous heuristic, this heuristic matches an edge at a time. One edge match is equivalent to matching two nodes, and therefore the aim is to construct node maps faster. The heuristic is shown in Figure 1.

An edge cluster E_i^H is formed by an edge $e_i^G \in E_G$ in Step 1. We shall refer to e_i^G as the *seed edge* of E_i^H. The cluster E_i^H consists of edges from H whose weights are within ϵ fraction of the weight of the seed edge. The parameter ϵ is borrowed from the ϵ-edge similarity measure defined in Section 3.1. The edges from the edge cluster will be considered for potential matches with its seed edge. The edge cluster E_i^H is further refined on the basis of the node invariant property. If the difference between the node invariant values of the source node of the seed edge e_i^G and that of an edge $e \in E_i^H$ is high, then e is discarded from the cluster E_i^H. Similar refinement is done for sink nodes as well.

The edge clusters are sorted in ascending order of their cardinality. Edges occurring in a cluster at the top of the sorted list gains preference for matching over an edge occurring at the bottom. An edge occurring in a cluster toward the tail of the ordered list $\mathcal{S}^H$ may be eliminated in Step 8, if the node map it implies clashes with the node-map already achieved. In the proposed heuristic we sort E_i^H in ascending order of their cardinality. Smaller clusters at the top of the recursion tree implies less permutations to check, as edges at the bottom clusters are expected to be eliminated by the edge matching from the top of the tree. However, this sorting method is not guaranteed to work well for all types of graphs. We have implemented other sorting methods, which include ascending/descending order sorting on the edge-weights of the seed edge, and descending order sorting of the cardinality of the clusters. A combination of these techniques gives better results.

The parameter f_d, in the algorithm described in Figure 1, represents the factor by which each of the node invariant values of two nodes at most differ for the nodes to be considered for potential match. As $f_d \to 0$, the matching criterion becomes tighter, and as a result the edge cluster E_i^H becomes smaller. This reduces the number of permutations to be checked, but may miss some potential better matches.

Input: Two weighted directed graphs G and H.
Output: m: Similarity measure between G and H, $(0 \le m \le 1)$

1. For each edge $e_i^G = (u, v) \in E_G$:

$$
\begin{aligned}
E_i^H = \{ e^H = (p, q) : e^H \in E_H \\
\wedge \ |W(e_i^G) - W(e^H)| \le (\epsilon \times W(e_i^G)) \\
\wedge \ |indegree(u) - indegree(p)| \le f_d \times indegree(u) \\
\wedge \ |indegree(v) - indegree(q)| \le f_d \times indegree(v) \\
\wedge \ |outdegree(u) - outdegree(p)| \le f_d \times outdegree(u) \\
\wedge \ |outdegree(v) - outdegree(q)| \le f_d \times outdegree(v) \}
\end{aligned}
$$

2. $\mathcal{S}^H = sort\left(\{E_i^H\}\right)$, /* in ascending order of cardinality of the sets */
   where $\mathcal{S}^H = \left(S_1^H, S_2^H, \ldots S_{|E_G|}^H\right)$ such that $(i \le j) \Leftrightarrow (|S_i^H| \le |S_j^H|)$;
3. $m = EdgeMatch(\mathcal{S}^H, \Phi, 1)$;
4. Return m;

FUNCTION: **EdgeMatch**

Input: $\mathcal{S}^H$: A set of edge clusters. Π: A set of ordered pair of nodes, representing node map between G and H. i: Index into the list $\mathcal{S}^H$.
Output: m: Similarity measure between G and H, $(0 \le m \le 1)$

---

1. $\mathcal{P} = \Pi$; $m = 0$;
2. If $(i > |\mathcal{S}^H|)$
3. $C_G = (u_1, u_2, \ldots, u_d)$, List of unmatched nodes of G;
4. $C_H = $ Unmatched nodes of H;
5.   For all permutations $(v_1, v_2, \ldots, v_d)$ of the nodes in C_H
        $\Pi = \Pi \bigcup \{(u_1, v_1), (u_2, v_2), \ldots (u_d, v_d), \}$;
        If $(\mathcal{I}_\Pi^\epsilon (G, H) > m)$ $m = \mathcal{I}_\Pi^\epsilon (G, H)$;
        $\Pi = \mathcal{P}$;
6.   Return m;

7. $(u, v) = seed(S_i^H)$; $count = 0$;
8. For each $e = (p, q) \in S_i^H$:
        /* Check for node-map clashes */
9.   If $(\forall x \ne p : (u, x) \notin \Pi) \ \wedge \ (\forall x \ne u : (x, p) \notin \Pi)$
        $\wedge \ (\forall x \ne q : (v, x) \notin \Pi) \ \wedge \ (\forall x \ne v : (x, q) \notin \Pi)$
        $\Pi = \Pi \bigcup \{(u, p), (v, q)\}$;
        $s = EdgeMatch(\mathcal{S}^H, \Pi, i + 1)$;
        If $(s > m)$ $m = s$;
        $count = count + 1$; $\Pi = \mathcal{P}$;   /* restore old node map */
10. /* A value of 0 of $count$ indicates that no node-map was possible in this recursion. Then we have to initiate the next recursion */
11. If $(count = 0)$ $m = EdgeMatch(\mathcal{S}^H, \Pi, i + 1)$;
12. Return m;

Fig. 1. Edge-match based heuristic

In the worst case the running time of the heuristic is exponential. But an upper bound on the number of node maps to be checked is imposed to keep the runtime within practical limit. In order to avoid computation for useless node maps, branch-&-bound technique is used.

3.3   The Splicing Algorithm

The representation of an entire communication pattern as a single graph does not contain any temporal information, and two entirely different communication patterns having the same number of messages exchanged between the same pairs of nodes, will be declared as similar. To capture the temporal properties of the communication pattern, both the reference and the application communication patterns are divided into small time slices, called *splices*. A pattern is spliced in a way such that the start of a splice boundary is either the start of the pattern if it is the first splice, or it is the same as the end boundary of the previous splice. The ith splice of the reference pattern and that of the application pattern are then converted into their corresponding weighted directed graphs and similarity between them are computed. The measures obtained from all pairs of splices are then combined to give a combined communication pattern similarity measure as discussed in Section 3.4.

In the splicing technique we first splice the reference pattern such that all the splice durations are the same. The level of temporal information captured depends on the duration of the splices. Splices with larger durations loose more temporal information, and hence there is more chance of two dissimilar patterns being classified as similar. Splices with shorter durations means more number of splices and hence more number of graph similarity measure computations, resulting in an increase in the running time of the scheme. The application pattern is then spliced in reference to the splices of the reference pattern such that the graph similarity measure between the splice pair is maximized. The end-boundary of the ith splice in the application pattern is obtained in the following manner. The end boundary of the splice is initially the start boundary. The end-boundary is then progressively advanced in time, while calculating the similarity measure between application splice thus achieved and the ith splice of the reference pattern. The end-boundary is chosen at a point where this measure is maximum.

The splicing algorithm, shown in Figure 2, is divided into four phases. In the first phase the reference communication pattern is spliced. In phase II of the algorithm, it determines whether two applications are likely to be similar. The estimation is based upon the observation that if two patterns are similar then the splice durations should have the same proportions and also should have similar values. The *splice duration ratio* is defined as the ratio of the time duration of the application and that of the reference splice. If the splice duration ratio fluctuates too much (deviation, δ_r, is high) the patterns are considered to be dissimilar and a sequence of 0's is returned. At the end of phase II, we have an estimation of the splice duration ratio. In phase III the rest of the application pattern is spliced based on this estimation, such that the new splices have approximately the same

Input: A reference communication pattern (R) and
         an application communication pattern (A).
Output: A sequence of graph similarity measure, $\mathbb{M}$, one for each splice pair.

Phase I:
The reference pattern is spliced arbitrarily into a list of splices: $\mathbb{P}^R = (R_{\bullet}, R_{\bullet}, \ldots)$,
such that $\forall i, j : duration(R_i) = duration(R_j)$;

Phase II:
1. $LOG = \Phi$;
2. For all $R_i : 1 < i \leq L$
   c = number of messages in R_i;
   $start(A_i) = end(A_{i-\bullet});$ $T = start(A_i);$ $m = 0$;
   For each message m, starting from $(c - f_m \times c)^{th}$ message
   to $(c + f_m \times c)^{th}$ message (from $start(A_i)$),
      $end(A_i) = receive\_time(m)$;
      $G_r = graph(R_i);$ $G_a = graph(A_i)$;
      $(s, \Pi) = \mathcal{I}^\epsilon(G_r, G_a)$;
      If $(s > m)$ $T = end(A_i);$ $m = s$;
   if $(m > f_\mathcal{I})$ $LOG = LOG \bigcup \{$node map corresponding to $m\}$;
   $end(A_i) = T;$ $r_i = duration(A_i)/duration(R_i)$;
3. μ_r = mean of $(r_i : 1 \leq i \leq L);$ δ_r = deviation of $(r_i : 1 \leq i \leq L)$;
4. If $(\delta_r > f_r)$ then return a sequence of $|\mathbb{P}^R|$ $0's$ and abort;

Phase III:
5. For all $R_i : L < i \leq l$
   $start(A_i) = end(A_{i-\bullet});$ $T = start(A_i)$;
   $\Delta_i = duration(R_i);$ $m = 0$;
   For each message m :
      $receive\_time(m) \in [(start(A_i) + \Delta_i(\mu_r - \delta_r)), (start(A_i) + \Delta_i(\mu_r + \delta_r))]$
      $end(A_i) = receive\_time(m)$;
      $G_r = graph(R_i);$ $G_a = graph(A_i)$;
      For all $\Pi \in LOG$ If $(\mathcal{I}^\epsilon_\Pi(G_r, G_a) > m)$ $m = \mathcal{I}^\epsilon_\Pi(G_r, G_a)$;
      If $(s > m)$ then $T = end(A_i),$ $m = s$;
   $end(A_i) = T;$ $r_i = duration(A_i)/duration(R_i)$;
   if $(m > f_\mathcal{I})$ $LOG = LOG \bigcup \{$node map corresponding to $m\}$;
6. $\mathbb{P}^A = (A_{\bullet}, A_{\bullet}, \ldots)$;

Phase IV:
7. Π = The highest occurring node-map in LOG;
8. For all $R_i : 1 \leq i \leq l$
   $start(A_i) = end(A_{i-\bullet});$ $T = start(A_i)$;
   $\Delta_i = duration(R_i);$ $m = 0$;
   For each message m :
      $receive\_time(m) \in [(start(A_i) + \Delta_i(\mu_r - \delta_r)), (start(A_i) + \Delta_i(\mu_r + \delta_r))]$
      $end(A_i) = receive\_time(m)$;
      $G_r = graph(R_i);$ $G_a = graph(A_i)$;
      $s = \mathcal{I}^\epsilon_\Pi(G_r, G_a)$;
      If$(s > m)$ $T = end(A_i);$ $m = s$;
   $end(A_i) = T;$ $\mathbb{M} = (\mathbb{M}, m);$ /* Concatenation of m with $\mathbb{M}$ */
9. Return $\mathbb{M}$;

Fig. 2. The splicing algorithm

splice duration ratio. The node maps that give the maximum similarity measures above $f_\mathcal{I}$ for the splices are logged.

In phase IV, we first determine the highest occurring node map in the log and the whole of the application pattern is respliced based on that node-map, and the similarity measures for all the splice pairs are returned.

The parameter f_m in phase II defines a window in which the splice boundaries are placed. A wider window (larger f_m) implies more similarity measure computation, and a narrow window implies a very tight boundary which may exclude the best point to place the boundary. The variable L suggests the number of splices we take to estimate the mean stretch factor μ_r. Higher value of L gives a better estimate of stretch factor, but require more computation. The parameter $f_\mathcal{I}$, defines a threshold for the similarity measure. Node-maps corresponding to similarity measures above this threshold are logged, and are used in later phases of the algorithm. The parameter f_r defines a threshold for splice duration ration deviation. If δ_r is above the threshold then the patterns are considered to be different. A low value of f_r implies a strict cut-off value.

3.4   Similarity Measure for Communication Pattern

The splicing algorithm returns a series of ϵ-similarity measures for the given pair of communication patterns. If there are l splices, we get a series of l measures $\mathbb{M} = \{\mathcal{I}^\epsilon_1, \mathcal{I}^\epsilon_2, \ldots \mathcal{I}^\epsilon_l\}$. Let the mean value of the series $\mathbb{M}$ be μ^ϵ_m and deviation be δ^ϵ_m. Since $0 \leq \mathcal{I}^\epsilon_i \leq 1$, therefore $0 \leq \mu^\epsilon_m \leq 1$. If an application pattern is similar to a reference communication pattern, $\mu^\epsilon_m \to 1$ and $\delta^\epsilon_m \to 0$. We define similarity between two communication patterns as follows:

Definition 5. *Given a set of l ϵ-graph similarity measures between splices of the reference and the application communication patterns, let μ^ϵ_m and δ^ϵ_m be the mean and deviation of the graph similarity measure respectively. Then, we define an (ξ, ϵ)-communication pattern similarity measure, $\mathcal{C}_{\xi,\epsilon}$, between the communication patterns, as follows:*

$$\mathcal{C}_{\xi,\epsilon} = \mu^\epsilon_m \qquad if\ (\delta^\epsilon_m \leq \xi)$$
$$= 0.0 \qquad otherwise.$$

A smaller value of ξ implies a very tight sequence of similarity values in $\mathbb{M}$.

The communication pattern of the application running in the system is captured by the decision system. Since the computation of the similarity between two communication patterns is computationally expensive, the system can first determine, from the CR performance database, the reference patterns which have system and application characteristics within ϕ-factor close to those of the application (as defined in Definition 1). Then checkpoint and recovery characteristics are reported for those reference patterns where $\mathcal{C}_{\xi,\epsilon} \geq \psi$. In Section 4 we present some experimental results of splicing on different communication patterns.

4   Experimental Results

Test Suite: We consider fourteen different types of communication patterns for this part of the experiments. Three of the communication patterns are taken from three different scientific applications namely, Jacobi's algorithm for the solution of a set of simultaneous equations (J) [4], large matrix multiplication (M) [5], and Gram-Schmidt algorithm for vector normalization (GS) [3]. A set of three more communication patterns were generated from these three patterns, by randomly introducing 20% of the total number of messages present in them. We call these patterns as JJ, MM, and GSGS respectively. Three communication patterns, namely Tree2, Tree3, and Tree4 are generated on network of tree topologies with of out-degrees of 2,3, and 4 respectively. We consider a communication pattern of token ring (Ring), a communication pattern based on line graph (Line), and three randomly generated patterns namely RAND1,RAND2, and RAND3. These 14 types of patterns were generated for each of the two varieties, with 10 and 17 computation nodes. Therefore, there are a total of 28 communication patterns. These patterns are consider as reference communication patterns.

Configuration: The value of the parameter ϵ for the graph similarity measure is taken as 0.1. We take $f_d = \psi$. A similarity measure ψ implies a node-map where approximately ψ fraction of the total edge must match. So, in-degree/out-degree of a pair of nodes differing by more than ψ fraction implies a bad choice for node-map and such node pairs are excluded. Experimentally, we found $f_m = 0.5$ to be a conservative value, which results in reasonable runtime for the automatic identification algorithm. Since, we assume communication pattern are different if the mean similarity measure of the splices are less that ξ, $f_{\mathcal{I}}$ is set to the value of ξ. For our experiments, we found that no new node maps are added after after 20 iterations. So we choose $L = 20$. The factor f_r defines the threshold of the current deviation of splice ratio. If it crosses the threshold the communication patterns are considered different. The value is chosen as 0.5 and ξ is taken as 0.8.

Table 1. Communication pattern similarity measures with different applications

	J	M	GS	RAND1	Tree2	Line	Ring
J	**1.000000**	0.168806	0.133637	0.103700	0.283030	0.349200	0.278817
M	0.136302	**1.000000**	0.239273	0.000000	0.185106	0.119355	0.139130
GS	0.138721	0.343614	**0.488954**	0.000000	0.200745	0.108712	0.076051
RAND1	0.089770	0.104031	0.070969	**1.000000**	0.097608	0.087814	0.072520
Tree2	0.294210	0.186387	0.221988	0.000000	**1.000000**	0.472473	0.269599
Line	0.523768	0.177908	0.119128	0.000000	0.519761	**1.000000**	0.473040
Ring	0.382260	0.231233	0.090583	0.000000	0.196764	0.387908	**0.998479**

Results and Discussions: A communication pattern similarity measure of 1 implies that the communication pairs are similar. Table 1 shows similarity measures between a subset of the 14 reference patterns of 10 processes with the same set of patterns. When an application is compared with itself the similarity measure is 1.0 or very close to 1.0 and also the measure is low when compared with other patterns. The only exception is the GS pattern where the similarity measure is very low even when compared with itself. The average computation time to compare two patterns with ~ 8000 receive events is ~ 2 min.

The pattern GS has a star type communication topology. A star graph has $(n - 1)!$ automorphisms, which makes it difficult to discover the actual node map though graph similarity computation. If the correct node map is not found, the splice boundaries cannot be placed correctly, and therefore, splice duration estimation made at the initial phases of the pattern matching algorithm becomesswrong.

5   Conclusion

This paper presents a method for comparing two distributed applications. Several assumptions have been made in the process. We assume that the number of processes in both the communication patterns are same. If this assumption is removed, the graph similarity problem transforms to maximum subgraph similarity one, where we would like to find the largest subgraph in the bigger graph which closely matches with the smaller graph. However, if the number of nodes in the application pattern differs largely from that of the reference pattern, then we may consider the patterns to be dissimilar, because with the different number of nodes the performance of checkpoint and recovery protocol varies wildly.

Two communication patterns generated by the same application on two different systems may not be stretched uniformly, since processes may have different speed-up factors. In such a cases we can not make any reliable estimation of splice stretch factor, μ_r, which is used in the later phases of the splicing heuristic to reduce graph similarity computation. Rather, we have to use a thorough computation for the whole pattern.

References

1. E N Elnozahy, L Alvisi, Y M Wang, and D B Johnson. A survey of rollback-recovery protocols in message-passing systems. 34(3):375–408, September 2002.
2. S Fortin. The graph isomorphism problem. Technical Report 96-20, University of Alberta, CS dept., July 1996.
3. G H Golub and C F Van Loan. *Matrix Computations*. The John Hopkins University Press, 2 edition, 1989.
4. L Hageman and D Young. *Applied Iterative Methods*. Academic Press, New York, 1981.
5. F T Leighton. *Introduction to Parallel Algorithms and Architecture: Arrays, Trees, Hypercubes*. Morgan Kaufmann, San Mateo, California, 1992.
6. H S Paul, A Gupta, and R Badrinath. Performance comparison of checkpoint and recovery protocols. *Journal of Concurrency and Computation: Practice and Experience*, 15(15):1363–1386, December 2003.
7. J R Ullmann. An algorithm for subgraph isomorphism. *Journal of the ACM*, 23(3):31–42, July 1976.

Distributed Computation for Swapping a Failing Edge[*]

Linda Pagli[1], Giuseppe Prencipe[1], and Tranos Zuva[2]

. Dipartimento di Informatica, Università di Pisa, Italy
{pagli, prencipe}@di.unipi.it
. Department of Computer Science, University of Botswana, Gaborone
Zuvat@mopipi.ub.bw

Abstract. We consider the problem of computing the *best swap edges* of a shortest-path tree T_r rooted in r. That is, given a single link failure: if the path is not affected by the failed link, then the message will be delivered through that path; otherwise, we want to guarantee that, when the message reaches the edge (u, v) where the failure has occurred, the message will then be re-routed using the computed swap edge. There exist highly efficient serial solutions for the problem, but unfortunately because of the structures they use, there is no known (nor foreseeable) efficient distributed implementation for them. A distributed protocol exists only for finding swap edges, not necessarily optimal ones.

In [6], distributed solutions to compute the swap edge that minimizes the distance from u to r have been presented. In contrast, in this paper we focus on selecting, efficiently and distributively, the best swap edge according to an objective function suggested in [13]: we choose the swap edge that minimizes the distance from u to v.

Keywords: Fault-Tolerant Routing, Point of Failure Rerouting, Shortest Path Spanning Tree, Weighted Graphs, Distributed Algorithms, Data Complexity.

1 Introduction

Fault tolerance is a very important feature for distributed systems. When faults occur, programs may produce incorrect results or may stop before they have completed the intended computation. In many distributed systems the routing of messages is performed through a *shortest path* strategy. For this purpose, the shortest path trees (SPT's for short) starting from each node of the network, are computed in a preprocessing phase and stored in the so called *routing tables*. These tables specify, for each node in the network and for all possible destinations, the next hop that a message has to follow to reach its destination along the shortest path route; they contain also additional information such as the length of the path. The routing tables as a whole contain, in a distributed manner,

---

[*] This work has been supported in part by the University of Pisa and by "Progetto ALINWEB: Algoritmica per Internet e per il Web", MIUR Programmi di Ricerca Scientifica di Rilevante Interesse Nazionale.

A. Sen et al. (Eds.): IWDC 2004, LNCS 3326, pp. 28–39, 2004.
© Springer-Verlag Berlin Heidelberg 2004

the shortest path trees rooted at each node; they can be computed by several distributed known algorithms with different degree of complexity and cost (e.g., see [3, 4, 7, 9]), starting from the distributed representation of the network, where the only knowledge of a node consists in its neighbors and their distance from it.

In these systems, a single link failure is enough to interrupt the message transmission by disconnecting one or more SPT's. Assuming that there should be at least two different routes between two nodes in the network[1] – otherwise nothing can be done – several approaches are known to recover from such situation.

One approach consists in recomputing the new shortest path trees from scratch and rebuilding the routing tables accordingly; clearly, this approach is rather expensive and causes long delays in the messages transmission [10, 15]. Another approach uses dynamic graph algorithms (e.g., those of [5]) but the difficulties arising in finding an efficient distributed approach have not yet been successfully overcome (e.g., see [14]).

A different strategy is suggested in [11]: k independent (possibly) edge-disjoint spanning trees are computed for each destination; hence at each entry of the routing table k additional links, specifying the next hop in each spanning tree, are inserted. To compute edge-disjoint spanning trees there exist also distributed algorithms (e.g. [12]). However, even if this strategy is k-fault tolerant, it is quite expensive in term of space requirements; in addition it is not shortest path.

The last approach, which will be also ours, starts from the observation that sooner or later each link will fail and from the idea of selecting for each link failure, a single non-tree link (the *swap edge*) able to reconnect the network [8, 13]. This approach does not compute the new shortest path tree, but the selection of the swap edge is done according to some optimization criteria and allows, with a single global computation, to know in advance how to recover from any possible failure. In addition, in [16] experimental results show that the tree obtained from the swap edge is very close to the new SPT computed from scratch.

Consider in particular a message with destination the root r of the SPT, arriving to node u where the link to the next hop v (as specified by the routing table) has just failed. The SPT is now divided into two disconnected subtrees, one of root r, say T'_r, and one of root u, T'_u. The swap edge can be selected, among the possible ones reconnecting the tree, to minimize different functions. For instance, it can be the one minimizing the distance from u to r, or the distance from u to v, (called *one-to-one* problems in [13]) or the total or the average distances from each node in T'_u to r (called *one-to-many* problems) in the tree obtained by substituting the failed edge (u, v) with the chosen swap edge. In [13] efficient sequential algorithms solving different one-to-one and one-to-many problems are given. In [8] the complexity of the selection of the swap edge minimizing the average distance, called there *average stretch factor*, is improved. In [6] it has been shown how the computation of swap edges can be efficiently performed in a distributed way. The routing table stored at a node is then designed to contain the new information needed to bypass any failed link.

---

[*] That is, the underlying graph must be 2−connected.

However, the only problem considered in [6] is the one-to-one swap problem which minimizes the distance from u to r, called there *point-of-failure shortest-path rerouting* strategy. This corresponds to the situation in which, after a failure, the message in u must be delivered as soon as possible to the root of the SPT (or, viceversa, from r to u).

Different situations can suggest a different selection of the swap edge. In particular, as suggested in [13], in this paper we consider the following problem (BEST NEAR SWAP, shortly BNS):

> Select any swap edge such that the distance from u to v is minimized, with v the parent of u in the original SPT.

This problem is of type one-to-one: it can be useful when the node u, once the failure has been detected, needs to deliver the message as soon as possible to its parent v in the original SPT [13]. In this paper, given an SPT T_r, we propose an efficient distributed algorithm which determines, for the failure of each possible edge e, a swap edge *optimal* for the BNS problem.

The solution we propose uses as starting point the structure of one of the algorithms presented in [6]. In addition, as will be observed later, the time needed to compute all the swap edges of an SPT, is less than the time required by the distributed computation of the SPT itself.

The paper is organized as follows. In the next section we give some definitions, terminology and we recall the computing paradigm. In Section 3, we propose and analyze the specific solutions for the considered problem. The concluding remarks are in Section 4.

2   Basic Definitions and Previous Results

Let $G = (V, E)$ be an undirected graph, of $n = |V|$ vertices and $m = |E|$ edges. A *label* $l(x)$ of length $|l(x)| \leq \log n$ is associated to each vertex of G. A *subgraph* $G' = (V', E')$ of G is any graph where $V' \subseteq V$ and $E' \subseteq E$. If $V' \equiv V$, G' is a *spanning* subgraph. A *path* $P = (V_p, E_p)$ is a subgraph of G, such that $V_p = \{v_1, \ldots, v_s\} | v_i \neq v_j$, for $i \neq j$, and $(v_i, v_{i+1}) \in E_p$, for $1 \leq i \leq s - 1$. If $v_1 = v_s$ then P is a *cycle*. A graph G is *connected* if, for each pair $\{v_i, v_j\}$ of its vertices, there exists a path connecting them. A graph G is *biconnected* if, after the removal of anyone of its edges it remains connected. A *tree* is a connected graph with no cycles. A non negative real value called *weight* (or *length*) and denoted by $w(e)$ is associated to each edge e in G. Given a path P, the length of the path is the sum of the lengths of its edges. The *distance* $d_G(x, y)$ between two vertices x and y in a connected graph G, is the length of the shortest path from x to y in G – computed according to the weights of the edges in the path. In the following we will denote $d_G(x, y)$ by $d(x, y)$, when it is clear from the context to which graph is referred.

For a given vertex r, called *root*, the *shortest path tree* (*SPT*) of r is the spanning tree T_r rooted at r such that the path in T_r from r to any node v is the shortest possible one; i.e., $\forall v \in V$, $d_{T_r}(v, r) = d(v, r)$ is minimum.

After the removal of an edge $e = (u, v)$, T_r will be disconnected in two components T'_r and T'_u, rooted in r and u, respectively. Since G is biconnected, there will always be at least an edge $e' \in E(G) \setminus E(T_r)$ that will join the two disconnected components. An edge is called a *feasible swap edge* (or simply a *swap edge*) for a node x if after the failure of edge $e = (u, v) \in T_r$, it can be utilized to reconnect T'_u to the other disconnected component rooted at r, thus forming a new spanning tree T' of G. It is easy to see that an edge $(x, y) \in E \setminus E(T_r)$ is feasible for u *if and only if* only one of x and y is a descendant of u. In the following, we will denote by $S(x)$ the set of swap edges for x, and by $InS(x) \subseteq S(x)$ the set of edges incident in x that are also swap edges for x.

We will assume that a node x knows the weight of all its incident links, and can distinguish those that are part of the spanning tree T_r from those that are not; moreover, among the links that are part of T_r, x can distinguish the one that leads to its parent $p(x)$ from those leading to its children. We assume also that each node knows its distance from the root and the distance from the root of its adjacent nodes in G.

The considered system is *distributed* with communication topology G. Each process is located at a node of G, knows the weight of its incident edges, and can communicate with its neighboring processes. A node, an edge, a label, a weight, and a distance are all unit of data. The system is *asynchronous*, and all the processes execute the same protocol. In the following, the term node or vertex will be also used to indicate a process and the term edge or link to indicate a communication line.

Algorithm 1 Overall Structure of the Algorithm

[Preprocessing]

1. DFS for labelling the tree according to [2].

[Broadcast.]

1. Each child x of the root starts the broadcast by sending to its children a list containing its name and its distance from the root.
2. Each node y, append x to the received list and sends it to its children.

[Convergecast.]

1. Each leaf z first computes its best swap. It then computes the best feasible swap edge for each of its ancestors, and sends the list of those edges to its parent (if different from r).
2. An internal node y waits until it receives the list of best swap edges from each of its children. Based on the received information and on $InS(y)$, it computes its best swap edge. It also computes the best feasible swap edge for each of its ancestors, and sends the list of those edges to its parent (if different from r).

As already mentioned, we will utilize as general paradigm, one of the algorithms of [6] for the *point-of-failure shortest path problem*. The algorithm consists of two phases: *broadcast* and *convergecast*. With the first phase (up-down in the SPT T_r) each node x receives the list of its ancestors along with their distances

from the root. The phase is started by the children of the root because no swap
edge is computed for the root r. In the second phase (bottom-up) each node
computes the best swap edge for itself and the best swap edge, among the edges
examined so far, for each of its ancestors. The general structure of this algorithm
is shown in Algorithm 1.

From [6], it derives that the message complexity of the above algorithm is
$O(n)$, if long (that is $O(n)$ unit of data) messages are allowed. Otherwise, it
becomes $O(n_r^*)$, where n_r^* is the size of the transitive closure of $T_r \setminus \{r\}$ and
$0 \leq n_r^* \leq (n-1)(n-2)/2$. Clearly, swap edges must be selected in order to be
optimal with respect to the BNS problem; this will be the focus of next section.

3   The Algorithm

In the problem we consider, the *optimal* swap edge e' for $e = (u, v)$ is any
swap edge for e such that the distance from u to node v in the new tree $T' = T \setminus \{e\} \cup \{e'\}$ is minimized. More precisely, the optimal swap edge for $e = (u, v)$
is a swap edge $e' = (u', v')$ such that $d_{T'}(u, v) = d_{T_r}(u, u') + w(u', v') + d_{T_r}(v', v)$
is minimum.

As an example, consider the biconnected weighted graph G shown in Figure (1),
with the minimum SPT (marked by a thick line) rooted in A. Consider vertex D
after the failure of edge (D, B): the best swap edge for the BNS problem is (F, B).

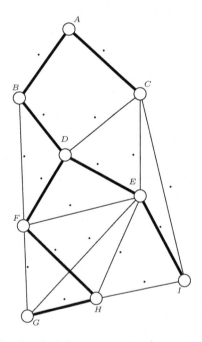

Fig. 1. An example: the thick line represents the starting SPT, rooted in A

Solving the BNS problem for a given T_r, means determining an optimal swap edge for each edge in T_r. We will design a distributed solution for the above problem, for which sequential solutions have been already studied [8, 13]. Starting from the overall structure described in Algorithm 1, we need to specify how the convergecast part is done. In particular, we will detail

(i) the computation of the best swap edge in the convergecast phase, and
(ii) the additional information, of constant size, to be communicated to the ancestors together to the swap edge.

All techniques described here are new and totally different from those adopted to design sequential solutions; furthermore, to our knowledge, this is the first distributed solution for the BNS problem.

Let us denote by $u_j, 1 \leq j \leq h$ the children of node u, and by $ANC(u)$ the set of ancestors of u in the original spanning tree T_r. Moreover, let $SL(u)$ be the list containing the set of pairs *(edge, distance)* of the feasible swap edges for u and their distance values, and $ASL(u)$ be the list of triples *(edge, distance, node)* indicating for each node $a_k \in ANC(u)$ the best feasible swap edge for a_k and the distance between a_k and $p(a_k)$ via the specified swap edge.

The details of the operations executed by node u are reported in Algorithm 2 (to compute its best swap edge) and Algorithm 3 (to compute its ancestors' swap edges). In particular, node u computes its best swap edge by considering all its feasible swap edges; that is, $InS(u)$ and the swap edges transmitted to it from its children. Then it computes, among the ones in T'_u, the best feasible swap edge for each one of its ancestors. Note that, the swap edges it computes for its ancestors can be worse than the final swap edges computed by its ancestors when *they* execute Algorithm 2.

Algorithm 2 Compute My Best Swap Edge

The protocol is described with respect to node u, with (u, v) the edge that fails.

1. Determine which of u's incident edges are feasible for u; i.e., u constructs the set $InS(u)$.
2. For each swap edge $s_i = (u, y_i) \in InS(u)$, compute the value of the distance $d_{i_{T'}}$ between u and v in T' via s_i, and insert it in $SL(u)$ the pair $(s_i, d_{i_{T'}})$.
3. If u is not a leaf, from each $ASL(u_j)$ received from child u_j, extract (s_i, d_i, u) (or NIL), and insert (s_i, d_i) in $SL(u)$ (or NIL, if no such pair exists).
4. Sort $SL(u)$ in non decreasing order of d_i. The minimal element of $SL(u)$ gives one of the best swap edges for u and the value of the minimal distance.

In the next section, we will introduce some properties that will be needed in order to show how node u can locally efficiently compute the operations in Algorithms 2 and 3.

3.1   Basic Properties

The first thing a node has to be able to do locally is to check the *feasibility* of an edge, i.e. if an edge can be considered a swap edge: this operation can be

---

Algorithm 3 Compute My Ancestors' Best Swap Edge

The protocol is described with respect to node u.

For each ancestor node $a_k \in ANC(u)$:

1. Consider the swap edge $s_i \in SL(u)$ feasible for a_k, with the minimal value of d_i, if any. If such an edge exists, compute the new value of the distance d_i for a_k, otherwise set it to NIL.
2. For all $1 \leq j \leq h$, let $\{(s_j, d_j, a_k)\}$ be the set of triples from $ASL(u_j)$, and consider the set $\{(s_j, d_j, a_k) \cup (s_i, d_i, a_k)\}$, $1 \leq j \leq h$, where (s_i, d_i, a_k) is the triple computed in Step 1. Select from this set the triple $(\overline{s}, \overline{d}, a_k)$ such that the distance $\overline{d}$ between a_k and $p(a_k)$ is minimal, if any, and insert it, in $ASL(u)$ (to be sent to u's parent); if no triple can be selected, insert NIL in $ASL(u)$.

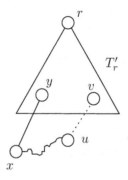

Fig. 2. Property 1

easily done during the convergecast phase, through the information collected in the broadcast phase. We state the following

Property 1. *A swap edge $(x, y) \in E \setminus E(T_r)$ with $x \in T'_u$ and $y \in T'_r$ is feasible for node u if y does not belong to the path connecting x to u.*

Property 1, derives immediately from the fact that an edge (x, y) is feasible for u *if and only if* only one of its endpoints is a descendant of u (refer to Figure 2). Furthermore, we have

Property 2. *Feasibility of swap edge $(x, y) \in E \setminus E(T_r)$ with $x \in T'_u$ and $y \in T'_r$ for node u can be checked at node x, and no communication is needed.*

Property 2, immediately derives from the fact that node x is descendant of u and neighbor of y in $\in E \setminus E(T_r)$, and that after the broadcast phase x has locally the list of all nodes between the root and itself, hence it knows which nodes are its ancestors. Therefore, the feasibility test of Step 1 in both Algorithm 2 and 3 can be locally performed. Note that, even if the global complexity does not change, this feasibility test is simpler than that used in [6], which required additional labeling of the tree nodes, with two labels to be transmitted in the two phases.

We also observe that if an edge is not feasible for x, it is not feasible for none of its ancestors.

In order to solve BNS problem, we need to compute in the convergecast phase the *nearest common ancestor* of pairs of nodes $x, y \in T_r$ (called $nca(x, y)$). Recall that the $nca(x, y)$ is the common ancestor of x and y, whose distance to x and y is smaller than the distance of any other common ancestor of x and y. In a recent work [2], it has been shown that this information can be locally computed in constant time, through a proper labeling of the tree that requires labels of $O(\log n)$ bits, denoted in the following as $l(x)$, that can be p recomputed by a depth first traversal of the tree. Therefore, Algorithm 1, needs to be slightly modified to transmit, for each node x, $l(x)$ instead of its name x. When such a labeling is computed for T_r, each node can be distinguished by its label. Therefore, we can state that

Property 3. *Let $(x, y) \in E \setminus E(T_r)$, with $x \in T'_u$, and $y \in T'_r$ be a swap edge for u after the failure of edge (u, v). Then, $nca(y, v)$ can be computed at x, and no communication is needed.*

Property 3 follows from the results shown in [2], and noting that $l(v) \in ANC(u)$, hence $l(v) \in ANC(x)$, and that $l(y)$ is accessible at x since x is directly connected to y.

3.2   Correctness

In the BNS problem, the *optimal swap edge* for the failure of the edge $e = (u, v)$ is an edge which minimizes the distance $d'_T(u, v)$ from u to v in the new spanning tree T' obtained after the removal of the failed edge. In this section, we show that the computation of the best swap edge can be accomplished by each node, in the convergecast phase, without requesting additional information to any other node in the SPT, which is not a neighbor; that is without additional message complexity, obtaining the same complexity of Algorithm 1.

First of all we have to define how the distance $d_{T'}(u, v)$ along a given swap edge $e = (u, y) \in InS(u)$ is computed (Step 2 of Algorithm 2). The possible cases that we can have are:

- v and y lay on the same path from the root to a leaf, hence one node is ancestor of the other one (Figure 3.a, and nodes B an F in Figure 1), or
- v and y have a nearest common ancestor (Figure 3.b), such as nodes H and I in Figure 1, having D as nca.

The following lemma states how correctly compute this distance.

Lemma 1. *Let $(u, y) \in InS(u)$. We have:*

(i) $d_{T'}(u, v) = w(u, y) + |d_T(v, r) - d_T(y, r)|$, if $nca(y, v) = v$ or $nca(y, v) = y$.
(ii) $d_{T'}(u, v) = w(u, y) + d_T(v, r) - d_T(z, r) + d_T(y, r) - d_T(z, r)$, if $nca(y, v) = z$.

Proof. First note that $d_{T'}(u, v) = w(u, y) + d_T(y, v)$. We distinguish the two possible cases.

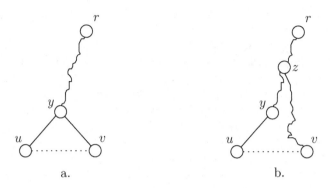

Fig. 3. (a) Case (i) of Lemma 1.(b) Case (ii) of Lemma 1

(i) y and v lay on the same path from the root to a leaf; hence, $d_{T'}(y, v)$ can be computed as the difference of their distances from the root.
(ii) In this case y and v lay on different paths which intersect in z. Their distance is easily computed by their distances from the root and from the distance of z from the root, possibly equal to 0.

Note that, each node knows its distance from r and the distance from r of each of its neighbors in G (this information can be obtained during the broadcast phase); hence, $d_{T'}(u, v)$ in the above lemma can be locally computed at u.

In the convergecast phase of Algorithm 1, a node (either a leaf or an internal node) has to be able to locally compute the best feasible swap for an ancestor. The following lemma states how distance in Step 1 of Algorithm 3 can be computed (refer to Figure 4.a and 4.b).

Lemma 2. *Consider a subset $a_1, \ldots, a_l$ of the ancestors of u, with $p(u) = a_1$, and a_k adjacent to a_{k+1}, $1 \le k < l$. Furthermore, let (x, y) be a feasible swap edge for (u, a_1) and for (a_k, a_{k+1}), $1 \le k < l$. Consider the two trees $T' = ((T_r \setminus (u, a_1) \cup (x, y))$ and $T'' = ((T_r \setminus (a_k, a_{k+1}) \cup (x, y))$; then, $d_{T''}(a_k, a_{k+1}) = d_{T'}(u, a_1) + w(u, a_1) - w(a_k, a_{k+1})$.*

Proof. Since (x, y) is feasible for a_k, by Property 1 it follows that y is not descendant of a_k, and that $nca(y, a_1) = nca(y, a_k)$. Thus, in T', the path p' from u to a_1 along the swap edge (x, y) includes $a_k, \ldots, a_2$ (see Figure 4.a). Moreover, the path p'' from a_k to a_{k+1} in T'' results to be the same as p', except for edge (u, a_1), that is substituted with (a_k, a_{k+1}) (Figure 4.b), and the lemma follows.

Also in this case, similarly to Lemma 1, the computation of $d_{T''}$ can be performed locally at u, because of the information retrieved during the broadcast phase of Algorithm 1. Finally, we can state that problem BNS is correctly solved by Algorithm 2 and 3.

Theorem 1. *Each node $u \ne r$:*

(i) *correctly computes its best swap edge;*

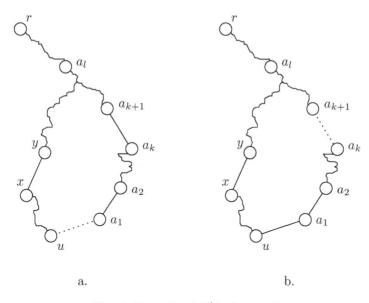

a.   b.

Fig. 4. Trees T and T' in Lemma 2

(ii) *correctly determines for each ancestor $a_k \neq r$ the best swap edge feasible for a_k in T'_u.*

Proof. First observe that, as result of the broadcast, every node receives the label of its ancestors (except r) and it can compute the feasibility of each available swap edge for itself and its ancestors (Property 1 and 2). The proof is by induction on the height $h(u)$ of the subtree T_u.

Basis. $h(u) = 0$; i.e., u is a leaf. In this case, one component contains only u, while the other contains all the other nodes. In other words, the only possible swap edges are incident on u. Thus, u can correctly compute its best swap edge computing the value of the distance as stated in Lemma 1, proving (i). It can also immediately determine the feasibility of any of those edges with respect to all its ancestors and, in case they are feasible, compute for them the value of the distance as stated in Lemma 2 and select, for each ancestor, the best feasible one.

Induction Step. Let the theorem hold for all nodes x with $k - 1 \geq h(x) \geq 0$; we will now show that it holds for u with $h(u) = k$. By inductive hypothesis, it receives from each child y the best feasible swap edge for each ancestor of y, including u itself. Hence, based on these lists and on the locally available set $InS(u)$, u can correctly determine its optimal swap edge, as well as its best feasible swap edge for each of its ancestors.

We can pose the following:

Theorem 2. *Problem BNS can be solved with the $O(n)$ message complexity and $O(n_r^*)$ data complexity.*

Proof. The theorem follows immediately from Properties 2 and 3, the computation of the *nca*, from Lemma 2, and from the fact that all the needed computation to determine the best swap edge of a node and of its ancestors can be done locally, thus not changing the complexity of Algorithm 1.

Example. Consider in the example of Figure 1, the computation of node D. Assume that nodes F and E have already correctly computed the lists $ASL(F) = \{((F, B), 4, D), NIL\}$ and $ASL(E) = \{((E, C), 5, D), ((E, C), 5, B)\}$ and sent them to their parent D. D has only one feasible swap edge (D, C), for which $d_{T'}(D, B) = 5$, then it receives $(F, B), 4$ from F and $(E, C), 5$ from E. Therefore (F, B) is the best swap edge for D. Now D selects the best feasible swap for its parent B, by considering the best one among its swap edges feasible for B, that is (D, C) and considering the edges coming from its children, in this case only (E, C) from E. The value $d_{T'}(B, A)$ via (E, C) is already known, while D has to compute $d_{T'}(B, A)$ via (D, C), which is equal to 5. $\{((D, C), 5, B)\}$ is then transmitted to B.

4   Concluding Remarks

In this paper we have presented an efficient distributed algorithm to solve the BNS problem: given a shortest path tree T_r rooted in r, we want to select the swap edge e' for any edge (u, v) in T_r so that the distance between u and v is minimized in $T_r \setminus \{(u, v)\} \cup \{e'\}$. To make the routing table 1-fault tolerant, the computation of the swap edges must be repeated for all possible shortest path trees; that is, for all nodes of the graph.

We note that the proposed algorithm allows for the efficient construction of a rerouting service. To do so, the proposed computation must be carried out for the n shortest path trees, each having as root a different vertex of the graph G. In this regards, an interesting open problem is whether it is possible to achieve the same goal in a more efficient way than by performing n independent computations.

An immediate possible development of this study, would be to study how to recover from multiple link failures, following the same strategy of storing in the routing tables the information useful for finding alternative paths. Other possible studies involve the analysis of the *one-to-many* problems presented in Section 1, such as choosing the swap edge so to minimize the sum of the distances from each node in T_u' to r.

References

1. Y. Afek, M. Ricklin. Sparser: a paradigm for running distributed algorithms. *Journal of Algorithms*, 14:316-328, 1993.
2. S. Alstrup, C. Gavoille, H. Kaplan, T. Rauhe. Nearest Common Ancestor: A survey and a new distributed algorithms. *14th Annual ACM Symposium on Parallel Algorithms and Architecture (SPAA)*, 258-264, 2002.

3. B. Awerbuch, R. Gallager. A new distributed algorithm to find breadth first search trees. *IEEE Transactions on Information Theory, 33 (315–322) 1987.*
4. K. M. Chandy, J. Misra. Distributed computation on graphs: shortest path algorithms. *Communication of ACM, 25 (833–837) 1982.*
5. D. Eppstein, Z. Galil, G.F. Italiano. Dynamic graph algorithms. *CRC Handbook of Algorithms and Theory, CRC Press, 1997.*
6. P. Flocchini, A. Mesa Enriquez, L. Pagli, G. Prencipe, N. Santoro. Efficient protocols for computing the optimal swap edges of a shortest path tree. *Proc. of 3-th IFIP International Conference on Theoretical Computer Science* (TCS@2004), 153–166, 2004.
7. G. N. Frederikson. A distributed shortest path algorithm for planar networks. *Computer and Operations Research, 17 (153–151) 1990.*
8. A. Di Salvo, G. Proietti. Swapping a failing edge of a shortest paths tree by minimizing the average stretch factor. *Proc. of 10th Colloquium on Structural Information and Communication Complexity* (SIROCCO 2004), 99–104, 2004.
9. P. Humblet. Another adaptive distributed shortest path algorithm. *IEEE/ACM Transactions on Communications*, 39(6):995–1003, 1991.
10. H. Ito, K. Iwama, Y. Okabe, T. Yoshihiro. Polynomial-time computable backup tables for shortest-path routing. *Proc. of 10th Colloquium on Structural Information and Communication Complexity* (SIROCCO 2003), 163–177, 2003.
11. A. Itai, M. Rodeh. The multi-tree approach to reliability in distributed networks. *Information and Computation*, 79:43-59, 1988.
12. H. Mohanti, G. P. Batthacharjee. A distributed algorithm for edge-disjoint path problem. *Proc. of 6th Conference on Foundation of Software Technology and theoretical Computer Science*, (FSTTCS), 344-361, 1986.
13. E. Nardelli, G. Proietti, P. Widmayer. Swapping a failing edge of a single source shortest paths tree is good and fast. *Algoritmica*, 35:56–74, 2003.
14. P. Narvaez, K.Y. Siu, H.Y. Teng. New dynamic algorithms for shortest path tree computation. *IEEE Transactions on Networking*, 8:735–746, 2000.
15. L. L. Peterson, B. S. Davie. *Computer Networks: A Systems Approach, 3rd Edition.* Morgan Kaufmann, 2003.
16. G. Proietti. Dynamic maintenance versus swapping: An experimental study on shortest paths trees. *Proc. 3-rd Workshop on Algorithm Engineering (WAE 2000).* Lecture Notes in Computer Science, Springer, (1982) 207–217, 2000.

Flexible Cycle Synchronized Algorithm in Parallel and Distributed Simulation

Xuehui Wang[1], Lei Zhang[2], and Kedi Huang[1]

· School of Mechatronics Engineering and Automation,
· School of Computer,
National University of Defense Technology, Changsha 410073, China
yzmailbox2003@163.com

Abstract. Large complex system simulation in various fields of science and engineering requires tremendous computational resources; however sequential execution algorithms badly limited its performance. So recently there has been a great deal of interest in parallel and distributed simulation, which runs on multiple processors to accelerate simulation. This paper begins with introduction of synchronization mechanisms. The emphasis of this paper is to provide and describe the implementation of the flexible cycle algorithm. This improved algorithm solves some fatal problems of conservative or optimistic algorithms, resulting in the best of both methods. Finally we also analyze how to compute the performance parameter M of this algorithm in detail.

1 Introduction

There is an increasing interest in the application of parallel and distributed simulation (PDS) to the study of large-scale complex dynamic systems. One of the fundamental is that cut down the computational time, and on geographically distributed computers interconnected via a local area and/or wide area network is the exploitation of inherent parallelism.[1] In this paper we first give an overview of two main approaches synchronization mechanisms in PDS execution. Then we emphatically expatiate on the implementation of flexible cycle algorithm, which is an improved synchronization algorithm. In the end, we provide how to analyze the efficiency parameter M of this algorithm at length.

2 Synchronization Mechanisms

The goal of the synchronization mechanism is to make all LP processed events accord with the local causality constraint (LCC) or else doubtless results in *causality violations*. A parallel simulation consists of a number of *Logical Processes* (LP) that communicate by exchanging time-stamp messages or events, typically each one running on a separate processor. The simulation progress is ensured by the processor scheduling new events to be executed in the future,

A. Sen et al. (Eds.): IWDC 2004, LNCS 3326, pp. 40–45, 2004.
© Springer-Verlag Berlin Heidelberg 2004

and executing these events in the time-stamp order. A process can schedule an event for itself, locally thus (self-initiation), or remotely, for another process. In the latter case, a message is sent via the network to the remote process. Each process maintains a separate time clock, called the *Local Virtual Time* [2].

Synchronization algorithms can be classified as being either conservative or optimistic. In brief, conservative algorithms take precautions to avoid the possibility of processing events out of time stamp order, i.e., the execution mechanism avoids synchronization errors. For another, optimistic algorithms use a detection and recovery approach. Events are allowed to be processed out of time stamp order, however, a rollback mechanism is provided to recover from such errors. [3]

3   The Flexible Cycle Algorithm

3.1   The Event Horizon

The event horizon is a concept that can first be understood without referring to parallel processing.

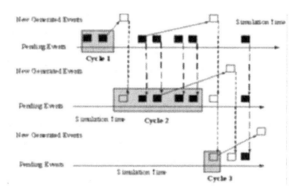

Fig. 1. Figure 1 illustrates the relationship of event horizon and event queue. Here, three event horizon cycles are shown. Each cycle processes its pending events while collecting newly generated events in an auxiliary event queue. When the next event to be processed is in the auxiliary event queue, the auxiliary event queue is sorted, merged into the primary event queue, and then the next cycle begins. Cycle 3 shows that even when an event schedules a new event for the same time as itself, the event horizon algorithm always processes at least one event. Thus, there is no way for a deadlock situation to occur when processing events in cycles defined by the event horizon [4]

Imagine first that all pending events are mapped into a single event queue. As each event is processed, it may generate zero or more new events with arbitrary time stamps. To maintain complete generality, it is assumed that the simulation engine has no way to predict what each event will do until it is processed. All newly generated events are maintained in a special auxiliary event queue. At some point in time, the next event to be processed will be in the auxiliary event queue. This point in time is called the event horizon. [5]

One of the key features of the event horizon is that, by definition, events in a given cycle are not disturbed by other events generated in the same cycle. If the events were distributed to multiple processors and if the event horizon was known before hand, it would be possible to process events in parallel without ever receiving a straggler message. The event horizon is not determined, however, until the events in the current cycle are actually processed.[6]

Optimistic event processing is used to determine the global event horizon. However, messages are released only after the true event horizon is determined. This means that messages are sent without risk. At the end of each cycle, garbage collection is performed to clean up the state-saving information required in case of rollback. It should be noted that we uses incremental state-saving techniques implemented in software for efficient support of rollback.

3.2   Implementation of the Flexible Cycle Algorithm

The flexible cycle algorithm (FCA) resolved this dilemma by merging optimistic processing with risk-free message sending. Each node determines its local event horizon using its own set of pending events and generated messages. This value is called T_{min}. When the node's next event has a time value greater than T_{min}, the node defines its local event horizon to be T_{min}. The true global event horizon is the minimum of each node's local event horizon. Once the global event horizon is determined, the FCA safely releases all messages generated by events with time stamps less than or equal to that value.[7]

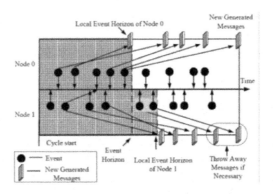

Fig. 2. The basic algorithm is shown in Figure 2. Each node starts the cycle using the same global time value (GTV). Events are then processed optimistically without releasing any of their generated messages. As shown for Node 0, it is still possible for events to be rolled back by stragglers. When this occurs, state information is restored and unsent messages are thrown away. Anti-messages are never necessary because messages are only released when events are committed

3.3   Local Rollback

Once a node crosses its local event horizon, it then broadcasts its local event horizon time to the other nodes. This may cause other nodes to realize that they have also crossed the event horizon. If another node later determines that its local event horizon has an earlier time value, then it will broadcast its local event horizon to the other nodes.[5]

Once all of the nodes have crossed the event horizon, they simultaneously break out of their optimistic event processing and begin to safely release all unsent messages generated by events with time tags less than or equal to the event horizon. This step is where events are committed. A coordinated message-sending algorithm ensures that each node receives all of its incoming messages before beginning the next cycle. Rollbacks may occur as straggler messages arrive, but their effect on rollbacks is limited locally. Events that are rolled back simply restore their state and then discard their unsent messages. In other words, rollbacks only happen in the local node without impacting others. They partly roll back so that it is possible for simulations to avoid excessive numbers of rollbacks, which could produce an explosion of cascading anti-messages. Thus, the "thrashing" phenomenon can drastically be eliminated.

4   Analyze Performance of Algorithm

4.1   Modeling

For this analysis, assume that each event generates a single new event as it is processed (i.e., the hold model).[8] The time-tag of the generated event is described by a random distribution function $f(t)$. With this model, the total number of events n in the simulation is constant. For the sake of without loss of generality, we assume that each event generates two new events when processed; the goal is to determine the average number of events M processed in a cycle. We define the variables and expressions as below:

N: the number of available nodes;
t: the simulation time, $t = 0$ is the start of the cycle.
n: the total number of events at the start of cycle.
M: Average number of events processed in a cycle.
$\rho(t)$: Density of pending events, $\rho(0) = P$.
$P(t)$: Probability of the next cycle boundary exceeding time point$t$.
$f(t)$: Random distribution for event generation.
$h(t)$: Average time interval between events, $h(t) = 1/\rho(t)$.
$F(t)$: Cumulative probability distribution of $f(t)$.
$G(t) = 1 - F(t)$: the probability that the event has a time-tag greater than t

4.2   Reason

Now that the event density has been found, the next step is to determine the probability $P(t)$ that an event with time stamp t is processed in the current cycle. Consider the first event. It is always safe to process the first event. Thus

$P(t_0) = 1$ the next event occurs at time $t_1 = t_0 + h(t_0)$. The probability of this event being processed in the current cycle is just the probability that the first event scheduled its new event with a time-tag greater than t_1. Since $F(t)$ is the probability of the event being generated with a time-tag less than or equal to t (relative to the generating event's time tag), $G(t) = 1 - F(t)$ is the probability that the event has a time-tag greater than t. This means that $P(t_1) = G(t_1 - t_0)$. In general, an event at time t will be in the current cycle if all the previous events in the cycle generate their events with time tags greater than or equal to t.

The probability for the $n'th$ event being processed in the current cycle can be constructed in a general way. Defining $t_{n+1} = t_n + h(t_n)$ as the time-tag of the $(n + 1)'th$ event from the start of the cycle (note that the $0'th$ event is actually the first event of the cycle), the probability of this event being in the current cycle is the product of all the probabilities of the previous events generating their events with time tags greater than t_{n+1}. This is described mathematically as

$$P(t_{n+1}) = P(t_n)G(t_{n+1}) \tag{1}$$

A more general form for (1) is

$$P(t + h(t)) = P(t)G(1 + h(t)) \tag{2}$$

Using

$$P(t + h(t)) \approx P(t) + h(t)P'(t) = P(t) + P'(t)/\rho(t) \tag{3}$$

and

$$P(t)G(1 + h(t)) \approx P(t)(G(t) + G'(t)h(t)) \tag{4}$$

$$P(t)(G(t) + G'(t)h(t)) = P(t)G(t) + P(t)G'(t)/\rho(t) \tag{5}$$

The equation (2) may now be transformed into

$$P(t) + P'(t)/\rho(t) = P(t)G(t) + P(t)G'(t)/\rho(t) \tag{6}$$

Using the fact that $G(t) = 1 - F(t)$ and $G'(t) = -f(t)$, the (2) equation may be simplified to the form

$$P(t) = -\int_0^t P(t)[\rho(t)F(t) + f(t)] \tag{7}$$

The solution to the (3) equation is

$$P(t) = e^{-F(t) - \int_0^t \rho(\tau)F(\tau)d\tau} \tag{8}$$

The average number of events processed in a cycle M can be computed as the sum of the probabilities of each individual event being in the current event cycle. So we can get the M

$$M = \sum_{i=0}^{n-1} P(t_i) = \int_0^\infty P(t)\rho(t)dt \tag{9}$$

Because P(t) is the probability of the next cycle boundary exceeding time point t, so $0 \leq P(t) \leq 1$, the simplified the (5) equation becomes

$$M = \int_0^\infty P(t)\rho(t)dt \leq \int_0^\infty P(t)dt \tag{10}$$

Finally, using that $f(t) = e^{-t}$, then a very good approximation to M can computed

$$M \approx \sqrt{2\pi n}(1 + 1/2n)(1/2 - 1/\sqrt{2\pi n}) \tag{11}$$

When $n > 10$ the error introduced by approximating in the above expression is much less than 1 percent, this expression simply reduces to

$$M \approx \sqrt{\frac{(n+1)\pi}{2}} - 1 \tag{12}$$

5   Conclusion

Over the past years, techniques for parallel simulation have been developed greatly within the academic research community. What's more, the advent of cluster computing and desktop multiprocessors have made it feasible to bring these results to bear on the simulation of large, complex engineering systems. The synchronization is one of most key problems, which ensure that the execution of the parallel simulation is proper. In this paper we emphatically expatiate on the implementation of flexible cycle algorithm, which is an improved synchronization algorithm. In the end, we provide how to analyze the efficiency parameter M of this algorithm at length.

References

1. Jenny Ulriksson, *et al.*, A Web-based Environment for building Distributed Simulations, 02S-SIW-036, *Euro Simulation Interoperability Workshop*, 2002
2. Kamil Iskra, Parallel Discrete Event Simulation Issues with Wide Area Distribution, *ASCI course a9*, March 7, 2003.
3. Jenny Ulriksson, *et al.*, A Web-based Environment for building Distributed Simulations, 02S-SIW-036, *Euro Simulation Interoperability Workshop*, 2002
4. Jeff S, Steinman, DISCRETE-EVENT SIMULATION AND THE EVENT HORIZON
5. Metron, Inc., SPEEDES User's Guide, http://www.speedes.com
6. Steinman, J. *Breathing Time Warp*, in *Proc. of the 7th Workshop on Parallel and Distributed Simulation*. 1993.San Diego. p. 109–118.
7. C.D. Carothers, and R.M. Fujimoto, Efficient Execution of Time Warp Programs on Heterogeneous, NOWPlatforms, *IEEE Transactions on Parallel and Distributed Systems*, vol. 11, no. 3, pp. 299–317, March 2000.
8. Chou C., Bruell S., Jones D.1993. "A Generalized Hold Model." *In Proceedings of the 1993 SCS Winter simulation Conference*. Pages 756-761.

Rule Mining for Dynamic Databases

A. Das and D. K. Bhattacharyya

Department of Information Technology,
Tezpur University, Napaam 784 028, India
dkb@tezu.ernet.in, anjan_sh@rediffmail.com

Abstract. *Association* rules identify associations among data items and were introduced in [1]. A detailed discussion on association rules can be found in [2], [8]. One important step in Association rule mining is to find *frequent* itemsets. Most of the algorithms to find frequent itemsets deal with the static databases. There are very few algorithms that deal with dynamic(incremental) databases. The most classical algorithm to find frequent itemsets in dynamic database is *Borders* algorithm [7]. But the *Borders* algorithm is suitable for centralized databases. This paper presents a modified version of the *Borders* algorithm, called *Distributed Borders*, which is suitable for *Distributed Dynamic* databases.

Keywords: Rule mining, itemsets, candidate sets, frequent items, support, confidence, border, promoted border.

1   Introduction

Association Rule mining is one of the most vital areas of research in data mining and was introduced by Agarwal et. al. in [1] The terms most frequently used in relation to association rules are *itemset, support, confidence, frequent itemsets* and *large itemsets*. For explanation of the terms, readers may refer to [2], [8]. The first and most important step of the association rule generation is to find the frequent(large) itemsets. *Apriori* [2] is the most classic algorithm to find frequent itemsets and association rule. Some other important algorithms to find frequent itemsets are *FP-Tree,DIC, Pincer-Search* etc. [8]

There are some algorithms like *FUP* [4], *FUP2* [3],*MAAP* [9] to find frequent itemsets in dynamic databases. One recent algorithm for dynamic database can be found in [6]. Above all, there is one popular and important algorithm for dynamic(incremental) database called *Borders* algorithm [7]. This paper presents a modified version of *Borders* algorithm, called *Distributed Borders*, to find frequent itemsets in *Dynamic Distributed* databases.

2   Distributed Borders Algorithm

Feldman *et. al.* [7] proposed *Borders* algorithm to find frequent itemsets for dynamic databases. The algorithm based on the concept of *border* set and *promoted border* sets. The algorithm is robust enough but cannot be used directly

A. Sen et al. (Eds.): IWDC 2004, LNCS 3326, pp. 46–51, 2004.
© Springer-Verlag Berlin Heidelberg 2004

Table 1. Symbols Used in Distributed Borders

Symbol		Definition	Symbol		Definition
S_i	=	The site i	T_{old}^i	=	Old database at the site i
T_{new}^i	=	Incremental database at site i	T_{new}	=	$\bigcup T_{new}^i$
			α	=	Minimum support in %
T_{old}	=	$\bigcup T_{old}^i$	T_{whole}^i	=	$T_{old}^i \cup T_{new}^i$
T_{whole}	=	$\bigcup T_{whole}^i (T_{old} \cup T_{new})$	L_{old}	=	Frequent itemsets in T_{old} with the local support
B_{old}	=	Border itemsets in T_{old} with the local support	L_{whole}	=	Frequent itemsets in T_{whole}
B_{whole}	=	Border itemsets in T_{whole}	F^i	=	Frequent itemsets at the site i
B^i	=	Promoted border itemsets at the site i	F	=	$\bigcup F^i$
B	=	$\bigcup B^i$ (Global promoted border)	$S(X)$	=	Support of X
			$S(X)_Y$	=	Support of X in the database Y
$X.sup.new^i$	=	Support of X at T_{new}^i	$X.sup.new$	=	Support of X at T_{new}
$X.sup^i$	=	Support of the itemset X at the site i	$X.sup$	=	Global support of X
$S(X)_Y^i$	=	Support of X at the site i for the database Y	$|D|$	=	Number of records in the database D

in distributed environment. So we present the *Distributed Borders* algorithm, to be used for distributed dynamic databases. Here, we assume that databases of similar structure are distributed in different sites which are networked. This algorithm also can be used to a centralized database by partitioning the database and placing the partitions in different nodes of a distributed system.

2.1 Distributed Algorithm for Maintaining Frequent Itemsets in Dynamic Database

Here, we have examined the *Borders* algorithm in the distributed environment, where old data are distributed in n sites and new(incremental) data are added to all the sites. Please refer to Table 1 for the details of the symbols used to describe the algorithm. For a given minimum support threshold α, an itemset X is globally large in the old database(updated database) if $X.sup \geq \alpha|T_{old}|(X.sup \geq \alpha|T_{whole}|)$. Similarly an itemset X is locally large in the old database(updated database) at some site i, if $X.sup^i \geq \alpha|T_{old}^i|(X.sup^i \geq \alpha|T_{whole}^i|)$. Like the *Borders* algorithm, this algorithm also uses the concept of *border* set and *promoted border* set. The only difference is that all the concepts have been used in the context of the distributed environment. An itemset X is a *global border* , if X is not globally large but all its subsets are globally large. An itemset X becomes *global promoted border* on adding the new transactions, if X is a global border in the old database and globally large in the updated database. Given L_{old} and B_{old}, the problem is to find the updated large itemsets L_{whole} and border sets B_{whole} for the updated database T_{whole}. The algorithm is presented in Fig.1.

2.2 Generation of Candidate Sets

The main purpose of the *Distributed Borders* algorithm is to reduce the number of candidate sets and in turn reduce the number of messages to be passed across the network and execution time. To reduce number of messages, we used the polling technique as used in *DMA* [5]. In addition to that, some interesting

Input: L_{old} ,B_{old}, T^i_{new}, T^i_{old} and α;
Output: Updated L_{whole} and B_{whole};
Repeat the following steps at each site i distributively.

1. Scan T^i_{new} and count the support of all the itemsets $X \in \{L_{old} \cup B_{old}\}$ and find
   (a) $F^i = \{X | X \in L_{old}$ and $S(X)^i_{Twhole} \geq \alpha|T^i_{whole}|\}$(by observation 1)
   (b) $B^i = \{X | X \in B_{old}$ and $S(X)^i_{Tnew} \geq \alpha|T^i_{new}|\}$(by observation 5)
2. Broadcast the local support of all $X \in \{F^i \cup B^i\}$ to other sites and receive the support for $X \in \{F^i \cup B^i\}$ from other sites and find the global support for all $X \in \{F^i \cup B^i\}$.
3. Prune F^i and B^i
   $F^i = \{X \in F^i$ and $S(X)_{Twhole} \geq \alpha|T_{whole}|\}$
   $B^i = \{X | X \in B^i$ and $S(X) \geq \alpha|T_{whole}|\}$
4. Broadcast $\{F^i \cup B^i\}$ to other sites and receive from other sites; Compute $F = \bigcup F_i$ and $B = \bigcup B_i$
5. Generate the set C of candidate sets from $B_{k-}.$, $C_{k-}.$ & $F_{k-}.$ using the technique as discussed in [7]
6. *Prune C*: Scan T^i_{new} and find $X.sup.new^i$ for all $X \in C$.
7. Remove any candidate set $X \in C$, which is or at least one of its immediate subsets is not large in any T^i_{new}.(by observation 7)
8. Scan T^i_{old} and find the support $X.sup^i$ for all $X \in C$ (T^i_{new} has already been scanned).

9. *Prune C*: $C = \{X \in C | Y \subset X, |X| - |Y| = 1, \{Y \in (F \cup B)$ or $Y.sup^i \geq \alpha|T^i_{whole}|\}\}$(by observation 8)
10. Find the global support for all $X \in C$ as $X.sup = \sum X.sup^i$
11. Calculate L_{whole} and B_{whole} as follows.
    (a) $L_{whole} = \{X | X \in 'C$ and $S(X) \geq \alpha|T_{whole}|\} \cup \{\cup F^i\} \cup \{\cup B^i\}$
    (b) $B_{whole} = \{X | X \in C$ and $S(X)$<$\alpha|T_{whole}|$ and all its subsets are in $L_{whole}\} \cup \{X | X \in L_{old}/\cup F^i$ and all its subsets are in $L_{whole}\} \cup \{X | X \in B_{old}/\cup B^i$ and all its subsets are in $L_{whole}\}$
12. Return L_{whole} and B_{whole}

Fig. 1. Distributed Borders Algorithm

observations have been made relating to large, border and promoted border sets in distributed environment. Some of these observations have been discussed in [5]. Following are the observations which can be used to reduce the candidate sets to a great extent.

1. Every global large itemset X must be large in at least one site S_i.
2. If an itemset X is locally large at some site S_i, then all its subsets are also locally large in the site S_i.
3. If an itemset X is globally large at some site S_i, then all its subsets are also globally large at the site S_i.
4. If an itemset X is globally large or promoted border, then X must be large in at least one site i.
5. If an itemset X is a global promoted border set, then X must be large in T^i_{new} for some site S_i.

6. If X is global border set, then there exists $Y \subset X$ so that Y is local border in some site S_i.

7. If a new candidate set C in T_{whole} has to be large or border in T_{whole}, then either C or one of its immediate subsets must be locally large in one T_{new}^i.

8. If a candidate set X in the updated database is either large or border set, all of its immediate subsets must be either $\in F \cup B$ or large in at least one site i.

3   Experimental Results

We simulated the algorithm on a share-nothing environment. A 10/100 Mb LAN was used to connect six PIII machines running WindowsNT. Each machine had 20GB disk space and 256MB memory. The dataset used in the experiments were T20I4200K and T20I6200K, which were generated using the technique given in [2]. Each datasets contained 200K tuples(transactions). The corresponding datasets were loaded in the machines before the experiments started.

We carried out three experiments. In the first experiment, we used three machines(sites). The purpose of the experiment was to find the execution time and number of candidate sets for different minimum support. Each machine initially contained 63K transactions and 3K transactions were added to each machine as incremental database. The results are given in Fig. 2. The second experiment was the scaleup experiment. The testbed of the second experiment was same as that of first experiment. Here also we used three machines(sites). The purpose of the second experiment was to find the effect of the database size on the execution time. Three machines initially contained 30%, 30% and 25% transactions respectively. Size of incremental database was 5% for each of the machines and minimum support was 1%. The results are given in Fig. 3. The third experiment was the speedup experiment. Here, we increased the number of machines(sites) from 1 to 6. Sizes of initial database and incremental database were taken as 80% and 20% respectively. Initial and incremental database were divided equally among the machines and minimum support was taken as 1% .

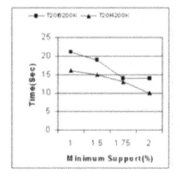

Fig. 2. Execution Time

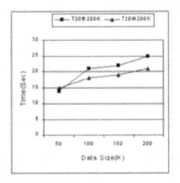

Fig. 3. Execution Time For Different Database Size

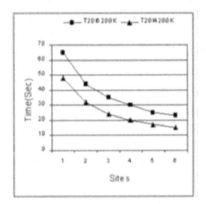

Fig. 4. Execution Time For Different Number of Sites

When we used 1 machine(site), it was the sequential run time of the *Borders* algorithm. The results are given in Fig. 4.

Discussion
The result of the first experiment was obvious and straightforward. In some cases execution time did not decrease significantly with the increase of minimum support. This was because whole scan of the database might be required in some sites. It was evident from the second experiment that execution time increased with the increase of the size of initial database and incremental database. . But, it increased linearly. Third experiment measured *speedup* and *efficiency* of the algorithm. The *speedup factor* is defined as $S(n) = T(1)/T(n)$ and *efficiency* is defined as $S(n)/n$, where $T(n)$ is the execution time with n sites. We found the average efficiency of 63% and 67% for T20I6200K and T20I4200K respectively, which showed that the algorithm achieved sublinear speedup. This speedup is acceptable for any distributed algorithm. But, as with other distributed algorithms, performance of this algorithm also depends on the factors such as database types,

distribution of data, skewness of data, network speed and other network related problems.

4   Conclusion

This paper presents one enhanced versions of the *Borders* algorithm called *Distributed Borders*, which is suitable for *Distributed Dynamic* databases . The paper has also presented experimental results to show the scalability and speedup of the algorithm.

References

1. Agarwal R, Imielinski T and Swami A, "Mining Association rules between Sets of Items in Large Databases", *Proc. ACM SIGMOD Conf. on Management of Data*,pp 207-217,Washington D C, May,1993.
2. Agarwal R, Mannila H, Shrikant R, Toivonen H and Verkamo A I, *Fast Discovery of Association Rules*, U M Fayyad, G Piatsky-Shapiro, P Smyth and R Uthruswamy, editors, Advances in Knowledge discovery and Data Mining,pp 307-328. MIT Press, 1996.
3. Cheung D W, Lee S D, Kao B, "A Genreral Incremental Technique for Maintaining Discovered Association Rules", *Proc. of the 5th Intl Conf. on Database System for Advanced Applications*, Melbourn, Australia, 1997.
4. Cheung D W, Han J, Ng V T and Wong C Y, "Maintenance of discovered association rules in large databases: An incremental updating technique", *Proc. of 12th Intl Conf. on Data Engineering*, New Orleans, Louisiana, 1996.
5. Cheung D W, Ng V T, Ada W Fu and Fu Y, "Efficient Mining of Association Rules in Distributed Databases", *IEEE Transactions on Knowledge and Data Engineering*, Vol 8,No 6,pp 911-921, Dec, 1996.
6. Ezeife C I and Y Su, " Mining Incremental Association Rules with Generalized FP Tree", *Proc. of 15th Canadian Conf. on Artificial Intelligence, AI2002*,pp 147-160, May, Calgary, Canada, 2002.
7. Feldman R, Aumann Y, Lipshtat O and Mannila H., "Borders: An Efficient Algorithm for Association Generation in Dynamic Databases",*Journal of Intelligent Information System*, 61-73,1999
8. Pujari A K , *Data Mining Techniques*, University Press, Hyderabad, India,2001.
9. Zhou Z and Ezeife C I, "A Low-Scan Incremental Association Rule Maintenance Method Based on Apriori Property", *Proc. of 14th Canadian Conf. on Artificial Intelligence, AI2001*,pp 26-35, June, Ottawa, Canada,2001.

APPLE: A Novel P2P Based e-Learning Environment*

Hai Jin, Zuoning Yin, Xudong Yang, Fucheng Wang, Jie Ma,
Hao Wang, and Jiangpei Yin

Cluster and Grid Computing Lab,
Huazhong University of Science and Technology, Wuhan, 430074, China
hjin@hust.edu.cn

Abstract. With the rapid development of information technology, dramatic changes have been taken place in the fundamental ways that people acquire and disseminate knowledge. Various e-Learning systems have been designed to help people take full advantage of the benefit brought by the technology. The newly emerged *Peer to Peer* (P2P) and grid computing will serve as the key driven forces to bring revolutionary impact on the future society. This paper evaluates the potential contribution of the P2P and grid technology into the e-Learning system and introduces a novel P2P based e-Learning environment, called APPLE. With the help of Gnutella-like P2P network, APPLE provides live broadcasting services to share services of education resources. We build a virtual classroom service based on WSRF.NET, which exposes the service as a grid service that could be accessed by all the users among the grid.

1 Introduction

e-Learning has been a topic of increasing interest in recent years [1]. Many e-Learning platforms and systems have been developed and commercialized. However, these e-Learning systems are mainly web-based [2][3]. Web-based courses and other education applications are in nature nothing more than a network of static hypertext pages [2]. Such paradigm is an information transfer paradigm, which focuses on content, and its goal is just to produce more and more static pages for the interested students. Learning is then considered to be an activity that helps instructors to produce, and students to consume, multimedia materials on the Web. This paradigm has been popular in earlier e-Learning systems, not because it is effective, but because it is easy to implement with basic Internet facilities, and it need not to change the traditional roles of the participants.

The deficiency of this paradigm only hinders it to receive more popular adoption from the public, but also can not reach a promising pedagogic result as expected. It is simple, humdrum and can not reflect the versatility and ampleness of education. People need an innovative paradigm to be adopted in e-Learning environment that can support higher-level interactions between the system, and its users, and sharing, even reusing course material between different applications.

---

* This paper is supported by research funding from Microsoft Research Asia and ImagineOne project from National Science Foundation of China.

A. Sen et al. (Eds.): IWDC 2004, LNCS 3326, pp. 52–62, 2004.
© Springer-Verlag Berlin Heidelberg 2004

To build cooperative e-Learning systems is a basic idea. The knowledge and information are not only from instructors, but also from other students with the same interest. When explanations for one question are transferred to all relative students, they also provide more constructive answers to requestor and exchange information with each other. More and more people are attempting to combine peer-to-peer computing and e-Learning together aiming for business, academic and individual use. The development of grid [4] also endows e-Learning with a promising future. With the help from grid computing, e-Learning can benefit a lot from the massive computing and storage capacity as well as various grid services. Some preliminary works have been done to use grid technology in e-Learning environment.

Most of the existing works only use one of these two technologies into their e-Learning system design. However, the combination of P2P and grid is very significant. There are many different application scenarios in e-Learning environment, such as message transmission, file data transferring, and live stream transferring, need high efficiency. P2P technology can be a good choice to solve such problem. While in an e-Learning environment, we also need some stable and powerful services to provide such functionalities as the storage of educational resource, the indexing and information service. In these occasions grid technology can achieve amazing results. And if we further this issue to a philosophical layer, some learning processes are individual-centric, and some are group centric, which just accord with the characteristics of P2P and grid. Therefore, the combination of P2P and grid technology can cope with most of e-Learning scenarios and enable e-Learning environment to be more powerful, efficient, scalable, mobile and versatile.

We have developed an e-Learning environment using Microsoft .NET, called APPLE. We use P2P and grid technology to build APPLE. We made some modifications on Gnutella protocol to make it to be more suitable for our system. With the support of this platform, we can broadcast the live class on the internet. Students who are not geographically together can not only watch the live from the screen of their desktops, but can interact with each other as if they were in the same real classroom simultaneously. Teacher can ask the students to reply a question and the video of the student's reply can be seen by all the participants of this virtual class. Hence our broadcast is based on a P2P network to offer more accesses to users than the traditional client-server paradigm.

We employ multicast when users are in the same subnet, which greatly reduce the cost of the host and network bandwidth. We also adopt an IP-locality strategy to let peers connecting to their adjacent (with low latency) father peers so as to provide good quality videos to users.

WSRF.NET [5] is also used in APPLE. We developed a virtual classroom service and published it through WSRF.NET. This approach made our P2P platform linked and integrated with the grid, therefore achieving a mutual benefit: on one hand our P2P based e-Learning environment can utilize grid's enormous computing and storage power to greatly extend the magnitude and promote the quality of the service capacity; on the other hand, grid can draw more public attention as it provides such an applicable application, which will accelerate the worldwide acceptance and popularization of grid computing.

The rest of this paper is organized as follows. In section 2, we present the system architecture of the environment. Section 3 discussed our design considerations. In section 4, we describe the experimental environment. In section 5, we introduce the state of art of related works of e-Learning systems. Finally, we draw the conclusions and point out our future research directions on section 6.

2 System Architecture

An e-Learning system is comprised of two primary categories of applications. The first category needs fixed and reliable server as the hardware supporting platform on which services are running. The other category usually pays more attention on efficiency of data transmission since the number of users is very large. For the first category of services, grid technology is a good solution to provide a reliable platform because servers running in the grid system are usually constant and not be shut off except that failures occur. For the second category of applications, the server cost maybe high if the data transmission method is based on traditional client/server model. Thus, P2P technique is exactly the graceful solution for this scalable problem.

In order to utilize these two kinds of technologies in the e-Learning system effectively, we use the following system architecture (shown in Fig.1), which has been divided into three layers from bottom up: resource layer, service layer, and grid application layer.

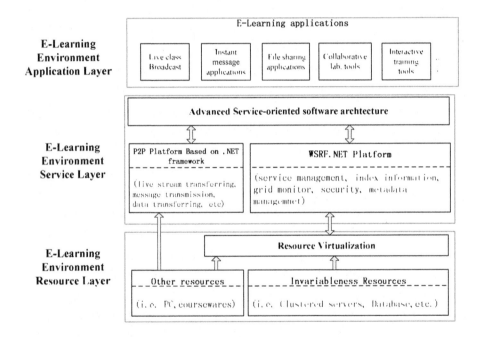

Fig. 1. e-Learning environment architecture based on WSRF.NET

2.1 Resource Layer

There are two parts in resource layer: resource domain and resource virtualization. Resource domains consist of physical resources (PC, servers, storage, and etc.) and logic resources (database, software tools, and etc) organized in resource virtualization way. According to the characteristics of different resources, those resources can be divided into two parts. One is the stable resources, such as dedicate servers and associated server software, which are often available anytime and anywhere. The other is changeable resources, such as client PCs and associated file resources, which can join and depart the e-Learning system dynamically.

This resource service environment provides a set of resources located within a single administrative domain that supports native facilities for service management, such as a J2EE application server, Microsoft .NET system, or other Linux cluster.

2.2 Service Layer

Service layer is built upon resource layer. A series of management toolkits and protocol criterions are defined to realize the sharing, integration and interoperation of all the resources in resource layer. At the same time, the transparent and unified access interfaces of resources and services are afforded to support the application in application layer. This layer is comprised of three kinds of functional components: WSRF.NET component, .NET Framework based P2P platform, and advanced service-oriented software architecture.

First, recent advances in the Internet technologies mark the trends of development towards resource sharing with grid computing [7] and service-oriented Internet by web services [6]. *WS-Resource framework* (WSRF) [8] is a set of proposed web services specifications to define a rendering of the WS-Resource approach in terms of specific message exchanges and related XML definitions. These specifications allow the programmer to declare and implement the association between a web service and one or more stateful resources.

WSRF.NET [5], based on Microsoft .NET Framework, is an independent hosting environment to be fully WSRF-compliant. It provides a container framework to perform WSRF-compliant grid computing in the .NET environment. It provides tools and supports for an attribute-based development model in which a service is transformed into a grid service by annotating it with meta-data. WSRF.NET also includes class libraries to perform common functions needed by both services and clients.

Secondly, live streaming, message, and file data transferring need high efficiency. The existing P2P systems, such as Gnutella [10] and Kazza, show a convincing proof of P2P computing technologies to solve such problems in the e-Learning environment. This technology provides a high efficiency transmission method. Hence we design a P2P platform module in the service layer.

Finally, a service-oriented architecture realizes a corresponding prototype infrastructure to support application processing and analysis. In our work, with the functionalities provided by WSRF.NET platform and peer-to-peer platform based on .NET framework, we handle the problem at both the grid platform and application levels, and address the grid scheduling and management issues for various applications. At the platform level, we investigate and design the whole architecture of the platform for series of applications upon WSRF.NET, the methods of data distribution, task partition and other related kernel functions.

2.3 Application Layer

On application layer, applications are mainly e-Learning applications. With the support of the underlying layers, we can develop various powerful and useful applications easily. These applications can be live class broadcast, instant message, file search, collaborative lab, and etc. To design useful, transparent, reliable, scalable, and secure applications and services for users is the main consideration for this layer.

3 Design Consideration

Figure 2 gives the overview of APPLE. There are two roles in the system, teacher and student. The teacher can teach either in a real classroom or in his own place. In APPLE, the capacity of a classroom is greatly extended, which enables more students to join the class and interact with the teacher.

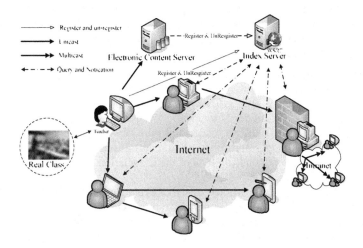

Fig. 2. The overview of APPLE

To make APPLE successful, the following issues should be taken into consideration: the efficiency and transmission quality of underlay P2P platform; the recording and replaying of the live of a class; the management of the virtual class; and the interaction approach between students and the teacher.

3.1 Overlay Broadcast in APPLE

Internet broadcast systems [9] are popular in both industrial and academic fields, but they are not widely used in e-Learning systems. In the following paragraphs, we will discuss the overlay broadcast in our system.

3.1.1 Scheduling Strategy
In APPLE, we set up a relay tree to support unlimited access to a live class. Scheduling strategy should be deliberately designed in order to yield good efficiency. Therefore the following principle should be followed when selecting father node:

Principle: the schedule strategy should make relay tree achieve appropriate clustering. If the link between two nodes has the characteristics of low latency, the two nodes can be a parent-child pair.

As the network topology is usually static, we can study the network topology to get the latency and bandwidth information between different sites. After studying the network topology in CERNET (China Education and Research Network), we develop a mechanism called landmark to represent the network status of a node. We map a subnet to a landmark and establish a landmark database containing those mappings. The nodes which have adjacent landmark ID will have low latency between each other. When a node is performing father selection, the landmark ID will be compared and a node holding an adjacent landmark ID will be chosen as father. This approach guarantees child node receiving good quality of audio and video from its father.

We use IP matching rule to schedule the nodes whose IP addresses are not located in the database. Fig. 3 shows the scheduling strategy of the relay tree. The nodes from the same university usually have the similar landmark IDs, hence they are scheduled to cluster together.

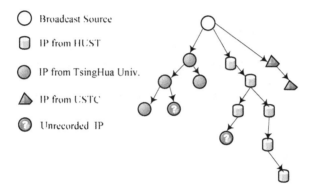

Fig. 3. Schedule strategy of the relay tree

The fact that many nodes are behind firewall cannot be ignored. When a new node which is behind the NAT is scheduled to the leaf node that has no ability to provide relay function because of his own firewall, the scheduling failure will occur. To prevent such situation from happening, we use trace back scheduling. By sending a certain message to the father of the inadequate node, the node which did not receive rely message from the inadequate node will be scheduled to another child of its father node. This mechanism avoids scheduling failure in most of situation except all children of the father node are behind the different NAT and firewalls.

Considering that many nodes which are behind the same NAT or firewall would join the same live class, setting up relay paths in those nodes is not efficient. Although lots of routers in Internet are not designed to support multicast, multicast in LAN is a good choice. The participants in the same class from the same LAN will form a multicast group, which will greatly reduce the overhead of the network transfer.

3.1.2 Transfer Policy

In order to make full use of bandwidth and improve the quality of live class, a prioritized packet forwarding scheme is used to exploit the available bandwidth. There are four kinds of packets in APPLE: a) *control command packet*: the packet transferred among the nodes on the relay tree to control and maintain the tree, sometimes bringing the message information from teacher to students; b) *powerpoint control packet*; c) *audio stream packet*; and d) *video stream packet*.

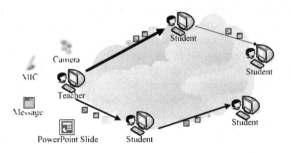

Fig. 4. Relay different streams in the system

Control command packet and powerpoint control packet are prioritized over audio and video stream packets, and audio is prioritized over video. The node dynamically selects proper type of the packet to transfer based on the loss rate to relay user (as shown in Fig.4). Thus, control command and message from teacher to students are highly protected. This ensures that in the case of network congestion or poor selection of parent node, students are still able to join the live class with low bit rate stream automatically.

3.2 Virtual Classroom Service

We develop a stateful grid service called virtual classroom service. This service is deployed and published in a server running WSRF.NET. This service is in charge of the management of the virtual class. The information of virtual classroom service is registered in an index server. All nodes in the environment acquire information of the classes and electronic learning contents by searching in index server.

The virtual classroom service maintains the up-to-date status of the live class. It uses WS-Notification mechanism to notify participants the status change of a class. People who join the class will automatically subscribe this notification. The WSRF.NET handles the whole process of notification which facilitates us concentrate on the design of other parts of the application.

3.3 Replay of Live Classes

It is possible that students miss some classes they are interested in. So how to replay the previous class is very significant in e-Learning system. During the period of the live class, the live of the class, including audio, video and PowerPoint action, is recorded and stored in the content server.

Adding timestamps to audio and video stream is a common and efficiency way to make them synchronized. But the problem of synchronization with the audio, video and PowerPoint control message is a still remained. We solve this problem by insert the control message into the send queue when the action takes place. Then control information and multimedia information are kept in the same file. This can offer the synchronization of the audio, video data and PowerPoint action.

Interaction message is another element that should be recorded. Those recorded message may help reviewers understanding the content of the class more thoroughly. Considering the loose coupled with the time, we record these messages without timestamps. We do not record all the chat messages during the class, instead recording those messages that were signed by teacher or teaching assistant.

3.4 Interaction Between Teacher and Students

Interaction is a very important part of e-Learning system. We provide the following interaction approaches in APPLE.

Sharing PowerPoint is the basic interaction pattern of a live class. APPLE does not convert the slides into pictures, but transfers the PowerPoint file and its control command to achieve the sharing of PowerPoint. The display of PowerPoint slide is controlled by teacher, and control command is forwarded on the overlay tree. The slides are synchronized with the audio and video streams. When the command is transferred, some restrictions are added to play the PowerPoint slide at student side. Allowing students only to view the slides the teacher have been played and not allowing student to copy the PowerPoint file are such restrictions. On the teacher side, it is designed to modify these restrictions easily.

Instant Message is another method to communicate with each other in live class. Here exits two ways to send messages, one is based on the overlay tree; the other is a distributed way to send messages among class participates.

The tree relays the control and chat messages from teacher to each participate in the class. The chat messages from teacher are always the important messages like answers of questions and announcement of class. They have little chance to loss as the relay path is based on TCP. The messages deliver to the teacher is set to broadcast to all participates in class by default, more like a real class interaction.

4 Scenario Description

We install WSRF.NET on a server and use it as the grid service provider. There could be multiple grid service providers in a grid domain. This can offer better service capacity and availability. There is a virtual classroom service running on each WSRF.NET server. These providers register its services to an index service server (or an information service server). Services with same functions usually conform to the same port-type, which enable the index service to aggregate the physical services of the same kind to a virtual service. We can also employ multiple index service servers in a grid domain. These servers cooperate with each other in a peer to peer fashion.

For an ordinary user, he/she just needs accesses to a web portal. Certain mechanism will automatically redirect him/her to an index service server which has the least latency from him/her. Then he/she can see all the virtual services published on the server node including the virtual classroom service. When he/she chooses to access the virtual classroom service, the index service will choose a best suitable physical service of virtual classroom for him/her.

We install our P2P application on about one hundred PCs distributed in several different sub nets. Everyone can act as teacher or students, which is decided in the initial configuration. The teacher uses virtual classroom service to establish a virtual classroom. Students access the virtual classroom service to retrieve the classroom lists. Then he/she selects the interested class to join the virtual classroom. A camera is used to capture the teacher's video and a P2P based network is used to broadcasting the audio and video data. A snapshot of APPLE user interface is shown in Fig. 5.

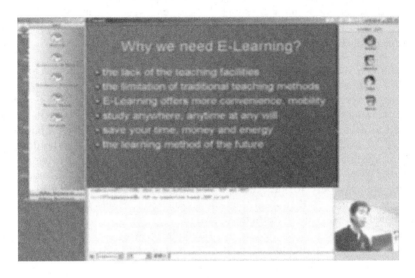

Fig. 5. The user interface of APPLE

5   Related Works

Many of the existing e-Learning products are content based and employing an information transfer paradigm. SOUL [11] (the SPACE On-line Universal Learning) Project is a famous project of such kind. SOUL is now serving over 20,000 users. Compare to other off-the-shelf e-Learning solutions, SOUL is tailored for students and teachers. To help organizations leverage technology and resources to achieve their e-Learning initiative, SOUL has developed a comprehensive set of e-Learning tools to streamline the process of e-course development, delivery, learner assessment as well as e-course evaluation and enhancements. Although SOUL has achieved some success, it lacks of live learning and synchronized collaboration.

Neal [12] studies how technology supports interactive, seminar-style distance learning classes where students learn from personal computers. Audio conference and internet relay chat support communication, and students feel that videoconferencing is necessary to create a classroom community. Gloster [13] employs synchronous and asynchronous learning components in its two-site distance education course program. They are concerned about the effect of the pedagogic process, but we are interested in the quality of the learning environment.

ConferenceXP [14] is an initiative of Microsoft Research's Learning Sciences and Technology group. It is aiming to explore how to make wireless classrooms, collaboration, and distance learning a compelling, rich experience. It is similar to our e-Learning environment. It supports the development of real-time collaboration and video conferencing applications. It also serves as an open research platform by providing a flexible, common framework for designing and implementing collaborative learning applications. ConferenceXP uses multicast to transfer audio and video data, though it claims supporting unicast where multicast is not supported, but now it is solely multicast based. It does not take grid technology into its design.

Access Grid (AG) [15] is an ensemble of resources including multimedia large-format displays, presentations and interactive environments, and interfaces to grid middleware and visualization environments. These resources are used to support group-to-group interactions across the grid. AG can be used for large-scale distributed meetings, collaborative work sessions, seminars, lectures, tutorials, and other e-Learning related scenarios. AG is now used at over 150 institutions worldwide, and it can be regarded as an enormous e-Learning resource warehouse. To maximum the benefit AG to us, we need develop applications that can take full use of the resource provides, which is just the aim of our project.

6 Conclusions and Future Works

In this paper, we present a P2P based e-Learning environment together with grid technology. To our knowledge, our effort is among the first several reports on experience with real application deployment which combine P2P and grid into the design of e-Learning system. Our work has proved that the adoption of P2P and grid in e-Learning is applicable and can achieve optimistic effect. APPLE also proves that a P2P overlay can be a cost-effective alternative for enabling the live broadcast over internet. APPLE copes with the advanced needs for both teachers and students, and yields a good result in the pedagogic process.

With the experiences and lessons accumulated from our preliminary work, we plan to conduct further researches in the following areas:

Enhancement of the P2P Platform. we will seek approaches to enhance the stability and reliability of the platform, reduce the loss rate of stream data transfer, in order to provide a high quality and availability e-Learning environment.

Enhancement of the Grid Service. we plan to design more sophisticated services which can take full use of the advantages of grid technology.

Standardization of Learning Materials. we will consider implement the SCORM [16] specification to describe the educational resources in APPLE, which will provide the interoperability with other system as well as the reusability of learning materials.

Artificial Intelligence. we will try to employ AI in APPLE and make the environment smarter. The initial AI attempt will be conducted in the phase of the aggregation and filter of the knowledge.

References

1. H. H. Adelsberger, B. Collis, and J. M. Pawlowski (eds.), *Handbook on Information Technologies for Education and Training*, Springer-Verlag, Berlin, 2002.
2. P. Brusilovsky, "Adaptive and Intelligent Technologies for Web-based Education", *Künstliche Intelligenz 4, Special Issue on Intelligent Systems and Teleteaching*, pp.19-25, 1999.

3. P. Brusilovsky and P. Miller, "Course Delivery Systems for the Virtual University", *Access to Knowledge: New Information Technologies and the Emergence of the Virtual University*, Elsevier Science, pp.167-206, 2001.

4. I. Foster and C. Kesselman (eds.), *The Grid: Blueprint for a New Computing Infrastructure*, Morgan Kaufmann, 1999.

5. WSRF.NET, http://www.cs.virginia.edu/~gsw2c/wsrf.net.html

6. S. Graham, S. Simeonov, T. Boubez, G. Daniels, D. Davis, Y. Nakamura, and R. Neyama, *Building Web Services with Java: Making Sense of XML, SOAP, WSDL, and UDDI*, SAMS, 2001.

7. I. Foster, C. Kesselman, J. Nick, and S. Tuecke, "The Physiology of the Grid: An Open Grid Services Architecture for Distributed Systems Integration", Globus Project, 2002. Available at http://www.globus.org/research/paper/ogsa.pdf.

8. WS-Resource Framework, http://www.globus.org/wsrf/specs/ws-wsrf.pdf.

9. Y. Chu, A. Ganjam, T. S. E. Ng, S. G. Rao, K. Sripanidkulchai, J. Zhan, and H. Zhang, "Early Experience with an Internet Broadcast System Based on Overlay Multicast", *Proceedings of USENIX 2004 Annual Technical Conference*.

10. M. Ripeanu, "Peer-to-peer architecture case study: Gnutella network", *Peer-to-Peer Computing*, 2001.

11. B. S. N. Cheung, "The Story of e-Learning in HKU SPACE", *Proceedings of the 13th International Workshop on Database and Expert Systems Applications (DEXA'02)*.

12. L. Neal, "Virtual Classrooms and Communities", *Proc. of International ACM SIGGROUP Conference on Supporting Group Work*, 1997, pp.81-90.

13. C. Gloster, Jr. and C. Doss, "A Distance Education Course in Computer Engineering at NC State University", *Computers in Education Journal*, Vol.10, No.3, 2000, pp.22-26.

14. ConferenceXP, http://www.conferencexp.com/

15. Access Grid, http://www.accessgrid.org/

16. ADL Technical Team, *Sharable Content Object Reference Model (SCORM)*, 2004.

Heuristic-Based Scheduling to Maximize Throughput of Data-Intensive Grid Applications

Souvik Ray and Zhao Zhang

Department of Electrical and Computer Engineering,
Iowa State University,
Ames, Iowa 50011
{rsouvik, zzhang}@iastate.edu

Abstract. Job scheduling in data grids must consider not only computation loads at each grid node but also the distributions of data required by each job. Furthermore, recent trends in grid applications emphasize high throughput more than high performance. In this paper, we propose a *centralized scheduling scheme, which uses a* scheduling heuristic called *Maximum Residual Resource* (MRR) that targets high throughput for data grid applications. We have analyzed the performance potentials of MRR, and have developed a simulator to evaluate it with typical grid configurations. Our results show that MRR brings significant performance improvements over existing online and batch heuristics like MCT, Min–min and Max-min.

1 Introduction

Grid computing is an emerging computing paradigm wherein authorized users can access and use distributed computing resources (e.g CPU cycles and large repositories of data) by submitting jobs to the grid and getting results back from the grid. A grid is a distributed collection of computing and data resources, which is shared by entities in a virtual organization. Computational grids address computationally intensive applications that deal with complex and time consuming computational problems on relatively small data sets. Data grids address data intensive applications that deal with the evaluation and mining of large amounts of data in the terabyte and petabyte range (e.g. future high energy physics experiments will require petabyte data storage and huge computational power that may only be efficiently supported by grids). Job scheduling in these grids would be influenced not only by the required computing power but also by the data intensiveness of the applications.

Historically, users of computing facilities have been mainly concerned with the response time of applications while system administrators have been concerned with throughput. However, a growing community of IT managers, researchers and scientists are now concerned about the throughput of their applications [1],[2]. Increasing grid throughput can be accomplished by scheduling the maximum number of tasks to the grid in a certain period of time. However, scheduling tasks in an optimal fashion has been shown to be NP complete [3].

A. Sen et al. (Eds.): IWDC 2004, LNCS 3326, pp. 63–74, 2004.
© Springer-Verlag Berlin Heidelberg 2004

Although previous work in this area has emphasized job scheduling for high performance computing, to the best of our knowledge no systematic attempt has been made in studying the scheduling of jobs in a data grid for maximizing the grid throughput (high throughput computing).

The proposed scheme is a centralized scheduling scheme, in which a central node or cluster collects the information about available computational resources and data replicas at all sites, makes scheduling decisions, and informs other sites the scheduling output. When comparing them with distributed schemes, one would think centralized schemes are inferior because of a potential performance bottleneck and the single point of failure at the central node. The former issue is negligible for our scheme, because the scheme is very efficient and the scheduling time is trivial when compared with grid job execution time. The latter one can be addressed by using backups of the central scheduling node.

Our scheme is different from existing scheduling schemes, such as those based on economic models, scheduling for computational grids, and decoupled computational and data scheduling. Scheduling for computational grids [9] considers only job execution but not data locations and movements. Economic models [18] are suitable when resources are owned by organizations of self-interests, while we target grids that dedicate resources to non-profit, high -performance and high-throughput computing. Decoupled computational and data scheduling [4] arranges job and data replication independently to reduce user response time, and uses various scheduling algorithms (e.g. scheduling at the least loaded site and random scheduling). Our scheme is different in that by using residual resources we consider job scheduling and data movements at the same time, and we target high-throughput of the grid.

From the viewpoint of scheduling, a data grid consists of heterogeneous sites, which have both computational and data resources. If a job can be executed at a site, which also has the required data, then the job is an instance of (Local data and Local execution) with respect to the site. Thus the different job execution scenarios can be Local data and Local execution (LDLE), Remote data and Local execution (RDLE), Local data and Remote execution (LDRE), Remote data and Same Remote execution (RDSRE) and Remote data and Different Remote execution (RDDRE).

We propose a scheduling heuristic, which takes into account both job completion time and processing power available at a site to guide the scheduling process. The main objective is to distribute jobs over sites in such a manner so as to lower the probability of RDLE executions. For data-intensive applications, where data transfer time can be appreciably higher than job execution time, this scheduling heuristic reduces the makespan for a task-set. In our system model, users submit jobs to a metascheduler. The metascheduler then schedules the jobs at different sites using a scheduling algorithm. Each site has a local scheduler, which only decides how to allocate resources to jobs submitted to the site by the metascheduler. Thus, we use a centralized scheduling policy. To evaluate the performance of our heuristic and to compare it with existing heuristics for online and batch scheduling modes, we have developed a discrete event simulator. Our results have been encouraging and show an appreciable improvement in makespan when compared with both online and batch heuristics. Moreover, a better load balance in job distribution is also achieved.

The paper is organized as follows. Section 2 discusses the related work. Section 3 gives the outline of our scheduling model. Section 4 presents the performance metrics for evaluating job scheduling for data grids, and Section 5 describes our scheduling method. Section 6 gives the experimental environment, and Section 7 presents the simulation-based experimental results. Finally, Section 8 concludes our work.

2   Related Work

Scheduling in grids has been extensively studied in different contexts e.g. scheduling for computational grids [9] [10], decoupled computational and data scheduling [4] and scheduling based on economic models [18]. Economic models (e.g. scheduling model used in Nimrod-G [18]) use factors like resource cost, user priority, job deadline, user preference, resource architecture etc. in making scheduling decisions. Ranganathan et. al. [4] propose a scheduling framework which considers data scheduling and computation scheduling separately. They emphasize high performance computing. Takefusa et. al. [19] present a performance analysis of scheduling and replication algorithms on grid datafarm architecture for high energy physics applications. Takefusa et. al. [20] study deadline scheduling for client-server systems on the Computational Grid. Casanova et al [10] describe heuristics for scheduling parameter sweep applications in computational grids. Park et al. [5] describe cost models to schedule jobs on the grid to minimize response time for the user and again they emphasize user response time optimization. Stockinger et al. [6] describe a cost model for distributed and replicated data stores. Min et. al. [7] and Smith et. al. [8] discuss advance reservation of resources (resource co-allocation problem) in their scheduling algorithms to satisfy the QoS requirements of the user. Subramani et.al. [9] evaluate some centralized and distributed scheduling decisions for a computational grid and propose a scheme which uses redundant distribution of a job to different sites to reduce average job slowdown and turn-around time. Scheduling of independent tasks to heterogeneous computing systems has been described in [15].

3   Scheduling Model

We use a system model in which the grid consists of sites which have both computing and data storage resources. The sites are connected by a wide area network (WAN), while the nodes in a site are connected by a local area network (LAN). We consider the data transfer time within the local LAN (intra-site data transfer) at a site to be negligible in comparison to both job execution time and inter-site data transfer time. We also ignore the time to transfer the output dataset from the site executing the job back to the user, since this does not influence the grid throughput. Our scheduling model uses a **Metascheduler** for scheduling of jobs at the different sites. The users submit jobs to the metascheduler. The Metascheduler decides the grid site for job submission using a **heuristic-based scheduling algorithm**. Once a job is submitted to a site, the Local Scheduler at the site manages scheduling using local scheduling algorithm, which may vary from one site to another. Thus, our model is somewhat similar to the model used in [4], the difference being that all users are associated with a single Metascheduler and sites do not have a Dataset Scheduler, since no dynamic replication takes place. Once a job is submitted to a site, it occupies the resources assigned to it until job completion i.e. there is no job preemption. The Metascheduler interacts with the Information and Monitoring service (e.g., the Globus MDS [11], NWS [12]) and Replica Location Service to determine the various possible resource allocations, which can satisfy the job requirement.

4   Performance Metrics

We use **makespan** as the primary performance metric. Before giving a formal definition of makespan, let us look into some other job execution terms in the context of a data grid. A data grid is characterized by a distribution of heterogeneous computing and storage nodes. A job requires an input data set (some form of data product), on which an algorithm is applied to generate a the output product (time to derive). Once this is done, this output product is analyzed (time to analyze). Thus the total execution time (if the input data set is present at the site, where the job is submitted) is given by (derivation time + analysis time). Hence, the **expected execution time** e_{mn} of job j_m on site s_n is given by (time to derive(j_m)+time to analyze(j_m)), given that the input data set is present at site s_n. The **expected completion time** c_{mn} of job j_m on site s_n is defined as the wall-clock time at which s_n completes j_m (includes the time to transfer the input data set from some other site, if it is not present at s_n.) Let us consider a batch of J jobs, which have to be scheduled. If a job j_m arrives at time t_a and begins execution at time t_b, then $c_{mn} = t_b + e_{mn}$. The **makespan** for the complete schedule is then given by: $Max_{j_m \in J}(c_{mn})$. In a data-grid, an input data set required by a job may or may not be present at the site, where the job is submitted for execution. Thus the size of the input data set and the network bandwidth available can have a significant influence on the makespan.

5   Scheduling Algorithm and Heuristics

A scheduler can schedule jobs in two different modes: _online_ and _batch_. In the online mode, the scheduler maps a job to a site and schedules it for execution immediately. Thus this mapping and scheduling is a one-time event. On the other hand, in the batch mode, when scheduling requests arrive at the scheduler, they are not mapped immediately. Instead the mapping is done for a set of tasks (meta-task) at a prescheduled time and this is called a mapping event. The frequency of mapping events is called scheduling frequency. The benchmark heuristic for online mode is Minimum Completion Time (MCT). Batch mode scheduling heuristics include Min-min [14] and Max-min [14]. Figure 1 outlines the Min-min and Max-min heuristics. Min-min heuristic is used as the benchmark for the batch mode. In the

Min-min heuristic, the minimum completion time for each job (over all sites which have the necessary processing power for job execution) is predicted. Then the job which has the least MCT is scheduled (by mapping it to the site which completes job execution in the minimum time) and then deleted from the meta-task. The process is repeated with the remaining jobs in the meta-task until all jobs have been scheduled. The motivation behind this heuristic is to complete job execution at a site at the earliest possible time and have resource available for future job submissions. Max-min uses the maximum value of MCT as the heuristic. The idea is to overlap execution of short tasks with long tasks.

5.1 Our Approach

In a data grid, job execution time is not only influenced by the processing speed at different sites, but also the presence or absence of the input data-set at the job execution site. We know that a job, when submitted to a site(say A), can be an instance of $LDLE_A$ or an instance of $RDLE_A$. The job completion time in the first scenario is always less than the second because of the overhead due to data transfer from a remote site (remote w.r.t site A).

We propose a **Min-MRRmin heuristic** (Figure 2), which not only uses MCT, but also the **Residual Resource** at each site to guide the scheduling process. We define **residual resource** of a site as the processing units available at the site after a job is submitted for execution. For each job, if there exists even a single job execution, which is an instance of LDLE, it is given preference over all other instances of RDLE. If multiple instances of LDLE (or multiple instances of RDLE and no instance of LDLE) exist, then the following objective function is used to select the best instance.

1) **while**	there are jobs (in metatask J) to be scheduled
2)	**for** each job j $\in$ J,
3)	calculate c_{js} for all sites (s $\in$ S: sites)
4)	calculate $c_j(\min)$
5)	**end for**
6)	schedule the job which has the (min/max) value of $c_j(\min)$ at the corresponding site s.
7)	delete the job from J.
8)	update the resource(processing units) at the corresponding site s.
9) **end while**	

1) **while**	there are jobs (in metatask J) to be scheduled
2)	**for** each job j $\in$ J,
3)	calculate W_{js} for all sites (s $\in$ S: sites)
4)	calculate $\underline{W_{js}(\max)}$ and record the corresponding c_{js}
5)	**end for**
6)	schedule the job which has the minimum value of c_{js} in step 4.
7)	delete the job from J.
8)	update the resource (processing units) at the corresponding site s.
9) **end while**	

Fig. 1. Min-min/Max-min heuristic   **Fig. 2.** Min-MRRmin heuristic

$$W_{js} = \alpha R_{js} - \beta c_{js}$$

where

R_{js}: Residual resource of site s after submission of job j;

c_{js}: Job completion time for job j at site s;

α, β: Weights s.t. $\alpha + \beta = 1$.

The motivation behind using this heuristic is to find an optimum balance between the job completion time and the residual resource available at a site after a job submission. A site which has a high residual resource and low job completion time is always given preference in step 4 of the algorithm. Instead of overloading sites with short jobs, this heuristic tries to distribute jobs over sites (achieving a better load balance) and decreases the probability of RDLE job executions. Weights are used to assign priorities to residual resource and expected completion time. A value of α greater than 0.5 (and correspondingly β less than 0.5) means that greater weight is given to residual resource. Residual resource should be given a higher priority if data transfer time is appreciably higher than job execution time and files are distributed in a non-uniform manner with some files available at specific sites. One example of this scenario can be the high energy physics experiments [17], where initially all data would be located at the central site at CERN. There would be a good number of RDLE job executions in such a scenario and hence higher weight must be given to residual resource. On the other hand, if the data files required for a job are small in size and the data transfer time is significantly smaller than job execution time, then the execution time becomes the major component of the job completion time. In this case, a higher weight should be assigned to job execution time. The value of α at which the minimum makespan is achieved depends on file access pattern, distribution of files at different sites and average job size.

From our simulations, we have observed that for typical data grid configurations the makespan decreases with an increase in α and reaches a minimum in the (0.5 - 0.8) range and then increases again. We have run simulations for different configurations and observe a trend which is close to that shown in Figure 3. In a data grid, the major component of the job completion time is the data transfer time and initially all the files are located at the central or root

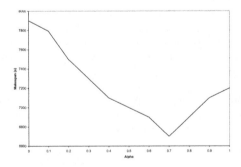

Fig. 3. Variation of makespan with alpha for a workload of size 1000

node. Therefore, a significant number of RDLE executions take place and the makespan decreases with increase in α. For values of α higher than 0.8, since the weight associated with job execution time is very low, the job allocations are decided mainly on the basis of residual resource available at a site. This can result in high values of job execution time for some jobs, thereby increasing the makespan.

5.2   Analysis

We first analyze how RDLE job execution affects the makespan of a set of jobs and the utilization of computing resources (processors[1])at each site. We then compare our heuristic with existing online and batch heuristics. In our scheduling model, the metascheduler uses either online or batch processing of jobs in the job queue. Thus, a job is submitted to a site only when it has the necessary processing units to execute the job. The local scheduler only decides how to schedule the jobs on its local resources. Hence a job can only be in a queue at a site, while it is waiting for transfer of the required input dataset from a remote site. Thus, whenever a job execution belongs to RDLE, the following happen:

1. The job completion time is high. Moreover, computing resources at the site are occupied for a longer period of time because of the waiting time due to data transfer. Thus the probability of LDLE at this site decreases and the probability of RDLE at other sites increases. This increases the makespan.
2. Since the processors remain idle during data transfer time, the processor utilization is reduced.

The online scheduling heuristic, MCT schedules a job at a site, where the job can be completed in a minimum amount of time. In our approach, we use the maximum value of W_{js} to select the site. Thus, preference is given to a site that has a higher residual resource and lower job completion time. Batch scheduling heuristics like Min-min tries to minimize the makespan by scheduling jobs at sites which can result in the the minimum job completion time. Step 4 in the Min-min algorithm filters out all possible execution scenarios (for each job), which are instances of RDLE, if there exists at least one scenario, which is an instance of LDLE. Thus, if there are two or more sites which have both the necessary processing units for the job execution as well as the input dataset in their data storage, then the site with the faster processors is selected. So, if there are frequent requests for a particular dataset (step 6), a site which has that dataset and has comparatively faster processors, gets flooded with job submissions resulting in insufficient computing resources for subsequent jobs (requiring different input datasets). This increases the probability of RDLE for those subsequent jobs. Max-min uses the same strategy in step 4 but gives priority to longer jobs in step 6. Thus two jobs requiring the same input dataset for job processing will be mapped to the same site and will run for a longer period of time, thereby worsening the performance even further than Min-min. Min-MRRmin selects the site which has the highest value of W_{js} for each job (step 4) and then gives priority to jobs which have lower job completion time (step 6).

---

[*] we use the terms processing units and processors interchangeably.

6   Simulation Setup

We have developed a discrete-event simulator (written in Java) to evaluate the different heuristics. The main components of the simulator are the **scheduler**, **network manager**, **resource manager** and the **replica manager**. The scheduler interacts with the network manager, resource manager and replica manager for information about network bandwidth, computing resources and file replicas respectively. Each site has computing (processing units) and storage (data sets) resources. The processing speed and storage capacity can vary from site to site. The job arrivals are modeled by a Poisson process. We use data from [17] to select the value of λ (job arrival rate). A job is represented by the tuple { arrival-time,job-id,user-id, processing-units,dataset-id }. The dataset request pattern from each user (the number of users used in our simulations = 50) is modeled using zipf distribution.

GRID TOPOLOGY	FLAT
NUMBER OF SITES	10
NUMBER OF DATASETS	200
DATASET SIZE(GB)	1-200
NETWORK BANDWIDTH (GB/s)	0.32,0.64
JOB ARRIVAL RATE (jobs/day)	250-10000
WORKLOAD SIZE	100,500,1000

Fig. 4. Simulation Parameters

We do not model any particular grid test-bed. A flat grid topology containing 10 sites is used for the simulation. Each site has a certain amount of processing units (100-2000) and storage capacity (7-80). We use data from [17] and appropriately scale them to suit our simulation needs. The grid consists of a central site (similar to CERN in EU data grid testbed), which contains the entire dataset and has the highest processing capacity. The datasets are distributed randomly at the other sites. When a dataset has to be fetched from a remote site, it is cached at the local site and LRU file replacement is used. No dynamic replication takes place. The network bandwidth is modeled using data from [17].

We assume that each dataset is represented by a file and different files have different file sizes. Each job requires a single file and the processing time and the number of processing units required is proportional to the size of the file. Figure 4 shows the different simulation parameters.

7   Results and Discussions

A data grid is characterized by the presence of input data sets, which are present at a central site and replicated at other sites. We know that the job completion time for a job j_m submitted to a site s_n, such that the input data set for the job is present at the site is much less than the case when the data set has to be fetched from a remote site. Therefore, the degree of replication of the data sets can significantly influence the makespan of a batch of jobs. We evaluate the different heuristics for random distribution of replicas at sites other than the central site (which has all the datasets). We have run simulations to compare the performance of the different heuristics in both online and batch mode.

Online Scheduling

The benchmark heuristic for online scheduling is Minimum Completion Time (MCT). We compare the performance of MRR-min with MCT for workload size of 100 and 1000 (Figure 5). MRR-min is the online version of Min-MRRmin. In the online mode, each job is scheduled immediately and this mapping occurs once. For each job, MRR-min calculates the maximum value of W_{js} and selects the corresponding site for job submission. We observe a significant performance improvement (average improvement of 45%) over MCT at high job arrival rates. We also compared the number of LDLE and RDLE executions for both cases (workload size of 1000). MRR-min has about 21% less RDLE executions than MCT (Figure 6).

The aforementioned statistics represent the case when the data transfer time for a dataset is appreciably higher than the job execution time and replicas are randomly distributed at sites other than the central site. In this case, we found best results are achieved using $\alpha = 0.5$ and $\beta = 0.5$. We also collected statistics for the cases when data transfer time is comparable to execution time and data transfer time is appreciably smaller than job execution time. In both cases, we get a percentage improvement of about 7%. Thus, the percentage improvement in performance of MRR-min is the highest when data transfer time is much higher than job execution time. As the job execution time becomes comparable to or larger than data transfer time, even though there might be instances of RDLE, these get overlapped by instances of LDLE at other sites and therefore the increase in makespan due to RDLE instances is appreciably smaller.

Batch Scheduling

To start with, we use a small set of jobs, which are mapped to different sites using a single mapping event. With a small set of jobs, we can effectively study

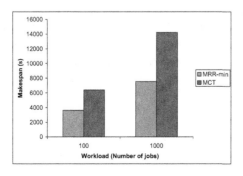

Fig. 5. Comparison of MRR-min and MCT (online mode)

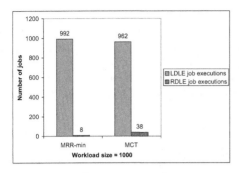

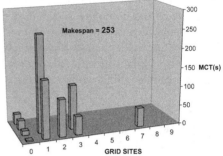

Fig. 6. Comparison of LDLE and RDLE executions (Online mode)

Fig. 7. Makespan for Min-min (batch mode)

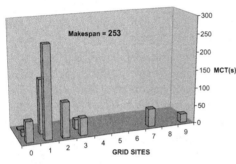

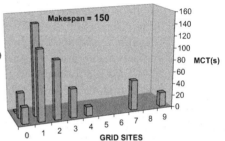

Fig. 8. Makespan for Max-min (batch mode)

Fig. 9. Makespan for Min-MRRmin (batch mode)

load-balancing issues for each heuristic besides analyzing the factors affecting the makespan in each case. Figures 10, 6 and 7 show the makespan for the three heuristics for the case, where the file replicas are randomly distributed. The makespan for the meta-task using MMR-min heuristic is about 40% less than that of the Min-min and Max-min heuristics. Moreover, a better load balance is achieved in the case of Min-MRRmin. Jobs are scheduled at 7 different sites in Min-MRRmin, whereas Min-min and Max-min schedule jobs at 5 and 6 sites respectively. Min-MRRmin achieves a better distribution of jobs and by giving priority to a job which can be scheduled at the site which has the maximum processing units (maximum residual resource). It tries to maximize the probability of a job being executed at a site which also has the required input dataset. This has a significant impact on the makespan, because the overhead due to dataset transfers (for instances of RDLE) is minimized.

For the batch mode, we compare the performance of Min-MRR, Min-min and Max-min heuristics for different scheduling frequencies and different job arrival rates (λ). We vary the value of λ from 200 jobs/day (0.003 jobs/s) to 10000 jobs/day (0.116 jobs/s). We use scheduling frequencies of 20, 50 and 100 seconds and also vary the values of the weights, α and β.

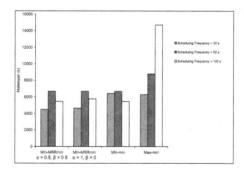

Fig. 10. Comparison of heuristics for different scheduling frequencies

Figure 8 shows the makespan in each case (for a workload size of 500). Min-MRRmin has the lowest makespan for lower frequencies and always performs at least as good or better than Min-min and better than Max-min. A performance gain of about 30% and 28.5% is achieved over Min-min and Max-min respectively for a scheduling frequency of 20 seconds. The best results are obtained for high data transfer time (in comparison to execution time), lower scheduling frequencies and high job arrival rates. We also observe that Max-min performs better than Min-min at low scheduling frequencies.

8   Conclusions

Job scheduling for data grid applications must take into account not only job execution times but the distributions of required data. Existing scheduling methods such as Min-min and Max-min only consider the former factor. We proposed a new scheduling heuristic called MRR, which systematically considers the execution time and data transfer time for the current job as well as minimizing the probability of future job assignments that require remote data transfer. By including the residual resource into the evaluation of a site for running a given job, our method may maximize the number of local-data, local-execution job assignments. Our simulations results show that in both the online and batch modes of scheduling, our method performs significantly better than the existing methods in the same category.

References

1. M. Livny and R. Raman, *High Throughput Resource Management*, chapter 13 in The Grid: Blueprint for a New Computing Infrastructure, Morgan Kaufmann, San Francisco, California, 1999.
2. R.F. Freund and T.D. Braun, *Production Throughput as a High-Performance Computing Meta-task*, The 2002 International Conference on Parallel and Distributed Processing Techniques and Applications (PDPTA 02).

3. E.G. Coffman, Jr. (ed.), *Computer and Job-Shop Scheduling Theory*, John Wiley and Sons, New York, NY, 1976.
4. K. Ranganathan and I. Foster, *Decoupling Computation and Data Scheduling in Distributed Data-Intensive Applications*. in 11th IEEE International Symposium on High Performance Distributed Computing (HPDC-11), 2002.
5. S. Park and J. Kim, *Chameleon: A Resource Scheduler in a data grid environment*, in Proceedings of the 3rd IEEE/ACM International Symposium on Cluster Computing and the Grid (CCGRID03).
6. H. Stockinger, K. Stockinger, E. Schikuta and I. Willers, *Towards a Cost Model for Distributed and Replicated Data Stores* , 9th Euromicro Workshop on Parallel and Distributed Processing (PDP01).
7. R. Min and M. Maheswaran, *Scheduling advance reservations with priorities in grid computing systems*. Thirteenth IASTED International Conference on Parallel and Distributed Computing Systems (PDCS '01).
8. W. Smith, I. Foster and V. Taylor, *Scheduling with Advanced Reservations*, International Parallel and Distributed Processing Symposium (IPDPS00).
9. V. Subramani, R. Kettimuthu, S. Srinivasan and P. Sadayappan, *Distributed Job Scheduling on Computational Grids using Multiple Simultaneous Requests*, Proceedings of 11th IEEE Symposium on High Performance Distributed Computing (HPDC02).
10. H. Casanova, A. Legrand, D. Zagorodnov and F. Berman, *Heuristics for Scheduling Parameter Sweep Applications in Grid Environments*, Heterogeneous Computing Workshop (HCW 2000).
11. K. Czajkowski, S. Fitzgerald, I. Foster and C. Kesselman, *Grid Information Services for Distributed Resource Sharing*, 10th IEEE International Symposium on High Performance Distributed Computing (HPDC-10, 2001).
12. R. Wolski, *Forecasting Network Performance to Support Dynamic Scheduling Using the Network Weather Service*, Proceedings of 6th IEEE Symposium on High Performance Distributed Computing, Portland, Oregon, 1997.
13. P. Busetta, M. Carman, L. Serafini, F. Zini and K. Stockinger, *Grid Query Optimisation in the Data Grid*, Technical Report, TR-01 09-01, IRST, Trento, Italy, Sept. 2001
14. O.H. Ibarra and C.E. Kim, *Heuristic algorithms for scheduling independent tasks on nonidentical processors*. Journal of the ACM, April. 1977.
15. M. Maheswaran, S. Ali, H.J. Siegel, D. Hensgen, and R. Freund, *Dynamic Matching and Scheduling of a Class of Independent Tasks onto Heterogeneous Computing Systems*. 8th Heterogeneous Computing Workshop (HCW), 1999.
16. M. Pinedo. *Scheduling: Theory, Algorithms, and Systems*. Prentice Hall, Englewood Cliffs, NJ, 1995.
17. K. Holtman. *HEPGRID2001: A Model of a Virtual Data Grid Application*. Lecture Notes in Computer Science, 2001.
18. R. Buyya, D. Abramson, J. Giddy and H. Stockinger, *Economic Models for Resource Management and Scheduling in Grid Computing*. Journal of Concurrency and Computation: Practise and Experience (CCPE), 2002.
19. A. Takefusa, O. Tatebe, S. Matsuoka and Y. Morita, *Performance Analysis of Scheduling and Replication Algorithms on Grid Datafarm Architecture for High-Energy Physics Applications*, HPDC, 2003.
20. A. Takefusa, H. Casanova, S. Matsuoka and F. Berman, *A Study of Deadline Scheduling for Client-Server Systems on the Computational Grid*, HPDC, 2001.

Failure Recovery in Grid Database Systems

Sushant Goel[1], Hema Sharda[2], and David Taniar[3]

[1,2] School of Electrical and Computer Systems Engineering,
Royal Melbourne Institute of Technology, Australia
s2013070@student.rmit.edu.au
hema.sharda@rmit.edu.au
[3] School of Business Systems, Monash University, Australia
David.Taniar@infotech.monash.edu.au

Abstract. Failure is unavoidable in any computing environment and hence any computing architecture must address recovery issues. Recovery becomes more complicated when sites are distributed, autonomous and heterogeneous. Grid architecture is such an evolving distributed architecture. Databases operating in Grid architecture have different recovery issues than their other distributed counterparts – distributed and multidatabase. In this paper we focus on maintaining correctness of data in case of site failure in Grid database.

1 Introduction

With continuously evolving computing infrastructure the need for data management has also changed. To maintain correctness and consistency of data in the database, transaction management techniques should be modified to accommodate these infrastructural changes. Initially data was centrally stored and managed but development of distributed computing infrastructure required distributed management of data. A transaction is a program unit that access and updates the data in central/distributed database [1,2]. Transaction must preserve the consistency of database. Atomicity, Consistency, Isolation and Durability (ACID) properties [2] are used to ensure correctness of data. Technique used to achieve these properties differs depending on the underlying hardware infrastructure, e.g., atomicity (transaction runs to its entirety or not at all) in centralized database management systems (DBMS) can be achieved only by log entry but achieving atomicity in distributed DBMS needs communication with all cohorts of the global transaction. Two-phase commit (2PC) [2] is used to meet requirement of atomicity in distributed environment.

Grid computing [5,6,9,10,11] is a new and evolving computing infrastructure that promises to support collaborative, autonomously evolved, heterogeneous and data intensive applications. There is a need to revisit and address transaction management issues in Grid databases. Our earlier work has addressed the concurrency control issues [8] and atomic commitment issues [7] in Grids. In this paper we mainly address the problem of failure recovery in Grid environment to maintain atomic commitment. 2PC [2] is the most widely accepted Atomic Commit Protocol (ACP) in distributed systems. It involves two phases- *voting phase* and *decision phase*. Grid database, due

A. Sen et al. (Eds.): IWDC 2004, LNCS 3326, pp. 75–81, 2004.
© Springer-Verlag Berlin Heidelberg 2004

to autonomy and heterogeneity, cannot assume implementation of common protocol among all participating sites.

The remainder of the paper is organized as follows. Section-2 explains Atomic Commitment in Grids and log files required to maintain consistency of data in case of site failure. Section-3 explains the proposed recovery algorithm in detail. Finally section-4 concludes the work.

2   Grid Atomicity and Maintaining Logs for Recovery

Grid databases will have different working environment than traditional distributed databases. We argue that Grid databases will not have the leverage of global logs and thus recovery issues have to be revisited. We briefly explain the state diagram of Grid-ACP from [7] for better understanding in this paper.

State Diagram of Grid-ACP: There is an *originator* of the transaction and may be one or more participant(s). To handle heterogeneity and autonomy features of Grid databases we introduce a new state, *sleep* state, in transaction execution. Any transaction that accesses more than one data sites is known as a *global transaction*. State diagram of global transaction executing at originator and participant(s) are shown in figure 1.

Working of Grid-ACP: As soon as the global transaction arrives at the originator, the transaction is divided in various subtransactions depending on location of data and enters *running* state. Grid's *data location service* may be used for splitting the transaction. Subtransactions are then submitted to corresponding participants. If the originator finishes execution of its cohort it enters *wait* state and waits for response from other participants. If all response is to 'commit' the originator enters *commit* state and informs participants accordingly. If any of the participants decided to 'abort' the originator decides to abort, enters *pre-abort* state and waits for acknowledgement from participants. On receiving acknowledgements the originator enters *abort* state.

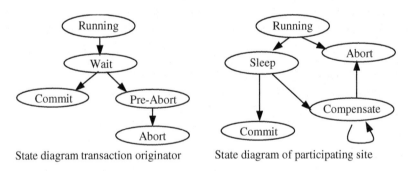

State diagram transaction originator   State diagram of participating site

Fig. 1. State diagram of transaction executing at different sites

Sleep state helps in avoiding requirement of a common protocol as well as requirement of communication between participants. The participant in *sleep* state indicates that the subtransaction has decided to *commit* but is awaiting originator's response. Effects of the *sleep*ing subtransaction have to be made visible to other local/global transactions due to control autonomy requirement of Grid databases.

Model for Storing Log Files at Originator and Participating Sites: Due to inherent nature of grid infrastructure like autonomy, heterogeneity, high volume of data handling etc. it may not be possible to maintain global log records, unlike traditional distributed and multidatabase systems. At the same time Grids will not have top-layer management system like distributed or multidatabase management systems. Thus we use a model where logs are stored at local sites. In absence of global logs, recovery procedure will have to be modified accordingly. We propose the recovery algorithm for this model in next section.

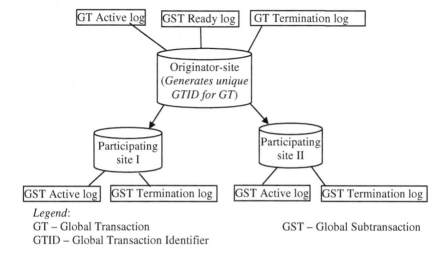

Legend:
GT – Global Transaction   GST – Global Subtransaction
GTID – Global Transaction Identifier

Fig. 2. Various logs at originator and participants

Though same site can act as an originator for some transaction and participant for some other transaction, but for pedagogical simplicity here we distinguish between logs stored in originator-site and participating-site. Figure 2 shows the log files required at originator and participant(s).
Logs required at originator site: (i) Global transaction active log, (ii) Global subtransaction ready log and (iii) Global transaction termination log. *Logs required at participating site*: (i) Global subtransaction active log and (ii) Global subtransaction termination log. Any transaction can have one or more subtransaction(s). Participating site doesn't need ready log, this could be figured out from the combination of GST active and termination log. Since *sleep* is updated in the active log and depicts that the participant decided to commit.

3 Proposed Failure Recovery Algorithm

Earlier we discussed various states of executing transaction at originator as well as participating sites. Sites may fail in any of the states of transaction execution. There could be different scenarios in site failure e.g. failure of only participants, failure of only originator and simultaneous failure of participant and originator. In this section we propose *recovery procedure* for participating as well as originating site. The recovery procedure can handle failure of transaction at various states.

3.1 Participant Recovery Procedure

Step-1: Restart the participating DBMS.

Step-2: Recover local transactions by using information stored in the log.

Step-3: The participating-site then checks in *Global subtransaction active log* whether it is executing subtransaction of any global transaction.

  Step-3A: If the site does not have any cohort of global transaction then the site can recover independently by using local logs.

  Step-3B: If the site is executing local subtransactions of any global transaction, originator-site of the global transaction is informed.

  (1) Participating site failed in *running* state: Abort the global subtransaction, remove the GTID from Global subtransaction active log, append *abort* in Global subtransaction termination log and inform the originator.

  (2) Participating site failed during *compensate* state: If the GST termination log contains abort but GTID still exists in GST active log then the participant knows it failed during compensate state. Compensating transaction is then rerun to completion. After successful compensation GTID is removed from GST active log and originator is informed.

  (3) Participating site failed during *sleep* state: If GTID exists in the GST active log and no decision (*commit* or *abort*) could be found in GST termination log regarding that GTID then the participant knows that it failed during it was in *sleep* state.

  (i) GT termination log at originator contains *commit*: Originator replies with 'commit', the participant recovers and updates the GST termination log and removes GTID from GST active log.

  (ii) GT termination log at originator contains *abort*: Originator replies with 'abort' and participant executes the compensating transaction. GST termination log is then appended with 'abort' and GTID is removed from the GST active log.

  (iii) GT active log at originator contains *wait*: Originator replies with 'active' and the participant can safely recover to the state where it failed i.e. *sleep*. No new entry in the participant's log is required.

  (iv) GT termination log at originator contains *pre-abort*: This indicates the global decision to abort has been made and the originator is waiting for acknowledgements. If 'abort' is not found in GST termination log at participant then it appends 'abort' in GST termination log. The participant should then execute the compensation rules and acknowledge the abortion of subtransaction and removes GTID from the GST active log.

  Originator makes the final decision after response from all participants is received.

Step-4: Decision is made depending on the message that the participant receives in *step-2* or *step-3* from the originator. Participant's logs are updated accordingly.

Step-5: The participating DBMS regains normal operations and starts accepting external requests.

Step-6: Participant's recovery process is terminated.

3.2 Originator Recovery Procedure

Though the originator is also a data site, failure of originator site has different impact than failure of participating database site. The originator should restart and then determine state of all participating sites. Next we discuss recovery procedure for the originator.

Step-1: Restart the originator site and restore the values from the log.

Step-2: Determine the status of outstanding subtransactions executing in multiple participants.

Case-I. Originator is in *running* state: If the subtransaction of the global transaction executing at the originator is active during the failure, the originator decides to abort, and appends 'abort' in GT termination log.

Case-II. Originator is in *wait* state (subtransaction executing at the originator has successfully executed but waiting for response of other participants), i.e. GTID can be found in GT active log and no entry regarding the GTID in GT termination log. Number of 'ready' entries in the GST ready log is also less than the number of subtransactions.

(i)   If the participating subtransaction is in *running* state then the originator allows it to continue normally.

(ii)   If the participating subtransaction is in *sleep* state then the originator records the information in GST ready log and leaves the participant in *sleep* state till the final decision is made.

(iii) If the participating site is either in *abort* or *compensate* state, this signifies that the originator failed after the global decision to abort the transaction was made but could not update the log. The GT termination log is updated with 'pre-abort', originator then informs all participants and it waits for acknowledgement from the participant.

Case-III. Originator is in *commit* state, i.e. 'commit' entry found in GT termination log. Since the originator decided to commit, this indicates that all subtransactions executed to successful completion. Hence all subtransactions can only be in *sleep* or *commit* state.

(i) If the participant is in *sleep* state then the originator instructs the participant about successful completion of the global transaction and updates the originator's log. Participant then enters the commit state.

(ii) If the participant is already in *commit* state then originator has to just update its log.

Case-IV. Originator is in *pre-abort/abort* state, i.e. 'pre-abort' or 'abort' entry found in the GT termination log. Since the originator decided to abort this indicates that any of the subtransactions must have decided to abort. If the originator is in *pre-abort* state then it is waiting for acknowledgement from some of the participants and thus the participants can be either in *sleeping* state or *abort* state. If the originator is in *abort* state then all participants must be in *abort* state, since it enters *abort* state only after receiving all acknowledgements.

(i) If the participant is in *sleeping* state, communicate *abort* decision to it. The participant then sends an acknowledgement to the originator.

(ii) If the participant is in *abort* state, acknowledgement from the participant is updated in the originator-site. When all acknowledgements are received, originator moves from *pre-abort* to *abort* state and the log is updated.

Step 3: Depending on above-mentioned scenario, response from all participants is collected. If all participants' response was to commit i.e. they are in *sleep* state then global decision is to *commit*, which is conveyed to all participants. If any of the participants decided to abort then the global *abort* decision is conveyed to all participants. GT termination log is updated accordingly.

Step-4: The global recovery process terminates.

4 Conclusion

In this paper we have presented a recovery algorithm for Grid databases. We have argued that due to changing architectural needs of distributed computing, e.g. Grid architecture, various database issues, e.g. concurrency control and failure recovery, need to be revisited. Unlike traditional distributed databases Grid database doesn't have the leverage to use global log files. Major challenge in maintaining consistency in case of site failure is to handle heterogeneity, autonomy, distribution and high volume of data in Grid architecture.

References

[1] T,Ozsu, P.Valduriez, "*Distributed and Parallel Database Systems*", *ACM Computing Surveys,* vol.28, no.1, pp 125-128, March '96.

[2] P. A. Bernstein, V. Hadzilacos, N. Goodman, *Concurrency Control and Recovery in Database Systems,* Addision-Wesley, 1987.

[3] K. Barker, "Transaction Management on Multidatabase Systems", PhD thesis, Department of Computer Science, The university of Alberta, Canada, 1990.

[4] I. Keidar, D. Dolev, "Increasing the Resilience of Atomic Commit, at no Additional Cost", *ACM-SIGMOD Symposium on Principles of Database Systems*, pp 245-254, 1995.

[5] I. Foster, C. Kesselman, S.Tuecke, "The Anatomy of the Grid", *International Journal of Supercomputer Applications,* vol. 15, no. 3, 2001.

[6] P. Watson, "*Databases and the Grid*", Technical Report, CS-TR-755, University of New Castle, 2002

[7] S. Goel, H. Sharda, D. Taniar, " Atomic Commitment in Grid Database Systems", *Inter. Conf. on Network and Parallel Computing, LNCS,* Springer-Verlag (accepted), 2004.

[8] S. Goel, H. Sharda, D. Taniar, "Preserving Data Consistency in Grid Databases with Multiple Transactions", *Grid and Cooperative Computing, LNCS,* Springer-Verlag, Dec 03

[9] I. Foster, C. Kesselman, J. M. Nick, S.Tuecke, "The Physiology of the Grid", http://www.globus.org/research/papers/ogsa.pdf

[10] A. Chervenak, I. Foster, C. Kesselman, C. Salisbury, S. Tuecke, "The Data Grid: Towards an architecture for the Distributed Management and Analysis of Large Scientific Datasets", *Journal of Network and Computer Applications*, vol. 23, pp 187-200, '01

[11] H. Stockinger, "Distributed Database Management Systems and the Data Grid", *18th IEEE Symposium on Mass Storage Systems* '01.

On Design of Cluster and Grid Computing Environment Toolkit for Bioinformatics Applications*

Chao-Tung Yang[1], Yu-Lun Kuo[1], Kuan-Ching Li[2], and Jean-Luc Gaudiot[3]

[1] High Performance Computing Laboratory,
Dept. of Computer Science and Information Engineering,
Tunghai University, Taichung 40744 Taiwan ROC
ctyang@mail.thu.edu.tw
[2] Parallel and Distributed Processing Center,
Dept. of Computer Science and Information Management,
Providence University, Taichung 43301 Taiwan ROC
kuancli@pu.edu.tw
[3] Parallel and Scalable Computer Architecture Laboratory,
Dept. of Electrical Engineering and Computer Science,
University of California – Irvine, Irvine, CA 92697 USA
gaudiot@uci.edu

Abstract. In this paper, we present BioGrid, a novel computing resource that combines advantages of grid computing technology with bioinformatics parallel applications. The grid environment permits the sharing of a large amount of idle computing resources and data. The investigation of bioinformatics demands orders of magnitude of computing resources and in parallel, the biological data are growing in such a high speed. By using BioGrid, we plan to integrate and share resources and biological data using the grid computing technology. Still in this paper, the well-known FASTA application is performed as matter of testing and analysis in our grid computing platform, as goal to show the improved efficiency and reduced computation time.

1 Introduction

Grid computing, most simply stated, is distributed computing taken to the next evolutionary level. The goal is to create the illusion of a simple yet large and powerful self managing virtual computer, a large collection of heterogeneous systems interconnected by sharing various combinations of resources and data. It is the standardization of communications between heterogeneous systems created with the internet explosion. The emerging standardization to share resources, along with the availability of higher bandwidth, is driving to an evolutionary step as large as grid computing [7, 8, 9].

---

* This research is supported in part by the National Science Council, Taiwan, under grant NSC93-2213-E-126-010.

A. Sen et al. (Eds.): IWDC 2004, LNCS 3326, pp. 82–87, 2004.
© Springer-Verlag Berlin Heidelberg 2004

There are available parallel versions of bioinformatics applications [1], which can be installed and performed on PC-based clusters; for example, HMMer [11], FASTA [12], mpiBLAST [13], ClustalW-MPI [2], Wrapping-up BLAST [3], and TREE-PUZZLE [4], among others. Using these parallel versions to work on sequence alignment always can save much time and cost. Especially for some biotechnology and high-tech companies, PC-based clusters are already replacing mainframe systems or supercomputers, by saving large amount of hardware cost.

Recent advances in computer technology, especially in the development of grid tools, make them excellent option for performing parallel application programs and resources usage. Computational grids enable sharing a wide variety of geographically distributed resources and allow selection and aggregation of distributed resources across multiple organizations for solving large-scale computational and date intensive problems in science. BioGrid is a large-scale distributed computing environment, including computer systems, storage systems, and other devices. BioGrid system can improve performance more than parallel computing on PC-based clusters. There are several BioGrid research projects under development in the world, such as, EuroGrid BioGrid [15], Asia Pacific BioGrid [14], UK BioGrid [17, 18], North Carolina BioGrid [19, 20], Osaka University BioGrid, Indiana University BioGrid, Minnesota University [6] and Singapore BioGrid [2], and others.

In this paper, FASTA bioinformatics application software is added and ported to a grid system, and recompiled with MPICH-G2. There are several other MPI based biology software applications that can be easily added to a grid system, for example, mpiBLAST [13], ClustalW [2] etc. BioGrid systems are important and necessary, in order to accelerate the sequence alignment experiment process. The use of parallel version softwares and cluster systems are excellent good way to achieve high efficiency and with reduced cost. As we already know, bioinformatics tools can speed up, by several orders of magnitude, analysis the large-scale sequence data, especially about sequence alignment.

The organization of this research paper is as follows. In section 2, we introduce the FASTA software and our hardware and software configurations, also, the user interface. Also in this section, it is discussed the proposed grid computing environment built over multiple Linux PC Clusters by using Globus Toolkit and SUN Grid Engine. The experimental results using FASTA software on this grid environment is discussed in section 3, and finally, conclusions are discussed in section 4.

2 System Environments and User Interface

We built three PC-based clusters to form a grid computing environment. Each master node executes SGE master daemon. SGE execute daemon to run, manage, and monitor incoming job. Each slave node executes SGE slave daemon to execute incoming job only. These PC-based clusters are located in three different sites of a building to form a BioGrid system, as shown in Figure 1, in the High-Performance Computing Laboratory, Department of Information Engineering and Sciences at Tunghai University, Taiwan. We use SCMS monitor to monitor our grid system and the status of our BioGrid system are shown in Figures 2 and 3.

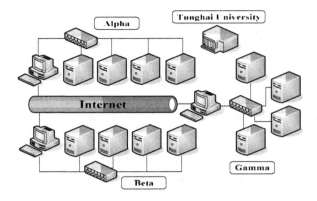

Fig. 1. The BioGrid hardware system architecture

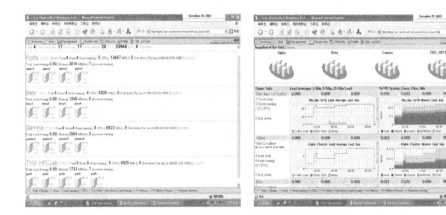

Fig. 2. The BioGrid's system status window   **Fig. 3.** The BioGrid's status summary page

In the entire software structure of this system, the grid environment available is a basic environmental construction, where Globus Toolkit serves as middleware to take care of message communication and information exchange in the grid environment. As of job allocation, SGE (Sun Grid Engine) is selected to assign tasks to the computers on the rear. We have developed graphic user interface supported by JAVA, which is highlighted with its inter-platform characteristics, the newly debuted interface suits all systems for successful operations. There, we have a program named as CoG, which is to link JAVA and the Linux environment for communication. We have to select the files for mapping. We can locate the files in the upper right of Figure 4 or just type in the file name in the space, the program will search in the portfolio by the name of Update in its own menu for matched files. After selecting files for mapping, we have to select the database for mapping. As shown in Figure 5, we can select the function parameters for mapping. After verified the selection, we start mapping the orders. After execution, reminder messages will appear to notify the user that mapping is completed.

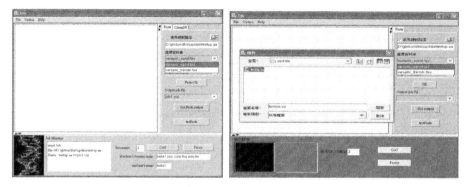

Fig. 4. Query sequence and database selection   **Fig. 5.** FASTA function selection

3 Experimental Results

We performed parallel version of FASTA application program in our BioGrid environment. In order to make the software execute flawlessly in the grid structure; we have edited it using MPICH-G2 to success in its operations. During this test, we have used two databases, namely tremble_new.fas and trembl.fas. The size of the former database is 23MB, while the latter one is of 153MB.

Figure 6 shows the result, by gradually increasing the number of processors, we can observe that the time consumed for execution decreases significantly. As tremble_new.fas is smaller, the time consumed does not change, once a specific number of processors are reached.

When the larger database is used for experiment, we would realize the time consumed does go down remarkably while more processors are added. Therefore, the larger and more complex the database becomes, better is the BioGrid environment's performance.

During our experimental test, we have used np3 (2 CPUs are used), np5 (4 CPUs are used), np7 (6 CPUs are used), np9 (8 CPUs are used), np11 (10 CPUs are used) and np13 (12 CPUs are used) for the order mapping. The performance analyses are shown in Figures 6 and 7.

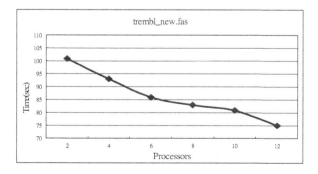

Fig. 6. Execution time of FASTA using 2 to 12 processors (trembl_new.fas)

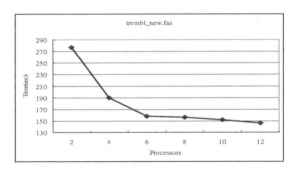

Fig. 7. Execution time of FASTA using 2 to 12 processors (trembl.fas)

4   Conclusions

In this paper, we have built the basic platform for the grid computing environment using the Linux PC-based cluster. In the grid environment, Globus Toolkit (GT) as middleware is used for message transfer and communication between grid platforms, while Sun Grid Engine (SGE) is responsible for task distribution. Still during experiments, we have installed the order mapping software of FASTA parallel version and have selected two databases of difference capacities for experiments. The results show that BioGrid can save significantly time in mapping, as well as improving its efficiency. Thus, it performs much better, in average, in any computer system. Naturally, BioGrid is not only suitable for FASTA software, it can show performance improved for all existing parallel bioinformatics software, such as mpiBLAST, TREE-PUZZLE and ClustalW-MPI, among others.

We are aiming at bioinformatics grid, where grid platforms would be used to build a super bioinformatics grid by integrating major bioinformatics bases to provide relevant bioinformatics to the users on the bioinformatics Grid for query.

References

1. Trelles, O., 2001. On the Parallelization of Bioinformatics Applications. *Briefings in Bioinformatics.* May, vol. 2. Available form: http://www.ac.uma.es/~ots/papers/survey.pdf
2. Li, Kuo-Bin, 2003. ClustalW-MPI: ClustalW Analysis Using Distributed and Parallel Computing. *Bioinformatics.* 19 (12), pp. 1585-1586.
3. Hokamp, K., Denis C. Shields, Kenneth H. Wolfe and Daniel R. Caffrey, 2003. Wrapping up BLAST and other applications for use on UNIX clusters. *Bioinformatics.* Feb. 19(3), pp. 441-442.
4. Heiko A. Schmidt, Korbinian Strimmer, Martin Vingron and Arndt von Haeseler, 2002. TREE-PUZZLE: maximum likelihood phylogenetic analysis using quartets and parallel computing. *Bioinformatics.* Mar, 18(3), pp. 502-504.
5. Michael Karo, Christopher Dwan, John Freeman, Jon Weissman, Miron Livny, Ernest Retzel, 2001. Applying Grid Technologies to Bioinformatics. *10th IEEE International Symposium on High Performance Distributed Computing (HPDC-10'01).* IEEE Computer Society.

6. Global Grid Forum. Available form: http://www.ggf.org
7. I. Foster, C. Kesselman, 1999. *The Grid: Blueprint for a New Computing Infrastructure.* Morgan Kaufmann.
8. I. Foster, 2002. The Grid: A New Infrastructure for 21st Century Science. *Physics Today,* 55(2), pp. 42-47.
9. SETI@home: Search for Extraterrestrial Intelligence at home. Available form: http://setiathome.ssl.berkeley.edu/
10. The Globus Project. Available form: http://www.globus.org/
11. HMMER: profile HMMs for protein sequence analysis. Available form: http://hmmer.wustl.edu/
12. The FASTA main page. Available form: ftp://ftp.virginia.edu/pub/fasta/
13. mpiBLAST main page. Available form: http://mpiblast.lanl.gov/index.html
14. Asia Pacific BioGRID Initiative, Available form: http://www.apbionet.org/apbiogrid/
15. BioGRID - European grid for molecular biology. Available form: http://biogrid.icm.edu.pl/
16. BioGrid: Construction of a supercomputer network main page. Available form: http://www.biogrid.jp/
17. L. Moreau and et. al. (2003) On the Use of Agents in a Bioinformatics Grid, In S. Lee, S. Sekguchi, S. Matsuoka, and M. Sato, editors, *Proc. of the 3rd IEEE/ACM CCGRID 2003.* IEEE Computer Society.
18. The UK MyGrid project site. Available form: http://www.mygrid.org.uk
19. North Carolina Bioinformatics Grid (BioGrid) web site. Available form: http://www.ncbiogrid.org
20. North Carolina Genomics and Bioinformatics Consortium web site. Available form: http://www.ncgbc.org

Study of Scheduling Strategies in a Dynamic Data Grid Environment

R.A. Dheepak, Shakeb Ali, Shubhashis Sengupta, and Anirban Chakrabarti

Software Engineering and Technology Laboratory,
Infosys Technologies Ltd.,
Electronics City, Bangalore 560 100, India
{dheepak_ra, shakeb_ali, shubhashis_sengupta,
anirban_chakrabarti}@infosys.com

Abstract. Data grids seek to harness geographically distributed resources for large-scale data-intensive problems. Such problems involve loosely coupled jobs and large data sets mostly distributed geographically. Data grids have found applications in scientific research, in the field of high-energy Physics, Life Sciences etc. The issues that need to be considered in the data grid research area include: resource management including computation management and data management. Computation management include scheduling of jobs, scalability, response time involved in such scheduling, while data management include data replication in selected sited, data movement when required. Therefore, scheduling and replication assumes great importance in a data grid environment. In this paper, we have developed several scheduling strategies based on a developed replication strategy. The scheduling strategies are called Matching based Scheduling (MJS), Cost base Scheduling (CJS) and Latency based Scheduling (LJS). Among these, LJS and CJS perform similarly and MJS performs worse than both of them.

1 Introduction

In an increasing number of scientific and enterprise applications, large data collections are emerging as important resources that need to be shared and accessed by research teams dispersed geographically. In domains as diverse as global climate change, high energy physics, and computational genomics, the volume of interesting data will soon total petabytes[1]. The combination of large data size, geographic distribution of users and resources, diverse data sources, and computationally intensive analysis results in complex and stringent performance demands that are not satisfied by any existing data management infrastructure. The literature offers numerous point solutions that address the issues of data management, data distribution and job scheduling (e.g., [2]). However, no integrating architecture exists that allows one to identify requirements and components common to different systems and hence apply different technologies in a coordinated fashion to a range of data-intensive application domains. Motivated by these considerations, researchers have launched a collaborative effort called *Data Grids* to design and produce such an integrating architecture.

A. Sen et al. (Eds.): IWDC 2004, LNCS 3326, pp. 88–94, 2004.
© Springer-Verlag Berlin Heidelberg 2004

Most previous scheduling work has considered data locality/storage issues as secondary to job placement [3,4]. Paper [5] talks about combining the replication and scheduling strategies in a more organized manner. The authors assumed three components: an External Scheduler (ES), which determines where (i.e. to which site) to send jobs that originate at that site; a Local Scheduler (LS), which determines the order in which jobs that are allocated to that site are executed; and a Data Scheduler (DS), responsible for determining if and when to replicate data and/or delete local files. The Grid architecture considered in this paper is similar to one proposed in [5]. In Data Grid, both scheduling and replication aim at reducing the latency for job execution. While scheduling does that by directing the jobs to certain sites so that the latency involved in data movement and job processing is reduced, replication moves the data around so that the data access time during scheduling is reduced. The key contribution of the paper lies in the study of effect of replication strategies on scheduling strategies. An integration approach is presented in [6] by the same authors.

2   Job Scheduling (JS) Problem

In a data grid G = <V, E>, where V form the set of vertices and E form the set of edges, we model a job request as a 3-tuple $J = <S, \tilde{F}, \tilde{C}>$, where Sj is the site from which the job is fired, $\tilde{F}$ is the list of files needed by the job and $\tilde{C}$ is the computation time required by the job J. A site is modeled as a 3-tuple $S = <\hat{F}, V, P_s>$, where $\hat{F}$ is the set of files stored in the site S, V is the storage capacity at that site and P_s is the computation capacity at that site.   The **Job Scheduling (JS)** problem states that: Let J_i be a job, and $\hat{S} = \{S_1, S_{2......} S_n\}$ be the set of sites, then the problem is to schedule the job J_i to a site S_j, where $S_j \in \hat{S}$, such that the latency between submitting the job and job execution is minimized. In this paper the strategies to solve the JS problem are proposed and studied. A simple history based strategy to solve the DR problem is proposed. It is to be noted that in a data grid scenario, the solution to JS problem is complicated as the data locations get changed due to data movements because of the underlying data replication strategy. Therefore, solutions to the JS problem need to be studied with the underlying replication strategy.

2.1   Job Scheduling Strategies

In this section, three Job Scheduling strategies are proposed which solves the JS problem mentioned in the previous section. First one is Matching based Job Scheduling (MJS) and the second one is Cost Based Job Scheduling (CJS).

Matching Based Job Scheduling (MJS): In MJS, the jobs are scheduled to those sites which have the *maximum match* in terms of data. If a job requests for F files, and in a site f of those are already present, then the amount of data in bytes corresponding to those f files represent the *match* corresponding the job request. The job is scheduled to the site which has the maximum match corresponding to the job request. If there is a tie then the tie is broken by reducing the latency involved in moving the data which is not present in the scheduled site from the site(s) containing the data. It is possible that MJS may distribute the jobs to the same site resulting in the queue size increase in that site. To distribute the jobs to different sites the scheduling is done based on $v = m.\dfrac{\overline{q}}{q_i}$ factor, where m is the maximum match, $\overline{q}$ is the average queue size of all PEs in the Grid and q_i is the queue size at the site. In the Performance Studies section, α is varied to see its effect on the simulation. MJS schedules based on the maximum v value. Figure 1 (a) shows an example of a topology of a data grid. S1, S2, S3 and S4 are the different sites in the Data Grid. In this example the $\dfrac{\overline{q}}{q_i}$ factor is considered to be equal to 1. The example just illustrates the running of the job scheduling strategies. The numbers and the arrows show the latency to move a file from one data site to the other. The elements in each site indicate the files that are present in each of those sites. Let a job comes which requires files D1, D3 and D6. According to the JSA algorithm, both S2 and S4 are candidate sites where the job can be scheduled. If the job is scheduled in S2, then it takes 7 secs to move the file D6 from S3 (File Originating Site) to S2. On the other hand, if the job is scheduled onto S4, then it takes 4 secs. Therefore, the job is scheduled onto site S4.

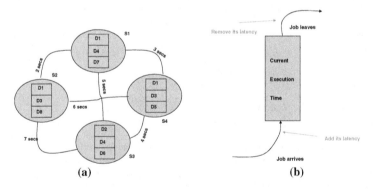

Fig. 1. (a) Topology of a Data Grid (b) Strategy for computing δ_i^q

Cost Based Job Scheduling (CJS): Another alternative to matching based job scheduling, a cost based job scheduling strategy is proposed. Cost ($C_{ij}^{\ s}$) of scheduling a job J_i onto a site S_j is defined as the combined cost of moving the data into the site S_j, latency to compute the job J_i in the site S_j and the wait time in the queue in the site S_j. The job is scheduled onto the site which has the minimum $C_{ij}^{\ s}$.

$$C_{ij}^s = \Delta_{ij}^s . \frac{\overline{q}}{q_i} \tag{1}$$

where, Δ_{ij}^s is the latency involved in moving the data files for the current jobs and $\overline{q}$ and q_i are as described earlier. Referring back to the example shown in Figure 1 (a), we assume that in this case the computational time is 0 and queues at each site is also 0. Therefore C_{ij}^s is composed of only the data latency. The values of C_{ij}^s for j=1,2,3,4 are: $C_{i1}^s = 7$ secs, $C_{i2}^s = 7$ secs, $C_{i3}^s = 8$ secs, $C_{i4}^s = 4$ secs. Therefore, the job is scheduled onto site S4, same as MJS. Though both the algorithms provide similar performance in this example, generally CJS will be better if instantaneous queue information is available. However, in case of stale or partial information the comparison between these algorithms can be an interesting future study.

Latency Based Job Scheduling (LJS): LJS is another interesting strategy studied in this paper. LJS takes the latency experienced into account before taking the scheduling decision. Cost (C_{ij}^s) of scheduling is defined as:

$$C_{ij}^s = \alpha.\Delta_{ij}^s + (1-\alpha).\delta_i^q \tag{2}$$

where Δ_{ij}^s is the latency involved in scheduling the current job based on the current data locations, and δ_i^q is the latency involved due to the current queue. δ_i^q is the sum of execution time of all jobs currently present in the queue. Equation (2) also has α which is the uncertainty parameter used. The uncertainty comes because of the replication process which changes the data localities. This factor brings into account the amount of relative importance that needs to be given to the current job vis-à-vis the jobs in the queue. δ_i^q is calculated based on the strategy mentioned in Figure 1(b). The strategy is employed at each site. As soon a job is scheduled at that site, the execution time is added to δ_i^q. Whenever a job leaves the site the execution time of the job (including the data movement latency) is removed from δ_i^q.

Comparing between the proposed algorithms: MJS, and CJSalgorithms run in the O(nfs) and O($n^2 f$) respectively where n is the number of sites, f is the number of files in each job request and s is the number of files stored in each site. From the expression is it clear that CJS is a more expensive algorithm than MJS by an order of n. However, the running time of CJS algorithm can be reduced to O(nfr) where r is the number of times a file is replicated if the information about the current data location is stored. Therefore, to reduce the running time an O(Fn) storage is required, where F is the total number of files in the data grid environment. This also requires that as soon a replication is carried out the information need to be stored. The LJS algorithm has the same running time as CJS, however the strategy mentioned in Figure 1(b), O(1) has to be employed whenever a job is scheduled and executed.

3 Performance Studies

To evaluate the performance of the proposed strategies, the OptorSim [7] simulator
was used, which is a commonly used simulator for the simulation of data Grid environment. The simulation runs are taken with jobs arriving average exponential
inter-arrival time of 0.25 seconds, the processing speed at the nodes are considered
constant at 10 second/Gb of data. Number of jobs requesting a particular file is distributed exponentially. This gives an elliptical file distribution per job with an average
of 7 and total files in the system (F) as 20. The initial file distribution in the Grid is
random.

3.1 Variation of Latency

In Figure 2 (a) , the variation of job latency with storage capacity is studied. As a
general trend with the increase in storage capacity, the job latency decreases. This is
because with the increase in storage capacity more files are stored in each site resulting in less time in actual data transfer. Among the different algorithms, the interesting
trend is that with increase in storage capacity, the difference between the performance
of the algorithms go down and all the algorithms perform similarly when the storage
capacity is very high (above 10GB). This is because at high storage capacity, the data
movement is minimized because of the replication algorithm. Among the different
algorithms CJS performs the best, closely followed by LJS algorithm. MJS performs
30% worse than CJS at low bandwidths. In Figure 2(b), the comparison among the
different versions of LJS are made. LJS with $\alpha = 0.7$ performs the best, closely
followed by LJS with $\alpha = 0.5$ .In Figure 2(b), the variation of job latency with computational capacity is illustrated. The computational capacity is indicated by the number of CPUs in each site. With the increase in computational capacity the job latency
decreases, however the decrease is not as significant as that of the storage capacity
variation because most of the jobs are data intensive jobs, and data movement latency
account for most of the job latency. Among the different algorithms, CJS and LJS
perform almost similarly. However, both of them perform at least 30% better (latency
is 30% lower) than MJS. Among the different versions of LJS, LJS with
$\alpha = 0.7$ performs the best. Figure 2(c) shows the variation of job latency with
bandwidth. With the increase in bandwidth, the latency decreases because it takes less
time to transfer files between sites. MJS and CJS perform consistently better than
LJS.

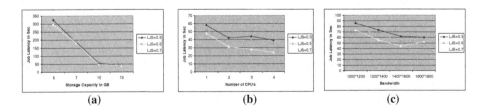

Fig. 2. Variation of Job Latency with (a) Storage, (b) Computational Capacity, (c) Bandwidth

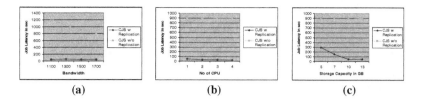

Fig. 3. Variation of Job Latency with Bandwidth

The effect of replication on CJS is studied in Figure 3. Figure 3a, b and c show the variation of job latency with bandwidth, computational capacity and storage capacity respectively. In all the figures, CJS strategy performs much better with the DRS replication strategy working in the background. The performance improvement is in the multiplicative order. The latency is 10-15 times more without replication than with it. Replication is also able to take advantage of the more storage space and pack in more files in each site than no replication scheme as illustrated in Figure 3(c). These sets of experiments show that replication is surely a better strategy to employ with any scheduling strategy.

4 Conclusions

Scheduling in a dynamic grid scenario is different from traditional scheduling because of the complications introduced due to data location, movement and replication. In this paper, this fact is reiterated and studied. Three scheduling strategies have been proposed for the ES viz. Matching Based Scheduling (MJS), Cost Based Scheduling (CJS) and Latency Based Scheduling (LJS). Extensive simulation studies were carried out using OptorSim, which is widely used for data grid simulations. Simulation results show that: (i) CJS and LJS perform similarly under most circumstances. (ii) Both CJS and LJS perform significantly better than MJS especially under constrained circumstances i.e., low storage, low bandwidth etc. (iii) Replication strategy when employed with the scheduling strategies significantly improve the performance and the performance also is better under low bandwidth case as more latency is required to move the files in low bandwidth scenario. As part of our future work, we intend to develop a distributed replication strategy which can work with the developed scheduling strategies in an efficient manner.

References

1. Chervenak, I. Foster, C. Kesselman, C. Salisbury, S. Tuecke, "The Data Grid: Towards an Architecture for the Distributed Management and Analysis of Large Scientific Datasets," *Journal of Network and Computer Applications*, 23:187-200, 2001.
2. Foster, C. Kesselman, "The Globus Project: A Status Report," *Proc. IPPS/SPDP '98 Heterogeneous Computing Workshop*, pp. 4-18, 1998.

3. H. Casanova, G. Obertelli, F. Berman and R. Wolski, "The AppLeS Parameter Sweep Template: User-Level Middleware for the Grid," in *Proceedings of SuperComputing'00*, 2000.
4. A.H. Alhusaini, V.K. Prasanna and C.S. Raghavendra, "A Unified Resource Scheduling Framework for Heterogeneous Computing Environments," in *Eighth Heterogeneous Computing Workshop*, 1999.
5. Ranganathan and I. Foster, "Identifying Dynamic Replication Strategies for a High Performance Data Grid," in *Proceedings of the Second International Workshop on Grid Computing*, 2001.
6. A. Chakrabarti, Dheepak R.A., and S. Sengupta, "Integration of Scheduling and Replication in Data Grids," in *Intl. Conf. on High Perf. Computing (HiPC)*, Dec. 2004.
7. W.H. Bell, D.G. Cameron et al., "Simulation of Dynamic Grid Replication Strategies in OptorSim," in Proc. Third Int'l Workshop on Grid Computing, 2002.

Virtual Molecular Computing – Emulating DNA Molecules

Sanjay Goswami[1] and Susmita Sur-Kolay[2]

[1] Narula Institute of Technology, Agarpara, West Bengal
[2] ACM Unit, Indian Statistical Institute, Kolkata
ssk@isical.ac.in

Abstract. Inherent complementary nature of double-stranded DNA molecules has led to the DNA computing model which provides massive parallelism. In order to facilitate study of this model without test-tubes and their associated laboratory errors, this paper proposes a scheme for software emulation of a well-known test tube algorithm, the first NP-complete problem SAT. Multi-threading is employed to obtain the effect of simultaneous test-tube reactions.

1 Introduction

The power of DNA computing [1, 2] lies in the striking features of DNA molecules, viz. *Massive Parallelism* in reactions among DNA strands, and the a vital property of *Watson-Crick Complementarity*.

A DNA molecule is a polymer, strung together from monomers called *deoxy-ribonucleotides*. There are four different bases in DNA molecules, namely, *Adenine* (A), *Guanine* (G), *Cytosine* (C), and *Thymine* (T); i.e., *{A, C, T, G}.* When *bonding* takes place between two DNA single strands, the bases opposite to each other are complementary, i.e., **A** always bonds with **T,** and **C** with **G**. This is called *Watson-Crick Complementarity*[5]. Since this is the *bio-equivalent* of binary logic, there is a great potential as a possible tool for computing.

Computing paradigms with DNA molecules are different from those of classical von Neumann style, thereby requiring new data structures or operations on classic ones (strings, languages). The massive parallelism of DNA reactions has inspired the design of different algorithms for solving NP-hard problems, but all *in vitro!*

Since building real DNA based computers are not yet feasible in the current scenario due to problems in automating (error prone) primitive test tube based bio-operations on DNA molecules; the alternative is **emulation** of them in the silicon framework. Our objective in this paper is to develop *representation* and *computational* techniques using *multithreading* to emulate the structure and parallel computing behavior of DNA molecules and execute the *in vitro* bio-algorithms for solving computational problems in the *in silico* model.

2 Preliminaries for DNA Computing

The deoxyribonucleotides (or simply nucleotides) in a DNA molecule [5] consist of three components – a *Sugar*, a *Phosphate* group, and a *Nitrogenous base* (or simply

A. Sen et al. (Eds.): IWDC 2004, LNCS 3326, pp. 95–101, 2004.
© Springer-Verlag Berlin Heidelberg 2004

base). The sugar called *deoxyribose* has *five* carbon atoms. Since the nitrogenous base also has carbons, the carbons of the sugar are numbered from 1' to 5', rather than 1 to 5. The Phosphate group is attached to the 5' carbon atom, and the base to 1' carbon. Within the sugar structure, there is a Hydroxyl group (OH-) attached to the 3' carbon. These nucleotides differ only by their four possible bases mentioned above. Nucleotides can link with each other in the following two ways:

- a strong covalent phosphodiester bond (-POH-) between the 5'–phosphate group of one nucleotide and the 3'- hydroxyl group of the other. This bonding is responsible for DNA single strand structure consisting of nucleotides with directionality 5'-3' or 3'-5'.
- a weak Hydrogen bond between the base of one strand and that of the other, subject to *Watson-Crick Complementarity*. This bonding is responsible for DNA double strand structure.

In a double stranded DNA the two single strands have opposite directions: the nucleotide at the 5' end of one strand is bonded to the nucleotide at the 3' end of the other strand. It is a standard convention that when a double strand is drawn, then the upper strand runs from left to right in the 5'– 3' direction, and consequently the lower strand runs from left to right in the 3'– 5' direction.

The primitive bio-operations that can be performed on DNA molecules are: (1) Shortening, (2) Cutting, (3) Hybridization, (3) Melting (4) Linking or Ligation, and (5) Multiplication. Of these, the molecules undergo hybridization, melting and ligation in parallel, thereby enhancing the power of bio-computing.

3 *In silico* Representation of DNA Molecules

We propose the following data structures to represent DNA molecules virtually:

- Doubly Linked List represents a Single Strand
- Laterally Linked Pair of doubly linked lists represents a Double Strand
- 1-D Array represents an *in vitro* test tube containing DNA strands.

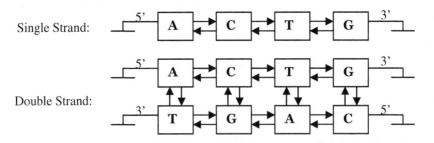

Fig. 1. Representation of DNA using linked lists

4 Emulation of Bio-operations

We propose emulation techniques for the following most frequently used bio-operations on the strands of DNA:, *Hybridization, Melting, Complementing and Ligation.* Each operation has been implemented as a function using *C* language.

• **Hybridization:** Two single strands, which are WC-complement of each other, are joined laterally through H-bond to form a double strand. Our virtual model implements this reaction as a *C* function **hybridize (S_1*, S2*)** which takes two DNA strands, i.e., two linked lists, as input and checks the WC-Complementarity for each nucleotide. If all the nucleotide pairs satisfy complementarity, it joins them by lateral linking (H-Bonds) forming a *laterally-linked list pair* (Figure 2).

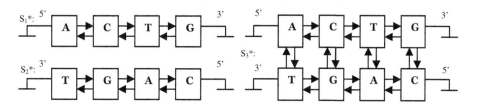

Fig. 2. Hybridization of two Single strands into a Double strand

• **Melting:** The weak H-bonds between complementary bases are broken by heating a double strand, yielding two single strands. This reaction is emulated by the *C* function **melt (S*)** which takes a double strand, i.e., a pointer to a laterally linked list pair, as input, and removes lateral links (the H-Bonds) between the corresponding nodes of the two lists as shown in Figure 3.

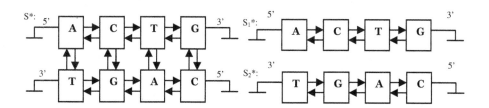

Fig. 3. Melting of a Double strand into two Single strands

• **Complementing:** This reaction is required to generate a complementary strand of a given strand. The **complement (S*)** routine implements this reaction by taking a strand (a linked list) as input, reading the name of the nucleotide in each node and writing out its WC-Complement. Then the 5' and 3' pointers are swapped.

• **Ligation (Linking):** This reaction involves head to head joining of single strands by phosphodiester bonds in presence of a certain class of enzymes called *Ligases*. The emulation is done by **ligate (S_1*, S2*)** which takes two single strands as input and joins the 3'-end of one strand with the 5'-end of the other strand by establishing links as depicted in Figure 4.

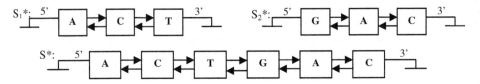

Fig. 4. Ligation of two strands into one strand

5   Problem Solving on This Platform

The approach adopted in emulating the parallel bio-operations on a test-tube full of DNA molecules is *Multithreading*. The concurrency in the events of H-bonding and melting among the corresponding nodes can be achieved to some extent by multithreading where different node-pairs (nucleotide-pairs) may be assigned to separate threads for linking and de-linking. To start with, the problems chosen for this virtual platform were (i) *evaluation of arithmetic and Boolean expressions* and (ii) the SAT*isfiability* problem. Algorithms of Gupta et. al. [3] for the first problem were implemented and tested with an improved encoding scheme and the bio-operation functions described in Section 4. Due to dearth of space, the next section discusses only the emulation of the algorithm to solve the satisfiability problem.

6   Solving SAT*isfiability* with DNA Molecules

As suggested by Lipton [4], the process of solving an instance of the SAT*isfiability* problem involves DNA strands encoding all possible combinations of Boolean values that the variables can assume. The encoding is done according to a scheme suggested by Lipton. The emulation of Lipton's algorithm in our virtual model is demonstrated through the following example (for simplicity of demonstration, a 2-CNF is taken).

Example 4: $\beta = (x_1 \vee x_2) \,\&\, (\sim x_1 \vee \sim x_2)$

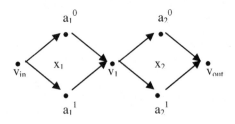

Fig. 5. Lipton Graph: a_i^0 represents assignment 0, a_i^1 represents assignment 1

The encoding of the 7 nodes and 8 edges of this Lipton graph are done in the following way:

- Each *node* is represented by a unique DNA strand:
  V_{in} : 5'-**AAAA** ; a_1^0 : 5'-**AGTG**; a_2^0 : 5'-**AGTC**;
  V_1: 5'-**AATT**; a_1^1 : 5'-**ACTC**; a_2^1 : 5'-**ACTG**; V_{out} :5'-**GGGG**;
- Each *directed edge* is represented as:
  V_{in}—a_1^0 : 3'-**TTTC**, V_{in}—a_1^1: 3'-**TTTG**, a_1^0—V_1 : 3'-**ACTT**,
  a_1^1—V_1: 3'-**AGTT**, V_1—a_2^0: 3'-**AATC**, V_1—a_2^1: 3'-**AATG**,
  a_2^0—V_{out}: 3'-**AGCC**, a_2^1—V_{out} : 3' – **ACCC**

The first two nucleotides of the edge strand are WC-complements of last two nucleotides of the first of the node strands-pair, while the last two nucleotides of the edge strand are complements of the first two nucleotides of the second of the node strands-pair. After creating the virtual node and edge strands, these are stored in two 1-D arrays representing the test tubes T_N and T_E. The single strands contained in the arrays T_N and T_E which have partial WC-Complementarity between them are subjected to virtual hybridization and ligation reactions (implemented as C functions, as presented earlier). In this reaction, the edge strands bring the two corresponding node strands together through hybridization and ligation joins those node strands head to head leading to formation of long double strands (Figure 6).

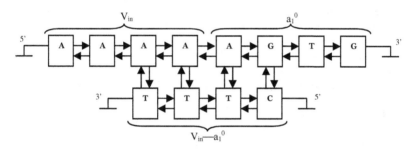

Fig. 6. An edge strand hybridizes two node strands (upper ones) for ligation

By this step, a set of double strands is formed which are then melted to obtain the single strands, each of which represents a path from a certain node to another in the Lipton graph. The problem reduces to finding out all those strands which contain strand segments representing all the nodes $a_i^x \in (a_i^0, a_i^1)$. These strands encode all the possible assignments to the variables (Figure 7).

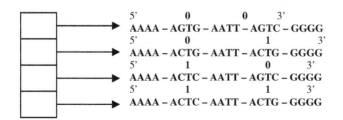

Fig. 7. An array holding strands encoding all the possible assignments

The next stage is to search for the satisfying assignments, which follows the molecular algorithm given below:

1.	input (No)	00,01, 10, 11
2.	$N_1 \leftarrow S$ (No, 1, 1)	10, 11
3.	$N_1' \leftarrow S^-$ (No, 1, 1)	00, 01
4.	$N_2 \leftarrow S (N_1, 2,1)$	01
5.	merge $(N_1, N_2) \rightarrow N_3$	10, 11, 01
6.	$N_4 \leftarrow S (N_3, 1, 0)$	01
7.	$N_4' \leftarrow S^- (N_3, 1, 0)$	10, 11
8.	$N_5 \leftarrow S (N_4', 2, 0)$	10
9.	merge $(N_4, N_5) \rightarrow N_6$	01, 10
10.	detect (N_6)	

The function S $(N_i, n, 1/0)$ searches the array (test tube) N_i for the strands satisfying n^{th} variable in a clause by either 1 or 0. Then it stores those strands in a test tube N_{i+1} to be fed to the next step. This involves parallel extraction of all relevant strands, which is implemented by *multiple threads* simultaneously examining all the strands.

Merge (N_i, N_{i+1}): takes input two arrays (test tubes) and merges their strands to form a *union* of the contents of the two. The resulting union is stored in another array (test tube) to be made input to next step.

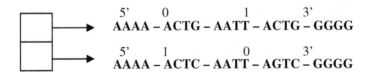

5'   0   1   3'
AAAA – ACTG – AATT – ACTG – GGGG

5'   1   0   3'
AAAA – ACTC – AATT – AGTC – GGGG

Fig. 8. Array holding strands encoding the assignments

At the end, decoding the strands contained by the tube N_6 (Figure 8) yields the following assignments satisfying the example problem: 01 and 10, *which is true!*

7 Concluding Remarks

The emulation routines for the algorithms mentioned above have been tested on randomly generated inputs including SAT instances with 5 or 6 variables. The results have been validated. The major challenges are scalability and space management. It may be pointed out that polynomial time complexity for NP-complete problems is attained with exponential number of DNA molecules. Thus, further work is required to be done to enhance space efficiency, which includes determining an appropriate management strategy for threads.

References

[1] Adleman, L. M.: Molecular Computation of Solutions to Combinatorial Problems. Science, Vol. 266 (1994), 1021-1024.
[2] Adleman, L. M.: On the Potential of Molecular Computing. Science, Vol. 268 (1995), No. 5210, 483-484.
[3] Gupta, V., Parthasarathy, S., and Zaki, M. J.: *Arithmetic* and Logic Operations with DNA. DIMACS Series in Discrete Mathematics and Computer Science, Vol. 48, (1999).
[4] Lipton, R. J.: DNA Solution of Hard Computational Problems. Science, Vol. 268 (1995), 542-545.
[5] Paun, G., Rozenberg G., Salomaa, A.: DNA Computing: New Computing Paradigms. Springer Verlag, (1998).
[6] Goswami, S.: Virtual Molecular Computing – emulating DNA Molecules. MCA Dissertation, IGNOU, (2004).

Complexity of Compositional Model Checking of Computation Tree Logic on Simple Structures

Krishnendu Chatterjee[1], Pallab Dasgupta[2,*], and P.P. Chakrabarti[2,*]

[*] EECS, University of California, Berkeley
[*] Dept. of Computer Science & Engg., Indian Institute of Technology, Kharagpur
c_krish@cs.berkeley.edu, {pallab, ppchak}@cse.iitkgp.ernet.in

Abstract. Temporal Logic Model Checking is one of the most potent tools for the verification of finite state systems. Computation Tree Logic (CTL) has gained popularity because unlike most other logics, CTL model checking of a single transition system can be achieved in polynomial time. However, in most real-life problems, specially in distributed and parallel systems, the system consist of a set of concurrent processes and the verification problem translates to model check the composition of the component processes. Since explicit composition leads to state explosion, verifying the system without actually composing the components is attractive, even for possibly restrictive class of systems. We show that the problem of compositional CTL model checking is PSPACE complete for the class of systems composed of components that are tree-like transition structure and do not interact among themselves. For the simplest forms of existential and universal CTL formulas model checking turns out to be NP complete and coNP complete, respectively. The results hold for both synchronous and asynchronous composition.

1 Introduction

Temporal logic model checking [2, 7] has emerged as one of the most powerful techniques for verifying temporal properties of finite-state systems. The correctness property of the system that needs to be verified is specified in terms of a temporal logic formula. Model checking has been extensively studied for two broad categories of temporal logics, namely *linear time temporal logic* (LTL) and *branching time temporal logic* [3]. The branching time temporal logic, *Computation Tree Logic* (CTL) [2], is one of the most popular temporal logics in practice. CTL allows us to express a wide variety of branching time properties which can be verified in polynomial time (that is, the time complexity of CTL model checking is polynomial in the size of the state transition system times the length of the CTL formula). CTL is also a syntactically elegant, expressive logic which makes CTL model checking computationally attractive as compared to the other logics like LTL and CTL* which are known to be PSPACE complete [7].

---

[*] Pallab Dasgupta and P.P.Chakrabarti thank the Dept. of Science & Tech., Govt. of India, for partial support of this work.

A. Sen et al. (Eds.): IWDC 2004, LNCS 3326, pp. 102–113, 2004.
© Springer-Verlag Berlin Heidelberg 2004

Given an explicit representation of a state transition system, M, CTL model checking is polynomial in the size of M times the length of the formula. In practice systems are seldom represented explicitly as a single transition structure. Generally a large system consists of several concurrent components that run parallely or in a distributed environment. Hence for verification of parallel and distributed systems it is important to be able to verify systems that are described as a set of concurrent processes. Given a set of concurrent components the complete transition system can be a synchronous [1], [7] or asynchronous composition of the components [7]. The composition of the components into a single transition structure is accompanied by the state-explosion problem as the size of the complete state transition structure will be the product of the size of the component transition structures. Therefore the ability to perform model checking without explicit composition is an attractive proposition, even for possibly restrictive class of systems. There have been several approaches to this sort of compositional model checking [7].

Model checking of logics like LTL and CTL* are known to be PSPACE complete for a state transition system. So the complexity of compositional model checking for such logics will be computationally hard as well. CTL model checking is known to be polynomial for a state transition system [2]. Given a set of k concurrent transition systems of size $|S|$, where k is a constant, CTL model checking on the global system which is a composition of the component systems can be achieved in time polynomial in $|S|^k$ times the length of the formula. This is done by composing the components into a single system (of the size $O(|S|^k)$) and applying the *CTL model checking algorithm* on it. If k is not an constant this approach of model checking does not produce a polynomial time solution.

In this paper we study complexity of model checking of CTL properties of a set of concurrent processes considering several modes of composition, namely synchronous and asynchronous composition. We show that the problem is hard even for a very restrictive class of concurrent systems. We consider system composed of components that tree-like transition systems, i.e., the components are trees with leaves having self-loops. Moreover, the components do not communicate among themselves and all these components are specified as an explicit representation of the system. We prove that the problem of CTL model checking is PSPACE complete. However, a PSPACE-upper bound can be proved for a more general class of concurrent systems. We also show that the problem of checking simple *existential* CTL formulas like $E(B\ U\ B)$ and *universal* formulas like $A(B\ U\ B)$, where B is a Boolean formula, is NP complete and coNP complete, respectively. We also show that the problem of reachability of two states of such tree-like structures can be answered in time linear in the size of the input. All the results hold for both synchronous and asynchronous composition. Our result proves that the compositional model checking for CTL is hard for very restrictive classes of systems and the problem is inherently computationally hard.

This paper is organized as follows. In Section 2 we define *tree-like* kripke structures and the synchronous, asynchronous composition of a set of tree-like kripke structures; and also describe the syntax and semantics of CTL in Section 2. In

Section 3 we study the complexity of model checking of CTL on a system which is the composition of a set of tree-like kripke structures. In Section 4 we analyze the complexity of reachability of two states.

2   Tree-Like Kripke Structure

We formally define a tree-like kripke structure and the composition of a set of tree-like kripke structures below.

Definition 1 (Tree-Like Kripke Structure). *A tree-like kripke structure, $T_i = \langle S_i, s_{0i}, \mathcal{R}_i, \mathcal{L}_i, \mathcal{AP}_i \rangle$, consists of the following components:*

- *S_i : finite set of states and $s_{0i} \in S_i$ is the initial state.*
- *$\mathcal{AP}_i$ is the finite set of atomic propositions.*
- *$\mathcal{L}_i : S_i \to 2^{\mathcal{AP}_i}$ — labels each state $s \in S_i$ with a set of atomic propositions true in s.*
- *$\mathcal{R}_i \subseteq S_i \times S_i$ is the transition relation with the restriction that the transition relation graph is a tree with leaves having self-loops. The transition relation is also total, i.e., for every state $s_i \in S_i, \exists\ s'_i \in S_i$ such that $\mathcal{R}_i(s_i, s'_i)$.*   ■

Definition 2 (Composition). *Let $T = \{T_1, T_2, \ldots, T_m\}$ be a set of m tree-like kripke structures. The synchronous, asynchronous and strict asynchronous composition of the tree-like kripke structures in T is denoted by T_S, T_A and T_{SA}, respectively. The set of states, initial state, the set of atomic proposition and the labeling function is same for T_S, T_A and T_{SA} and is defined as follows:*
1. *$S = S_1 \times S_2 \times \ldots \times S_m$ and $s_0 = (s_{01}, s_{02}, \ldots, s_{0m})$ is the initial state;*
2. *$\mathcal{AP} = \bigcup_{i \in \{1,2,\ldots,m\}} \mathcal{AP}_i$;* 3. *$\mathcal{L}(s = (s_1, s_2, s_3, \ldots, s_m)) = \bigcup_{i \in \{1,2,\ldots,m\}} \mathcal{L}_i(s_i)$.*

   The transition relation for T_S, T_A and T_{SA} is defined as follows:

- Synchronous composition T_S: $\mathcal{R} \subseteq S \times S$ such that given $s = (s_1, s_2, s_3, \ldots s_m)$ and $t = (t_1, t_2, t_3, \ldots, t_m)$, $\mathcal{R}(s, t)$ *iff* $\forall\ i \in \{1, 2, \ldots, m\}$ we have $\mathcal{R}_i(s_i, t_i)$, *i.e., every component T_i make a transition.*
- Asynchronous composition T_A: $\mathcal{R} \subseteq S \times S$ such that given $s = (s_1, s_2, s_3, \ldots s_m)$ and $t = (t_1, t_2, t_3, \ldots, t_m)$, $\mathcal{R}(s, t)$ *iff* $\exists\ i \in \{1, 2, \ldots, m\}$ we have $\mathcal{R}_i(s_i, t_i)$, *i.e., one or more component T_i make a transition.*
- Strict asynchronous composition T_{SA}: $\mathcal{R} \subseteq S \times S$ such that given $s = (s_1, s_2, s_3, \ldots s_m)$ and $t = (t_1, t_2, t_3, \ldots, t_m)$, $\mathcal{R}(s, t)$ *iff for some i we have $\mathcal{R}_i(s_i, t_i)$ and for all j such that, $j \neq i$, we have $s_j = t_j$, i.e., exactly one of the components is allowed to make a transition.*   ■

We now present the syntax and semantics of CTL [2, 7].

Syntax of CTL. The syntax of CTL is as follows:

$$S ::= p \mid \neg S \mid S \wedge S \mid AX(S) \mid EX(S) \mid A(S\ U\ S) \mid E(S\ U\ S) \text{ where } p \in \mathcal{AP}.$$

In the syntax of ECTL the rules $AX(S)$ and $A(S\ U\ S)$ are not allowed. Similarly, in ACTL the rules $EX(S)$ and $E(S\ U\ S)$ are not allowed.

Semantics of CTL. The semantics of CTL is as follows:
- $s_0 \models p$ iff $p \in \mathcal{L}(s)$; • $s_0 \models \neg f$ iff $s_0 \not\models f$;
- $s_0 \models f_1 \wedge f_2$ iff $s_0 \models f_1$ and $s_0 \models f_2$;
- $s_0 \models AX(f)$ iff for all states t such that $\mathcal{R}(s,t)$, $t \models f$;

The semantics for $EX(f)$ and $E(f_1 \ U \ f_2)$ is similar to the semantics of $AX(f)$ and $A(f_1 \ U \ f_2)$ with the for all states and for all paths quantifier changed to there exists a state and there exists a path, respectively.

3 Complexity of Compositional CTL Model Checking

In this section we study the complexity of CTL model checking on the composition of a set of tree-like kripke structures. We show that CTL model checking is PSPACE hard by reducing the QBF, that is, the truth of *Quantified Boolean Formulas* (QBF) [6], to the model checking problem. A QBF formula is of the following form: $\phi = \exists x_1 \forall x_2 \exists x_3 .... \forall x_n . C_1 \wedge C_2 ... \wedge C_m$. In the formula ϕ all C_i's are clauses which are disjunction of literals (variables or negation of variables). We restrict each clause to have exactly three distinct literals. QBF is PSPACE complete with this restriction [6]. We reduce the QBF problem to the model checking of CTL formulas on synchronous/asynchronous composition of tree-like kripke structures. We present our reduction in steps as follows. We first present the idea of constructing a tree-like kripke structure for a given clause. Given a QBF formula ϕ with m clauses $C_1, C_2, ... C_m$ we construct m tree-like kripke structures $T_1, T_2, ..., T_m$, one for each clause. We define a CTL property ψ on the composition of $T_1, T_2, ..., T_m$ (denoted as T_S) and show that ψ is true in the start state of T_S iff the QBF formula ϕ is true.

3.1 Construction of Tree-Like Kripke Structure for a Clause

Let ϕ be a QBF formula on a set of variables $X = \{x_1, x_2, ..., x_n\}$ and a clause C_j with exactly three variables from X. We construct a tree-like kripke structure T_j, where T_j is a tree of depth n, as follows:

1. The root of the tree T_j is at depth 0. The root is the initial state of T_j.
2. If a node is at depth i then the depth of its child (successor) is $i + 1$.
3. A node s at level i has two children if variable x_{i+1} appears in C_j, else s has only one child.
4. The root is marked by the atomic proposition r_j.
5. If a variable x_i appears in C_j then for a node s at depth i then: if s is a left child of its parent it is labeled with p_{ji0}, and if s is a right child of its parent it is labeled with p_{ji1}.
6. If x_i does not appear in C_j then every node at depth i is labeled with both p_{ji0} and p_{ji1}.

The number of nodes at level n is 8 for any tree as exactly three variables occur in any clause. Let the variables for the clause C_j be x_i, x_k, x_t where $i < k < t$. Let the nodes at the level n be numbered from 0 to 7 in order as they

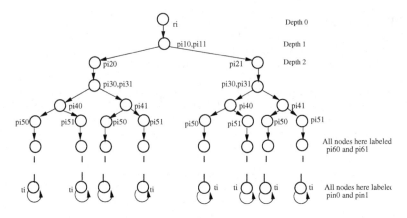

Fig. 1. Tree-like kripke structure for clause $C_i = (x. \vee \neg x. \vee x.)$

will appear in an in-order traversal of T_j. The nodes at depth n are labeled with the proposition t_j as follows : Consider a node s at depth n such that it is numbered i. Let $B_1 B_2 B_3$ be the *binary representation* of i. If assigning $x_i = B_1, x_k = B_2, x_l = B_3$ makes C_j false then s is not labeled by t_j, otherwise it is labeled by t_j. (B_1, B_2, B_3 are $0, 1$ respectively and 0 represents false and 1 represents true). Intuitively the idea is as follows: the assignment of truth value 0 to variable x_{i+1} in C_j is represented by the choice of the left child at depth i in T_j and right child represents the assignment of truth value 1. We refer to the tree-like kripke structure for clause C_j, denoted by T_j, as the *clause tree kripke structure* for clause C_j. The tree structure corresponding to a clause is illustrated in the Figure 1.

The next Lemma follows from construction of tree-like kripke structures.

Lemma 1. *Let variables x_i, x_k, x_t occur in C_j. Given a truth assignment to variables x_i, x_k, x_t we can construct a path (state sequence) $(s_{j0}, s_{j1}, ..., s_{jn})$ in T_j such that s_{jn} is marked with t_j iff the truth assignment makes C_j true. The state sequence is constructed as follows:*

- *If x_ℓ is assigned false then $s_{j\ell}$ is the left child of $s_{j,\ell-1}$ and if x_ℓ is assigned true then $s_{j\ell}$ is the right child of $s_{j,\ell-1}$, where $\ell \in \{ i, k, t \}$.*

3.2   CTL Model Checking of Synchronous Composition

Given m clauses $C_1, C_2, ..., C_m$ we construct the corresponding tree-like kripke structures $T_1, T_2, ..., T_m$ for the respective clauses. The synchronous composition of the tree-like structures is denoted as T_S. We define the properties $p_i, 1 \leq i \leq n$ as follows : $p_1 = (\wedge_{j=1}^m p_{j10}) \vee (\wedge_{j=1}^m p_{j11})$, $p_2 = (\wedge_{j=1}^m p_{j20}) \vee (\wedge_{j=1}^m p_{j21})$ and in general, $p_i = (\wedge_{j=1}^m p_{ji0}) \vee (\wedge_{j=1}^m p_{ji1})$. Given a QBF formula with m clauses an *inconsistent* assignment of truth value to a variable x_i occurs if different truth values are assigned to variable x_i in different clauses.

Lemma 2. *Consider a state sequence $\langle \nu_0, \nu_1, ... \nu_n \rangle$ in T_S where $\nu_0 = s_0$ and each ν_i is the immediate successor of ν_{i-1}. Let ν_i be represented as $(s_{i1}, s_{i2}, ..., s_{im})$. Let $O_i = \{k \mid x_i \text{ occurs in } C_k\}$. Then $\nu_i \models p_i$ iff one of the following conditions are satisfied:*

1. *for all $k \in O_i$ we have s_{ik} is the left child of $s_{i-1,k}$.*
2. *for all $k \in O_i$ we have s_{ik} is the right child of $s_{i-1,k}$.*

Proof. We prove the result considering the following cases:

1. If for all $k \in O_i$ we have s_{ik} is the left child of $s_{i-1,k}$ in T_k then $\nu_i \models \wedge_{j=1}^{m} p_{ji0}$. This is because for any clause C_k in which x_i occurs a node at depth i in T_k which is a left child satisfies p_{ki0}. In any clause C_l such that x_i does not occur a node depth i is the only child of its parent in T_l and satisfies p_{li0}. Similar argument can show that if for all $k \in O_i$ we have s_{ik} is the right child of $s_{i-1,k}$ in T_k then $\nu_i \models \wedge_{j=1}^{m} p_{ji1}$.
2. If $\exists\, t, l$ such that $t, l \in O_i$ and s_{it} is the left child of $s_{i-1,t}$ in T_t and s_{il} is the right child of $s_{i-1,l}$ in T_l then $\nu_i \not\models \wedge_{j=1}^{m} p_{ji0}$ as $\nu_i \not\models p_{li0}$ and $\nu_i \not\models \wedge_{j=1}^{m} p_{ji1}$ as $\nu_i \not\models p_{ti1}$. Intuitively, the state ν_i which does not satisfy p_i actually shows that in one component, T_t, the left branch is followed at depth $i-1$ (representing the assignment of truth value 0 to x_i in C_t) and in other component, T_l, the right branch is followed at depth $i-1$ (representing the assignment of truth value 1 to x_i in C_l) which is represents a inconsistent truth value assignment to x_i.   ∎

Given a QBF formula : $\phi = \exists x_1 \forall x_2 \exists x_3 .... \forall x_n . C_1 \wedge C_2 ... \wedge C_m$ where each C_j is a clause with exactly three variables, for every clause we construct tree-like kripke structure as described in Section 3.1. Given the clauses $C_1, C_2, ..., C_m$ we have $T_1, T_2, ..., T_m$ as the respective tree-like kripke structures. Let T_S denote the parallel synchronous composition of the m kripke structures. We consider model checking the CTL property ψ on T_S, where ψ is defined as follows:

$$EX(p_1 \wedge AX(\neg p_2 \vee (p_2 \wedge EX(p_3 \wedge AX(\neg p_4 \vee (p_4 \wedge ....$$
$$EX(p_{n-1} \wedge AX(\neg p_n \vee (p_n \wedge (t_1 \wedge t_2 .... \wedge t_m)) ...)))))))).$$

We will prove that ϕ is true iff ψ is true in the start state of T_S.

Example 1. We illustrate the whole construction through a small example. Given the following QBF formula ϕ_1 with four variables and two clauses, the corresponding formula ψ_1 is as follows:

$$\phi_1 = \exists x_1 \forall x_2 \exists x_3 \forall x_4 . [(x_1 \vee x_2 \vee x_4) \wedge (x_2 \vee \neg x_3 \vee \neg x_4)]$$

$$\psi_1 = EX(p_1 \wedge AX(\neg p_2 \vee (p_2 \wedge EX(p_3 \wedge AX(\neg p_4 \vee (p_4 \wedge (t_1 \wedge t_2)))))))$$

Given the clauses the corresponding tree-like kripke structures are shown in the figures, Figure 2 and Figure 3.   ∎

Solution Tree. Given a QBF formula ϕ that is true there is a solution tree defined as follows to prove that ϕ is true. The solution tree can be described as:

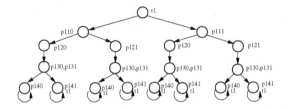

Fig. 2. The tree corresponding to the clause $(x. \vee x. \vee x.)$

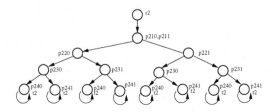

Fig. 3. The tree corresponding to the clause $(x. \vee \neg x. \vee \neg x.)$

- A node at depth $2*i$ has a one child that represents a truth value assignment of 0 or 1 assigned to x_{2*i+1}.
- A node at depth $2*i-1$ has two children: left child represents the truth value 0 and the right child represents the truth value 1 assigned to x_{2*i}.

A path from the root to a leaf represents an assignment of truth values to each variable $x_1, x_2, ..., x_n$. A solution tree proves the truth of ϕ iff for all paths from the root to a leaf the corresponding truth assignment satisfy each clause in ϕ.

Lemma 3. *If ϕ is true then ψ is true in the start state of T_S.*

Proof. Given a truth value assignment for variables $x_1, x_2, ..., x_n$ we follow the state sequence $(\nu_0, \nu_1, \nu_2, ..., \nu_n)$ with $\nu_0 = s_0$ as follows : (ν_i is represented as $(s_{i1}, s_{i2}, ..., s_{im})$)

- If x_i is assigned true then in all clauses C_k where x_i occurs s_{ik} is the right child of $s_{i-1,k}$, else if x_i is false then s_{ik} is the left child of $s_{i-1,k}$. In all the other clauses C_l in which x_i does not occur s_{il} is the only child of $s_{i-1,l}$.

It follows from Lemma 2 that in this state sequence ν_i satisfies p_i . It also follows from Lemma 1 that ν_n satisfies t_j iff the valuation of the variables makes C_j true. Given a solution tree to prove ϕ we construct a proof tree P_T, that proves that ψ holds in the start state of T_S, as follows:

1. For a node ν_{2*i} at depth $2*i$ in P_T its immediate successor is defined as follows:
   - If ν_{2*i} satisfies $\neg p_{2*i}$ it has no successor.
   - Else ν_{2*i} satisfies p_{2*i} and if x_{2*i+1} is assigned true then in all T_j's such that x_{2*i+1} is in C_j choose the right child in T_j and if x_{2*i+1} is assigned false then choose the left branch in T_j. In all T_r's such that x_{2*i+1} is not in C_r choose the only immediate successor in T_r.

2. For a node at depth $2 * i + 1$ in P_T its immediate successors are all its successors present in T.

Note that for any node at any depth i only two of its successor can satisfy p_{i+1}, one representing the assignment of truth value 0 to x_{i+1} where in all components left branches are taken and the other representing the assignment of truth value 1 to x_{i+1} where in all components right branches are taken. A proof tree has been sketched in It follows that in P_T a node at depth $2 * i + 1$ from the start state will satisfy p_{2*i+1}. Hence the node at depth $2 * i$ will satisfy $EX(p_{2*i+1})$. For a node at depth $(2 * i - 1)$ if in all the T_j's for clause C_j in which x_{2*i} occurs left branches or right branches are followed (consistently in all T_j's) then the next state satisfy p_{2*i}. All the other successors satisfy $\neg p_{2*i}$. By the construction of P_T it follows any leaf node which is at a depth i where $i < n$ it satisfies $\neg p_i$. Since for the given solution tree $C_1 \wedge C_2 \wedge .... \wedge C_m$ is satisfied any leaf at depth n will either satisfy $\neg p_n$ or will satisfy $t_1 \wedge t_2 \wedge ...t_m$. Hence P_T proves that ψ is satisfied in the start state of T_S. ∎

Lemma 4. *If ψ is true in the start state of T_S then ϕ is true.*

Proof. If the formula ψ is true in the starting state of T_S then there is a proof tree P_T to prove ψ to be true. We construct a solution tree to prove ϕ. For a node $\nu_{2*i} = (s_{2*i,1}, s_{2*i,2}, ..., s_{2*i,m})$ at depth $2 * i$ in P_T let $\nu_{2*i+1} = (s_{2*i+1,1}, s_{2*i+1,2}, ..., s_{2*i+1,m})$ be its successor such that p_{2*i+1} is satisfied at ν_{2*i+1}. From Lemma 2 we have that one of the following two conditions hold:

1. in every T_j such that x_{2*i+1} occurs in C_j, $s_{2*i+1,j}$ is the left child of $s_{2*i,j}$.
2. in every T_j such that x_{2*i+1} occurs in C_j, $s_{2*i+1,j}$ is the right child of $s_{2*i,j}$.

If the former condition is satisfied then we construct the solution tree assigning truth value 0 (false) to x_{2*i+1} and if the later is satisfied then we assign the value 1 (true) to x_{2*i+1}. As ψ is true in the start state it follows that in P_T any leaf at depth n which satisfy p_n must satisfy $t_1 \wedge t_2... \wedge t_m$. Hence the choice of the truth values for the odd variable as constructed above from the proof tree P_T ensures that the solution tree thus constructed will prove ϕ (will satisfy all clauses). Hence if ψ is true in the start state then $\phi = \exists x_1 \forall x_2 \exists x_3 .... \exists x_{n-1} \forall x_n. [C_1 \wedge C_2... \wedge C_m]$ is true. ∎

It follows from Lemma 3, 4 that the CTL model checking is PSPACE-hard. A DFS model checking algorithm that performs on-the-fly composition requires space polynomial in the size of the depth of the proof tree. This gives us the following result.

Theorem 1. *CTL model checking of synchronous composition of tree-like kripke structures is PSPACE complete.*

Theorem 2. *Model checking of formulas of the form $E(B\ U\ B)$ and $A(B\ U\ B)$, where B is an Boolean formula, is NP complete and coNP complete respectively, for synchronous composition of tree-like kripke structures.*

Proof. Given a SAT formula in CNF (Conjunctive Normal Form) $\psi = C_1 \wedge C_2 \wedge \ldots \wedge C_m$ where each C_i is a clause with exactly three variables from the set of variables of $\{x_1, x_2, \ldots, x_n\}$. For each clause C_j we construct a clause tree-like kripke structure T_j as described in Subsection 3.1. Let synchronous composition of the component kripke structures be T_S. We will prove that the SAT formula ψ is satisfiable iff the following formula φ is true in the start state of T_S, where φ is defined as $\varphi = E(r \vee p_1 \vee p_2 \vee \ldots \vee p_n U(t_1 \wedge t_2 \wedge \ldots \wedge t_m))$, where $r = r_1 \wedge r_2 \wedge \ldots \wedge r_n$. Note that for every T_j the root of T_j is marked with proposition r_j. Hence the staring state of T will satisfy r.

Suppose ψ is satisfiable, then there is a satisfying assignment A. Given A we construct the following path (state sequence) $\nu_0, \nu_1, \nu_2, \ldots, \nu_n$, where $\nu_i = (s_{i1}, s_{i2}, \ldots, s_{im})$, to satisfy φ. We construct the immediate successor ν_i of ν_{i-1} as follows:

- if x_i is assigned false by A then in all T_j such that x_i occurs in C_j the left branch is followed.
- if x_i is assigned true by A then in all T_j such that x_i occurs in C_j the right branch is followed.

It is evident that ν_i satisfies p_i (from Lemma 2) and ν_0 satisfies r. Since ψ is satisfiable we have ν_n satisfies $t_1 \wedge t_2 \wedge \ldots \wedge t_m$. So φ is true in the start state.

If φ is true at the start state then there is a path P in T to satisfy $(r \vee p_1 \vee p_2 \vee \ldots \vee p_n U(t_1 \wedge t_2 \wedge \ldots \wedge t_m))$. Let the path be $\nu_0, \nu_1, \nu_2, \ldots, \nu_n$. Then in this path ν_i must satisfy p_i. For a node $\nu_i = (s_{i1}, s_{i2}, \ldots, s_{im})$ at depth i in P let $\nu_{i+1} = (s_{i+1,1}, s_{i+1,2}, \ldots, s_{i+1,m})$ be its successor such that ν_{i+1} satisfy p_{i+1}. It follows from Lemma 2 then one of the following two conditions must hold:

- in every T_j such that x_{2*i+1} occurs in C_j, $s_{2*i+1,j}$ is the left child of $s_{2*i,j}$.
- in every T_j such that x_{2*i+1} occurs in C_j, $s_{2*i+1,j}$ is the right child of $s_{2*i,j}$.

If the former condition is satisfied then assign x_{i+1} to be 0 (false) and if the later is satisfied assign x_{i+1} to be 1 (true). As $t_1 \wedge t_2 \wedge \ldots t_m$ is satisfied in the last state we have ψ satisfied for the given assignment. This proves that the model checking of a simple formula of the form $E(B \ U \ B)$ is NP hard.

To prove the model checking is in NP we note that in T any infinite path is path from the start state which is a state sequence of the form : $\nu_0, \nu_1, \nu_2, \ldots, \nu_i, \nu_i, \nu_i, \ldots$ where i is bounded by the maximum of the depth of the component tree-like kripke structure. Hence for any infinite path of the form: $\nu_0, \nu_1, \nu_2, \ldots, \nu_i, \nu_i, \nu_i, \ldots$ which satisfies $E(B \ U \ B)$, $(\nu_0, \nu_1, \nu_2, \ldots, \nu_i)$ can be a proof. This proof is polynomial in size of the input. A NP algorithm guesses the state sequence and then verifies that the state sequence satisfies the formula $E(B \ U \ B)$, which can be achieved in P. The desired result follows.

To prove that the model checking problem is coNP hard for formulas of the form $A(B \ U \ B)$ we reduce the *validity* problem to it. Consider the problem of *validity* of a formula ψ expressed in DNF (Disjunctive Normal Form) as follows: $\psi = F_1 \vee F_2 \vee \ldots \vee F_m$ where each F_i is a *term* (conjunction of literals) with exactly three variables from the set of variables of $\{x_1, x_2, \ldots, x_n\}$. We construct the clause tree-like kripke structure T_j for every term F_j as mentioned in Section 3.1. The only difference is that every node in T_j at depth i is marked with a proposition d_i. Also the nodes at depth n are marked with t_i according to the following condition: Consider a node s at depth n such that it is numbered i. Let $B_1B_2B_3$ be the *binary representation* of i. If assigning $x_i = B_1, x_k = B_2, x_l = B_3$ makes F_j true then s is labeled by t_j, otherwise it is not labeled by t_j. (B_1, B_2, B_3 are $0, 1$ respectively and 0 represents false and 1 represents true). Let the synchronous composition of $T_1, T_2, \ldots, T_M$ be T_S. Consider the formula:

$$\varphi = A(r \vee p_1 \vee p_2 \ldots \vee p_n \ U \ (t_1 \vee t_2 \vee \ldots t_n) \vee (d_1 \wedge \neg p_1) \vee (d_2 \wedge \neg p_2) \ldots \vee (d_n \wedge \neg p_n))$$

where $r = r_1 \wedge r_2 \wedge \ldots \wedge r_n$. Similar argument as above with minor modifications for the *universal* nature of the A operator and the validity problem we can show φ is true in the start state of T_S iff the formula ψ is valid. The proof of the model checking problem of formulas of the form $A(B \ U \ B)$ is in coNP is similar. ∎

3.3 CTL Model Checking of Asynchronous Composition

Given m clauses $C_1, C_2, ..., C_m$ we construct $T_1, T_2, ..., T_m$ as m tree-like kripke structures for the respective clauses. Let T_A denote the asynchronous composition of the tree-like structures. We prove that the CTL model checking of asynchronous composition is PSPACE complete. In this section we refer to p_i's, ψ, ϕ as defined in the Subsection 3.2. The construction of the tree-like kripke structure in Subsection 3.1 gives us the following result.

Lemma 5. *Given a state $\nu_i = (s_{i1}, s_{i2}, \ldots s_{in})$ in T_A such that ν_i satisfies p_k then for all j, depth of s_{ij} in T_j is k.*

Theorem 3. *CTL model checking of asynchronous composition of tree-like kripke structures is PSPACE complete.*

Proof. Consider the formula ϕ and ψ as described in the Subsection 3.2. Consider the start state s in T_A. It follows from Lemma 5 that any successor s_1 of s in T_A which satisfies p_1 follows from a transition in which all the components make a transition (which corresponds to a transition of the synchronous composition). Similarly consider any successor s_2 of s_1, a transition in which all the components does not make a transition will cause s_2 to satisfy $\neg p_2$. For a transition which satisfies p_2 it will have to be a transition in which all the component T_j's make a transition (which again corresponds to a transition of the synchronous composition). This argument can be extended for any depth $2 * i$ and $2 * i + 1$. Hence the construction of the proof tree P_T from a given solution tree of truth values to variables to prove ψ and the construction of a solution tree from the proof tree P_T is similar as in the Lemmas and Theorems in the Subsection 3.2. This proves that CTL model checking of T_A is PSPACE hard. The PSPACE upper bound argument is similar to Theorem 1. ∎

Lemma 5, Theorem 3 and arguments similar to to Theorem 2 gives us the following Theorem.

Theorem 4. *Model checking of formulas of the from $E(B \cup B)$ is NP complete and model checking of formulas of the form $A(B \cup B)$ is coNP complete, where B is a Boolean formula, for asynchronous composition of tree-like kripke structures.*

3.4   CTL Model Checking of Strict Asynchronous Composition

Given m clauses $C_1, C_2, ..., C_m$ we construct $T_1, T_2, ..., T_m$ as m tree-like kripke structures for the respective clauses. We denote by T_{AS} the strict asynchronous composition of the tree-like structures. For every node s in T_j such that the depth of s is d it is marked with an atomic proposition l_{jd}. In this section we refer to p_i's , ϕ as defined in the Subsection 3.2. We define properties l_i, l_i' at a node in T, for $1 \le i \le n$ as follows: $l_i = \wedge_{j=1}^m (l_{ji} \vee l_{j,i-1})$, $l_i' = \wedge_{j=1}^m (l_{ji})$. We define ψ as follows:

$$\psi = E(l_1 U(p_1 \wedge A(l_2 U(\neg l_2 \vee (\neg p_2 \wedge l_2') \vee (p_2 \wedge E(l_3 U(p_3 \wedge$$
$$...A(l_n U(\neg l_n \vee (\neg p_n \wedge l_n') \vee (p_n \wedge (t_1 \wedge t_2... \wedge t_m))))...)))))))$$

We briefly sketch the idea of the proof of the reduction of QBF to CTL model checking of strict asynchronous composition. The property l_i is true at a state if the depth of every component node is either i or $i-1$. Consider a path $\pi = (s_0, s_1, ...)$ which satisfy $l_1 U p_1$, where s_0 is the start state of T. In the path π in no component more than one transition is taken. When p_1 is reached all components must have taken one transition each. Hence it corresponds to a single transition of a synchronous composition. Consider a state which satisfy $s' \in T$ such that s' satisfies p_1. The state s' is a state in T_{AS} such that depth of all the component nodes is 1. We consider the truth of the formula $A(l_2 U(\neg l_2 \vee (l_2' \wedge \neg p_2) \vee p_2)$ in s'. The part $(\neg l_2 \vee (l_2' \wedge \neg p_2))$ ensures the following :

- If there is more than one transition in a component then $\neg l_2$ is satisfied.
- If in all components one transition is made and there are components such that in one component the left branch transition is followed whereas in the other component the right branch transition is followed then we have $l_2' \vee \neg p_2$ satisfied.

So in the above cases $A(l_2 U(\neg l_2 \vee (l_2' \wedge \neg p_2) \vee p_2)$ cannot be false. So any l_2 path to a state with more than one transition for any component or to a state which is a representative of inconsistent truth values to variable x_2 (a state which satisfy $\neg p_2$) in different clauses will not cause $A(l_2 U(\neg l_2 \vee (l_2' \wedge \neg p_2) \vee p_2)$ to be falsified. A l_2 path to a state satisfying p_2 again corresponds to a single synchronous transition. Similar arguments can be extended to depth $2 * i$ and $2 * i + 1$ respectively. The rest follows arguments similar to those i Lemmas and Theorems in the Subsection 3.2 and 3.3 to prove that the model checking of strict asynchronous composition of tree-like kripke structure is PSPACE complete.

Theorem 5. *CTL model checking of strict asynchronous composition of tree-like kripke structures is PSPACE complete.*

Remark 1. The PSPACE-upper bound for CTL model checking holds for synchronous, asynchronous and strict asynchronous composition even if the component structures are arbitrary kripke structure. (i.e., underlying transition relation is a graph rather than a tree).

4   Reachability Analysis

The reachability problem asks given two states s and t in the composition of m tree-like kripke structure whether there is a path from s and to t.

Synchronous Composition. Let $s = (s_1, s_2, ..., s_m)$ and $t = (t_1, t_2, ..., t_m)$ be two states. It can be shown that t is reachable from s if and only if the following two conditions hold: (a) for all non-leaf nodes t_i and t_j we have $depth(t_j) - depth(s_j) = depth(t_i) - depth(s_i) = d$, and (b) for all leaf nodes t_k we have $depth(t_k) - depth(s_k) \leq d$. The values for $depth(t_i) - depth(s_i)$ can be computed by a simple BFS algorithm linear in the size of the input.

Theorem 6. *Given two states $s = (s_1, s_2, ..., s_m)$ and $t = (t_1, t_2, ..., t_m)$ whether t is reachable from s can be determined in time linear in the input size for synchronous composition of tree-like kripke structures.*

Asynchronous Composition. For asynchronous and strict asynchronous composition reachability analysis is linear even if the individual components are arbitrary kripke structures. Given m kripke structures $G_1, G_2, ..., G_m$ let G be their asynchronous composition (or strict asynchronous composition).

Theorem 7. *Given two states $s = (s_1, s_2, ..., s_m)$ and $t = (t_1, t_2, ..., t_m)$ whether t is reachable from s can be determined in time linear in the input size for asynchronous and strict asynchronous composition of arbitrary kripke structures.*

References

1. Burch, J.R., Clarke, E.M., Long, D.E., McMillan, K.L., and Dill, D.L., Symbolic model checking for sequential circuit verification. *IEEE Trans. on Computer Aided Design*, **13**, 4, 401-424, 1994.
2. Clarke, E.M., Emerson, E.A., and Sistla, A.P., Automatic verification of finite-state concurrent systems using temporal logic specifications. *ACM Trans. on Program. Lang. & Systems*, **8**, 2, 244-263, 1986.
3. Clarke, E.M., and Kurshan, R.P., Computer aided verification. *IEEE Spectrum*, **33**, 6, 61-67, 1996.
4. Cormen, T.H., Leiserson, C.E., and Rivest, R.L., *Introduction to Algorithms*. The MIT Press, Cambridge and McGraw-Hill, 1990.
5. Emerson, E.A., Mok, A.K., Sistla, A.P. and Srinivasan, J., Quantitative temporal reasoning, In *First Annual Workshop on Computer-Aided Verification*, France, 1989.
6. Papadimitriou, C.H., *Computational Complexity*, Addison-Wesley, 1994.
7. Clarke, E.M., Grumberg, O., and Peled, D.A., *Model Checking*, MIT Press, 2000.

A Multi-agent Framework Based on Communication and Concurrency

M. Jamshid Bagherzadeh and S. Arun-Kumar

Indian Institute of Technology Delhi, 110016, New Delhi, India
{jamshid, sak}@cse.iitd.ernet.in

Abstract. Multi-agent systems are receiving attention nowadays, as they can be applied in a variety of disciplines like industry, e-commerce, control systems, etc. As the areas of usage are more crucial the matter of assurance of correctness of programs is important. However, verification of these systems has received attention only very recently. Hitherto such systems have been programmed without a clearly defined formal semantics and with very little idea about formally expressed verifiable properties to be satisfied by such systems. In this paper a new multi-agent programming language, called ECCS is defined. Its operational semantics is defined and a model checking algorithm is described which verifies properties expressed in the logic ACTL.

Keywords: Multi-agent systems, Verification, Model checking, CCS, CTL.

1 Introduction

A multi-agent system consists of various agents, which communicate with each other through an agent communication language (ACL), to fulfill their individual goals (intentions). Each agent may also have its own set of beliefs, about other agents and the environment. However each agent is *rational* and *logically consistent* with regard to its beliefs, goals and uncertainties and is capable of deriving the logical consequences of its attitudes. The problem of agent communication verification is to check whether agents that use ACL, conform to its semantics, i.e. when an agent sends a message (communicative act) to other agents, whether it complies with the semantics of the message or not. For example when agent a sends a message $inform(\omega)$ to agent b, it has to conform with the semantics of $inform$ or simply satisfy the conditions of the message.

In this document we define a framework for agent programming and communication. We use CCS [12] as an agent programming language, and extend it with some primitive communicative acts (message types) from FIPA-ACL [8]. We define a structural operational semantics [14] of the language. We then introduce a variant of the logic CTL [2,3] called ACTL[6], to define the properties of agent systems. Finally we use a model checking algorithm to verify whether programs comply with the defined specifications.

A. Sen et al. (Eds.): IWDC 2004, LNCS 3326, pp. 114–125, 2004.
© Springer-Verlag Berlin Heidelberg 2004

This document is organized as follows. In section 2 we show the structure of the information store. Section 3 defines the syntax of programming language ECCS. We define the semantics of ECCS in section 4 and the syntax and semantics of the logic ACTL in section 5. In section 6 we present our model checking algorithm. In section 7 we give a small example, and section 8 is the conclusion.

2   Information Store (IS)

Let $Ag = \{1, ..., n\}$ be a set of agents. We use three modal operators B, I and U standing for belief, intention and uncertainty respectively, which represent the attitudes of the individual agents. We assume the formal semantics of beliefs and intentions are defined in a Kripke structure $M = (S, B_1, \ldots, B_n, I_1, \ldots, I_n, L)$ where S is the set of states and L is a labeling of states. B_i and I_i are belief and intention accessibility relations for agent i defined as $B_i \subseteq S \times S$ and $I_i \subseteq S \times S$. Agent i, in state s, believes ϕ, i.e. $s \models B_i\phi$, iff for all s' s.t. $(s, s') \in B_i$, $s' \models \phi$. The semantics for intention modal operator is defined in a similar fashion. As usual, we assume B_i is serial, transitive and euclidean, and I_i is serial for any $i \in Ag$. U_i is not defined as a separate relation, but is interpreted in terms of B_i. In FIPA, $U_i\phi$ is defined as, "i is uncertain about ϕ, but thinks ϕ is more likely than $\neg\phi$". Assuming this and discussions in [9], we formally interpret uncertainty in the Kripke structure based on belief relations. Consider $S' = \{t|(s, t) \in B_i\}$. We define $s \models U_i\phi$, if $s' \models \phi$ for a majority of states $s' \in S'$, and at least one state $s' \in S'$, $s' \not\models \phi$. Here **majority** means, more than half of S' if S' is finite, and all but a finite number of S' if S' is infinite. The belief relations satisfy the axioms of the logic KD45 and intention relations satisfy those of the logic KD. These axioms for an attitude O_i are:

K: $\vdash O_i(F \Rightarrow G) \Rightarrow (O_iF \Rightarrow O_iG)$ **4:** $\vdash O_iF \Rightarrow O_iO_iF$
D: $\vdash O_iF \Rightarrow \neg O_i\neg F$ **5:** $\vdash \neg O_i\neg F \Rightarrow O_i\neg O_i\neg F$.

When $O_i = B_i$ all axioms **K, D, 4** and **5** hold. For $O_i = I_i$ only axioms **K** and **D** hold. Based on the above definition we can see that when $O_i = U_i$ only axiom **D** will hold. Also based on the definition of belief relations, $\vdash B_iB_iF \Rightarrow B_iF$ and $\vdash B_i\neg B_i\neg F \Rightarrow \neg B_i\neg F$ hold for any $i \in Ag$.

Let $\mathcal{O} = \{B, U, I, \neg B, \neg U, \neg I\}$ be a set of symbols. Let **V** be the set $(\mathcal{O} \times Ag)^*$, i.e., the set of finite strings of the form $M_{1i_1} \ldots M_{ni_n}$ with $M_k \in \mathcal{O}$ and $i_k \in Ag$. We call any $v \in$ **V**, a view. Intuitively, each view in **V** represents a possible nesting of mental attitudes. For example, the view B_i contains beliefs of agent i, B_iB_j contains beliefs of i about beliefs of j, and so on. Considering this definition, $B_iB_jI_k\omega$ shows that agent i believes that agent j believes that agent k intends to make ω true. The Information store of each agent is like a tree, and any view is a node of the tree. The IS of a multi-agent system is a collection of trees (Figure 1). We define **AtomProp** as a set of atomic propositions. A **literal** is an atomic proposition or its negation. The set **ModFor** of *modal formulas* is defined by the following grammar:

$$\omega ::= p \mid O_i\omega \mid \neg p \mid \neg O_i\omega$$

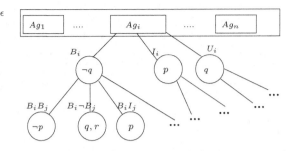

Fig. 1. Information store as a tree, with nodes representing views

where $O \in \{B, I, U\}$. We associate a subset of **ModFor** to each view $v \in \mathbf{V}$. Note that literals are stored explicitly in any view of the agent's information tree except the view $v = \epsilon$. $O_i\omega$ ($\neg O_i\omega$) is an implicit formula of view v if ω is a formula of view vo_i ($v\neg o_i$). We may imagine the information store of a multi-agent system as a function Ψ, where

$$\Psi : \mathbf{V} \longrightarrow \wp(\mathbf{ModFor})$$

Some of the notations which are used in the paper are: Ψ denotes IS of multi-agent system, $\Psi_i = \Psi_i(\epsilon)$ denotes IS of agent i, $\Psi_{O_i} = \Psi_i(O_i) = \Psi(O_i)$ is the subtree of agent i, rooted at O_i. We assume ψ is any subtree of Ψ, and $\psi_{O_i}(v) = \psi(O_iv)$ (for example $\Psi_{B_i}(B_j)$ and $\Psi(B_iB_j)$ denote the same subtree).

We have views $\neg O_i$ as well as views O_i. It must be noted that at the top level (Ψ_i), we have assumed a closed world and only three nodes B_i, U_i and I_i are present, and we don't have $\neg B_i$, $\neg U_i$, and $\neg I_i$. At this level, we assume $\Psi_i \models \neg O_i\omega$ iff $\Psi_i \not\models O_i\omega$. At the lower levels of tree however, we have $\neg O$ nodes also. Thus for example $\Psi_{B_i} \models \neg O_j\omega$ iff $\Psi_{B_i\neg O_j} \models \omega$.

2.1   The Satisfaction Relation

Based on the preceeding discussion, we may derive the following relationships between the various modalities. These relationships merely emphasize the rationality and the logical consistency of the mental attitudes of each agent.

1. $B_i\omega \Rightarrow B_i\omega'$ if $\omega \Rightarrow \omega'$
2. $I_i\omega \Rightarrow I_i\omega'$ if $\omega \Rightarrow \omega'$
3. $B_i\omega \Rightarrow \neg B_i\neg\omega$
4. $I_i\omega \Rightarrow \neg I_i\neg\omega$
5. $U_i\omega \Rightarrow \neg U_i\neg\omega$
6. $B_i\omega \Rightarrow \neg U_i\omega$
7. $U_i\omega \Rightarrow \neg B_i\omega$
8. $B_i\omega \Rightarrow \neg U_i\neg\omega$
9. $U_i\omega \Rightarrow \neg B_i\neg\omega$
10. $B_i\omega \Leftrightarrow B_iB_i\omega$
11. $\neg B_i\omega \Leftrightarrow B_i\neg B_i\omega$

Rules 1 to 4 and 10 and 11 follow from **K, D, 4** and **5**. Rules 5-9 follow from the definition of U_i modality. The IS of a multi-agent system should not violate the above rules. So when updating the information store, its consistency must be maintained somehow.

Definition 1. *Each node of the IS represents a view $v \in \mathbf{V}$. A node or view is said to be of **uncertain parity** if some U or $\neg U$ ocuurs in v. All other nodes* are of **certain parity**. *Further a node of certain parity is* **even** *if there are an even number of $\neg B$ and $\neg I$ modalities in v, and is* **odd** *otherwise.*

Theorem 2. *If $F \Rightarrow G$. Then for any view $v = O_1 \dots O_k \in \mathbf{V}$, of certain parity, $vF \Rightarrow vG$ if v is even, and $vG \Rightarrow vF$ if v is odd.* $\qquad\square$

Let **For** (which we call *local formulas*) be the set of formulas ϕ defined as:

$$\phi ::= O_i\omega \mid \phi \wedge \phi' \mid \phi \vee \phi' \mid \neg\phi \qquad where \; \omega \in \mathbf{ModFor}$$

Definition 3. *A formula ω is* **accessible** *from information tree Ψ_i, i.e., $\Psi_i \models_{acc} \omega$, if it is stored explicitly in Ψ_i. This relation is formally defined as:*

$$
\begin{array}{lll}
\Psi_i \models_{acc} \omega & iff \; \Psi_i, \epsilon \models_{acc} \omega & \\
\Psi_i, v \models_{acc} l & iff \; l \in \Psi_i(v) & where \; l \; is \; a \; literal \\
\Psi_i, v \models_{acc} O_i\omega & iff \; \Psi_i, vO_i \models_{acc} \omega & where \; O \in \{B, I, U, \neg B, \neg I, \neg U\}
\end{array}
$$

Definition 4. *A formula ω is* **derivable** *from Ψ_i, i.e., $\Psi_i \vdash \omega$, iff there is a formula ϕ s.t. $\Psi_i \models_{acc} \phi$, and $\phi \Rightarrow \omega$ using rules 1-11 and theorem 1. Note that Any accessible formula is also derivable.*

Definition 5 (Satisfaction). *A formula ϕ is satisfiable in Ψ_i, iff ϕ is derivable by Ψ_i. Satisfaction relation $\models$ for different formulas is defined as:*

- $\Psi_i \models O_j\omega \; iff \; \Psi_i \vdash O_j\omega$
- $\Psi_i \models \phi_1 \wedge \phi_2 \; iff \; \Psi_i \models \phi_1 \; and \; \Psi_i \models \phi_2$
- $\Psi_i \models \phi_1 \vee \phi_2 \; iff \; \Psi_i \models \phi_1 \; or \; \Psi_i \models \phi_2$
- $\Psi_i \models \neg\phi \; \; \Psi_i \not\models \phi$

2.2   Information Revision

Belief and goal revision is an important subject in light of non-monotonicity in the behaviour of agents in their interaction with other agents. Agents need to add new information and remove the old information and they like to have consistent information.

Any agent is capable of updating its own local information but not that of any other agent. However, an agent may seek to influence the attitudes of other agents by communication. As discussed earlier, we like properties 1-9 to be satisfied in information store. So when updating the information store, we will regard them as consistency rules.

Definition 6. *The information store of agent i (Ψ_i) is consistent if the following holds*

$$\mathbf{r}: \quad If \; \Psi_i \models O_i\omega \; then \; \Psi_i \not\models O_i\neg\omega \quad (O \in \{B, I, U\})$$

Information store of the multi-agent system is consistent if the information store of individual agents are consistent. To update the information store, we define function $upd(\Psi_i, v, \omega)$, where Ψ_i is the information store of agent i, v is a view of Ψ_i and $\omega \in \mathbf{ModFor}$ is a formula. This function is given in table 1.

We assume $O \in \{B, U, I\}$, l is a literal, $cond \equiv$ $"if\ v\ contains\ only\ B\ and\ I$ $modalities"$, and $M, N \in \{B, U\}$ s.t. in any formula including M and N either $M = B$ and $N = U$, or $M = U$ and $N = B$. The table includes two parts, first part shows adding of a formula and the second part shows deletion of a formula from IS. We prefix a formula with the symbol $\sim$ to denote its deletion. It is

Table 1. IS revision

command	primary update	if cond Secondary update
$upd(\Psi_i, v, l)$	$= \Psi_i(v) \cup \{l\};$	if $cond$ then $\Psi_i(v) - \{\neg l\}.$
$upd(\Psi_i, v, B_j B_j \omega)$	$= upd(\Psi_i, v, B_j \omega).$	
$upd(\Psi_i, v, B_j \neg B_j \omega)$	$= upd(\Psi_i, v, \neg B_j \omega).$	
$upd(\Psi_i, v, M_j \omega)$	$= upd(\Psi_i, v M_j, \omega);$	if $cond$ then [$upd(\Psi_i, v, \sim \neg M_j \omega);$ $upd(\Psi_i, v, \sim N_j \omega);$ $upd(\Psi_i, v, \sim N_j \neg \omega)$]
$upd(\Psi_i, v, I_j \omega)$	$= upd(\Psi_i, v I_j, \omega);$	if $cond$ then $upd(\Psi_i, v, \sim \neg I_j \omega).$
$upd(\Psi_i, v, \neg O_j \omega)$	$= upd(\Psi_i, v \neg O_j, \omega);$	if $cond$ then $upd(\Psi_i, v, \sim O_j \omega).$
$upd(\Psi_i, v, \sim l)$	$= \Psi_i(v) - \{l\}.$	
$upd(\Psi_i, v, \sim M_j \omega)$	$= upd(\Psi_i, v M_j, \sim \omega);$	if odd then [$upd(\Psi_i, v, \sim \neg M_j \neg \omega);$ $upd(\Psi_i, v, \sim \neg N_j \omega);$ $upd(\Psi_i, v, \sim \neg N_j \neg \omega)$]
$upd(\Psi_i, v, \sim I_j \omega)$	$= upd(\Psi_i, v I_j, \sim \omega);$	if odd then $upd(\Psi_i, v, \sim \neg I_j \neg \omega).$
$upd(\Psi_i, v, \sim \neg M_j \omega)$	$= upd(\Psi_i, v \neg M_j, \sim \omega);$	if $even$ then [$upd(\Psi_i, v, \sim M_j \neg \omega);$ $upd(\Psi_i, v, \sim N_j \omega);$ $upd(\Psi_i, v, \sim N_j \neg \omega)$]
$upd(\Psi_i, v, \sim \neg I_j \omega)$	$= upd(\Psi_i, v \neg I_j, \sim \omega);$	if $even$ then $upd(\Psi_i, v, \sim I_j \neg \omega).$

supposed $upd(\Psi_i, \omega)$ denotes $upd(\Psi_i, \epsilon, \omega)$. This function satisfies consistency rule r, when it updates the IS. We can extend the function upd to update a sequence of modal formulas as $upd(\Psi_i : \omega_1, \omega_2, ..., \omega_n) = upd(...upd(upd(\Psi_i, \omega_1), \omega_2)..., \omega_n)$. Finally we have the following theorem. Its proof is omitted because of space limit.

Theorem 7. *The function upd preserves property r.*

3   Syntax of Agent Programming Language

We use CCS [12] as the basis of our agent language and extend it with some new features, to obtain ECCS. The formal syntax of ECCS (Extended CCS) is as follows:

$$P = 0 \mid \bar{c}(\alpha).P \mid c(\alpha).P \mid update(O_i \omega).P \mid query(\phi).P \mid observe(p).P \mid P_1 + P_2 \mid A$$

The intuitive meaning of different constructs are as in CCS [12]. In the above definition, P, P_1 and P_2 are ECCS agents. Operators $\bar{c}(\alpha)$ and $c(\alpha)$ are used for sending and receiving information between agents respectively, where c is an unidirectional communication channel between two agents (with an input port c and output port $\bar{c}$) and α is one of { $inform(\omega)$, $confirm(\omega)$, $disconfirm(\omega)$, $request(a)$}. These performatives will be explained in the sequel. Operators $update(O_i \omega)$ and $query(\phi)$ are used for updating and querying $O_i \omega$ and ϕ in the information store, where $\omega \in$ **ModFor** and $\phi \in$ **For**. $observe(p)$ is used to observe some information from the environment and p is an atomic proposition.

The meaning of the composition operators is as usual. $a.P$ is an agent that can perform action a and then become the agent P, $P_1 + P_2$ is choice, which means either P_1 or P_2 will be executed. Finally we assume *Labels* is a set of labels and $A \in Labels$ is a name which stands for an ECCS program. Labels are used for defining recursive procedures.

A multi-agent system is defined as a parallel composition of various agents which can communicate with each other. In the following $P_i (i \in Ag)$ are agents, and Ψ_i are information stores.

$$M = < P_1, \Psi_1 > \mid < P_2, \Psi_2 > \mid ... \mid < P_n, \Psi_n >$$

3.1   FIPA's Performatives and Axioms

We consider four FIPA [8] primitive performatives. The syntax of each is of the form $< s, act(r, \alpha) >$, where s is the sender, r is the receiver, act is the type of action, and α is the content of the message, which can be for example an action a asking r to do something specific, or a proposition ω. The semantics of each communicative act consists of Feasibility Preconditions (FP), which need to be satisfied before the act is performed, and Rational Effect (RE), which is the effect expected after the act is performed. In this definition $Bif_r(\omega) = B_r\omega \vee B_r\neg\omega$, and $Uif_r(\omega) = U_r\omega \vee U_r\neg\omega$. $FP(a)[s\backslash r]$ denotes the part of the FPs of a which are mental attitudes of s. $Agent(r, a)$ means that agent r can perform action a, and $Done(a)$ means that action a is done (if $B_iDone(a)$) or intended to be done (if $I_iDone(a)$). These terms will be discussed later in section 4.1.

In addition to the performatives, in FIPA some axioms have been defined too. We don't discuss these axioms here, but as discussed in [13] there are some problems using only the set of performatives and axioms defined by FIPA. We don't explain these problems here, but the interested reader may refer to [13].

perf.	syntax	semantics	
inform	$\langle s, inform(r, \omega)\rangle$	FP : $B_s\omega \wedge \neg B_s Bif_r\ \omega \wedge \neg B_s Uif_r\ \omega$	RE: $B_r\omega$
confirm	$\langle s, confirm(r, \omega)\rangle$	FP : $B_s\omega \wedge B_s U_r\omega$ RE: $B_r\omega$	
disconf	$\langle s, disconf(r, \omega)\rangle$	FP : $B_s\neg\omega \wedge (B_s B_r\omega \vee B_s U_r\omega)$ RE: $B_r\neg\omega$	
request	$\langle s, request(r, a)\rangle$	FP : $(FP(a)[s\backslash r]) \wedge B_s Agent(r, a) \wedge \neg B_s I_r Done(a)$ RE : $Done(a)$	

4   Semantics of ECCS

The semantics of ECCS is defined by Structural Operational Semantics (SOS) [14]. Many of the semantic rules are extensions of those for CCS [12]. We assume every agent of the system is honest and reliable. Let

$$Act_\tau = \{\tau\} \cup \{c(\alpha), \bar{c}(\alpha) \mid \alpha \ is \ a \ communicative \ act\} \cup \{p, \neg p \mid p \in AtomProp\}$$

In addition let $\Psi_i = (\Psi_{B_i},\ \Psi_{U_i},\ \Psi_{I_i})$ be the complete information store of i. The operational semantics of *update, query* and *observe* operators are as:

$$\frac{\Psi_i' = upd(\Psi_i, O_i\omega)}{\langle update(O_i\omega).P_i, \Psi_i\rangle \xrightarrow{\tau} \langle P_i, \Psi_i'\rangle} \qquad \frac{\Psi_i \models \phi}{\langle query(\phi).P_i, \Psi_i\rangle \xrightarrow{\tau} \langle P_i, \Psi_i\rangle}\ ,\ \phi \in \mathbf{For}$$

$$\frac{\Psi_i \not\models (B_i p \vee B_i\neg p),\ \Psi_i \models (I_i B_i p \vee I_i B_i\neg p),\ Env \models l}{\langle observe(p).P_i, \Psi_i\rangle \xrightarrow{l} \langle P_i, \Psi_i'\rangle}$$

where $l \in \{p, \neg p\}, p \in AtomProp$, and $\Psi_i' = upd(\Psi_i : B_i l, \sim I_i B_i l, \sim I_i l, \sim I_i B_i \neg l, \sim I_i \neg l)$.

It is assumed $\omega \in \mathbf{ModFor}$ and $\Psi_i' = (\Psi_{B_i}',\ \Psi_{U_i}',\ \Psi_{I_i}')$ is the information store of agent i after performing an *update* or *observe*. Observe(p) is used for updating the information of an agent by observing some proposition from the environment. As *observe* is a communicative action (communication with environment), we define $FP(observe(p)) = \neg B_i p \wedge \neg B_i \neg p$ and $RE(observe(p)) = B_i p \vee B_i \neg p$. We assume Env (environment) contains the truth value of a set of related atomic propositions. After observe we will remove $I_i B_i l$ or $I_i l$ or $I_i B_i \neg l$ or $I_i \neg l$ as the intended proposition is believed. Query is used to ask ϕ from the information store and it is executed if ϕ is satisfied by information store of agent i.

4.1   Communication Operators

As mentioned before, we have two operators for communication of agents: $c(\alpha)$ and $\bar{c}(\alpha)$ for receiving and sending information respectively. We use four primitive communicative acts: $inform(\omega), confirm(\omega), disconfirm(\omega)$ and $request(a)$. We define the semantics of *inform* and *request* here. The semantics of *confirm* and *disconfirm* are similar to that of *inform* (only FP and RE is different as shown in section 3.1). Semantics of sending messages is shown in table 2. We

Table 2. Semantics of sending a message

$$\frac{\Psi_i \models B_i\omega \wedge \neg B_i Bif_j\omega \wedge \neg B_i Uif_j\omega,\ \ \Psi_i \models I_i B_j\omega \vee I_i Done(a)}{\langle \bar{c}(inform(\omega)).P_i, \Psi_i\rangle \xrightarrow{\bar{c}(inform(\omega))} \langle P_i, \Psi_i'\rangle}$$

where $a \in \{\bar{c}(inform(\omega)),\ \bar{c}(inform\_if(\omega))\}$ and $\Psi_i' = upd(\Psi_i, B_i B_j\omega, \sim I_i B_j\omega, \sim I_i Done(a))$.

$$\frac{\Psi_i \models FP(a)[i\backslash j] \wedge B_i Agent(j,a) \wedge \neg B_i I_j Done(a),\ \ \Psi_i \models I_i Done(a) \vee I_i\omega}{\langle \bar{c}(request(a)).P_i, \Psi_i\rangle \xrightarrow{\bar{c}(request(a))} \langle P_i, \Psi_i'\rangle}$$

where $RE(a) = \omega$ and $\Psi_i' = upd(\Psi_i, B_i I_j Done(a), \sim I_i Done(a), \sim I_i\omega)$

suppose i is the sender and j is the recipient. Both the transitions have three parts. Firstly, FP of performative must be satisfied. This is known from section 3.1. Second is the intention which are the reason to send the message, and the third is updating of IS to obtain Ψ_i'. Note that in FIPA, $inform\_if(\omega) \equiv inform(\omega) \mid inform(\neg\omega)$, where $\mid$ is the non-deterministic choice operator. In the semantics of inform we have deleted $I_i B_j \omega$ and $I_i Done(a)$, because the intended proposition is likely to be satisfied with the execution of the action. In the semantics of $request$, $Agent(j, a)$ is a function $Agent : Ag \times Act \rightarrow \{true, false\}$, which given an agent and an action, specifies whether the agent can do the action or not. $FP(a)[i \backslash j]$ is not defined clearly in the FIPA. It is defined in FIPA as the feasibility preconditions of the action a relating only to the sender i. We suppose a in the $\bar{c}(request(a))$, is either an internal action or one of $S = \{\bar{d}(inform(\omega)), observe(p), \bar{d}(confirm(\omega)), \bar{d}(disconfirm(\omega)), \bar{d}(inform\_if(\omega)) \}$ where d is a channel name. Finally If c is a channel from i to j and d from j to i, Then $FP(a)[i \backslash j]$ for actions of S in order is: $\neg Bif_i \omega \wedge \neg Uif_i \omega$, $\{\}$, $U_i \omega$, $B_i \omega \vee U_i \omega$, and $\neg Bif_i \omega \wedge \neg Uif_i \omega$. If d is not a channel from j to i then $FP(a)[i \backslash j] = \{\}$.

Table 3. Semantics of receiving a message

$$\Psi_j' = upd(\Psi_j, \; B_j \omega, \; \sim B_j I_i Done(a), \; \sim I_j B_j \omega, \; \sim I_j Done(a))$$
$$\langle c(inform(\omega)).P_j, \Psi_j \rangle \xrightarrow{c(inform(\omega))} \langle P_j, \Psi_j' \rangle$$

where $a \in \{c(inform(\omega)), \; c(inform\_if(\omega))\}$.

$$\Psi_j' = upd(\Psi_j, I_j Done(a))$$
$$\langle c(request(a)).P_j, \Psi_j \rangle \xrightarrow{c(request(a))} \langle P_j, \Psi_j' \rangle$$

Semantics of receiving a message is defined in table 3. Intuitively j after receiving the $inform(\omega)$ which is sent by i, would believe the contents of inform, because agents trust each other. The second argument removes $B_j I_i Done(a)$, as the action is beleived to be done by i. Actually, $B_j I_i Done(a)$ might be added after a request and we know it is satisfied if $c(inform(\omega))$ is done. $I_j B_j \omega$ and $I_j Done(a)$ will be removed because of the same reasons.

4.2   Summation and Parallel Composition

Semantics of summation $P_1 + P_2$ is defined as usual. Let $a \in Act_\tau$ then:

$$\frac{\langle P_{i_1}, \Psi_i \rangle \xrightarrow{a} \langle P_{i_1}', \Psi_i' \rangle}{\langle P_{i_1} + P_{i_2}, \Psi_i \rangle \xrightarrow{a} \langle P_{i_1}', \Psi_i' \rangle} \qquad \frac{\langle P_{i_1}, \Psi_i \rangle \xrightarrow{a} \langle P_{i_1}', \Psi_i' \rangle}{\langle P_{i_2} + P_{i_1}, \Psi_i \rangle \xrightarrow{a} \langle P_{i_1}', \Psi_i' \rangle}$$

In the semantics of parallel composition there are two cases: First for any $l \in \{\tau\} \cup literals$ and the second for any communication γ,

$$\frac{\langle P_i, \Psi_i \rangle \xrightarrow{l} \langle P_i', \Psi_i' \rangle}{[...|\langle P_i, \Psi_i \rangle|...] \xrightarrow{l} [...|\langle P_i', \Psi_i' \rangle|...]}$$

$$\frac{\langle P_i, \Psi_i \rangle \xrightarrow{\bar{\gamma}} \langle P_i', \Psi_i' \rangle , \; \langle P_j, \Psi_j \rangle \xrightarrow{\gamma} \langle P_j', \Psi_j' \rangle}{[...|\langle P_i, \Psi_i \rangle|...|\langle P_j, \Psi_j \rangle|...] \xrightarrow{\tau[\gamma, \bar{\gamma}]} [...|\langle P_i', \Psi_i' \rangle|...|\langle P_j', \Psi_j' \rangle|...]}$$

In the second rule $\tau[\gamma, \bar{\gamma}]$ means the action is silent action but γ and $\bar{\gamma}$ have produced it. This will be useful in model checking when we use action expressions in the formulas.

5   ACTL Logic

In this section we define a logic which is like the branching time temporal logic CTL, but it has action operators for handling actions [6]. In addition the logic has operators for expressing mental properties like beliefs, uncertainties and intentions. The formal syntax of ACTL is defined as:

$$\mu ::= true \mid \phi \mid \neg\mu \mid \mu \wedge \mu \mid EX_x\mu \mid EG_x\mu \mid E\mu_x U_{x'}\mu'$$
$$\mid E\mu_x U\mu' \mid AX_x\mu \mid AG_x\mu \mid A\mu_x U_{x'}\mu' \mid A\mu_x U\mu'$$

Where $\phi \in \mathbf{For}$ and $x, x' \subseteq Act_\tau$ are sets of actions. When x or x' include only one action, we omit the set brackets. The other operators can be defined using those of above. For $P \in \{E, A\}$, $PG\mu_x = \mu \wedge PG_x\mu$, $PF_x\mu = P\ true\ U_x\mu$. Many of the operators have their traditional meaning as in CTL. Semantics of ACTL is defined in terms of Labelled Transition Systems (LTS) with labelling in the transitions as well as states. Let $\mathbf{IS} = \{\Psi \mid \Psi\ is\ information\ store\ of\ multi-agent\ system\}$, and LTS structure M be a tuple of four elements as $< S, R, L, s_0 >$ where S is the set of states, $R \subseteq S \times Act_\tau \times S$ is the transition relation , $L : S \to \mathbf{IS}$ is the state labelling function which assigns an information store Ψ for any state s, and $s_0 \in S$ is the initial state. We suppose $L(s_0) = \{\ \}$, or information store initially is empty. Formal semantics of ACTL is defined in table 4. Satisfaction of local formulas in each state ($L(S) \models \phi$) has been defined in section 2. Note that ACTL extends CTL and we can express CTL formu-

Table 4. Satisfaction of ACTL formulas in labelled transition systems

$s \models true$	for any state s holds.
$s \models \phi$	iff $L(s) \models \phi$ which means information store in state s must satisfy local formula ϕ.
$s \models \neg\mu$	iff $s \not\models \mu$
$s \models \mu_1 \wedge \mu_2$	iff $s \models \mu_1$ and $s \models \mu_2$
$s_0 \models EX_x\mu$	iff there is a path $\pi = s_0 \xrightarrow{a_1} s_1 \xrightarrow{a_2} s_2 \to \ldots$ such that $s_1 \models \mu$ and $a_1 \in x$.
$s_0 \models E(\mu_x U_{x'}\mu')$	iff $s_0 \models \mu$ and there is a path $\pi = s_0 \xrightarrow{a_1} s_1 \xrightarrow{a_2} s_2 \to \ldots$ and $\exists j \geq 1$, $s_j \models \mu'$ and $a_j \in x'$ and for all $1 \leq i < j$, $s_i \models \mu$ and $a_i \in x$.
$s_0 \models E(\mu_x U\mu')$	iff there is a path $\pi = s_0 \xrightarrow{a_1} s_1 \xrightarrow{a_2} s_2 \to \ldots$ and $\exists j \geq 0$ such that $s_j \models \mu'$ and for all $0 \leq i < j$, $s_i \models \mu$ and $a_{i+1} \in x$.
$s_0 \models EG_x\mu$	iff there is a path $\pi = s_0 \xrightarrow{a_1} s_1 \xrightarrow{a_2} s_2 \to \ldots$ such that $s_{i+1} \models \mu$ and $a_i \in x$, for all $i \geq 0$.
$s_0 \models A\ldots$	iff for all paths $\ldots$ (same as existential counterpart) $\ldots$

las by using Act_τ to express action expression x in any formula. For example $EX_{Act_\tau}\mu \in ACTL$ is like $EX\mu \in CTL$, because $a \in Act_\tau$ for any action a.

6   Model Checking

Model checking of multi agent systems is a process of verifying correctness of agent systems. In these systems we not only deal with traditional concepts of concurrent systems like safety and liveness properties [19] but the mental properties of the system must be satisfied as well [22].

As we saw before, ECCS programs can be modeled as LTSs (as defined by the operational semantics). We may transform LTSs to Kripke models [11] and ACTL formulas to CTL formulas, then we may use existing model checkers. The other alternative is to define algorithms to check properties expressed in ACTL, directly on LTS. Algorithms for direct model checking of ACTL is omitted here because of space limit.

Our algorithm is similar to that of checking CTL formulas in the Kripke structures [3]. The algorithm contains various procedures to deal with different kinds of ACTL formulas. We assume some global data structures such as: M=(S, R, L, s_0) is the LTS to be checked, $labels = \{label(s_i) \mid label(s_i)$ is set of labels of $s_i \}$. We will store any subformula which is satisfied in a state s_i in the variable $label(s_i)$. In addition we assume $ListOfSub(\mu)$ is an ordered list of subformulas of a formula $\mu \in ACTL$ from shortest to longest length.

Our main procedure is Check-ACTL which, for any subformula $f \in ListOfSub(\mu)$, calls the appropriate model checking procedure based on the structure of the subformula. The list of subformulas are ordered from shortest to longest, and it guarantees whenever we check a subformula (like $f_1 \wedge f_2$), all of its subformulas (like f_1 and f_2) already have been checked. After checking all subformulas of the set, labels of any state shows the set of subformulas, satisfied by that state. If a state contains μ, it satisfies μ. If labels of initial state $label(s_0)$ contains μ then we say μ is satisfied in LTS structure M.

7   An Example

We implement a very small example using ECCS and define its properties with the ACTL logic. In this example we assume there are two agents, one is *Provider* agent and the other is *Salesman* agent. Provider is responsible to provide an item and salesman is responsible for finding customer. Every time, if provider believes that there is no item, it will provide a new item from the environment and salesman can sell the item. We assume every time there is an item in the environment. When item is sold then provider will provide a new item. In the following example we have assumed ps is a channel from *Provider* to *Salesman* and sp from *Salesman* to *Provider*, $inform\_if(s, \phi)$ is feasible if either $inform(s, \phi)$ or $inform(s, \neg\phi)$ is feasible, $c\_r = customer\ is\ ready$ and $i\_r = item\ is\ ready$. Also we have assumed $\langle s, query\_if(r, \phi)\rangle \equiv \langle s, request(r, \langle r, inform\_if(s, \phi)\rangle)\rangle$, This operator allows s to query p from r.

Prvdr $=$ update($I_p B_p$ i_r). Loop
Loop $=$ {query($I_p B_p$ i_r). observe(i_r). update($I_p B i f_p c\_r$). Loop}
        $+$ {query($I_p B i f_p c\_r$). $\bar{ps}\langle$query_if(c_r)$\rangle$.
            {$sp\langle$inform(c_r)$\rangle$. Loop } $+$ {$sp\langle$ inform($\neg$ c_r)$\rangle$. update($I_p B i f_p c\_r$).
                                update($\neg B_p \neg$ c_r). Loop} }
        $+$ {query(B_p c_r). update($\neg B_p$ i_r). update($\neg B_p c\_r$). update($I_p B_p$i_r). Loop}

Slman $=$ update($I_s(B i f_s c\_r)$). Loops
Loops $=$ query($I_s B i f_s c\_r$). ps$\langle$query_if(c_r)$\rangle$.
        {observe(c_r). $\bar{sp}\langle$inform(c_r)$\rangle$. update($\neg B_s c\_r$).
            update($\neg B_s B_p c\_r$). update($I_s B i f_s c\_r$). Loops }
    $+${observe($\neg$c_r). $\bar{sp}\langle$inform($\neg$c_r)$\rangle$. update($\neg B_s \neg c\_r$).
            update($\neg B_s B_p \neg c\_r$). update($I_s B_s c\_r$). Loops }

Here are some properties of the system, written in ACTL. For reasons of simplicity we don't write action expression indexes in formulas.

$AG[(B_p i\_r \wedge B_p c\_r) \Rightarrow AFI_p B_p i\_r]$. $AG[B_s c\_r \Rightarrow AFI_s B i f_s c\_r]$.
$AG[B_s \neg c\_r \Rightarrow EFB_s c\_r]$. $AG[I_p B i f_p c\_r \Rightarrow AFB_p c\_r]$.

8   Conclusion and Future Work

In this paper we have defined a language ECCS, with its syntax and semantics. We defined the structure of information store, which is a tree like structure with multiple views. A logic ACTL was defined for defining specifications of the system and a model checking algorithm was proposed for verification of agents.

Most of the work in the verification of multi-agent systems try to define a theory of rational agency [4, 16], but they suffer from lack of computationally grounded semantics [21]. There are some frameworks [23, 1] which attempt model checking on agent programs. One of the most relevant works to ours is Meyer's et.al. [20] work on defining a multi-agent framework using CSP [10] and CCP [17]. Authors have given a proof method for proving the properties of the system as well. In addition there are some other agent programming languages which are inspired by logic programming languages [5, 18, 15], and for few of them verification issues are specified.

Our work uses an abstract functional language CCS with a well defined operational semantics and we can simply check FIPA compliance properties in the semantics of the language (as we have done). Also, the model checking algorithm is easy and straightforward to implement in this framework.

The reason we have omitted disjunction in our information store is due to problems that crop up with disjunction. One of these problems is inconsistency checking, which is NP-complete.

One possible extension which we plan to try, is to add disjunction to our framework and use clausal resolution for inferring formulas from information store [7]. Also we plan to extend our framework to include some more performatives from FIPA-ACL. Finally we will use these ideas in an abstract rules based agent programming language.

References

1. R. H. Bordini, M. Fisher, C. Pardavila, and M. Wooldridge. Model checking AgentSpeak. In *AAMAS 2003*, pages 409–416, 2003.
2. E. M. Clark, E. A. Emerson, and A. P. Sistla. Automatic verification of finite-state concurrent systems using temporal logic specifications. *ACM Trans Programming Lang Syst*, 8(2):244–263, 1986.
3. E. M. Clarke, O. Grumberg, and D. Peled. *Model Checking*. MIT Press, 1999.
4. P. R. Cohen and H. J. Levesque. Intention is choice with commitment. *Artificial Intelligence*, 42(2-3):213–261, 1990.
5. M. Dastani, B. van Riemsdijk, F. Dignum, and J.-J. Ch. Meyer. A programming language for cognitive agents: Goal Directed 3APL. In M. Dastani and et.al., editors, *Proc. of the First Workshop on Programming Multi-agent Systems: Lang., Frameworks, Techs. and Tools (ProMAS03)*, pages 9–15, Melbourne, 2003.
6. R. De Nicola, A. Fantechi, S. Gnesi, and G. Ristori. An action-based framework for verifying logical and behavioral properties of concurrent systems. *Computer Networks and ISDN Systems*, 25(7):761–778, 1993.
7. C. Dixon, M. Fisher, and A. Bolotov. Clausal resolution in a logic of rational agency. *Artif. Intell.*, 139(1):47–89, 2002.
8. Foundation for Intelligent Physical Agents(FIPA). Fipa97 agent specification, http://www.fipa.org.
9. J. Y. Halpern. A logical approach to reasoning about uncertainty: a tutorial. In X. Arrazola, K. Korta, and F. J. Pelletier, editors, *Discourse, Interaction, and Communication*, pages 141–155. Kluwer, 1998.
10. C. A. R. Hoare. *Communicating Sequential Processes*. Prentice Hall, 1985.
11. S. A. Kripke. Semantical considerations on modal logic. In *A Colloquium on Modal and Many-Valued Logics*, Helsinki, 1962.
12. R. Milner. *Communication and Concurrency*. Prentice-Hall, 1989.
13. J. Pitt and A. Mamdani. Some remarks on the semantics of FIPA's agent communication language. *Aut. Agents and Multi-Agent Systems*, 4:333–356, 1999.
14. G. D. Plotkin. A structural approach to operational semantics. Technical report, DAIMI, FN 19, Department of Comp. Sci., University of Aarhus, Denmark, 1981.
15. A. S. Rao. AgentSpeak(L): BDI Agents speak out in a logical computable language. In W. Van de Velde and J. Perram, editors, *Proc. of MAAMAW'96*, number 1038 in LNAI, pages 42–55, The Netherlands, 1996. Springer-Verlag.
16. A. S. Rao and M. P. Georgeff. BDI-agents: From theory to practice. In *Proceedings of the First Intl. Conf. on Multiagent Systems(ICMAS-95)*, San Francisco, 1995.
17. Vijay A. Saraswat. *Concurrent Constraint Programming*. The MIT Press, 1993.
18. Y. Shoham. Agent-oriented programming. *Artif. Intell.*, 60(1):51–92, March 1993.
19. C. Stirling. *Modal and Temporal Properties of Processes*. Springer-Verlag, 2001.
20. R. M. Van Eijk, F. S. De Boer, W. Van Der Hoek, and J.-J. Ch. Meyer. A verification framework for agent communication. *Autonomous Agents and Multi-Agent Systems*, 6(2):185–219, 2003.
21. M. Wooldridge. Computationally grounded theories of agency. In E. Durfee, editor, *Proc. of the 4th Intrl. Conf. on Multi-Agent Systems (ICMAS 2000)*. IEEE Press.
22. M. Wooldridge. Verifiable semantics for agent communication languages. In Y. Demazeau, editor, *Proceedings of the 3rd International Conference on Multi Agent Systems*, pages 349–356. IEEE Computer Society, 1998.
23. M. Wooldridge, M. Fisher, M.-Ph. Huget, and S. Parsons. Model checking multi-agent systems with MABLE. In *Proc. of the first intrl. joint conf. on Autonomous agents and multiagent systems*, pages 952–959. ACM Press, 2002.

Statistical Analysis of a P2P Query Graph Based on Degrees and Their Time-Evolution

Jean-Loup Guillaume, Matthieu Latapy, and Stevens Le-Blond

LIAFA – CNRS – Université Paris 7,
2 place Jussieu, 75005 Paris, France
(guillaume, latapy, stevens)@liafa.jussieu.fr

Abstract. Despite their crucial impact on the performances of P2P systems, very few is known on peers behaviors in such networks. We propose here a study of these behaviors in a running environment using a semi-centralised P2P system (eDonkey). To achieve this, we use a trace of the queries made to a large server managing up to fifty thousands peers simultaneously, and a few thousands queries per second. We analyse these data using complex network methods, and focus in particular on the degrees, their correlations, and their time-evolution. Results show a large variety of observed phenomena, including the variety of peers behaviors and heterogeneity of data queries, which should be taken into account when designing P2P systems.

1   Introduction

In P2P systems, the exchanges between peers are not random: if someone has a data of interest to someone else (a music file for example) then he/she probably has other data of interest for the same person (musics from the same artist for example). Likewise, the peer behaviors (tendency to provide many or few data, for example) has crucial consequences on the way a P2P system will work, in particular on its efficiency. Despite this, very few is nowadays known on P2P exchanges properties and on how peers behave [9, 11].

The distributed nature and the large size of P2P systems are the main reasons for this lack of knowledge. However, some of the main P2P systems currently running use a mid-term between the centralised and the fully distributed approaches [5]: a small set of servers is used for the processing of the queries and data transfers are managed directly between peers.

In this paper, we analyse a large trace of queries and exchanges processed in such a system, which gives new insight on the properties of exchanges and peer behaviors. To achieve this, we mainly use the methods from the recent field of complex network analysis, in particular the study of node degrees, their correlations and their time-evolution. In section 2, we describe the P2P protocol under concern, the trace we use, the statistical tools used to analyse it, and the context into which our work lies. We then study the peers point of view (how do peers behave? what is a typical peer load?) and the data point of view (are there various kinds of data in the system?) in sections 3 and 4 respectively.

A. Sen et al. (Eds.): IWDC 2004, LNCS 3326, pp. 126–137, 2004.
© Springer-Verlag Berlin Heidelberg 2004

2   Preliminaries

In this section, we describe the P2P protocol we use for our analysis, namely eDonkey. We then describe the trace we will study and the way it has been collected. We will represent and analyse these data using graphs and statistical properties of graphs, which will prove to be very efficient tools for this purpose. We introduce and discuss them later in this section. Finally, we describe the context in which our work lies.

The eDonkey Protocol
As already pointed out, an eDonkey system relies on dedicated servers whose only purpose in to manage queries and bring peers into contact. To achieve this, a server has to process various kinds of commands:

- login/logout commands correspond to arrival/departure of peers. Once a peer is connected to the server (using a login command), it sends metadata to the server which describe the files it provides. The server stores these metadata into a local table for the processing of later queries.
- filesearch commands are entered interactively by the end-user. They generally contain one or a few words describing the wanted data, but they can be much more complex (including logical operations on words, size of the requested file, its type, etc). The server answers such commands with metadata (mainly hashcodes of the files) fitting the given description.
- sourcesearch commands allow a peer to know other peers providing a file (or parts of it) given its hashcode (obtained through a filesearch query in general). The server answers such a command with a list of peers providing the data, the list may be incomplete (it gives a bounded number of sources, not all the ones which have the data). Notice that each peer keeps its sourcesearch commands in a buffer and sends them every 5 minutes. Moreover, it automatically sends them again every 15 minutes to get new sources, if any.

There are various other details in the protocol (TCP vs UDP connexions, HighId vs LowId for peers, etc) but they do not play a significant role in the following, therefore we do not detail them. For more detailed information, we refer to [5].

The Measurement and the Trace
In this paper, we focus on the exchanges between peers and on the properties of data. Therefore, we will mainly consider the sourcesearch commands. We record the answers of the server to such commands in the following form:

$$[T] \quad Q \quad H \quad "S_1, S_2, \ldots, S_n"$$

where T is a timestamp (in seconds from the beginning of the trace), Q is the peer which has emitted the query, H is the hashcode of the data queried by Q, and $(S_i)_{i=1\ldots n}$ is a list of peers which has registered the data. The server chooses these peers from its knowledge of which one provides which data, and only gives a bounded number of such peers ($n < N$ for a given N independent of the query).

We studied several traces, during up to more than two days. During such a period, the server typically processed 1.5 million `login` commands, nearly the same amount of `logout` commands, and around 210 million `sourcesearch` commands. The results presented hereafter are qualitatively the same for all these traces. We therefore chose to present them using a single typical trace (of 800 minutes).

Notice that the trace has been started simultaneously with the server reboot, therefore we can observe the startup phase of the server. Moreover, it is long enough to ensure that the server as reached a steady state, as will be shown in the following.

We argue that these traces are representative of the exchanges actually processed in a typical P2P system, mainly because of three points:

- the observed queries depend mainly on peer behaviors, not on the underlying protocol,
- the observed phenomena do not significantly vary from one trace to another,
- the huge size of the trace ensures that we capture most of the behaviors which indeed occur.

The Query Graph $\mathcal{Q}$

There are several ways to conduct statistical studies on the data collected on queries as described above. In this paper, we propose to use tools from the recent field of complex network analysis. We will show that they make it possible to give strong insight on some important properties of the trace. However, this approach might be completed using tools from other fields, like signal processing for example.

A first way to encode the gathered data into a complex network is to define a labeled weighted bipartite graph $\mathcal{Q} = (P, D, E, w)$ where

- P is the set of peers in the network, D is the set of data (hashcodes),
- $E \subseteq (P \times D) \cup (D \times P)$ is the set of directed edges where $(p, d) \in E$ if the peer p has made a query for the data d, and $(d, p) \in E$ if p has been cited by the server as a provider of d,
- w is a weight function over E where $w(x, y)$, for all $(x, y) \in E$, is the number of times x has requested y or the number of times y has been cited as a provider for x.

We will call this graph *the query graph*, since it mainly encodes which peer queried which data and who is cited in the answer to these queries.

Notice that, despite this graph encodes much information on the exchanges captured by the trace, it does not contain *all* the information. However this graph is essential to put some properties into light, which would not appear without it. For example, one can immediately see on this graph which data are queried most often by looking at their number of incoming edges.

Statistical Properties of Graphs

Complex network analysis is a scientific area in full development aiming at describing very large graphs met in practice and extracting some relevant information from them. Is is based on various statistical properties which can be measured on graphs. See [2, 4, 10] for surveys on this field.

In this paper, we will in particular study the time-evolution of degrees in $\mathcal{Q}$. Notice that this cannot be done simply by plotting the time-evolution of the average degree, since, as we will see, the degree distributions in $\mathcal{Q}$ follow power laws. Therefore, the average degree is a very poor indicator. However, this power law structure gives an original way to study the evolution of degrees. The nodes may be separated into two very different classes: low degree nodes, which represent the vast majority of the whole, and the few very high degree nodes, which play a particular role in the system. One may then study these two classes with two orthogonal approaches: one may plot the time-evolution of the proportion of nodes of degree i for small values of i whereas one may plot the time-evolution of the degree of the few nodes with the highest final degree. This is what we will do in the following.

Context

In the last few years, various measurements of P2P networks have been carried out. Some used active measurement [11, 12], others used passive measurement and flow analysis [1, 3, 7, 9, 13, 14]. We briefly present these previous works here, with a special emphasis on the ones based on passive measurements.

Adar and Huberman [1] studied the Gnutella 0.4 traffic over a 24 hours period of time from a given client. The main point of the analysis was to discriminate users between free-riders (no sharing at all), and active peers (lot of sharing). It turns out that 70% of the users are free-riders, while 1% of the clients answer to 50% of the queries.

In [3], Gnutella traffic is observed during 35 hours from a client point of view with the objective to study the amount and type of signaling traffic. In particular the authors observed the distribution of TTL for the search queries, in order to evaluate the distance from their client to others peers. Similarly, [9, 14] studied Gnutella traffic from various traces with different duration (or geographic location) in order to study queries caching strategies to decrease signaling traffic.

Data from various P2P systems (Fastrack, Gnutella, Directconnect) have also been collected directly from routers of some Internet Service Providers [7, 13]. These study are mainly aimed at finding strategies for ISP to reduce the P2P traffic. In particular [7] showed that P2P data contain enough redundancy to use efficient caching strategies.

More recently, [6, 8] used passive measurement based on KaZaA and KaZaA Lite (Fastrack). In [8] it is confirmed that KaZaA traffic is mainly composed of a few very popular files. Their results show that this tendency is even more pronounced than supposed before, which increase the advantages of caching strategies. Finally, [6] innovated using 3 KaZaA clients within NY Polytechnic network to get strong insight on KaZaA protocol (which is not open source). Their measurements allowed to estimate the number of privileged clients in KaZaA to 30 000, each client having from 40 to 60 connections to others privileged clients and from 100 to 200 connections to ordinary clients.

All these studies, and others, have therefore been based on the use of clients or routers to understand the traffic itself, the main conclusion being that, independently of the P2P system in concern, most of the traffic is concentrated on few very popular files. In this context, the use of caching strategies might therefore be very efficient.

Our approach is quite different since it is based on measurements from the server side. This makes it possible to confirm and improve some of the previous results, but our main aim is to deepen the study of peers behaviors. Indeed, one may consider that the queries we observe are weakly influenced by the underlying protocol (we will discuss this in the following where it may not be true): these queries mainly depend on the users interests, culture, etc. Our study is therefore directed towards the analysis of peer behaviors, which certainly play an important role in the efficiency of P2P systems and their design. Moreover, the use of tools from the recent field of complex network analysis provides some new and original insights on the topic.

3   The Peers Point of View

In this section, we study the query graph $\mathcal{Q}$ from the peers point of view. More precisely, we will focus on the degrees of the nodes in P, the set of peers. Recall that the peer p in P has an outgoing edge to the data d if and only if p has made a query for d, and that p has an incoming edge from d if and only if p has been pointed out as a provider of d. Therefore, we may look at the following values:

- *the out-degree* of a peer is the number of (distinct) data it has looked for,
- *the weighted out-degree* of a peer is the number of queries sent by the peer (including several queries for the same data),
- *the in-degree* of a peer is the number of data for which it has been pointed out as a provider,
- *the weighted in-degree* of a peer is the number of times it has been pointed out
- *the in- and out- weight* express the number of times a given peer is cited for a given file, or request a given file.

All these degrees play an important role in describing a given peer. For example, a peer with a high out-degree is a peer seeking many data, a peer with a high in-degree certainly has many data to provide, and a peer with high weighted in-degree is a peer which is solicited very often (it may shares many data or very popular ones), and therefore may be overloaded. We will use all these notions in the section to describe peer behaviors.

Let us first consider the unweighted in- and out-degree distributions of peers, and the weight distribution (Figure 1). As expected, they show that the node degrees are very heterogeneous, with a power law shape: whereas most peers have a small degree, some have a high one (several orders of magnitude more). This means that there is no *typical* behavior of peers. In other words, they cannot be properly modeled nor simulated using a notion of *mean* peer, which could not capture the variety observed in practice. Let us emphasize on the fact that this has significant importance for the design of P2P systems, which should certainly take this heterogeneity into account.

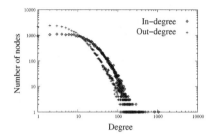 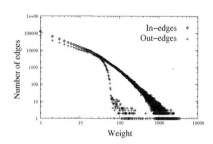

Fig. 1. Left: the in- and out-degree distributions of peers. Right: the in- and out-degree weight distributions on the edges

One may also notice that the out-weight distribution has a cutoff (Figure 1, right). This can be interpreted as a consequence of the fact that a peer should not request a given file more often than once every 15 minutes. Therefore, there is a maximal number of queries a peer may send, which corresponds to the cutoff. The peers which have a degree lower than the cutoff are the ones which send few queries or have joined the server later. The ones which reach the cutoff are the ones with classical client software and use it at its maximal rate. The ones which are above the cutoff certainly correspond to peers with modified client software, which allows them to query the server more frequently. Therefore, this plot makes it possible to evaluate the number of unfair peers which may endangered the system by overloading it, and even detect them.

A natural continuation of the analysis is to study the correlations between in- and out-degrees, as displayed in Figure 2 (left). These plots do not display strong correlations, but they show several things. First, it appears clearly that high in-degree nodes are not the ones with high out-degree, and conversely. This means an important thing: peers which provide many data do not in general send many queries, whereas the peers which make most queries provide only few data. This indicates that some peers are installed to serve mainly as data repositories from which other peers get data, whereas some peers do not behave fairly in the system since they get many data while providing very few. Finally, this tendency, despite it is not strongly pronounced, is general: if a peer has a high in-degree (out-degree), then it tends to have a low out-degree (in-degree, respectively).

One may observe different phenomena on the weighted in- and out-degree correlations (Figure 2, right). For example, the nodes with highest weighted out-degree tend to send very few queries. This seems to confirm our hypothesis that there are peers which mainly play the role of data providers.

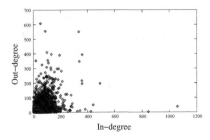
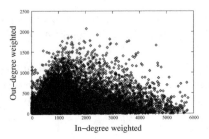

Fig. 2. Left: correlation between in- and out-degrees. Right: correlation between weighted in- and out-degrees. The in- and out-degrees are on the x- and y-axis respectively

Let us now turn to the time-evolution of degrees. The first natural ideas certainly are to plot the in- and out-degree distributions at several dates, as well as the time-evolution of mean in- and out-degrees, see Figure 3. The plots of degree distributions show that it is very stable, which may be surprising but is quite typical of large complex networks. The time-evolution of the average degree shows that on average the nodes have a higher in-degree than their out-degree, which means that on average they are more often contacted than they make requests. This is a consequence of the fact that, in most client software, a data retrieved from the P2P system is automatically made available on the corresponding peer for others.

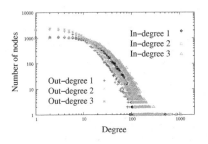
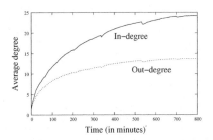

Fig. 3. Left: the in- and out-degree distributions at various dates. Right: time-evolution of the average in- and out-degrees (the irregularities in the plots correspond to peaks in the arrival and departure of peers, due to reboot of other large servers in the system)

However, as already pointed out, this mean behavior is not very meaningful. This is particularly clear here, since we have shown above that peers have very different natures. Therefore, this average over all the peers has to be taken very carefully, and certainly does not mean that there is a notion of *average peer* which would have the average in-degree and the average out-degree: most peers do not have the average in-degree nor the average out-degree, and if their in- or out-degree is high then the other tends to be low. The evolution of the average in- and out-degrees must be viewed as a property of the whole system, not of its components.

To obtain more precise information, we now study separately low and high degree nodes. To achieve this, we plotted the proportion of nodes of (weighted or not, in- or out-) degree i for small values of i (typically $i \leq 10$). This proportion is very stable, as one may have guessed from Figure 3 (left), therefore we do not reproduce these plots here. On the contrary, we will focus on high degree nodes, for which it is possible to plot the time-evolution of their degree. This is what we do in Figure 4.

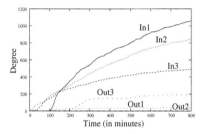
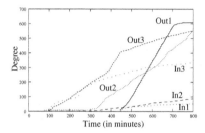

Fig. 4. Time-evolution of in- and out-degrees for the three peers with maximal final in-degree (left) and out-degree (right)

Let us first notice that these plots confirm that nodes with highest in-degree tend to have a low out-degree, and conversely. Moreover, these plots show that the high degree nodes are not nodes which have a low degree during a long time and then experience an abrupt grow up in their degree. On the contrary, they are among the highest degree nodes for a long time, and their degree grows quite regularly. Moreover, they all behave in a similar fashion, therefore one may consider that there is a *typical* behavior for high degree nodes, or, equivalently, for very active peers. This gives hints for their accurate modeling and simulation.

If we now consider the time-evolution of the *weighted* in-degrees of the nodes with the maximal final in-degrees, we obtain Figure 5 (left). We observe several things on this plots. First, as before, the nodes with the highest weighted in-degrees have in general a low weighted out-degree. Moreover, the time-evolution of the weighted in-degree is very regular and homogeneous, which shows that it is possible to introduce a relevant model.

One may also consider that the weighted in-degree of a peer is a measure of its load. We can then use this plot to try to understand why the server fails in distributing fairly the load among peers (which is proved by the weighted in-degree distribution). The protocol ensures that the queries for given data will be distributed fairly among the peers providing them. Two causes may make this fail: the corresponding peers may provide rare data (therefore the server has no choice when these data are queried but to cite these peers), or they may provide many (different) data and are most likely to be cited.

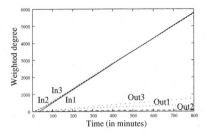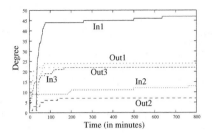

Fig. 5. Left: time-evolution of weighted in-degrees for the three peers with maximal final weighted in-degree. Right: time-evolution of the (unweighted) in-degree of the *same* nodes

In order to decide between these two hypothesis, let us observe, for the peers under concern, the time-evolution of their unweighted in-degree (Figure 5, right). This plot shows that these nodes reach very quickly their maximal in-degree. In other words, we know very quickly *all* the data they will provide; the growing in their in-degree simply means that they will be queried frequently for these data. Because of the load-balancing managed by the server, this makes us conclude that a large weighted in-degree is actually due to the fact that the corresponding peer provides rare but very popular data, which certainly correspond to newly introduced data.

We may now study the time-evolution of weighted out-degree of largest final weighted out-degree peers in a similar way, see Figure 6. The weighted out-degree of a peer is a measure of the load it induces on the server. It appears that the nodes with the highest weighted out-degree also have a high weighted in-degree, which is due to the fact that when a peer retrieves some data it also makes them available on its machine. This is a good point for the protocol, which induce that a greedy peer also has to serve the community. The stairs in the plots are due to technical specificities of the protocol which we do not detail here.

If we look at the time-evolution of the unweighted out-degrees for these nodes (Figure 6, right) we again see that either they converge quite quickly to a value which is not very large, either they converge very slowly. This means that some high weighted out-degree are due to the fact that peers send many queries for

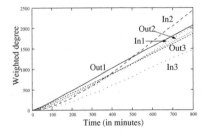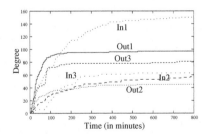

Fig. 6. Left: time-evolution of weighted out-degrees for the three peers with maximal final weighted out-degree. Right: time-evolution of the (unweighted) out-degree of the *same* nodes

the same data, or that some peer are continuously looking for new files. As already discussed, the first point may be induced by unfair modifications of client software, and these plots show that, despite they induce a significant overload for the server, these modifications have little benefit, if any, for the unfair peers.

4 The Data Point of View

In the previous section, we studied precisely the peers behaviors using their degrees in the query graph Q. The same kind of study may be conduced with benefit from the *data* point of view, which constitute the other part of this bipartite graph. We present rapidly our main observations concerning this here.

Recall that the data d in D has an incoming edge from the peer p if and only if p has made a query for d, and that d has an outgoing edge to p if and only if p has been pointed out as a provider of d. Because of the lack of space, we will focus on the unweighted degrees here. Therefore, we may look at the following values:

- *the in-degree* of a data is the number of (distinct) peers which have looked for it,
- *the out-degree* of a data is the number of (distinct) peers which provide it,

We show in Figure 7 the in- and out-degree distributions for data at different dates (left) as well as the time-evolution of the average in- and out-degrees. As previously, the degrees display a very high heterogeneity (the plots fit surprisingly well power laws), therefore the average degrees should be considered as global properties of the system which are not relevant for its components. They show however that the average in- and out-degrees converge to a steady value, and that the average out-degree is larger than the average in-degree. This is due to the fact that when a peer is downloading some data, it generally provides them (after the download, but also during it, since the data are divided into blocs).

We can observe the effect of this strategy more precisely by plotting the correlations between in- and out-degrees, weighted or not, of data (Figure 8): it clearly appears that data which are queried often by peers are also provided by many peers. This is a very good point for the protocol, which avoids this way the overload of peers which provide data wanted by many other peers.

This plot also shows that, in almost all the cases, a data has a larger out-degree than its in-degree (most points are above the diagonal), which is another effect of this strategy. This means that the difference observed in the average in- and out-degrees (Figure 7, right) may be representative of what actually happens for most data.

We may now look more precisely at the data with highest final in- and out-degree, see Figure 9. Like in the case of peers, these plots show that the highest in-degree data clearly have a typical behavior. Therefore, in this case too, it is possible to give a general description of properties of very popular data, despite the global heterogeneity of data in general.

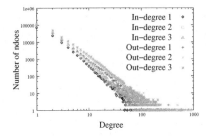
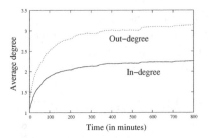

Fig. 7. Left: the in- and out-degree distributions of data at different dates. Right: time-evolution of the average in- and out-degrees of data

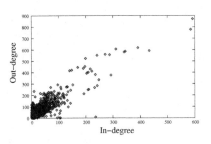
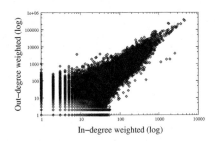

Fig. 8. Left: correlations between in- and out-degrees of data. Right: correlations between weighted in- and out-degrees of data

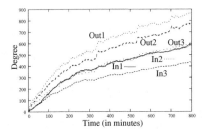
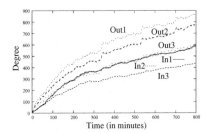

Fig. 9. Time-evolution of in- and out-degrees for the three data with maximal final in-degree (left) and out-degree (right)

5 Conclusion and Discussion

We present in this paper an in-deep study of peer behaviors using their degrees in the query graph, their correlations and their time-evolution. We also give some insight on the properties of the exchanged data using similar techniques. We use for this a representative trace of queries processed by a large eDonkey server during a significant period of time.

Our analysis gives evidence for several phenomena. Some of them are induced by the protocol properties, but most are mainly related to peer behaviors. Notice that some properties belong to both classes. For example, we pointed out a phenomenon due to the fact that unfair peers use modified client software. Evaluating the amount of such peers and their impact on the system may be crucial.

Besides the precise details of our results and the description we obtained of peers and data, two main points strongly appear in our study:

- Both peers and data are highly heterogeneous, which makes irrelevant any notion of *typical* peer having a mean behavior,
- On the contrary, peers may be separated into several classes (peers which mainly provide data, peers with rare data, peers which send many queries, etc) which correspond to well-defined behaviors.

The first point has already been noticed in previous studies, and both are also true for data. These results may certainly be deepen, but we already point out basic properties for an accurate modeling and simulation of a wide variety of peers. We believe that these facts are of high relevance for the design of efficient P2P systems, and should be taken into account in further research. They should lead to accurate description and modeling of classes of behaviors in P2P systems.

References

1. E. Adar and B.A. Huberman. Free riding on gnutella. *First Monday*, September 2000.
2. R. Albert and A.-L. Barabási. Statistical mechanics of complex networks. *Reviews of Modern Physics 74, 47*, 2002.
3. K. Anderson. Analysis of the traffic on the gnutella network. 2001.
4. S.N. Dorogovtsev and J.F.F. Mendes. Evolution of networks. *Adv. Phys. 51, 1079-1187*, 2002.
5. A.-M. Kermarrec F. Le Fessant, S. Handurukande and L. Massouli. Clustering in peer-to-peer file sharing workloads, 2004.
6. K. W. Ross J. Liang, R. Kumar. Understanding kazaa. 2004.
7. N. Leibowitz, A. Bergman, R. Ben-Shaul, and A. Shavit. Are file swapping cacheable? characterizing p2p traffic. In *7th International Worshop on Web Content Caching and Distribution (WCW'03)*, 2002.
8. N. Leibowitz, M. Ripeanu, and A. Wierzbicki. Deconstructing the kazaa network. In *3rd IEEE Workshop on Internet Applications (WIAPP'03)*, 2003.
9. E.P. Markatos. Tracing a large-scale peer to peer system : an hour in the life of gnutella. Technical Report 298, 2001.
10. M.E.J. Newman. The structure and function of complex networks. *SIAM Review*, 45(2):167–256, 2003.
11. M. Ripeanu, I. Foster, and A. Iamnitchi. Mapping the gnutella network: Properties of large-scale peer-to-peer systems and implications for system design, 2002.
12. S. Saroiu, P. Krishna Gummadi, and S.D. Gribble. A measurement study of peer-to-peer file sharing systems. In *Proceedings of Multimedia Computing and Networking 2002 (MMCN '02)*, San Jose, CA, USA, January 2002.
13. S. Sen and J. Wang. Analysing peer to peer traffic accross large networks. In *Internet Measurement Workshop (IMW 2002), Marseille, France*, 2002.
14. K. Sripanidkulchai. The popularity of gnutella queries and its implications on scaling. 2001.

t-UNITY – A Formal Framework for Modeling and Reasoning About Timing Constraints in Real-Time Systems

Sumit Kumar Basu

Honeywell Technology Solutions Laboratory,
Bangalore, India
sumit.basu@honeywell.com

Abstract. This paper proposes a timed extension to the UNITY framework, for modeling, specification and reasoning about timing constraints in real-time systems. The UNITY formalism of Chandi and Misra [1] is extended by introducing timing constraints in the definition of safety and liveness properties and in the proof logic. The proposed t-UNITY framework enables specification of both time independent logical properties and real-time properties, without any specific assumptions on scheduling and constraints imposed by implementation environments. The application of t-UNITY formalism to specification and reasoning about real-time systems is illustrated by an example.

1 Introduction

Implementation of real-time systems are often distributed and inherently concurrent. Most real-time design methods that are used in practice, such as the Vienna Definition Method (VDM) [2], Z [3] and structured analysis (SA) [4], are based on approaches that have been basically developed for terminating, non-reactive and sequential systems. For application systems with real-time constraints, it is not enough for software systems to be logically correct. Such systems must also satisfy timing constraints, which are determined by the characteristics of the physical system being controlled, and task executions must meet deadlines to prevent their failure. Hence, for formal specification of real-time systems, it is important to use a general framework that allows formal modeling of all concerns of a real-time system such as functionality, timing and co-ordination as different aspects of system design.

The motivation for our work is to extend the Chandi and Mishra's UNITY formalism [1] so that it can be used for modeling and verification of timed real-time systems. Such an extension is useful since it permits us to model systems with timed behavior, for example, "temperature above 250 degrees is followed by an alarm within a delay of 7 time units" or "in any interval of 8 time units, fuel flow to the engine can not remain at the maximum level for more than 2 time units". The proposed generalization of UNITY by introducing timing constraints establishes a robust

A. Sen et al. (Eds.): IWDC 2004, LNCS 3326, pp. 138–143, 2004.
© Springer-Verlag Berlin Heidelberg 2004

theoretical foundation that allows formal analysis and verification both real-time and non-real times properties of timed designs.

This paper is organized as follows: Section 2 gives a brief overview of the UNITY formalism. Section 3 introduces the proposed t-UNITY formalism and explains the various logical constructs that can be used in t-UNITY for specifying and reasoning about real-time behavior of systems. Section 4 describes a case study on modeling a safety critical system for controlling traffic on a junction of a farm-road with a highway. The paper ends with conclusions in section 5.

1.1 The UNITY Formalism

The UNITY formalism consists of a simple language for specifying programs, a logic for expressing properties that a program must satisfy, and a proof system for proving assertions about program behavior. A typical UNITY program consists of three sections: a *declare* section, which contains declaration of variables; an *initially* section, in which all or some of the variables are initialized, and an *assign* section, which is a set of guarded assignment statements or actions. Each action is a relation over program states. An execution of a system is an infinite sequence of the form $\sigma_0 A_0 \sigma_1 \ldots \sigma_i A_i \sigma_{i+1}$ where each σ_i is a program state and A_i is an action or program statement. The state σ_0 satisfies the initial condition. The program actions are written as guarded commands, preceded optionally by a label, as in $\alpha :: g \rightarrow s$ where g is the guard, s is the statement and α is the label. In each step of execution, any action is non-deterministically selected from the set of enabled actions. The selection of actions is assumed to be weakly fair, which means that an action, which is enabled and waiting to be executed, will eventually be executed.

The basic UNITY operator for expressing safety properties is **co** (short for **constraints**). For every execution of a given UNITY program F that satisfies p **co** q, a state satisfying p is immediately followed by a state satisfying q. UNITY provides three operators for specifying progress properties: **transient, ensures** and $\rightarrow$ (pronounced 'leads to'). The most fundamental progress property of UNITY logic is **transient**. In UNITY, p **transient** means that p holds initially and there is a statement in F.assign after whose execution, p doesn't hold anymore. The second progress property **ensures** can be defined in terms of **co** and **transient**. In UNITY, p **ensures** q means that if p holds at some point during execution, it will continue to hold as long as q doesn't hold; and q is guaranteed to hold eventually. Another commonly used progress property that is defined using co is **unless**. In UNITY, p **unless** q means that if p holds at some point during execution, it will continue to hold as long as q doesn't hold; however, unlike **ensures** property, it is not guaranteed that q will hold eventually. The most powerful operator for specifying progress properties in UNITY is 'leads to', denoted as $\rightarrow$. Formally, p $\rightarrow$ q denotes that if p holds at some point, q will hold at this or some later point during program execution.

Space restrictions do not permit a detailed overview of UNITY formalism here and interested readers may refer to [1] and [5] for this purpose. For current research on applications and extensions of UNITY formalism by various authors, please refer to [7]-[8].

2 The t-UNITY Formalism

Similar to UNITY, in t-UNITY a program execution is an infinite sequence of the form $\sigma_0 A_0 \sigma_1 \ldots \sigma_i A_i \sigma_{i+1}$ where each σ_i is a program state and A_i is an action or program statement. However, in t-UNITY, with each predicate p defined over the values of the program variables, we define a time instant p.start and a time interval p.interval, such that p.start denotes the instant at which the predicate p becomes true and p.interval denotes the time interval during which the predicate p remains true. The only assumptions about time flow in t-UNITY are the following: time progresses as computation proceeds and the progression of time is uniform. In UNITY, a program action is enabled when a certain predicate becomes true in the program. In t-UNITY, an action can also become enabled when a certain temporal relation such as$<$, $\leq$, $=$, $\neq$, $\geq$, $>$ between p.interval and a given time interval [a,b] is satisfied. For every predicate p and a given time interval [a,b], we define a boolean function life(p,R,[a,b]) which returns true when p.interval satisfies relation R with the given time interval [a,b]. Thus, for example, life(p,=,[a,b]) is true if p becomes true at instant a, and remains true till instant b. Similarly, life $((p, \geq, [a,b])$ is true if p becomes true at instant a, and remains true till an instant $\geq$ b. With every action A, we associate a duration A.d which is the interval during which the action must be scheduled for execution, once it is enabled and another duration $A.\tau$, which is the time taken by A to complete its action. In other words, an action A is guaranteed to complete its execution within a duration $A.d + A.\tau$ of it being enabled in the program. Thus in t-UNITY, we impose additional real time constraints over the fair transition system of UNITY. The program actions in t-UNITY are written as guarded commands, preceded optionally by a label, followed by specification of A.d as in α : delay $= \tau$: g $\rightarrow_\Delta$ s, where α is the statement label, τ is the maximum time interval within which the statement must be taken up for execution once it is enabled, Δ is the time required by the statement to complete its action, g is the guard and s is the statement that is executed after the guard g becomes true. The delay part is omitted if the statement is scheduled for execution as soon as it is enabled.

In t-UNITY, we define the same fundamental safety operator **co** as in UNITY. However, we generalize the definition of the liveness properties to incorporate our knowledge of real-time constraints on the system in the definition of those operators. In t-UNITY, the liveness operator **transient**$_{[a,b]}$ is defined in the following way: p **transient**$_{[a,b]}$ means that p becomes true at instant p.start = a and there is a statement in F.assign after whose execution, p doesn't hold anymore, and this happens at some time within the interval [a,b]. Formally,

$$p \text{ transient}_{[a,b]} \equiv\, <\text{p.start} = a : \exists s : s \in \text{F.assign} : \{p\}\, s\, \{\neg p\} \wedge (a \leq (\neg p).\text{start} \leq b) >$$

As in UNITY, the second progress property **ensures** can be defined in terms of **co** and **transient**. In t-UNITY, p **ensures**$_{[a,b]}$ q means that if p becomes true at some instant p.start = a during execution, it will continue to hold as long as q doesn't hold; and q is guaranteed to hold at some time within time interval[a,b]. Formally speaking,

$$\frac{(p \wedge \neg q) \text{ co } (p \vee q),\ (p \wedge \neg q) \text{ transient}_{[a,b]}}{p \text{ ensures}_{[a,b]} q}$$

In a similar fashion, $p \rightarrow_{[a,b]} q$ denotes that if p becomes true at some instant p.start = a during execution, q will hold at time a or some later time $\leq b$ during program execution. Formally, $\mapsto$ is defined as the transitive, disjunctive closure of the **ensures** relation.

$$\frac{p \text{ ensures}_{[a,b]} q}{p \rightarrow_{[a,b]} q} \qquad \text{(basis)}$$

$$\frac{p \rightarrow_{[a,b]} q , q \rightarrow_{[b,c]} r}{p \rightarrow_{[a,c]} r} \qquad \text{(transitivity)}$$

$$\frac{<\forall p : p \in S : p \rightarrow_{[a,b]} q>}{<\exists p : p \in S : p> \rightarrow_{[a,b]} q} \qquad \text{(disjunction)}$$

where S is any set of predicates.

In the above definitions and formulas , when the timing constraints are omitted, they have their usual non-real-time interpretations as in UNITY. Also, in many applications, real-time behavior depends on relative time constraints, rather than absolute time constraints. For such cases, we adopt another notation in which we use a subscript d to denote the interval a – b. In such cases, p **transient**$_d$ means that p becomes true at some instant and $\neg p$ becomes true within a duration d of p becoming true. Also, p **ensures**$_d$ q means that q is guaranteed to become true within a duration d of p becoming true and p continues to be true as long as q doesn't hold. In a similar manner, we define p $_d$ q.

We can also define the life predicate for duration d in the following way: life(p,=, d) is true if p becomes true at some instant and continues to be true for a duration d. Similarly, life(p, $\geq$, d) is true if p becomes true at some instant and continues to hold for a duration $\geq$ d, and life(p, $\leq$, d) is true if p holds at some instant and continues to hold for a duration $\leq$ d.

The following relationship holds for life of a predicate p.

$$\frac{\text{life}(p,R, [a,b]) \text{ ensures}_{[c,d]} q}{p \rightarrow_{[a,d]} q} \qquad \text{(l-basis)}$$

$$\frac{\text{life}(p, R, [a,b]) \rightarrow_{[c,d]} q, \text{life}(q, R, [e,f]) \rightarrow_{[g,h]} r}{p \rightarrow_{[a,h]} r} \qquad \text{(l-transitivity)}$$

$$\frac{<\forall p : p \in S : \text{life}(p, R, [a,b]) \rightarrow_{[c,d]} q >}{<\exists p : p \in S : \text{life}(p, R, [a,b])> \rightarrow_{[c,d]} q} \qquad \text{(l-disjunction)}$$

For systems having relative time constraints, the corresponding relations are

$$\frac{\text{life}(p,R, d1) \text{ ensures}_{d2} q}{p \rightarrow_{d1+d2} q} \qquad \text{(ld-basis)}$$

$$\frac{\text{life}(p, R, a-b) \rightarrow_{c-d} q, \text{life}(q, R, e-f) \rightarrow_{g-h} r}{p \rightarrow_{[a-h]} r} \qquad \text{(ld-transitivity)}$$

$$\frac{<\forall p : p \in S : \text{life}(p, R, d1) \rightarrow_{d2} q >}{<\exists p : p \in S : \text{life}(p, R, d1)> \rightarrow_{d2} q} \qquad \text{(ld-disjunction)}$$

3   Formal Specification of a Traffic Light Controller

As an example of application of t-UNITY framework for modeling and specification of real-time safety critical systems, we consider the case of a traffic light controller that control traffic through a highway cutting across a farm road. This example is adapted from [6]. There is a car sensor on the farm road, that sends a Boolean signal (frd) to the controller the moment it detects a car waiting on the farm road on either side of the highway. Once frd is true, the highway signal turns from green to yellow after 25.01 seconds (while the farm road signal stays red), and yellow is followed by red after 4.01 seconds. The transition action from one signal state to another in not instantaneous, and takes a finite time of 0.01 seconds. When the highway signal turns red, the farm road signal turns green simultaneously. The system continues in this state for 20 seconds. Then, the farm signal turns yellow while the highway signal stays red. After 4.01 seconds, the farm signal turns red and the highway signal turns green again. If another car appears on the farm road anytime during this cycle, it will not affect the state transitions described above in any way.

The states space of the system consists of the following four states:

HGFR $\equiv$ highway signal green and farm road signal red
HYFR $\equiv$ highway signal yellow and farm road signal red
HRFG $\equiv$ highway signal red and farm road signal green
HRFY $\equiv$ highway signal red and farm road signal yellow

The safety properties of the system are the following:

Initially HGFR $\wedge$ ¬frd
HGFR **co** HGFR $\vee$ HYFR
HYFR **co** HYFR $\vee$ HRFG
HRFG **co** HRFG $\vee$ HRFY
HRFY **co** HRFY $\vee$ HGFR

The liveness properties are the following:

life(HGFR $\wedge$ frd, =, 25) ensures$_{0.01}$ HYFR   (14)
life(HYFR, =, 4) ensures$_{0.01}$ HRFG   (15)
life(HRFG, =, 20) ensures$_{0.01}$ HRFY   (16)
life(HRFY, =, 4) ensures$_{0.01}$ HGFR$\wedge$ ¬frd   (17)

Using these properties, and proof logic of t-UNITY described above, we can easily prove assertions such as:

HGFR $\wedge$ frd **ensures**$_{30}$ HRFG   (18)
HGFR $\wedge$ ¬frd $\mapsto$ HGFR   (19)
HRFG **ensures**$_{25}$ HGFR   (20)

If highway signal is green and farm road signal is red and frd becomes true, then highway signal will turn yellow and farm road signal will turn red after 25.01 seconds (Property (14)). If highway signal turns yellow and farm road signal is red, highway signal will turn red and farm road signal will turn red after 4.01 seconds (Property (15)). If highway signal turns red and farm road signal turns green, farm road signal will turn yellow after 20.01 seconds and highway signal will remain red(Property (16)). If highway signal is red and farm road signal is yellow, highway signal will turn green, farm road signal will turn red and frd will be reset to false after 4.01

seconds(property(17)). Property (18) states that if there is a car waiting on farm road, and highway signal is green, it will turn to red and farm road signal will turn green within 30 seconds. Property (19) ensures that when there is no car on the farm road, the highway signal always stays green and the farm road signal always stays red. Property (20) guarantees that the highway signal will never be red for more than 25 seconds at a time.

4 Conclusion

Frameworks for specifying real-time systems are often considered to be incompatible with those that are found useful for behavioral specification of non-real-time systems. This makes it quite difficult to deal with both kinds of properties and separate their treatment into successive design steps. For this reason, there is a need for practical specification framework and language that has a well defined logical basis, and at the same time, has sufficient expressive power to model real-time reactive behavior. This is the motivation of our work. The main contribution of this paper is to propose a framework for requirements engineering and design of real-time systems based on the mathematical approach of the UNITY formalism. The proposed t-UNITY framework has sufficient expressive power to reason about both real-time and non-real-time properties of a system under a common logical framework.

References

1. Mani Chandy, K and Misra, Jayadev: Parallel Program Design : A Foundation, Addison Wesley, 1988.
2. Jones, C.B.: Systematic Software Development Using VDM, Prentice-Hall, Englewood Cliffs, NJ, 1986.
3. Abrial, J. R.: Programming As a Mathematical Exercise. Mathematical Logic and Programming Languages,, C. A. R. Hoare and J. C. Shepherdson, Eds. Prentice-Hall, Englewood Cliffs, NJ, 1985.
4. Ward, P. and Mellor S.: Structural Development for Real-Time Systems, Yurdon Press, Englewood Cliffs, NJ, 1985.
5. Jayadev Misra: A Logic For Concurrent Programming, April 12,1994.
6. Mead, Carver and Conway, Lynn: Introduction to VLSI systems, Addison Wesley, 1979.
7. Picco, G. P., Roman, G., and McCann, P. J.:Reasoning About Code Mobility With Mobile UNITY. ACM Trans. Software Engng. and Methodology, Vol.10, No.3, pp. 338-395, July 2001.
8. Klavins, E. and Murray, Richard, M.: Distributed Algorithms for Cooperative Control, IEEE Pervasive Computing, Vol.3, No.1, pp. 56-65, Jan. 2004.

Finding Pareto-Optimal Set of Distributed Vectors with Minimum Disclosure

Satish K. Sehgal and Asim K. Pal

Indian Institute of Management Calcutta, Kolkata, India*
sehgal.satish@gmail.com, asim@iimcal.ac.in

Abstract. A set of alternatives along with their associated values is available with individual parties who do not want to share it with others. Algorithms to find the feasible set (i.e. common subset) X and the pareto-optimal subset of X with minimum disclosure in presence or absence of a third party are explored. These are useful in multiparty negotiations.

1 Introduction

Let there be m parties (decision making agent (DMA)). Each DMA^i; $i = 1, \ldots, m$, has a ***decision set*** $X^i \subset U$, the universal set of ***alternatives*** (or options or decision vectors). A ***value vector*** $v(x) = (v^1(x) \ldots v^m(x))$ represents the valuation of the alternative x by all DMAs. $X = X^1 \cap X^2 \cap \ldots \cap X^m$ is the ***feasible set***. $PO \subset X$ is the subset of all ***pareto-optimal (p.o.)*** alternatives. $v^i(x)$ is known only to DMA^i who does not want to share it with any other DMA. Hence, $v(x)$ is distributed among m DMAs. The motivation of the problem comes from that PO is the set of alternatives which the negotiators would like to negotiate on. This allows the negotiators to avoid the alternatives for which better alternatives will always exist in PO for all the DMAs.

The two steps involved in finding PO are: 1) Find X; 2) Find PO. The objective of the algorithms is that DMAs will learn only about X and PO, and MA (mediator agent) should not learn anything about X, PO or $v(x), x \in X$.

2 Finding the Feasible Set (Finding the Intersection)

Three algorithms to compute $X = X^1 \cap \ldots \cap X^m$ where X^i is available only with DMA^i; $i = 1, \ldots, m$, have been developed.

2.1 Double Encryption Based Algorithm: Two Parties (DMA^1 and DMA^2). The algorithm [1] (similar to the algorithm in [2]) is based on ***commutative encryption***. The algorithm:

1. Each DMA^i randomly chooses a secret key: $e_i \in_r$ Key $\mathcal{F}^1$.

---

* The work is partly funded by the AICTE project ISISAMB.

[1] In all the algorithms "Each DMA^i performs the task T" means that "Each DMA^i performs the task T in parallel with other DMAs". If any task is to be performed in sequence, it will be specifically mentioned in the text.

A. Sen et al. (Eds.): IWDC 2004, LNCS 3326, pp. 144–149, 2004.
© Springer-Verlag Berlin Heidelberg 2004

2. DMA^1 sends $Y_1 = f_{e_1}(X^1)$ to DMA^2; and similarly does DMA^2.
3. DMA^1 sends $f_{e_1}(Y_2)$ to DMA^2; and similarly does DMA^2.
4. Each DMA finds the intersection X.

Double encryption based algorithm: Multiple parties. Here any one of the DMAs takes up the central control and first finds individually the intersection of the decision set of its own with those of others and then finds X by intersecting these sets and finally sends X to all.

Disclosure. The central DMA learns the alternatives which are common with each of the other DMAs and the other DMAs learn those which are common with the central DMA. The latter however can be avoided if in Step 3, the central DMA does not send the encrypted alternatives to other DMAs.

2.2 Randomization Based Algorithm. This algorithm is communication intensive, but leads to reduced disclosure compared to Double encryption based algorithm. Here, each DMA distributes its decision set X^i among other DMAs. To increase ambiguity each DMA adds random noise at random positions.

Phase-I: Random noise is appended before the intersection is computed.

1. Each DMA^i performs ($k \leftarrow 0$):
   (a) Finds $X_0^i = X^i \cup R_0^i$ s.t. $R_0^i \cap X^i = \phi$, where R_0^i is random noise.
   (b) Splits X_0^i into disjoint parts, s.t. $X_0^i = \bigcup\limits_{j=1;j\neq i}^{m} s_j^i$ and $|X_0^i| = \sum\limits_{j=1;j\neq i}^{m} |s_j^i|$.
   (c) Sends s_j^i to $DMA^j, j = 1, \ldots, m$, and $j \neq i$. Finds $S_0^i = \bigcup\limits_{j=1;j\neq i}^{m} s_i^j$.
   (d) **while** $k < m$ **does**
       i. Sets $k \leftarrow k + 1$.
       ii. Finds $S_k^i = (S_{k-1}^{i-1} \cap X^i) \cup R_k^i$; R_k^i is random noise, s.t. $S_{k-1}^{i-1} \cap R_k^i = \phi$
       iii. **if** $k \neq m$ **then** sends S_k^i to DMA^{i+1} (DMA^m sends to DMA^1).
   (e) Sends S_m^i to central DMA (say DMA^1).
2. DMA^1 finds $X_R = \bigcup\limits_{i=1}^{m} S_m^i$.

Phase-II: The noise appended in the previous phase is removed.

1. Each DMA^i (starting from the central DMA, i.e. DMA^1) sequentially sends
$$X_R^i = X_R^{i-1} - \left(\bigcup\limits_{k} R_k^i\right) \text{ to } DMA^{i+1}. \text{ For } DMA^1, X_R^{i-1} \text{ is } X_R.$$
2. The last DMA (DMA^m here) sends X_R^i ($= X$) to all other DMAs.

2.3 Single Encryption Based Algorithm with Semi-honest Mediator. Each DMA's decision set is encrypted (using the same key which is generated by the DMAs through consensus) and sent to MA who finds the intersection. There is no disclosure as MA does not know the encryption function used.

3   Finding the Pareto-Optimal Frontier, PO

Algorithm for finding the pareto-optimal set PO: 1) DMAs (with consensus) choose a Comparison scheme C and a Preference hiding scheme P, and 2) DMAs together (in parallel) perform C adopting P. The final algorithm for finding PO $\subseteq$ X would therefore depend on both P and C. C would be selected based on the number of comparisons required for a given X and on disclosure requirements. P will depend on availability of MA.

Definitions. Let a and b belong to X. a dominates b (a $\succ$ b) if $v^i(a) \geq v^i(b)$, for all $i = 1, \ldots, m$, and $\exists j, 1 \leq j \leq m$ s. t. $v^j(a) > v^j(b)$. a is dominated by b (a $\prec$ b) if b $\succ$ a. a is incomparable to b (a $\sim$ b) if neither a $\succ$ b nor a $\prec$ b.

3.1 Comparison Schemes. In CS_a comparisons are performed in sequence. In CS_b all pairs are compared simultaneously in parallel. Scheme CS_c is a compromise between the two.

CS_a: One comparison at-a-time. A pair of alternatives is compared. Any alternative which is found dominated is marked *excluded* and is not considered for comparison in future. Let us put the alternatives of X in an ordered list L. We scan L in sequence. Let the *current alternative* be denoted by c, *comparison alternative* by p, the next unmarked alternative after c by c' and that after p by p'. **For simplicity, the updation of c' and p' has not been shown explicitly, i.e. whenever c is updated c' will also be updated, and similarly for p and p'.** Three strategies of comparisons are proposed.

CS_a - Strategy 1. This is a modification to the *Approach 1* in [3] except that here we mark p if it is dominated.

1. Set $c \leftarrow$ first alternative in L and $p \leftarrow$ second alternative in L.
2. Repeat until there is no unmarked alternative in L after c:
    (a) Compare c and p:
        i. $c \succ p$: Mark p *excluded* and set $p \leftarrow p'$.
        ii. $c \sim p$: Set $p \leftarrow p'$.
        iii. $c \prec p$: Set $c \leftarrow c'$ and $p \leftarrow c'$ (note, c' is updated after updating c).
    (b) If there is no unmarked alternative in L after p: Mark c *p.o.*, set $c \leftarrow c'$ and $p \leftarrow c'$.
3. Mark c *p.o.* The alternatives marked *p.o.* form PO.

CS_a - Strategy 2. This is the *Basic block-nested-loops algorithm* [4] (*Approach 2* in [3]). A growing *window* w of non-dominated alternatives is maintained. A new alternative p in L is compared with the alternatives in w.

1. For each $c \in$ L, compare c with the alternative d in w (one at-a-time).
    (a) $\nexists\, d \in w$ s.t. $d \succ c$: c is appended to w.
    (b) $\exists\, d \in w$ s.t. $c \succ d$: d is deleted from w.
2. The alternatives in w form PO.

CS_a - Strategy 3. Motivated by a variant (call it *self organizing list variant*) of the Basic block nested loops algorithm this strategy adaptively prioritizes the alternatives which dominate other alternatives.

1. Set $c \leftarrow$ first alternative in L and $p \leftarrow$ second alternative in L. Set $flag \leftarrow 0$.
2. Repeat until there is no unmarked alternative in L after c:
   (a) If $c \prec p$ then mark c *excluded*, set $c \leftarrow p$, $flag \leftarrow 1$ else mark p *excluded*.
   (b) Set $p \leftarrow p'$.
   (c) If $flag = 0$ and there is no unmarked alternative in L after p then mark c *p.o.*, set $c \leftarrow c'$ and $p \leftarrow c'$ (note, c' is updated before p is updated).
   (d) If $flag = 1$:
      i. If there is no unmarked alternative in L after p then mark c *p.o.*, set $p \leftarrow$ first unmarked alternative from start in L.
      ii. If there is no unmarked alternative in L between p and c, (note p is prior to c in L) then mark c *p.o.*, set $c \leftarrow$ next unmarked alternative from the start in L, $p \leftarrow c'$ and $flag \leftarrow 0$.
3. Mark c *p.o.* The alternatives marked *p.o.* form PO.

Analysis of comparison strategies. It can be proved that the number of comparisons for Strategy 1 and Strategy 2 are same, but they are different from that for Strategy 3. Earliest announcement of a *p.o.* alternative is possible in Strategy 3 where the first announcement occurs after $|X| - 1$ comparisons. In Strategy 2, PO is known only at the end, while in Strategy 1 a *p.o.* is announced whenever an alternative has been compared with all the unmarked ones.

CS_b: All comparisons together. The comparisons are performed in parallel and the results are announced simultaneously. The alternatives which are found dominated in any pair are marked *excluded*. The unmarked alternatives form PO. Here, each DMA needs to perform $^{|X|}C_2$ comparisons. Thus, computation and communication costs are high compared to CS_a which takes the advantage of early comparisons. CS_b however, takes only one communication cycle.

CS_c: Comparisons in batch. A set (batch) of pairs are evaluated at-a-time. The result for all the pairs in the batch is found and announced at one go. The new pairs having any alternative found dominated are not considered.

Disclosure. If in any comparison, a $\succ$ b (or vice versa), each DMA knows the preference ordering on a and b for everybody else. Note, a and / or b may not belong to PO. Similarly, when a $\sim$ b, DMAs can deduce that there is at least one other DMA who has a preference ordering opposite to their own.

In CS_a and CS_c DMAs would not learn about the preference between members of the pairs for which comparisons are not performed. In CS_b all comparisons are performed together and would lead to relatively more disclosure.

3.2 Preference Hiding Schemes. These schemes comprise two processes: **Setup process** and **Comparison process**. The schemes do not apply to the two DMA case as, from the final result a DMA can deduce the preference of the other. Four cases arises: 1) MA not available, 2) MA available and does not know X, 3) MA available, knows X and alternative order is preserved and; 4) MA available, knows X and alternative order does not matter.

Encrypted output based mechanism (MA not available). The output of each DMA is kept secret by performing multiple XORs. This is motivated from mechanisms in [5, 6].

Setup process:

1. One of the DMAs generates m pairs of binary random vectors (all unique and same size, sufficiently large) and sends one pair (e_1^i, e_2^i) to each DMA^i.
2. Each DMA^i performs:
   (a) Generates $(m-1)$ random binary vectors $r_1^i \ldots r_{m-1}^i$.
   (b) Finds $r^i = e_1^i \oplus r_1^i \oplus \ldots \oplus r_{m-1}^i$ ($\oplus$ is the bit wise XOR operator between two binary vectors at a time).
   (c) Sends randomly one vector $p^{ij} \in_r \{r_1^i \ldots r_{m-1}^i, r^i\}$ to DMA^j ($j = 1, \ldots, m$; $j \neq i$) retaining one with itself. No vector is sent to more than one DMA.
   (d) Sends $\alpha^i = \oplus_j p^{ji}$ to all other DMAs.
   (e) Finds $h_+ = \oplus_i \alpha^i = \oplus_i e_1^i$ (this intuitively represents a $\succ$ b).
3. Repeats Step 2 (a) - 2 (d) for e_2^i giving h_- (this implies b $\succ$ a).

Comparison process: Let the two alternatives to be compared be a and b. Each DMA^i performs:

1. Finds e^i: if $v^i(a) \geq v^i(b)$ then $e^i = e_1^i$ else $e^i = e_2^i$.
2. Performs Steps 2(a) - 2(d) of the Setup Process with new parameters.
3. If $h = h_+$ then a $\succ$ b else (if $h = h_-$ then b $\succ$ a else a $\sim$ b), where $h = \oplus_i \alpha^i$.

Note that there is a non-zero chance of occurrence of $h = h_+$ even if a $\succ$ b is not true. But, the probability of this can be brought arbitrarily close to zero by using suitably long random pairs [7].

Disclosure: Since, each DMA receives a random vector it cannot make out the preference structure of the other DMAs.

Straight comparison based mechanism (MA available, does not know **X).** No extra mechanism is required to hide the information from MA. Thus, *Setup process* is redundant here.

Comparison process: Let the two alternatives to be compared be a and b.

1. Each DMA^i sends z^i to MA: if $v^i(a) \geq v^i(b)$ then $z^i = 0$ else $z^i = 1$.
2. MA sends z' to all DMAs: if $z^1 = \ldots = z^m$ then $z' = 1$ else $z' = 0$.
3. Each DMA^i finds: if $z' = 0$ then a $\sim$ b else (if $z^i = 0$ then a $\succ$ b else a $\prec$ b).

Disclosure: Knowing the dominance between the alternatives does not help MA who does not have the identity of the alternatives.

Output randomization based mechanism (MA available, knows **X** ***and alternative order to be preserved).*** If it is a priori known that the first few alternatives dominate a large number of alternatives, retaining the order of alternatives could be useful. This algorithm is motivated from [7]. A random list R contains binary elements -1 and +1. For each comparison DMAs observe an element in sequence from R and alter output coding accordingly.

Setup process: One of the DMAs (say DMA^1) generates a random list R of binary elements -1 and +1 of length $^{|X|}C_2$, and sends it to all DMAs.

Comparison process: Let a and b be compared in the kth comparison:

1. Each DMA^i sends z^i to MA: if R_k is -1 then (if $v^i(a) \geq v^i(b)$ then $z^i \leftarrow 0$ else $z^i \leftarrow 1$) else (if $v^i(a) \geq v^i(b)$ then $z^i \leftarrow 1$ else $z^i \leftarrow 0$).
2. MA sends z' to all DMAs: if $z^1 = \ldots = z^m$ then $z' = 1$ else $z' = 0$.
3. Each DMA^i finds: if $z' = 0$ then a $\sim$ b else
   (if $((R_k = $ -1 & $z^i = 0)$ OR $(R_k = 1$ & $z^i = 1))$ then a $\succ$ b else
   b $\succ$ a).

Disclosure : Same as Straight comparison based scheme.

Permutation based mechanism (MA available, knows X and alternative order need not be preserved). The *Comparison process* is same as that for *Straight comparison based mechanism.*

Setup process: DMAs permute randomly elements in X. Thus, when a particular comparison is made MA cannot ascertain the identity of the alternatives being compared. The generation of new indices for all the alternatives by random permutation can be undertaken by any DMA.

Disclosure : Same as Straight comparison based scheme.

4   Conclusions

Algorithms requiring minimum disclosure (in presence and absence of a mediator) to compare two distributed vectors and to find the intersection of sets of vectors and the p.o. subset of a set of vectors have been explored here. Detailed analysis of computaion and communication costs as well as some proofs have been ommitted due to shortage of space.

References

1. Huberman, B.A., Franklin, M., Hogg, T.: Enhancing privacy and trust in electronic communities. In: 1st ACM Conference on Electronic Commerce, Colorado (1999) 78–86
2. Agrawal, R., Evfimievski, A., Srikant, R.: Information sharing across private databases. In: 2003 ACM SIGMOD International Conference on Management of Data, ACM Press (2003) 86–97
3. Deb, K.: Multi-Objective Optimization using Evolutionary Algorithms. John Wiley & Sons, Ltd. (2001)
4. Börzsönyi, S., Kossmann, D., Stocker, K.: The skyline operator. In: Seventeenth International Conference on Data Engineering, Heidelberg, Germany (2001)
5. Madore, D.A.: A method of free speech on the Internet: random pads. http://www.eleves.ens.fr:8080/home/madore/misc/freespeech.html (11/06/04) (2000)
6. Atallah, M.J., Du, W.: A multi-dimensional Yao's millionaire protocol. http://dependability.cs.virginia.edu/bibliography/2001-09.ps (17/02/04) (2001)
7. Du, W.: A Study of Several Specific Secure Two-Party Computation Problems. PhD thesis, Purdue University (2001)

Lean-DFS: A Distributed Filesystem for Resource Starved Clients

Shyam Antony and Gautam Barua

Dept. of CSE, IIT Guwahati,
Guwahati 781039, India
gb@iitg.ernet.in, antony@cs.ucsb.edu

Abstract. Devices which have limited computing resources but are capable of networking have become increasingly important constituents of distributed environments. In order to maximize the advantages of their networking capability, it is important to provide efficient methods to access modify and share data. In this paper we position distributed filesystems as a possible solution to this problem. We discuss the constraints imposed by such environments on traditional distributed filesystem design parameters. We describe the design and implementation of a distributed filesystem (lean-dfs) for such environments.

1 Introduction

Devices which have limited resources in terms of computational power, memory etc. form vital components of 'intelligent' environments. Such resource starved machines are increasingly capable of networking. In order to maximize the benefits of networking, it is necessary to provide efficient methods to access, modify, and share data. A Personal Digital Assistant (PDA) cum cell phone needs to store information it gathers, in a server. Current PDAs have applications that "synchronise" files between the PDA versions and the server versions. A general purpose distributed file system will be a better vehicle for providing support for all these activities than piecemeal, machine and OS specific solutions for each of the different usages. Embedded systems need to communicate with "Master" nodes to get commands and parameters that change its behaviour from time to time. The use of configuration files to control the behaviour of processes is a well understood and time tested technique So a distributed file system could be the vehicle of communication in an embedded system network, rather than specific protocols for specific needs. Distributed Filesystems (DFS) form an integral part of distributed environments and have been adapted for a variety of research goals. General information on DFS can be found in [1, 2]. NFS [3, 4, 5] is the most widely used distributed filesystem. There has been some work on DFS for mobile clients, notably, CODA and Odyssey ([6, 7]). Recent work by Atkin and Birman and by Muthitacharoen et. al, have focussed on a low bandwidth environment ([8, 9]). Both works do not put constraints on resource availability other than bandwidth. Software for PDAs devote attention to the building of

A. Sen et al. (Eds.): IWDC 2004, LNCS 3326, pp. 150–155, 2004.
© Springer-Verlag Berlin Heidelberg 2004

file systems on flash memory with its specific characteristics and these have no direct relationship with a distributed file system. The PalmOS, a popular PDA OS, has facilities for file synchronisation and file copying as a result, but no distributed file system interface is provided ([10]).

2   Constraints and Implications

Memory Constraint: Resource starved clients usually have very limited main memory. This rules out implementation choices that involve high memory usage such as a large main memory file cache or a highly sophisticated protocol the implementation of which will involve a large code size.

Lack of Non-Volatile Storage: Since resource starved clients usually do not have access to significant local non-volatile storage, distributed filesystem design paradigms which implicitly convert a remote file into a local file, as in [8], are not possible.

CPU and Power Issues: Unlike normal clients which are designed to multiplex a number of applications, resource starved clients are designed to execute one or two applications at a time. As a result, no process can execute on behalf of the distributed filesystem in the background. For example it is not possible to execute a daemon which lazily updates a cache. Further, features such as callbacks, delayed writing and read-ahead, relying on background processes cannot be used.

Network Issues: Earlier work on mobile file systems have included a lack of bandwidth as a constraint. Even though network bandwidth is limited, it is not a constraint nowadays. So a tradeoff by using more network bandwidth to preserve other resources is feasible. This translates into the reduction of caching resulting in more network traffic.

Application Characteristics: Unlike normal clients, in a resource starved client, files are not manipulated directly by users but indirectly by applications. Hence the workload for distributed filesystems for resource starved clients is different from conventional file workloads.

TCP Vs UDP: This is not a constraint but more of a implementation choice. The recent trend among distributed filesystem implementations is to use TCP. However since UDP is more lightweight than TCP, our implementation uses rpc over UDP.

3   Lean-Dfs Filesystem

Typical Workloads In the case of resource starved clients, we have identified two most common workloads: *Workload I:* This workload consists of very short reads and writes with long periods of inactivity between successive operations. Typical examples include reading configuration and startup files from the remote server and writing to remote files to indicate some change in the client's environment. The long interval between operations occurs because changes in the environment happens only occasionally. In order to be useful it is necessary to provide rapid response time to such reads and writes. *Workload II:* This is the large file workload which usually consists of large files which are read or written sequentially in fairly large chunks. A typical example of this workload is the processing of multimedia files.

3.1   Optimisations

In the following paragraphs we outline a few optimizations for workload I to provide a rapid response time. Conventional features of NFS are sufficient for workload II since such a workload cannot benefit from caching due to sequential flooding.

Mounting: Since resource starved clients often suffer long periods of inactivity between periods of activity, it is necessary to allow a rapid 'mount-operate-umount' paradigm. The client sends an rpc request called MOUNT to the server. In response the server returns the root filehandle and server side parameters such as maximum allowed file name etc. No security checking is done at this point and hence any client can execute the mount request. In order to reduce the time taken by the server to browse the server exports, we insist that the server export a single, unified filesystem tree. As a result of these changes we were able to achieve rapid mount times of around 100 ms with a server under moderate load.

Truncate-on-Write and Consistency Issues: When a write is intended to overwrite a file completely and the length of the new write is shorter than the original file size, a write request carries an extra variable called truncate which as suggested by its name, truncates the file before writing. The consistency provided by this scheme is extremely weak but quite sufficient for workload I.

Limited Batching with Compound Requests: Since the constraints of resource starved clients force the distributed filesystem to be an 'on-demand' system, we can ensure a rapid response time by batching requests which are related into a single request. This is similar to the batching in nfs version 4 ([5]) and the 'andx' feature in cifs ([11]). However since we use udp rather than tcp, arbitrary batching of requests cannot be accommodated in a single datagram. Hence we have created new requests which are compounded versions of selected requests. The advantages of these compounded requests and the subtle changes in semantics they introduce, are discussed below.

Lookup Path: Experiments show that the LOOKUP request is the most executed of all requests. The LOOKUP request implicitly shifts the burden of pathname traversal logic to the client and consequently generates a lot of extra traffic. While this approach is reasonable for normal clients, it is unacceptable for resource starved clients. For this purpose our implementation introduces a new request called LOOKUP-PATH. The pathname is included in the request and the file handle corresponding to the file is returned. Restrictions that are imposed include use of only absolute path names and conforming to the separator syntax of the server (obtained during a mount).

Lookup-Read and Lookup-Write: Lookup-Read combines the lookup-path request with the read request so that read operations typical of workload I can be satisfied with one or two network transmissions. Lookup-write is also similar and the truncate-on-write which is used by normal write requests is also allowed.

Lookup-Readdir and the Readdir Cache: The LOOKUP-READDIR request is very similar to the lookup-read request but is used for reading directory entries. This is particularly efficient for small directories. The most frequent directory operation is the readdir operation. Since most filesystem semantics do not provide any guarantee about the order in which the different files occur within a single directory, applications that do readdir based operations typically read all the entries of the directory sequentially. In order to optimize for such workloads while satisfying the constraints imposed by resource starved clients, whenever an application reads a directory entry, we do a read-ahead using two or three READDIR requests and cache the two or three UDP datagram worth of directory entries (usually around 50 directory entries) in a time-to-live (TTL) based cache. Since a resource starved client typically supports only one or two processes, there is very little chance for heavy cache contention. Also the size needed is very small (around 25 KB). Further, since the cache is TTL based, no background work is needed for cache management. Thus all the constraints of resource starved clients are satisfied while providing good performance for subsequent readdir requests. A similar cache implementation for files will not be efficient since the nature of file workloads is fundamentally different from directory workloads.

Security: In this paper we ignore sophisticated security requirements. Such an assumption is not unreasonable since resource starved clients are not expected to handle sensitive data.

3.2   The Remote Procedure Calls

Based on the discussion above, the following RPC calls comprise the interface of the distributed file system. Details of the data structures are omitted. They are similar to what is used in NFS. It may noted that a client need not implement all the calls if space constraints are severe, as the compound calls *lookup_** subsume the functionalities of the simple calls. Implementing all the calls are however desirable. It is also to be noted that the *create* and *delete* calls apply to both files and directories (unlike NFS), with a parameter specifying which.

Mount, lookup, lookup_path, readdir, lookup_readdir, read, lookup_read, write, lookup_write, create, setattr, delete.

4   Implementation and Results

The above design was implemented under Linux with the server implemented as a user level process. For the client, part of the implementation was in the kernel (as a Linux kernel module) and part in user space. Essentially, the kernel module was used to intercept file system calls and to divert them to the user process which implemented the remote file access using a standard RPC library. Since most of the implementation was in user space, no Linux-specific kernel features were used. The client code size is about 120 KB with 30KB comprising the kernel module and 90KB the user space code. The maximum variable memory usage per request is restricted to twice the maximum size of an UDP packet, that is, 16KB. So a total of 136KB on an Intel system is required to implement the client. Lean-dfs has been tested with file accesses of different sizes and using both reads and writes. The results show that the file system performs adequately under different loads. As the table below shows, performance is quite good. The tests were run with 1 Ghz CPU PCs as a client and a server, with Redhat Linux 8.0. Read performance is better or comparable to the performance of a local file system. Sequential writes performance is worse than the local case because there is no delayed write and so write-through is implemented. The "Updatedb" benchmark builds a database from a file. It is an I/O intensive benchmark with both reads and writes. Again because there is no advantage of caching, the performance of lean-dfs is quite good. Finally the program "fstree" copies an entire file system. Given that there is read and write involved with no advantage for caching, the results are consistent with the earlier results. The poor results for a large filesystem, though not important for the environments we envisage, could not be explained adequately. It is to be noted that while there is no caching at the client, caching with read-ahead and write-behind is implemented at the server side. So the advantage of server side caching is available to lean-dfs. This reinforces the case that absence of caching and asynchronous operations at the client side is not a big disadvantage for sequential accesses.

Table 1. Experimental Results

Sequential Read with 1KB per Read		
Read Size	amp; Local Filesystem (in ms)	amp; Lean-dfs (in ms)
1 KB	amp; 0.194	amp; 6.211
512 KB	amp; 514.88	amp; 510.14
1 MB	amp; 1033.46	amp; 1018.53
Sequential Write with 1KB per write		
Write Size	amp; Local Filesystem (in ms)	amp; Lean-dfs (in ms)
1 KB	amp; 0.16	amp; 0.61
512 KB	amp; 69.48	amp; 651.12
1 MB	amp; 139.42	amp; 874.11
Updatedb Performance		
No. of Objects	amp; Local Filesystem (in ms)	amp; Lean-dfs (in ms)
100	amp; 5.0	amp; 11.0
2000	amp; 17.0	amp; 43.0
33000	amp; 39.0	amp; 94.0
Fstree Performance		
Filesystem Size	amp; Local Filesystem (in ms)	amp; Lean-dfs (in ms)
90 MB	amp; 19,323	amp; 36,847
200 MB	amp; 78,263	amp; 114,361
900 MB	amp; 100,595	amp; 1944,310

5   Conclusions and Future Work

This paper has described the design and implementation of a simple distributed file system, lean-dfs, for an environment where the clients are resource starved. A distributed file system is seen as an useful abstraction for implementing a wide variety of communication needs of such environments. The design has emphasised on low memory usage and the lack of adequate power at the clients. The implementation has demonstrated the feasibility of such a system meeting the goals. A number of extensions and future work can build on this prototype. *Surrogate Servers* : By using surrogate servers for a group of resource starved clients, a number of potential benefits could be realized. The clients can communicate with the surrogate server using the protocol explained above while the surrogate server can communicate with the remote server using a much more sophisticated protocol. *Heterogeneous Set of Clients* : We have assumed all clients to be resource starved. A more realistic environment would involve both resource starved and resource rich clients interoperating together. Further they could be spread over different locations involving different network conditions and security requirements.

References

1. Levy, E., Silberschatz, A.: Distributed File Systems: Concepts and Examples. Computing Surveys (December 1990)
2. Braam, P.J., Nelson, P.A.: Removing Bottlenecks in a Distributed File System. Proceedings of the Linux Expo (1999)
3. Sandberg, R., et.al.: Design and Implemenation of the Sun Network File System. Proceedings of the USENIX Summer Conference (1985)
4. Pawloski, B., et.al.: NFS Version 3 Design and Implementation. Proceedings of the USENIX Summer Conference (1994)
5. Pawloski, B., et.al.: NFS Version 4 Protocol. Proceedings of SANE-2 (2000)
6. Satyanarayanan, M., et.al.: CODA: A Highly Available File System for a Distributed Workstation Environment. IEEE Transactions on Computers (April 1990)
7. Satyanarayanan, M., Kistler, P., et.al.: Experience with Disconnected Operations in a Mobile Computing Environment. Proceedings of the USENIX Symposium on Mobile and Location-Independent Computing (1993)
8. Atkin, B., Birman, K.P.: MFS: An Adaptive Distributed File System for Mobile Hosts. Technical Report Cornell University www.cornell.edu/batkin/doc/mfs/ps (2003)
9. Muthitacharoen, A., Chen, B., Mazieries, D.: A Low-Bandwidth File System. Proceedings of the Eighteenth ACM Symposium on Operating Systems Principles (2001)
10. PalmOS: PalmOS (Cobalt) Documents on Files and High-Level Communications. www.palmos.com/dev/support/docs/protein_books/memory_databases_files.pdf www.palmos.com/dev/support/docs/protein_books/highlevel_comms.pdf (2004)
11. French, S., et.al.: Exploring Boundaries of CIFS. Proceedings of the CIFS Conference (2002)

A Fair Medium Access Protocol Using Adaptive Flow-Rate Control Through Cooperative Negotiation Among Contending Flows in Ad Hoc Wireless Network with Directional Antenna

Dola Saha[1], Siuli Roy[1], Somprakash Bandyopadhyay[1],
Tetsuro Ueda[2], and Shinsuke Tanaka[2]

[1] Indian Institute of Management Calcutta,
Diamond Harbour Road, Joka, Kolkata – 700104
{dola, siuli, somprakash}@iimcal.ac.in
[2] ATR Adaptive Communication Research Laboratories,
2-2-2 Hikaridai, Seika-cho Soraku-gun, Kyoto 619-0288 Japan
{teueda, shinsuke}@atr.jp

Abstract. Medium Access Control protocols proposed in the context of ad hoc networks primarily aim to control the medium access among contending nodes using some contention resolution schemes. However, these protocols do not necessarily guarantee a fair allocation of wireless medium among contending flows. Our objective in this paper is to adaptively adjust the flow-rates of contending flows, so that each gets fair access to the medium. This adaptive adjustment will also ensure high packet delivery ratio and optimal utilization of wireless medium. We use a deterministic approach to adaptively improve the performance of the suffered flows in the network through mutual negotiation between contending flows. In this paper we have also suggested the use of directional antenna to further reduce the contention between the flows in the wireless medium. The proposed scheme is evaluated on QualNet network simulator to demonstrate that our scheme guarantees fairness to all contending flows.

1 Introduction

Fairness is one of the most important properties of a computer network: when network resources are unable to satisfy demand, they should be divided fairly between the clients of the network [1]. In ad hoc network environment, the wireless medium is a shared resource. Thus, the applications of ad hoc wireless networks raise the need to address a critical challenge: How to manage this shared resource in an efficient manner among the contending flows in the network, so that each flow gets fair chance to access the medium? MAC protocols proposed in the context of ad hoc networks aim to control the medium access among contending nodes using some contention resolution schemes [2]. However, these protocols do not necessarily guarantee a fair allocation of wireless medium among contending flows [3].

A. Sen et al. (Eds.): IWDC 2004, LNCS 3326, pp. 156–167, 2004.
© Springer-Verlag Berlin Heidelberg 2004

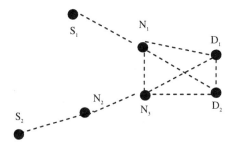

Fig. 1. Flow (S_1-D_1) is disturbing Flow (S_2-D_2) because of route coupling. Dotted Lines show omni-directional connectivity among nodes

For example, in Figure 1, both N_3 and D_2 are aware of the communication between N_1-D_1 through exchange of RTS/CTS between N1 and D1. But, node N2, being unaware of this communication, sends an RTS packet for N_3 to reserve the channel. N3 cannot send a CTS packet in reply to that RTS, as it has heard of the communication N_1-D_1. So, N_2 backs off with increasing back-off time as a result of unsuccessful attempt to communicate with N_3. The data transmission between N_1 and D_1 may be over during this time. Since N_2 has chosen a larger back off, so, N_1-D_1 communication has higher chance to reserve the channel again than N_2-N_3 communication. Moreover, the source node S_2 of flow S_2-N_2-N_3-D_2, being unaware of the contention at the intermediate node N_3 on the flow, will continue injecting packets at a predefined rate. This will lead to an unnecessary packet drop at node N_2, who is getting less chance to forward packets. As a result of that, the packet delivery ratio of that flow will suffer a lot. Our goal is to resolve the unfairness between contending flows rather than contending nodes, which is radically different from other existing approaches. In the situation shown in figure 1, if the flow-rate of S_1-N_1-D_1 can be optimally reduced, then the flow S_2-N_2-N_3-D_2 will get more chances to access the medium they share, which eventually reduces the congestion and improves the packet delivery ratio of both the flows. This, in turn, will also improve the overall network throughput.

We use a deterministic approach rather than a probabilistic approach to adaptively improve the performance of the suffered flows in the network through mutual negotiation between contending flows. Each node continuously monitors the packet arrival rate of other flows in its vicinity. As soon as a node belonging to, say flow 1, senses that another flow, say flow 2, in its vicinity has a lower flow-rate than its own flow-rate, indicating that flow 2 is not getting fair access, then flow 1 will decide to reduce its flow rate adaptively so that flow 2 can get chance to access the medium and uniform performance can be achieved by each flow. The scheme is based on mutual cooperation between contending flows. In other words, *our objective is to adaptively adjust the flow-rates of contending flows, so that each gets fair access to the medium. This adaptive adjustment will also ensure optimal utilization of wireless medium.*

For example, let us assume that flow 1 is operating at a flow-rate p and flow 2 at flow-rate q where p>q. Flow 1 detects flow-rate of flow 2 and decides to reduce its flow-rate p to accommodate higher flow-rate of flow 2. Flow 2 in turn detects the flow-rate of flow 1 and decides to increase its flow-rate in anticipation that Flow 1 will reduce its flow-rate to accommodate higher flow-rate of flow 2. This control-action will continue till flow-rate of flow 1 becomes less than that of flow 2(p<q). Then, the same process is repeated with reversed control-action i.e. flow 1 will now increase its flow-rate and flow 2 will reduce its flow-rate. Eventually both of them will settle down to a common flow-rate. Figure 2 shows the flow control decision of Flow 1. This simulation is done in QualNet network simulator, as will be detailed in section 5.

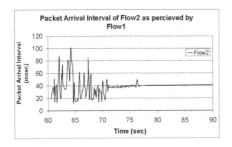
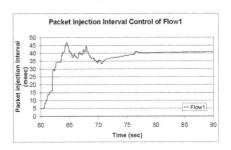

Fig. 2. Flow Control by Flow1 on detection of Flow 2 in the vicinity

2 Related Work

A number of fair-scheduling algorithms have been proposed to address the fairness issues in wireless network. An online scheduling policy for providing fair allocation of bandwidth is described in [10]. The policy can detect whether the traffic demand of a flow is consistently less than its fair share, and in such cases distribute the excess bandwidth among other flows. A centralized packet-scheduling algorithm that achieves optimal channel utilization and fairness for each flow is designed in [11]. It uses some kind of predictions about maximum achievable channel utilization, which provide essential guidelines during the design of new fairness-aware scheduling protocols. Much research has been performed on "fair queuing" algorithms for achieving a fair allocation of bandwidth on a shared link. By design, these fair queuing algorithms are centralized, since they are executed on a single node which has access to all information about the flows. It has been observed that fairness achieved by these algorithms may suffer in presence of location-dependent errors [14]. Many approaches for improving fairness in presence of location-dependent errors have been developed [15, 16]. These approaches are centralized and require the base station to coordinate access to the wireless channel to "compensate" hosts whose packets are corrupted due to the presence of location-dependent errors.

In [17], a Distributed Fair Scheduling (DFS) approach is proposed for wireless LAN, by modifying the Distributed Coordination Function (DCF) in IEEE 802.11 standard. This protocol allocates bandwidth in proportion to the weights of the flows sharing the channel. In [18], a general mechanism is presented for translating a given fairness model into a corresponding contention resolution algorithm. Using this, a back-off algorithm is derived for achieving proportional fairness in shared wireless channel.

Our proposal of adaptive flow rate control through cooperative negotiation among contending flows in the context of fairness is radically different from the earlier proposals in the sense that, it deals with the two major issues discussed above: i) Flow-wise fairness and ii) Unproductive congestion due to packet-drop. The key features of our proposed scheme are:

- it is *deterministic,* not probabilistic;
  - ➤ The degradation of performance of each flow found in the vicinity of a flow is detected and measured.
  - ➤ Depending on the measured value of degradation, proper rate control decision is taken by the source node of privileged flows so that the suffered flow may get more access to the medium through reduction in flow rate of privileged flow.
  - ➤ The situation is getting monitored continuously, the information about any degradation in performance of a flow as perceived by each of the other contending flows in its vicinity is propagated back to their respective sources and the flow-rates are regulated accordingly. So, whenever a privileged flow will sense that a flow, which was suffering earlier, has improved substantially then it will automatically increase its flow rate so that *all the flows can be operated uniformly with full utilization of the medium.*
- *Continuous mutual negotiation and collaboration* between flows helps to achieve fairness in the truest sense of the term.
- Since the contention-information is back-propagated at the source node who will regulate the flow, the packet delivery ratio of the entire flow improves substantially, resulting in less congestion in the medium due to packets that are going to be lost anyway.
- Use of directional antenna will improve the individual throughput and fair medium access further, when the traffic density is high.

3   Implementation of Flow Control Scheme

In order to illustrate our scheme, let us refer back to the example shown in figure 1. There are basically three parts in this scheme: i) Contention detection and measurement at each node of a flow, ii) Back propagation of the knowledge of contention to source node, and iii) Adaptive regulation of flow rate at source using the knowledge of contention. Part i) and ii) i.e., contention detection, measurement and back propagation of the knowledge of contention to source node are implemented with the help of traditional RTS and CTS exchange scheme, with a minor change in the format of existing RTS, CTS packets. From the RTS transmitted by N_1 and CTS transmitted by D_1, both N_3 and D_2 detect the presence of flow S_1-D_1 in their neighborhood. This remains unknown to the source S_2, which is far away from the flow S_1-D_1. So, with the help of CTS packet, D_2 transmits the knowledge to N_3. When N_3 has to send a CTS packet to N_2, it combines its own detection of contention with the received knowledge from D_2 and considers the maximum contention in the flow and transmits it with the CTS packet. N_2 lastly sends this information back to S_2 through a CTS packet. The source node, S_2, then considers the contention in the medium of the flow and adaptively takes a decision of adjusting its packet injection rate. Hence, with no extra packet, the information of contention in the medium as perceived by a flow is transmitted to the source node, which adaptively controls the packet injection rate.

To implement the above scheme, we assumed that each flow in the network is identified by a unique communication-id and we have introduced a special type of RTS and CTS packets. An extra field is attached to the original format of RTS packet, which denotes the *communication-id* of the flow for which the current RTS is being sent. Similarly, CTS packet has got two extra fields now. The first field is exactly similar to the extra-field of RTS packet, and is required to convey the *communication-id* of the flow for which the current CTS is being sent. The second field contains *the packet-arrival-interval of the most suffered flow* among the flows contending for the medium in the neighborhood of the flow for which current CTS is being sent. So, in presence of more than one contending flow in the neighborhood of a flow, back-propagation of the maximum packet arrival interval of the flows is done. This indicates that the privileged flow can adaptively adjust itself repeatedly, so that the suffered flows can get maximum chance to the medium and their packet arrival interval at the region of contention is improved. A control theoretic approach is adopted in this context to adjust the flow-rate at the source node according to the feedback of contention acquired from the affected nodes on a flow. The adaptive flow-rate control scheme, suggested in this paper, is based on conventional Proportional-Integral-Derivative (PID) Control mechanism. The control mechanism will be explained elaborately in the subsequent section.

3.1 Use of Directional Antenna

So far, we have considered omni-directional neighbors using omni-directional antenna. But, to modify the scheme using directional antenna, we have to consider a directional MAC and its directional neighbors. We have used a receiver-oriented rotational-sector based directional MAC protocol [19, 20], and a network-aware, directional routing protocol [8] to implement the proposed scheme. Here, each node is aware of its directional neighbors and this information is recorded in its Angle-Signal Table (AST). RTS and CTS packets are omni-directional, whereas data and acknowledgement packets are directional. Use of directional antenna in the context of ad hoc wireless networks can largely reduce radio interference, thereby improving the utilization of wireless medium [8,19,20]. This property of directional antenna is utilized to improve the efficiency of our protocol. This is shown in Figure 3, where S_1-D_1 and S_2-D_2 flows of figure 1, can co-exist without disturbing each other, using directional antenna, which would not have been possible using omni-directional antenna (Figure 1). So, with directional antenna, it is not necessary to control the packet injection rate of S_2-D_2 even in presence of S_1-D_1. Using directional antenna, the detection of contention in medium is also directional in the sense, that even if there are multiple contending flows in the vicinity, only the contention from communication in the direction of flow is considered. MAC detects the directional contention in medium consulting its AST. Since directional antenna improves SDMA (Space Division Multiple Access) efficiency, it enhances the packet injection rate of suffered flow with minimally disturbing other flows in the medium and hence leads to increased throughput of all the flows in the network. At the same time, chance of multiple flows getting coupled is reduced, leading to improved network performance.

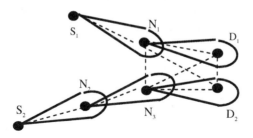

Fig. 3. Using directional antenna flow S_2-D_2 can coexist with flow S_1-D_1

3.2 Contention Detection and Measurement of Flow-Rates by Other Flows

When a flow is initiated, packets are sent through multiple hops to the destination and at MAC layer, the packet delivery at each intermediate node is ensured by RTS/CTS/DATA/ACK exchange. These RTS and CTS packets are utilized to detect and back-propagate the flow-related information on which packet injection rate control decision is taken at source nodes. In the context of directional transmission, two flows will interfere with each other, only if the direction of flows overlaps. In figure 3, although N_1 and N_3 are within the omni-directional transmission range of each other, the flow from N_1 to D_1 will not interfere with the flow from N_3 to D_2 during directional data communication. In order to detect the contention faced by a flow using directional antenna, it is imperative that each node in that flow should sense whether its directional transmission zone in the direction of flow contains any node handling any other flow. If it does, it implies that a contention is expected to occur at that node during directional data communication. So it is necessary to control the flow-rate of the flow that has detected the contention to protect the flow rate of the other contending flow.

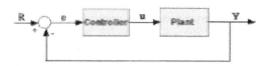

Fig. 4. Basic Feedback Controller

3.3 Flow-Control Mechanism

A feedback controller is designed to generate an output u that causes some corrective effort to be applied to a process so as to drive a measurable process variable Y towards a desired value R known as the set-point (Figure 4). The controller uses an actuator to affect the process and a sensor to measure the results. Virtually all feed-back controllers determine their output by observing the error e between the set-point (R) and a measurement of the process variable (Y). Errors occur when a disturbance or a load on the process changes the process variable. The controller's mission is to eliminate the error automatically [21]. Earlier feedback control devices implicitly or explicitly used the idea of proportional, integral and derivative (PID) actions in their control structure. The general form of the PID control algorithm is:

$$u = K_p e + K_i \int e\, dt + K_d \frac{de}{dt}$$

The variable (e) represents the tracking error, the difference between the desired input value (R) and the actual output (Y). This error signal (e) will be sent to the PID controller, and the controller computes both the derivative and the integral of this error signal. The signal (u) just past the controller is now equal to the proportional gain (K_p) times the magnitude of the error plus the integral gain (K_i) times the integral of the error plus the derivative gain (K_d) times the derivative of the error. Proportional gain (K_p) will have the effect of reducing the rise time and will reduce, but never eliminate, the steady-state error. An integral gain (K_i) will have the effect of eliminat-ing the steady-state error, but it may make the transient response worse. A derivative gain (K_d) will have the effect of increasing the stability of the system, reducing the overshoot, and improving the transient response. The above equation is a continuous representation of the controller and it must be converted to a discrete representation. There are several methods for doing this, the simplest being to use first-order finite differences. So the discrete representation of the equation is:

$$m(n) = k_p * e(n) + k_i * \sum_{k=n-w}^{n} e(k) * \Delta t + k_d * \frac{[e(n) - e(n-1)]}{\Delta t}$$

Thus it will be necessary to find the current error, the sum of the errors, and the recent change in error in order to calculate desired output.

In order to provide fairness to all the contending flows in the network, each flow, on detecting contention in the medium, is adaptively changing its flow-rate u at its source using PID control strategy. According to our control strategy, a flow will de-tect error in other flows in terms of reduction in flow-rate and accordingly adjust its own flow-rate to allow an improved flow-rate for the deprived flows. This kind of requirement is absent in conventional PID control and, therefore, our approach is a derivative of conventional PID control, which we will illustrate subsequently. In subsequent discussion, we have considered Packet Injection Interval (PII) at source node as a measure to controlling flow-rate. The Packet Injection Rate (PIR) of flow (in packets/sec) at a source node is computed at: PIR = 1/ PII. In order to take any control decision, first we have to compute the *error* term in PID controller.

Error e at any flow F_i at its source node $S = (PII^{Fi} - PAI(S)^{Fi})$,

where PII^{Fi} is the Packet Injection Interval of the flow F_i and $PAI(S)^{Fi}$ is the maxi-mum packet-arrival-interval of other contending flows in the neighborhood of F_i , detected by nodes in F_i and propagated back to the source node S of F_i.

Once the error e(n) and the time interval between two successive error Δt is calculated, the PII of $F_i(S)$ is calculated as

$$\text{PII}(new) = \text{PII}(old) - [k_p * e(n) + k_i * \sum_{k=n-w}^{n} e(k) * \Delta t + k_d * \frac{[e(n) - e(n-1)]}{\Delta t}]$$

The value of k_p, k_i and k_d needs to be tuned for optimal performance. The performance of the controller is shown in the next section. The value of kp, ki, kd and w has been chosen to 0.2, 0.08, 0.08 and 5 respectively in the simulation.

4 Performance Evaluation

We have evaluated the performance of our proposed scheme on QualNet simulator [9]. We have considered IEEE 802.11 based directional MAC [19] and implemented the proposed protocol with directional antenna only. We have simulated ESPAR antenna [20] in the form of a *quasi-switched beam antenna*, which is steered discretely at an angle of 30 degree, covering a span of 360 degree. We have done the necessary changes in QualNet simulator to implement the proposed protocol. The set of parameters used is listed in Table I.

Table I. Parameters used in Simulation

Parameters	Value
Transmission Power	15 dBm
Receiving Threshold	-81.0 dBm
Sensing Threshold	-91.0 dBm
Data Rate	2Mbps
Packet Size	512 bytes
Simulation Time	5 minutes

4.1 Performance in Static Scenario

We have used static routes in order to avoid the effects of routing protocols to clearly illustrate the gain obtained in our proposed protocol. When two flows are coupled with each other and contend to access the shared medium, unfair medium access may result in variable performance of the coupled flows. In this situation, our proposed protocol of packet injection rate control is required for fair medium access. So, in all the static topology, instead of random selection of source destination pair, we have chosen the source destination pairs in such a way, that they are coupled with each other to artificially create a situation so that we can demonstrate the effect of Packet Injection Interval Control. We have evaluated the performance in string topology and under three settings of grid topology. We have compared our proposed protocol, captioned as "Fair Media Access" with the scheme, where no fairness scheme is applied, captioned as "Unfair Media Access".

4.1.1 String Topology

Our initial string topology, with "Flow1" and "Flow2" using directional antenna is shown in Figure 5(a). Without any fairness mechanism, the throughput (Figure 5(b)) of Flow1 is even less than one-third of the throughput of Flow2. This is the effect of unfair medium access. With the introduction of fair medium access, the throughput of the two flows nearly becomes equal and the throughput of each flow is even more than that of Flow2 without any fairness scheme. So, the average throughput doubles in our proposed protocol than it was without any fairness scheme. Without any fairness scheme, Flow2 gets most chance to the medium and Flow1 suffers. Also, the contention of the two flows is not in a single node, rather all the links of the two flows are tightly coupled with each other. Due to this strong coupling, even the best-performed flow has lesser throughput without any fairness scheme than that of each flow after introduction of packet injection rate control.

4.1.2 Grid Topology

We have evaluated the packet injection rate control algorithm for fair media access in the following grid topology setting: six flows crossing each other along three horizontal rows and three vertical columns of a grid as shown in Figure 6(a). The transmission zone of each flow is similar to that shown with fig. 5(a). All the flows selected are 4 hop. Flows are captioned as "Flow1" to "Flow6". Our proposed fairness scheme yields improved uniform throughput, as evident from Figure 6(b).

4.2 Performance Under Mobility

We have evaluated the proposed protocol under average mobility of 0-10mps with 6 flows in 100 nodes in a bounded region of 1500×1500 sq. m. area. Mobility of nodes indulges each flow to operate at various scenarios at different point of time. The scenarios may be 1) operating alone, when there is no requirement of fair media access, 2) operating just beside another flow and contend with that flow to get access to the shared media, where flow-rate controlling is necessary, and 3) operating just beside multiple flows and contend with those flows to get access to the shared media, where drastic flow-rate controlling is done to give fairness to each contending flow. In each scenario, the throughput of any flow is widely different from other scenarios. Fair media access is ensured only between the contending flows during the contention. So, we do not show throughput of the flows under mobility. Packet delivery ratio and average end-to-end delay of the 6 flows is shown in Figure 7(a) and 7(b) respectively. With the implementation of our proposed protocol, packet delivery ratio of each flow increases two to three times more than its value without any fairness scheme. As shown, end-to-end delay of each flow with flow control is nearly one-third to one-fifth than that without flow control. Also, the variation of end-to-end delay among the contending flows is diminished after the implementation of flow-rate control scheme. All these indicate that the flow-rate control scheme gives a fair access of the shared medium to all the contending flows.

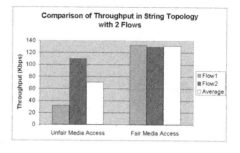

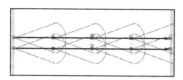

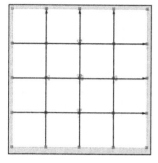

Fig. 5(a). String Topology

Fig. 5(b). Comparison of Throughput

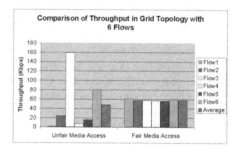

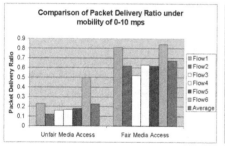

Fig. 6(a). Grid Topology

Fig. 6(b). Comparison of Throughput

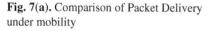

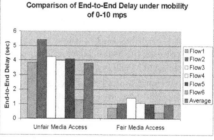

Fig. 7(a). Comparison of Packet Delivery under mobility

Fig. 7(b). Comparison of End-to-End Ratio Delay under mobility

5 Conclusion

In this paper, we adaptively adjust the flow-rates of the contending flows, so that each flow gets fair access to the medium. Flow rates are adjusted in anticipation that other contending flows will also adjust their flow-rates accordingly. Thus, continuous mutual negotiation and collaboration between flows helps to achieve fairness in the truest sense of the term. We have tuned the K_p, K_i and K_d values in different scenarios, and the values have great impact on improving the fairness scheme. Currently, we are trying to adjust the K_p, K_i and K_d values dynamically according to the application scenarios.

Acknowledgements

This research was supported in part by the National Institute of Information and Communications Technology (NICT) of Japan.

References

1. Jangeun Jun, Mihail L. Sichitiu, "Fairness and QoS in Multihop Wireless Networks", IEEE Semiannual Vehicular Technology Conference, VTC2003-Fall, October 6-9, 2003 Hyatt Orlando Hotel Orlando, Florida, USA.
2. S. Bandyopadhyay, Tetsuro Ueda and Kazuo Hasuike, "A Review of MAC and Routing Protocols in Ad Hoc Wireless Networks", The Transactions of The Institute of Electronics, Information and Communication Engineerings (IEICE), Vol.J85-B, No.12, December 2002 (Special issue for ad hoc networks).
3. Timucin Ozugur, Mahmoud Nagshinch, Parviz Kermani, John A. Copeland, "Fair media Access For Wireless LANs", in Proc. of IEEE GLOBECOM '99, 1999
4. IEEE, IEEE std 802.11 - wireless LAN mediumaccess control (MAC) and physical layer (PHY)speci_cations," 1997.
5. C. E. Koksal, H. Kassab, and H. Balakrishan "An Analysis of Short-Term Fairness in Wireless Media Access Protocols", ACM SIG-METRICS 2000, Santa Clara, CA.
6. Somprakash Bandyopadhyay, M.N. Pal, Dola Saha, Tetsuro Ueda, Kazuo Hasuike, "Improving System Performance of Ad Hoc Wireless Network with Directional Antenna" Accepted in IEEE International Conference on Communications (ICC 2003), Anchorage, Alaska, USA, May 11-15, 2003.
7. Tetsuro Ueda, Shinsuke Tanaka, Dola Saha, Siuli Roy, Somprakash Bandyopadhyay, "An Efficient MAC Protocol with Direction Finding Scheme in Wireless Ad Hoc Network Using Directional Antenna", Proc. of the IEEE Radio and Wireless Conference RAWCON 2003, Boston, MA, August 10-13, 2003.
8. Siuli Roy, Dola Saha, Somprakash Bandyopadhyay, Tetsuro Ueda, Shinsuke Tanaka, "A Network-Aware MAC and Routing Protocol *for Effective Load Balancing in Ad Hoc Wireless Networks with Directional Antenna" Proc. of the Fourth ACM International Symposium on Mobile Ad Hoc Networking and Computing (MobiHoc 2003) Annapolis, Maryland, USA, June 1-3, 2003*
9. QualNet Simulator Version 3.1, Scalable Network Technologies, www.scalable-networks.com.
10. L. Tassiulas and S. Sarkar, "Maxmin Fair Scheduling in Wireless Networks," Technical Report Institute for Systems Research and Electrical and Computer Engineering Department, University of Maryland, 2001; Available at http://www.seas.upenn.edu/_swati/publication.htm.
11. Xinran Wu, Clement Yuen, Yan Gao, Hong Wu, Baochun Li,"Fair Scheduling with Bottleneck Consideration in Wireless Ad-hoc Networks", 10th IEEE International Conference on Computer Communications and Networks, Phoenix, Arizona, Oct. 2001.

12. J. C. R. Bennett and H. Zhang, "Wf2q: Worst-case fair weighted fair queueing," in INFOCOM'96, March 1996.

13. S. Keshav, "On the efficient implementation of fair queueing," Journal of Internetworking: Research and Experience, vol. 2, pp. 57-73, September 1991.

14. T. S. Ng, I. Stoica, and H. Zhang, "Packet fair queueing: Algorithms for wireless networks with location-dependent errors," in INFOCOM, March 1998.

15. S. Lu, T. Nandagopal, and V. Bharghavan, "A wireless fair service algorithm for packet cellular networks," in ACM MobiCom, 1998.

16. T. Nandagopal, S. Lu, and V. Bharghavan, "A unified architecture for the design and evaluation of wireless fair queueing algorithms," in ACM MobiCom, August 1999.

17. Nitin H. Vaidya, Paramvir Bahl, Seema Gupta, "Distributed Fair Scheduling in a Wireless LAN" Sixth Annual International Conference on Mobile Computing and Networking, Boston, August 2000.

18. T. Nandagopal, T. Kim, X. Gao and V. Bharghavan, " Achieving MAC Layer Fairness in Wireless Packet Networks." Proceedings of ACM Mobicom 2000, Boston, MA, August 2000.

19. Tetsuro Ueda, Shinsuke Tanaka, Dola Saha, Siuli Roy, Somprakash Bandyopadhyay, "A Rotational Sector-based, Receiver-Oriented Mechanism for Location Tracking and Medium Access Control in Ad Hoc Networks Using Directional Antenna", Proc. of the IFIP conference on Personal Wireless Communications PWC 2003, Venice, Italy, September 23-25, 2003.

20. T. Ueda, K. Masayama, S. Horisawa, M. Kosuga, K. Hasuike, "Evaluating the Performance of Wireless Ad Hoc Network Testbed Smart Antenna", Fourth IEEE Conference on Mobile and Wireless Communication Networks (MWCN2002), September 2002.

21. Vance J. VanDoren, Understanding PID Control: Familiar examples show how and why proportional-integralderivative controllers behave the way they do, Control Engineering on line www.controleng.com, June 1, 2000.

Analytical-Numerical Study of Mobile IPv6 and Hierarchical Mobile IPv6*

Myung-Kyu Yi and Chong-Sun Hwang

Dept. of Computer Science & Engineering Korea University,
1,5-Ga, Anam-Dong, SungBuk-Gu, Seoul 136-701, South Korea
{kainos, hwang}@disys.korea.ac.kr

Abstract. In this paper, we investigate performance of the Hierarchical Mobile IPv6 (HMIPv6) and compare it with that of the Mobile IPv6 (MIPv6). It is well known that HMIPv6 can reduce considerable number of signaling messages to handle Mobile IP registration locally [1]. For the more detailed performance analysis, we propose an analytic mobility model based on the random walk to take into account various mobility conditions. Based on this analytic model, we studied the impact of subnet residence time, packet arrival rate, and various mobility conditions on total signaling cost. The simulation results shows that HMIPv6 can has superior performance to MIPv6 when the packet arrival rate is low and the mobile node's mobility is high.

1   Introduction

Mobility support in IP network has been an area of active research and development. In IP networks, routing is based on stationary IP addresses. Thus, the generic problem with IP mobility is that when an IP node roams away from its home network and is no longer reachable using normal IP routing. This causes the active sessions of the device to be terminated. Mobile IPv6 (MIPv6) allows an IPv6 node to be mobile to arbitrarily change its location on the IPv6 Internet and still maintain existing connections [2, 3]. However, MIPv6 results in a high signaling cost to update the location of an Mobile Node (MN) if it moves frequently[3]. Thus, the Hierarchical Mobile IPv6 (HMIPv6) is proposed by IETF to reduce signaling cost [1, 4]. It uses a new MIPv6 node called the Mobility Anchor Point (MAP) to handle Mobile IP registration locally. It is well known that performance of HMIPv6 is better than that of MIPv6 [1, 4]. Some works have already investigated performance evaluation of Mobile IP in terms of bandwidth, signaling load, CPU processing overhead, and so on [5, 6]. However, previous works do not reflect the properties of MN's mobility pattern. For example, when an MN moves quickly back and forth between MAP domains (i.e. ping-pong effect), this would generate a several number of Binding Update (BU) messages in HMIPv6. Also, let us consider the case where the internal

---

* This research was supported by University IT Research Center Project.

A. Sen et al. (Eds.): IWDC 2004, LNCS 3326, pp. 168–179, 2004.
© Springer-Verlag Berlin Heidelberg 2004

Correspondent Node (CN) that is inside of an MN's visiting MAP domain in HMIPv6. In this case, an MN sends a BU to the internal CN using the MN's on-link Care-of Address (LCoA) whenever it moves within a MAP domain. After the MN leaves the MAP domain, the internal CN is outside of an MN's visiting MAP domain (i.e., external CN). Thus, the MN sends a BU to the external CN whenever it moves to a new MAP domain using the Regional Care-of Address (RCoA). For the more detailed performance analysis, as mentioned above, an analytic model of Mobile IP must take into account various mobility conditions. In this paper, thus, we propose an analytic mobility model based on the random walk to take into account various mobility conditions for performance analysis of MIPv6 and HMIPv6.

The rest of the paper is organized as follows. Section 2 introduces an analytic mobility model for performance evaluation and Section 3 formulates location update cost and packet delivery cost using the analytic model. Section 4 shows the numerical results based on the analytic model. Finally, conclusions are presented in Section 5.

2   Analytic Mobility Model

Inspired by the initial idea in [7], we describe a two-dimensional random walk model for mesh planes. Our model is similar to [7, 8] and considers a regular MAP domain/subnet overlay structure. In this model, the subnets are grouped into several n-layer MAP domains. Every MAP domain covers $N = 4n^2 - 4n + 1$ subnets. As shown in Fig. 1 (where n = 4), the subnet at the center of a MAP domain is called *layer 0*. An n-layer MAP domain consists of a subnet from layer 0 to layer $n - 1$. Based on this domiain/subnet structure, we derive the number of subnet crossings before an MN crosses a MAP domain boundary.

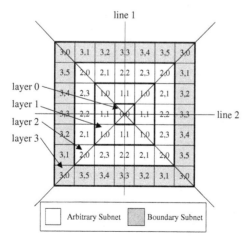

Fig. 1. Type Assignments of the mesh 4-layer MAP domain

According to the equal moving probability assumption (i.e., with probability $1/n$), we classify the subnets in a MAP domain into several subnet types based on the type classification algorithm in [8]. A subnet type is of the form $< x, y >$, where x indicates that the subnet is in layer x and y represents the $y + 1$st type in layer x.

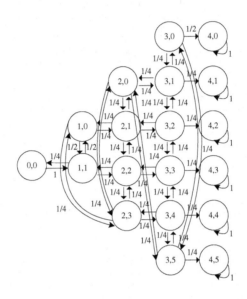

Fig. 2. The State Diagram for a 4-layer MAP domain

Based on the type classification and the concept of absorbing states, the state diagram of the random walk for an n-layer MAP domain is shown in Fig. 2. In this state diagram, state (x, y) indicates that the MN is in one of the MAP domain of type $< x, y >$, where the scope of x and y is

$$0 \leq x \leq n, \quad \begin{cases} 0 \leq y \leq 2x - 1 & , if \quad x \geq 1 \\ y = 0 & , if \quad x = 0. \end{cases} \tag{1}$$

State (n, y) indicates that the MN moves out of the MAP domain from state $(n - 1, y)$, where $0 \leq y \leq 2n - 3$. For $x = n$ and $0 \leq y \leq 2n - 3$, the states (n, y) are absorbing, while the others are transient. For $n > 1$, the total number $S(n)$ of states for n-layer MAP domain random walk is $n^2 + n - 1$. The transition matrix of this random walk is an $S(n) \times S(n)$ matrix $P = (p_{(x,y)(x',y')})$. Therefore, $P = (p_{(x,y)(x',y')})$ can be defined as the one-stop transition probability from state (x, y) to state (x', y') (i.e., which represents the probability that the MN moves from a $< x, y >$ subnet to a $< x', y' >$ subnet in one step). We use the Chapman-Kolmogorov equation to compute $p_{(x,y)(x',y')}^{(r)}$, which is the probability that the random walk moves from state (x, y) to state (x', y') with exact r steps. We define $p_{r,(x,y)(n,j)}$ as the probability that an MN initially resides at an $< x, y >$

subnet, moves into a $< n - 1, j >$ subnet at the $r - 1$ step and then moves out of the MAP domain at the r step as follows:

$$p_{r,(x,y)(n,y)} = \begin{cases} p_{(x,y)(n,y)} & , for \quad r = 1 \\ p_{(x,y)(n,y)}^{(r)} - p_{(x,y)(n,y)}^{(r-1)}, & for \quad r > 1. \end{cases} \tag{2}$$

3   Signaling Cost Functions

To investigate performance of MIPv6 and HMIPv6, the total signaling cost given to the Home Agent (HA), CN, and Mobility Anchor Point (MAP) to handle mobility of MNs are analyzed. We assume that performance metric is the total signaling cost which consists of the location update cost and packet delivery cost.

3.1   Location Update Cost in HMIPv6

We define the costs and parameters used for performance evaluation of location update as follows:

- C_{hm} : The transmission cost of BU between the HA and the MAP
- C_{nc} : The transmission cost of BU between the MN and the CN
- C_{mn} : The transmission cost of BU between the MAP and the MN
- a_h : The processing cost of location update at the HA
- a_m : The processing cost of location update at the MAP
- l_{hm} : The average distance between the HA and the MAP
- l_{mn} : The average distance between the MAP and the MN
- l_{nc} : The average distance between the MN and the CN
- δ_U : The proportionality constant for location update

Fig. 3 shows the control signaling message for BU with CN, MAP and HA in HMIPv6. According to signaling message flows for BU, each location update cost can be calculated as follows [6]:

$$C_{HA} = a_h + 2(C_{hm} + C_{mn}) \tag{3}$$
$$C_{MAP} = a_m + 2C_{mn}$$
$$C_{CN} = C_{nc}$$

For simplicity, we assume that the transmission cost is proportional to the distance in terms of the number of hops between the source and destination mobility agents such as HA, MAP, CN and MN. Using the proportional constant δ_U, each location update cost can be rewritten as follows:

$$C_{HA} = a_h + 2(l_{hm} + l_{mn})\delta_U \tag{4}$$
$$C_{MAP} = a_m + 2l_{mn}\delta_U$$
$$C_{CN} = l_{nc}\delta_U$$

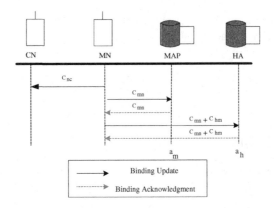

Fig. 3. The Cost of Location Update in HMIPv6

We derive the number of MAP domain/subnet crossings and location updates between the beginning of a session and the beginning of the next session. Similar to [7], we define the additional costs and parameters used for performance evaluation of location update as follows.

- r : The number of the MN's subnet crossings
- d : The number of subnet crossings before an MN leaves the first MAP domain
- K : The number of the MN's MAP domain crossings
- t_d : The time interval between the beginning of a session and the beginning of the next session
- $r(t_d)$: The number of the BUs for the MAP during t_d
- l : The number of subnet crossings before an MN leaves the first MAP domain during t_d
- $K(t_d)$: The number of the BUs for the external CN and HA during t_d
- $q(t_d)$: The number of the BUs for the internal CN during t_d
- N : The total number of subnets within a MAP domain.
- L : The number of boundary edges for that boundary subnet in an n-layer MAP domain
- $1/\lambda_m$: The expected value for the subnet residence time
- $1/\lambda_d$: The expected value for the t_d distribution
- η_1 : The number of the external CNs that have a binding cache for the MN
- η_2 : The number of the internal CNs that have a binding cache for the MN

Assume that an MN is in any subnet of a MAP domain with equal probability. This implies that the MN is in subnet $< 0, 0 >$ with a probability of $1/N$ and is in a subnet of type $< x, y >$ with a probability of $4/N$, where $N = 4n^2 - 4n + 1$ is the number of subnets covered by an n-layer MAP domain. From (2), we derive d as the number of subnet crossings before an MN leaves the first MAP domain as follows:

$$d = \frac{1}{N}\left(\sum_{k=1}^{\infty} k \cdot \sum_{j=0}^{2n-3} p_{k,(0,0)(n,j)}\right) + \frac{4}{N}\left(\sum_{k=1}^{\infty} k \cdot \sum_{x=0}^{n-1}\sum_{y=0}^{2x-1}\sum_{j=0}^{2n-3} p_{k,(x,y)(n,j)}\right) \quad (5)$$

We denote $\pi(r)$ as the probability that an MN will leave the MAP domain at the rth step provided that the MN is initially in an arbitrary subnet of the MAP domain as follows:

$$\pi(r) = \frac{1}{N}\left(\sum_{j=0}^{2n-3} p_{r,(0,0)(n,j)}\right) + \frac{4}{N}\left(\sum_{x=1}^{n-1}\sum_{y=0}^{2x-1}\sum_{j=0}^{2n-3} p_{r,(x,y)(n,j)}\right) \quad (6)$$

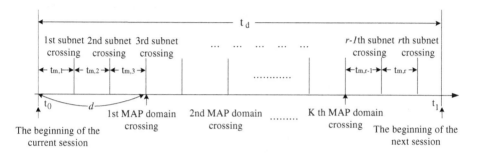

Fig. 4. Time diagram for subnet and MAP domain crossings

Similarly, we denote $\widehat{\pi}(r)$ as the probability that an MN will leave the MAP domain at the rth step provided that the MN is initially in a boundary subnet of the MAP domain. It is well known that the probability that after an MN enters a MAP domain, it leaves the MAP domain is proportion to the number of boundary edges for that boundary subnet [8]. In our random walk model (i.e., n=4), the number of boundary edges for that boundary subnet can be represented as $L = 4*(2n-1)$. Thus, we can get

$$\widehat{\pi}(r) = \frac{2\cdot4}{L}\left(\sum_{j=0}^{2n-3} p_{r,(n-1,0)(n,j)}\right) + \frac{1\cdot4}{L}\left(\sum_{y=1}^{2n-3}\sum_{j=0}^{2n-3} p_{r,(n-1,y)(n,j)}\right) \quad (7)$$

We denote $\Pi(r,K)$ as the probability that the MN crosses K MAP domain boundaries after r subnet movements provided that the MN is initially in an arbitrary subnet of a MAP domain as follows:

$$\Pi(r,K) = \begin{cases} 1, & \text{for } K = r = 0 \\ \sum_{i=r+1}^{\infty} \pi(i), & \text{for } K = 0, r > 0 \\ \sum_{i=1}^{r} \pi(i) \times \widehat{\Pi}(r-i, K-1) & \\ & \text{for } K \geq 1, r \geq K \\ 0, & \text{for } r < K \end{cases} \quad (8)$$

From (6) and (7), we denote $\widehat{\Pi}(r, K)$ as the probability that the MN crosses K MAP domain boundaries after r subnet movements provided that the MN is initially in a boundary subent of a MAP domain as follows:

$$
\widehat{\Pi}(r, K) = \begin{cases} 1, & \text{for } K = r = 0 \\ \sum_{j=r+1}^{\infty} \widehat{\pi}(j), & \text{for } K = 0, r > 0 \\ \sum_{j=1}^{r} \widehat{\pi}(j) \times \widehat{\Pi}(r - j, K - 1) & \\ & \text{for } K \geq 1, r \geq K \\ 0, & \text{for } r < K \end{cases} \tag{9}
$$

Note that the above derivation are based on the equal moving probability assumption, thus, we derive the number of subnet/MAP domain updates between the beginning of a session and the beginning of the next session. Fig. 4 shows the timing diagram of the activities for an MN. Assume that the previous session of the MN ends at time t_0 and the next session begins at time t_1. Let $t_1 - t_0$, which has a general distribution with density function $f_d(t_d)$, expect value $1/\lambda_d$, and Laplace Transform

$$
f_d^*(s) = \int_{t_d=0}^{\infty} e^{-st_d} f_d(t_d) dt_d \tag{10}
$$

We denote $r(t_d)$ as the number of location updates for the MAP during period t_d. Since an MN needs to register with the MAP whenever it moves in HMIPv6, $r(t_d)$ is equal to the number of subnet crossings during t_d. Assume that the subnet residence time $t_{m,j}$ at j-th subnet has an Erlang distribution with mean $1/\lambda_m = m/\lambda$, variance $V_m = m/\lambda^2$, and density function as follows:

$$
f_m^*(t) = \frac{\lambda e^{-\lambda t} (\lambda t)^{m-1}}{(m-1)!} \quad (where \ \ m = 1, 2, 3, \cdots) \tag{11}
$$

Notice that an Erlang distribution is a special case of the Gamma distribution where the shape parameter m is a positive integer. From (10) and (11), we can get the probability mass function of the number of subnet crossings $r(t_d)$ within t_d as follows:

$$
\begin{aligned}
Pr[r(t_d) = k] = \ & \frac{1}{m} \left\{ \sum_{j=km}^{km+m-1} \left[\frac{(km + m - j)(-\lambda)^j}{j!} \right] \left[\frac{d^j f_d^*(s)}{ds^j} \right] \bigg|_{s=\lambda} \right\} \\
& - \frac{1}{m} \left\{ \sum_{j=km-m}^{km-1} \left[\frac{(j - km + m)(-\lambda)^j}{j!} \right] \left[\frac{d^j f_d^*(s)}{ds^j} \right] \bigg|_{s=\lambda} \right\}
\end{aligned} \tag{12}
$$

$(where \ k = 1, 2, \cdots)$

$$
Pr[r(t_d) = 0] = \frac{1}{m} \left\{ \sum_{j=0}^{m-1} \left[\frac{(m - j)(-\lambda)^j}{j!} \right] \left[\frac{d^j f_d^*(s)}{ds^j} \right] \bigg|_{s=\lambda} \right\}
$$

We denote l as the number of subnet crossings before an MN leaves the first MAP domain during t_d. From (5) and (12), we can get l as follows:

$$l = \frac{1}{N} \left(\sum_{k=1}^{\infty} k \cdot \sum_{j=0}^{2n-3} p_{k,(0,0)(n,y)} \cdot Pr[r(t_d) = k] \right) \tag{13}$$

$$+ \frac{4}{N} \left(\sum_{k=1}^{\infty} k \cdot \sum_{x=0}^{n-1} \sum_{y=0}^{2x-1} \sum_{j=0}^{2n-3} p_{k,(x,y)(n,j)} \cdot Pr[r(t_d) = k] \right)$$

We denote $q(t_d)$ as the number of location updates for the internal CN during period t_d. Recall that an MN sends a BU to the internal CN for the first MAP domain crossing whenever it crosses subnets and then sends a BU whenever it crosses MAP domain boundaries during t_d in HMIPv6. From (8),(9), and (12), the probability mass function for $q(t_d)$ is

$$Pr[q(t_d) = j] = \begin{cases} Pr[r(t_d) = j], & \text{for } j < l \\ \sum_{k=j}^{\infty} Pr[r(t_d) = k] \\ \times \Pi(k - l, j - l), & \text{for } j \geq l \end{cases} \tag{14}$$

Finally, we denote $K(t_d)$ as the number of location updates for the external CN and HA during period t_d. Since an MN sends a BU to the external CN and HA whenever it crosses MAP domain boundaries during t_d, $K(t_d)$ is equal to the number of MAP domain crossing during t_d. Therefore, the probability mass function for $K(t_d)$ is

$$Pr[K(t_d) = j] = \sum_{k=0}^{\infty} Pr[r(t_d) = k] \times \Pi(k, j) \tag{15}$$

Thus, we can get the total location update cost during t_d in HMIPv6 from (4), and (12)-(15) as follows:

$$C_{LU} = C_{HA} + C_{CN} + C_{MAP} \sum_{j=0}^{\infty} j Pr[r(t_d) = j] \tag{16}$$

3.2   Packet Delivery Cost in HMIPv6

The packet delivery cost consists of transmission and processing cost. First of all, we define the additional costs and parameters used for performance evaluation of packet delivery cost as follows:

- T_{hm} : The transmission cost of packet delivery between the HA and MAP
- T_{mn} : The transmission cost of packet delivery between the MAP and MN
- T_{nc} : The transmission cost of packet delivery between the CN and MN
- v_h : The processing cost of packet delivery at the HA

- v_m : The processing cost of packet delivery at the MAP
- λ_α : The packet arrival rate for each MN
- δ_D : The proportionality constant for packet delivery
- δ_h : The packet delivery processing cost constant at the HA
- δ_m : The packet delivery processing cost constant at the MAP

Similar to [6], the packet delivery cost during t_d in HMIPv6 can be expressed as follows:

$$C_{PD} = v_h + v_m + T_{hm} + T_{mn} + T_{nc} \tag{17}$$

We assume that the transmission cost of packet delivery is proportional to the distance between the sending and receiving mobility agents with the proportionality constant δ_D. Therefore, T_{hm}, T_{mn}, and T_{nc} can be represented as $T_{hm}=l_{hm}\delta_D$, $T_{mn}=l_{mn}\delta_D$ and $T_{nc} = l_{nc}\delta_D$. Also, we define a proportionality constant δ_h and δ_m. While δ_h is a packet delivery processing constant for lookup time of binding cache at the HA, δ_m is a packet delivery processing constant for lookup time of binding cache at the MAP. Therefore, v_h can be represented as $v_h=\lambda_\alpha\delta_h$ and v_m can be represented as $v_m=\lambda_\alpha\delta_m$. Finally, we can get the packet delivery cost during t_d in HMIPv6 as follows:

$$C_{PD} = (l_{hm} + l_{mn} + l_{nc})\delta_D + \lambda_\alpha(\delta_h + \delta_m) \tag{18}$$

Based on the above analysis, we introduce the total signaling cost function in HMIPv6 from (16) and (18) as follows:

$$C_{TOT}(\lambda_m, \lambda_d, \lambda_\alpha) = C_{LU} + C_{PD} \tag{19}$$

3.3   Location Update and Packet Delivery Costs in MIPv6

To investigate performance of MIPv6, we define the additional costs and parameters used for performance evaluation of location update as follows.

- l_{hn} : The average distance between the HA and the MN

In MIPv6, an MN sends a BU message whenever it changes its point of attachment transparently to an IPv6 networks. From (15), we can get the total location update cost during t_d in MIPv6 as follows:

$$C'_{LU} = \left(C_{HA} + (\eta_1 + \eta_2) \cdot C_{CN}\right) \cdot \sum_{j=0}^{\infty} j \, Pr[r(t_d) = j] \tag{20}$$

From (18), we can get the total packet delivery cost during t_d in MIPv6 as follows:

$$C'_{PD} = (l_{hn} + l_{nc})\delta_D + \lambda_\alpha \cdot \delta_h \tag{21}$$

Based on the above analysis, we introduce the total signaling cost function in MIPv6 from (20) and (21) as follows:

$$C'_{TOT}(\lambda_m, \lambda_d, \lambda_\alpha) = C'_{LU} + C'_{PD} \tag{22}$$

4   Numerical Results

In this section, we demonstrate some numerical results. Table 1 shows the some of parameters used in our performance analysis that are discussed in [6, 7]. For simplicity, we assume that the distance between mobility agents are fixed and same number of distance in terms of the number of hops. We define the relative signaling cost of HMIPv6 as the ratio of the total signaling cost for HMIPv6 to that of MIPv6. A relative cost of 1 means that the costs under both schemes are exactly the same. We can see that relative signaling cost is less than 1, which indicates HMIPv6 offers better performance than MIPv6.

Table 1. Performance Analysis Parameters

Parameter	N	L	a_h	a_m	$\lambda_d, \lambda_m, \lambda_\alpha$	δ_U	δ_D	δ_h	δ_m	η_1/η_2
Value	25-81	20-36	30	20	0.01-100	0.1	0.05	15	10	1-20

Fig. 5 (a) shows the effect of packet arrival rate λ_α for $\lambda_m = 1$, $\lambda_d=0.001$, and η_1 and η_2 =5. We can see that performance of HMIPv6, on the whole, is better than that of MIPv6. As the packet arrival rate λ_α increases, relative signaling cost increases. This is because as the packet arrival rate increases, the system requires a larger processing cost for tunnelling at the MAP in HMIPv6. Note that packets addressed to the RCoA are intercepted by the MAP, encapsulated and routed to the MN's LCoA in HMIPv6. For the fixed value of λ_α, performance of HMIPv6 for the four layer MAP domain is better than that of the three layer. Similarly, performance of HMIPv6 for the five layer MAP domain is better than that of the four. Fig. 5 (b) shows the effect of mobility rate λ_m for $\lambda_\alpha = 0.1$, $\lambda_d=0.001$, and η_1 and η_2 =5. As the mobility rate λ_m increases, relative signaling cost decreases. These results are expected because HMIPv6 tries to reduce the

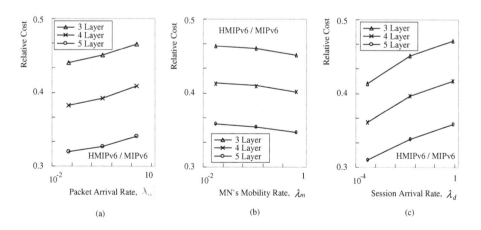

Fig. 5. Effect of $\lambda_\alpha, \lambda_m, \lambda_d$ on Relative Signaling Cost

number of BU messages when an MN moves within a MAP domain. Fig. 5 (c) shows the effect of session arrival rate λ_d for $\lambda_\alpha = 0.1$, $\lambda_m = 0.1$, and η_1 and $\eta_2 = 5$. As shown in Fig. 5 (c), we can see that HMIPv6 results in the lowest total cost compared with MIPv6. As the session arrival rate λ_d increases, relative signaling cost increases. A large λ_d implies small session interval period. Thus, performance of HMIPv6 is better than that of MIPv6 for the small value of λ_d.

Fig. 6 shows that the effect of the Call-to-Mobility Ratio (CMR) on relative signaling cost. Similar to performance analysis in Personal Communication Service (PCS) [6], we define the CMR as the ratio of the packet arrival rate to the mobility rate (i.e. CMR $= \lambda_\alpha$ / λ_m). As shown in Fig. 6, we found that relative signaling cost increases as the CMR increases. For the small value of CMR, performance of HMIPv6 is better than that of MIPv6. From the above analysis of results, HMIPv6 has superior performance to MIPv6 when an MN's mobility is high and packet arrival rate is low.

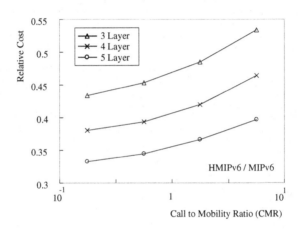

Fig. 6. Effect of CMR on Relative Signaling Cost

5   Conclusions

In this paper, we studied performance of HMIPv6 and compare it with that of MIPv6. For the more detailed performance analysis, we proposed an analytic mobility model based on the random walk to take into account various mobility conditions. The simulation results shows that HMIPv6 can has superior performance to MIPv6 when the packet arrival rate is low and the MN's mobility is high.

References

1. C. Castelluccia, "HMIPv6: A Hierarchical Mobile IPv6 Proposal, ACM Mobile Computing and Communications Review," vol.4, no.1, pp.48-59, January 2000.

2. C. Perkins,"IP Mobility Support for IPv4," IETF Request for Comments 3344, August 2002.
3. D. B. Johnson, C. E. Perkins, and J. Arkko,"Mobility support in IPv6," IETF Request for Comments 3775, June, 2004.
4. Hesham Soliman, Claude Castelluccia, Karim El-Malki, Ludovic Bellier, "Hierarchical Mobile IPv6 mobility management (HMIPv6)," IETF Internet draft, draft-ietf-mipshop-hmipv6-02.txt (work in progress), June 2004.
5. Sangheon Pack and Yanghee Choi, "Performance Analysis of Hierarchical Mobile IPv6 in IP-based Cellular Networks," In Proc. IEEE International Symposium on Personal, Indoor and Mobile Radio Communications (PIMRC), September 2003.
6. Jiang Xie and I.E. Akyildiz, "A Novel Distributed Dynamic Location Management Scheme for Minimizing Signaling Costs in Mobile IP," *IEEE Transactions on Mobile Computing*, vol. 1 , Issue 3, pp 163 - 175, July-September 2002.
7. Yi-Bing Lin, Shun-Ren Yang, "A Mobility Management Strategy for GPRS," *IEEE Transactions on Wireless Communications*, vol. 2 ,pp. 1178 - 1188, November. 2003.
8. Akyildiz. I.F, Yi-Bing Lin, Wei-Ru Lai, Rong-Jaye Chen, "A New Random Walk Model for PCS Networks," *IEEE Journal on Selected Areas in Communications* , vol. 18, pp1254 - 1260, July 2000.

An Adaptive Transmission Power Control
Protocol for Mobile Ad Hoc Networks

Kyung-jun Kim, Nam-koo Ha, and Ki-jun Han*

Department of Computer Engineering, Kyungpook National University
{kjkim, adama}@netopia.knu.ac.kr, kjhan@bh.knu.ac.kr

Abstract. In this paper, we propose the possibility of bringing the concepts of power control and route relay functions together in the MAC design in mobile multi-channel ad hoc networks. Our protocol makes use of multi-channel route relay function with power control capability to cope with inter-channel interference and path breakage caused by mobility in multi-channel mobile ad hoc networks. We provide simulation results showing a good performance for re-establishing a path.

1 Introduction

In ad hoc networks, there are usually more than one non-interfering channels available. So, proper channel allocation and power control should be considered at the same time. Various studies on Medium Access Control (MAC) protocols which assume a multi-channel or single common channel to be shared by mobile hosts have been proposed [3, 4, 5, 6, 7, 8, 9, 10]. Both power control and channel allocation schemes have to be implemented in a distributed manner [1, 2].

Narayanaswamy et al. [3] has proposed a protocol called COMPOW. This power control protocol is conceptualized as a network layer problem. The COMPOW relies completely on routing-layer agents to converge to a common lowest power level for all network nodes. In Wu et al. [1] approach, each terminal decides the appropriate transmission power level based on the distance between two terminals in a distributed manner. Kawadia et al. [7] consider the problem of power control when nodes are non-homogeneously dispersed in space. In this approach, network utilization reducing since all communications have to go through the cluster header.

Our protocol, inspired by previous work [1, 10], dynamically negotiates channels with power control to allow multiple communications in the same region simultaneously, each in a different channel without any interference problem. Our protocol offers a higher throughput, and a more enhanced quality for service capability as well as less transmission delay than the Chang's [5] scheme.

The remainder of this paper is organized as follows: In Section 2, we propose an adaptive power control protocol. In Section 3, we present analytical and simulation models for performance evaluation. Finally, Section 4 contains conclusion, reveals

---

* Correspondent author.

A. Sen et al. (Eds.): IWDC 2004, LNCS 3326, pp. 180–185 2004.
© Springer-Verlag Berlin Heidelberg 2004

that our protocol improves the performance and effectively deal with the breakage of communication of ad hoc networks.

2 Adaptive Transmission Power Control Protocol

2.1 Basic Concept of the Power Control

As shown in Fig. 1, if we can properly tune each transmitter power level, a communication pairs can coexist without any interference.

Fig. 1. The need for power control: in case when there is no power control (dotted line) and power control (solid line)

A simple power control mechanism is suggested in [4, 5, 13]. Suppose mobile hosts X and Y want to exchange with one packet each other. Let X sends a packet with power $p_{Tx}^{(X)}$, which is heard by Y with power $p_{Rx}^{(Y)}$. And then, Y's transmission power satisfies $p_{Rx}^{(Y)}$, where $p_{Rx}^{(X)}$ and $p_{Rx}^{(Y)}$ are given by

$$p_{Rx}^{(Y)} = p_{Tx}^{(X)}\left(\frac{\lambda}{4\pi d}\right)^{n} g_{Tx} g_{Rx} \qquad p_{Rx}^{(X)} = p_{Tx}^{(Y)}\left(\frac{\lambda}{4\pi d}\right)^{n} g_{Tx} g_{Rx} \qquad (1)$$

respectively, where g_{Tx}, g_{Rx} denote the antenna gains at the sender and the receiver, respectively, and d is the distance between source host X and destination host Y, and can be obtained by

$$d = \frac{\lambda}{4\pi}\left(\frac{p_{Tx}^{(X)} g_{Tx} g_{Rx}}{p_{Rx}^{(Y)}}\right)^{\frac{1}{n}} \qquad (2)$$

where λ is the carrier wavelength, n is the path loss coefficient that may vary between 2 and 6 depending on the physically environment such as the existence of obstacles [1]. Note that λ, g_{Tx} are constants in normal situations. Then Y can determine its transmission power, $p_{Tx}^{(Y)}$, if the other powers are known.

2.2 Adaptive Power Control Protocol with Routes Relay Capability

In this section, we now describe the channel assignment strategy for the adaptive power control routes relay protocol. Consider the early stage of network topology shown in Fig. 1, where a small circle node represents a host and a larger circle represents power ranges. Host pairs C-D indicates that they are within the communicative range of mobile host A in the Fig. 2(a).

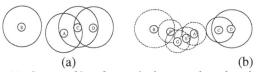

(a)   (b)

(a) Impact of interference in the case where there is no power control
(b) Large and dotted small circles indicate case with power control

Fig. 2. Transmission scenarios

Consider that the destination host A gradually moves away from the source host B, as shown in the Fig. 2(a). For example, host A moves towards host C. Then there will be a communication breakage between the source host B and the destination host A as well as issuing inter-channel interference with neighbor host by mobility. In our previous work [10], the problem above discussed has been investigated, but not in the context of collision avoidance MAC protocols with power control. And, each mobile node maintains a communications states table (CST) with assigned power that includes source/destination node and the channel used by source node or not.

We will assume that each mobile host A keeps an array called $p^{(i)}$, each node i keeps a transmission power value within CST table of all one hop neighbors that are within the maximum transmission power of node i. Also, let $P_{\min}^{(i)}$ be the minimum power level at which a mobile host can distinguish signals from noises. The value of $P_{\min}^{(i)}$ is the minimum power that any node i must use for data transmission in order for node j to correctly decode the data packet at the current level of interference. The value of transmission power can be dynamically adjusted if any host always monitors the communications around itself on the control channel since in our protocol the control channel is to serve this purpose. Generally, in our scheme, the transmission power can be found by replacing the parameter $P_{Tx}^{(i)}$ in (1) by the constant $P_{\max}^{(i)}$. We assume that each node i has N transmission power levels, $P_N^{(i)}$, where $N = (1, 2, 3, ..., 10)$. The actions taken by a node are as follows:

Step 1: As mobile node A causes inter-channel interference as well as channel breakage, it immediately stops communication, which helps to prevent other communicating hosts from being affected by the inter-channel interference.

Step 2: Node A computes distance between host A and C, say d. If $d < d_{\min}$, (where d_{min} is minimum distance where can be applicable to power control), then it concludes that the power control of the node i has failed.

Step 3: If $d > d_{\min}$, then it concludes that the amount of interference is tolerable at node i. Also, if $P_{\max}^{(A)} < P_{\max}$, power scaling should be implemented in a distributed manner. In other words, node A uses its connectivity power, (transmitting power used by host A and B, $P_{conn}^{(A)}$) which has been dynamically computed to get the maximum scaling constant $P_\alpha^{(A)}$. In [9], we should note that the transmission power at a node A is given by

$$P_\alpha^{(A)} = \frac{P_{\max}}{P_{conn}^{(A)}} \tag{3}$$

where it can communicate directly with neighbors using the power $p_\alpha^{(A)}$. This power is typically much smaller than P_{max}.

Step 4: When node A computes $p_\alpha^{(A)}$ successfully, it immediately transmits $p_\alpha^{(A)}$ to node C.

Step 5: Once the node C receives a control packet with $p_\alpha^{(A)}$, node A computes distance between host A and C. The node C computes the complement of $p_{Tx}^{(C)}$ which is used for deciding whether or not it could cause an unacceptable interference with node A's ongoing reception [9].

Step 6: If node C is acceptable to the transmission power and distance between node C and D, it broadcasts the computed $p_\alpha^{(A)}$.

As shown in Fig. 1, if we can properly tune each transmitter power level, a communication pair can coexist without any interference. Suppose mobile hosts X and Y want to exchange one packet with each other. Let X send a packet with power $p_{Tx}^{(X)}$, which is heard by Y with power $p_{Rx}^{(Y)}$. The following four functions are defined to formally describe the route relay with power control in the Fig. 3.

(1) OneHop(x) is defined to be the set of hosts located in communicative range of host x.

(2) FreeChannel(x) is a function that seeks a free (idle) channel to establish communication link.

(3) Neighbor(OneHop(x)) computes the set of hosts located in communicative range of *OneHop(x)*.

(4) Connect(x) computes the number of channels which have been connected.

```
repeat for ever
  When host x wants to communicate with host y.
  if FreeChannel (x) not NULL  /* Host x process FreeChannel(x) */
    send CRM message to host y;
  if CRM message received      /* Host x (idle channel check) */
    CHECK CST table;
  if FreeChannel (y) not NULL && /* Host x */
      Connect (y) > maximum number of channels {
    send CRM_ACK to host x;
    call OneHop(y);
  }
  else {
      call Power control process;
      if (acceptable) { execute Power control; end loop;}
      else {
        call Channel negotiation process; /* see Fig 3 */
        exchange host y and host x;  /* their information */
        end loop;
      }
  }
  if CRM_ACK message received call OneHop(x);  /* Host x */
  else end loop;
  if Neighbor(OneHop(y) ∩ OneHop(x) ) is available ) /* Host y */
  {
    if (FreeChannel(y) ∩ FreeChannel(x) ) /* All channel are used */
      discard CRM message request;
    else  {
      call Power control process;
      if (acceptable) { execute Power control; end loop;}
      else   call Channel negotiation process;
  }
  broadcast update message; /* update CST table */
  end loop;
```

Fig. 3. Pseudocode for saturated route relay with power control

3   Analysis and Simulations Results

Simulations have been done with some parameters used in our previous work [10]. Suppose that we are given a fixed channel bandwidth. Let the bandwidth of the control channel be B_c, the number of data channels be n, and that of each data channels B_d. Let the lengths of control packet and data packet be denoted by L_c and L_d, respectively. The number of data channels should be limited by the scheduling capability of the control channel. Since the control channel can schedule a data packet by sending at least k control packets, the maximum number of data channels should be limited by

$$n \leq \frac{L_d / B_d}{k L_c / B_c} \tag{4}$$

Here, we define success ratio as a function of the lengths of control and data packets. We can see that decreasing the length of control packets or increasing the length of data packets will improve the success ratio. Hence, the success ratio can be rewritten by

$$s_b = \frac{L_d}{k * L_c + L_d} = \frac{n * B_d}{n * B_d * B_c} = \frac{B_c}{n * B_d} \tag{5}$$

Therefore, the total success ratio S_t can be obtained by

$$S_t = \frac{k L_c}{L_d} \tag{6}$$

Fig. 4 shows the success ratio versus the number of nodes. The curves labeled as random refers to performance by the conventional channel assignment scheme [7], and the curves labeled as 'channels 2', 'channels 3', and 'channels 4' indicate performance by our protocol with 2, 3, and 4 channels available, respectively. Fig. 4 shows that our protocol offers a higher success ratio than Chang [5] and Wo [1] that randomly select a channel from the set of available channels.

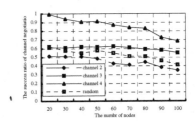

Fig. 4. Success ratio of channel negotiation process when there is inter-channel interference between two communicating pairs

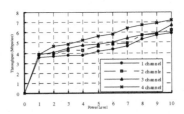

Fig. 5. Throughput with power control

Fig. 5 depicts network throughput with power control, we can see that our protocol provides a higher throughput although it may create more control messages than the randomly assigned protocol. The improvement is dominantly observed when four channels are used in our protocol.

4 Conclusions

The goal of power control is to properly reduce transmission power so as to increase channel reuse. In this paper, we propose a route relay protocol with power control capability to alleviate problems due to inter-channel interference and path breakage. Simulation results show that our protocol improves the capacity of ad hoc networks by effectively dealing with the breakage of communication in a mobile ad hoc network.

References

[1] S. L. Wu, Y. C. Tseng and C. Y. Lin, "A Multi-channel MAC Protocol with Power Control for Multi-hop Mobile Ad Hoc Networks," The Computer Journal, Vol. 45, No. 1, 2002.
[2] A. Muqattash and M. Krunz, "Power Controlled Dual Channel(PCDC) Medium Access Protocol for Wirelesss Ad Hoc Networks," in *IEEE INFOCOM*, 2003
[3] S.Narayanaswamy and V.Kawadia, R.S.Sreenivas and P.R.Kumar, "Power Control in Ad Hoc Networks: Theory, Architecture, Algorithm and Implementation of the COMPOW Protocol," in *European Wireless Conference,* 2002
[4] J.M. So and N.H. Vaidya, "A Multi-channel MAC Protocol for Ad Hoc Wireless Networks," Technical Report, University of Illinois at Urbana Champaign, 2003.
[5] C.Y. Chang, P.C. Huang, C.T. Chang, and Y.S. Chen, "Dynamic Channel Assignment and Reassignment for Exploiting Channel Reuse Opportunities in Ad Hoc Wireless Networks," *in IEICE TRANS. COMMUN., Vol.E86-B*, No.4, April 2003.
[6] G. Aggelou, "On the Performance Analysis of the Minimum-Blocking and Bandwidth-Reallocation Channel-Assignment (MBCA/BRCA) Methods for Quality-fo-Service Routing Support in Mobile Multimedia Ad Hoc," *in IEEE Transactions on Vehicular Technology Vol.53 No. 3*, May. 2004.
[7] V. Kawadia and P.R. Kumar, "Power Control and Clustering in Ad Hoc Networks," in *Proceedings of IEEE INFOCOM* 2003
[8] S. Agarwal and S.V.Krishnamurthy, "Distributed Power Control in Ad Hoc Wireless Networks," in *Proceedings of IEEE PIMRC '01, Vol. 2*, pp.59-66, Oct. 2001.
[9] A. Muqattash and M.M. Krunz, "A Distributed Transmission Power Control Protocol for Mobile Ad Hoc Networks," *in IEEE TRANSACTIONS ON MOBILE COMPUTING, VOL. 3, NO. 2*, 2004
[10] K.J. Kim and K.J. Han, "A Multi-Channel MAC Protocol with Route Relay Capability for Mobile Ad Hoc Networks ", *International Conference on Embedded and Ubiquitous Computing 2004*, Aizu-Wakamatsu City, Japan, pp.429-438, August 2004.

A Macro-Mobility Scheme for Reduction in Handover Delay and Signaling Traffic in MIPv6

Basav Roychoudhury[1] and Dilip Kr. Saikia[2]

[1] St. Anthony's College, Shillong 793001, India
basavrc@sancharnet.in
[2] Tezpur University, Napaam, Tezpur 784028, India
dks@tezu.ernet.in

Abstract. Mobile IP, a macro-mobility solution, is often criticized for its handover latency, and the number of registration messages it generates to support mobility. Several micro-mobility protocols have been defined as improvements – Hierarchical Mobile IP, Fast Handover and Cellular IP, etc. While these micro-mobility protocols help in reducing handover delay, they bring along the requirement of some sort of predefined security association between various entities. Implementing these may be difficult, and Mobile IPv6 actually tried to eliminate such requirements. In this paper, we propose certain modifications to Mobile IPv6 by introducing the mobile agents to take care of the mobility management. Moreover, the scheme does not assume any security association between entities belonging to different networks. We also present simulation results to prove the performance improvement.

1 Introduction

With every passing day, the popularity of wireless network access is increasing. This is due to the fact that it allows movement while being connected, without a disruption in communication. When the mobile node (MN) moves across different subnets, the layer 3 (L3) protocols get into action. This is because the MN's IPv6 address is not topologically valid any more [1] after the inter-subnet movements.

Of the various mobility management mechanisms at the network layer level, Mobile IP is comparatively a more complete solution [2]. Mobile IPv6 (MIPv6) provides undisrupted connectivity as the MN moves from one subnet to the other. However, the MN cannot receive IP packets immediately after getting attached to an access router (AR) in the new subnet. This is possible only after the process of *handover* is completed. The *handover latency* (t_{ho}) can be defined as

$$t_{ho} = t_{pd} + t_{CoA} + t_{regd} + t_{ack} + t_{rrp} + t_{bu} \qquad (1)$$

where t_{pd} is the time for prefix discovery in visited network, t_{CoA} is the time to establish the care-of-address, t_{regd} is the time to register the new care-of-address with the Home Agent (HA), t_{ack} is the time for the registration acknowledgement to reach MN from HA, t_{rrp} is the time to set up a key with the correspondent node (CN), and t_{bu} is the time to send the binding update (BU) to CN.

A. Sen et al. (Eds.): IWDC 2004, LNCS 3326, pp. 186–191, 2004.
© Springer-Verlag Berlin Heidelberg 2004

The predecessor of MIPv6 – Mobile IPv4 had *Route Optimization* [3] extension, required pre-configured security associations among the entities. As having pre-configured security association among the various entities in a large scale would not be easy, MIPv6 [4] removed such requirements by incorporating *Return Routability Procedure* (RRP). The RRP mechanism, however, adds significant amount of signaling traffic and delay to the handover process. Many extensions to MIPv6 has been proposed – Hierarchical Mobile IPv6 (HMIPv6), Fast Handover, Cellular IP (CIP) – to name a few. These attempt reduction in handover latency, in number of lost packets due to the handover process, and in signaling load on the network. However, these extensions bring back the requirement for pre-configured security association [5,6,7].

In this paper, we propose modifications to MIPv6 which aims at reducing handover latency and the signaling traffic, but does not involve setting up of pre-configured security associations among entities belonging to different administrative domains. Moreover, this is a macro-mobility scheme, unlike the extensions that provide mobility support at the local level. This is achieved through the use of *Mobile Agents* (MA) which proxy for the home agent of the mobile node at the foreign networks.

The rest of the paper is organized as follows. We propose our scheme in section 2. In section 3, we present the results of experiments carried out to estimate the improvement in performance through the proposed scheme vis-à-vis original MIPv6. Section 4 concludes the paper.

2   Proposed Scheme

In this proposed scheme, we envisage a mobile agent to proxy for the HA in the foreign networks. Mobile Agents are processes dispatched from a source computer to accomplish a specified task. Each mobile agent is a computation along with its own data and execution state. After its submission, the mobile agent proceeds autonomously and independently of the sending client [8].

2.1   Basic Protocol

When a given mobile node MN moves out of its home network, it attaches itself to an access router AR1 after acquiring a care-of-address and sends this binding information to its home agent HA. The HA then sends a mobile agent MA1 to the access router AR1 to proxy for itself. If a mobile agent proxying for the HA already is present at AR1 (serving any other MN from the same home network), then the HA will send only the information specific to MN to the MA. The same mobile agent shall serve all the mobile nodes belonging to a home network. When a CN gets interested in communicating with the MN, it sends the packets to the home address of the MN. The HA intercepts the same and forwards it to the MN. The MN then initiates the RRP for setting up a key in order to send an authenticated BU to CN. After setting up a communication with CN, MN will stop sending regular BUs to its HA. Instead, the BUs will be sent regularly to the CN. However, the MA shall update the HA from time to time and in this it will update the HA on all the mobile nodes under its service. As MA does this (using the wireline network), this does not contribute to the handover latency.

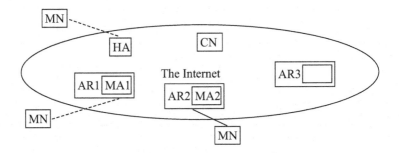

Fig. 1. Modified scheme for enhancement of Mobile IPv6

When the MN moves and goes out of reach of AR1, it will get attached to another access router AR2. If this happens, the MN sends a BU to the MA1 at AR1. On receiving this BU, MA1 will authenticate MN on behalf of HA for the registration of MN at AR2. It will record the binding and its lifetime and shall dispatch a mobile agent MA2 with information about MN to AR2 along with the binding acknowledgement. As before, if there already exists a MA from the home network, only the relevant information about MN is sent by MA1. The MN then sends new BU(s) to the CN(s). Meanwhile the packets in transit reaching AR1 will be forwarded by MA1 to MA2 at AR2. While the MN remains attached to AR2 it keeps sending regular binding updates to MA1 at AR1 and MA1 continues to maintain the information about MN. When the MN moves to access router AR3, it sends binding updates to MA1 (at AR1) and MA2 (at AR2). MA1 on receiving such a binding update will either delete all information about the MN (if it is also serving some other MN) or destroys itself (if it is not serving any other MN). To reduce traffic over the wireless interface, the binding update will be sent to MA2 (at AR2), which in turn, will inform MA1. In situations where no binding update is received by the MA1 at AR1, MA1 assumes a network failure and sends the information about MN back to HA. On being acknowledged, it either deletes all information pertaining to the MN or destroys itself. After recovering from a network failure, the MN will have to send binding update directly to HA which then shall send a new MA to the concerned AR. The MN shall then repeat the RRP with the CNs to setup the authentication keys and then send the BUs to the CNs.

2.2 Security Related Aspects

As in MIPv6, each mobile node must have a security association with its HA. The MA (which belongs to the home network) should also have a security association with the HA. Thus the MN and the MA from a given home network can share a security association. This makes the communication between the HA and the MN, as well as between the MA and the MN secure and authentic. The MA stores the information about the previous care-of address of the MN, the current care-of address, security associations, and the time for which the services of the given network is used. To make the system fault tolerant, the MA will periodically send these information to the HA.

While it is possible to set up pre–configured security associations among the HA, the MN and the MA — as they all belong to the same administrative domain, such a thing may not be possible for the CN. The CNs will often belong to different administrative domains, and setting up pre–configured security association across various entities in diverse administrative domains will be next to impossible. A security key between the MN and the CNs to authenticate the BU is set up on the fly using RRP.

Apart from registering the MN, the MA at the previous AR is also involved in RRP. In the MIPv6 protocol, the RRP involves the MN sending two messages (HoTI and CoTI) to the CN, one via the HA and the other directly. The CN replies with HoT and CoT messages, one via the HA and the other straight to the MN. These messages contains one token each (Home Keygen and Care-of Keygen Tokens respectively), which are used to generate the key between the CN and MN. In this scheme, the HoTI message and the response HoT message passes through the HA only the first time. From the next time onwards, these are send via the MA in the previous AR. Thus, when MN moves to AR2, the HoTI and the HoT messages should travel via MA1 at AR1. As the path between the CN and MN at AR1 was optimized, the path to CN via AR1 will be shorter than via the HA. Hence, t_{rp} will be shortened.

When the MN moves to another access router AR2, it sends a binding update to the MA1 at AR1. This is a secure communication due to the shared security association existing between the MN and the MA1. On this being acknowledged, the original MIPv6 suggests setting up a new key between the MN and CN through RRP. However, to reduce the signaling traffic, we suggest that there be a lifetime for the key generated by RRP. If this lifetime is still valid when MN connects to AR2, it will use the same key to inform the CN about the new care-of address.

2.3   Interoperability with Other Micro-Mobility Protocols

This scheme can also be made to operate over micro-mobility protocols. Fast Handover is claimed to work with HMIPv6. In HMIPv6, a MN entering a domain make regional registration with Mobility Anchor Point (MAP) and informs the HA and CN(s) about this regional CoA. Movement of MN within the domain requires registration only with the MAP and is transparent to others. When MN moves to a new domain, it needs to update HA and also the CN following the RRP. We suggest that MA can be stationed at the MAP. When MN moves to a new domain, the MA at the previous MAP can assist in RRP, thereby reducing the handover delay. The same idea is applicable in CIP, as CIP Gateways function somewhat similar to the MAPs of HMIPv6.

3   Simulation and Results

In today's Internet, there is wide heterogeneity in the network interconnectivity. To have an experimental estimate of the performance improvement through the proposed scheme, we considered two simple cellular like topology for the access routers. In one case we considered the routers to be connected to each other in a grid along with diagonal connectivity (*topo 1*), while in the other we took a network of the routers connected in a grid without diagonal connectivity (*topo 2*).

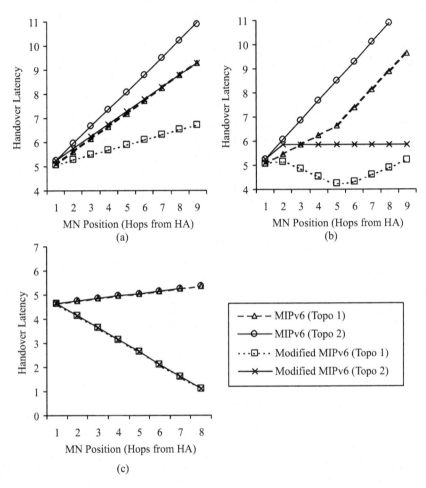

Fig. 2. Plots of simulation results. Fig (a) depicts the case where MN is moving perpendicularly away from the line joining HA and CN. Fig (b) shows where MN is moving diagonally away from the line joining HA and CN. Fig (c) is the plot when MN is moving along the line joining HA and CN towards CN. We consider the simulation both using *topo1* and *topo2*

We have estimated the handover latency in terms of number of hops the packets have to make in the wired network through the shortest paths in the various steps of the handover process. To make a comparison, we compute this handover latency for both, the original MIPv6 and the proposed scheme assuming three different movements for the MN. These are- i) MN moving perpendicularly away from the line joining HA and CN, ii) MN moving diagonally away from the line joining HA and CN, and iii) MN moving along the line joining HA and CN towards CN. The experimental results show significant improvement in all the three cases for the modified scheme vis-à-vis MIPv6 which are shown figure 2 (a), (b) and (c).

4   Conclusion

We have proposed the introduction of a Mobile Agent for mobility management in MIPv6. The scheme has several advantages. One, the subsequent RRP does not involve the HA. This reduces the network path traversed, and thus reduce handover latency as well as overall network traffic. This also makes the scheme more immune to home agent failure. Second, the MA and the MN share a security association. As either the home agent or the mobile agent handles all the signaling, no separate process is needed to set up keys (except for RRP). For example, MIPv6 suggests setting up of security association with a home agent in previous network (not its home network) to allow forwarding the packets in transit to the new CoA. Third, the MN, at many times, need not send binding updates to its home agent, which may be far away. Fourth, the envisaged existence of a security association between the MN and the MA ensures that the scheme does not bring in any more security threats than those present for MIPv6.

References

1. Montavont, N.: Handover Management for Mobile Nodes in IPv6 Networks. IEEE Comm. Mag. (August 2002) 38-43
2. Henderson, T.R.: Host Mobility for IP Networks: A Comparison. IEEE Network (Nov-Dec 2003) 18-26
3. Perkins, C. E.: IP Mobility Support for IPv4. Request for Comments 3344, (Aug 2002)
4. Johnson, D., Perkins, C., Arkko, J.: Mobility Support in IPv6. Request for Comments 3775, (June 2004)
5. Soliman, H., Catelluccia, C., El-Malki, K., Bellier, L.: Hierarchical MIPv6 Mobility Management. Internet Draft, Work in Progress, (June 2004)
6. Koodli, R.: Fast Handovers for Mobile IPv6. Internet Draft, Work in Progress, (July 2004)
7. Campbell, A.: Cellular IP. Internet Draft, Work in Progress, (Dec 1999)
8. Samaras, G., :Mobile Agents: What About Them? Did They Deliver What They Promised? Are They Here to Stay? Proc. Of 2004 IEEE Intl. Conf. On Mobile Date Management (2004)

QoS Support in TLMM: Three Level Mobility Model for IP-Based Networks

Mohuya Chakraborty[1], Iti Saha Misra[2], Debasish Saha[3], and Amitava Mukherjee[4]

[1] Netaji Subhash Engineering College, Garia, Kolkata 700084, India
mohuyacb@yahoo.com
[2] Department of Electronics and Telecommunication Engineering, Jadavpur University,
Kolkata 700032, India
itimisra@cal.vsnl.net.in, bitihotra_ju22@yahoo.com
[3] MIS & Computer Computer Science Group, Indian Institute of Management (IIM),
Calcutta, Joka, D.H.Road, Kolkata 700 104, India
ds@iimcal.ac.in
[4] IPresently at Microelectronics and Information Technology KTH,
Royal Institute of Technology, 164 40 Kista, Sweden
amitava@imit.kth.se

Abstract. TLMM, a three level mobility model for IP-based mobility management has been recently proposed as an architecture for managing global mobility in an IP-based network. This paper evaluates the performance of TLMM's Quality of Service (QoS) framework using a combination of DiffServ and Int-Serv architectures with the concept of Bandwidth Broker for admission control and resource reservation for different service classes. The most important contribution in this paper is a dynamic handoff policy using the concept of Boundary Location Area, for performing location updates for inter-domain roaming of mobile nodes, which helps in maintaining proper QoS. The performance evaluation of the proposed protocol is provided by simulation results using Network Simulator (ns-2).

1 Introduction

Notwithstanding the amazing rate at which network capacity is growing, we find ourselves challenging with congested networks today and can be doing so for the near future. Network researchers all over the world are experimenting with several technologies to reduce congestion. It is unlikely that the promised proliferation of high bandwidth connectivity will assuage congestion problems any time soon. For these reasons network quality of service (QoS) promises to become increasingly important. QoS is a set of technologies that enables network administrators to manage the effects of congestion on application traffic by using network resources optimally, rather than by continually adding capacity.

---

[1] The author is thankful to NSEC, Techno India Group, India.
[2] The author is financially supported for this research by the CAYT project of AICTE, India.

A. Sen et al. (Eds.): IWDC 2004, LNCS 3326, pp. 192–197, 2004.
© Springer-Verlag Berlin Heidelberg 2004

In this paper, we describe the development of an integrated QoS framework for our Three Level Mobility Model (TLMM), which has been recently proposed as an optimal hierarchical mobility model for IP-based networks with respect to network parameters like handoff latency, signaling overhead and frequency of location updates [1]. We have designed and implemented the QoS framework for TLMM in this paper as an integrated approach for supporting advanced mobility management for NG mobile wireless networks that guarantees efficient QoS and scalability among end users by using a combination of IntServ [2] [3] and DiffServ [4], [5], [6] models. An efficient dynamic handoff policy with the concepts of bandwidth broker (BB) (for resource reservation and admission control) and boundary location area (BLA) has been proposed that takes care of false handoff.

The rest of the article is organized as follows. Section II describes QoS-related TLMM functional elements and provides the dynamic handoff policy. Section III provides the performance evaluation of the proposed protocol using ns-2 [7]. Finally we conclude the paper in section IV.

2 QoS-Related TLMM Functional Elements

Essentially TLMM consists of IntServ capable routers at the boundaries and DiffServ capable routers within the interior of a domain. The architecture of TLMM [8] consists of a three level hierarchical structure with foreign agents (FA) at the lowermost level, mobility agents (MA) at the middle level and gateway mobility agents (GMA) at the topmost level (Fig. 1). FAs and MAs are DiffServ capable routers but GMA is an IntServ capable router placed at the boundary of two overlapping domains and works as a gateway to a domain. In TLMM, whenever an MN enters a subnet, it obtains a local care-of-address (LCoA) of the FA, a regional care-of-address (RCoA) of the MA and a global care-of-address (GCoA) of the GMA. GMA consists of a routing database register called a Boundary Location Register (BLR), which is a database cache maintaining the roaming information of the mobile nodes (MNs) moving between different domains. The roaming information is captured when an MN requests a location registration to the GMA and is called Service Level Application (SLA) [5], which is an agreement with the Internet Service Provider (ISP). An SLA basically specifies the service classes supported and the amount of traffic allowed in each class.

Various QoS parameters for IP mobility scenarios may be pointed out for understanding and estimating the performance criteria of a protocol. Among them, packet loss, handoff delay, signaling overhead, signaling cost and bandwidth find importance in evaluating a system operation. Regarding signaling overhead, handoff latency and packet loss, it has been established that TLMM suffices MIP and TeleMIP in many cases [1]. Regarding bandwidth, a Boundary Location Area (BLA) based BB algorithm has been adopted in TLMM that allocates bandwidth to a mobile user dynamically as and when required during an MN's transition from one domain to another. The flowchart of the algorithm for the case when an MN in domain A moves towards domain B is represented in Fig. 2. The scheme proposed in this paper shall prove the ability of a BB using efficient QoS management to provide a modified form of Differentiated services to a Mobile IP user. This technique also removes the possibility of false handoffs, lowers signaling costs and packet loss rate [8].

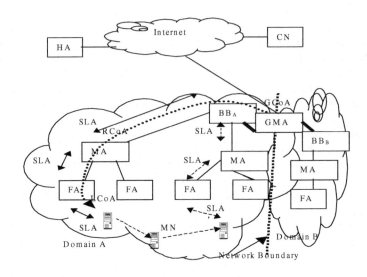

Fig. 1. QoS-Related TLMM Functional Elements

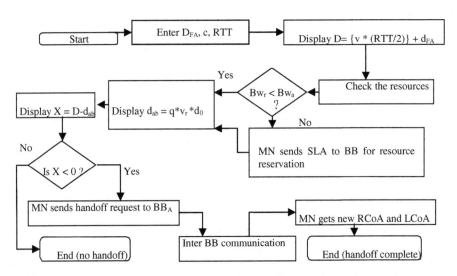

D_{FA}: Distance of FA in domain B from the boundary   c: velocity of light   RTT: Round trip time
D: Distance of MN from the boundary d_{ab}: BLA

Fig. 2. Flowchart of BLA-Based BB Algorithm in TLMM

For achieving the BB arrangement of inter-system (interdomain) handoff and QoS maintenance simultaneously, we define BLA of an MN to be the region in which the MN sends location registration request to the new access network (or domain) to-wards which it moves [9] and is found to be proportional to the QoS factor (q) times velocity ratio (v_r), where q is the ratio of bandwidth required by the MN (Bw_r) to the available bandwidth in the new system (Bw_a) and v_r is the ratio of velocity of the MN to the average velocity of all the MNs moving in the existing domain. The proportionality constant is d_0 and depends on network parameters.

For the purpose of maintaining QoS while moving between different domains managed by different ISPs, an MN transforms and transmits the previously negotiated SLA with HA to FA of the visited domain. The BB that controls the foreign network (FN) then configures the network according to the SLA of the user and reserves bandwidth accordingly. The bandwidth broker in GMA is mainly responsible for automating the process of SLA negotiation. The GMA actually has two BLRs corresponding to the two domains that it controls. Presently a client-server oriented protocol that uses a TCP connection between neighboring BBs is used [6].

Bicasting employed here is not initiated by HA but by GMA. A change of GMA for an MN causes an initiation of an update registration up to HA. So when an MN moves from one domain to another and comes under the scope of a different GMA, both new incoming packets and packets in progress must wait for processing till the inter domain handoff and location registration is finished. As a result, the packets may be lost due to waiting for handoff and location registration for GMA change. By using the concept of BLA, MNs are allowed to request handoff and location registration before they arrive at the new domain, which means, BLA provides extra time Δt for a packet to wait for processing. In the absence of BLA, a packet will be lost if the waiting time $W_t > 0$. However, when the BLA is used, the packet will not be lost if $W_t <$ or $= \Delta t$ due to the fact that this packet acquires extra time Δt to obtain its required bandwidth.

3   Performance Evaluation

In this section we compare the signaling costs resulted from using BLA with that in a conventional IP network without using BLA. Simulation experiments through ns-2 using relatively heavy traffic load have been deliberately used to emulate the situation on a highly congested link where our architecture is supposed to work well. In this section, a comparative study of TLMM with MIP and TeleMIP (without QoS support) [10] has also been made with regard to parameters such as packet loss, total network delay and throughput with respect to bandwidth. Fig. 3a shows that signaling cost increases with velocity of MN at a slow rate for q <1 but at a faster rate for q >1 by using BLA. The cost is independent of velocity of MN in the absence of BLA as expected. But one important aspect that becomes noticeable is that using BLA the signaling cost remains at a much lower value compared to the corresponding cost without BLA for MNs having lower velocity and q <1. This is advantageous for slow moving MNs whose bandwidth requirement is less. But for faster MNs whose bandwidth requirement is more than the network capacity, the increase in signaling cost is pronounced as expected. Fig. 3b shows packet loss vs packet flow rate for a fixed bandwidth (ns-2 simulation). From the figure it is clear that as number of flows per second increases, the packet loss increases at a very rapid rate for MIP. TeleMIP shows better result than MIP but for TLMM the packet loss is the least. Figs. 3c, 3d and 3e show the total network delay with bandwidth for 10%, 50% and 90% global users (MNs moving around more than five subnets surrounding their home subnet) respectively.

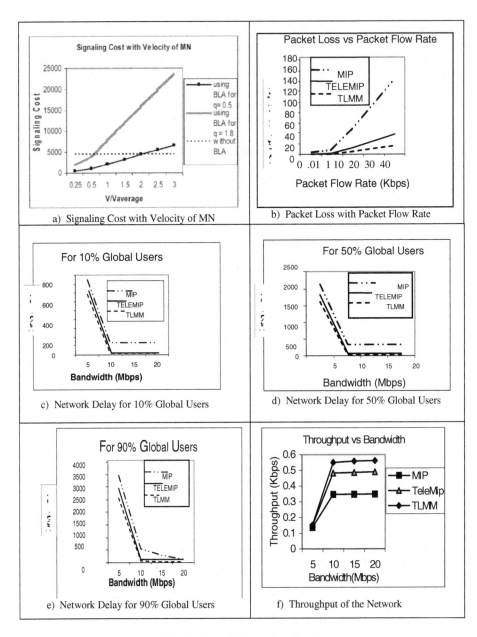

Fig. 3. Plots of Simulation Results

Fig. 3f sketches the throughput of a network for MIP, TeleMIP and TLMM. It shows that as bandwidth increases, rate of increase of throughput is much pronounced in TLMM as compared to MIP and TeleMIP.

4   Conclusion

In this paper, we presented a performance study of TLMM's Bandwidth Broker-based architecture with a dynamic handoff policy using BLA concept for providing QoS support in an IP-based network. Simulation results show the advantage of TLMM over MIP and TeleMIP for large network and number of global users. Packet loss for TLMM is much less as compared to others. Throughput of TLMM is large as compared to MIP and TeleMIP. Network delay for 10% global users is almost same for TeleMIP and TLMM but for 50% and 90% global users TLMM show much improvement over MIP and TeleMIP as the number of MNs and network size increases.

We finally conclude that the architecture of TLMM is able to provide scalable global QoS support especially over the bandwidth controlled wireless links. For future NG wireless networks, increased bandwidth is a must for supporting real-time multimedia and TLMM proves to be the right choice as it is seen to provide higher throughput.

References

1. I.S.Misra, M.Chakraborty, D.Saha, A. Mukherjee, "A Three Level Mobility Management Architecture for IPv4 Networks", International Conference on Mobile Communication Summit 2004.
2. R. Braden, D. Clark, and S. Shenker, "Integrated Services in the Internet Architecture: an Overview", Internet RFC 1633, June 1994.
3. S. Blake, D. Black, M. Carlson, E. Davies, Z. Wang, and W. Weiss, "An architecture for differentiated services, RFC 2475, IETF, December 1998.
4. P. Ferguson and G. Hutson, Quality of Service, John Wiley & Sons, 1998.
5. S. Blake, D. Black, M. Carlson, E. Davies, Z. Wang, and W. Weiss, "An architecture for differentiated services, RFC 2475, IETF, December 1998.
6. S. Jha and M. Hassan, Engineering Internet QoS, Artech House, 2002.
7. ns-2 home page, http://www.isi.edu/nsnam/ns.
8. I.S.Misra, M.Chakraborty, D.Saha, A. Mukherjee, Billawdeep Deb, Bitihotra Chatterjee, "Global Mobility Management: A Three Level Architecture for Next Generation Wireless Networks",5th International Workshop on Distributed Computing (IWDC), Kolkata, India, December 2003, Springer Verlag publication, pp. 184-193.
9. F. Akhyldiz and W. Wang, "A Dynamic Location Management Scheme for Next Generation Multi-tier PCS Systems", IEEE Transaction on Wireless communication, January 2002.
10. Subir Das, Archan Misra, Prathima Agrawal, and Sajal K. Das, "TeleMIP: Telecommunications-Enhanced Mobile IP Architecture for fast Intradomain Mobility," IEEE Personal Communications, Aug 2000, pp 50-58.

Path Stability Based Adaptation of MANET Routing Protocols

Sandeep Choudhary[1,*], M M Gore[2], and O P Vyas[3]

[1] Wireless People(M) SDN. BHD. Kuala Lumpur-60000, Malaysia
sandeepchoudhary_be@yahoo.com
[2] Department of Computer Science and Engineering,
M N National Institute of Technology, Allahabad-211004, India
mmgore@ieee.org
[3] School of Studies in Computer Science,
Pt. Ravi Shankar Shukla University, Raipur-492010, India
vyas2k2@yahoo.co.in

Abstract. This paper proposes adaptation of Mobile Ad-hoc Network (MANET) [13] routing protocols taking stability of links as primary consideration. The presented scheme can be associated with a resource reservation strategy to ensure Quality Of Service (QoS). Packets routed through stable routes have very low waiting time in queue which reduces end to end delay. The overall performance shows that the developed adaptation can support a higher degree of QoS as compared to the conventional version of MANET routing protocol.

Keywords: Path stability, Ad-hoc networks, Stable link.

1 Introduction

Ad-hoc routing protocols discover path between mobile nodes in an ad-hoc network. Most of the proposed ad hoc routing protocols try to find out shortest paths. Now suppose there is a need to support real time application like video conferencing which needs QoS guarantee viz. a path with a maximum specified delay and a minimum specified bandwidth. A resource reservation strategy can be used, along with ad hoc routing protocol, to provide QoS guarantee. But as nodes move an established route may break. This will result in interruptions perceived by the users of real time applications. To avoid this the approach should be towards finding durable paths.

There exists a lot of literature for finding stable paths in ad-hoc networks. SSA [5], RABR [7], FORP [8], and ABR [9] routing protocols discover stable paths. For details on related work refer [1]. This paper proposes adaptation for DSDV [4], [6] and AODV [4], [15] routing protocols, to consider stability of link during route formation. This work relies on stability metrics developed in [2],[3]. The adaptation involves changes in packet formats, messages and routing algorithm itself.

---

* Work conceived and completed during authors' association with IIIT Allahabad, India.

A. Sen et al. (Eds.): IWDC 2004, LNCS 3326, pp. 198–203, 2004.
© Springer-Verlag Berlin Heidelberg 2004

The rest of the paper is organized as follows. Section 2 presents the proposed adaptation. Simulation results are presented in section 3. Section 4 concludes the paper and describes future possibilities.

2   Path Stability Based Adaptation

This section describes the proposed adaptation for DSDV and AODV. The modifications are stated in *italics*.

2.1   DSDV Adaptation

The information in the route tables is similar to that found in route tables with conventional DSDV. Except the *Metric field is the path stability metric [3]. The metric field for a zero hop entry, i.e. a path from a node to itself, is equal to N-1. Here N is the size of link life time array [2].*

1. Each node broadcasts RUPD, periodically or immediately when significant new information is available. The two cases are described as follows:
   (a) Periodic update: Each mobile node periodically advertises its view of the interconnection topology with other mobile nodes within the network Nodes forms the RUPD by increasing its own sequence number by two and then copying all the entries of route table in RUPD. The nodes then broadcast this RUPD packet.
   (b) Triggered update: Significant new information immediately triggers the update. Following are two cases of triggered update:
      i. When a link to next hop has broken, any route through that next hop is immediately assigned   *Zero Metric* and a sequence number incremented by one. This updated route table is copied in a RUPD packet and immediately broadcasted.
      ii. If a new route is recorded in the route table then it also immediately triggers a update. The formation of RUPD is same as periodic update.
2. When a node receives a RUPD packet, it executes following steps:
   (a) *The first step is to update the link life time data structure as described in [2].*
   (b) *Node calculates the link stability metric [2]. Then it calculates the new path stability metric [3] for each of the destination in the packet and also for each destination in the routing table. The metric so calculated includes the updated link stability metric of the link on which the advertisement was received.*
   (c) It compares this update information to its own routing table. Following are the rules to update routing table information:
      i. Select route with higher destination sequence number.
      ii. Select the route with greater metric when sequence numbers are equal.

2.2   AODV Adaptation

The routing table structure and routing packets are same as that of conventional AODV. Except the *Metric field is the path stability metric [3]. In RREQ and RREP, metric field contains the path stability metric of path yet traversed. The metric field for a zero hop entry, i.e. a path from a node to itself, is equal to N-1 where N is size of link life time array [2].*

1. Each node exchanges HELLO packets periodically with neighboring nodes to maintain neighborhood information. *Each time a node receives a HELLO packet, it updates the link life time data structure [2].*
2. When node wants to send a data packet to a destination and it has no route to the desired destination then it broadcasts a RREQ packet with *metric field initialized by N-1.*
3. Any node that receives a RREQ does the following:
   (a) *Node will calculate the link stability metric for the link on which RREQ is received. Then it will calculate the path stability metric and will assign it to metric field of RREQ.*
   (b) If the node has already received the RREQ (which is identified using the unique identifier), *node will compare the metric of old and new RREQ. If metric of new RREQ is greater, then this new RREQ is also broadcasted and the reverse route entry is updated to use this new link. Otherwise this RREQ is discarded.*
   (c) Else the reverse route entry is updated to use the link on which RREQ was received.
   (d) If the node recognizes its own address as the destination, the request has reached its target. So RREP is formed by copying the source address, destination address and the current sequence number of destination. *Metric field is set to N-1.*
   (e) Else it checks cache to have a valid route to destination. If such a route is found, RREP is formed.
   (f) If a RREP is formed during steps d or e then this RREP is unicasted back to the source by using the reverse route entry i.e. on the link from which RREQ was received.
   (g) Otherwise, the node broadcasts this updated RREQ.
4. When a node receives a RREP it updates the metric field of RREP and executes the following steps:
   (a) If it is a new RREP then node forms forward route entry and simply forwards the route reply using the reverse route entry if it is not the destination i.e. the originator of RREQ.
   (b) If it is a old RREP then it checks whether the route reply has a new sequence number or a greater metric in case of same sequence number. If this is the case then it updates its forward route entry. If it not the originator of RREQ then it forwards the route reply by using the reverse route entry.
5. When a link in some active path is broken, then the node upstream to it sends RERR to the nodes in the routes precursor list. When a node receives RERR it marks the path as invalid and similarly sends RERR.

3   Evaluation

The simulations were carried out by modifying the MANET routing protocol code of NS [16]. Refer [1] for detailed description of simulation setup. The original and modified protocols are compared in terms of three metrics namely *Fraction of total data packets received, Routing overhead*, and *End-to-end delay*. The total number of packets received [1] for modified version is always less than the old one. Most of the packets are dropped in modified version. Unavailability of route is the reason behind this. A route needs to satisfy the criteria of stability for becoming a valid route. If it fails to do so the packets are queued or dropped if queue is full. Routes discovered by adapted algorithm are generally longer than the conventional algorithm. This results in increased routing overhead [1].

The end to end delay for a packet is considerably reduced in the modified version as seen in Fig. 1 and Fig. 2 for DSDV and AODV respectively. Reduced waiting time in queue is the reason for this. In conventional version the packets

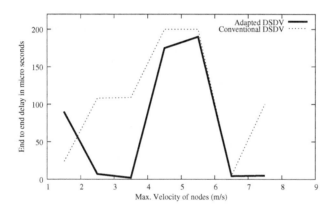

Fig. 1. Comparison graph for average end to end delay in network for DSDV

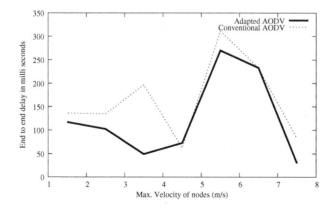

Fig. 2. Comparison graph for average end to end delay in network for AODV

are dispatched from the source in very less time as the delay in finding a route is very less. But as the nodes move the path discovered become invalid. The packets which were on the path need to wait in queues of intermediate nodes. The next path to destination is searched and the packets again start flowing. But the frequent interruptions make the overall waiting time large. But in the modified version the packets arrived do not have to wait in queue for long time as the path is more stable and remains up for more amount of time. The initial waiting time is although more than the conventional protocol, but as soon as a path is discovered the flow is seamless. Thus the overall waiting time is less.

4   Conclusion and Future Work

The designed adaptation is rather restrictive in its operation and not suited for general purpose applications due to reduced throughput and increased overhead. But in case of real time applications the adaptation will outperform the traditional protocols. The protocol will be able to serve soft real time systems like video conferencing with a resource reservation strategy, which the traditional one cannot. The performance of protocol in such a real time environment is yet to be tested, but the simulation statistics indicate that it will perform better than the traditional version. This adaptation is a step forward for development of QoS support in ad hoc networks.

Future possibilities include, using a weighted average of hop count and stability metric as the selection criteria. This will be a mid way between the traditional version and the modified one. A running weighted average can be expected to adapt according to the network characteristics. Also, a resource reservation strategy is to be developed to be used along with the proposed scheme to support QoS.

References

1. Sandeep Choudhary: Path Stability Based Adaptation Of MANET Routing Protocols. Master's thesis, Indian Institute of Information Technology, Allahabad, India, June 2004 $http : //wcc.iiita.ac.in/thesis2004/sandeepc\_wc02.pdf.zip$
2. Michael Gerharz , Christian de Waal, Matthias Frank and Peter Martini : Link Stability in Mobile Wireless Ad Hoc Networks. Proceedings of the 27th Annual IEEE Conference on Local Computer Networks (LCN.02), pp. 30-39, Tampa, FL, November 2002.
3. Michael Gerharz , Christian de Waal and Peter Martini : Strategies for Finding Stable Paths in Mobile Ad Hoc Networks. Proceedings of the 28th Annual IEEE Conference on Local Computer Networks (LCN), pp. 130-139, Bonn /Koenigswinter, Germany, October 2003.
4. Charles E. Perkins : Ad Hoc Networking. Addison-Wesley, 2000.
5. R. Dube, C. D. Rais, K.-Y. Wang, and S. K. Tripathi : Signal Stability based Adaptive Routing (SSA) for Ad-Hoc Mobile Networks IEEE Personal Communication, Volume:4, Issue: 1, pp.36-45 February 1997.

6. Charles E. Perkins and Pravin Bhagwat : Highly Dynamic Destination-Sequenced Distance-Vector Routing(DSDV) for Mobile Computers. SIGCOMM 1994. pp.234-244.

7. S. Agarwal, A. Ahija, J. P. Singh, and R. Shorey : Routelifetime Assessment Based Routing (RABR) Protocol for Mobile Ad-hoc Networks. In Proc. IEEE International Conference on Communications 2000 (ICC00), volume 3, pp. 16971701.

8. W. Su, S. Lee, and M. Gerla : Mobility Prediction and Routing in Ad Hoc Wireless Networks. International Journal of Network Management, Wiley & Sons, 11:330, 2001.

9. C.-K. Toh : Associativity Based Routing For Ad Hoc Mobile Networks. Wireless Personal Communications Journal, Special Issue on Mobile Networking and Computing Systems,(2):103139, March 1997.

10. Christian Huitema : Routing in the Internet. Prentice Hall PTR 1999.

11. Jaroslaw Malek : NS trace files analyzer. $http://www.geocities.com/tracegraph/$

12. M. Gerharz and C. de Waal : Bonnmotion: A mobility scenario generation and analysis tool. $http://web.cs.unibonn.de/IV/BonnMotion/$

13. Mobile Ad-hoc Networks (MANET): $http://www.ietf.org/html.charters/manet-charter.html$.

14. M. Scott Corson and Joseph Macker : Mobile Ad Hoc Networking (MANET): Routing Protocol Performance Issues and Evaluation Considerations. Internet-Draft no.2501, January 1999.

15. C. Perkins, E. Belding-Royer and S. Das : Ad hoc On-Demand Distance Vector (AODV) Routing. Internet-Draft no. 3561, July 2003.

16. The Network Simulator - ns-2 : $http://www.isi.edu/nsnam/ns/$

17. Elizabeth M. Belding-Royer and Chai-Keong Toh : A review of current routing protocols for ad hoc mobile wireless networks. Personal Communications, IEEE,Volume: 6 , Issue:2 , April 1999, pp. 4655.

18. Chenxi Zhu and M. Scott Corson : QoS routing for mobile ad hoc networks. INFOCOM 2002. Twenty-First Annual Joint Conference of the IEEE Computer and Communications Societies. Proceedings. IEEE , Volume: 2 , 23-27 June 2002 pp. 958-967 vol.2

19. Understand for C++ : A reverse engineering, documentation and metrics tool for C and C++ source code. $http://www.scitools.com/ucpp.html$

Computational Biology - The New Frontier of Computer Science
(Arun K. Choudhury Memorial Lecture, Kolkata, Dec.27, 2004)

Amar Mukherjee

School of Computer Science, University of Central Florida,
Orlando, FL USA 32816-2362

In 1952, the transistor was invented. In 1953, the double helix structure of DNA was discovered. These two milestones have revolutionized the respective fields of computer science and biology. Biology is now on the verge of another revolution in which computation is playing a central role.

1   Biological Landmarks

Gregor Mendel, the father of modern genetics, published a paper in 1886 that pioneered the experimental study of genetics. His famous laws are called **Mendel's laws**. Prior to Mendel's discovery, it was conjectured that some discrete physical entities present in all living organisms control hereditary characteristics and that these entities are passed from parents to offspring of organisms. By early 20th century, these entities were called **genes**. It was recognized that that the genes are carried by **chromosomes**. Chromosomes were discovered in 19th century as threadlike structures in the nucleus of a eukaryotic cell that could be observed under a microscope as the cells begin to divide. While the laws of life were still mostly unknown in the early 1930's, scientists theorized that like all particles in the human body, genes must be composed of molecules. Two famous physicists Niels Bohr in 1932, and Erwin Schrodinger in 1944, attempted to explain the nature of life based on a molecular theory. Their theories had errors, but the involvement of these two famous names with biology inspired other young physicists like Max Delbruck and Paul Brenner to attempt to understand the chemical nature of the gene.

Biochemical analysis of molecules concluded that chromosomes contain both DNA (Deoxyribonucleic acid) and protein. The fundamental question was: which element of the chromosome constitutes hereditary genetic material? DNA or protein? In view of the varieties of proteins and species found in nature, proteins as carriers of genetic information seemed to make more sense. However, this hypothesis was overturned by a famous experiment by Griffith in 1942 and interpreted by Avery. Avery discovered a fundamental principle of biology, called the **transforming principle**. The search for the molecular structure of DNA also attracted several well known scientists such as George Gamow and Linus Pauling.

The search for the molecular structure of DNA culminated with the discovery of the double helix by James Watson and Francis Crick in 1953. This discovery was preceded by several other important discoveries in biology: (1) Erwin Char-

A. Sen et al. (Eds.): IWDC 2004, LNCS 3326, pp. 204–218, 2004.
© Springer-Verlag Berlin Heidelberg 2004

gaff found experimentally that in DNA the number of **adenine** (A) residues equals the number of **thyamine** (T) residues and that the number of **guanine** (G) equals the number of **cytosine** (C). This is sometimes stated as A=T and C=G. But this does not mean that A+T equals C+G. In fact, the AT and CG contents of different species vary considerably. For example, the malaria parasites are very AT rich. (2) In 1952, Rosalind Franklin of King's College, London, discovered using X-ray diffraction analysis that DNA has a helical structure. In fact, she showed that DNA exists in two forms, the A-form and the B-form. The Watson-Crick structure was the B-form of which she obtained an amazingly clear X-ray photograph.

It is now well known that a DNA (deoxyribonucleic acid) consists of two strands of nucleotides each consisting of a sugar-phosphate backbone strung together by what is called a phosphodiester covalent bond and a string of nitrogenous bases A, T, C and G attached to the backbone. The two strands are complimentary in the sense that A or C of one strand is always attached to T or G, respectively, of the other strand by hydrogen bond(s) and the two strands are wrapped up in the form of a double helix. The DNA or the polynucleotide has two distinct ends. One end has the triphosphate group that does not participate in forming the phosphodiester bond. This is called the 5'-terminus. At the other end the 3'-hydroxyl group does not participate in the bond formation. This is called the 3'-terminus. These two distinct ends imply that the polynucleotides have a directionality: going from the 5'-3' direction would be considered going 'downstream'; the 3'-5' direction 'upstream'. Apparently, there is no limit to the number of nucleotides that can be joined together or no strict specificity as to the ordering of these nucleotides. Thus, the number of possible 'strings' that can be formed using this four letter alphabet grows exponentially with the length of the string.

The total DNA content in the cell that carries the hereditary information of an organism is called its **genome**. The human genome has an approximate size of 3 billion base pairs. The biological information of the genome is essentially contained in what is called the coding region of the gene. The coding region is the template from which an enzyme or protein molecule is generated. The coding region constitutes about 10% of the entire genome. This region contains **genes** which encodes via combinations of DNA triplets (**the genetic code**) all possible amino acids, the basic ingredients of all proteins and hormones that a living organisms need to function, to live and to die. The human genome has approximately 40000 genes, but a much larger number of encoded proteins are generated through alternative splicing and post-translational modification. The process of interpreting the instructions provided in the genes to produce the proteins is called **gene expression** and involves a host of biochemical processes involving transcription (via messenger RNA) and translation (via transfer RNA) and an 'assembly' line of chemical factory via ribosomal RNA.

The above description is a brief summary of the basic biological processes that takes place at the lowest level of hierarchy which sustains an organism whose description is infinitely more complex. We will discuss a much simplified model of this pyramid of complexity.

2   Multilevel Hierarchy

"I think the next century will be the century of complexity" Stephen Hawkins

Scientists attempt to analyze any complex system, natural or artificial, by decomposing it into constituent subsystems and trying to formulate the rules of interactions of these subsystems in terms of multilevel hierarchy of abstractions. Let us consider first an artificial system like a VLSI microchip which is today the end product of the transistor revolution (See Figure 1). At the lowest level of hierarchy, we have the atoms and electrons which by themselves are very complex systems worthy of study by physicists for the most part of 20th century. At the transistor or semiconductor device level, we are interested in the nature of the current flow constituted by the cloud of electrons which move under the control of externally applied voltages to its 'terminals'. When this device is used as a digital switch, the current flow is turned on or off. An abstraction of this device is to say that it acts like a switch which can be in any of the two binary states '0' or '1'. In the next level of abstraction, the concern is how to interconnect these switches to realize logical gates like AND, OR and NOT gates. When describing the function of a logical network, which is an interconnection of logical gates, the details of electron flow and current flows have been hidden from the model. The language and tools used to describe and analyze the behavior of the logical networks are quite distinct from those used in the lower levels. The abstraction is now pushed upwards to build subsystems out of logical networks, and a complete system out of an interconnection of subsystems. Without the use of this hierarchical approach, it will be practically impossible to build a complex VLSI chip that may have more than a billion transistors [[Mead and Conway, 1980, Mukherjee, 1986]].

A biological system [[Brown, T. 1998, Alberts et al., 2000]] may be infinitely more complex than a VLSI system but the multilevel abstraction paradigm is still a powerful approach to understand such a system (See Figure 2).At the lowest level of hierarchy we have the molecules of DNA that are glued together by electrical, thermodynamic and chemical forces. In the next level of abstraction we deal with sequences, in particular sequences of strings created from a four letter alphabet A, T, C and G. The Genome project whose goal was to sequence the entire human genome, was essentially concerned with this second layer of abstraction. A whole set of biotechnology was developed in the 80's and 90's to sequence whole genomes of organisms, beginning with the fruit fly and reaching a milestone in 1996 when the entire genome of humans was sequenced. Several technologies were crucial to these developments and include : 1) recombinant DNA technology techniques where DNA sequences are cut with restriction enzymes and recombined with segments of DNA derived from different species; 2) electrophoresis which can separate the DNA segments according to size; 3) PCR (Polymerase Chain Reaction) technology which allows amplification of DNA sequences resulting in the production of multiple copies of a DNA fragment; 4) and microarrays for fast sequencing as well as for measuring the expression levels of genes. A parallel development along with these technologies is the emergence

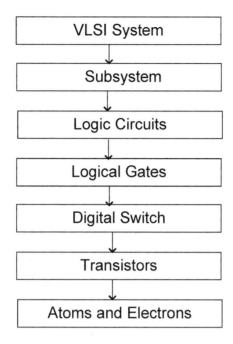

Fig. 1. Hierarchy of VLSI abstraction levels

of the field of computational molecular biology by mathematicians, statisticians and computer scientists who contributed to the discovery of new and efficient algorithms to compare sequences for similarity, multiple sequence alignment problems, new genes and pattern discovery and cross species genome analysis. All of these are now contributing to our knowledge of how genes function, diagnosis of inherited diseases and evolutionary biology.

The third level of abstraction is concerned with gene regulation, gene-protein interaction, and signaling and gene expression. A DNA sequence is not only an instruction set for producing a particular protein, it also encodes conditions under which the instructions are activated. A gene may be spliced with intervening introns with promoter or suppressor sequences flanked upstream near or even very far from the gene clusters. The DNA sequence forms loops with itself so that certain regulatory proteins can bind to these control sites to produce chemical signals that act like signals in an electric network to control the transcriptional activity. There are also transcription factors that have been highly preserved through millions of years from yeast to human that can bind to enhancer sequences to initiate the transcription process. The next three levels of abstractions are proteomics, cell function and biological pathways and system biology. The primary structure of a protein is a linear sequence of amino acids. All proteins in their stable natural states fold into characteristic three dimensional structures which determine their functions in the living organisms. The

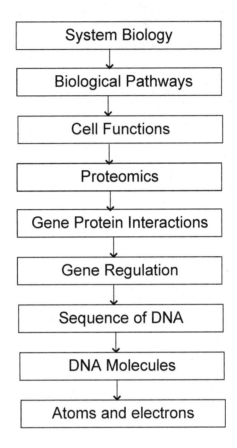

Fig. 2. Multi-Level Hierarchy for Biological Systems

linear structure can fold unto itself to create protein-protein or protein-ligand interaction sites. The folded structures are called secondary structures, the most common examples of which are the α-helix or β-sheet. A tertiary structure is formed when groups of α-helices or β-sheets further bind by hydrogen bonds to a more complex protein structure. The number of possible secondary and tertiary structures grows exponentially with the length of the linear structure and traditional methods of using x-ray crystallography and nuclear magnetic resonance to study these structures is very difficult and costly. Protein lengths in organisms may vary from 50 to several thousands of polypeptides. Because the number of possible proteins of length l could be as large as 20l, the number of possible protein structures is enormous. There are also quaternary protein structures when more than one polypeptide chain interacts via both hydrogen and ionic bonds and hydrophobic reactions. The largest known quaternary protein structure involves 40 separate polypeptide chains. Prediction of protein structure using mathematical models or by computer simulation of molecular dynamics has become a very active and challenging research area. Structural similarities between proteins also imply functional similarities. Algorithms to determine structural similarities and multiple alignments of proteins have also become another major challenge in proteomics. Understanding the structures of proteins is fundamental to the understanding of cell life cycle and metabolism, and biological pathways which control the functions of life of the organism at the systems level. The protein structure determines its functions. Understanding this relationship might lead to the discovery of new drugs and treatment procedures. The complexity and varieties of proteins are really mind boggling. In a human cell, there are about 100 million proteins of about 30,000 different types. Each cell contains the genetic code for every possible protein. What function a particular cell will assume (viz. muscle, neuron, ligaments, liver etc), depends on the expression levels of genetic codes in that particular cell.

In the next level of abstraction, the object of study is cell - how it functions as an almost autonomous entity, how it interacts with its environment, how biological pathways maintain its functions and nutrients, what enzymatic signals control multicellular development, cell to cell communication, cell division and a host of other complex phenomena involved in morphogenesis and morphologic evolution. Needless to say, these are core biology problems which are now being addressed by teams of interdisciplinary researchers.

At the highest level of abstraction we are dealing with the whole organism which is the model of life. In recent years, several hundred microbial genomes have been sequenced. More than 50% of the genes found in these genomes have unknown functions. Within several years, this number of such genes might jump to hundreds of millions if we include higher organisms. Since genes, proteins, regulatory processes and cells do not work in isolation, a systems approach to derive the basic principles of working of life has to be developed. We might take several centuries to begin to understand it or perhaps we will never be able to understand it because of its deep philosophical and cosmological dimensions.

3   Exponential Growth of Biological Data

The human genome contains about 3.1647 billion base pairs. Improvements in sequencing technology and the increased use of special purpose computer algorithms for sequencing are major factors that lead to completion of human genome and genomes of several other species. It is estimated that the number of nucleotide bases double approximately every 14 months, while genomes are being sequenced at a rate of 15 complete genomes per month (see Figure 3). In February 2002, GENBANK contained approximately 17,089,000,000 bases in 15,465,000 sequence records. Within a period of two months, the total number recorded was 23,099,919,533. A similar trend in growth has been observed for other databases that house biological data such as the SWIS_PROT (for protein sequences) and PDB (for protein 3D structures).

An important new challenge facing researchers is to make sense out of this huge mass data. This has heightened need for efficient and effective algorithms for

Growth of GenBank

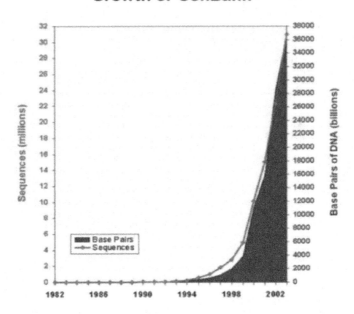

Fig. 3. Exponential growth of biological data

the analysis, annotation, interpretation and visualization of biological sequences. The revised goal of the Human Genome Project emphasizes research in the development of tools for genome-scale analysis of proteins and for improved representation and analysis of sequence variations and sequence similarity. Clearly, this challenge has implications not only for the Human Genome Project, but also for other genome-scale projects, such as those for microbial genomes, plant genomes, and genomes of other organisms, such as the mouse, puffer fish etc. We now have the prerequisite technologies to create massive biological data sets. In order to be able assimilate this data and make biological sense out of it, data management, modelling and simulation tools along with faster computer and networks connecting research laboratories world wide will be absolutely essential. The community of distributed and parallel processing researchers has thus been uniquely challenged to participate in this development.

4   Computational Challenges

Fortunately, some of the foundational work on mathematical biology and algorithm developments were undertaken in the 70s and 80s long before the technology for rapid sequencing was in place. Some of the basic classes of algorithms that have found significant applications are listed as follows:

4.1 Algorithms for Exact String Matching

These include the famous Knuth-Morris-Pratt linear time pattern matching algorithm, BoyerMoore algorithm and multiple pattern matching algorithm of AhoCorasick and those based on suffix trees. These algorithms can be used to find known patterns such as sequence tagged sites (STS), expressed sequence tags (ETS) and CpG islands. STS and ETS have been used for mapping genomes at low resolution. CpG islands corresponds to infrequent occurrences of the dinucleotides CG (across the strand as opposed to a base pair) around promoter or start regions of many genes where the natural tendency of C being chemically modified by methylation is suppressed. Besides these, exact pattern matching algorithms are useful to locate binding sites, promoter sequences and other gene regulatory sequences. Exact pattern matching algorithms also find application in determining overlapping DNA segments in shotgun sequencing methods, analysis of repetition structures, finding DNAbinding protein motifs.

4.2 Pattern Discovery in DNA Sequences

Pattern discovery in DNA sequences is a fundamental problem in computational biology. Typical problems in this class include finding exact or approximate matches in the DNA sequences for gene regulatory elements, finding transcription factor binding sites in the promoter regions, finding gene clusters that are co-regulated or coexpressed or finding specialized motifs. The most commonly used approach to finding regulatory patterns is to look for what is called a monad pattern which is a contiguous short string. A more precise description of the problem is to find patterns of the form (l,d)-k , where l is the length of the pattern, d is the maximum number of mismatches allowed, and k is the minimum number of times the pattern is repeated in t samples. Earlier approaches to this problem used a greedy CONSENSUS algorithm the stochastic GibbsDNA algorithm and MEME all of which have a high probability of success only for sequences of length 100, falling drastically to 10% probability of success when the sequence length is about 800. Several authors proposed algorithms base on branch-and-bound approach [[Marsan and Sagot, 2000, Eskin and Pevzner, 2002]] which have high computational cost, particularly for longer motifs. These motivated several researchers to develop combinatorial approaches to the problem [[Pevzner and Sze, 2000, Eskin and Pevzner, 2002]]; see [[Pevzner, P.A., 2000]] for other references and a complete treatment of this topic]. The time-complexity of some of the best known algorithms in the last class of algorithms is $O(nt^2 l^d (|\sigma|)^d)$, where t is the number of input sequences, and n is the length of each input sequence and $|\sigma|$ is the size of the alphabet, which is 4 for DNA sequences. We have developed two new algorithms (VijayaSatya and Mukherjee, 2004] for this problem. The first algorithm takes $O(n^2 t^2 l^{\frac{d}{2}} |\sigma|^{\frac{d}{2}})$ and space $O(ntl^{\frac{d}{2}} |\sigma|^{\frac{d}{2}})$, and the second algorithm takes $O(n^3 t^3 l^{\frac{d}{2}} |\sigma|^{\frac{d}{2}})$ time using $O(l^{\frac{d}{2}} |\sigma|^{\frac{d}{2}})$ space. In practice, our algorithms have much better performance provided the $\frac{d}{l}$ ratio is small. The second algorithm performs very well even for large values l and d as long as the $\frac{d}{l}$ ratio is small. Both the algorithms performed extremely well on the "challenge" problem posed by Pevzner of (15,4) on 20 input sequences of 600 nucleotides. Many of the actual regulatory signals are composite patterns that are groups of monad patterns that occur relatively near each other. These patterns are responsible for co-regulating genes that share two or more transcription factors. A difficulty that arises in finding the composite pattern is that one component monad pattern may be too weak (implying more mismatch distance) which makes the monad based approach unsuitable. Real examples of this kind of scenario has been found by [[Guha Thakutha and Stormo, 2001]] in a set of yeast S. cerevisiae genes. Finding efficient algorithms for composite patterns remains an open challenge.

4.3   Sequence Similarity Algorithms

The biological motivation for studying this problem comes from the fact that high degree of similarity of bimolecular sequences usually implies significant structural and functional similarity. After the first successful sequencing of the genome of a living organism in 1995 of the bacterium Haemophilus influenza, researchers identified 1743 sites as prospective gene sites. In order to determine whether these sites are actually involved in protein synthesis, the coding regions were translated into amino acid sequences using the genetic code. The resulting amino acid sequences were then compared with a protein database that contains for each known protein the corresponding amino acid sequences. The search identified about 1007 close matches. Since the protein database is annotated with functions, the close matches allowed coming up with strong conjectures about the functions of these genes. Similarity of two sequences can be expressed by their edit distance which is the minimum number of mutations (deletion, insertion or substitution operation) in the DNA sequence that will transform one sequence to the other sequence and vice versa. This is also sometimes expressed by biologists by showing an alignment of the two sequences as illustrated below for two sequences ATAGCCAT and AAGTCTAT ([T,-], [-,T] and [C,T] stand for deletion, insertion and substitution, respectively).

ATAGCCAT-
A- AGTCTAT

Let $f(i,j)$ denote the number of alignments of one sequence of i letters with another of j letters. Then, it has been proved that $f(n,m) \approx (1+\sqrt{(2)})^{2n+1}n^{-\frac{1}{2}}$. For $n = 1000$, $f(1000, 1000) = 10^{767.4}$ alignments! The number of elementary particles in the universe is about 10^{80} and Avogadro's number is 10^{23}. Needleman and Wunsch [1970] proposed a dynamic programming algorithm and a more efficient version was developed by Gotoh[1980] to find *global* alignments of two strings on length m and n taking $O(nm)$ time. A much more useful problem is to find local alignments of subsequences of two sequences. Surprisingly, a similar dynamic programming algorithm taking $O(nm)$ time was proposed by Smith and Waterman [1981] to find all the local alignments. These two seminal work has opened up a floodgate of new sequence similarity algorithms using probabilistic and more complex and realistic models of cost (alignment with affine gap scores, PAM and BLOSUM scoring matrices) as well as algorithms for finding repeated and overlapping matches. In practical situations where a data base having 100 million protein residues have to be searched against sequence lengths of a few thousands, the dynamic programming algorithms, although mathematically elegant and correct, takes hours of computation time even with fastest machines. For this reason, a set of very efficient heuristic algorithms have been proposed by several researchers in the 90s Lawler and Chang 1990, Wu and Manber, 1992 and Myers 1994] which have been incorporated in commonly used web based search tools such as BLST and FASTA. The BLAST finds high scoring local alignments for both DNA and protein sequences. It works by preprocessing the database to obtain an index table to find short stretches or 'q-gram's of exact matches. For a particular query sequence, the algorithm then quickly finds the regions of locally maximum match areas and then extends these regions in both directions to look for ungapped alignment or gapped alignments. FASTA is also a widely used search tool. The underlying idea is similar to that of BLAST at the first step. After finding the short exact matches, it looks for best diagonal matches with ungapped extension and then joins the ungapped regions by gapped extensions. In the final step, this approximate match region is then subjected to a full fledged dynamic programming algorithm.

4.4   Multiple Sequence Alignment

The idea of alignment can be easily generalized to multiple numbers of DNA or protein sequences. The purpose of multiple alignment is to extract faint or widely dispersed commonalities of a set of strings rather than a pair of strings. This might be due to common ancestral string from which all the strings have evolved. The multiple sequence similarity is thus relevant for understanding the molecular basis of evolution. It is well known that the closely related organisms have high similarity between their genomes. Conserved sequences among the organisms reveal past speciation, the structure of ancestral family trees and the role of mutation in the evolution of these trees. Family trees constructed on the basis of gene similarity is called gene tree. For example, by studying the similarity of the gene 16S ribosomal RNA which turns on translation process of the nucleotide sequence to a protein is conserved in almost all living organisms. Another kind of tree called phylogenetic tree which depicts possible mutational events that caused a past ancestral species to diverge into extant species, has been successfully used to classify groups of species into closely related sub-species. The time line of evolution can also be inferred from this tree. Studying similarities within the individual organisms in a species might also reveal whether certain individuals are prone to inherited diseases. For multiple alignments of proteins, homologous residues are usually aligned together in the same columns. Proteins are called homologous if they have both three-dimensional structural as well as functional similarities. (The study of protein structures and functions, prediction of protein folding mechanisms using experimental and theoretical models and application of this knowledge to drug design has evolved into a new field called proteomics which we will not discuss in this lecture.) A scoring model for a multiple sequence alignment is complicated by the facts that it depends not only on conserved positions but also by the history of evolution. These two aspects can be addressed by a very complex idealized model which estimates the probabilities of all the evolutionary events in the ancestral sequences. Simpler models based on sum-of-pairs, consensus function and tree functions have used instead. The proposed solutions use multidimensional dynamic programming approach which becomes very unwieldy if the number of sequences and the length of the sequences is not very small. A host of other simpler heuristic algorithms such as progressive alignment, profile alignment and iterative refinement and hidden Markov model training methods have been reported in the literature. The reader is referred to two excellent texts [[Gusfield, 1997]] and [[Durbin et al., 1998]] for further details.

4.5   Phylogenetic Trees

All species of organisms on our planet undergo slow transformation throughout ages. This process has been identified by the biologist as evolution. One central problem in biology is to explain the evolutionary history of species and in particular, how species are related to each other and whether or not they shared a common ancestor. This is depicted by constructing a tree whose leaves represent the present day species and whose internal nodes represent possible ancestors. Such a tree is called a phylogenetic tree. With the advent of molecular biology, the evolutionary processes have been linked to several basic processes at the genome level such as insertion, deletion, substitution, inversion and transposition of its DNA. All these operations are grouped under a common name called mutation. In the past, biologists used morphology data (the so-called phenotypes: color of hair, skin, eye, physical characteristics like presence of wings, length of arms, legs etc) or biochemistry data (such as amino acid synthesis pathways) to come up with taxonomy and ancestral relationship. In recent times, use of molecular sequence data has g iven rise to a more precise science of phylogenies which incorporates mathematical and algorithmic approaches. There are also many software tools that have been designed based on these algorithms to re-create phylognetic trees. There is a vast amount of literature and competing theories of evolutionary biology and classification of species. The phylogenetic tree construction algorithms have been classified into two broad classes: maximum parsimony based methods and distance-based methods. The detailed description of these algorithms appear in standard text [[Gusfield, 1997]]. In view of the availability of genomic data for both human and other species, the evolutionary biologists have renewed their research and have come up with new and exciting insights.

4.6   Haplotype Inference Problem

One important goal of Genomic research is to identify the mutations that cause common diseases, such as diabetes, cancer, stroke, heart disease, depression and asthma. Inherited genes and environmental factors cause these diseases. Two unrelated individuals might have the same 99.9% of their DNA sequences, but the remaining 0.1% may be responsible for phenotypic differences such as color of skin or eyes and, more ominously, risk factors for these fatal diseases. Sites in the genome where the DNA sequences of at least 10% of the population differ by a single base are called single nucleotide polymorphisms (SNPs). The nucleotides involved in a SNP are called alleles. Almost all observed alleles are biallelic, that is, only two nucleotides are involved in any SNP. In diploid organisms such as human, each chromosome is made of two distinct copies of double stranded DNA and each copy is called a haplotype. A child inherits exactly one haplotype from each parent in the absence of any recombinant event. If recombination happens, a haplotype of the child may have parts of both haplotypes of parents. To understand an individual's variation, including susceptibility to inherited diseases, we must determine the individual's haplotypes. This has been a major undertaking for research (http://www.hapmap.org/abouthapmap.html.en) by the International HapMap project . Separating two chromosomes of an individual to analyze its haplotype content is possible but not practical. Current technology is suitable for large scale polymorphism screening which identifies the genotypes only. The genotype gives the base information at each SNP but does not say which base occurs in which haplotype. For example, if the bases A and G are alleles in a SNP, and if A or G occurs in both haplotypes, these correspond to two cases of homozygous genotypes (denoted by '0' for no mutation and '1' for mutation), whereas if A occurs in one and G in the other it is called heterozygous genotype but we cannot infer on which chromosome each appear (denoted by symbol φ). The haplotype inference problem is as follows: Given a set $G = (g_1, g_2, ..g_i, , g_n)$ of n genotypes where g_i is a vector of m elements from $0, 1, \varphi$, resolve the genotype by finding for each genotype a pair ¡h,k¿ of haplotypes $h = (h_1, h_2, h_j, , , h_m)$ and $k = (k_1, k_2, .., k_j, k_m)$ such that $h_j = k_j$ equals 0 or 1 if the corresponding element in g_i is 0 or 1, respectively and h_i,k_i is 0 or 1, $h_i \neq k_i$ if the corresponding element g_i is φ and the number of total distinct haplotypes in the resolution is minimum. The combinatorial resolution algorithms proposed by several researchers [[Gusfield, D. 2000, Eskin et. al, 2003]] are based on two observations: first, the human genome contains blocks that contain only a few different haplotypes; second, it is reasonable to assume that haplotypes that occur within a block have evolved according to a perfect phylogeny in which at most one mutation event occurred at any site and no recombinant event has occurred at any site. The algorithms have $O(nm^2)$ complexity and it still remains an open problem whether a $O(nm)$ algorithm exists. Several other algorithms for the family of haplotype problems using statistical and dynamic programming approaches have also been reported in the literature.

4.7   Molecular Simulation

plus .1em The biological system is an incredibly complex system. In order to discover basic principles of biology from the molecular points of view mathematical modelling and simulation tools are absolutely essential. IBM's Blue Gene project (http://www.research.ibm.com/journal/sj/402/allen.html) is an example of such a large scale simulation initiative. In 1999, IBM announced the building of a massively parallel computer to study bimolecular phenomena such as protein folding and to explore novel ideas in massively parallel machine architecture and software. IBM also plans to link up with teams of experimental biophysicists of protein dynamics and mathematicians worldwide to validate the simulation results. The study of protein folding involves prediction of three-dimensional secondary and tertiary structures from the given linear sequence of amino acids. Out of millions of possibilities, in its natural state the sequence takes a unique reproducible three-dimensional structures in seconds whereas in laboratory test tube it might fold into a random coil. Understanding the mechanism behind this behavior is interesting from scientific point of view and might have practical significance in drug design and drug therapy. Biophysicists have studied the protein folding phenomena from thermodynamic points of view involving free-energy, temperature and physical parameters. The simulation of molecular dynamics at different points of transitions of protein from the linear to the stable three-dimensional structures involves computation of forces on atoms of the simulated model of the protein at increments of 10-4 seconds of simulated times for each increment of 10-15 real time. To simulate a real life phenomenon of 100 microseconds, this might take several years. The hardware configuration projected for a "cellular" Blue Gene architecture is a petaflop/s (1015 floating-point operations per second) computer, with about 50 times the computing power of all supercomputers in the world put together. For further details of the simulation project, the reader is referred to the IBM website cited earlier. The US Department of Energy has recently undertaken a big initiative called GTL (Genome to Life) program for the 21st century. The project is to develop over a period of 10 to 20 years providing facilities for whole genome analysis, production and characterization of proteins, analysis and modeling of cellular system and characterization and imaging of molecular machines [Frazier et. al., 2003]. The project will fund research for collecting high-throughput data, advances in mathematical modeling, algorithms and data management techniques and environmental microbiology.

4.8   Bionetworks

It will be appropriate to conclude this paper with a topic that brings back the memories of Late Professor Arun K. Choudhury. In the early sixties, Professor Choudhury and I started an investigation on switching networks. A few years earlier in the late 50's, Professors Choudhury and Mahalanabis started a research effort on the study of non-linear feedback control systems with the help of the analog computer that Profs. Choudhury and B.R.Nag built at the Institute of Radio physics and Electronics. Both of these topics have emerged to be relevant again in molecular biology.

One of the simplest mathematical models to analyze gene expression is a Boolean network [[Tozeren and Byers, 2003]]. A bionetwork consists of a set of nodes, each of which represents either a gene or a biological stimulus. The stimulus could be physical factors like temperature, pressure, ion concentration etc. The value associated with a node is either the amount of gene activity (viz. amount of mRNA available in the cytoplasm of the cell) or the level of a stimulus. For each of these quantities a threshold can be defined such that if the amount equals or exceeds the threshold, the node is turned ON (state '1') and if the amount is below the threshold value, the node is turned OFF (state '0'). The state of the bionetwork is a configuration of states of some of the nodes in the network. Obviously, if there are s nodes, the possible number of states in the network is 2s. In living organisms, genes interaction of two nodes via proteins can be depicted by a directed arrow connecting the stimulus gene to the active gene. The network can have cycles and can be looked upon as a sequential network or a feed back control system with analog input signals.

As an example of gene regulation in, biologists have studied in detail a cluster of 3 genes (jointly called an operon) that control utilization of lactose (milk sugar) in E.coli. lacZ: encodes an enzyme that splits lactose into glucose and galactose. lacY : encodes for a protein that helps pump lactose from outside environment to inside of the cell. lacA : encodes for an enzyme that degrades carbon compounds to extract energy.There is also an additional gene lacI with its own promoter and terminator which acts as a repressor which prevents RNA polymerase to attach to the DNA sequence stopping transcription of the operon. lacI acts as a regulatory gene. If there is no lactose, transcription of lac operaon does not occur because the Lac suppressor attaches to the operator region preventing RNA polymerase to bind. If there is also sufficient glucose within the cell, a second regulatory gene called catabolic activator protein (CAP) just upstream the operator, prevents RNA polymerase to bind inactivating the operon. Thus, the regulation of lac is a classic example a feedback control system. The abundance of glucose in the environment suppresses the transcription of the enzyme which is required to convert lactose to glucose and lack of glucose in the environment stimulates production of the enzymes needed for its conversion. In more complex situations, there could be groups of suppressors and enhancers which act in response to varieties of biochemical sensory inputs in seconds to change the rate of expression of a gene or groups of genes. Metabolic pathways are also examples of complex bionetworks which involve thousands of gene products . It can be said that the living cells are nothing but a network of signaling pathways controlled by chemical reactions and enzymes. Researchers have developed data bases of pathways and gene networks of several organisms. One of the best known of such knowledge repositories is the Kyoto Encyclopedia of Genes and Genomes (KEGG: http://www.genome.ad.jp/kegg/).

5 Conclusions

With the advent of new automated sequencing and assembly tools, the capabilities to acquire genomic data have become very powerful. This has given rise to an exponential growth of genomic information. The need to process this data for further scientific advances and to understand its role in heredity, chemical processes within the cell, drug discovery, evolutionary studies, sequence analysis etc have created new problems that are of interdisciplinary nature. The computer scientists, mathematicians, statisticians and bio-medical engineers will play key roles in this development in the 21st century. For computer scientists, the challenge is to discover efficient algorithms, combinatorial or probabilistic, mathematical modelling and simulation tools and computer architectures and software that the new bio-technologies to develop for the good of human beings and help understand the basic principles of life on earth.

Acknowledgments

I would like to thank Dr. Mita Mukherjee for her careful review and suggestions.

References

[Alberts et al., 2000]Alberts, B., Johnson, A., Lewis, J., Raff, M., Roberts, K., and Walter, P. (2000). Garland Science, 4th edition.

[Brown, T. 1998]Brown, T. (1998) *Genetics: A Molecular Approach*. Chapman and Hall, 3 edition.

[Durbin et al., 1998]Durbin, R., Eddy, S., Krogh, A., and Mitchison, G. (1998). *Biological Sequence Analysis*. Cambridge University Press.

[Eskin et. al, 2003]Eskin, E., Halperin, E. and Karp, R. M. Large Scale Reconstruction of Haplotypes from Genotype Data. In *Proceedings of RECOMB'03*. Berlin, Germany.

[Eskin and Pevzner, 2002]Eskin, E. and Pevzner, P. A. (2002). Finding composite regulatory patterns in dna sequences. In *Proceedings of the Tenth International Conference on Intelligent Systems for Molecular Biology(ISMB-2002)*, Edmonton, Canada.

[Guha Thakutha and Stormo, 2001]Guha Thakutha, D. and Stormo, G. D. (2001). Identifying dna and protein patterns with statistically significant alignments of multiple sequences. *Bioinformatics*, 10:1205–1214.

[Gusfield, 1997]Gusfield, D. (1997). *Algorithms on Strings, Trees and Sequences: Computer Science and Computational Biology*. Cambridge University Press.

[Gusfield, D. 2000]Gusfield, D. (2000). A practical Algorithm for Optimal Inference of Haplotypes from Diploid Populations. In *Proceedings of ISMB'00*.

[Marsan and Sagot, 2000]Marsan, L. and Sagot, M. (2000). Algorithms for extracting tsructured motifs using suffix tree with applications to promoter and regulatory sit consensus identification. *Journal of Computational Biology*, 7:345–360.

[Mead and Conway, 1980]Mead, C. and Conway, L. (1980). *Introduction to VLSI systems*. Addison-Wesley, Reading, Massachusets.

[Mukherjee, 1986]Mukherjee, A. (1986). *Introduction to nMOS and cMOS VLSI Systems Design*. Prentice Hall.

[Pevzner, P.A., 2000]Pevzner, P.A. (2000). *Computational Molecular Biology: An Algorithmic Approach*. Bradford Book.

[Pevzner and Sze, 2000]Pevzner, P. A. and Sze, S. (2000). Combinatorial approaches to finding subtle motifs by branching from sample strings. In *Proceedings of the eighth international conference on Intelligent Systems for Molecular Biology*, pages 269–278.

[Tozeren and Byers, 2003]Tozeren and Byers (2003). *New Biology for Engineers and Scientists*. Pearson International.

Cryptanalysis of "Wavelet Tree Quantization" Watermarking Scheme

Tanmoy Kanti Das and Subhamoy Maitra

Applied Statistics Unit, Indian Statistical Institute,
203 B T Road, Kolkata 700 108, India
{das_t, subho}@isical.ac.in

Abstract. Here we study a recently proposed watermarking scheme based on "Wavelet Tree Quantization" (WTQ) which has been presented by Wang and Lin in IEEE Transactions on Image Processing, February 2004. In the scheme, the wavelet coefficients corresponding to same spatial locations are grouped together. Two such groups, selected at random, are merged to form a super tree. Some of these super trees are quantized to embed the watermark signal in the image. In the process of cryptanalysis we can identify the groups which are quantized during watermark insertion process. We then select the non-quantized groups and quantize them to remove the watermark. Experimental results show that the watermark is completely removed by this attack. The cryptanalysis falls under cipher text only jamming attack which requires a single watermarked copy.

Keywords: Cryptanalysis, Digital Watermarking, Information Security, Multimedia Systems, Wavelet Transform.

1 Introduction

Lot of interest have been generated in past few years in the field of copyright protection of digital contents. Researchers are coming up with new watermarking schemes frequently. Most of these schemes are robust against signal processing attacks and employ complicated signal processing techniques to gain user confidence. However, most of the existing schemes have seldom been tested for their security against serious cryptographic analysis other than routine signal processing attacks like rotation, cropping, random geometric bending (Stirmark) [15, 16], etc.. It is well known that the correlation based watermarking schemes are vulnerable against collusion attack [5], but that may require large number of watermarked copies which may not be available in practice. Recently the most successful attacks are the ones that use a single watermarked copy for cryptanalysis [2, 3, 4, 7, 10, 11, 14]. In the same line, here we present a successful single copy attack against the watermarking scheme presented in [18], which we will refer as WTQ in short.

Invisible digital watermarking system adds a signal $s^{(i)}$ to the host image I to get the watermarked copy $I^{(i)} = I + s^{(i)}$ which is visually indistinguishable

A. Sen et al. (Eds.): IWDC 2004, LNCS 3326, pp. 219–230, 2004.
© Springer-Verlag Berlin Heidelberg 2004

from I. This watermarked copy $I^{(i)}$ is given to the ith buyer. The watermark $s^{(i)}$ can be made buyer specific for forensic tracking if required. Now the watermark retrieval algorithm works in the following way. The available image (may be attacked using image processing or cryptanalytic techniques) $I^{\#}$ is compared to the original image I and a signal $s^{\#} = I^{\#} - I$ is recovered. From $s^{\#}$, the buyer i is suspected if $s^{(i)}$ possesses some significant correlation with $s^{\#}$.

Let us now briefly discuss the security concept of a digital watermarking scheme from cryptographic viewpoint. We consider that the algorithm will be known to the attacker as it is accepted in the field of cryptology and information hiding [1, 8]. Thus, a scheme is considered to be secured if an attacker, who has access to the algorithmic principle of the scheme but has no access to the key, should not be able to tamper with the watermark [1, 8]. This cryptographic principle was first introduced by Kerckhoffs [9] in 1883. There are several examples to prove that "Security by Obscurity" (the assumption that opponent will remain ignorant about the system being used) can't work – latest one being the Secure Digital Music Initiative (SDMI) challenge [19]. In the challenge, the algorithmic principle of watermarking technologies were kept secret. In spite of this, authors of [2] were able to successfully cryptanalyse the scheme. Thus while analyzing a watermarking scheme, it is assumed that the scheme is known to the attacker but the keys are unknown.

The existing watermarking models need to be analyzed using cryptanalytic techniques as it is done for standard cryptographic schemes. We here look into the watermarking scheme as a cryptographic model and provide an attack which can be considered as a cipher text only jamming attack since the proposed attack removes/invalidates the secret watermark using a watermarked copy only. Before the deployment of a digital watermarking scheme in practice, it is required to analyze the scheme in detail and it seems that the most of the existing schemes are not robust with respect to customized cryptanalytic attacks. Here we mount the attack on the WTQ scheme [18] and provide successful results by removing the watermark. The robustness of the watermarking strategy is primarily evaluated on the following two criteria: (i) how well the malicious buyer is identified (who has intentionally attacked the watermarked image) and (ii) how infrequently an honest buyer is wrongly implicated.

In the process of cryptanalysis one needs to construct an attacked image $I^{\#}$ from the available image $I^{(i)}$ in a manner that there is no significant correlation between $s^{\#}$ and $s^{(i)}$. Thus it will be impossible to identify the malicious buyer i anymore. Moreover, $I^{(i)}, I^{\#}$ need to be visually indistinguishable. Note that to the attacker only a single copy of the image is available and he has no knowledge about the watermark signal $s^{(i)}$ or the key. Though he may have access to algorithmic principle of watermark embedding but he has no way to directly verify that the watermark has been erased. He needs to convinced indirectly that the correlation between $s^{(i)}$ and $s^{\#}$ has been removed.

Let us now explain how our contribution positions itself with respect to some recent 'single copy' attacks. The research in [10, 14] show an optimal way of estimating a watermark given only a watermarked signal without any access to the decoder. Our scheme is different to what has been explained in [10, 14]. In [10], it has been considered that the watermark is replicated several times, which is not the case in WTQ scheme. In a similar direction, in [14], a specialized attack has been mounted on a discrete sequence spread spectrum (dsss) audio watermarking. Both the watermarking and the attack have been analyzed on audio signals and it is clear that these attacks are not directly applicable on WTQ scheme. The replacement attack [11] exploits the repetition of similar kind of signal in the watermarked multimedia content. Hence this attack may be placed in the category of collusion attack instead of 'single copy attack'.

Another kind of attack, where the decoder is available in public domain, needs to be mentioned in similar context [7]. In this model it is assumed that the attacker has access to the decoder and he tries to gain knowledge about the watermark by using the decoder as an oracle. However, in our attack, we do not consider that this kind of facility is available. On the other hand, our methodology, by itself, justifies that the watermarking signal in the WTQ scheme can be completely removed. In [17, Page 122], a statistical removal attack has been pointed out. The attack involves rewatermarking (watermarking the watermarked copy further using the same or different watermarking algorithm) the watermarked image several times and then trying to remove each of the rewatermarks using some image transformations. It should be noted that rewatermarking an image several time degrades the image quality. Moreover, the exact image transformations that are required to remove the rewatermarks have not been discussed in [17]. Further, it has not been identified how the attacker will be convinced that the watermark has been removed.

It is pointed out in [18] that the WTQ scheme is an extension of "Optimal Differential Energy Watermarking (DEW)" [12] scheme in wavelet domain. In [3], cryptanalysis of DEW scheme has been presented. The basic idea in the attack was to remove the energy difference created by the DEW scheme between two set of blocks. Similar to DEW, the WTQ scheme creates statistical difference between two super trees during embedding. Here we present an attack methodology whose basic philosophy is similar to that of of [3] but actual implementation is quite different to that of [3]. In fact, the attack presented here is different in the sense that we are able to identify the wavelet groups affected due to watermarking, unlike that in [3].

In this paper we present a complete watermark removal strategy on the scheme proposed in [18]. The scheme is described in the next section. In section 3, we present the attack techniques in detail. In section 4 experimental results are presented to support the claim.

2   The WTQ Scheme

The "Wavelet Tree Quantization (WTQ) for Copyright Protection Watermarking" scheme [18] introduces the watermark in wavelet domain. The host image is subjected to Discrete-time Wavelet Transform and wavelet coefficients corresponding to same spatial location are grouped together. Let the number of such groups be $4m$. Super trees are formed by merging two randomly selected groups. Then the number of super trees is $2m$. Let us enumerate the super trees by T_k, for $k = 1 \ldots 2m$. Consider that the watermarking signal is a binary sequence of m many ± 1's, $w = w_1 w_2 \ldots w_m$. A watermark bit w_k is embedded using two such super trees T_{2k-1}, T_{2k}. That is, given a super tree T_l, it is related to the bit $w_{\lceil \frac{l}{2} \rceil}$. Depending on the watermark bit w_k, one of the two super trees T_{2k-1}, T_{2k} is quantized with respect to quantization index q_k. The quantization index q_k is chosen in such a manner that the two super trees used to embed the watermark bit, exhibit large enough statistical difference after quantization. Normalized cross correlation between the extracted watermark $w^{\#}$ and embedded watermark w is used as the confidence measure during verification.

The host image I is subjected to four levels of wavelet transform [13]. As mentioned earlier, the wavelet coefficients corresponding to same spatial location form a group. Figure 1 shows three such grouping. So the number of available groups is equal to the total number of coefficients in the wavelet band $C_{4,1}$, $C_{4,2}$, $C_{4,3}$. A group will contain 21 wavelet coefficients as follows: one coefficient from $C_{4,3}$, 4 coefficients from $C_{3,3}$ and 16 coefficients from $C_{2,3}$. Two such groups are combined to form a super tree, thus there will be 42 wavelet coefficients in a super tree. Embedding procedure uses two such super trees (i.e., four groups) to embed a single bit of watermark.

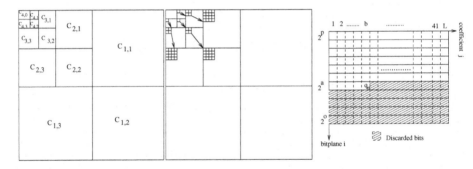

Fig. 1. (i) Four Level Wavelet Transform (left), (ii) Grouping of Wavelet Coefficients (middle), (iii) Bit matrix of a super tree (right)

Quantization of a super tree T_{2k} involves removal of some of the bits from the LSBs of the constituent wavelet coefficients of the super tree. Let us consider that each wavelet coefficient is represented by a $(p+1)$ bit number. Thus we can interpret a super tree as a two dimensional matrix of bits, having $(p+1)$ rows and L columns. Each column (of bits) represents a wavelet coefficient value and is denoted by $x_{2k}(j)$. In the specific case mentioned in Figure 1, $L = 42$, the number of constituent wavelet coefficients in a super tree. First row of the matrix represents the MSBs of all wavelet coefficients in a super tree. Similarly last row represents the LSBs. Each row also known as *bit plane* and bit plane 0 is the LSB. The sign bit is not considered in this discussion. The quantization index q_k is related to w_k, and it is same for both the super trees T_{2k-1}, T_{2k}. Now quantizing the super tree with respect to index $q_{\lceil \frac{2k}{2} \rceil}$, i.e., q_k (q_k gives the count up to the coordinate (a, b) in the bit matrix) means all the bits after the location (a, b) get removed. The process of quantizing a specific wavelet coefficient $x_{2k}(j)$ (i.e., jth column) in the selected super tree is denoted by $Q[x_{2k}(j)]_{q_k}$. The quantization step size is denoted by Δ_{2k} which means, $\Delta_{2k}(j) = 2^a$ if $j \leq b$, otherwise $\Delta_{2k}(j) = 2^{a+1}$.

The quantization index q_k represents the number of bits discarded during quantization. The quantization error is given by $e_{2k}(j) = Q[x_{2k}(j)]_{q_k} - x_{2k}(j)$. The total quantization error $\mathcal{E}_{2k}(q_k)$ of the selected super tree is the sum of absolute differences between wavelet coefficients before and after quantization and is given by $\mathcal{E}_{2k}(q_k) = \sum_{j=1}^{L} |e_{2k}(j)|$. It is apparent that larger the value of q_k larger the value of quantization error. Also the value of q_k directly influences the quality of the watermarked image and it should be less than certain pre-defined maximum q_{max}.

During embedding, two super trees T_{2k-1} and T_{2k} are used to encode a single watermark bit w_k. Smallest quantization index is calculated in such a manner that $\mathcal{E}_{2k-1}(q_k)$ and $\mathcal{E}_{2k}(q_k)$ should be greater than some predefined threshold $\mathcal{E}$, known as *reference error*. Reference error $\mathcal{E}$ provides a trade-off between the watermarking strength and watermarked image quality. Thus, depending on the watermark bit w_k, one of the two super tree is quantized with respect to q_k.

Algorithm 1

1. *Generate a pseudo random sequence w of length m using a secret seed S.*
2. *Compute the wavelet coefficient of the host image I.*
3. *Group the coefficients and arrange them randomly using the same seed S.*
4. *Merge two groups to form a super tree T_k, for $k = 1 \ldots 2m$.*
5. *For $k = 1 \ldots m$ do*
   (a) *$q_k = 1$, $\mathcal{E}_{2k-1}(q_k) = 0$, $\mathcal{E}_{2k}(q_k) = 0$*
   (b) *While $((\mathcal{E}_{2k-1}(q_k) < \mathcal{E}$ or $\mathcal{E}_{2k}(q_k) < \mathcal{E})$ and $(q_k < q_{max}))$*
       i. *Calculate $\mathcal{E}_{2k-1}(q_k)$, $\mathcal{E}_{2k}(q_k)$.*
       ii. *$q_k = q_k + 1$.*
   (c) *If $(w_k == 1)$ quantize T_{2k-1}, otherwise quantize T_{2k}.*
6. *Compute inverse wavelet transform to get watermarked image I^w.*

Extraction algorithm is correlation based, i.e., correlation between the embedded and extracted signals is used as the confidence measure in verification procedure. The (attacked) watermarked image is subjected to wavelet transform and super trees are generated using the same seed S used during embedding. Quantization error is re-calculated for super trees T_{2k-1} and T_{2k}. For this, q_k has to be estimated. We denote this estimated q_k by q'_k. Now the number of coefficients having very little quantization error with respect to q'_k (see algorithm below) in each of the super trees will determine the decoded bit. Let us denote number of coefficients in T_{2k-1} having $|e'_{2k-1}(j)/\Delta'_{2k-1}(j)| < \epsilon$ by N_{2k-1}. Similarly number of coefficient in T_{2k} having $|e'_{2k}(j)/\Delta'_{2k}(j)| < \epsilon$ is denoted by N_{2k}. Here ϵ is a predefined threshold. Now let us describe the watermark extraction algorithm in detail.

Algorithm 2

1. *Generate a pseudo random sequence w having length m using the same secret seed S taken at the time of embedding.*
2. *Wavelet transform the (attacked) watermarked image $I^{\#}$.*
3. *Group the coefficients and arrange them at (pseudo) random using the same seed S.*
4. *Merge two group to form a super tree $\mathcal{T}_k$, $k = 1 \ldots m$.*
5. *For $k = 1 \ldots m$ do*
   (a) $q'_k = 1$, $\mathcal{E}_{2k-1}(q'_k) = 0$, $\mathcal{E}_{2k}(q'_k) = 0$.
   (b) *While* $((\mathcal{E}_{2k-1}(q'_k) < \mathcal{E}$ *and* $\mathcal{E}_{2k}(q'_k) < \mathcal{E})$ *and* $(q'_k < q_{\max}))$
      i. *Calculate* $\mathcal{E}_{2k-1}(q'_k)$, $\mathcal{E}_{2k}(q'_k)$.
      ii. $q'_k = q'_k + 1$.
6. *Calculate N_{2k-1}, N_{2k} and if $N_{2k-1} > N_{2k}$ then $w^{\#}_k = 1$, else $w^{\#}_k = -1$.*
7. *Compute normalized correlation coefficient $\rho = \frac{\sum_{k=1}^{m} w_k w^{\#}_k}{m}$.*
8. *If $(\rho > \rho_T)$ watermark present; otherwise it is absent. Here ρ_T is a predefined threshold.*

In [18], ρ_T has been taken as low as 0.23 for experimental set up. We show that after our attack (presented in the next section) this value comes to be at most 0.04, thus the watermark extraction fails.

3   Cryptanalysis of the WTQ Watermarking Scheme

It is evident from the exhaustive experimentation in [18] that the WTQ watermarking scheme is robust against the signal processing attacks. Authors claimed that the scheme is robust against certain kind of bit removal attack. It is also pointed out that the exact knowledge of constituent groups of a super tree is required to remove the watermark, otherwise the quality of the attacked image gets affected. However, we show that it is possible to identify those groups from which bits are removed during watermark embedding. Thus one can identify the groups that remained unaltered during watermark embedding and quantize those groups also. This is the basic strategy of our cryptanalytic technique. We are also able to calculate the reference error $\mathcal{E}$ quite accurately from the watermarked image. Before presenting the exact attack, let us highlight the following points regarding WTQ watermarking scheme.

(1) It is hard to reconstruct the super trees as existed during watermark embedding without the knowledge of the secret seed S, but we will show that identification of quantized and non-quantized groups are possible.

(2) Extraction of watermark exploits the information that one set of super trees are quantized and another set is not quantized. If one quantizes the non-quantized super trees also, it is clear from the nature of watermark extraction algorithm that the process gets unreliable. However, proper quantization requires proper estimate of reference error $\mathcal{E}$. We will show that estimation of the reference error $\mathcal{E}$ is possible from the set of quantized groups.

(3) The verification stage is correlation based, i.e., correlation between the extracted and embedded bit string is used as the confidence measure. If one removes this correlation without affecting the image quality then the attack becomes successful.

(4) Randomly selected groups are used to construct a super tree. This randomness fails to provide any security as attacker do not require the knowledge of super trees for a successful attack. Knowledge of groups, which is image dependent, but not dependent on secret seed S, is enough for successful removal of correlation.

Let us first present the algorithm to find the nature of a group, i.e., whether a particular group belongs to a quantized super tree or not. To the attacker, only a single watermarked copy of the image is available and he possesses no other information regarding the secret seed used during watermark embedding. Let us denote the group quantization index by $\hat{q}_r$, which is the quantization index applicable to the group G_r. The idea is similar to quantization index of a super tree but here it is applicable to a group. Similarly we define quantization error $\hat{e}_r(j)$ and total quantization error $\hat{\mathcal{E}}_r(\hat{q}_r)$ and are given by

$$\hat{e}_r(j) = Q[x_r(j)]_{\hat{q}_r} - x_r(j), \ \hat{\mathcal{E}}_r(\hat{q}_r) = \sum_{j=1}^{n} |e_r(j)|.$$

Here $x_r(j)$ is a constituent wavelet coefficient of the group G_r and n is the number of wavelet coefficients in a group.

If we consider each group as a two dimensional matrix of bits, like that of a super tree, we actually need to inspect the last row (LSBs of constituent wavelet coefficients) of the bit matrix to get an idea whether the group is already quantized or not. If almost all the bits at the last row are absent, one can conclude that the group is quantized. However, to reduce the chance of false identification, we inspect the last two rows of the bit matrix, i.e., we set $\hat{q} = 2n$. Here n is the number of wavelet coefficients in a group, i.e., number of bits in a row as explained in Figure 1(iii) for a super tree. Let us denote the set of groups containing quantized and non-quantized groups by S_1 and S_2 respectively. The proposed algorithm to distinguish between the quantized and non-quantized groups are as follows.

Algorithm 3

1. *Compute the wavelet coefficients from the watermarked image I^w.*
2. *Generate the group information. Let us denote the groups by G_r, $r = 1 \ldots \beta$, where β is the total number of available groups.*
3. *For $r = 1 \ldots \beta$ do*
   (a) Quantize G_r with respect to quantization index $\hat{q}$.
   (b) Calculate quantization error $\hat{\mathcal{E}}_r(\hat{q})$ of the group G_r.
   (c) If $(\hat{\mathcal{E}}_r(\hat{q}) \leq \tau)$ group G_r belongs to a quantized super tree, i.e., $G_r \in S_1$. How to fix the value of τ will be discussed in Section 4.
   (d) Otherwise the group G_r comes from a non-quantized super tree, i.e., $G_r \in S_2$.

Our strategy of cryptanalysis mainly depends on quantization of non quantized groups. Thus during attack, we like to find out all the groups which are non quantized and quantize them. One strategy could be to quantize all the groups, irrespective of whether they are quantized or not. That will work perfectly for removal of the watermark signal. However, on the other hand, we need that the attacked image should have good image quality. This requires the knowledge regarding the amount of quantization that has been incorporated during watermark embedding. Thus, we like to over estimate the set S_2, such that it should contain all the non quantized groups. In the process S_2 may contain some quantized groups also. That means S_1 should not contain many non quantized group (it is underestimated and miss some quantized groups in the process). The quantization error is estimated by studying the number of bit planes removed most frequently. So even if S_1 is underestimated, the estimation of quantization error (see Algorithm 4) will not suffer if S_1 contains a sizeable amount of quantized groups. See Table 1 for the estimation of S_1 and Table 2 for the success of our strategy in the estimation.

Extraction of watermark depends on the premise that the wavelet coefficients belonging to a quantized super tree will have little quantization error upon re-quantization and those belonging to non-quantized super tree will have large quantization error. Thus quantizing the non-quantized groups leads to a situation where all wavelet coefficients belonging to any two different super trees will have similar quantization error making it difficult to decide the watermark bit. Thus if the value of reference error is known to the attacker, he can quantize the non-quantized groups which will render the watermark extraction algorithm ineffective. A super-tree consists of two wavelet groups which are operated on a similar way, thus reference error $\mathcal{E}^G$ for a group should be half of $\mathcal{E}$. As the value of reference error is not known to the attacker, he needs very good estimation of that for a successful removal attack.

Let us now discuss how bit plane removal affects individual wavelet coefficients. A wavelet coefficient $x(j)$ can be written as $x(j) = a_1 2^0 + a_2 2^1 + \ldots + a_{p+1} 2^p$, where a_i is the bit at bit plane (a row) $i-1$. Now if one removes the LSB, i.e. bit at bit plane 0, it will reduce the value of $x(j)$ by 1 if $a_1 = 1$. Similarly if one removes the bit at bit plane i the value of $x(j)$ will be reduced by 2^i, if $a_{i+1} = 1$. Now if one considers that the numbers of 0's and 1's are almost equal at some bit plane i, then the sum of reduction due to removal of bit plane i is given by $\frac{L}{2} 2^i$. We have experimented exhaustively and found this assertion true for $i < 5$. Thus if one removes α many bit planes, total reduction in values of wavelet coefficients is given by $\delta = \frac{L}{2}(2^0 + 2^1 + \ldots + 2^\alpha)$. The amount of reduction

Table 1. Quantized Group Identification

Image	# IQG	# CIG
Lena	843	756
Goldhill	958	904
Peppers	875	802

Table 2. Reference Error Estimation

Image	Actual $\mathcal{E}$	Estimated $\mathcal{E}_{est}$
Lena	100	105
Goldhill	100	105
Peppers	100	105

δ is termed as the reference error $\mathcal{E}$ in the watermark embedding and extraction algorithm. Thus the knowledge of α provides the knowledge of reference error $\mathcal{E}$. In fact, one can determine the value of α (and hence δ) for each group and take the average of those δ's as a reference error $\mathcal{E}^G$. Alternatively one can choose a few most prevalent values of α and corresponding values of δ. Then take the average of those δ's as reference error $\mathcal{E}^G$, which we use here. Reference error estimation algorithm is as follows.

Algorithm 4

1. *Let the number of element in S_1 be s.*
2. *Let us use an array of integers $P[1 \ldots s]$.*
3. *For $r = 1 \ldots s$ do*
   (a) *Consider the bit matrix corresponding to group $G_r \in S_1$.*
   (b) *For bit plane $i = 0 \ldots \max$*
       − *Let the number of ones and zeros at bit plane i be b_i^1 and b_i^0 respectively.*
       − *If ($b_i^1 \approx b_i^0$), i.e., the bit plane is not removed, go to Step 3.*
       − *$P[r] = i$.*
4. *Let us denote the distinct numbers with highest and second highest frequency in $P[1 \ldots s]$ by α_1, α_2 respectively.*
5. *$\mathcal{E}_1 = \frac{n}{2}(2^0 + 2^1 + \ldots + 2^{\alpha_1})$, $\mathcal{E}_2 = \frac{n}{2}(2^0 + 2^1 + \ldots + 2^{\alpha_2})$, where n is the number of wavelet coefficients in a group.*
6. *Estimated reference error of a group $\mathcal{E}_{est}^G = \frac{\mathcal{E}_1 + \mathcal{E}_2}{2}$.*

After the estimation of the reference error $\mathcal{E}_{est}^G$ (see Table 2 for experimental results regarding estimation of reference error) applicable to each group, we will quantized each non-quantized group (in S_2) in such a manner that quantization error is always greater than or equal to $\mathcal{E}_{est}^G$. Actual algorithm for quantization is presented in Algorithm 5 as follows.

Algorithm 5

1. *Read the watermarked image I^w and perform forward wavelet transform up to four level to get I_T^w.*
2. *Generate List of quantized and non-quantized groups from I_T^w using Algorithm 3.*
3. *Compute (estimated) reference error $\mathcal{E}_{est}^G$ applicable to a group using Algorithm 4.*
4. *Quantize the non-quantized groups such that quantization error $\mathcal{E}^G \geq \mathcal{E}_{est}^G$.*
5. *Compute inverse wavelet transform to get the attacked image $I^\#$.*

Now consider the following scenario. One needs to extract the watermark from the attacked image $I^\#$. From the seed one could generate the super trees $\mathcal{T}_{2k-1}$ and $\mathcal{T}_{2k}$ but instead of one super-tree both of them are now quantized. Thus the number of coefficients having quantization error less than ϵ in the super-tree $\mathcal{T}_{2k-1}$, $\mathcal{T}_{2k}$ will be almost equal, which makes it difficult to determine the watermark bit and the recovered string $w^\#$ will be a random binary string having almost no correlation with the watermarking signal w. The claim is further supported by the experimental result presented in Table 3.

Table 3. Results presenting the success of Cryptanalysis

Image	Length of Watermark	Value of $\mathcal{E}$	Correlation	PSNR(w,a)
Lena	512	100	0.02	42.75 dB
GoldHill	512	100	-0.01	39.31 dB
Peppers	512	100	0.04	41.23 dB

4   Experimental Results

Now we present the experimental results in support of our claim. To have proper comparison, we use the same set up as given in [18]. Host images having size 512×512 are watermarked using WTQ watermarking scheme and the length of watermark m is taken to be 512. The host image is subjected to four levels of wavelet transform. The value of reference error $\mathcal{E}$ is 100 and that of largest quantization index q_{max} is 336. Correlation threshold ρ_T is set at 0.23. As mentioned earlier that the number of groups quantized is twice the length of watermark, i.e., number of quantized groups will be $2m = 1024$, out of available 3072. Also there are 1024 more non quantized groups which are used in the algorithm. The rest of the groups are non quantized and not considered during watermark embedding.

We run Algorithm 3 to generate the list of quantized and non-quantized groups. As mentioned in the Algorithm 3, we inspect last two bits of each wavelet coefficient, i.e., bit planes 0 and 1, to decide the nature of the group. If two bit planes are removed then the total reduction of values in a group will be $\delta = \frac{21}{2}(2^0 + 2^1) = 31.50$ under the assumption that the number of ones and zeroes in a bit plane are almost equal. Now the value of τ in step 3c of Algorithm 3 is set at 15% of δ. Our aim is to fix the value of τ in such manner that the set S_1 contain only quantized groups and very few non quantized groups (underestimated), which will ensure proper estimation of reference error $\mathcal{E}_{est}^G$. Also setting the value of τ very low will include some of the quantized groups in S_2, the set of non-quantized groups. Inclusion of some of the quantized groups in set S_2 will not degrade the image quality at a non acceptable level as re-quantizing an already quantized group with similar value of reference error will lead to very few bit removal, if any. Results for estimation of S_1 are presented in Table 1 below (in this table, #IQG denotes "number of Identified Quantized Groups" and #CIG denotes "number of Correctly Identified Groups").

There are 1024 many quantized groups. It is evident from Table 1 that the Algorithm 3 works well to identify the quantized groups against the non quantized groups. Successful identification of quantized groups will help us to estimate the reference error $\mathcal{E}^G$. Next we present simulation results regarding estimation of reference error in Table 2. The estimated reference error $\mathcal{E}_{est} = 2\mathcal{E}_{est}^G$.

It is evident from Table 2 that the estimated value of reference error $\mathcal{E}_{est}$ is very close to actual value, in fact estimation error is always less than 10%. The reason it is same for all the three of the above mentioned images is that the values of α_1, α_2 are always found to be 2, 1 respectively. Thus the values of $\mathcal{E}_1$,

$\mathcal{E}_2$ in Algorithm 4 comes out be 73.5, 31.5 respectively, which leads to the value of $\mathcal{E}^G_{est} = 52.5$.

We use the value of $\mathcal{E}^G_{est}$ in the Algorithm 5 to generate the attacked image $I^\#$. In Table 3, we present the values of correlation coefficient ρ for different images and the value is always less than the threshold $\rho_T = 0.23$ mentioned in [18]. In fact, it is almost close to zero.

In Table 3, we also present PSNR values of attacked image with respect to watermarked image. Note that the attacked image is of high visual quality as evident from the PSNR values. Here PSNR(w,a) indicates PSNR value of the attacked image with respect to the watermarked image.

In [18, page 163] the authors also consider bit removal attack. They have presented the experimental result that when fewer number of bit planes are removed, then the correlation does not fall below the threshold 0.23. On the other hand they claimed that the correlation becomes less than the threshold only when more number of bit planes are removed, resulting in poor quality of the attacked image. However, our strategy shows that the correlation can be made very close to 0 with removal of only 3 bit planes after proper estimation. This also keeps the quality of the attacked image very well as evident form the PSNR values.

5 Conclusion

In this paper we cryptanalyse the WTQ watermarking scheme with just one copy of watermarked image. The key to the attack is identification of non-quantized wavelet coefficients in the watermarked image and to quantize them for removal of the watermarking signal. Our method raises serious question on practical use of the WTQ watermarking scheme. It would be of interest to see whether the scheme can be modified so that the attack presented here can be resisted.

References

1. R. J. Anderson and F. A. P. Petitcolas. On The Limits of Steganography. *IEEE Journal of Selected Areas in Communications. Special Issue on Copyright and Privacy Protection*, 16(4):474-481, May 1998.
2. J. Boeuf and J. P. Stern. An Analysis of One of the SDMI Candidates. *Information Hiding 2001*, pages 395-410, vol 2137 of Lecture Notes in Computer Science. Springer-Verlag, 2001.
3. T. K. Das and S. Maitra. Cryptanalysis of Optimal Differential Energy Watermarking (DEW) and a Modified Robust Scheme. In *Indocrypt 2002*, volume 2551 in Lecture Notes in Computer Science, pages 135-148, Springer-Verlag, December 2002. A revised version is to be published in IEEE Transactions on Signal Processing, February, 2005.
4. T. K. Das and S. Maitra. Cryptanalysis of Correlation Based Watermarking Schemes using Single Watermarked Copy. *IEEE Signal Processing Letters*, pages 446-449, 11(4), April 2004.

5. F. Ergun, J. Kilian and R. Kumar. A note on the limits of collusion-resistant watermarks. In *Eurocrypt 1999*, volume 1592 in LNCS, pages 140–149, Springer Verlag, 1999.

6. R. C. Gonzalez and P. Wintz. *Digital Image Processing*. Addison-Wesley Publishing (MA, USA), 1988.

7. T. Kalker, J. P. M. G. Linnartz and M. v. Dijk. Watermark Estimation through Detector Analysis. In *International Conference on Image Processing*, 1998.

8. S. Katzenbeisser, F. A. P. Petitcolas (edited). Information Hiding Techniques for Steganography and Digital Watermarking. Artech House, USA, 2000.

9. A. Kerckhoffs. La Cryptographie Militaire. *Journal des Sciences Militaires*, 9th series, IX(Jan 1883):pages 5-38, FEB(1883):pages 161-191.

10. D. Kirovski and H. S. Malvar. Embedding and Detecting Spread-Spectrum Watermarks under the Estimation Attack. In *IEEE International Conference on Acoustics, Speech, and Signal Processing*, 2002.

11. D. Kirovski and F. A. P. Petitcolas. Replacement Attack on Arbitrary Watermarking Systems. In *ACM Workshop on Digital Rights Management*, 2002.

12. G. C. Langelaar and R. L. Lagendijk. Optimal Differential Energy Watermarking of DCT Encoded Images and Video. *IEEE Transactions on Image Processing*, 10(1):148–158, 2001.

13. S. G. Mallet. A theory of multi resolution signal decomposition : the Wavelet representation. *IEEE Transactions on PAMI*, 11:674–693, 1989.

14. M. K. Mihcak, R. Venkatesan, M. Kesal. Cryptanalysis of Discrete-Sequence Spread Spectrum Watermarks. In *Workshop on Information Hiding 2002*, Lecture Notes in Computer Science, volume 2578, pages 226–246, Springer-Verlag, 2003.

15. F. A. P. Petitcolas, R. J. Anderson, M. G. Kuhn and D. Aucsmith. Attacks on Copyright Marking Systems. In *2nd Workshop on Information Hiding*, pages 218–238 in volume 1525 of Lecture Notes in Computer Science. Springer Verlag, 1998.

16. F. A. P. Petitcolas and R. J. Anderson. Evaluation of Copyright Marking Systems. In *IEEE Multimedia Systems*, Florence, Italy, June 1999.

17. J. O. Ruanaidh, H. Petersen, A. Herrigel, S. Pereira and T. Pun. Cryptographic copyright protection for digital images based on watermarking techniques. *Theoretical Computer Science* 226:117–142, 1999.

18. S.-H. Wang and Y.-P. Lin. Wavelet Tree Quantization for Copyright Protection Watermarking. *IEEE Transactions on Image Processing*, 13(2):154–165, Feb 2004.

19. http://www.hacksdmi.org

A Multisignature Scheme for Implementing Safe Delivery Rule in Group Communication Systems

S. Rahul and R.C. Hansdah

Dept. of Computer Science & Automation, Indian Institute of Science,
Bangalore 560012, India
{srahul, hansdah}@csa.iisc.ernet.in

Abstract. The safe delivery rule guarantees that any message delivered to the application by the group communication system has been received and acknowledged by all group members. In this paper, we present a new multisignature scheme which can be used in client-server model of group communication systems to deal with certain problems that arise while implementing safe delivery rule in such systems. If security is incorporated into safe delivery rule by encrypting the acknowledgement messages from each group member using group-key (to ensure message integrity) or by requiring each member to digitally sign these messages (to prevent malicious members from disrupting the system), the sender of a message which receives these messages would have to decrypt or verify all these messages. The proposed multisignature scheme enables the group communication server to combine acknowledgements of a message from all group members into a single group-acknowledgement message of constant size and send it to the sender of the message. This single acknowledgement can be verified by any member in constant time and thereby avoids the problem of having to perform $n - 1$[1] cryptographic operations.

Keywords: Distributed systems; Secure group communication; Ack implosion; Safe delivery rule; Multisignature.

1   Introduction

There are two important models for implementing group communication systems. One is the peer-to-peer model [1, 2, 3] in which a library linked to the application implements the two main services of a group communication system - the multicast service and the group membership service.

The other model for group communication is the client-server model[4, 5]. In this model, the application is linked to a library which, together with a set of group communication servers(GCSs), provides the multicast and the group membership service to the application. Every group member is connected to the GCS nearest to it. In order to send a message to the group, a member has to

---

[1] n is the size of the group.

A. Sen et al. (Eds.): IWDC 2004, LNCS 3326, pp. 231–239, 2004.
© Springer-Verlag Berlin Heidelberg 2004

unicast the message to the GCS to which it is connected. The GCS will then relay the message to the other GCSs. Every GCS will then forward the message to all the group members connected to it. This model for group communication is highly scalable. When a member sends a message, it only needs to wait for a single acknowledgement from the GCS to which it is connected. The GCS will send the acknowledgement(ack) only after it *knows* that all other group members have acknowledged the receipt of the message. Thus, the sender of a message does not have to deal with an *ack implosion*. The ack implosion is handled by the GCSs. The GCSs can handle it more efficiently because every GCS receives acknowledgements from a subset of the group members.

In the client-server model for group communication, since the group members are separate from the servers, there is a scope for a *third party* to provide group communication services to a group. While designing security in such a system, it becomes necessary to consider the possibility of the GCSs intentionally disrupting the synchrony within a group.

Most groups follow the safe delivery rule for group communication. According to this rule, only those messages which are stable in the current group view are delivered at any member in the current group view. Implementation of the safe delivery rule requires the following three rounds of communication.

1. Application message from sender to group members.
2. Acknowledgement messages from group members to sender.
3. Safe indicator message from sender to group members.

The integrity of all these message can be verified by using message authentication codes(MACs) keyed by a secret key shared only by the group members. A member accepts a received message only if it has not been tampered with. If the system model has to take into account the presence of malicious members also in the group, then every message must be accompanied by a digital signature on it by its sender so that the receiving member can verify the identity of the sender. Digitally signed messages are used in Rampart [6] to manage group communication in the presence of corrupt group members.

The safe delivery rule allows only those messages to be delivered which are stable in the group. Therefore, every group member must verify the stability of a message before delivering it. The stability of a message m can be verified after verifying the n acknowledgements for m. In Rampart [6], a message is delivered after verifying only $\frac{2n+1}{3}$ acknowledgements. The necessity to verify the authenticity of n acknowledgements and the $O(n)$ size of safe indicator messages makes this scheme unscalable if MACs are used and, more so, if digital signatures are used.

In order to cope with this problem, there is a requirement for a multisignature scheme which can combine n signatures over a message into a single *multisignature* which can be verified in constant time. The *(n,n) Threshold signature scheme* proposed in [7] and the multisignature schemes proposed in [8, 9] are not efficient solutions to this problem as explained in the next section. The *(t,n) Threshold signature scheme* proposed in [7] cannot be used in group communication systems supporting dynamic group membership. The multisignature scheme for broadcast architecture proposed in [10] is also not suitable for group communication because the scheme requires a trusted third party to generate the public and private keys of all group members. The sequential signature aggregation schemes [11] are also not useful because of the long delay incurred in signature aggregation. In this paper, we propose a new multisignature scheme which can be used in group communication systems for generating secure group acknowledgements of a message efficiently.

The rest of the paper is organized as follows. Section 2 gives a brief explanation of why most of the existing multisignature schemes are not suitable for combining acknowledgements of group members. In section 3, we present our multisignature scheme, and describe how it can be used to implement safe delivery rule for GCSs. In section 4, we discuss the security aspects of the scheme. Section 5 describes how the scheme is adaptable for use in GCSs supporting dynamic membership. Section 6 concludes the paper.

2   Related Work

The generation of group acknowledgements can be done using the *(n,n) Threshold signature scheme* proposed in [7]. This scheme uses a modified version of the ElGamal signature scheme [12] to produce a group signature on a message. The size and verification time of this signature is constant and is independent of the size of the group. Such signatures can be used as safe indicators for messages as follows.

1. A member sends a message m to the GCS which sends it to every member in the group.
2. Each member generates his partial signature on m and sends it to the GCS.
3. The GCS verifies each of the partial signatures, combines them into a single group signature and sends it to the sender of m.
4. The sender of m signs and sends this group signature as the safe indicator message for m to the GCS which sends it to every member in the group.
5. Every member verifies the group signature before delivering m.

The problem with using the *(n,n) Threshold signature scheme* in the above algorithm is that the generation of group signature in step 2 requires three rounds of communication between the GCS and the group members.

Round 1. Each members M_i selects a random integer r_i and sends $g^{r_i} \bmod p$ [2] to the GCS.
Round 2. GCS computes $r = \prod g^{r_i} \bmod p$ and sends it to the members.
Round 3. Each member computes the partial signature s_i over m and sends it to the GCS.

The GCS then combines all the s_i's into a multisignature and sends it to the sender of m. Because of three rounds of communication, it is not possible for each

---

[2] p is a prime number and $g(1 \leq g < p)$ is a generator of Z_p^*.

GCS to independently compute a *partial* multisignature. Ideally, we would like to have a scheme in which step 2 is completed in single round of communication. Hence, the above scheme is inefficient to be used in *GCS*s. The multisignature scheme proposed in [13] also requires three rounds of communication between the GCS and the group members. The *(t,n) Threshold signature scheme* presented in [7] can generate a multisignature in a single round. But this scheme has the drawback that whenever the group changes, the trusted key authentication center(KAC) will have to generate new keys and distribute them to the group members. This is necessary to ensure that past members cannot sign messages sent in the current view.

There are other multisignature schemes and signature aggregation schemes proposed in literature. The sequential signature aggregation schemes [11] are not useful for group communication because they require $O(n)$ causally ordered messages to be passed for generation of aggregate signatures. What is required for secure group communication systems is a signature scheme which works as follows.

1. As soon as a group member receives a message m, he signs it using his private key and sends the signature to the GCS.
2. The GCS then combines these signatures into a multisignature *without any more rounds of communication* with the group members and sends the multisignature to the sender of m.
3. The sender of m must be able to verify the authenticity of the multisignature in the same time as required for verifying an ordinary digital signature.

The only multisignature scheme which has all of the above features uses elliptic curve cryptography and is presented in [14]. This scheme makes use of the elliptic curve digital signature scheme presented in [15] which makes use of elliptic curves on which the decision DH[3] problem is easily solvable, but the computational DH problem is hard.

The multisignature scheme proposed in this paper can be used by the GCSs to *combine* all the acknowledgements for a group message efficiently and return this combined acknowledgement to the sender of the message. The sender can then verify that *every* member in the current group view has acknowledged the message. Our signature scheme does not make use of elliptic curves. The generation of the combined acknowledgement is achieved using a single round of communication as compared to the three rounds of communication required for the *(n,n) Threshold signature scheme.* Since a single round of message passing is used, the generation of authentic group acknowledgements introduces neither any communication delay nor any increase in the number of messages as compared to the normal safe delivery algorithm. Also, the time taken to verify the group signature is the same as the time taken to verify a single digital signature.

3   The Algorithm

The following are the variables used in the algorithm.

---

[3] Diffie-Hellman.

1. pq : It is a product of two primes and is public. The factorization of pq is not known to anybody.
2. α_i : The private key of party M_i.
3. g : $g < pq$ and has a large order. It is public.
4. $x_i \equiv g^{\alpha_i} \bmod pq$: The public key of party M_i.

3.1 Generation of Partial Signatures

The partial signature of member M_i on a message m is generated as follows.

1. M_i selects a random number r_i.
2. $s_i = \alpha_i + H(m)r_i$ where H is a hash function.
3. $t_i = g^{r_i} \bmod pq$
4. (s_i, t_i) is the partial signature of M_i over m.

The member M_i sends (s_i, t_i) to the GCS. The GCS verifies the partial signature by checking that the following holds.

$$g^{s_i} \equiv x_i t_i^{H(m)} \bmod pq$$

3.2 Aggregation of Partial Signatures

The following are the variables known to the GCS.

1. $x \equiv \prod_{i=1}^{n} x_i \bmod pq$: The public key of the group $M_1, M_2, \ldots, M_n$.
2. (s_i, t_i) : The signature of party M_i over m.

The GCS combines the partial signatures from the group members into a multisignature (s, t) as follows.

1. $s = \sum_{j=1}^{n} s_i$
2. $t = \prod_{i=1}^{n} t_i \bmod pq$

The GCS then sends (s, t) to the sender of m. The authenticity of the group multisignature (s, t) over m is verified by checking that the following holds.

$$g^s \equiv xt^{H(m)} \bmod pq$$

The correctness of the signature verification step is proved as follows.

$$g^s \equiv g^{\sum_{i=1}^{n} s_i} \bmod pq$$
$$\equiv \prod_{i=1}^{n} g^{s_i} \bmod pq$$
$$\equiv \prod_{i=1}^{n} g^{\alpha_i + H(m)r_i} \bmod pq$$
$$\equiv \prod_{i=1}^{n} x_i t_i^{H(m)} \bmod pq$$
$$\equiv xt^{H(m)} \bmod pq$$

3.3   Implementation of Safe Delivery Rule

The three rounds of message passing carried out for implementing the safe delivery rule for a message msg are given below. These messages assume a client-server model of group communication system. In the following, GCS denotes the group communication server(s). The actual message m that is sent contains a few fields in addition to the message msg, and only one of these fields is shown below for explanation purposes.

- $type[m] = \begin{cases} gm & \text{if } msg \text{ is a group message} \\ safe & \text{if } msg \text{ is a safe indicator message} \end{cases}$
- $text[m]$: The text of the message being broadcast.

1. Round 1: Sending of group message
   (a) M_i : $type[m] \leftarrow gm$; $text[m] \leftarrow msg$
   (b) M_i computes signature (s_i, t_i) over m.
   (c) $M_i \longrightarrow GCS$: $\{m, (s_i, t_i)\}$
   (d) $GCS \longrightarrow M_j (M_j \in G \wedge i \neq j)$: $\{m, (s_i, t_i)\}$
   (e) M_j checks that the sender of m is a group member, $type[m] = gm$ and verifies the signature (s_i, t_i) over m.
2. Round 2: Generation and verification of acknowledgement
   (a) M_j computes signature (s_j, t_j) over m.
   (b) $M_j \longrightarrow GCS$: (s_j, t_j)
   (c) GCS combines the partial signatures $\{(s_k, t_k) \mid (M_k \in G)\}$ into a multisignature (s, t).
   (d) $GCS \longrightarrow M_i$: (s, t)
   (e) M_i verifies the multisignature (s, t) over m.
3. Round 3: Sending of safe indicator for msg.
   (a) M_i : $type[m'] \leftarrow safe$; $text[m'] \leftarrow msg$
   (b) M_i : $sign \leftarrow$ signature of M_i over m'
   (c) $M_i \longrightarrow GCS$: $\{sign, (s, t)\}$
   (d) $GCS \longrightarrow M_j$: $\{sign, (s, t)\}$ $(\forall M_j \in G \wedge i \neq j)$
   (e) M_j creates m' and verifies that $sign$ is a valid signature of M_i over m' and (s, t) is a valid multisignature of the group over m before delivering $text[m]$.

4   Security of the Algorithm

The algorithm's security hinges on the fact that the factorization of pq is not known to *anybody*. The values for p, q and g must be selected by a third party who can be trusted not to reveal the values of p and q to anybody. The algorithm therefore has a weakness which is not present in the signature scheme of [14]. Unlike the (t,n) multisignature scheme given in [7], our scheme does not require a trusted third party to be online during group communication.

The algorithm assumes that every member knows the value of the public key x_i of every other group member. In practice, these keys must be certified as belonging to its owner by a certifying authority. So, every member will have

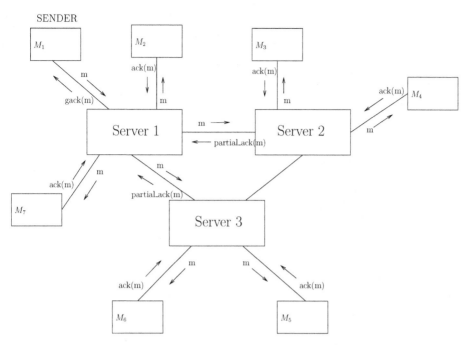

Fig. 1. GCS Servers Returning Group Acknowledgement to the Sender of a Message

to verify the other members' identity before computing the value of the group public key x.

In order that s_i does not reveal information about α_i, α_i should be a prime or a product of large primes and the size of α_i must be less than the size of $H(m)r$. The values of the primes p and q are chosen to be of the form $2r + 1$ and $2s + 1$ respectively, where r and s are primes. This is done to ensure that neither $p - 1$ nor $q - 1$ is b-smooth for a small number. This ensures that pq cannot be factored in polynomial time using any of the known algorithms. The one-way function $H(m)$ used in the algorithm must be preimage resistant and collision resistant. Popular hash algorithms like SHA-1 and MD5 may be used.

In this signature scheme, the operations are performed modulo pq instead of modulo a prime n. This is because, if the operations were performed modulo a prime n, an attacker could find $H(m)^{-1} \bmod \phi(n)$ for any m, and the following would be a valid group signature over m for any s.

$$\left(s, g^{sH(m)^{-1} \bmod \phi(n)} \left(x^{-1} \bmod n \right)^{H(m)^{-1} \bmod \phi(n)} \bmod n \right)$$

The validity of this signature can be proved as follows.

$$xt^{H(m)} \equiv x \left(g^{sH(m)^{-1} \bmod \phi(n)} \right)^{H(m)} \left(\left(x^{-1} \bmod n \right)^{H(m)^{-1} \bmod \phi(n)} \right)^{H(m)} \bmod n$$

$$\equiv xg^s \left(x^{-1} \bmod n \right) \bmod n$$

$$\equiv xg^s x^{-1} \bmod n$$
$$\equiv g^s \bmod n$$

5   Communication in Dynamic Groups

The algorithm presented in section 3 can be easily integrated into group communication systems supporting dynamic membership. On a group change, after all group members have installed the new *view*, the new value of x can be computed as follows.

$L \leftarrow \{M \mid M \in G \wedge M \text{ is leaving the group}\}$
$J \leftarrow \{M \mid M \notin G \wedge M \text{ is joining the group}\}$
for all $M_i \in L$, x_i being the public key of M_i **do**
    $x \leftarrow xx_i^{-1} \bmod pq$
end for
for all $M_i \in J$, x_i being the public key of M_i **do**
    $x \leftarrow xx_i \bmod pq$
end for

The overhead incurred by the group members during group change is due to $(|L| + |J|)$ multiplications and computation of $|L|$ inverses which is not much since $|L|$ and $|J|$ are usually small.

6   Conclusion

In this paper, we have presented a digital multisignature scheme which can be used for carrying out authenticated group communication while making use of the power of client-server model of group communication system. The scheme can be used for carrying out group communication even in the presence of malicious group members. It enables a group of members who want to communicate with each other to make use of the services of group communication servers managed by an untrusted third party. We have identified the necessity of signed acknowledgements in secure group communication systems supporting the safe delivery rule. The naive solution to this problem requires each group member to perform a lot of computation before delivering a message and also requires $O(n)$ sized safe indicator messages. Using the proposed scheme, the group communication servers can combine the signed acknowledgements for a message into a single group acknowledgement after receiving acknowledgements from group members *without any further rounds of communication* with them. This signed group acknowledgement can be verified by any group member by performing only two modular exponentiation operations.

References

1. Birman, K.P.: Isis: A system for fault-tolerant distributed computing. Technical Report TR86-744, Cornell University, Department of Computer Science (1986)

2. Renesse, R.V., Birman, K.P., Glade, B.B., Guo, K., Hayden, M., Hickey, T., Malki, D., Vaysburd, A., Vogels, W.: Horus: A flexible group communications system. Technical Report TR95-1500, Cornell University (1995)
3. Moser, L.E., Melliar-Smith, P.M., Agarwal, D.A., Budhia, R.K., Lingley-Papadopoulos, C.A.: Totem: A fault-tolerant multicast group communication system. Communications of the ACM **39** (1996) 54–63
4. Amir, Y., Dolev, D., Kramer, S., Malki, D.: Transis: A communication subsystem for high availability. In: FTCS-22: 22nd International Symposium on Fault Tolerant Computing, Boston, Massachusetts, IEEE Computer Society Press (1992) 76–84
5. Amir, Y., Stanton, J.: The spread wide area group communication system. Technical report, CNDS (1998)
6. Reiter, M.K.: Secure agreement protocols:reliable and atomic group multicast in rampart. In: Proceedings of the 2nd ACM Conference on Computer and communications security, New York, NY, USA, ACM Press (1994) 68 – 80
7. Harn, L.: Group-oriented (t, n) threshold digital signature scheme and digital multisignature. IEE Proceedings - Computers and Digital Techniques **141** (1994) 307–313
8. Chang, Y.S., Wu, T.C., Huang, S.C.: Elgamal-like digital signature and multisignature schemes using self-certified public keys. Journal of Systems and Software **50** (2000) 99 – 105
9. Wu, T.S., Hsu, C.L.: Threshold signature scheme using self-certified public keys. Journal of Systems and Software **67** (2003) 89 – 97
10. Huang, H.F., Chang, C.C.: Multisignatures with distinguished signing authorities for sequential and broadcasting architectures. Computer Standards and Interfaces (2004) (in press).
11. Boneh, D., Gentry, C., Lynn, B., Shacham, H.: A survey of two signature aggregation techniques. CryptoBytes Technical Newsletter **6** (2003)
12. ElGamal, T.: A public key cryptosystem and a signature scheme based on discrete logarithms. In: Proceedinds of Crypto '84, LNCS 196. (1984) 10–18
13. Micali, S., Ohta, K., Reyzin, L.: Accountable-subgroup multisignatures. In: Proceedings of CCS 2001. (2001) 245–54
14. Boldyreva, A.: Efficient threshold signature, multisignature and blind signature schemes based on the gap-diffie-hellman-group signature scheme. In: Proceedings of PKC 2003. (2003)
15. Boneh, D., Shacham, H., Lynn, B.: Short signatures from the weil pairing. In: Proceedings of Asiacrypt '01. (2001)

Agent-Based Distributed Intrusion Alert System

Arjita Ghosh and Sandip Sen

University of Tulsa, Tulsa OK 74104, USA
{arjita-ghosh, sandip}@utulsa.edu

Abstract. Intrusion detection for computer systems is a key problem in today's networked society. Current distributed intrusion detection systems (IDSs) are not fully distributed as most of them centrally analyze data collected from distributed nodes resulting in a single point of failure. Increasingly, researchers are focusing on distributed IDSs to circumvent the problems of centralized approaches. A major concern of fully distributed IDSs is the high false positive rates of intrusion alarms which undermine the usability of such systems. We believe that effective distributed IDSs can be designed based on principles of coordinated multi-agent systems. We propose an Agent-Based Distributed Intrusion Alert System (ABDIAS) which is fully distributed and provides two capabilities in addition to other functionalities of an IDS: (a) early warning when pre-attack activities are detected, (b) detecting and isolating compromised nodes by trust mechanisms and voting-based peer-level protocols.

1   Introduction

Work on securing networks and hosts from malicious attackers have concentrated on two areas: i) Intrusion prevention mechanisms that include cryptographic techniques to safeguard sensitive information from unauthorized access and manipulation, ii) Intrusion detection mechanisms that recognize an ongoing attack and respond appropriately to thwart such intrusive, disruptive behaviors. Over the last decade, research in the latter of this two approaches has been leaning towards a distributed framework to circumvent the demerits of centralized intrusion detection systems(IDS), e.g. [9]. But currently available distributed intrusion detection system (DIDS) are not fully distributed in design: they collect data from distributed nodes but analyze them centrally. In this framework the first problem is the transfer of raw data which can lead to security breaches. The second drawback is that an intruder can take control over the whole network in a if it can compromise the central server. Hence, it is preferable to have distributed IDS. However, several problems with current distributed IDSs, e.g., the high rate of false positive rates, insufficient protection against compromised nodes, etc. prevent them from being deployed.

We are interested in enhancing the mechanism of distributed intrusion detection with a layer of active, vigilant, monitoring defense mechanism. This layer will detect precursive activities to actual attacks with the help of a large number of distributed, loosely-coupled, computational units. We believe the requirements

A. Sen et al. (Eds.): IWDC 2004, LNCS 3326, pp. 240–251, 2004.
© Springer-Verlag Berlin Heidelberg 2004

of this layer can be effectively met by a distributed computational framework. In this paper, we discuss our proactive agent-based early warning system that uses coordinated surveillance by incorporating inter-agent communication and distributed computing in decision making to identify early signs of attack and recognize situations that are likely to predate an actual attack (e.g., systematic scanning activity) and alert the system administrator. Our ABDIAS system has two primary goals:

Early, Distributed Threat Detection: We want our system to be an early warning system that, in addition to its ability to respond to ongoing attacks, should be able to alert the system administrator to signs of pre-attack activities. By local monitoring and sharing individual belief-estimates, agents can recognize and preempt security threats and pre-attack activities, thus responding to attacks before the system is endangered.

Effectively Handle Compromised Nodes: To address a key problem in current distributed IDSs, we want our system to be capable of detecting and isolating compromised nodes. We tackle this problem by incorporating trust mechanism including the application of majority voting among agents in neighborhood.

To effectively model the inherent domain and environmental uncertainty that must be handled by IDSs, our agents represent their knowledge about the possible attack scenarios in the form of Bayesian networks[5]. This knowledge is derived offline from analysis of repositories of network attack related data. Our research emphasis is to distribute this knowledge such that each agent is required to monitor relatively few aspects of the local network neighborhood but, together, the system is still able to reliably detect security threats through timely coordination with agents. To enable such distributed inference, we use multiply-sectioned Bayesian Networks [19] for representing domain knowledge and clique-tree propagation algorithm [7] for reasoning. To reduce network congestion, we group agents into localities and then design the intrusion detection protocol to limit the significant majority of communications within localities.

The organization of this paper is as follows: Section 2 describes the background of this work, Section 3 outlines the distributed agent-based IDS, Section 4 depicts the distributed intrusion detection mechanism, Section 5 presents the trust model among peer nodes, Section 6 shows the experimental framework and result, and section 7 summarizes our work and discusses future scope.

2   Background

2.1   Intrusion Detection Systems

The process of monitoring events occurring in a computer system or network and analyzing them for sign of intrusions is known as *Intrusion Detection*. Based on data source Intrusion Detection Systems (IDS) can be characterized as follows:

Host Based: uses system call data from an audit process that tracks all system calls made on behalf of each user on a particular machine.

Multihost Based: collects audit data from multiple hosts and analyzes them centrally to detect intrusions.

Network Based: typically uses network traffic data from a network packet sniffer,e.g., TCP-dump, along with audit data from one or more hosts.

Host-based IDSs examine the activities on a specific host. This allows them the advantage of having greater access to the logs and files of a particular computer, while being limited in what external activities they can see. Network-based IDSs placed into a sensor on a segment see only the traffic of that segment. To circumvent these problems several researchers focus on the field of multihost based IDSs or distributed IDSs. Besides the above categorization, IDSs can be classified into two types based on the model of intrusions, namely *misuse intrusion detection* and *anomaly intrusion detection*.

Misuse Detection Model: detects intrusions by identifying activities that correspond to known intrusion techniques or system vulnerabilities. It uses well-defined attack patterns to identify intrusions. Its merit is relatively low false positive rate. But it can detect only well-known attacks, leaving vulnerable to new attacks.

Anomaly Detection Model: detects intrusions by identifying activities distinct from a user's or system's normal behavior. Its demerits are i) high false positive rates which makes the system unreliable, and ii) a susceptibility to being compromised when malicious activities disguise as acceptable behaviors.

2.2   Current Distributed IDSs

AID (Adaptive Intrusion Detection system) is a multihost based misuse detection system that proposes a client-server architecture consisting of a central monitoring station and several agents on the monitored hosts. The audit data collected by agents are transferred to the central monitoring station, buffered in a cache and analyzed by a real-time expert system. AID is being developed at Brandenburg University of Technology at Cottbus, Germany.

AAFID (Autonomous Agents For Intrusion detection)[16] is a distributed anomaly detection system that employs autonomous agents at the lowest level for data collection and analysis. At the higher levels of the hierarchy transceivers and monitors are used to obtain a global view of activities.

DIDS (Distributed Intrusion Detection system)[11] is the first intrusion detection system that aggregates audit reports from a collection of hosts on a single network. The architecture consists of a host manager, a monitoring process or collection of processes running in background.

EMERALD (Event Monitoring Enabling Responses to Anomalous Live Disturbances) [10] is an analysis and response system that is able to address unanticipated misuse in large network-based enterprises, within an interoperable and scalable modular system framework.

CSM (Cooperating Security Managers)[17] is designed for a distributed network environment. The goal of CSM is to detect intrusive activities in a distributed environment without the use of a centralized director.

AID, *AAFID*, *DIDS* and *EMERALD* have tried to implement the concept of distributed intrusion detection either by capturing misuse or anomaly or both. But their common drawback is that each of them is, to a varying degree, hierarchical in nature. Hence, raw data must be transferred up to the highest level to be analyzed, which gives opportunity to the intruder to intercept the data. Moreover, the analysis of this huge amount of data consumes a significant amount of time and resources, creating system bottlenecks. CSM presents a different approach that makes the system fully distributed in nature. We adopt the same approach and enhance the functionality by differing from CSM in the following aspects: allowing the agent to pass their decision (not the raw data) to neighboring agents (not to everyone). It is safer since a malicious entity cannot get raw data and is quicker because decision is made within a local neighborhood of the hosts being monitored. Another novel characteristic of our system is to identify a compromised agent by incorporating trust mechanism and majority voting.

3   ABDIAS Architecture

We envisage a distributed, lightweight agent-based intrusion alert mechanism that leverage of our previous experience with developing coordinated multiagent systems[13, 14]. In this approach we view our agents as autonomous, reflexive, proactive and cooperative entities. They are responsible for collecting data, analyzing them and making appropriate inference from the analysis. Their inference process uses the collected data as evidence in the Bayesian network. Monitoring and analysis work is duplicated for accuracy and fault tolerance, e.g., handle the problem of some agents getting compromised.

In this paper we present an architecture (see Figure 1) where several autonomous agents form a layer of defense that surrounds the internal system network. Agents are grouped into several islands/neighborhoods, N_i, inside this layer to focus communication within the neighborhood[1]. Inter-neighborhood communication is used only when consensus cannot be arrived within a neighborhood. Agents are responsible for alerting system/network administrator with any possible attack-related activities. Agents are cognizant of a Bayesian network model of the structure of well-known attack types and as well as normal usage pattern which is constructed offline from data repositories containing system logs from ongoing attacks[2]. This network has been partitioned into multiple sub-nets based on the spatial location of the agents. And each of these subnets is common knowledge to agents in same neighborhood. Each agent performs a certain predefined security monitoring function at a peer host. In addition, some agents are responsible for monitoring network traffic data for possible network

---

[1] Our restriction of communication refers only to the communication for the purpose of intrusion detection, and does not restrict normal communication between nodes.

[2] It is easy to confuse the term "network" between the physical network hosting the system and the Bayesian network model of intrusion detection. Unless otherwise specified, we will use *network* and related terms to refer to the Bayes net model.

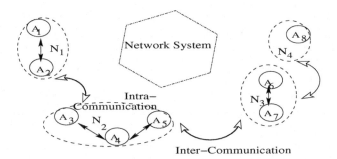

Fig. 1. ABDIAS: Architecture

attack signatures. Agents may collect data locally, i.e., from audit trail, or over the entire network, i.e. from TCPdump data.

We use Bayesian networks to represent existing knowledge of different security threats [4]. A Bayes net captures the mutual influence of different domain variables on target attributes. Using a Bayes net model we can infer the probabilities of the occurrence of different intrusion types, which are easy for human security investigators to interpret. Moreover, this representation can easily accommodate prior domain knowledge. We believe that the Bayesian net representation is the best currently available approach for handling intrinsic uncertainties in intrusion detection. A Bayes net based approach also allows for combining competing intrusion detection methods such as anomaly detection and signature recognition [12]. To facilitate this, we generate one Bayes net whose target node classifies several known attack types and normal system behavior. Using this agents can detect either normal behavior or a known attack type. If none of the probability of target nodes, given input feature values, cross the threshold, anomalous behavior is suspected.

The Bayes net attack model is updated by distributed incremental inference process based on dynamically arriving incomplete information. Such local model updates may necessitate coordination with peers in the neighborhood and, more infrequently, inferences will be communicated to peers in different neighborhoods. An agent can request others to re-confirm their inference and also request updates about network properties that are not monitored locally. If the requesting agent, R, suspects a problem with the information received from another peer, because of inconsistencies with local inference, the agent may check the status of the sender agent, S. If such a suspicion is raised, R can poll its neighborhood agents, using a majority voting mechanism, to confirm the suspicion. On confirmation, steps are taken to tag the sending agent as a possibly compromised node, and then isolate it from the network. If the neighborhood agents fail to confirm the suspicion and does not provide a convincing argument, R, can ask for confirmation from agents beyond its immediate neighborhood. Thus by introducing distributed trust mechanisms and majority voting, we make our system robust against situations where a security breach has comprised some nodes.

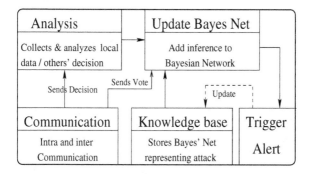

Fig. 2. Architecture of an agent embedded in a node

Figure 2 depicts the ABDIAS agent architecture. The agent tasks are:

Data Collection and Analysis: Each agent collects audit or network data from its own domain, analyzes them and draws inference from the analysis.

Network Update: Agent updates the belief associating the node and distributes its belief to all neighboring nodes.

Communication: The inference is passed to peers either in same locality or greater neighborhood. If any agent is not satisfied with the received inference, it may ask the sender to verify its inference. An agent may also ask other agents, including those from a different neighborhood, to vote on the inference submitted by another agent to evaluate whether this latter agent has been compromised.

Trigger Alert: When an agent recognizes that target node exceeds threshold of one known attack, it triggers an alert for that particular attack, and communicates it to the system administrator. Besides this misuse detection, we allow the agents to trigger an alert representing "something is wrong" when the activated target node does not belong to those representing normal behavior or any of the known attack types considered while creating Bayes net. The administrator can confirm the attack and take necessary responses, or otherwise reject the alert. Thus our agents can detect both anomaly and misuse intrusions.

Update Knowledge Base: If the system administrator confirms an anomaly alert, a Bayes net is modified to accommodate this new attack in the knowledge base which will allow this attack to be recognized as a known attack in future. Thus our system is adaptive to the discovery of new types of network intrusions.

4   Forecasting Attack Using Bayesian Hypothesis

4.1   Bayesian Network

A Bayesian network (BN) is a graph-based modeling approach to represent dependencies among domain variables [5]. A BN is a directed acyclic graph with nodes representing the variables and each directed edge representing a dependency between the corresponding variables. The effect of the parents of a node on a node is represented by conditional probabilities of that variable given values of its parent nodes in the form of a conditional probability table (CPT). We represent attack structures as Bayesian network for the following reasons:

• BNs can readily handle incomplete data sets. Agents in ABDIAS have limited view of the network and may receive only partial information about an attack.

• BNs can represent causal relationships which can help IDSs predict the consequences of intervention by combining a priori knowledge and observed data.

• BNs allow updating of the belief or the probability of occurrence of the particular event for the given causes and several networks can be used by IDSs to recognize the possibility of new attacks.

In ABDIAS, a Bayes tree is first learned from a database of known attacks. This tree is then partitioned into several subtrees following the principle of Multiply Sectioned Bayesian Networks (MSBNs) [19], and distributed among agents. Though Bayes trees have been used for centralized IDSs, we are not cognizant of any work in the field of computer security where agents combine distributed local inference from partitioned trees to form a proactive distributed IDS.

4.2   Inference with Multiply Sectioned Bayesian Networks

A Multiply Sectioned Bayesian Network (MSBN) consists of interrelated subnets each of which encode an agent's knowledge of a sub-domain. Exact, distributed probabilistic inference can be performed using MSBNs: a perfect match of for our ABDIAS requirements where each agent have knowledge of only a sub-domain.

Existing methods for inference in MSBNs are extensions of a class of methods for inference in single-agent Bayesian networks: message passing in junction trees [5]. We have used the *exact* Bayesian network inference algorithm [3], namely, *linked junction forest* (LJF) method [19] on MSBN. It first transforms each subnet of a multiply connected network (here, a Bayes tree) into a clique tree or junction tree by clustering the triangulated moral graph of the underlying undirected graph, and then performs message propagation over the clique tree. Interneighborhood (i.e., between two junction trees in Linked Junction Forest (MSBN)) message passing is performed through a *linkage tree* between a pair of peer nodes in adjacent neighborhood. Though exact belief update is NP-hard [2, 15] we can still use it for IDS domains as the subnet sizes are manageable.

In our architecture, agents in the same neighborhood first find the junction tree of associated Bayes sub-tree (discussed in Section 6). Each agent monitors one/more cluster(s) and when they find any evidence, they update the belief tables at that node, and pass the message to neighboring agents for updating their tables. The clique propagation algorithm (part of *LJF* algorithm) works efficiently for sparse networks. Our approach exploits the structure of the problem to gain efficiency in computing *exact* probabilities. As we divide our entire Bayes network into several subparts, the clique-size of subnets is not large, and hence inferences can be made in real-time.

Figure 3 shows a MSBN. We denote by N_i the group of agents $A_1, \ldots, A_k$ whose knowledge is encoded in subnet D_i. The peers of each N_i can only observe locally. Once a multiagent MSBN is constructed, agents may perform probabilistic inference by computing the query $P(x|e)$, where x is any variable within the sub-domain of a group of agents and e denotes the observations made by all agents. The key computation is to communicate the impact of observations to all agents. Often agents in N_i computes the query $P(x|e_i, e'_i)$, where e_i is the local observations made by N_i and e'_i is the observations made by agents of other groups up to the latest communication. Each subnet, D_i, formed by a group of peer nodes may be multiply connected. To facilitate exact inference with message passing, the LJF method compiles each subnet into a JT, called a local JT, and converts each d-sepset (analogous to separator in JT) into a JT,

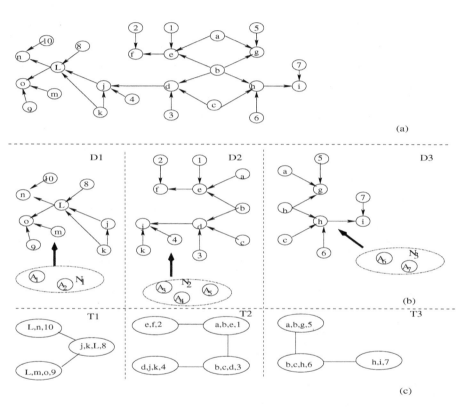

(a)

(b)

(c)

Fig. 3. (a) A Bayes network (b)The DAGs of three subnets of a MSBN; each DAG is under supervision of each group of agents (c) JTs converted from the subnets

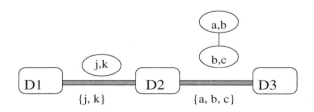

Fig. 4. Linkage trees for JTs of Figure 3

called a linkage tree. Figure 4 illustrates the three local JTs and two linkage trees of the original Bayes network. Since reduction of network congestion is a desirable goal, we chose the LJF method as it has been shown that among different distributed multiagent inferences in MSBNs, LJF requires least amount of system-wide messages during communication [18].

5   Trust Among Peers

We now present the use of trust mechanism among peer agents, a relatively novel concept in computer security, but in our estimation a key, integral feature of any distributed IDS. Our prior research in multiagent systems have shown the pros and cons of believing others [14]. In ABDIAS, each agent is limited in the things it can monitor. Hence each agent needs to rely on other agents for non-local data. As intruders will try to breach any network node, agents must continually monitor their trust on other agents to quickly identify compromised nodes in the system. While compromised nodes inside a locality may attempt to influence the JT, such activities also provide detection clues. If any agent finds that received messages from an agent does not tally with the anticipated trends, it may take any or all of the actions: i) ask sender to resend the message, ii) check its own belief matrix with that of the sender, iii) ask for vote to identify and subsequently eliminate the suspicious agent from the system.

Each agent, i, in ABDIAS maintains a belief table, B_i about other agents, which it updates whenever it receives any message. The entry for the jth agent, is dependent on the nature of the last m messages received from that agent, and is defined as $B_i[j] = \frac{S_j - R_j}{m}$, where S_j and R_j is respectively the number of messages coming from agent j that does or does not match with agent i's anticipation. When agent i is not satisfied with agent j's response for corroborating an inference, it checks its belief matrix entry for the sender agent. If the corresponding entry is less than a threshold, i asks other neighborhood agents to vote on j's trustworthiness. When an agent is asked for vote on another peer, it checks its belief table for its trust in that peer and votes for or against the agent if it finds the value above or below, respectively, of the trust threshold. If the vote difference between total for and against votes is small, i asks vote from agents in a larger neighborhood. If the candidate agent supervises a node in the linkage tree, it has connections with remote agents whose vote can be used to break the tie. If a tie still exists, the local group takes the decision randomly. Such a procedure is robust in removing not only single, but multiple, compromised nodes from the system.

Each agent in one neighborhood knows the structure of subnets and CPTs associated with each node. If the probability of a particular node given specific states of its parents, was gradually increasing but this observation is countered by another agent, the latter's response is marked as inconsistent.

Thus ABDIAS can detect compromised nodes and maintain its performance, reliability and availability to users which makes ABDIAS resilient in the situation where the intruder has already captured some nodes. We believe, this robustness is unique to ABDIAS among Distributed IDSs.

6   Experimental Setup and Results

We used the KDD Cup 1999 Intrusion detection contest data [6] in our experiments. This data was prepared by the 1998 DARPA Intrusion Detection Evaluation program by MIT Lincoln Labs [8]. Lincoln labs set up an environment consisting of a local-area network simulating a typical U.S. AirForce LAN. They acquired nine weeks of raw TCPdump data that was processed into connection records. The original data contains 744MB of data with 4.94 million records. The dataset has 41 attributes for each connection record plus one class label specifying one of 24 attacks or normal condition. All these attacks fall into four major categories: i) Denial of Service (DoS), ii) Remote to User (R2U), iii) User to Root (U2R) and iv) Probing (Probe).

We have also processed the original data from 24 attacks to the above-mentioned four major attack classes. The dataset for our experiments contain 11800 records, randomly selected from the original dataset. This dataset has five different classes: 4 attacks and 1 normal. We ensured that the number of data instances selected from from each class was proportional to their frequency in the original data set. The only exception is that all instances of classes with significantly small frequency are selected. This dataset is used to generate the diagnostic Bayesian network. We have used 17 of the 41 attributes as these are considered the most important variables for intrusion detection by researchers in this field. Bayesian Network Power Constructor (BNPC) [1] has been used to generate Bayes network from this dataset of 11800 records and 17 attributes. Then we section into two subnets as described in figure. 5 maintaining the rules for sound sectioning in MSBN literature [19]. Thereafter we used LJF method [19] to detect intrusions. To test our network, a new dataset consisting of 37 attacks has been considered. Some of these attacks do not come under the four

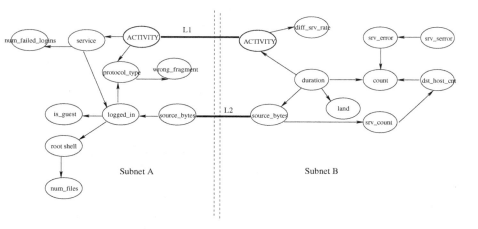

Fig. 5. Subnets A and B are locally computed in two neighborhoods. L1 and L2 depict the connection between them. ACTIVITY is the target node; it has 5 classifications: 4 attacks and 1 normal situation

Table 1. Performance of USBN and MSBN on DARPA Intrusion detection data set

	Training data: 11800 records		Test data: 15000 records	
Activity Type	amp; USBN	amp; MSBN	amp; USBN	amp; MSBN
Normal	amp; 96.67%	amp; 94.37%	amp; 97.11%	amp; 95.71%
Probe	amp; 92.37%	amp; 89.50%	amp; 92.37%	amp; 88.12%
DoS	amp; 91.85%	amp; 90.78%	amp; 91.20%	amp; 89.30%
U2R	amp; 85.00%	amp; 84.70%	amp; 81.00%	amp; 79.08%
R2U	amp; 89.16%	amp; 86.07%	amp; 85.43%	amp; 82.73%

major attack classifications mentioned above, in which case ABDIAS detects it as a new attack or anomalous behavior of the network. Table 1 compares the detection rate for each activity classification (4 attacks and 1 normal) between unsectioned BN (USBN) and MSBN on training and test data. Though a centralized IDS, using USBN, can be seen to have performed better, performance of ABDIAS, using MSBN, is encouraging given its fully distributed nature.

7   Conclusion

This paper presented ABDIAS, a peer level distributed intrusion alert system. Using distributed computation and message passing between distributed agents, ABDIAS recognizes pre-attack activities in the system and can alert the system administrator for taking appropriate actions. The two novel feature of ABDIAS is (a) the ability to form completely distributed inference based on partitioned Bayesian networks to provide early warning of possible future attack, and (b) recognition of compromised nodes by peer-level collaboration.

ABDIAS improves on existing distributed IDSs by using distributed monitoring and diagnosis techniques for early detection of imminent attacks and compromised nodes in the network. The use of Bayesian networks enable our system to track misuse as well as anomalous behavior in the system. Estimation of trust by applying majority voting makes the system intrusion-tolerant.

Currently, we ran experiments considering one USBN having n-ary classification (here, 4 attacks and 1 normal situation). In future we want to compare the performance of ABDIAS considering one BN for each attack type and performing binary classification. The false positive rate of ABDIAS is low, but needs to be compared with other DIDSs. We also want to enhance the system so that it can update its knowledge base with newly discovered attack which has been recognized as an anomalous situation.

Acknowledgments. This work has been supported in part by NSF award IIS-0209208.

References

1. J. Cheng, D. Bell, and W. Liu. Learning bayesian networks from data: An efficient approach based on information theory. Technical report, University of Alberta, Canada, 1998.
2. G. F. Cooper. The computational complexity of probabilistic inference using bayesian belief networks. *Artificial Intelligence*, 42:393–405, 1990.
3. H. Guo and W. H. Hsu. A survey of algorithms for real-time bayesian network inference. In *AAAI/KDD/UAI-2002 Joint Workshop on Real-Time Decision Support and Diagnosis Systems*, Edmonton, July 2002.
4. M. Y. Huang and T. M. Wicks. A large-scale distributed intrusion detection framework based on attack strategy analysis. In *Web proceedings of the First International Workshop on Recent Advances in Intrusion Detection*, Louvain-la-Neuve, Belgium, September 1998.
5. F. V. Jensen. *An Introduction to Bayesian Networks*. Springer Verlag, New York, NY, 1996.
6. Kddcup   99   intrusion   detection   data   set.   URL: http://kdd.ics.uci.edu/databases/kddcup99/kddcup.data_10_percent.gz. DARPA Intrusion data repository.
7. S. L. Lauritzen and D. J. Spiegelhalter. Local computations with probabilities on graphical structures and their applications to expert systems. In *Proceedings of the Royal Statistical Society, Series B., 50*, pages 154–227, 1988.
8. Mit lincoln laboratory. URL: http://www.ll.mit.edu/IST/ideval/. DARPA Intrusion data repository.
9. B. Mukherjee, T. L. Heberlein, and K. N. Levitt. Network intrusion detection. *IEEE Network*, 8(3):26–41, May/June 1994.
10. P. A. Porras and P. G. Neumann. Emerald: event monitoring enabling responses to anomalous live disturbances. In *20th National Information Systems Security Conference*, October 1997.
11. J. B. S. Snapp and G. D. et al. Dids (distributed intrusion detection system) motivation, archi-tecture, and an early prototype. In *Fourteenth National Computer Security Conference*, Washington, DC, October 1991.
12. S. L. Scott. A bayesian paradigm for designing intrusion detection system. *Computational Statistics and Data Analysis*, 45(1):69–83, February 2004.
13. S. Sen. Developing an automated distributed meeting scheduler. *IEEE Expert*, 12(4):41–45, July/August 1997.
14. S. Sen. Believing others: Pros and cons. *Artificial Intelligence*, 142(2):179–203, 2002.
15. S. Shimony. Finding maps for belief networks is np-hard. *Artificial Intelligence*, 68:399–410, 1994.
16. E. H. Spafford and D. Zamboni. Intrusion detection using autonomous agents. *Computer Networks*, 34(4):547–570, October 2000.
17. G. White, E. Fisch, and U. Pooch. Cooperating security managers: A peer-based intrusion detection system. *IEEE Network*, 10(1):20–23, 1996.
18. Y. Xiang. Comparison of multiagent inference methods in multiply sectioned bayesian networks. *International Journal of Approximate Reasoning.*, 33(3):235–254, August 2003.
19. Y. Xiang, D. Poole, and M. Beddoes. Multiply sectioned bayesian networks and junction forests for large knowledge-based systems. *Computational Intelligence*, 9(2):171–220, 1993.

SCIDS: A Soft Computing Intrusion Detection System

Ajith Abraham[1], Ravi Jain[2], Sugata Sanyal[3], and Sang Yong Han[1]

[1] School of Computer Science and Engineering, Chung-Ang University, Korea
ajith.abraham@ieee.org, hansy@cau.ac.kr
[2] Land Operations Division, Defence Science & Technology Organisation (DSTO), Australia
[3] School of Technology and Computer Science,
Tata Institute of Fundamental Research, India
sanyal@tifr.res.in

Abstract. An Intrusion Detection System (IDS) is a program that analyzes what happens or has happened during an execution and tries to find indications that the computer has been misused. This paper evaluates three fuzzy rule based classifiers for IDS and the performance is compared with decision trees, support vector machines and linear genetic programming. Further, Soft Computing (SC) based IDS (SCIDS) is modeled as an ensemble of different classifiers to build light weight and more accurate (heavy weight) IDS. Empirical results clearly show that SC approach could play a major role for intrusion detection.

1 Introduction

Intrusion detection is classified into two types: misuse intrusion and anomaly intrusion detection [3][7]. Data mining approaches for IDS were first implemented in mining audit data for automated models [2]. Several data mining algorithms are applied to audit data to compute models that accurately capture the actual behavior of intrusions. This paper introduces three fuzzy rule based classifiers and compares the performance with Linear Genetic Programming (LGP) [1], Support Vector Machines (SVM) [8] and Decision Trees (DT) [5]. Further, we used Soft Computing (SC) [9] based IDS (SCIDS) as a combination of different classifiers to model light weight and more accurate (heavy weight) IDS. Rest of the paper is organized as follows. Section 2 provides the technical details of the three fuzzy rule based systems. Experiment results are presented in Section 3 and some conclusions are also provided towards the end.

2 Fuzzy Rule Based Systems

Let us assume that we have a n dimensional c-class pattern classification problem whose pattern space is an n-dimensional unit cube $[0, 1]^n$. We also assume that m patterns $x_p = (x_{p1},...,x_{pn})$, $p = 1,2,...,m$, are given for generating fuzzy *if-then* rules where $x_p \in [0,1]$ for $p = 1,2,..., m$.

A. Sen et al. (Eds.): IWDC 2004, LNCS 3326, pp. 252–257, 2004.
© Springer-Verlag Berlin Heidelberg 2004

2.1 Rule Generation Based on the Histogram of Attribute Values (FR₁)

In this method, use of histogram itself is an antecedent membership function. Each attribute is partitioned into 20 membership functions $f_h(.)$, $h=1,2,...,20$. The smoothed histogram $m_i^k(x_i)$ of class k patterns for the ith attribute is calculated using the 20 membership functions $f_h(.)$ as follows:

$$m_i^k(x_i) = \frac{1}{m^k} \sum_{x_p \in Class\ k} f_h\left(x_{pi}\right)$$

$$for\ \beta_{h-1} \leq x_i \leq \beta_h,\ h=1,2,...,20 \tag{1}$$

where m_k is the number of Class k patterns, $\left[\beta_{h-1},\beta_h\right]$ is the hth crisp interval corresponding to the 0.5-level set of the membership function $f_h(.)$

$$\beta_1=0,\ \beta_{20}=1,\ \beta_h=\frac{1}{20-1}\left(h-\frac{1}{2}\right)\ for\ h=1,2,...,19 \tag{2}$$

The smoothed histogram in (1) is normalized so that its maximum value is 1. A single fuzzy *if-then* rule is generated for each class. The fuzzy *if-then* rule for the kth class can be written as *If* x_1 is A_1^k and ... and x_n is A_1^k *then* class k $\tag{3}$

where A_i^k is an antecedent fuzzy set for the ith attribute. The membership function of A_i^k is specified as

$$A_i^k(x_i)=\exp\left(\frac{\left(x_i-\mu_i^k\right)^2}{2\left(\sigma_i^k\right)^2}\right) \tag{4}$$

where μ_i^k is the mean of the ith attribute values x_{pi} of class k patterns, and σ_i^k is the standard deviation. Fuzzy *if-then* rules for the two-dimensional two class pattern classification problem are written as follows:

If x_3 is A_3^1 and x_4 is A_4^1 *then* class 2 or *If* x_3 is A_3^2 and x_4 is A_4^2 *then* class 3.

Membership function of each antecedent fuzzy set is specified by the mean and the standard deviation of attribute values. For a new pattern $x_p = (x_{p3},x_{p4})$, the winner rule is determined as follows:

$$A_3^*(x_{p3}).A_2^*(x_{p4})=\max\left\{A_1^k(x_{p3}).A_2^k(x_{p4})|k=1,2\right\} \tag{5}$$

2.2 Rule Generation Based on Partition of Overlapping Areas (FR₂)

In this method m - dimensional pattern space is partitioned and a single fuzzy *if-then* rule is generated for each fuzzy subspace. Because the specification of each membership function does not depend on any information about training patterns, this approach uses fuzzy *if-then* rules with certainty grades. The local information about training patterns in the corresponding fuzzy subspace is used for determining the consequent class and the grade of certainty. In this approach, fuzzy *if-then* rules of the following type are used.

$$If \; x_1 \; is \; A_{j1} \; and \; .. \; and \; x_n \; is \; A_{jn} \; then \; class \; C_j, \; with \; CF = CF_j, \; j = 1, 2, .., N \quad (6)$$

where j indexes the number of rules, N is the total number of rules, A_{ji} is the antecedent fuzzy set of the ith rule for the ith attribute, C_j; is the consequent class, and CFj is the grade of certainty. The consequent class and the grade of certainty of each rule are determined by the following simple heuristic procedure:

Step 1: Calculate the compatibility of each training pattern $x_p = (x_{p1}, x_{p2}, ..., x_{pn})$ with the jth fuzzy *if-then* rule by the following product operation:

$$\pi_j(x_p) = A_{j1}(x_{p1}) \times ... \times A_{jn}(x_{pn}), \; p = 1, 2, ..., m. \quad (7)$$

Step 2: For each class, calculate the sum of the compatibility grades of the training patterns with the jth fuzzy *if-then* rule R_j:

$$\beta_{class \; k}(R_j) = \sum_{x_p \in class \; k}^{n} \pi(x_p), \; k=1,2,...,c \quad (8)$$

where $\beta_{class \; k}(R_j)$ the sum of the compatibility grades of the training patterns in class k with the jth fuzzy if-then rule R_j.

Step 3: Find Class A_j^* that has the maximum value $\beta_{class \; k}(R_j)$:

$$\beta_{class \; k_j^*} = Max\{\beta_{class \; 1}(R_j), ..., \beta_{class \; c}(R_j)\}.$$

If two or more classes take the maximum value or no training pattern compatible with the jth fuzzy *if-then* rule (i.e., if $\beta_{Class} \; k(R_j)=0$ for $k = 1,2,..., c$), the consequent class C_i can not be determined uniquely. In this case, let C_i be ϕ.

Step 4: If the consequent class C_i is 0, let the grade of certainty CF_j be $CF_j = 0$. Otherwise the grade of certainty CF_j is determined as follows:

$$CF_j = \frac{(\beta_{class \; k_j^*}(R_j) - \bar{\beta})}{\sum_{k=1}^{c} \beta_{class \; k}(R_j)}, \; where \; \bar{\beta} = \sum_{\substack{k=1 \\ k \neq k_j^*}} \frac{\beta_{Class \; k}(R_j)}{(c-1)} \quad (9)$$

2.3 Neural Learning of Fuzzy Rules (FR₃)

In a fused neuro-fuzzy architecture, neural network learning algorithms are used to determine the parameters of fuzzy inference system (membership functions and number of rules). We made use of the Evolving Fuzzy Neural Network (EFuNN) to implement a Mamdani type FIS [10].

3   Experiment Setup and Results

Certain features may contain false correlations, which hinder the process of detecting intrusions. Extra features can increase computation time, and can impact the accuracy of IDS. Feature selection is done based on the contribution the input variables made to the construction of the decision tree. Variable importance, for a particular variable is the sum across all nodes in the tree of the improvement scores that the predictor has when it acts as a primary or surrogate (but not competitor) splitter [11].

The data for our experiments was prepared by the 1998 DARPA intrusion detection evaluation program by MIT Lincoln Labs [6]. The data set has 41 attributes for each connection record plus one class label and they are named as *A, B, C, D, E, F, G, H, I, J, K, L, M, N, O, P, Q, R, S, T, U, V, W, X, Y, Z, AA, AB, AC, AD, AE, AF, AG, AH, AI, AJ, AK, AL, AM, AN, AO* and *AP* respectively. The data set contains 24 attack types that could be classified into four main categories *DoS*: Denial of Service, *R2L*: Unauthorized Access from a Remote Machine, *U2Su*: Unauthorized Access to Local Super User (root) and *Probing*. Our experiments have three phases namely input feature reduction, training phase and testing phase. In the data reduction phase, important variables for real-time intrusion detection are selected by feature selection. In the training phase, the different soft computing models were constructed using the training data to give maximum generalization accuracy on the unseen data. The test data is then passed through the saved trained model to detect intrusions in the testing phase. The training and test comprises of 5,092 and 6,890 records respectively [4]. All the training data were scaled to (0-1). The decision tree approach helped us to reduce the number of variables to 12 variables. The list of reduced variables is *C, E, F, L, W, X, Y, AB, AE, AF, AG* and *AI*. Using the original and reduced data sets, we performed a 5-class classification. We examined the performance of all three fuzzy rule based approaches (*FR₁, FR₂* and *FR₃*) mentioned in Section 2. When an attack is correctly classified the grade of certainty is increased and when an attack is misclassified the grade of certainty is decreased. A learning procedure is used to determine the grade of certainty. Triangular membership functions were used for all the fuzzy rule based classifiers. For FR_1 and FR_2 two triangular membership functions were assigned and 2 and 2^{12} rules were learned respectively for the reduced data set. For FR_3, 4 triangular membership functions were used for each input variable. A sensitivity threshold *Sthr* = 0.95 and error threshold *Errthr* = 0.05 was used for all the classes and 89 rule nodes were developed. For comparison purposes various other results were adapted from [1][7][11].

A number of observations and conclusions are drawn from the results illustrated in Table 1. Using 41 attributes, the FR_2 method gave 100% accuracy for all the 5 classes, showing the importance of fuzzy inference systems. Using 12 attributes most of the classifiers performed very well except the fuzzy classifier (FR_2). For detecting U2R attacks FR_2 gave the best accuracy. However, due to the tremendous reduction in the number of attributes (about 70% less), we are able to design a computational efficient (light weight) IDS. Since a particular classifier could not provide accurate results for all the classes, we propose to use a combination of different classifiers to detect different attacks.

Table 1. Performance comparison using full/reduced data set

Attack type	Classification accuracy on test data set (%)					
	FR$_1$	FR$_2$	FR$_3$	DT	SVM	LGP
Full Dataset						
Normal	40.44	**100.00**	98.26	99.64	99.64	99.73
Probe	53.06	**100.00**	99.21	99.86	98.57	99.89
DOS	60.99	**100.00**	98.18	96.83	99.92	99.95
U2R	66.75	**100.00**	61.58	68.00	40.00	64.00
R2L	61.10	**100.00**	95.46	84.19	33.92	99.47
Reduced Dataset						
Normal	74.82	79.68	99.56	**100.00**	99.75	99.97
Probe	45.36	89.84	99.88	97.71	98.20	**99.93**
DOS	60.99	60.99	98.99	85.34	98.89	**99.96**
U2R	**94.11**	**99.64**	65.00	64.00	59.00	68.26
R2L	91.83	91.83	97.26	95.56	56.00	**99.98**

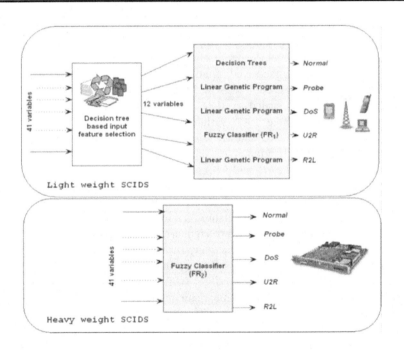

Fig. 1. Light/heavy weight SCIDS architecture

The Soft Computing Intrusion Detection System (SCIDS) using 41 attributes (heavy weight) and 12 attributes (light weight) are depicted in Figure 1. The proposed heavy weight model could detect with 100% accuracy while the light weight model could detect Normal, Probe, DOS, U2R and R2L class with 100.00%, 99.93%, 99.96%, 94.11% and 99.98% accuracies respectively.

4 Conclusions

In this paper, we have illustrated the importance of soft computing paradigms for modeling intrusion detection systems. For real time intrusion detection systems, LGP would be the ideal candidate as it can be manipulated at the machine code level. Overall, the fuzzy classifier (FR_2) gave 100% accuracy for all attack types using all the 41 attributes. The proposed hybrid combination of classifiers requires only 12 input variables. While the light weight SCIDS would be useful for MANET/distributed systems, the heavy weight SCIDS would be ideal for conventional static networks, wireless base stations etc.

Acknowledgements. This research was partially supported by the MIC, Korea, under the Chung-Ang University HNRC-ITRC support program supervised by the IITA.

References

[1] Abraham A., Evolutionary Computation in Intelligent Web Management, Evolutionary Computing in Data Mining, Ghosh A. and Jain L.C. (Eds.), Studies in Fuzziness and Soft Computing, Vol. 163, Springer Verlag Germany, 2004.

[2] Barbara D., Couto J., Jajodia S. and Wu N., ADAM: A Testbed for Exploring the Use of Data Mining in Intrusion Detection. SIGMOD Record, 30(4), pp. 15-24, 2001.

[3] Denning D., An Intrusion-Detection Model, IEEE Transactions on Software Engineering, Vol. SE-13, No. 2, pp.222-232, 1987.

[4] KDD Cup 1999 Intrusion detection data set:
<http://kdd.ics.uci.edu/databases/kddcup99/kddcup.data_10_percent.gz>

[5] Brieman L., Friedman J., Olshen R., and Stone C., Classification of Regression Trees. Wadsworth Inc., 1984.

[6] MIT Lincoln Laboratory. <http://www.ll.mit.edu/IST/ideval/>

[7] Peddabachigari S., Abraham A., Thomas J., Intrusion Detection Systems Using Decision Trees and Support Vector Machines, International Journal of Applied Science and Computations, USA, 2004.

[8] Vapnik V.N., The Nature of Statistical Learning Theory. Springer, 1995.

[9] Zadeh L. A., Roles of Soft Computing and Fuzzy Logic in the Conception, Design and Deployment of Information/Intelligent Systems, Computational Intelligence: Soft Computing and Fuzzy-Neuro Integration with Applications, O. Kaynak et al. (Eds.), pp 1-9, 1998.

[10] Kasabov N., Evolving Fuzzy Neural Networks-Algorithms, Applications and Biological Motivation, in Yamakawa T. et al. (Eds), Methodologies for the Conception, Design and Application of Soft Computing, World Scientific, pp. 271-274, 1998.

[11] Shah K., Dave N., Chavan S., Mukherjee S., Abraham A. and Sanyal S., Adaptive Neuro-Fuzzy Intrusion Detection System, IEEE International Conference on Information Technology: Coding and Computing (ITCC'04), IEEE Computer Society, Vol. 1, pp. 70-74, 2004.

Effect of Data Encryption on Wireless Ad Hoc Network Performance

Vijay K. Garg[1] and R.K. Ghosh[2]

[1] Electrical and Computer Engineering Department, University of Illinois at Chicago, Chicago, IL. USA 60607
vgarg@ece.uic.edu
[2] Department of CSE, IIT-Kanpur, Kanpur 208016, India
rkg@cse.iitk.ac.in

Abstract. In this paper we studied various routing algorithms for ad hoc networks to explain why Ad hoc On Demand Distance Vector (AODV) should be chosen over other possible rotuing algorithms. We then the effect of applying encryption over AODV [5] to data payload on different parameters such as delay, queue size, throughput, retransmission attempts, channel back-off etc.

1 Introduction

The routing protocols for ad-hoc networks can generally be categorized as: (a) table-driven, and (b) source-initiated on-demand-driven [6, 7]. Table-driven routing protocols attempt to maintain consistent, up-to-date routing information from each node to every node in the network. These protocols require each node to maintain one or more tables to store routing information, and they respond to changes in network topology by propagating route updates throughout the network to maintain a consistent network view. The Destination Sequenced Distance Vector (DSDV), Wireless Routing Protocol (WRP), and Cluster Switch Gateway Routing (CSGR) protocol belong to this category.

The source-initiated on-demand routing protocols create routes only when desired by a source node. When a node requires a route to a destination, it initiates a route discovery process within the network. This process is completed once a route is found or all possible route permutations have been examined. The Ad-hoc On-demand Distance Vector (AODV), Dynamic Source Routing (DSR), Temporally Ordered Routing Algorithm (TORA), and Cluster Based Routing Protocol (CBRP) belong to this category.

A comparison of the routing protocols for ad-hoc network is provided in Table 1.

Except for DSR all protocols assume links to be bi-directional. In DSR the route from a source to destination can consist of only uni-directional links. It can be seen that none of the protocols provide any degree of security; neither do they support power conservation or quality of service. None is proactive to take any smart routing decision when network load is taken into consideration.

A. Sen et al. (Eds.): IWDC 2004, LNCS 3326, pp. 258–263, 2004.
© Springer-Verlag Berlin Heidelberg 2004

Table 1. Comparison of Routing Protocols

	AODV	DSDV	TORA	DSR	CBRP
Loop-free	Yes	Yes	Yes	Yes	Yes
Multicast	Yes	No	No	No	No
Distributed	Yes	Yes	Yes	Yes	Yes
Reactive	Yes	No	Yes	Yes	Yes
Bi-directional link	Yes	Yes	Yes	No	Yes
Multiple Routes	No	No	Yes	Yes	Yes
Security	No	No	No	No	No
Power Conservation	No	No	No	No	No

AODV was selected for simulation, since it provides most of the features like freedom from loops, multicasting, distributed nature, reactive nature and so on.

2   Security

Possible security measures are authorization and encryption [4]. Errors may be introduced intentionally or unintentionally during transmission of data. Error detecting codes are used to determine such errors. In simulations, we use CRC on the payload data, and the check sum is appended to the data. To further secure the data, encryption is applied to the plain text data. We used RC4 stream cipher algorithm [1]. The RC4 key has a limitation of 40 bits as a result of export restrictions; it can also be used as a 128-bit key.

The plain text is XORed with the encrypting variable obtained from the key setup phase to generate the encrypted message. XOR is the logical operation of comparing two binary bits. If the bits are different, the result is 1. If the bits are the same, the result is 0. Once the receiver gets the encrypted message, it decrypts by XORing the encrypted message with the same encrypting variable.

3   Simulation Environment

We used NIST/AODV OPNET [2] model in our simulations. In our platform, the IP address is assimilated into the MAC address, which must be indicated before the simulation compilation.

We use the following assumptions:

- There can be no more than 40 mobile nodes in the given scenario at a time.
- The network activity is monitored over a radius of 250 meters.
- The nodes in the network are aware of the encryption.
- Data source includes constant bit rate information.
- RC4 algorithm is used for data encryption.

- Data payload includes: (1) No encryption data payload consists of 128-bit string, (2) With encryption; data payload consists of 128-bit string and an unsigned long integer representing the checksum.
- 16-bytes encryption key is used.

The input to mobility module used in simulations includes:

- Mobility attribute (enumerated values: Enable or Disabled): Indicates whether the current node is fixed or mobile
- Grid dimensions: Each mobile node moves around the specified area
- Speed limit: Maximum speed that a node in motion may reach
- Pause time: After reaching a target position, a moving node must pause during this period of time before reaching for a new target position.

The general motion of a particular node is simulated through a set of discrete small step intervals. A node is motion updates its position at every step interval. In simulations, the duration of each step is set to a value of 0.2 second. The simulations were conducted for 500 seconds of network activity. The speed of mobile nodes is set to 20 meters per second and a data rate of 1 Mbps is used.

4   Simulation Metrics

These include global and node metrics. The global metrics are the parameters that are obtained considering all the nodes in a scenario, including the effect of simulation on global environment and obtaining an average. Node metrics determine the effect of simulation on a particular mobile node. We selected node number 39 as it showed consistent behavior over a number of simulation runs.

- Global Metrics
  AODV Metrics
  1. AODV delay: It is the average routing delay.
  2. AODV average discovery time: It is average time taken to determine route from source to destination node.
  Wireless LAN Metrics
  1. Data dropped: The data bits dropped.
  2. Delay: It is the average wireless LAN delay experienced by the nodes in the network.
  3. Load: The network activity as number of bits per second
  4. Media access delay: It is the average time taken to access the transmission medium by the nodes in the network.
- Node Metrics
  1. Queuing delay: The delay experienced by a packet in a single node
  2. Queue size: The size of queue in a single node
  3. Back-off slots: Number of slots a node is prevented from transmitting data
  4. Channel reservation: The time during which the channel is reserved for a node to transmit

5. Control traffic received: Number of bits of control traffic received by a node 6.Control traffic sent: Number of bits of control traffic transmitted by a node
6. Delay: It is the data transfer delay experienced by a node
7. Dropped data packets: Number of data packets dropped by a node
8. Retransmission attempts: The number of attempts a node makes before successful transmission of data packet.

5 Simulation Results

Comparisons of AODV average delay and AODV average discovery time are shown in Fig. 1 and 2. The average delay and average discovery time are slightly higher for the encryption case and are attributed to the additional delay caused by encryption and checksum calculations. The routing delay and discovery times differ by less than 2 seconds leading to the conclusion that encryption does not introduce heavy delays in network.

Figures 3 to 7 show wireless LAN data dropped, wireless LAN delay, load, and media access delay. In all the cases, there seems an initial difference between two cases but it tends to converge as simulation progresses. The difference in number of bits dropped on an average for the two cases is less than 5000 bits. If we consider 512 bits packet then the number of data packets dropped is less than 10 extra packets in case of encryption, which can be tolerated if increased security can be achieved. The delay parameter also differs in practically insignificant measure. Thus the performance degradation can be considered tolerable.

Network load is calculated in terms of bits per second. High network loads tend to make the network unstable and performance degrades beyond acceptable levels. Considering the simulation output (Fig. 5) at the point indicating 5 minutes of network activity, we can see that the difference in load for the two cases is less than 50,000 bits. After 7.5 minutes of simulation the difference in load remains a constant at 50, 000 bits. This means the difference in load over 2.5 minutes interval is around 334 bits per second. If a data packet of 512 bits is chosen, the difference in load is less than one packet per second. Thus we conclude that increase in network load due to encryption is insignificant.

The wireless LAN delay difference in the two cases is obtained to be around 0.04 seconds maximum and around 0.005 seconds minimum. This is in compliance with wireless LAN delay that is obtained as a global parameter. A delay difference of 0.005 seconds is a tolerable difference.

We also noted the simulation results with respect to node metrics, as described in section 4, for the mobile node 39 and include queue size, queue delay, back-off slots, channel reservation, control traffic sent, control traffic received, delay, load, and retransmission attempts. However, the results are not included here due to the lack of space. Interested reader can find then in the detailed technical report [3].

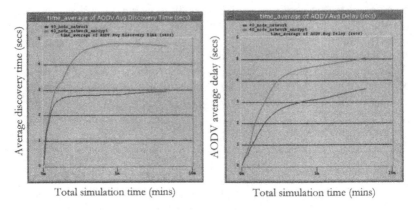

Fig. 1. Average discovery time and average delay

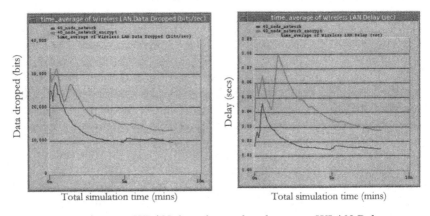

Fig. 2. Average WLAN data dropped and average WLAN Delay

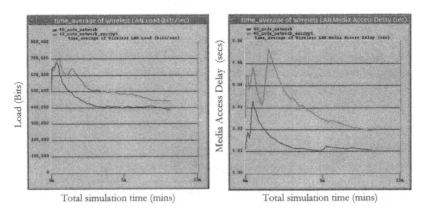

Fig. 3. Average WLAN load and average WLAN media access delay

6 Conclusions

Adding security to ad-hoc wireless network is a complex issue. Use of key encryption to data provides a certain degree of security. Analysis of critical parameters such as network load, network delay, queue size and so on shows that implementation of data encryption does not introduce significant service degradation but could improve security. The small degradation of service would be a worthy compromise for increased security.

References

1. Rc4 encryption algorithm, history and description. http://www.ncat.edu/grogans/algorithm_history_and_description.htm.
2. www.opnet.com.
3. V. Garg and R. K. Ghosh. Effect of data encryption on wireless ad hoc networks performance. Technical report, IIT-Kanpur, Department of CSE, 2003.
4. Z. L. and Z. J. Haas. Securing adhoc networks. *IEEE Network Magazine*, 13(6), 1999.
5. C. Perkins. Ad hoc on demand distance vector (aodv) routing. Internet draft, draft-ietf-manet-aodv-00.txt.
6. E. M. Royer and C.-K. Toh. A review of current routing protocols for ad-hoc mobile wireless networks. *IEEE Magazine on Personal Communication*, 17(8):46–55, 1999.
7. C.-K. Toh. *Ad Hoc Mobile Wireless Networks – Protocols and Systems*. Prentice Hall, Upper Saddle River, NJ, 2002.

On-Board RSVP: An Extension of RSVP to Support Real-Time Services in On-Board IP Networks

Muhammad Ali Malik[1,2], Salil S. Kanhere[1], Mahbub Hassan[1,2], and Boualem Benatallah[1]

[1] School of Computer Science and Engineering, The university of New South Wales
Sydney, NSW 2052, Australia
[2] National ICT Australia Ltd.** ,
Locked bag 9013,
Alexandria, NSW 1435, Australia

Abstract. The extension of Internet services to public transport passengers is slowly becoming inevitable. To this end, it is envisaged that high-speed local area networks will be deployed on-board public transport vehicles (e.g., buses, trains, ships and planes). The on-board LAN will be connected to the Internet via an on-board mobile router (MR). The passengers simply connect their devices to the on-board LAN and start enjoying Internet services. The mobility of the entire on-board network including the passenger devices is managed transparently by the MR. However, the mobility of the router (and the entire IP subnet) gives rise to several unique challenges for achieving end-to-end resource reservation. In this paper we propose a novel extension for RSVP, which addresses these issues. The proposed On-Board RSVP protocol can effectively, transparently, and scalably support end-to-end resource reservation in on-board IP networks. A key feature of On-Board RSVP is that it retains the basic building blocks of the original RSVP, minimising the changes required to existing RSVP infrastructure. The high level of dynamism associated with the QoS resource demand in an on-board communication system results in excessive signaling and processing overhead at the MR and the intermediate routers along the end-to-end paths. To address this issue, we propose and discuss two new aggregation schemes for handling the large number of RSVP setup messages: Cardinal Operating Policy (COP) and Temporal Operating Policy (TOP).

1 Introduction

In recent years we have witnessed an explosive growth in the availability of interconnected computing devices (e.g., PDAs, laptops, and 3G mobile phones)

** National ICT Australia is funded through the Australian Government's backing Australia's ability initiative, in part through the Australian Research Council.

A. Sen et al. (Eds.): IWDC 2004, LNCS 3326, pp. 264–275, 2004.
© Springer-Verlag Berlin Heidelberg 2004

and the deployment of more sophisticated wireless communication infrastructure (e.g., advanced data communication satellites). In order to achieve a truly pervasive computing environment it is imperative that we introduce Internet services in public transport systems. An on-board communication solution will enable transport operators to deliver value-added work, communication and entertainment services to their passengers. Indeed, providing limited on-board services such as access to entertainment and news is already a reality [1]. In recent years, this new paradigm of *Networks in Motion* is fast becoming an active area of research and development, and several commercial and research projects have been initiated to build such systems [2, 3, 4, 5, 6, 7]. The work in this paper is part of our larger goal of providing On-board Communication, Entertainment, And iNformation (OCEAN) [8] for public transport systems.

A typical on-board mobility architecture consists of three main components (see Fig.1) : high-speed on-board local area network (OBLAN), the Mobile Router (MR), and Mobile Wireless Internet Connection (MWIC) [1]. The OBLAN provides a local high-speed connectivity to the outside world for on-board passengers. The MR facilitates communication between the OBLAN and the global communication infrastructure (e.g., Internet). The QoS module attached to the MR is responsible for the management of all QoS functions such as admission control and resource reservation. The OBLAN may also be additionally equipped with data server and query manager to process on-board user requests. The MWIC connects the MR to a land-based wireless station (e.g., 3G cellular packet data service) or a satellite (e.g., Inmarsat Swift64 mobile packet data service) to maintain connectivity between the OBLAN and the outside world. The heart of the architecture is the MR [9] which provides global connectivity whereby all users can access information by simply plugging into the OBLAN.

Fig. 1. Architecture of on-board Network

IP networks are considered a viable candidate for on-board computing environment due to their flexibility and cost effectiveness. A key characteristic of the on-board IP network is that the entire IP subnet consisting of the MR and its associated user devices, is mobile and may rapidly change its communication point to the outside world while moving. Existing IP protocols are not appropriate to cope with the requirements of the mobile networks. New extensions are required to provide continuous connectivity while MR changes point of association to the Internet. To this end, the Internet Engineering Task Force (IETF) has recently charted a new Working Group, called Network Mobility or NEMO to address the issue of mobility management for networks in motion. In the NEMO basic protocol [10] none of the user devices behind the MR are aware of the network's mobility. The MR is responsible for preserving session continuity as the network moves making the mobility of the network transparent and seamless to the on-board users. In other words, the on-board IP networks appears to be *static* to all user devices. This mobility transparency posse several new challenges for providing QoS support. The existing RSVP extensions for mobility are designed to work with mobile IP but not with the NEMO basic protocol. Further, since the MR is responsible for managing the mobility of the user devices, it is natural for the MR to handle the resource reservation on behalf of these devices.

Another challenging aspect of the on-board communication system is the high level of dynamism associated with the QoS resource demand at the MR. The number of user devices connected to the OBLAN in a public transport vehicle will invariably be very large. Further, this number is expected to change frequently as travelers depart the vehicle and new riders board. Last but not least, due to the wide variety of applications available to the users, there is a high likelihood that a single user will access different real-time services at different times. As a result the QoS requirements of a single user may also vary significantly over the duration of his trip. This high level of QoS dynamics will result in massive processing and signaling overhead of setup messages at MR and the other routers along the end-to-end paths from senders to receivers. Hence, it is extremely critical to address this scalability issue.

The rest of the paper is organized as follows. Section 2 provides an overview of existing RSVP protocols that have been proposed for mobile networks. We also elaborate on the unique challenges raised by on-board communication systems which render these protocols to be inapplicable in the on-board context. The scalability issues associated with the RSVP signaling overhead are also discussed in greater detail. To overcome these limitations, we proposed a new on-board RSVP protocol, which builds upon the building blocks of the traditional RSVP and extends it to cater for the requirements of mobile networks. Section 3 presents the conceptual architecture of the on-board RSVP protocol. In Section 4 we present the temporal and cardinal aggregation policies to tackle scalability issues. Finally, Section 5 concludes the paper and outlines future work.

2   Overview of Existing RSVP Protocols

The original RSVP proposed by Zhang et al [11] is a receiver initiated signaling protocol for the Integrated Services architecture [12] for establishing QoS paths between senders and receivers. If the sender/receiver is mobile, part of the end-to-end path changes over time. Resources in the old path have to be released, and required resources must be reserved along the new path each time the mobile host moves. Several extensions [13, 14, 15, 16] of RSVP have been proposed to address host mobility and for gracefully integrating RSVP with Mobile IP. One common feature of these protocols is that they make advance reservations at future locations of mobile host.

We use MRSVP (a representative extension of RSVP for mobile communication) [13] as an example to illustrate the operation of RSVP extensions for unicast flows. In Fig.2 (a), we assume that a mobile node (MN) is receiving real-time data from a fixed sender. The path from sender to MN has a *fixed segment* from sender to HAoMN, and a *dynamic segment* from HAoMN to MN. The reservation over the dynamic segment is established through proxy agents at home (HAoMN) and foreign networks (FAoMNs) as shown in Fig.2 (a). The NEMO basic protocol proposed to handle mobility management for networks in motion requires the MR to maintain a bidirectional tunnel between its current location and its home network. All in-bound and out-bound on-board traffic is routed through this tunnel, making the mobility of the network transparent and seamless to the on-board users. The NEMO basic protocol bidirectional tunnel is not an issue since RSVP tunnel protocol [17] can provide signaling of RSVP messages in the tunnel. However, existing mobile RSVP protocols such as MRSVP posses certain fundamental drawbacks that make them inappropriate for on-board IP networks. Firstly, the dynamic segment (from HAoMN to MN) is now more complex in on-board IP networks due to the mobility of the router (MR). In NEMO basic protocol [10], the dynamic segment is broken into three sub-segments (see Fig.2 (b)), the first connecting the HAoMN and the HAoMR (home agent of mobile router), the second connecting the HAoMR and the FAoMR (foreign agent of MR), and the third, essentially a wireless link, connecting the MR to the FAoMR. Clearly MRSVP, is very limited in this environment, because it will reserve resources over the original dynamic segment (HAoMN and FAoMN), whereas all traffic mainly flows over the more circuitous NEMO basic protocol segment (see Fig.2 (b)).

Secondly, for MRSVP to function correctly (i.e., releasing resource over old path and converting passive reservation into active reservation over new path), MNs must be able to detect change of location (handoff). With NEMO, on-board MNs are incapable of detecting change of location (mobility is managed by MR). Thirdly, maintenance of individual RSVP flows (sessions) over the bi-directional tunnel between MR and HAoMR by periodic refresh messages can lead to serious scalability problems for the MR as well as the tunnel routers. Further the resources requested change dynamically with new sessions being established and existing ones being torn down quite frequently. Thus a change in the original reserved resources triggers the setup process [11]. Some of these issues, notably the scalability of refresh messages have been addressed elsewhere [18, 19, 20] in contexts which different from the on-board communication architecture. A scheme to aggregate the RSVP refresh messages has been proposed

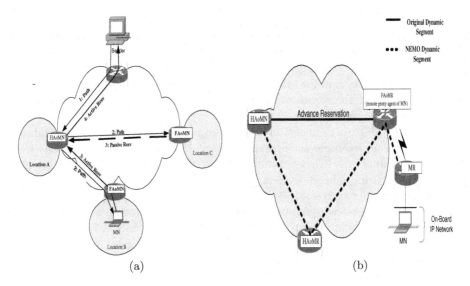

Fig. 2. (a) Overview of MRSVP, (b) Dynamic segment problem of MRSVP

which essentially combines all the refresh messages for the various sessions over a single refresh period into a single message. The aggregation of the refresh messages is much easier due to their periodic nature. However, handling the setup and tear down messages is much more difficult since they are triggered randomly based on user dynamics. This problem is further magnified due to the presence of a large number of users in the on-board system. A scheme to aggregate setup messages based on the bandwidth threshold has been briefly mentioned in [18]. However, to our knowledge, there has been no detailed analysis of aggregation schemes for setup messages.

3   Architecture and Operation of On-Board RSVP

Unlike most wireless end devices (e.g; mobile phones), whose mobility behavior is generally unpredictable, the routes of on-board IP network in public transport vehicle are known in advance. We can leverage this knowledge for making the advance reservations to the future locations. This important feature is used to design an effective and scalable On-Board RSVP protocol. This section presents the protocol architecture and operation of the proposed On-Board RSVP. We describe the QoS proxies, message formats, protocol operation, and handoff management.

3.1   QoS Proxies

On-Board RSVP requires three types of QoS proxies deployed at three different locations. A mobile proxy (MPX) is located at the on-board IP subnet, a home proxy (HPX) is located in the home network of the MR, and foreign proxies (FPXs) are located at subnets the MR visits during the trip.

The main tasks performed by MPX are: (1) to compress multiple individual outgoing RSVP (Path and Resv) messages into a single message and de-compress incoming messages into individual RSVP messages, (2) establish active reservations from MR to home of MR, (3) to acquire addresses of FPXs (which are pre-allocated CoAs of MR) using mechanisms such as service location protocol (beyond the scope of this paper) at predefined future locations of MR and send these addresses to HPX. Task (1) addresses the scalability issue by reducing bandwidth overhead of RSVP signaling over the wireless connection, Task (2) allows reservation of resources over the correct path (NEMO dynamic segment shown in Figure 2(b)), and Task (3) helps HPX to establish passive reservation between home of MR and all future visiting locations. Passive reservations will be converted to active reservations when MR reaches a new location (similar to MRSVP). HPX has the following responsibilities: (1) compress multiple MR-bound RSVP (Path and Resv) messages into a single message and de-compress messages from MR into individual RSVP messages, (2) establish active reservations between home of MR and MR, and passive reservations between home of MR and FPXs. On behalf of the MR, FPXs establish passive reservations between future locations of MR and MR home using pre-allocated CoA of MR at their respective locations.

3.2   On-Board RSVP Messages

To facilitate the above tasks of QoS proxies, On-Board RSVP uses six new messages in addition to the existing RSVP messages respectively. These messages are briefly described in Fig.3. Fig.4 and Fig.5 shows the format of OBPath and OBResv messages respectively.

These additional objects in Fig.4 and Fig.5 help in compression and decompression mechanism. For compression of RSVP Path messages to OBPath message, the additional object ACC_Sender has the destination (receiver) addresses with the corresponding Sender_TSpec objects of the received Path messages

Messages	Desciption
OBPath	All individual Path messages received in the last T sec are compressed into this message
OBResv	All individual Resv messages received in the last T sec are compressed into this message
OBRx	It contains the receiver specification and identification such as flow spec object and session object.
OBTx	It contains the sender specification such as sender Tspec and ADSpec object.
OBRls	asks the FPX of old location to release any reserved resources
OBLns	contains addresses of FPXs of future locations.

Fig. 3. On-Board RSVP messages

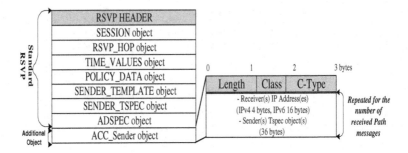

Fig. 4. OBPath message format

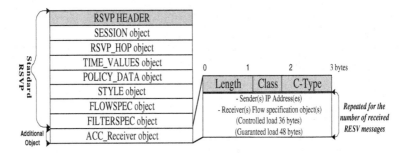

Fig. 5. OBResv message format

by the QoS proxy. Similarly for the compression of standard Resv messages to OBResv message, ACC_Receiver has the destination (sender) addresses with the corresponding flow specifications of the received Resv messages. The received Path and Resv messages are compressed by the QoS proxy depending on the aggregation policy in use. These aggregation policies will be explained in greater detail in the subsequent section.

To de-compress OBPath, the responsible QoS proxy will send the new standard RSVP Path messages to destinations using their respective Sender_TSpec specified in compress message. On the other hand, for the de-compression of OBResv, the responsible QoS proxy will send the standard Resv messages to the senders on behalf of the destinations (receivers) using their respective flow specifications stored in ACC_Receiver object.

3.3   Tunnel Operation

In RSVP tunnel protocol [17], data packets that require resource reservations within a tunnel are encapsulated by perpending an IP and UDP header and by using the UDP port number to distinguish packets of different RSVP flows. This is a layer violation problem because routers are designed to process data only at the network layer of OSI model. Other drawbacks with IP and UDP encapsulation are traffic control performance and IP level security problem. For the efficient operation of On-Board RSVP over bidirectional tunnel, the proposed protocol make use of flow label field of mobile IPv6 to distinguish between QoS and non-QoS data packets. Therefore in order to establish a proper On-Board RSVP session state in bidirectional tunnel routers, OBPath has a unique label in the sender template object and similarly OBResv must also contain that label in filter specification object. The packet classifier in the tunnel routers does not have to look at any port number but only at the pair of QoS proxy address and label in an encapsulated header.

3.4 Protocol Operation

Using proxies and messages described above, Fig.6 (a) illustrates the resource reservation process of On-Board RSVP. Initially, MPX sends the list of future locations (or addresses of FPXs) to HPX using the OBLns message (step 1). Let us assume that there are two senders, S1 and S2, sending data to two on-board receivers, R1 and R2 respectively. The periodic Path messages from senders go to the home agents of respective receivers, who then simply relay them to home network of MR (step 2). The HPX intercepts all these Path messages during a time period determined by the deployed aggregation policy. In this illustrative example, we assume that the TOP policy has been deployed wherein the HPX compresses all the Path messages in the last T sec, and sends a single compressed active OBPath (AOBPath) message to MPX and a passive OBPath (POBPath) to all FPXs contained in the OBLns message received earlier (step 3). Upon receiving the OBPath message, the MPX de-compresses it and delivers the individual Path messages to respective on-board receivers (step 4). The receivers respond with Resv messages with bandwidth requirements, in this case 2 Kbps and 3 Kbps (step 5). MPX compresses these two outgoing Resv messages into a single active OBResv (AOBResv) message and sends it to HPX over the wireless link (step 6). It also notifies the FPXs that the total bandwidth requirement is 5 Kbps using the OBRx message (step 7). The FPXs, upon receiving OBRx, establishes passive reservation to HPX using the passive OBResv (POBResv) message (step 8). Finally, the HPX de-compress active OBResv (AOBResv) message into individual Resv messages of 2 kbps and 3 Kbps and send them to S1 and S2 (step 9). In this case, the data packets, which require resources, are encapsulated by HPX with proper label (carried by OBPath and OBResv messages). While normal best effort oriented data packets are encapsulated with no label.

3.5 Handoff Management

Fig.6 (b) shows the dynamics of resource management of On-Board RSVP after a hand-off, i.e., after a MR changes its point of attachment from an old location to a new location. MPX sends an OBRls message to its old foreign agent (step 1). Upon receiving the OBRls message from MR, MR's old foreign agent will send standard RSVP RESV tear message to explicitly free up the resources reserved by MR on routers along the path to the home agent of MR (step 2). Finally MPX sends the updated list of its future FPXs (old FPX is removed from the list) to HPX (step 3).

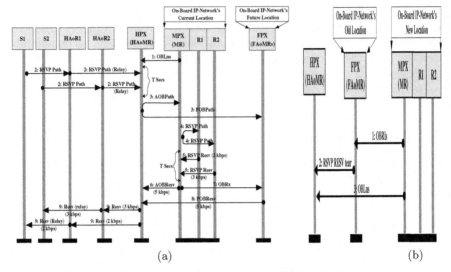

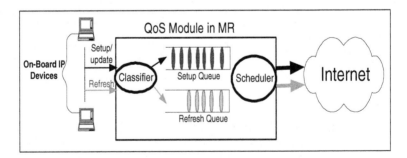

Fig. 6. (a) Resource reservation process, (b) Handoff scenario

4   Aggregation Schemes for Setup Messages

The QoS module at the MR and FAoMR are responsible for handling all the signaling messages. The refresh and setup/update messages are classified into two queues as shown in Fig.7. The incoming Path and Resv messages will be compared by the classifier to the existing Path state block and reservation state block respectively in order to determine whether they are new, updated, or refresh messages. Since new/update messages need different treatment to that of refresh messages, new and update messages are placed in the setup queue, while refresh messages are placed in the refresh queue.

Fig. 7. Setup and refresh messages handling at MR

One way to reduce the frequency of setup messages is the reservation threshold scheme [18]. In this scheme, the setup/update messages will only be sent when the reserved bandwidth changes by more than a certain threshold value

R. We will call this policy as Resource Threshold Operating Policy (ROP). The main advantage of the ROP is that the granularity of bandwidth request in setup messages can be controlled by setting R. But this scheme suffers from three problems. Firstly, the ROP policy provides no control over the waiting time of the messages in queue. This time duration is entirely dependent on the value of the threshold and the bandwidth requirements of the new setup requests. In particular, if the bandwidth requirements of the sessions are considerably small, as compared to the value of the threshold, it can easily result in a considerably large waiting time. Secondly with ROP, there is no control over the level of aggregation that can be achieved. In other words, we cannot control the number of messages that will be compressed. Lastly, ROP may result in unfairness in the waiting time duration for sessions with different resource requirements. For simplicity, assume that there are two categories of sessions with bandwidth requirements $r1$ and $r2$ respectively, where $r1$ is much less than R and $r2$ is approximately equal to R. One can readily see that sessions with bandwidth requirement $r1$ have to wait for a longer time in the queue before the threshold value is reached, as compared to the sessions with bandwidth requirement of $r2$.

As an alternative to ROP, we propose two new aggregation techniques to address the above problems: (1) Temporal Operating Policy (TOP), and (2) Cardinal Operating Policy (COP). The TOP is based on time interval. In this technique the QoS module takes a vacation of a fixed length T if there are no message(s) in queue. After the time period T, it scans the setup queue and if it finds message(s) waiting in the queue it starts the setup process (generating On-Board RSVP messages), otherwise it takes another vacation of length T. Unlike TOP, where the QoS module goes on vacation for a fixed duration of time, in COP the QoS module remains in the vacation state until a certain K request messages are accumulated in the queue. We assume that that there is no arrival during the setup process as the time for setup process is negligible. The problem of the waiting delay of setup messages can be managed by the TOP technique. Consequently, TOP may be used to aggregate real time sessions, which require defined minimum setup delay. The COP policy provides fine-grained control over the message aggregation factor by setting an appropriate value for K, and hence eliminates the second drawback of the ROP policy. As a result, with COP, it is possible to admit a defined number of sessions, which may be useful for situations where profit is based on number of admitted sessions. Contrary to ROP, the control parameters in TOP and COP are completely independent of the bandwidth requirement of sessions. As a result, these two schemes do not exhibit any unfairness towards the sessions with low bandwidth requirements, which is another limitation of ROP. However, unlike the ROP scheme, neither TOP nor COP provides any control over the granularity of the bandwidth aggregation.

In general, these aggregation policies will help to reduce the frequency of setup messages, which results in savings in terms of the signaling and processing overhead. However, since all these schemes aggregate several requests into one collective request, they will lead to a slight increase in the setup delay. It is important to note that the setup process delay is totally independent of the actual end-to-end delay experienced by flows. The control parameters of these policies can be adjusted based on passenger dynamics and the QoS requirements of the applications. For example, a non-real-time application may be able to sustain a longer setup delay. A hybrid QoS module could also be developed, wherein these three aggregation policies could be deployed simultaneously to cater to the varying requirements of different applications. However, there is a need to develop an analytical model for comparing the performance of these policies under different set of parameters such as setup delay and setup processing cost.

5   Conclusion and Future Work

We have identified three major limitations of existing RSVP protocols in the context of on-board IP networks. To overcome these limitations,, we have proposed an extension of RSVP, called On-Board RSVP. The architecture, protocol message formats and the operation of On-Board RSVP are described. One can readily see that On-Board RSVP requires minimum modifications to the existing RSVP protocol. The highly dynamic nature of the QoS reservations in an on-board communication system also introduces a scalability issue due to the large number of setup and tear-down messages that need to be processed by the MR and other routers along the bi-directional tunnel. To address this problem, we have also proposed two new aggregation schemes for setup messages : Cardinal Operation Policy (COP) and Temporal Operating Policy (TOP). As part of our on-going work, we are focusing on developing a mathematical model for analysing these schemes and comparing their performance characteristics under different scenarios.

Acknowledgment

The authors would like to acknowledge Dr. Debashish Saha and the entire OCEAN [8] team for their suggestions and feedback. The research was partly funded by Australian Research Council (ARC) Discovery Grant DP0452942.

References

1. K-D Lin and J-F Chang. Communications and entertainment onboard a high-speed public transport system. IEEE Wireless Communication, 9:8489, February 2002.
2. PointShot Wireless: http://www.pointshotwireless.com.
3. Icomera: Real-Time Internet Services Onboard Trains: http://www.railway-technology.com/contractors/entertainment/icomera/.
4. Connexion by Boeing: http://www.connexionbyboeing.com.
5. Nautilus6 Working Group: http://www.nautilus6.org/.
6. In Motion Technology Inc.: http://www.inmotiontechnology.com.
7. Overdrive: Spectrum Efficient Uni-and Multicast Services over Dynamic Multi-Radio Networks in Vehicular Environments: http://www.comnets.rwth-aachen.de.

8. Project OCEAN: On-board Communication, Entertainment, And iNformation: http://www.ocean.cse.unsw.edu.au.
9. CISCO 3200 Series Wireless and Mobile Access Routers: http://www.cisco.com/en/us/products/hw/routers/ps272.
10. V. Devarapalli, R.Wakikawa, A. Petrescu, and P. Thubert. NEMO Basic Protocol. Internet draft: http://www.ietf.org/internet-drafts/draft-ietf-nemo-basic-support-03.txt, June 2004.
11. L. Zhang, S. Deering, D. Estrin, S. Shenker, and D. Zappala. RSVP: A new resource ReSerVation Protocol. pages 818, September 1993.
12. R. Braden, D. Clark, and Shenker S. Integrated services in the internet architecture: an overview. RFC 1633, June 1994.
13. A. K. Talukdar, B. R. Badrinath, and A. Acharya. MRSVP: A Resource Reservation Protocol for an Integrated Services Network with Mobile Hosts. Wireless Networks, 7:519, 2001.
14. W-T. Chen and L-C. Huang. RSVP mobility support: a signaling protocol for integrated services Internet with mobile hosts. In Proc.IEEE INFOCOM 00, volume 3, pages 12801292, 2000.
15. C-C. Tseng, G-C. Lee, R-S. Liu, and T-P. Wang. HMRSVP: A Hierarchial Mobile RSVP Protocol. Wireless Networks, 9:95102, March 2003.
16. A. Mahmoodian and G. Haring. Mobile RSVP with Dynamic Resource Sharing. In Proc. IEEE Conference on Wireless Communications and Networking (WCNC00), volume 2, pages 896901, September 2000.
17. A. Terzis, J. Krawczyk, J. Wroclawski, and L. Zhand. RSVP Operation Over IP Tunnels. RFC 2746, January 2000.
18. A. Terzis, L. Zhang, and E. Hahne. Reservations for Aggregate Traffic: Experiences from an RSVP Tunnels Implementation. In Proc. IEEE International Workshop on Quality of Service (IWQoS98), May 1998.
19. F. Baker, C. Iturralde, F. Le Faucheur, and B. Davie. Aggregation of RSVP for IPv4 and IPv6 Reservations. RFC 3175, September 2001.
20. L.Berger, D. Gan, G. Swallow, P. Pan, F. Tommasi, and S. Molendini. RSVP Refresh Overhead Extensions. RFC 2961, April 2001.

A Secure PIM-SM Multicast Routing Protocol

Junqi Zhang[1], Vijay Varadharajan[1], and Yi Mu[2]

[1]Department of Computing, Macquarie University,
North Ryde, NSW 2109, Australia
[2] School of Information Technology and Computer Science,
University of Wollongong, NSW 2522, Australia
{janson, vijay}@ics.mq.edu.au,   ymu@uow.edu.au

Abstract. This paper presents a new secure scheme for Protocol Independent Multicast Sparse Mode (PIM-SM). PIM is the predominant
multicast routing protocol in use on the Internet today, where members
of the multicast group are distributed sparsely over a wide area. Security
issues are particularly important in such multicast routing protocols. In
this paper, we propose two distributed group key management schemes to
build a secure PIM-SM multicast routing protocol. With these schemes,
the network administrator can manage the secure PIM-SM multicast
more efficiently, and the management of groups is made more flexible.

1   Introduction

Multicasting invoves sending of data from one to many recipients, or many to
many recipients [1]. Multicast has become significant because it can be used to
service many users with reduced loading of the network and the server. The
prospective members initiate joining the multicast group using the Internet
Group Management Protocol (IGMP). Routers in a network employ multicast
routing protocols to optimally route the multicast packets through the network
from the source to the destinations. The multicast routing protocols can be
divided into three categories: distance vector, link state, and shared trees. Distance Vector Routing Protocol (DVRP) and Protocol Impendent Protocol-Dense
Mode (PIM-DM) are based on distance vector, Multicast Open Shortest Path
First (MOSPF)is based on link state, and Protocol Impendent Protocol-Sparse
Mode (PIM-SM) and Core-Based Tree (CBT) are based on shared trees. PIM-
SM is designed for the larger and sparser groups encountered on the Internet and
is probably the predominant multicast routing protocols in use on the Internet
today [2]. However security issues are still a major concern with multicasting
protocols for some of the applications that have confidential and high value content. Furthermore, there are issues with the system robustness as the malicious
users may attack the multicast routing system and disrupt the interactions.

In general, there are three main characterisitics of multicast: all members
receive all packets sent to the address, open group membership, and open access
to send packets [3]. Based on these properties, the components of the multicast

A. Sen et al. (Eds.): IWDC 2004, LNCS 3326, pp. 276–288, 2004.
© Springer-Verlag Berlin Heidelberg 2004

system that need to be secured include the following [4][3]: multicast distribution tree protection, end-to-end data protection through cryptographic operations and member access control. Researchers have developed many schemes for end-to-end data protection [5] [6] and the member access control [3][7][8]. In this paper, we present one multicast distribution tree protection scheme that uses a distribution algorithm to protect the control messages and authenticate the sending routers in PIM-SM multicast domain as well as another flexible end-to-end data protection scheme that uses a dynamic group key management method that we have proposed earlier.

The remainder of this paper is organized as follows. Section 2 introduces the PIM-SM Protocol and security issues. Section 3 describes the distributed algorithm, and then presents our new secure PIM multicast routing control messages scheme using the ID based distributed group key management. Section 4 introduces the dynamic group key management algorithm and then proposes the secure end-to-end data protection PIM-SM multicast scheme. Finally, the last section contains some concluding remarks.

2   PIM-SM and Security Issues

This section introduces PIM-SM protocol and its security issues. There are several related works such as [9] [10] [11] and [12].

In general, PIM-SM is designed for the larger and sparser groups encountered on the Internet. PIM uses an underlying topology-gathering protocol to develop a routing table. This routing table is called Multicast Routing Information Base (MRIB). MRIB is used to provide the next hop router to each destination subnet. PIM-SM takes three phases to route data packets from source to the receivers.

Phase one builds a shard tree rooted at the Rendezvous Point (RP) and then uses this shared tree to forward data to group members (Figure 1). A multicast receiver sends an IGMP join message to local Designate Router (DR). The DR sends (*, G) PIM Join message towards the RP for that group. The join message (*, G) reaches either the RP, or another router that already has a group member downstream for that group. If there are many members in that group, the join message will converge on the RP and form RP tree (RPT) (also called shared tree) for that group. Join message is sent periodically by the receiver's designated router as long as the receiver remains in the group. The multicast data sender sends a packet with multicast address as its destination to the DR. The sender's DR encapsulates the data packet (called registering) and sends them directly to the RP. After receiving the register packet, the RP decapsulates them, and forwards them on to the shared tree.

Phase two forwards the native (unencapsulated) packets from the sender to the RP, as the encapsulation and decapsualation is expensive. After the RP receives the registering packets, it will initiate an (S, G) source specific Join to S. All the routers along the path initiates the (S, G) multicast tree state; then the packets start to flow following the (S, G) tree to RP. If the packets reach a router with (*.G) state, then they can do a short cut to receivers. RP may receive

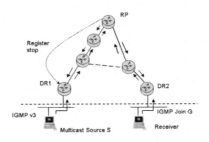

Fig. 1. PIM-SM Phase one: Shared Tree

both the original and the encapsulated packets. It discards the encapsulated one and sends a register stop message to the DR of source to prevent the unnecessary encapsulated packets.

In phase three, the receiver's DR initiates a transfer from a source specific shortest path tree (SPT) instead of the shared tree. It sends an (S, G) Join message toward the sender. On receiving this Join message, the sender DR forwards the multicast data to the receiver directly. As several receivers initiate the shortest path tree, these paths converge and create a shortest path tree (SPT). At this time, the receiver may get two copies: one from the RPT, and one from SPT. It will drop the one from RPT, and send an (S, G) prune message to RP (called (S, G, rpt) prune). After this, it forms the final shortest path tree (Figure 2).

We can note that PIM sparse mode has several interesting characteristics. First, PIM-SM has the transition property; that is, it transmits from the shared tree to source-based tree. After the receiver receives the multicast packets from the RP through the shared tree, it gets the other multicast packets directly from the source through the source-based tree if this tree is shorter. Moreover, RP is the core of PIM-SM; the senders report their existence to one or more RPs, and

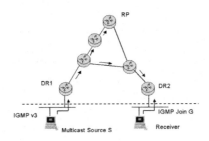

Fig. 2. PIM-SM Phase Three: Source-specific Shorted-Path Tree

the receivers find the multicast session by querying RPs. Furthermore, routers join the PIM-SM tree through explicit message when there are downstream receivers. These flexibility and scaling characteristics make PIM-SM more suitable for those groups where members are distributed sparsely across a wide area.

As mentioned earlier, security issues become significant in such an environment. One can envisage several attacks based on forged messages to the PIM-SM system (see for instance, IETF Draft). They include forged link-local messages (Join/Prune message, Hello message, and Assert message) and forged unicast messages (such as a Register message and a Register stop message). The forged register message can be used to inject illegitimate traffic onto the shared multicast tree. The forged register stop message can be used to prevent the legitimate DR from registering the packets to the RP. Currently, IETF Draft [12] recommends using the IPSec transport mode (AH) to prevent these attacks against the PIM. The PIM network administrator configures each PIM router with one or more Security Associations (SA) and associated SPI. The senders use it to sign PIM protocol messages and the receiver uses it to authenticate the received PIM protocol message.

There are two methods to protect the register and register stop messages in PIM-SM network. One involves configuring each DR to select a unique SA and SPI for the traffic sent to each RP. Another involves all DR in the same domain use same authentication method or authentication key. Note that the first method will create key management and distribution problem for the network administrator, and the second method has another problem that all routers must be changed when you want to change the authentication key or the method.

In the next section, we will propose a new secure distributed group management algorithm where each router in the domain has a unique key, and the RP can use a different key to authenticate the register message.

Other security issues in PIM-SM multicast include confidentiality and authentication. As we know, in the IP multicast model, any host can use the Internet Group Membership Protocol (IGMP) to join any multicast group. This open group model of the multicast is beneficial in many environments. Another property of the multicast is that any host can send data to the multicast group. However, these properties of the multicast might cause some serious security issues such as eavesdropping and denial of service. The group members have to verify the message received is really from the claimed source.

The solutions for these security problems include multicast group data encryption with group key management, multicast source authentication, multicast receivers and multicast sender access control. The Internet Engineering Task Force (IETF) in [13] has proposed a multicast security architecture reference framework. This framework classifies and specifies the functional areas, functional elements and their interfaces.

The three functional areas are multicast data handling, group key management, and the multicast security policies. Multicast data handling covers the issues concerning the security related treament of the multicast data by the sender and the receiver. Typically, the data is encrypted with a group key which mainly addresses the issues of confidentiality. The data authentication includes the data source authentication and the data integrity. The multicast policy provides rules of operation for the other elements of the Reference Framework.

Group key management is concerned with the secure distribution and refreshing of the keying material. The keying material refers to the cryptographic key belonging to the group, the state associated with the keys and the other security parameters related to the key. Group key management is one of the main aspects of the security multicast. The objective of a group key management protocol is to provide the group members with an up-to-date security association. In the Group Security Association Model [14], the Group Key Management Architecture consists of three protocols: the Registration Protocol, the Re-key protocol, and the Data Security protocol.

There are two types of group keys: the KEK (key-encrypting key) and the TEK (traffic-encrypting key). The KEK maybe a single key that encrypts the TEK or a vector of keys that encrypt the TEK and other TEKs. The TEK is established by the Registration Protocol and is used by the re-key protocol. The TEK is established by the Re-Key Protocol and used by the Data Security Protocol.

There are some challenges in designing secure multicast services in IP multicast for the dynamic group in large scale systems, in which the group members join and leave frequently. One is that we need to ensure the forward and backward secrecy. Forward secrecy implies that whenever a member of a group leaves the group, s/he must be prevented from having further access to the data and keys of the multicast group. Backwards secrecy requires that the data communicated within a group before a new member or members join(s) must remain secret to the new member or members. Other multicast security requirements include "1 affects all" scalability and data source authentication. The former requirement implies that the addition or removal of one or more members from a group should not affect other members of the group. The latter addresses the situation where an adversary or a group member poses as a member or another member of the group in sending the data.

There are a lot of research works on secure multicast communications in recent years, and several survey papers categorize these existing secure multicast protocols. According to these papers [15], the existing group key management protocol can be divided into two categories: the flat scheme and the hierarchical scheme. The flat schemes can be further divided in Centralized Flat schemes and Distributed Flat schemes. The Hierarchical schemes can be further divided into node based protocols and the key based protocols. As far as we know all of these existing protocols still suffer from at least one or more of the following problems: scalability, secrecy, dynamic subgroup/member move, unreliable multicast and high dynamics.

Based on the number of the senders, multicast is divided into two types: one-to-many (or 1-to-N) and many-to-many (or M-to-N). In a 1-to-N multicast, only one sender can transmit data to a group and in a M-to-N multicast, multiple (or all) group members can transmit data to a group. As we discussed before, PIM-

SM multicast suffers more than other routing protocols from these problems. In this paper, we will give two flexible group key management protocols, one for the one-to-many PIM-SM multicast and another for many-to-many PIM-SM multicast. These schemes will follow IEFE's multicast security architecture reference framework and the group security association model.

3   New Secure Distribution Tree Protection Scheme for PIM-SM

In this section, we introduce an ID based distributed group management algorithm, and then present our new secure distribution tree protection scheme for PIM-SM.

3.1   System Setup

We set up our systems using bilinear pairings due to Boneh and Franklin [16]. Let us define two cyclic groups G_1, G_2. G_1 is an additive group and G_2 is a multiplicative group. Both have a prime order q. Let e be a computable bilinear map $e : G_1 \times G_1 \to G_2$. For $a, b \in Z_q$ and $P, Q \in G_1$, we have $e(aP, bQ) = e(P, Q)^{ab}$.

Definition 1. (Decisional Diffie-Hellman Problem) *Given $P, aP, bP, cP \in G_1$ and $a, b, c \in Z_q$, decide whether $c = ab \in Z_q$.*

A decisional Diffie-Hellman problem (DDHP) is satisfied [17] since $e(aP, bP) = e(P, P)^{ab}$. The security of the pairing algorithm is based on the computational Diffie-Hellman problem (CDHP), which is given below.

Definition 2. (Computational Diffie-Hellman Problem) *Let a, b be chosen from Z_q at random and P be a generator chosen from G_1 at random. Given (P, aP, bP), compute $abP \in G$.*

G_1 is referred to as a Gap Diffie-Hellman (GDH) group and CDHP can be referred to as a Gap Diffie-Hellman problem – if DDHP can be solved in polynomial time and no polynomial algorithm can solve CDHP with non-negligible advantage within polynomial time.

An Identity-Based Signature Scheme. Let Alice be a server who is trusted by a group of users. Alice implements the following steps in order to set up the system.

- selects a master secret key s and then computes its corresponding public key $Y \leftarrow sP$;
- selects a hash function $H_1 : \{0, 1\}^* \to G_1$;
- extracts $Q_i \leftarrow H_1(ID_i)$;
- computes secret signing key for each user: $K_i \leftarrow sQ_i$.

To sign a message $m \in \{0,1\}^*$, user i selects a random number $r \in \mathbb{Z}_q$, a generator $P \in \mathbb{G}_1$, and a public hash function $H_2 : \{0,1\}^* \to \mathbb{Z}_q$ and computes $R_i \leftarrow rQ_i$ and

$$S_i \leftarrow (H_2(m, R_i) + r)K_i.$$

The signature is now a triple (R_i, S_i, m).

To verify the signature, the following is checked:

$$e(S_i, P) \stackrel{?}{=} e(H(m, R_i)H_1(ID_i) + R, Y).$$

3.2   Our Secure Tree Protection Scheme for PIM-SM

In this section, we present a new security scheme for the PIM-SM system. As we mentioned in the last section, each DRi has a unique identification ID_i. No matter which DRi sends the signed register message to the RP in Phase One or the RPi sends the register stop message to DRr in the Phase Two, both can use this scheme to authenticate the received message that comes from ID_i.

The scheme works as follows. The domain administrator sets up the system by following the algorithm presented in the preceding section and then distributes each DR's secret key via secure channels in the domain separately. At this stage, each DR in the domain has a public key Y, secret signing key K_i, a unique identification ID_i.

For the register message in the PIM-SM protocol Phase One, the DRi can sign the register message M_r using his secret signing key K_i and generate a signature triple (R_i, S_i, M_r), where $R_i \leftarrow rQ_i$, $S_i \leftarrow (H_2(M_r, R_i) + r)K_i$, and M_r is the register message.

When the RP receives the signing register massage, it can verify the signature using the public key Y and the sender DR ID_i.

$$e(S_i, P) \stackrel{?}{=} e(H(M_r, R_i)H_1(ID_i) + R, Y).$$

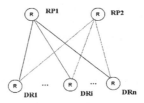

Fig. 3. Secure Tree Protection Scheme

Similarly, for the register stop message in the PIM-SM protocol Phase Two, similarly, the RP as a DR can also sign the stop register message M_{sr} and generate the signature (R_i, S_i, M_{sr}), and then it can be verified by the DR.

4   New Secure End-to-End Data Protection Scheme for PIM-SM

In this section, we describe an dynamic distributed group key management algorithm, and then present two new secure end-to-end data protection schemes based on one-to-many and many-to-many multicast for PIM-SM.

4.1   Key Generation Algorithm

Our approach involves the proposal of a dynamic group key management scheme that enables secure and efficient updating of group members. We achieve this by constructing a public key that is associated with several private keys. The proposal for secure multicasting is based on our earlier work on key distribution described in [18].

Preliminaries. The security of our scheme is dependent on the difficulty of computing discrete logarithms, and is based on the polynomial functions and a set of exponentials.

Let N be a product of p, q that are large primes, $\mathbb{Z}_N^*$ be a multiplicative group of order $\phi(N) = (p-1)(q-1)$, and $g \in \mathbb{Z}_{\phi(N)}$ be a generator. Let $x_i \in_R \mathbb{Z}_q$ for $i = 0, 1, 2, ..., n$ be a set of integers. A polynomial function of order n is constructed as follows: $f(x) = \prod_{i=1}^{n}(x - x_i) \equiv \sum_{i=0}^{n} a_i x^i \bmod \phi(N)$, where a_i are the coefficients: $a_0 = \prod_{j=1}^{n}(-x_j)$, $a_1 = \sum_{i=1}^{n} \prod_{i \neq j}^{n}(-x_j), ..., a_{n-2} = \sum_{i \neq j}^{n}(-x_i)(-x_j)$, $a_{n-1} = \sum_{i=1}^{n}(-x_j)$, $a_n = 1$. Note that $f(x_j) = \sum_{i=0}^{n} a_i x_j^i = 0$. We can use this property to construct a multicasting encryption system. With the set $\{a_i\}$, we can construct the corresponding exponential functions,

$$\{g^{a_0}, g^{a_1}, g^{a_2}, ..., g^{a_n}\} \equiv \{g_0, g_1, g_2, ..., g_n\}.$$

System Setup. The construction of the encryption and decryption keys is done as follows:

- Select n distinct random numbers $x_i \in \mathbb{Z}_{\phi(N)}$ for $i = 1, 2, \cdots, n$, which form a set X_n and a subset $X_m \subset X_n$.
- Compute $A = \prod_{j=1}^{n}(\prod_{i=0}^{n-1} g_i^{x_j^i}) \bmod N$. Note that A is computed only once. We will see later that dynamic updates of the system do not require re-computation of A.
- Select an integer $b \in \mathbb{Z}_{\phi(N)}$ and compute its multiplicative inverse b^{-1} such that $bb^{-1} = 1 \bmod \phi(N)$.
- Compute $\bar{x}_j = b^{-1} \sum_{i \neq j}^{n} x_i^n \bmod \phi(N)$, for $j = 1, 2, ..., n$.
- Compute $\hat{x}_j = s_j x_j^n$, where

$$s_j = s_1' s_2' \cdots s_n', \quad s_j s_j' = s_j' \bmod \phi(N), \quad s_j, s_j' \in \mathbb{Z}_{\phi(N)}.$$

These values satisfy the equality:

$$A^s g^{sb\bar{x}_j} g^{s\hat{x}_j} = 1 \bmod N, \quad \forall j \in \{1, 2, \cdots, n\}.$$

A is kept by the authorized server and will be used as the encryption key. Since the encryption key is not public, there is no need for us to protect it against any illegal modification.

$\bar{x}_j$ and $\hat{x}_j$ are given to user j as its secret decryption key during the process of its registration. Hence the private decryption key doublet is $(\bar{x}_j, \hat{x}_j)$. Note that the computation of A is a one-time task. The server does not need to modify this during a system update. This is an important feature, since it makes the encryption/decryption processes very efficient (a maximum of 2 or 3 exponential computations).

Multicasting Encryption Protocol. The encryption key A is used to encrypt a session key, which is then used to encrypt a message. All members of the group can decrypt the session key and then decrypt the message individually with their private keys. Let us suppose that M is the message to be encrypted and k is a session key. The protocol works as follows:

- Select an integer $r \in_R \mathbb{Z}_{\phi(N)}$.
- Compute $\bar{g} = g^{sr} \bmod N$ and $\hat{g} = g^{sbr} \bmod N$.
- Compute the ciphertext $c = E_k(M)$ and $k' = kA^{sr} \bmod N$, where $E_k(.)$ denotes a symmetric key encryption function.
- Broadcast the 4-tuple $(\bar{g}, \hat{g}, c, k')$ to all subscribers.

To decrypt the session key, the user j computes $k'\hat{g}^{\bar{x}_j}\bar{g}^{\hat{x}_j} = k \bmod N$. k is then used for the decryption of the message.

4.2   Security Scheme for One-to-Many PIM-SM Protocol

As mentioned before, the multicast can be divided into two categories: one to many (or 1-to-N)and many to many (or M-to-N). One-to-many multicast covers such scenarios where the multicast group has only one sender and multiple receivers. Only one sender can transmit the data and the transmission is unidirectional from the sender to other group members. The sender is the producer of the data and the receivers are the passive consumers of the data. Some examples of this multicast application include video-on-demand, Internet TV and other applications such as broadasting of stock quotes and news.

In one-to-many or many-to-many multicast, usually there are thousands or even millions of members, and the membership is dynamic. That is, the members join and leave the group frequently. In particularl, for the PIM-SM multicast routing protocol, the members can be sparsely distributed in a vast area. So it is a big challenge to ensure perfect secrecy to prevent the non-legitimate member from accessing the data. In some applications, the data source authentication is also required.

For one-to-many multicast, the sender is usually the group owner and the initiator of the group. More specifically, in the PIM-SM multicast routing protocol, the sender will be located in the root of the shared tree or the Rendezvous Point (RP) for the efficiency. Therefore, the sender can act as the Group Controller and Key Server (GCKS). We also discuss the case in which the sender is located in one of the branches of the shared tree.

In the rest of this section, we will propose a new security scheme for PIM-SM multicast routing protocol based on the distributed algorithm given in last section.

As we mentioned before, there are three protocols in the group key management architecture. The first one is the registration protocol. In this phase, the GCKS (sender) initiates the protocol by inviting the prospective member to join a multicast group. If the prospective member agrees to join the group, it can establish the security Association (SA). Then it can use the security channel such as the IPsec ot TLS/SSL to transmit the private key ($\bar{x}_j$ and $\hat{x}_j$) to the new member, which is generated as described in the previous section.

The second protocol is the re-keying protocol. To remove a member, the GCKS does not need to reconstruct the encryption key A. Instead, the GCKS only recomputes s such that s'_γ does not include the member to be removed; the computation is $s = \Sigma_{i=1,i\neq\gamma}^{n} s'_i$. We can still use the protocol above without any modification.

To add new members to the group, the GCKS makes use of an element in the spare set $X_n - X_m$. Recall that we have assumed that the actual number of members is less than the total set. That is, $m < n$ or $X_m < X_n$. Hence to add a new member, the GCKS simply moves one unused element from $X_n - X_m$ to X_m.

The third protocol is the data security protocol. Figure 4 shows this protocol in the PIM-SM multicast. As mentioned in Section 2, we have two types of group keys: the KEK and the TEK. KEK is used for the re-keying protocol and the TEK is used for the data transfer security protocol. In this scheme, there are two ways to encrypt the data. The multicast source or sender (GCKS) can use the encryption key (A) as both KEK and TEK. In the re-keying protocol, the sender (GCKS) recomputes s for an update of the group.

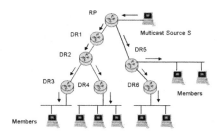

Fig. 4. Securing One-to-Many Multicast – Scheme One

One can also adopt a hybrid approach to reduce the encrypting and decrypting time. The sender's(GCKS) encryption key (A) is used for the KEK. The GCKS generates a symmetric key as the TEK to encrypt the message to be transmitted. The message to be transmitted is encrypted with the TEK that is encrypted with the KEK, and is then sent to the associated members. The members can decrypt it with their own private key ($\bar{x}_j$ and $\hat{x}_j$) to get the session key TEK, and then use it to decrypt the cipher message. The message data can be transmitted to the members along the shared tree just like the Core Based Tree (CBT), because this shared tree is also source-specific shortest-path tree (SPT).

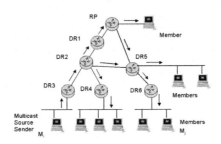

Fig. 5. Securing One-to-Many Multicast – Scheme Two

In some cases, the sender may not be located in the root of the shared tree or Rendezvous Point (RP). In particular, the sender may be a mobile node. Figure 5 depicts this protocol for PIM multicast. The multicast source or sender is still the group owner and can still act as the GCKS having the encryption key (A); it encrypts the data and sends it using the source-specific shortest-path tree (SPT). For instance, the message will be sent from multicast source (sender) to the member M_i following the path: DR_3, DR_2, DR_5, DR_6 to member M_j.

4.3   Security Scheme for Many-to-Many PIM-SM

Another category of the multicast is the Many-to-Many (or M-to-N). In many-to-many multicast protocols, some or all group members can disseminate messages in the multicast group. The many-to-many multicast applications include multimedia conferencing such as A/V and whiteboard, shared editing and collaboration, interactive distance learning, synchronized resources such as database updates, distributed interactive simulations (DIS) multi-player gaming and chat groups.

In some many-to-many multicast applications, the group owner needs to handle hundreds even thousands of members. Some or all of them may become the senders to distribute the messages. It needs a flexible scalable key management scheme.

We still use the distributed algorithm described earlier. By following the group key management architecture, it still has three protocols. The first and the second protocols are same as the ones for the one-to-many multicast. The third one is as follows (see Figure 6).

Here the GCKS can be located in the RP or at the root of the shared tree, while at the same time the sender could be any member of the multicast group. For example, the multicast source is in one branch of the shared tree (the member M_i). The GCKS will manage the KEK as described before to generate the KEK (A) and the TEK. When the multicast source M_i needs to send the data to the multicast group, it will get the TEK encrypted by the KEK (A) from the GCKS (in Figure 6, the path will be RP, $DR1$, $DR2$, $DR3$). Then it will decrypt the TEK with its private key pair ($\bar{x}_i$ and $\hat{x}_i$). After this, it can encrypt the data to be sent using the TEK, and transmit the encrypted data and the encrypted TEK to the multicast group members.

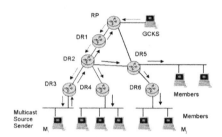

Fig. 6. Securing Many-to-Many Multicast Scheme

The sent data will follow the PIM source-specific shortest-path tree (SPT) from the sender to the multicast group members. For example, the encrypted data from the sender (M_i) to one of the multicast group members (M_j) will follow the source-specific shortest-path: DR_3, DR_2, DR_5, DR_6 to M_j (showed in Figure 6), and it will not detour to follow the path: DR_3, DR_2, DR_1, RP, DR_5, DR_6 to M_j. When the member M_j gets the encrypted TEK and message, it will use its private key pair (($\bar{x}_j$ and $\hat{x}_j$) to decrypt the TEK, and then use it to decrypt the encrypted message.

5   Concluding Remarks

We have presented a new security scheme for PIM-SM system. With this scheme, the PIM-SM domain administrator can manage the network more efficiently. Compared with the two currently used schemes, it does not need to update all the routers in the domain when the authentication key is changed, thereby making the scheme more flexible and efficient. We have proposed two secure end-to-end data protection schemes for PIM-SM. These schemes provide a flexible and scalable key management method for the dynamic multicast group. It also provides perfect secrecy and source authentication.

References

1. C. K. Miller, Multicast Networking and Applications. Addison Wesley Longman, Inc., September 1998.
2. JUNOS Internet Software Configuration Guide Multicast Release 6.0, Juniper Networks Inc.
3. P.Judge and M.Ammar, Security Issues and Solutions in Multicast Content Distribution: A Survey, IEEE Network Jan. 2003.
4. T. Hardjono and B. Cain, "Key establishment for IGKM authentication in IP multicast," in IEEE European Conference on Universal Multiservice networks (ECUMN), CREF, Colmar, France, 2000.
5. T. Hardjono and G. Tsudik, "IP multicast security: Issues and directions," Annales de Telecom, pp. 324-340, July- August 2000.
6. P. S. Kruus and J. P. Macker, " Techniques and Issues in multicast security," MILCOM 98, 1998.
7. C. Shields and J. J. Garcia-Auna-Aceves, "KHIP- a scalble protocol for secure multicast routing," in SIGCOMM, pp. 53-64,1999.
8. P. Q. Judge and M. H. Ammar, "Gothic: Group access control architecture for secure multicast and any cast," in IEEE INFOCOM, July 2002.
9. S.Deering, D.Estrin, D.Farinacci, Van Jacobson, C.Liu, L. Wei, Hierarchical PIM-SM Architecture for Inter-Domain Multicast Routing, draft-ietf-idmr-Hierarchical-pim.ps. December 18, 1995.
10. AR800 Series Modular Switching Router software Reference, Allied Telesyn.
11. B.Fenner, M.Handley, H.Holbrook, I. Kouvelas Protocol Independent Multicast - Sparse Mode (PIM-SM) Protocol Specification (Revised), IETF, Internet draft, draft-ietf-pim-sm-v2-new-08.txt, 1 October 2003.
12. O. Paridaens, A. Van Moffaert, Security Isses In PIM-SM, IRTF, GSEC meeting, Minneapolis, March 19, 2002.
13. T. Hardjono, B. Weis, MSEC Architecture, draft-ietf-msec-arch-00.txt, Oct 2002, Work in Progress.
14. M. Baugherand, R. Canetti, L. Dondeti, and F. Lindholm, "Group key management architecture, draft-ietf-msec-gkmarch-03.txt," Feb 2002, Work in Progress.
15. Lakshminath R. Dondeti, Sarit Mukherjee and Ashok Samal, Scalable Secure One-to-Many Group Communication Using Dual Encryption, Computer Communications Journal, November 2000.
16. D. Boneh and M. Franklin. Identity based encryption from the Weil pairing. SIAM J. of Computing, Vol. 32, No. 3, pp. 586-615, 2003. Extended abstract in proceedings of Crypto '2001, Lecture Notes in Computer Science, Vol. 2139, Springer-Verlag, pp. 213-229, 2001.
17. A. Joux, K. Nguyen, " Separating Decision Diffie-Hellman from Diffie-Hellman in cryptographic groups", Jan. 2001, available from eprint.iacr.org.
18. Y. Mu, and V. Varadharajan, "Robust and secure broadcasting," In Indocrypt 2001, Lecture Notes in Computing Science, Springer 2001.

Restoration of Virtual Private Networks with QoS Guarantees in the Pipe Model

Chittaranjan Hota[1], Sanjay Kumar Jha[2], and G. Raghurama[3]

[1] Computer Science and Information Systems Group,
Birla Institute of Technology and Science, Pilani, Rajasthan, 333031, India
c_hota@bits-pilani.ac.in
[2] School of Computer Science & Engineering,
University of New South Wales, Sydney, NSW 2052, Australia
National ICT Australia,
Bay 15, Australian Technology Park, Eveleigh 1431, NSW, Australia
sjha@cse.unsw.edu.au
[3] Electrical and Electronics Engineering Group,
Birla Institute of Technology and Science, Pilani, Rajasthan, 333031, India
graghu@bits-pilani.ac.in

Abstract. We propose heuristic algorithms to compute efficient restorable tunnel paths for IP Virtual Private Networks (IPVPNs). We first propose a Customer Premises Equipment (CPE) based solution to the problem and then optimize it by activating selectively few core ISP routers. We consider link cost as a function of bandwidth and loss over the link. The VPN tunnel paths are computed taking into account two parameters, the link cost and the cost of core routers that serve as end points of the tunnel. These paths we then call as Active Paths. Reliability of a VPN depends on the reliability of links in the Active path. To guarantee service quality and VPN availability to the Corporate users, seamless recovery from failures is mandatory. For the sake of survivability we propose heuristics for computing optimal backup path. We assume that the residual capacity available over the links for the VPN is sufficient to satisfy the Service Level Agreement (SLA). The problem of finding optimal paths for both Active and Backup is similar to constructing a directed steiner tree routed at source and spanning all the destinations which is NP-hard. Our heuristic algorithms provide an efficient solution to this problem with polynomial computation time.

1 Introduction

Corporations with branch offices and facilities across the globe wish to connect their subnetworks hundreds or even thousands of miles away. Traditional solutions based on dedicated leased lines are gradually being replaced by Vpns. A Virtual Private Network (VPN) is a logical network that is established on top of a physical network like the Internet in order to provide the behavior of a dedicated network with private lines to the users of the VPN [1]. As private networks built on using dedicated leased

A. Sen et al. (Eds.): IWDC 2004, LNCS 3326, pp. 289–302, 2004.
© Springer-Verlag Berlin Heidelberg 2004

lines offer guaranteed bandwidth, security, and latency, users demand similar guarantees from the IPVPNs [2].

The first generation IPVPNs focused on security issues ignoring Quality of Service guarantees. However, the recent IP-technologies like MPLS, Diffserv, RSVP deal with QoS issues. Quality of Service guarantee is becoming a significant challenge for the VPN service providers as VPN users want to have real time applications such as IP telephony, interactive games, teleconferencing, videos, and audios etc., over their VPN connections [3].

A variety of ways that tunnels can be formed are IP tunnels (IP over IP, IPSec, GRE), ATM VCs, and MPLS. The peer VPN model is one where paths are computed on a hop-by-hop basis, but in overlay VPN model the network layer-forwarding path is not done on a hop-by-hop basis, but rather the intermediate link layer is used as a cut-through to another edge node on the other side of the public network cloud [4]. The overlay model introduces serious scalability problems as network management to maintain routing information increases in direct proportion to the number of connected sites. A subtype of this overlay model is tunneling that allows tunnels between source and destination router, router to-router, or host-to-host. Tunnels encapsulate source packets with a new header, and forward them into a tunnel with a destination address of the end point.

Quality of Service in VPNs can be assured by employing either Pipe model or Hose model [5]. In Pipe model, the customer specifies the load between every pair of endpoints. In Hose model, the customer specifies the aggregate traffic requirements. Our work in this paper targets Pipe model VPNs.

There are two approaches for establishing VPN tunnels in Pipe model: Customer Premises Equipment (CPE) based and Network based [6]. In CPE based approach, tunnels are established only between the CPE devices (mainly border routers); whereas in the network-based approach, tunnels are established between the routers of core network.

In case of CPE based IPVPN, security may be applied from end to end [7]. As the traffic is IP traffic, the enterprise has the flexibility of adding and removing tunnels dynamically, instead of requiring the service provider to configure permanent virtual circuits (PVCs) within the network. This allows the enterprise to have the flexibility of a fully meshed network without having to pay for the numerous PVCs needed in frame relay or ATMs. As a result, the enterprise would bring up tunnels for video calls, overnight backups, file transfers, etc and take them down when not needed. In Network based approach, we have the tunnel end points within the ISPs core network, i.e. the routers in the core network can be strategically activated to make the path optimal between any two border routers or Customer edge routers, passing through core routers or provider routers. An example of this approach is described in Figure 1.

Figure 1 shows an Intranet/Extranet VPN scenario with four branch offices connected to the corporate headquarter through VPN. This situation models a single source and multiple destinations. Every link has a cost associated with it. The cost we assume here is a function of QoS parameters like bandwidth, and loss over a link. Every node in this network is associated with a weight function that measures the capability of the node in the form of hardware and software resources available at that node. We also assume another metric called *funds* that is defined as a limit on the number of core routers that can be activated. Our objective in this work is to find efficient tunnel path spanning from source to multiple destinations. Here, by activating few core routers, the overall routing cost can be reduced. For example, in figure 1, the total cost incurred when no core router is activated is 23 units; *S-C1-C3-D1(5)* plus *S-C1-C3-C4-D2(8)* plus *S-C1-C3-C5-D3(5)* plus *S-C1-C3-C5-D4(5)*. This is of course by traversing minimum distance. But, if we activate the core router C3, we get a cost benefit of 6 units for the same task. Activating C3, means it can act as a tunnel end point. So the tunnels that will be formed are S to C3, C3 to D1, C3 to D2, C3 to D3, and C3 to D4. The total cost in this arrangement is 17; *S-C1-C3(2)* plus *C3-D1(3)* plus *C3-C4-D2(6)* plus *C3-C5-D3(3)* plus *C3-C5-D4(3)*. This is because of the fact that in the later approach, we are able to save 2 units of cost each for D2, D3 and D4 as these three have a common path from source S up to C3. Activating two core routers (C3 and C5) gives a total cost of 15 units, saving again 2 units from the earlier. This is because of the provision of a tunnel between D3 and D4 as these have a common link C3 to C5 in the optimal path.

High availability of network connections is a key challenge to service providers to increase their revenue. When a path fails, the service provider must quickly re-establish another path so that the user can continue its VPN connectivity without interruption [8]. Restoration mechanisms help in this regard. Some work has already been done on optimal tunnel path finding [6][9][10]. However, the problem of computing optimal tunnel paths with restoration guarantees has not been studied extensively. Our work here is motivated by emerging trends in core networks or backbone networks towards fast provisioning of optimal restorable VPN tunnels in the case of link failures.

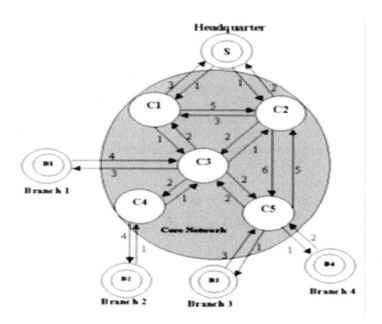

Fig. 1. Intranet/Extranet VPN Scenario

In a VPN tree, if any edge fails, this would definitely disrupt the service unless a backup path is established to reconnect the tree [8]. A restoration algorithm selects a backup path so that the traffic disrupted by failure of a tunnel can be rerouted via backup paths [11]. Our work in this paper presents heuristic algorithms for restoring VPN tree in case of link failures.

2 Restoration Schemes

The restoration techniques can be categorized into *link-based*, and *path-based*. Link restoration finds alternate paths between the nodes of the failed link. The optimal link restoration approach may involve circuitous restoration routes. Path restoration overcomes this problem by rerouting flow between the source and destination pairs affected by a link failure. This is illustrated in Figure 2. Figure 2(a) shows a network consisting of 6 nodes and 8 links without any link failure. It also shows one of the possible ways for reaching at node 4 starting from node 1. Figure 2(b) shows one way of recovery when link 2-3 fails. This is called as link restoration where we find another path for the failed link. Another way of restoration is shown in figure 2(c). In this case we do not find alternate path for the failed link. We do try to find an alternate path for the original source destination pair. We have used path based restoration approach in this paper.

The incorporation of restoration leads to a new QoS enabled traffic-engineering problem [12]. There are two approaches to handle this: First one is simultaneous formation or establishment of both active and backup paths, which aids in fast restoration by eliminating path computation and path setup signaling delays, and the other one is using a signaling protocol to re-establish the backup path only after active path fails. Our algorithms suit both scenarios.

The QoS requirement of a point-to-point connection can be specified using link constraints like bandwidth requirement or path constraint like delay for the entire path. But, we have considered here link constraints only, i.e., the QoS parameters are defined for each link individually. Here, link cost models bandwidth and loss over a link. As stated earlier, our objective in this paper is to compute optimal active and backup paths from headquarter to all the branch offices in an Intranet/Extranet VPN. This problem is analogous to finding a directed steiner tree spanning source to all the destinations. The QoS restorable path finding in a VPN is NP-hard and it is hard to approximate in polynomial time. So we propose new heuristics for computing both the paths.

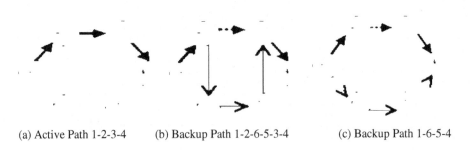

(a) Active Path 1-2-3-4   (b) Backup Path 1-2-6-5-3-4   (c) Backup Path 1-6-5-4

Fig. 2. Link/Path Restoration

The rest of the paper is organized as follows. In section 3, we discuss related work. In section 4, we define the Minimal Cost (MC) Restorable VPN problem. In section 5, we describe algorithms for restoring the optimal VPN tree. We compare our algorithms with Shortest Path Heuristic (SPH) [14]. Though the presented algorithms achieve no strict theoretic approximation ratios, in practice they perform better. This is shown in the simulation results for a range of scenarios described in section 6. Finally, in section 7, we conclude and discuss future work.

3 Related Work

Cohen et al. [6] have proposed an optimization algorithm for finding optimal VPN tunnel path by using Active Shortest Path heuristics and Active Double Tree heuristics. The cost of each link is considered as the administrative cost that is incurred in establishing a tunnel between the end points of the link. The optimal path is computed by activating core routers on the basis of cost profit ratio. The computational complexity of the algorithms is also high. Their work does not deal with restorability that we discuss here. Italiano et al. [8] have proposed fast restoration algorithms for VPNs in the hose model. Their algorithms are based on designing two reductions to convert the optimal restorable VPN problem into a 2-connected graph. The backup path that is constructed ensures the availability of minimum required bandwidth. Their algorithms are designed for single link failures. Their approach does not deal with restoration in *pipe* model VPNs that we discuss here. Also our algorithms handle multiple link failures. Kodialam et al. [12] have proposed heuristics for computing bandwidth guaranteed active and backup paths allowing sharing. The backup link cost is modeled separately. Their work focuses on optical networks. Their heuristic algorithm does not run in polynomial time and also does not deal with VPN scenario. Singhal et al. [15] have proposed four different algorithms SEGMENT, IMPROVED SEGMENT, PATH, and IMPROVED PATH for computing active and backup paths in a multicast scenario. These algorithms are based on shortest segment and shortest path computation. They have not considered any constraint-based selection as we have done in our approach. Also their work is not modeled for VPN scenario.

4 Minimal Cost (MC) Restorable VPN Problem

We have assumed a capacitated network, in which every link has a cost associated with it. The links are directed. We assume the cost over each link as function of link bandwidth and loss. Our model allows different costs on every direction in any link. Hence, the core network shown in Figure 1 is a directed graph. More formally, the link with less residual bandwidth and more loss is expected to be more costly than the link with more residual bandwidth and less loss. As the network links have different cost on each direction, our model resembles the behavior of a real network.

In Figure 1, we have S, D1, D2, D3, and D4 as border routers and C1 to C5 as core routers. If C3 is acting as an end of a tunnel, we call it as activated. To form a VPN between S and all destinations, by default, S and D1 to D4 must be active (VPN enabled). The objective is to minimize the network resources used for establishing the VPN connectivity between single headquarter and multiple destinations. The problem here can be viewed as obtaining a directed steiner tree starting with the source and spanning to all the branch office gateways. This is because VPN tunnels form a tree, as we can remove a tunnel to reduce the layout cost without the loss of connectivity. As our corporate headquarter node acts as source in Intranet/Extranet VPN, we seek a minimal cost spanning tree from S to all destinations. Considering the resource scarcity, we should only activate those many core routers that do not exceed the *funds* available. This will give us the set of *Active paths.*

For the purpose of restoration, when either a single link or multiple links of a tunnel fails, we construct a backup path for the tunnel, not for the failed link. This gives us an optimal backup tree starting with S and covering all the branch offices.

The problem can be mathematically formulated as: Given a directed graph G (V, E) representing a mesh network where V is the set of vertices and E is the set of edges with an edge weight function c: E →R+, a vertex weight function w: V→ R+, a bound on available funds F for active core nodes, a group M ⊆ V of border nodes, and a root (headquarter node) s ∈ M.

Our problem here is to find a set of directed paths both Active and Backup, and a set of active nodes A such that:

Minimize:

$$\sum_{AP \in T} \sum_{e \in AP} c(e) + \sum_{BP \in BT} \sum_{e \in BP} c(e)$$

such that:

$$\sum_{v \in A \setminus M} w(v) \leq F \qquad (1)$$

Where, for all AP ∈ T, BP ∈ BT, the end points in AP and BP are vertices in A, and for all v ∈ M \ s, there exists a sequence of one or more directed paths in T and BT that leads from s to v. Here, T represents the optimal VPN Active Tree, and BT represents the optimal VPN Backup Tree.

5   Proposed Algorithms

Algorithm 1: Heuristics for Active Path (APH)

Input: A directed network graph G (V, E) with edge costs and vertex weight functions, a source headquarter node s, a set of branch office nodes M, and available funds F

Output: A steiner tree rooted at s and spanning all the nodes in M

Step 1: Initializations: X ← M, T ← φ

Step 2: CPE based Solution to MC restorable VPN

While (X ≠ φ) do {

    a) Find the shortest path p from s to a node t ∈ X using DIJKSTRA

    b) T ←T ∪ {p}

    c) Update the cost of all the edges along p to 0

    d) X ←X − {t} }

    endwhile;

Step 3: A ←M

Step 4: Call Optimize(T,A).

Step 5: Report (T, A) as the desired solution.

Procedure 1. Optimize (T,A): *N/W Based Solution*

Step 1: Compute the benefit for each core router using predecessor chains, and then

the cost.

a) Depth_First(T)

    If (T ≠φ) {

        i.   S ←Root of T

        ii.   Depth_First (left subtree)

        iii.   Pred[LST] ← S

        iv.   Depth_First (right subtree)

        v.   Pred[RST] ←S}

b) For (every core router K ∉ A) do {

        i.   Compute No_Succ using Pred[] chains

        ii.   Profit = (No_Succ - 1) $* \sum_{i=S}^{j=K} Cost_{i,j}$

        iii.   Insert (K, Profit) into ActiveList

        iv.   Increase Size_of_ActiveList}

        endfor;

Step 2: Select the core routers that are to be activated.

While (F ≠ φ) do {

    If(Size_of_ActiveList == φ) then Exit;

    n ←Element from ActiveList with highest profit

If (Profit(n) == 0) {

    Delete 'n' from ActiveList;

    Decrease Size_of_ActiveList;}

Else {

    If (w(n) > F) {

        Delete n from ActiveList;

        Decrease Size_of_ActiveList;}

    Else {

        $A \leftarrow A \cup \{n\}$;

        $F \leftarrow F - w(n)$;

        Delete n from ActiveList;

        Decrease Size_of_ActiveList; }

    endif; }

endif; }

endwhile;

Step 3: Return (T, A).

Algorithm 2: Heuristics for Backup Path with Link Failures (BPH)

Input: A directed network graph G (V, E) with edge costs and vertex weight functions, a source headquarter node s, a set of branch office nodes M, the Optimal Active Path Tree (T), and active set A from Algorithm 1, the failure scenario set FS, and Funds (F)

Output: A minimal cost directed backup tree rooted at s and spanning all the nodes in M

Step 1: Initializations: BT←T

Step 2: Compute backup tree iteratively for all the failure scenarios

For (each f ∈ FS) do

    While (f ≠ϕ) do {

        i.   Select an element (t) from f

        ii.   Remove l ∈ t from graph G and from BT

        iii.   Find the shortest path p from s to destination node given in t using DIJKSTRA in graph G

iv.   BT ←BT ∪ {p}

v.   Update cost of all edges along p in BT to 0

vi.   f ← f- {t } }

endwhile;

endfor;

Step 3: Update BT such that it will be a source routed tree covering leaf nodes as destinations.

Step 4: Call Optimize (BT, A).

Step 5: Report (BT, A) as the desired solution.

We present two heuristic algorithms and a procedure for selecting the core routers. In [6], the Active Shortest Path and Active Double Tree heuristic algorithms were proposed for STP on directed graph. Our algorithm 1 is variant of ASPH. Algorithm 1 computes shortest path from S to all the destinations one by one. The core routers encountered during the tree creation (iteratively) are the intermediate nodes with shortest distance from S. So we update the cost of the links along that path as 0 for the next iteration. Hence, any new destination node that uses earlier explored nodes need not incur extra cost. This is repeated until the complete Active Tree is built. A similar approach is used in [6] except that in our algorithm there is no multiple usage of edges. Also in our case we do not recreate the optimal VPN tree for any new boarder router getting dynamically added to the set M. So, our approach has an edge in the sense that it takes less time to compute the paths and also ensures survivability.

An example of steps 1 and 2 of Algorithm 1 is as described in Figure 3. We consider the VPN in Figure 1 as the input to this algorithm. Here, *M={D1, D2, D3, D4}*. Dijkstra's shortest path algorithm is used to compute the shortest path between S and every member of M. Let the order in which the shortest paths computed be *S-C1-C3-D1, S-C1-C3-C4-D2, S-C1-C3-C5-D3,* and *S-C1-C3-C5-D4*. The VPN tree that is created is shown in Figure 3. Here, every edge is used once that differs from the heuristics used in [6] where edges are used for multiple times.

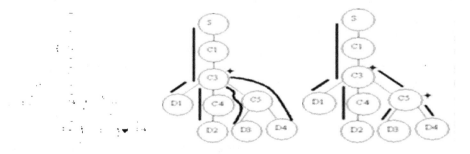

Fig. 3. VPN Tree with source and destinations

Fig. 4. Optimal VPN Tree with Funds = 1

Fig. 5. Optimal VPN Tree with Funds = 2

The Procedure 1 is used to find a network-based solution to the example VPN. This selects the core routers that are to be activated keeping in mind the limit on available funds. As stated earlier the weight function defines the resource capabilities of a core router. A depth first search is carried out on the tree as shown with a dotted line in Figure 3 to know the predecessor chains in the tree. Cost benefit for each core router is computed next.ActiveList is a list structure where each node represents a core and it's associated cost benefit. For example, C3 in Figure 3 has three successors. The profit for C3 is twice the cost of links from S to C3. This is because of the fact that out of three paths; we pay for only one path, the cost of common links. So, P[C3] = 2 * (1+1) = 4. This way the profit for rest all will be P[C4]=0, P[C5]=4, P[C1]=0. Hence, either C3 or C5 can be selected first. The selection of these core routers is carried out until the funds are exhausted. A core router whose profit is highest is selected iff the weight function of that node does not exceed Funds. At the end of this we get an optimal VPN tree. This is shown in Figure 4, and Figure 5 with funds = 1, and funds = 2 respectively. The set of active nodes (A) becomes [D1 to D4, C3] for funds = 1, and [D1 to D4, C3, and C5] for funds = 2. Nodes with asterisks represent active core routers. These two figures show the segments or tunnels that are required to be established to carry out a communication.

Fig. 6. Backup Tree for failure scenario f(S-C1, C3-C5)

Fig. 7. Optimal Backup Tree for failure scenario f with Funds =1

Algorithm 2 is used for computing backup tree in case of link failures. Let us consider an example of few failure scenarios for the optimal Active tree shown in Figure 5. The complete failure scenario set will be FS= f (l_{S-C1}, C3 ; l_{C3-C5}, C5), (l_{S-C1}, C3 ; l_{C1-C3}, C3), (l_{C1-C3}, C3 ; l_{C3-C5}, C5), (l_{S-C1}, C3), (l_{C1-C3}, C3), (l_{C3-C5}, C5), (l_{S-C1}, l_{C1-C3}, l_{C3-C5}, C3, C5)}. Here, our main objective is to compute a backup path for common segments or tunnels. We also assume that the optimal backup tree should connect the single source with all the destinations. Let us again consider the backup tree path computation for the first failure scenario i.e. f = (l_{S-C1}, C3 ; l_{C3-C5}, C5). Here, every element of f signifies the failed links and the tunnel end point in which it lies. For example first element says S-C1 is failed and it is in the tunnel path whose end point is C3. This is the destination node in the element. Step 1 to Step 3 with this as the input gives a backup tree as shown in Figure 6. The updating step removes any leaf node in the tree that is not a border router. Step 4 of algorithm 2 calls the Optimization procedure (Procedure 1) with Active set A= {C3, C5}, and the optimal VPN tree T produced from Algorithm 1. Let additional *funds* be 1 for backup tree. The set A already contains C3, and C5 inherited from Active path. Here we have two core routers whose profit is computed as P[C4]=0, and P[C2]=1. So, C2 is selected as the activating core. The result is the optimal backup VPN tree for the failure scenario f. This is shown in Figure 7 which has 7 tunnels shown as dark segments.

The run time of APH and BPH given in Algorithm 1 and Algorithm 2 is analyzed below. In APH, the while loop runs for every border router, and hence a total of |M| times. The Dijkstra's shortest path algorithm takes O(E+Vlog|V|) using an efficient heap implementation. Every other step in the while loop takes O(E) times. So, our APH runs in O(E|M| + V|M|log|V|). The BPH (Algorithm 2) can be run in O(|FS||f|(E+Vlog|V|)), where FS is the failure scenario set and f is independent failure scenario.

6 Simulation Results

The simulation run of our algorithms were made on a Metropolitan network topology that represents a big network as shown in Figure 8. Antisymmetric edges were assigned equal costs. We ran our algorithms with varied border group sizes. These groups were reselected at random. The available funds were also varied for different cases. The results are plotted in Figures 9-12.

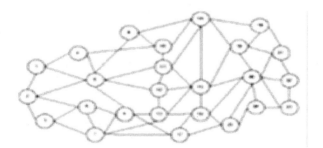

Fig. 8. A Metropolitan Network

We compared our results with the well-known SPH [14] which is an approximation algorithm for STP. SPH does not find a solution to MC restorable VPN problem. It constructs a spanning tree, and not an optimal active and backup path.

Figure 9 shows the plot between varying number of border routers and VPN cost for both Active and Backup paths when Funds are equal to 2. Both the costs increase linearly with the increase in number of border nodes. BPH with core routers, i.e., the optimal Backup path is better over the rest three. But, it is not similar to SPH as we have fewer funds. The worst-case performance is given by APH without optimization. As BPH uses the Active set (A) produced by APH, it further optimizes the tree; hence it gives a better reduced VPN cost than APH. Figure 10 shows the same plot with Funds equal to 13, a relatively higher value. In this scenario, both the APH with Core and BPH with Core are closer to SPH. Even BPH with Core gives better performance than SPH. This is possible because more destinations have common segments in this case. Figure 11 shows VPN cost for varying funds. We keep here the number of destination border nodes equal to 15. For low funds the cost of Active path with core is higher than the Backup. Increasing funds brings the backup path cost nearer to SPH, but the decrease in Active path cost is marginal. This is because of more core routers getting activated in case of BPH. In Figure 12, for small group sizes up to 9, both APH and BPH use same number of core routers. From group size between 11 to 26, the average number of core routers increased linearly. For above 26, it remains flat. This behavior results from the fact that when less number of destinations are to be reached from source, few common segments will be traversed in the path, and when the group size is large, the common segments will remain fixed. Also BPH activates more core routers than APH. This is because BPH creates few new tunnels than that of APH.

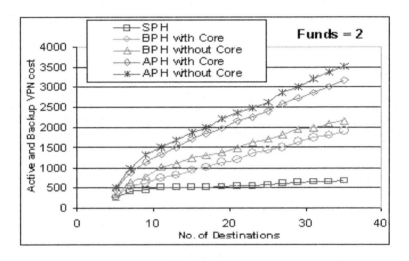

Fig. 9. Active and Backup Path Cost with Funds = 2

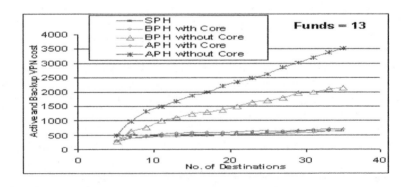

Fig. 10. Active and Backup Path Cost with Funds = 13

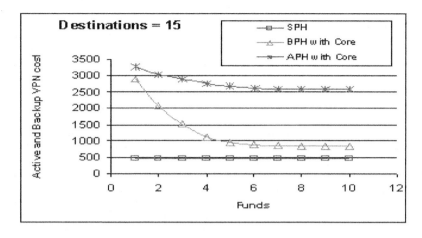

Fig. 11. Active and Backup Path Cost with Varied Funds for Group Size = 15

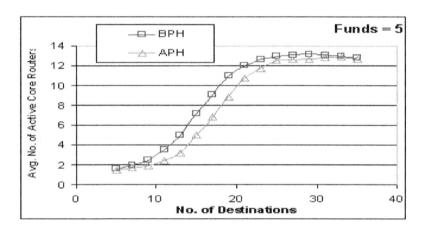

Fig. 12. Average Number of participating Core Routers with Group Size

7 Conclusion

In this paper we proposed heuristics for finding restorable paths for IPVPNs with QoS guarantees. The APH and BPH produced a better solution to MC Restorable VPN problem. Both the algorithms first used CPE based approach to find out VPN path and then used network-based optimization to strategically activate core routers to produce an optimal path. Our restoration algorithm is path based. We compared our results with well known approximation algorithm for STP, and found the results close to optimal performance. We do not consider here node failures. Also, we do not consider dynamic traffic, i.e. setting up optimal active and backup paths as and when new border nodes are added to the group. We plan to extend our work in this direction.

Acknowledgement

This work is supported by AVCC India Exchange program grant, The University of New South Wales, Australia.

References

1. Debasis Mitra, and Ziedins, "Hierarchical Virtual Partitioning: Algorithms for Virtual Private Networking," IEEE GLOBECOMM97.
2. T. Erlebach, and M. Ruegg, "Optimal Bandwidth Reservation in Hose-Model VPNs with Multipath Routing," in Proceedings of IEEE INFOCOM, 2004.
3. Juttner, Szabo, and Szentesi, "On Bandwidth Efficiency of the Hose Resource Management Model in VPNs," in Proceedings of IEEE INFOCOM, 2003.
4. McDysan, VPN Applications Guide, J. Wiley & Sons, Inc.
5. N. G. Duffield, P. Goyal, A. Greenberg, P. Mishra, and K. K. Ramakrishnan, "A Flexible Model for Resource Management in Virtual Private Networks," in Proc.ACM SIGCOMM, September 1999.
6. R. Kohen, and G. Kaempfer, "On the Cost of Virtual Private Networks," IEEE Transactions on Networking, Vol.8, No.6, Dec 2000.
7. C. Hota, and G. Raghurama, "A Heuristic Algorithm for QoS Path Computation in VPNs," International Conference on Information Technology (CIT), Bhubaneswar, India, December 2003.
8. G. Italiano, R. Rastogi, and B. Yener, "Restoration Algorithms for Virtual Private Networks in the Hose Model," in Proceedings of IEEE INFOCOM, 2002.
9. H. N. Gabow, Z. Galil, T. Spencer, and R. E. Tarjan, "Efficient Algorithms for Finding Minimal Spanning Trees in Undirected and Directed Graphs," Combinatorica, Vol.6-2, pp. 109-122, 1986.
10. Anna Hac, and K. Zhou, "A New Heuristic Algorithm for Finding Minimal Cost Multicast Trees with Bounded Path Delays," IJONM, pp. 265-278, 1999.
11. W. Lau, and Sanjay Jha, "Failure Oriented Path Restoration Algorithms for Survivable Networks," NOMS, Korea, 2004.
12. M. Kodialam, and T. V. Lakshman, "Dynamic Routing of Restorable Bandwidth-Guaranteed Tunnels Using Aggregated Network Resource Usage Information," IEEE Transactions on Networking, Vol. 11, No.3, June 2003.
13. Hyong, and Konstantopoulos, "Dynamic Capacity Resizing for Fair Bandwidth Sharing in VPNs," IEICE Transactions on Communications, Vol. E86-B, No.5, May 2003.
14. Takahashi, and Matsuyama, "An Approximate Solution for the Stenier Problem in Graphs," Math Japonica, Vol. 24, pp. 573-577, 1980.
15. N. K. Singhal, L. H. Sahasrabuddhe, and B. Mukherjee, "Provisioning of Survivable Multicast Sessions Against Single Link Failures in Optical WDM Mesh Networks," Journal of Lightwave Technology, Vol. 21, No.11, Nov 2003.
16. Chandra, and Anupam, "Building Edge Failure Resilient Networks," 9th IPCOC, Cambridge, MA.
17. A. Kumar, Rastogi, Silberschatz, and Yener, "Algorithms for Provisioning VPNs in the Hose Model," in Proceedings of ACM SIGCOMM 2001.
18. Hakimi, "Steiner Problem in Graphs and its' Implications," Networks, Vol. 1, 1971.
19. A. Bremler Barr, Y. Afek, H. Kaplan, E. Cohen, and M. Merritt, "Restoration by Path Concatenation: Fast Recovery of MPLS Paths," in Proceedings of ACM SIGMETRICS, 2001.

A User Level, Reliable, and Reconfigurable Transport Layer Protocol

Tan Wang and Ajit Singh

Department of Electrical and Computer Engineering,
University of Waterloo,
Waterloo, Ontario, Canada, N2L 3G1
t7wang@engmail.uwaterloo.ca, asingh@etude.uwaterloo.ca

Abstract. It is well known that TCP is not suitable for a number of environments such as wireless, satellite, and long-fat-pipe networks. At the same time, there is no other single transport protocol that would outperform TCP in all situations. In this paper, we explore an alternative transport layer protocol that is more suitable for today's mobile as well as other non-conventional network environments. The result is a user-level, reconfigurable, TCP-friendly (asymptotically converges to fairness as in the case of LIMD (Linear Increase Multiplicative Decrease) algorithms) transport layer protocol, called RRTP (Reliable and Reconfigurable Transport Protocol), which runs atop of UDP. We evaluate our protocol using the standard network simulation tool (ns2). Several representative network configurations are used to benchmark the performance of our protocol against TCP in terms of network throughput and congestion loss rate. It is observed that under normal operating conditions, our protocol has a performance advantage of 30% to 700% over TCP in lossy, wireless environments as well as high bandwidth, high latency networks.

1 Introduction

TCP is certainly an extremely well designed transport protocol in terms of its robustness and versatility. However, some important situations exist where the performance of TCP can be dramatically improved. For instance, Balakrishnan et al. [1] have pointed out, TCP treats all losses as signs of network congestion. Consequently, deploying TCP over wireless network, where wireless losses instead of congestion losses are commonplace, will result in poor performance. In addition to providing unsatisfactory performance in wireless environments, TCP is also ill suited for high bandwidth high latency networks (also known as long-fat-pipe networks) [2].

In this paper, we propose a solution that targets several non-conventional categories of network environments where the performance of TCP is known to be unsatisfactory. At the same time, our solution should provide competitive performance in other environments. Our approach differs from the traditional routes for improving the performance of TCP in several ways:

(1) We design and implement a reliable transport protocol that would meet or exceed the performance of TCP under various types of networks.

A. Sen et al. (Eds.): IWDC 2004, LNCS 3326, pp. 303–314, 2004.
© Springer-Verlag Berlin Heidelberg 2004

(2) Instead of requiring the algorithm to be implemented in the kernel of operating systems, the algorithm can be demonstrated at the user level. At the same time, OS developers can adopt the algorithm later for implementation at the kernel level.

(3) We suggest the approach of designing a single algorithm that is reliable, robust, and is configurable to provide better performance over different types of networks. For this, the research suggests a few key network characteristics that can be used to configure the algorithm.

(4) The approach can take advantage of an application developer's or an end-user's knowledge of the operating environment and provide better performance. However, it is capable of working well even in the absence of such knowledge.

The new algorithm is called RRTP. For the purpose of evaluating RRTP, we study its behavior under several representative network environments using the network simulation tool ns2 [3]. The simulation environments include: wireless last-hop topology, which is representative of CDMA and satellite network scenarios; wireless backbone topology, which corresponds well to wireless LAN such as 802.11 networks; as well as long fat pipe topology, which is often found in intercontinental, high bandwidth high latency networks. From these studies, the throughput of RRTP is compared to that of TCP's in each scenario.

Our simulation results demonstrate that significant improvements can be made to enhance a user's experience with wireless networking through the appropriate usage of parameters for congestion avoidance and loss differentiation. In addition, user re-configurability is shown to be of key importance for the superior performance of RRTP. This is especially evident in the case of long-fat-pipe networks. By allowing the user to reconfigure RRTP to adapt to high bandwidth high latency networks, the network utilization can be increased tremendously.

2   Related Work and Motivations

Many approaches to improve the performance of TCP over wireless have been presented in the data communications literature. The first category of approach uses link-layer retransmissions and thus shields wireless losses from TCP as proposed by DeSimone et al. [4]. Such approaches work well when the latency over the wireless link is small as compared to the coarse grain TCP timer. There are also TCP-aware snoop mechanisms that have a snoop-agent module at the wireless base station as proposed by Balakrishnan et al. [5]. The snoop-agent monitors every packet that passes through the TCP connection in both directions and maintains a cache of TCP segments sent across the link that have not yet been acknowledged by the receiver. On receipt of a negative ACK, it suppresses the ACK and sends the required packet from its cache. In WWAN environments, snoop does not work well because it exacerbates the problem of large and varying round trip times by suppressing negative ACKs.

In the past, a number of researchers have proposed end-to-end solutions to improve the performance of TCP in certain cases. Casetti et al. [6] proposed an end-to-end modification of the TCP congestion window algorithm, called TCP Westwood. TCP Westwood relies on end-to-end bandwidth estimation to discriminate the cause of packet loss. However, most of their evaluations are based on the wireless link being the last link to the receiver. This algorithm is also highly dependent on the TCP ACKing scheme, i.e., at least one ACK for every two packets received - a feature that often does not exist in a best-effort transport protocol, e.g., TFRC (TCP Friendly Rate Control).

Biaz and Vaidya have looked at two different approaches to the end-to-end loss differentiation for TCP connections. They first looked at a set of "loss predictors" based upon three different analytic approaches to congestion avoidance that explicitly model connection throughput and/or round-trip time (e.g., TCP Vegas) [7]. Their results were negative in that these algorithms, formulated to do loss differentiation, were poor predictors of wireless loss. In subsequent work, they proposed a new algorithm that uses packet inter-arrival time to differentiate losses. Using simulation, they show that it works well in a network where the last hop is wireless and is also the bottleneck link. But they failed to evaluate their algorithm when the wireless link is not the last hop and nor the bottleneck of the network. Sinha et al. proposed a rate-based reliable transport protocol called WTCP, which is able to differentiate between wireless and congestion losses [8]. But again, they did not evaluate their protocol on types of network configurations other than wireless last hop networks.

An important distinction between previous approaches and RRTP is the reconfigurable nature of the algorithm used in RRTP. The algorithm utilizes a couple of selected key characteristics of the underlying network to quickly attain its best performance under a given environment.

3 Algorithms and Implementation

Now, we describe the major aspects and characteristics of the RRTP protocol.

3.1 Congestion Control Mechanism

According to Chiu and Jain [9], the LIMD (Linear Increase Multiplicative Decrease) approach to congestion control is the only paradigm that will settle down to a state of fairness with an arbitrary starting send rate. The congestion control mechanism of RRTP, like many other TCP variants, follows the basic framework of LIMD approaches but with a significant difference. Instead of taking TCP's approach of flow control window ramping and adjustment, RRTP uses a rate-based algorithm that reacts to incipient congestion and consequently limits the rate of traffic flow below the maximum available bandwidth most of the time. RRTP implements a 4-way handshake connection establishment in order to avoid the DoS (Denial of Service) phenomenon suffered by TCP. During the handshaking process, the nominal value of network RTT (round trip time) is determined. This RTT value refers to the ideal situation in which no network congestions are present.

Once the connection is established, the sender will send out two successive packets for the purpose of probing the network capacity and determining the initial send rate. Here, we make the assumption that the two communicating machines are free of other CPU intensive tasks so that the RRTP processes are able to get the required CPU cycles for the purpose of initial capacity probing. Several other variants of TCP also depend on similar assumptions. Let us suppose the send interval of these two packets is X milliseconds. Once the receiver gets both packets, it will advertise to the sender the observed receive interval (Y milliseconds) for the two packets. The sender will calculate the initial send rate based on *max(X, Y)*.

After the initial send rate is determined, the upper layer applications will be able to start using RRTP to transfer information. In the ideal situation where the application user/programmer has an accurate knowledge of the network throughput capability and configures the send rate accordingly, RRTP should be able to instantaneously operate at just below the maximum network capacity. This ensures both minimum wasted bandwidth and stress-free network conditions.

Without user configuration, RRTP will make an educated guess as to the approximate network configuration based on the measured initial send rate and RTT. Each type of network configuration has a pre-defined set of parameter values associated with it. These values are summarized in Table 1 shown below:

Table 1. Send Rate Adjustment Parameters

Parameter	Purpose
$SendRate_{max}$	Upper bound
$SendRate_{min}$	Lower bound

$SendRate_{max}$ serves the purpose of preventing the newly computed send rate from exceeding the maximum network capacity. $SendRate_{min}$ prevents the underutilization of the network that sometimes occurs due to the downward fluctuations of the newly computed send rate.

In protocol design terminology, an epoch refers to a certain interval of packet interchange. In RRTP, we define an epoch to be the interval in which ten packets are sent or received. Since the packet interval time is a key network parameter that we use in RRTP's rate-based congestion control mechanism, we keep two running averages of it: the long-term and the short-term running average. The long-term packet interval average is used for calculating the send/receive rate ratio and adjusting the current send rate. The short-term packet interval average is computed during each epoch. If it significantly deviates from the long-term average, the network would most likely be under stress (congestion due to link failure or additional traffic). At such times, the short-term average is used for the purpose of send rate adjustment instead of the long-term average in order to accurately reflect the network conditions. If we observe the major discrepencies between long-term and short-term averages for ten consecutive epochs or more, we can safely assume that there has been a permanent change in network dynamics and the old long-term average is discarded. A new one is calculated based on the previous ten short-term averages. Inevitably, under circumstances like this, RRTP incurs quite a bit of overhead cost, but such a rare overhead cost is a justifiable price for RRTP's improved robustness.

Because of the fact that the send rate is only adjusted at the end of each epoch, constant fluctuation of network traffic is minimized. This results in a more stable network connection. At the time of send rate adjustment, the newly adjusted rate is subjected to comparison with two parameters listed in Table 1: $SendRate_{max}$ and $SendRate_{min}$. In other words, the new rate must fall within the range of $SendRate_{min}$ to $SendRate_{max}$. This is done to minimize the chance that an overshoot occurring when RRTP ramps up the send rate during the linear increase phases, and the occurrence of unnecessary reduction in the send rate during the multiplicative decrease phases.

$SendRate_{max}$ and $SendRate_{min}$ are not fixed values. They are re-calculated based on changes of network dynamics as discussed in the previous paragraph. The send rate adjustment is carried out using the following algorithm: first, we define an additive increase factor α with different initial values based on the type of network RRTP is operating on as well as a multiplicative decrease factor β with an initial value of 0.05. If the send/receive rate ratio is greater than 1.05, RRTP is operating at a level above the maximum network throughput capacity. Our protocol treats such situations as signs of incipient congestion and will carry out the following adjustment: $SendRate_{new} = SendRate_{prev} \times max((1-\beta), 0.5)$. The value of β is doubled for every consecutive multiplicative decrease phase until it reaches the upper bound of $1-\beta > 0$. Here, we take $max((1-\beta), 0.5)$ to be the adjustment factor to ensure that the rate reduction factor will never drop below 0.5. In other words, when RRTP first detects signs of incipient congestion, it gently reduces the send rate with a small value of β. If the incipient congestion persists over several epochs, the value of β will be doubled every epoch to more effectively suppress incipient congestions. Now on the other hand, if the send/receive rate ratio is less than 0.95, RRTP is operating well below the maximum network capacity. This results in a linear increase phase in which $SendRate_{new} = SendRate_{prev} + \alpha$. In addition, β is reset to its initial value of 0.05.

Since the purpose of send rate adjustment is to probe the current network capacity and to achieve near 100% network throughput utilization, a characteristic send rate can be chosen for maximum utilization of the available network bandwidth. Our protocol provides an estimate of this characteristic value by averaging the send rate during epochs in which the send rate stays constant (0.95 < send/receive ratio < 1.05). If the send rate stays constant for two or more epochs, this estimate is put into use as the new send rate.

With the rate-based congestion avoidance mechanism described above, RRTP is able to avoid several situations for congestion that would be encountered by TCP. However, there are situations that will result in congested network even with RRTP as the end-to-end transport mechanism. Such situations include temporary link failures and sudden surges of new traffic. Under ill-fated network conditions like this, packets may be lost due to severe congestion. RRTP aggressively reduces the send rate (by 50% for each congested epoch) in response to detected congestions. Such efforts are needed to avoid a total network collapse. When the signs of congestion disappear, instead of carrying out the slow start used in TCP, RRTP performs an instantaneous send rate recovery by using the last recorded characteristic send rate as the one for the next send/receive cycle.

For the case in which the user mis-configures the initial send rate, our algorithm is smart enough to detect that. Send rate convergence is still guaranteed in this scenario due to the nature of RRTP's rate control mechanism.

3.2 Reliability and Reconfigurability

The ability to reconfigure to adapt to different network platforms is the key feature that sets RRTP apart from most of the other protocols of its kind. Reconfigurability is built into RRTP by the means of the parameterization of a set of key network parameters. Our experiments indicate that only a small set of parameters is needed to design a re-configurable transport protocol algorithm that would provide a good performance on different types of networks. These parameters are listed in Table 2.

Table 2. User-configurable Parameters

Parameters	Meanings
$SendRate_{nominal}$	Normal channel capacity
$RoundTripTime_{nominal}$	Normal end to end latency
$LossRate_{nominal}$	Characteristic data loss rate

To ensure a reliable transport, the receiver sends two kinds of acknowledgement to the sender: cumulative acknowledgement, and negative acknowledgement. Negative acknowledgements are coupled with timeouts. Our timeout mechanism uses RTT. Cumulative acknowledgements serve as confirmation of received packets during normal network operations. When a cumulative acknowledgement is received by the sender, the sender can safely remove the corresponding acknowledged buffered packets. The cumulative acknowledgement interval is defined to be the period during which 32 packets are received.

3.3 Loss Differentiation Algorithm

Several published research works on the issue of TCP performance enhancement over wireless networks have considered sender-based loss differentiation. RRTP, on the other hand, is based on the intuition that the receiver usually has more accurate and timely knowledge of packet losses. Consequently, the receiver is responsible for figuring out the cause of a particular loss and informing the sender to take the appropriate action.

For wireless last hop networks, RRTP makes two assumptions regarding the path characteristics. The first assumption states that the wireless link has the lowest bandwidth and thus is the bottleneck of the network. Secondly, the wireless base station is assumed to serve strictly as a routing agent between the wired and the wireless network with no additional smart capabilities. As one can, quite easily, see, with the big difference in bandwidth between wired LAN (100 Mbps) and cellular wireless (around 19.2 Kbps), packets traveling on the wired network would get congested at the base station while adapting to the lower send rate imposed by the wireless network. As a result, the packets transmitted on the wireless connection tend to be clustered together. If a packet loss occurs due to random wireless transmission errors, the receiver should be able to observe a certain time interval in which the packet is expected but not received. Such an event can be interpreted to be the sign of wireless loss due to transmission errors. Following this reasoning, RRTP can distinguish between wireless losses form congestion losses using the following heuristics: let T_{min} be the minimum observed packet interval for the receiver and $T_{separation}$ be the interval between the time when the last correct packet is received and the time when the lost packet is detected by the receiver. Suppose n packets were lost, the loss is characterized as wireless loss if the following relation holds: $(n + 1) T_{min} < T_{separation} < (n + 1.75) T_{min}$. The number we choose are experimentally determined to cause the lowest misclassification rate between congestion and wireless losses.

For the wireless LAN topology, the assumptions that we made in the previous situation are usually not true. Conventional wired LAN is not much faster than high-speed wireless LAN. As a result, packets don't necessarily travel in close succession on the wireless LAN connection. Consequently, the previous LDA heuristic will not perform as well as in wireless last hop topology. As a result, an alternative approach is used in this case to distinguish between wireless loss and congestion losses.

In order to achieve good accuracy in distinguishing between the two types of packet losses for the wireless LAN topology, RRTP uses the ROTT (Relative One-way Trip Time) measurements as congestion indicators. ROTT is defined to be the time between the moment when the packet is sent and the moment when the packet is received. It is measured at the receiver end. During periods of smooth traffic flow, ROTT measurements will remain relatively stable. When the network starts to become congested, the receiver will detect rising ROTT values. The default behavior of RRTP in this situation is that the receiver will issue an explicit incipient congestion notification to the sender to throttle the send rate. In the event that the rise in ROTT values is coupled with packet losses, the receiver can be confident that the packet losses are caused by congestion. However, if the packet losses are not accompanied by a rise in ROTT value, the receiver will categorize these losses to be due to wireless errors. As it was discussed above, two different LDA schemes are used by RRTP. Depending on the actual wireless network in use, RRTP selects the appropriate LDA to achieve optimum performance.

4 Experimental Setup and Results

To evaluate the actual performance of RRTP, we have created various simulation scenarios using the ns2 simulator [3]. Tests were conducted under various environments with RRTP, TCP Reno, TCP New Reno and TCP Vegas. All the scenarios and their corresponding results are summarized in Table 3 and 4 shown below. Table 3 shows the relative performance of each of the four protocols evaluated on the various network platforms in terms of the total number of packets sent in a fix amount of time. The packet size used was 1 kilo-byte. The characteristics of the testing platforms are summarized in Table 4. As an example of cross referencing between the two tables, RRTP sends on average 3590 packets within 8.5 seconds in the high latency high bandwidth environment whereas TCP Vegas is able to send only 292 packets in equal time period.

Table 3. Comparative Performance in terms of Total Number of Packets Sent Per Connection Period

Environment	RRTP	Reno	New Reno	Vegas
High Latency & High Bandwidth	3590	492	581	292
CDMA	242	183	180	226
Satellite	3157	2755	2689	3060
LAN	1172115	920704	918655	1173222
Wireless LAN	1228150	913512	913497	1146950

Table 4. Testing Environment Specifications

Environment	Bandwidth	One-way Latency	% Loss	Test Interval
High Latency & High Bandwidth	100 Mbps	100 ms	1%	8.5 sec
CDMA	19.2 Kbps	100 ms	1%	98.5 sec
Satellite	256 Kbps	100 ms	1%	98.5 sec
LAN	100 Mbps	5 ms	0%	98.5 sec
Wireless LAN	11 Mbps	10 ms	1%	998.5sec

In a high latency high bandwidth topology, a typical protocol that relies on sender-receiver feedbacks will inevitably suffer from the slowness of its response to changing network condition. This is due to the fact that round trip return time is extremely large and consequently, it is difficult to rely on feedbacks to adjust the send rate. Fairness can be severely limited as newly entered traffic will almost always be starved by previously established traffic.However, because of the fact that RRTP is reconfigurable, good estimates of the network conditions can be provided to the application before the transfer starts, allowing a much higher throughput than conventional TCP as demonstrated in Figure 1.

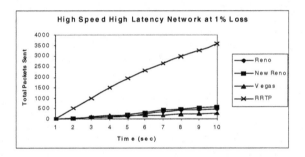

Fig. 1. Protocol Performance for High Speed High Latency Environment with 1% Data Loss Rate

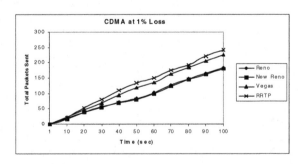

Fig. 2. Protocol Performance for CDMA Environment with 1% Data Loss Rate

Both CDMA and satellite network can be considered to be roughly wireless last hop topologies. As demonstrated in Figure 2 and Figure 3, RRTP performs much better than TCP Reno and TCP New Reno on both types of network platforms. This is expected since when losses are encountered, TCP invokes its congestion control mechanisms right away without making an effort to distinguish among the different types of losses. In this scenario, results are quite similar to the wireless last hop topology. The Spike LDA enables RRTP to differentiate between congestion losses and wireless losses, resulting in a superior performance in term of throughput as shown in Figure 4.In addition to three network platforms mentioned above in which RRTP demonstrates superior performance, the simulation result shown in Figure 5 also demonstrates that the performance of RRTP on conventional LAN closely matches that of TCP Vegas. This implies that not only could RRTP outperform TCP in certain network configurations, it could also serve as a viable substitute in the more traditional network settings.

5   Comparison with Related Work

One of the fundamental design decisions we made in the making of RRTP is the conscientious effort of congestion avoidance. By promoting congestion avoidance, network throughput can be significantly enhanced as less congestion related situations are encountered during the lifetime of the network connection. This design approach can also be seen in TCP Vegas. However, in the case of TCP Vegas, there is one significant drawback in its design. Lai and Yao [10] have shown in their study that when different traffic flows compete with each other in the same channel, traffic running under older and more widespread version of TCP such as TCP Reno and TCP Tahoe tends to be much more aggressive than the ones that are running under TCP Vegas in terms of competing for the available network bandwidth. RRTP, on the other hand, does not suffer from the same problem. In fact, it is observed to be as aggressive as TCP Reno and TCP New Reno in terms of bandwidth acquisition.

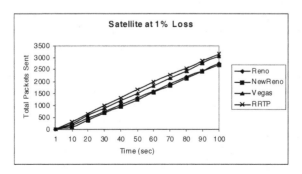

Fig. 3. Protocol Performance for Satellite Environment with 1% Data Loss Rate

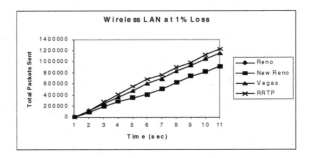

Fig. 4. Protocol Performance for Wireless LAN Environment with 1% Data Loss Rate

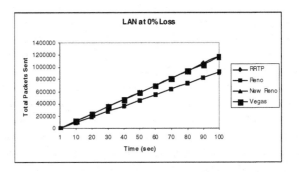

Fig. 5. Protocol Performance for LAN Environment with 0% Data Loss Rate

Another major advantage of RRTP is that it is reconfigurable in nature. The user does not have to restrict himself to any particular network configuration for optimum network conditions when RRTP is used as the underlying transport layer protocol. In a way, RRTP tries to be a generic protocol like TCP. The main deviation from TCP's design philosophy is that RRTP takes advantage of user's knowledge of the network. By doing so, RRTP can perform just as well as the various solutions discussed in the related work section in each individual special cases while still remaining insensitive to the varying network configurations.

The research done by Sinha et al. [8] on WTCP has significant commonality with the present work. WTCP is an end-to-end transport layer protocol that uses a rate-based mechanism for congestion control and the Biaz [7] LDA for differentiating between congestion losses and wireless losses. Although it is able to achieve good results on wireless last hop networks, the authors did not test WTCP on other types of wireless platforms such as wireless backbone network and wireless LAN. In fact, we believe that WTCP will likely perform poorly on the two latter network platforms. The reason is that the Biaz LDA is only optimized for wireless last hop networks. When we tested the Biaz LDA on networks with wireless LAN configuration, we found that the algorithm resulted in a lower throughput than the Spike [11] LDA. RRTP addresses this shortcoming of WTCP by designing a LDA mechanism that is closer to the Spike LDA for better performance on wireless backbone and wireless LAN networks.

Another advantage of RRTP over WTCP is its faster send rate convergence. Since RRTP allows the user to specify the ideal sending rate for the network platform of interest, accurate user inputs could potentially help RRTP to converge to the ideal send rate within the initial connection establishment period. This really translates into the avoidance of many unnecessary overshoots that would otherwise be encountered if WTCP were used as the transport layer protocol. For short-lived connections, RRTP will be able to out perform WTCP by several folds since the user inputs for the initial send rate essentially eliminate the need for network capacity probing phase.

6 Future Directions and Conclusions

The paper presents a novel reliable transport protocol called RRTP that not only achieves better performance on networks where performance of TCP is known to be unsatisfactory, it also provides a competitive performance when compared to the best known versions of TCP in other situations as well. Presently, the LDA (Loss Differentiation Algorithm) used in RRTP has not been exhaustively tested under conditions such as multiple heterogeneous network connections. More studies can be carried out to examine the fairness-related issues revolving around the usage of LDA in RRTP. We believe that the current LDA mechanisms used in RRTP have a very low misclassification rate when it comes to distinguishing between congestion packet loss and wireless packet loss. As a result, it is expected that RRTP will not act over aggressively in the process of bandwidth acquisition. Additional work should be done to add intelligence to RRTP in the form of keeping persistent state information of the network it is running on. This information facilitates a learning mechanism for the protocol to utilize temporal information for better adaptation to the network of interest.

References

1. H. Balakrishnan, V. Padmanabhan, S. Seshan, and R. Katz, "A comparison of mechanisms for improving TCP performance over wireless links," *IEEE/ACM Transactions on Networking*, Vol.5, no. 6, (1997), pp 756-769.
2. V. Jacobson, R. Braden, and D. Borman. TCP Extensions for high performance. RFC 1323, (1992).
3. ns-2 network simulator (ver 2). LBL, URL: http://www.isi.edu/nsnam/ns.
4. A. DeSimone, M. C. Chuah, and O. Yue. "Throughput performance of transport layer protocols over wireless LANs", *Proceedings of IEEE GLOBECOMM*, (1993).
5. H. Balakrishnan, S. Seshan, E. Amir, and R. Katz. "Improving TCP/IP performance over wireless networks". *Proceedings of ACM MOBICOM*, (1995).
6. C. Casetti, M. Gerla, S. Mascolo, M.Y. Sanadidi, and R. Wang. "TCPWestwood: Bandwidth Estimation for Enhanced Transport over Wireless Links," *Proc. ACM Mobicom 2001 Conference*, Rome, Italy, (2001), pp 287-297.
7. S. Biaz and N. Vaidya, "Distinguishing congestion losses from wireless transmission losses: A negative result," *Proc. 7th Intl. Conf. on Computer Communications and Networks*, Lafayette, LA, (1998).
8. P. Sinha, T. Nandagopal, N. Venkitaraman, R. Sivakumar, and V. Bharghavan. "WTCP: A Reliable Transport Protocol for Wireless Wide-Area Networks", *Wireless Networks 8*, (2002), pp 301-316.

9. D. Chiu, and R. Jain, "Analysis of the Increase/Decrease Algorithms for Congestion Avoidance in Computer Networks", *Journal of Computer Networks and ISDN Systems*, vol. 17, no. 1, (1989).

10. 10 Yuan-Cheng Lai, Chang-Li Yao, "The performance comparison between TCP Reno and TCP Vegas", *Proc. of Seventh International Conference on Parallel and Distributed Systems*, Iwate, Japan, (2000).

11. Y. Tobe, Y. Tamura, A. Molano, S. Ghosh, and H. Tokuda, "Achieving moderate fairness for UDP flows by path-status classification," in *Proc. 25th Annual IEEE Conf. on Local Computer Networks (LCN 2000)*, Tampa, FL, (2000), pp. 252–261.

The Notion of Veto Number
for Distributed Agreement Problems

Roy Friedman[1], Achour Mostefaoui[2],
and Michel Raynal[2]

[1] Computer Science Department, Technion, Haifa 32000, Israel
[2] IRISA, Campus de Beaulieu, 35042 Rennes Cedex, France
roy@cs.technion.ac.il
{achour, raynal}@irisa.fr

Abstract. This paper introduces the notion of *veto number* that can be associated with agreement problems. An agreement problem has veto number ℓ when ℓ is the minimal number of processes that control the allowed decision values, i.e., if each of them changes its mind on the value it proposes, then it forces deciding on a different value. The paper presents and investigates this concept.

Keywords: Agreement problem, Asynchronous system, Consensus, Distributed algorithm, One shot problem, Process crash, Failure detector.

1 Introduction

Agreement problems are central issues when one is interested in designing fault-tolerant applications in asynchronous distributed systems prone to failures. The most know of these problems is consensus: each process proposes a value, and (at least) the non-faulty processes have to decide a value (termination), such that no two different values are decided (uniform agreement), and a decided value has to be a proposed value (validity). Many results have been produced on this problem. The most famous of them is the so-called FLP impossibility [3] that states that consensus cannot be solved in asynchronous distributed systems as soon as even a single process can crash. An important concept that has been introduced to prove this result is the notion of *valence* that can be associated with a global state: a state is x-valent if the set of values that can be decided from it includes x different values. This means that a single value can be decided from a 1-valent state, while no definitive choice has yet been done in a x-valent state where $x > 1$.

Another notion of number that has been introduced in the context of agreement problems is the notion of *consensus number* [8]. This notion allows ranking the power synchronization primitives (or synchronization objects) in asynchronous shared memory systems prone to process crashes. An object has consensus number k if k is the greatest integer such that this object allows solving consensus among k processes in presence of up to $k-1$ crashes. It is shown

A. Sen et al. (Eds.): IWDC 2004, LNCS 3326, pp. 315–325, 2004.
© Springer-Verlag Berlin Heidelberg 2004

in [8] that (among other objects) *read/write* objects have consensus number 1, while *compare&swap* objects have consensus number $+\infty$.

This paper presents and investigates the notion of *veto number* (denoted ℓ) that can be associated with agreement problems. This notion captures the minimal number of processes that control the decision taking in the sense that, if each of these processes changes its mind on the value it proposes, then the decision can no longer be the same. The veto number notion is interesting to understand and solve agreement problems in asynchronous distributed systems where up to f processes can crash. Several results provided by the veto number notion are presented. Moreover, the paper introduces agreement protocols whose design is based on their veto number. Interestingly, this study shows a borderline separating the cases $f < \ell$ and $f \geq \ell$ (where f is the maximum number of processes that can crash).

The paper is made up of five sections. Section 2 presents the computation model and defines the agreement problems we are interested in. Section 3 presents the ℓ-veto concept. Then, Section 4 presents results obtained thanks to this concept. Section 5 presents protocols solving ℓ-veto problems.

2   Computation Model and Definitions

2.1   Asynchronous Distributed Systems with Process Crash Failures

We consider a system consisting of a finite set Π of n processes, namely, $\Pi = \{p, q, \ldots\}$. A process can fail by *crashing*, i.e., by prematurely halting. It behaves correctly (i.e., according to its specification) until it (possibly) crashes. By definition, a *correct* process is a process that does not crash. A *faulty* process is a process that is not correct; f denotes the maximum number of processes that can crash $(1 \leq f < n)$.

Processes communicate and synchronize by sending and receiving messages through channels. Every pair of processes is connected by a channel. Channels are assumed to be reliable: they do not create, alter or lose messages. There is no assumption about the relative speed of processes or message transfer delays.

Let $AS_{n,f}(\emptyset)$ denotes such an asynchronous distributed system.

2.2   One-Shot Agreement Problems

In a one-shot agreement problem, each process p starts with an individual input value v_p. The input values are from a particular value set $\mathcal{V}_{in}$. Moreover, let $\perp$ denote a default value (such that $\perp \notin \mathcal{V}_{in}$), and $\mathcal{V}_{in,\perp}$ denote the set $\mathcal{V}_{in} \cup \{\perp\}$. All the correct processes are required to produce outputs from a value set $\mathcal{V}_{out}$. We say that a process "decides" when it produces an output value.

Let $I = [v_1, \ldots, v_p, \ldots, v_n] \in \mathcal{V}_{in}^n$ be a vector whose pth entry contains the value proposed by process p. Such a vector is called an *input vector* [10]. Let $\mathcal{B}_{fail}$ be a subset of processes, and let $\mathcal{F}(I, \mathcal{B}_{fail})$ be a mapping from $\mathcal{V}_{in}^n$ into a non-empty subset of $\mathcal{V}_{out}$. The mapping $\mathcal{F}(I, \mathcal{B}_{fail})$ associates a set of possible output values with each input vector in runs in which the processes of $\mathcal{B}_{fail}$ fail. For simplicity, we denote $\mathcal{F}(I) = \mathcal{F}(I, \emptyset)$, or in other words, $\mathcal{F}(I)$ is the set of possible decision values from I when there are no failures. We also assume that for any $\mathcal{B}_{fail}^1$ and $\mathcal{B}_{fail}^2$, if $\mathcal{B}_{fail}^1 \subset \mathcal{B}_{fail}^2$, then for any vector I, we have $\mathcal{F}(I, \mathcal{B}_{fail}^1) \subseteq \mathcal{F}(I, \mathcal{B}_{fail}^2)$. Essentially, this means that having a certain number of failures cannot prevent a decision value that is allowed with fewer (or no) failures. $\mathcal{F}(I)$ is called the *decision value set* associated with I. If it contains x values, the corresponding input vector I is said to be *x-valent*. For $x = 1$, I is said to be *univalent*.

Definition. A one-shot agreement problem is characterized by a set $\mathcal{V}_{in}$, a set $\mathcal{V}_{out}$, and a particular mapping $\mathcal{F}(I, \mathcal{B}_{fail})$ with the following properties:

- *Termination:* Each correct process decides.
- *Agreement:* No two processes decide different values (sometimes called *Uniform Agreement*).
- *Validity:* In runs in which processes in $\mathcal{B}_{fail}$ fail, the value decided on from the input vector I is a value from the set $\mathcal{F}(I, \mathcal{B}_{fail})$. In particular, in failure free runs, the value decided on from the input vector I is a value from the set $\mathcal{F}(I)$.

Examples. We consider here three one-shot agreement problems. Each is defined by specific values of $\mathcal{V}_{in}$, $\mathcal{V}_{out}$, and a particular function $\mathcal{F}()$.

- Consensus:
  - $\mathcal{V}_{in} = \mathcal{V}_{out} =$ the set of values that can be proposed.
  - $\forall I$ (an input vector): $\forall \, \mathcal{B}_{fail} : \mathcal{F}(I, \mathcal{B}_{fail}) = \{x| \text{ where } x \text{ appears in } I\}$.
- Interactive Consistency:
  - $\mathcal{V}_{in}$ is the set of values that can be proposed, $\mathcal{V}_{out} = \mathcal{V}_{in,\perp}^n$.
  - $\forall \, I, \forall \, \mathcal{B}_{fail}$: $\mathcal{F}(I, \mathcal{B}_{fail})$ is the set of all vectors J that satisfy the following:
    $\forall \, k :$ if $k \notin \mathcal{B}_{fail}$ then $\forall J: J[k] = I[k]$,
    $\forall \, k :$ if $k \in \mathcal{B}_{fail}$ then $J[k] \in \{I[k], \perp\}$.
    In particular, this means that $\forall I : \mathcal{F}(I) = I$.
- Non-blocking Atomic Commit:
  - $\mathcal{V}_{in} = \{yes, no\}$, $\mathcal{V}_{out} = \{commit, abort\}$.
  - $\mathcal{F}([yes, \ldots, yes]) = commit$.
  - $\forall \, \mathcal{B}_{fail} \neq \emptyset : \mathcal{F}([yes, \ldots, yes], \mathcal{B}_{fail}) = \{commit, abort\}$.
  - $\forall \, \mathcal{B}_{fail}, \forall I$ such that I includes at least one abort : $\mathcal{F}(I, \mathcal{B}_{fail}) = abort$.

Thus, in the Consensus problem, there is no distinction between the allowed set of decision values in runs with and without failures. On the other hand,

Non-Blocking Atomic Commit and Interactive Consistency allow a different output when there are failures. Let us observe that not all agreement problems are one-shot. (As an example, the membership problem is an agreement problem that is not one-shot: its specification is not limited to a single invocation of a membership primitive, but rather involves the entire execution of the application in which it is used.)

3   The Concept of Veto Number

3.1   Irreconcilable Input Vectors

Let $\{I_i\}_{1 \le i \le k}$ ($k > 1$) be a set of input vectors, $\{V_i\}_{1 \le i \le k}$ the corresponding set of decision value sets, i.e., $V_i = \mathcal{F}(I_i)$ for $1 \le i \le k$.

Definition 1. *Set $\{I_i\}_{1 \le i \le k}$ is said to be made up of irreconcilable input vectors if $\bigcap_{1 \le i \le k} V_i = \emptyset$.*

Let us note that, when the set of decision values $\mathcal{V}_{out}$ is binary, only sets of univalent input vectors can be irreconcilable. The following lemma directly follows from the above definition:

Lemma 1. *Let $\{I_i\}$ be a minimal set of irreconcilable input vectors, and let $I_1 \in \{I_i\}$. For any decision value $v_1 \in V_1 = \mathcal{F}(I_1)$, there is a vector I_2 in $\{I_i\}$ such that $v_1 \notin V_2 = \mathcal{F}(I_2)$. (We then say that "$I_2$ counters I_1 on v_1".)*

3.2   Veto Number

The intuition that underlies the veto number notion is simple. It is defined for failure-free runs, and concerns the minimal number of processes such that the decided value can no longer be the same when each of these processes changes its mind on the value it proposes. So, the veto number ℓ of a one-shot agreement problem is the size of the smallest set of processes that, in worst case scenarios, control the decision value. For example, in the non-blocking atomic commit problem, as soon as a single process votes *no*, the decision is *abort* whatever the votes of the other processes. Hence, $\ell = 1$ for this problem. Similarly, the veto number of the interactive consistency problem is 1: if a single process changes its initial value, the decided vector changes accordingly. Differently, the veto number of the binary Consensus problem is n, since in failure-free runs, the only input vectors that enforce specific decision values are when all processes propose the same input value.

More formally, to have a veto number, a one-shot agreement problem P needs to have at least one set of irreconcilable input vectors. Given S_x a minimal set of irreconcilable input vectors of a problem P, let $\ell(S_x)$ be the number of distinct entries for which at least two vectors of S_x differ[1], i.e., the number of entries k such that there are two vectors I_a and I_b of S_x with $I_a[k] \neq I_b[k]$. As an example let $S_x = \{[a, a, a, a, e, b, b], [a, a, a, a, e, c, c], [a, a, a, f, e, b, c]\}$. We have $\ell_x = 3$.

Definition 2. *Let P be an agreement problem whose minimal sets of irreconcilable input vectors are S_x, $1 \leq x \leq m$. The veto number of P is the integer $\ell = \min(\ell(S_1), \ldots, \ell(S_m))$.*

When we consider the previous example, this means that there is a set of 3 processes that control the decision value. Therefore, intuitively, we show that no decision can be made without first consulting these processes, or knowing definitely that a failure has occurred.

If a one-shot agreement problem has no set of irreconcilable input vectors, we say that its veto number is $+\infty$ (by definition). We also say that a one-shot agreement problem is an ℓ-veto problem if its veto number is ℓ.

Lemma 2. *Let P be a one-shot agreement problem for which there is no set of irreconcilable input vectors (hence, its veto number is $+\infty$). Then P can be solved in $AS_{n,f}(\emptyset)$ with $f < n$.*

Proof. Since there is no set of irreconcilable input vectors, there is at least one value that appears in the decision sets of all possible input vectors. Therefore, it is always possible to deterministically decide on the smallest such value. $\square_{Lemma\ 2}$

4   Results Based on the Veto Number Concept

4.1   Results on Failure Detectors

Two classes of failure detectors with eventual accuracy Failure detectors have been formally defined by Chandra and Toueg who have introduced several classes of failure detectors [1]. A failure detector class is formally defined by two abstract properties, namely a *Completeness* property and an *Accuracy* property. In this paper, we are interested in the following properties:

- Strong Completeness: Eventually, every process that crashes is permanently suspected by every correct process.
- Eventual Strong Accuracy: There is a time after which no correct process is suspected.
- Eventual Weak Accuracy: There is a time after which some correct process is never suspected.

Combining the completeness property with every accuracy property provides us with the following three classes of failure detectors [1]:

---

[1] Let us notice that the Hamming distance is defined on pair of vectors: it measures the number of their entries that differ. Here we consider the whole set of vectors defining S_x.

- $\Diamond \mathcal{P}$: The class of *Eventually Perfect* failure detectors. This class contains all the failure detectors that satisfy strong completeness and eventual strong accuracy.
- $\Diamond \mathcal{S}$: The class of *Eventually Strong* failure detectors. This class contains all the failure detectors that satisfy strong completeness and eventual weak accuracy.

In the following, $AS_{n,f}(\mathcal{X})$ denotes an asynchronous distributed system made up of n processes communicating through reliable links, where up to f processes may crash, and equipped with a failure detector of the class $\mathcal{X}$ ($\mathcal{X}$ being $\Diamond \mathcal{S}$ or $\Diamond \mathcal{P}$).

On a limitation of $\Diamond \mathcal{P}$ The following theorem is proved in [4] using a proof that is centered around the concept of l-veto.

Theorem 1. [4] $\forall f$, *there is no one-shot agreement problem that can be solved in $AS_{n,f}(\Diamond \mathcal{P})$ and cannot be solved in $AS_{n,f}(\Diamond \mathcal{S})$.*

The corollary that follows is an immediate consequence of this theorem.

Corollary 1. $\Diamond \mathcal{P}$ *cannot be the weakest class of failure detectors that allow to solve one-shot agreement problems in asynchronous distributed systems prone to process crash failures.*

4.2   A Class of Non-wait-free Problems

Wait-free implementation The notion of wait-free implementation has been formalized by Herlihy in [8]. A wait-free implementation of an object solving a problem (e.g., a consensus object) is one that guarantees that any process can complete its operations in a finite number of steps, regardless of the execution speed of the other processes. Hence, in a wait-free computation, no process can be prevented from terminating by undetected process crashes or arbitrary variations in their speed [8]. This means that wait-free implicitly considers the case $f = n - 1$.

A class of problems that cannot have wait-free implementation. The next theorem characterizes a class of agreement problems that cannot have a wait-free implementation (and consequently cannot have a sequential specification [8, 9]).

Theorem 2. *Let P be a one-shot agreement problem with veto number $\ell < n$. P has no wait-free implementation.*

Proof. The theorem follows directly from the definition of ℓ-veto number. That is, such problems have distinct input vectors such that no decision can be safely taken by a process until its causal history includes at least $n - l + 1$ processes. In particular, no decision can be safely taken when more than ℓ processes crash.

$\square_{Theorem\ 2}$

The next corollary follows from the previous theorem and the fact that interactive consistency and non-blocking atomic commit have veto number 1.

Corollary 2. *The interactive consistency problem and the non-blocking atomic commit problem have no wait-free implementation. Consequently, they also cannot have sequential specifications.*

We would like to point out that ℓ-veto problems with $\ell < n$ have no wait-free implementation in an inherent and profound manner. That is, for many problems, having a wait-free implementation or not depends on the level of abstraction used for solving them. For example, in asynchronous shared memory systems, as mentioned before, consensus can be implemented in a wait-free fashion using *compare&swap* objects, but not with *read/write* objects, and definitely not in a pure message passing model. However, unless processes can guess the input values of each other, an ℓ-veto problem cannot have a wait-free implementation regardless of the communication abstraction used or failure detection capabilities. This is because wait-freeness means that a process can always terminate even if it is the only one currently participating in the protocol, be the other processes faulty or alive (i.e., wait-freeness implies $(n-1)$-fault tolerance, but not vice-versa).

5 Solving Agreement Problems with Veto Number

This section focuses on solving ℓ-veto problems when $\ell < n$ in asynchronous distributed systems equipped with a consensus black box[2]. More precisely, it presents protocols reducing ℓ-veto problems (with $\ell < n$) to the consensus problem. Two cases are considered according to the value of ℓ with respect to f. Let V' be a vector with no entry equal to $\bot$. The notation $V \leq V'$ means $\forall j \in \{1, \ldots, n\} : V[j] \neq \bot \Rightarrow V[j] = V'[j]$.

5.1 Solving ℓ-Veto Problems When $f < \ell < n$

When $f < \ell < n$ it is relatively simple to reduce an ℓ-veto problem to consensus. Such a reduction is described in Figure 1. It is made up of three parts.

- V_i is the local view p_i has of the actual input vector I. This view is built at lines 1-4.
- This part (lines 5-7) is the core of the reduction protocol. Each process p_i first computes the set $\mathcal{V}_i$ including all the input vectors from which its local view V_i can be obtained (line 5). Then, p_i computes the intersection of the values that can be decided from each of these possible input vectors (line 6). Finally, p_i takes arbitrarily one of these values and keeps it in w_i (line 7).

---

[2] Such a black box can be built in asynchronous message-passing systems equipped with a failure detector of the class $\Diamond \mathcal{S}$ when $f < n/2$ [1]. When $f < n$, it can be built in asynchronous message-passing systems equipped with a failure detector of the class $\mathcal{P}^f + \Diamond \mathcal{S}$ [2,5].

Function Reduction_1 (v_i)

(1) $V_i \leftarrow [\perp, \dots, \perp]$;
(2) **for** $1 \le j \le n$ **do** *send* VALUE (v_i) *to* p_j **enddo**;
(3) **wait until** (VALUE$(-)$ has been rec. from at least $(n - \ell + 1)$ processes);
(4) **for** $1 \le j \le n$ **do if** (VALUE(v_j) rec. from p_j) **then** $V_i[j] \leftarrow v_j$ **endif enddo**;
(5) **let** $\mathcal{V}_i = \{V_i' \mid V_i'$ has no entries equal to $\perp \wedge V_i \le V_i'\}$;
(6) **let** $X = \bigcap_{V_i' \in \mathcal{V}_i} \mathcal{F}(V_i')$;
(7) $w_i \leftarrow$ any value from X;
(8) $output_i \leftarrow$ Consensus (w_i);
(9) *return* $(output_i)$

Fig. 1. Reducing ℓ-veto Problems to Consensus when $f < \ell < n$

– The last part (lines 8-9) is a consensus invocation where p_i proposes the value w_i it has previously computed.

Theorem 3. *Let P be an ℓ-veto problem ($\ell < n$). Let us consider an asynchronous message-passing system where consensus can be solved and such that $f < \ell$. The protocol described in Figure 1 solves P.*

Proof. As $f < \ell$, we have $n - f \ge n - \ell + 1$, from which we conclude that no process can block forever at line 3. The termination property follows directly from this observation and the fact that consensus can be solved in the system. The agreement property follows directly from consensus agreement.

The validity property follows from the very definition of veto number. As the veto number is ℓ, it follows from the lines 5-6 that all the vectors in $\mathcal{V}_i$ are not irreconcilable. Moreover, due to the very construction of $\mathcal{V}_i$, the actual input vector I is a member of $\mathcal{V}_i$. As the vectors in $\mathcal{V}_i$ are not irreconcilable, it follows that the sets of values that can be decided from each vector of $\mathcal{V}_i$ have a non-empty intersection. Consequently, X is not empty and contains values that can be decided from the actual input vector I. Finally, due to the consensus validity, the value that is decided is one of these values, and the validity property follows.

$\square_{Theorem\ 3}$

5.2   Solving ℓ-Veto Problems When $n > f \ge \ell$

We now consider the case of ℓ-veto problems in systems where $f \ge \ell$. When we consider the protocol described in Figure 1, the new constraint $f \ge \ell$ creates two new problems we have to solve (these problems are implicitly solved when $\ell > f$). One is to prevent the permanent blocking that could appear at line 3 of Figure 1 (as now $n - f < n - \ell + 1$), and the second is the fact that some value has to be decided even when ℓ or more processes crash, i.e., when a set of processes that could change the decision value have crashed.

We solve the first of these problems by introducing an appropriate class of failure detectors, and the second by restricting the class of ℓ-veto problems.

The Failure Detector Class $?\mathcal{P}^\ell$ This class extends the class of *anonymously perfect* failure detectors (denoted $?\mathcal{P}$) that has been introduced in [6] to solve the non-blocking atomic commit problem (the class $?\mathcal{P}$ is actually $?\mathcal{P}^1$).

Let each process be equipped with a flag initialized to *false*. Any failure detector belonging to $?\mathcal{P}^\ell$ satisfies the following properties:

- Anonymous completeness: If at least ℓ crashes occur, eventually the flag of every correct process remains permanently equal to *true*.
- Anonymous accuracy: No flag is set to true, unless at least ℓ processes crash.

A sub-class of ℓ-Veto problems. The sub-class of the ℓ-veto problems we consider in the following includes the ℓ-veto problems for which a predetermined value can be decided in the runs where ℓ or more processes crash. That value is not necessarily related to the input vector. An example of such a problem is non-blocking atomic commit. This is a 1-veto problem where, in presence of one (or more) crash, the predetermined value *abort* can be decided even if all processes have proposed *yes*. Let predet_val the set of these predetermined values. In the non-blocking atomic commit problem, this set comprises a single value (namely, *abort*). In the general case, this set can contain several values.

Function Reduction_2 (v_i)

(1) $V_i \leftarrow [\bot, \ldots, \bot]$;
(2) **for** $1 \le j \le n$ **do** *send* VALUE (v_i) *to* p_j **enddo**;
(3) **wait until** (VALUE$(-)$ has been rec. from at least $(n - \ell + 1)$ proc. $\vee$ $flag_i$);
(4) **for** $1 \le j \le n$ **do if** (VALUE(v_j) rec. from p_j) **then** $V_i[j] \leftarrow v_j$ **endif enddo**;
(5) **if** (values have been received from at least $(n - \ell + 1)$ processes)
(6)   **then let** $\mathcal{V}_i = \{V_i' \mid V_i'$ has no entries equal to $\bot \wedge V_i \le V_i'\}$;
(7)   **let** $X = \bigcap_{V_i' \in \mathcal{V}_i} \mathcal{F}(V_i')$;
(8) $w_i \leftarrow$ any value from X
(9)   **else** $w_i \leftarrow$ any value taken from predet_val
(10) **endif**;
(11) $output_i \leftarrow$ Consensus (w_i);
(12) *return* $(output_i)$

Fig. 2. A $?\mathcal{P}^\ell$-Based Reduction of ℓ-veto Problems to Consensus when $f \ge \ell$

A $?\mathcal{P}^\ell$-Based Protocol The protocol described in Figure 2 enriches the protocol of Figure 1 in order to solve the ℓ-veto problems of interest.

A process p_i first sends its input value v_i to all (line 2) and then waits until it has received values from at least $(n - \ell + 1)$ processes or is informed by $?\mathcal{P}^\ell$

(through the boolean $flag_i$) that there are at least ℓ crashes (line 3). Then, there are two cases, according to the number x of processes from which p_i has received values. In each case, p_i sets a local variable w_i to a value that could be decided in this run, and then, as before, participates in a consensus where it proposes w_i.

- $x \geq n - \ell + 1$. This case is the same as the previous one: despite the fact that $f \geq \ell$, p_i has enough proposed values in its view.
- $x \leq n - \ell$. In that case, p_i sets w_i to a value taken from the set of predetermined values (e.g., the value $abort$ in the case of the non-blocking atomic commit problem).

The proof that this protocol is correct is left to the reader. It is a straightforward extension of the proof of the previous reduction protocol.

Remark. The protocol described in Figure 2 can be seen as a generalization of the non-blocking atomic commit protocol described in [6] that reduces atomic commit to consensus with the help of $?\mathcal{P}$ (which does correspond to $?\mathcal{P}^1$). Let us also remark that, differently from the non-blocking atomic commit problem, the interactive consistency problem does not belong to the class of ℓ-veto problems that the protocol of Figure 2 can reduce to consensus. (Let us also observe that, differently from the non-blocking atomic commit problem, the interactive consistency problem is equivalent to the construction of a *perfect* failure detector [7].)

An interesting problem that remains open is the following one: "Is $?\mathcal{P}^\ell$ the weakest failure detector to reduce ℓ-veto problems to consensus when $f \geq \ell$?". Other interesting questions concern the use of the ℓ-veto number to rank the difficulty of agreement problems.

References

1. Chandra T.D. and Toueg S., Unreliable Failure Detectors for Reliable Distributed Systems. *JACM*, 43(2):225-267, 1996.
2. Delporte-Gallet C., Fauconnier H. and Guerraoui R., Failure Detection Lower Bounds on Registers and Consensus. *Proc. 16th Int. Symposium on Distributed Computing*, Springer-Verlag LNCS #2508, pp. 237-251, 2002.
3. Fischer M.J., Lynch N. and Paterson M.S., Impossibility of Distributed Consensus with One Faulty Process. *Journal of the ACM*, 32(2):374-382, 1985.
4. Friedman R., Mostéfaoui A. and Raynal M., The Notion of Veto Number and the the Respective Power of $\Diamond\mathcal{P}$ and $\Diamond\mathcal{S}$ to Solve One-Shot Agreement Problems. *Proc. 18th Int. Symposium on Distributed Computing (DISC'04)*, Springer-Verlag LNCS, 2004.
5. Friedman R., Mostéfaoui A. and Raynal M., A Weakest Failure Detector-Based Asynchronous Consensus Protocol for $f < n$. *Information Processing Letters*, 90(1):39-46, 2004.
6. Guerraoui R., Non-Blocking Atomic Commit in Asynchronous Distributed Systems with Failure Detectors. *Distributed Computing*, 15:17-25, 2002.
7. Hélary J.-M., Hurfin M., Mostefaoui A., Raynal M. and Tronel F., Computing Global Functions in Asynchronous Distributed Systems with Process Crashes. *IEEE Transactions on Distributed and Parallel Systems*, 11(9):897-909, 2000.

8. Herlihy M.P., Wait-Free Synchronization. *ACM Transactions on Programming Languages and Systems*, 13(1):124-149, 1991.
9. Herlihy M.P. and Wing J.L., Linearizability: a Correctness Condition for Concurrent Objects. *ACM Transactions on Programming Languages and Systems*, 12(3):463-492, 1990.
10. Mostéfaoui A., Rajsbaum S. and Raynal M., Conditions on Input Vectors for Consensus Solvability in Asynchronous Distributed Systems. *Journal of the ACM*, 50(6):922-954, 2003.

Reliability of VLSI Linear Arrays with Redundant Links

Soumen Maity[1], Amiya Nayak[2], and Bimal Roy[3]

[1] Department of Mathematics, Indian Institute of Technology,
Guwahati, Assam, India
soumenmaity@yahoo.co.in
[2] School of Information Technology and Engineering,
University of Ottawa, Ontario, Canada, K1N 6N5
anayak@site.uottawa.ca
[3] Applied Statistics Unit, Indian Statistical Institute,
203 B. T. Road, Kolkata, India
bimal@isical.ac.in

Abstract. Reliability is one of the most important attributes of any system. Adding redundancy is one way to improve the reliability. In this paper, we consider linear VLSI arrays in which each processor has a set of redundant links to bypass faulty processor(s). It is known that patterns of faults occurring at strategic locations in such arrays can be catastrophic and may render the system unusable regardless of its component redundancy and of its reconfiguration capabilities. Assuming a number of faulty processors (i.e., a fault pattern which may or may not be catastrophic) and a set of redundant links (i.e., link configuration), we use combinatorial modelling to evaluate the reliability of the linear VLSI arrays. Moreover, we also discuss how the choice of a link configuration can play a role in reliability improvement.

1 Introduction

Systolic systems consist of a large number of identical and elementary processing elements locally connected in a regular fashion. Each element receives data from its neighbors, computes and then sends the results again to its neighbors. Few particular elements located at the extremes of the systems (these extremes depend on the particular system) are allowed to communicate with the external world. The simplest systolic model is the VLSI linear array. In such a system the processing elements (PEs) are connected in a linear fashion: processing elements are arranged in linear order and each element is connected with the previous and the following element (see Figure 1).

Fault-tolerant techniques are very important to systolic systems. Here, we assume that only processors can fail. Indeed, since the number of processing elements is very large, the probability that a set of processing elements becomes faulty is not small. In a linear array of N processing elements, one faulty element is sufficient to stop the flow of information from one side to the other. Without the provision of fault tolerance capabilities, the yield of VLSI chips for such an

A. Sen et al. (Eds.): IWDC 2004, LNCS 3326, pp. 326–337, 2004.
© Springer-Verlag Berlin Heidelberg 2004

Fig. 1. VLSI linear array

architecture would be so poor that the chip would be unacceptable. Thus, fault-tolerant mechanisms must be provided in order to avoid faulty processing elements taking part in the computation. A widely used technique to achieve reconfigurability consists of providing redundancy to the desired architecture [1].

The effectiveness of using redundancy to increase fault tolerance clearly depends on both the amount of redundancy and the reconfiguration capability of the system. It does, however, depend also on the distribution of faults in the system. There are sets of faulty processing elements for which no reconfiguration strategy is possible. Such sets are called catastrophic fault patterns. From a network perspective, such fault patterns can cause network disconnection.

Reliability is perhaps the most important attribute of any system. Almost all specifications for systems mandate that certain values for reliability be achieved and, in some way, demonstrated. The most popular reliability analysis techniques are the analytic approaches. Of the analytic techniques, combinatorial modelling is the most commonly used approach [12].

In this paper, assuming a fault pattern which may or may not be catastrophic and a set of redundant links, we use combinatorial modelling to evaluate the reliability of the linear VLSI arrays in cases where the links are unidirectional or bidirectional. We derive closed-form reliability expressions for link configurations with just one redundant link and also for the general link configuration. Moreover, we study the effect of redundant link on system reliability to find that the reliability improves with longer bypass links.

2   Preliminaries

In VLSI linear arrays the redundancy consists of additional processing elements, called spares, and additional connections, called bypass links. Bypass links are links that connect each processor with another processor at a fixed distance greater than 1. Figure 1 shows a linear array of processing elements.

We now recall the relevant definitions and concepts from the literature. The basic components of a linear array are the *processing elements*, or simply processors, and the *links*. There are two kind of links: *regular and bypass*. Regular links connect neighboring processors, while the bypass links connect non-neighbors. The bypass links are used only for reconfiguration purposes when faulty processors are detected; otherwise, they are considered to be the redundant links.

More precisely, let $A = \{p_1,\ p_2, \ldots,\ p_N\}$ denote a linear array of identical processing elements connected by regular links $(p_i,\ p_{i+1})$, $1 \leq i < N$.

Definition 1. Let $G = \{g_1,\ g_2,\ \ldots,\ g_k\}$ be an ordered set of integers such that $2 \leq g_1 < g_2 < \ldots < g_k$. We say that A has *link redundancy* or *link configuration* G if, the bypass links are (p_i, p_{i+g_t}) for $1 \leq i \leq N - g_t$ and $1 \leq t \leq k$.

Note that the set G does not contain the regular links even though they exist. We denote the length of the longest bypass link by g, i.e., $g = g_k$. At the extremities of the array, two special processors, called I (for input) and O (for output), are responsible for the I/O function of the system. We assume that I is connected to p_1, p_2, $\ldots$, p_g while O is connected to p_{N-g+1}, p_{N-g+2}, $\ldots$, p_N so that bottlenecks at the borders of the array are avoided.

Example 1. Figure 2 shows a linear array of 15 processors with redundancy $G = \{4\}$.

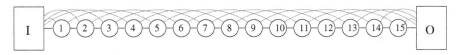

Fig. 2. A linear array of processors

We refer to this structure as a *redundant linear array* or as a *redundant array*. A redundant array is called *bidirectional* or *unidirectional* according to the nature of its links. We sometimes refer to a processor p_i as processor i.

Definition 2. A *fault pattern* $F = \{f_1, f_2, \ldots, f_m\}$ for A is the set of faulty processors which can be any non-empty subset of A.

Definition 3. The *width* ω_F of a fault pattern F is defined to be the number of processors between and including the first and the last fault in F. That is, if $F = \{f_1, f_2, \ldots, f_m\}$ then $\omega_F = f_m - f_1 + 1$.

Definition 4. A fault pattern F is *catastrophic* for an array A with link redundancy G if I and O are not connected in the presence of such an assignment of faults.

In other words, given a redundant linear array A, a fault pattern F is catastrophic for A if and only if no path exists between I and O, once the faulty processors, and their incident links are removed. For example, in a linear array of processing elements with no link redundancy, a single PE fault in any location is sufficient to stop the flow of information from one side to the other.

Example 2. Consider the following two fault patterns $F_1 = \{4, 5, 7\}$ and $F_2 = \{3, 5, 7\}$ for a linear array with link redundancy $G = \{3\}$. We see from Figure 3, that the input processor I and the output processor O are connected by a path $[I, 1, 2, 3, 6, 9, O]$. Hence F_1 is not a catastrophic fault pattern by Definition 4. It is easy to check that, F_2 is catastrophic.

We denote a fault pattern by FP and a catastrophic fault pattern by CFP. If we have to reconfigure a system when a fault pattern occurs, it is necessary to know if the fault pattern is catastrophic or not. Therefore, it is important

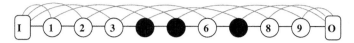

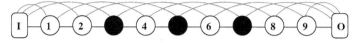

Fig. 3. Fault Pattern $F_1 = \{4,\ 5,\ 7\}$

Fig. 4. Fault Pattern $F_2 = \{3,\ 5,\ 7\}$

to study the properties of catastrophic fault patterns. A Characterization of catastrophic fault patterns was given in [8]. Nayak, Santoro, and Tan [8] proved that the number of faulty processing elements in any catastrophic fault pattern is greater than or equal to the length of the longest bypass link.

As done in [10], we consider only fault patterns of cardinality g_k, so, in general, $F = \{f_1,\ f_2,\ \ldots,\ f_{g_k}\}$. Also, the width of a fault pattern must fall within precise bounds for the pattern to be catastrophic; these bounds were established on the width ω_F of the fault pattern for different link configurations.

Proposition 1. [10] Let $F = \{f_1,\ f_2,\ \ldots,\ f_{g_k}\}$ be a fault pattern for a linear array A with link redundancy $G = \{g_1, g_2, \ldots, g_k\}$. Necessary condition for F to be catastrophic is

$$g_k \leq \omega_F \leq (\lceil \frac{g_k}{2} \rceil - 1)g_k + \lfloor \frac{g_k}{2} \rfloor + 1,$$

in the case of bidirectional links and

$$g_k \leq \omega_F \leq (g_k - 1)^2 + 1,$$

in the case of unidirectional links.

Nayak, Santoro and Tan [10] give an algorithm for constructing a catastrophic fault pattern with maximum width. Nayak, Pagli and Santoro [9] and De Prisco, Monti and Pagli [3] give algorithms for testing whether a fault pattern is catastrophic or not.

From now on, by catastrophic fault pattern we mean a catastrophic fault pattern having minimum number of faulty processing elements, i.e., with size equal to the length of the longest bypass link. Given a linear array with a set of bypass links, an important problem is to count the number of independent catastrophic fault patterns. The knowledge of this number enables us to estimate the probability that the system operates correctly.

Example 3. Figure 5 shows all mutually independent catastrophic fault patterns for a linear array with bidirectional link redundancy $G = \{4\}$. Links are not drawn in Figure 5. Figure 6 shows the only fault pattern $F = \{4, 7, 10, 13\}$ which is not catastrophic for bidirectional links but is catastrophic for unidirectional link redundancy $G = \{4\}$. Hence, the number of mutually independent CFPs for a linear array with unidirectional link redundancy $G = \{4\}$ is 5.

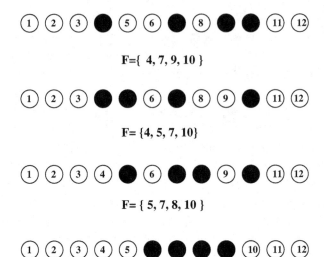

F={ 4, 7, 9, 10 }

F= {4, 5, 7, 10}

F= { 5, 7, 8, 10 }

F={ 6, 7, 8, 9 }

Fig. 5. Catastrophic Fault Patterns for bidirectional link redundancy $G = \{4\}$

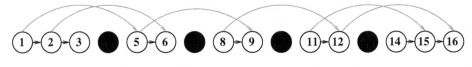

F= { 4, 7, 10, 13}

Fig. 6. Catastrophic Fault Pattern F for unidirectional link redundancy $G = \{4\}$

Enumeration of mutually independent catastrophic fault patterns for link redundancy $G = \{g\}$ has been done in [6] and [4] for bidirectional and unidirectional case respectively. Maity, Roy and Nayak [6] extended this to the case of link redundancy $G = \{2, 3, \ldots, k, g\}, 2 \leq k < g - 1$.

Theorem 1 ([6], [4]) The number of mutually independent CFPs for linear array with link redundancy $G = \{g\}$ is given by

$$F^B(g) = \sum_{n=0}^{\lfloor \frac{g-1}{2} \rfloor} \frac{1}{n+1} \binom{2n}{n} \binom{g-1}{2n}$$

in the case of bidirectional links and

$$F^U(g) = \frac{1}{g} \binom{2g-2}{g-1}$$

in the case of unidirectional links.

Theorem 2 [6]. The number of mutually independent catastrophic fault patterns for a linear array with with link redundancy $G = \{2, 3, \ldots, k, g\}$ for $k < g - 1$ is given by $F^B(2, 3 \ldots, k, g)$

$$= 1 + \sum_{n=1}^{\lfloor \frac{g-k}{2} \rfloor} \sum_{r=2}^{n} \left[\binom{n-1}{r-1}^2 - \binom{n-1}{r-2}\binom{n-1}{r} \right] \left(\frac{g - k - 2(n-r)(k-1)}{2n} \right).$$

in the case of bidirectional links and $F^U(2, 3, \ldots, k, g)$

$$= 1 + \sum_{n=1}^{\lfloor \frac{g-k}{2} \rfloor} \sum_{r=2}^{n} \left[\binom{n-1}{r-1}^2 - \binom{n-1}{r}\binom{n-1}{r-2} \right] \left(\frac{g - k - (n-r)(k-2)}{2n} \right).$$

in the case of unidirectional links.

3   Linear Array with Link Redundancy $G = \{g\}$

Combinatorial models use probabilistic techniques that enumerate the different ways in which a system can remain operational. Here, by a system we mean VLSI linear array with link redundancy $G = \{g\}$. A VLSI linear array with link redundancy $G = \{g\}$ remains operational even after some of its PEs have failed. More precisely the system remains operational if the number of faulty PEs is less then g and it fails only if the number of faulty PEs is more than or equal to g. Any fault pattern of size g or more may or may not cause system failure. It does, however, also depend on the distribution of faults in the system. We know that only catastrophic fault patterns can cause network disconnection. In [6, 7, 4], by (minimal) catastrophic fault pattern they mean catastrophic fault pattern having minimum number of faulty processing elements, i.e., with size equal to the length g of the longest bypass link. However, system may fail in the presence of $n > g$ defective processors though only g defective processors are responsible for network disconnection and rest $(n - g)$ defective processors are redundant. However, the reliability of the system depends on link structure G, the processor failure probability p and the size of the array N. Throughout this paper we mostly talk about bidirectional case. However, similar statement holds for unidirectional case as well.

Notation:

N total number of processors in the array

g length of the longest bypass link

FP fault pattern

CFP catastrophic fault pattern

p probability of processor failure

ω width of the fault pattern (same as ω_F)

G link configuration

Assumption:

Processor failure probabilities p are i.i.d.

The object is to compute the reliability of the system for given values of g, p, and N. These values are chosen by analyst. Given $G = \{g\}$, p, and N, the initial step is to compute the reliability of the system in the presence of g defective processors only. The system reliability is the probability of system being operational. Note that the probability of system failure is equal to the probability of occurrence of a catastrophic fault pattern. One has to be careful about the the necessary conditions for a fault pattern of size g to be catastrophic. We have already discussed that the width ω_F of a fault pattern must fall within precise bounds for the pattern to be catastrophic. More precisely, a fault pattern of size g and width more than $(\lceil \frac{g}{2} \rceil - 1)g + \lfloor \frac{g}{2} \rfloor + 1$ can not be catastrophic with respect to bidirectional link redundancy $G = \{g\}$. Thus we are interested in the fault patterns of size g which are of width less then $(\lceil \frac{g}{2} \rceil - 1)g + \lfloor \frac{g}{2} \rfloor + 1$ for bidirectional links. Hence, P(system failure in the presence of g defectives)

$$= P(\text{occurrence of a CFP of size } g)$$

$$= P(\text{occurrence of a FP of size } g \text{ and width } \leq (\lceil \frac{g}{2} \rceil - 1)g + \lfloor \frac{g}{2} \rfloor + 1) \times$$

$$P(\text{a FP of size } g \text{ and width } \leq (\lceil \frac{g}{2} \rceil - 1)g + \lfloor \frac{g}{2} \rfloor + 1 \text{ is catastrophic})$$

$$+ P(\text{occurrence of a FP of size } g \text{ and width } \geq (\lceil \frac{g}{2} \rceil - 1)g + \lfloor \frac{g}{2} \rfloor + 1) \times$$

$$P(\text{a FP of size } g \text{ and width } \geq (\lceil \frac{g}{2} \rceil - 1)g + \lfloor \frac{g}{2} \rfloor + 1 \text{ is catastrophic})$$

Note that P(a fault pattern of size g and width $\geq (\lceil \frac{g}{2} \rceil - 1)g + \lfloor \frac{g}{2} \rfloor + 1$ is catastrophic) = 0. Thus, we compute the above probability in two steps. The **first step** is to compute the probability that a fault pattern of size g and width $\leq (\lceil \frac{g}{2} \rceil - 1)g + \lfloor \frac{g}{2} \rfloor + 1$ is catastrophic for bidirectional link redundancy $G = \{g\}$. We introduce the following definition in attempting to compute the above probability.

Definition 5. Two fault patterns F_1 and F_2 are said to be *identical* if F_2 can be obtained from F_1 by adding an integer with each element of F_1; otherwise, they are *distinct*.

For example, consider the fault patterns $F_1 = \{1, 4, 6, 7\}$, $F_2 = \{2, 5, 7, 8\}$ and $F_3 = \{2, 5, 7, 9\}$ in a linear array of N processors. Clearly F_1 and F_2 are identical because F_2 can be obtained by adding 1 with each element of F_1, while F_1 and F_3 are two distinct fault patterns as are F_2 and F_3.

Now, we can write

P(a FP of size g and width $\leq (\lceil \frac{g}{2} \rceil - 1)g + \lfloor \frac{g}{2} \rfloor + 1$ is catastrophic)

$$= \frac{\text{Total number } F^B(g) \text{ of distinct CFPs of size } g}{\text{Total number of distinct FPs of size } g \text{ and width } \leq (\lceil \frac{g}{2} \rceil - 1)g + \lfloor \frac{g}{2} \rfloor + 1}$$

for bidirectional links and
P(a FP of size g and width $\leq (g-1)^2 + 1$ is catastrophic)

$$= \frac{\text{Total number } F^U(g) \text{ of distinct CFPs of size } g}{\text{Total number of distinct FPs of size } g \text{ and width } \leq (g-1)^2 + 1}$$

for unidirectional links.

Lemma 1. The total number of distinct fault patterns of size g and width less then or equal to ω is equal to $\binom{\omega-1}{g-1}$.

Proof. The required number of fault patterns is equal to the number of fault patterns $\{f_1, f_2, \ldots, f_g\}$ of size g, width $\leq \omega$ and $f_1 = 1$. The reason is this. Any fault pattern with $f_1 \neq 1$ is identical to a fault pattern with $f_1 = 1$. Suppose to the contrary that a fault pattern $F = \{f_1 \neq 1, f_2, \ldots f_g\}$ of width $\leq \omega$ is distinct from the collection S of fault patterns of size g, width $\leq \omega$ and $f_1 = 1$. It may be noted that fault pattern $F^* = \{1, f_2 - f_1 + 1, \ldots, f_g - f_1 + 1\} \in S$ is identical to F, a contradiction. Thus, the number of distinct fault patterns is equal to $\binom{\omega-1}{g-1}$. $\qquad\square$

Theorem 1 provides the number of distinct catastrophic fault patterns for linear array with link redundancy $G = \{g\}$. Thus, P(a fault pattern of size g and width $\leq (\lceil \frac{g}{2} \rceil - 1)g + \lfloor \frac{g}{2} \rfloor + 1$ is catastrophic)

$$= \frac{\sum_{n=0}^{\lfloor \frac{g-1}{2} \rfloor} \frac{1}{n+1} \binom{2n}{n} \binom{g-1}{2n}}{\binom{(\lceil \frac{g}{2} \rceil - 1)g + \lfloor \frac{g}{2} \rfloor}{g-1}} \tag{1}$$

in the case of bidirectional links, and
P(a FP of size g and width $\leq (g-1)^2 + 1$ is catastrophic)

$$= \frac{\frac{1}{g} \binom{2g-2}{g-1}}{\binom{(g-1)^2}{g-1}} \tag{2}$$

in the case of unidirectional links.

The **second step** is to compute the the probability of occurrence of a fault pattern of size g and width $\leq (\lceil \frac{g}{2} \rceil - 1)g + \lfloor \frac{g}{2} \rfloor + 1$. The idea here is to enumerate all fault patterns (not necessarily distinct) of size g and width $\leq (\lceil \frac{g}{2} \rceil - 1)g + \lfloor \frac{g}{2} \rfloor + 1$. Then, multiplying this quantity with $p^g(1-p)^{(N-g)}$ yields the probability of occurrence of a fault pattern of size g and width $\leq (\lceil \frac{g}{2} \rceil - 1)g + \lfloor \frac{g}{2} \rfloor + 1$. The number of fault patterns of size g, width ω (i.e., WLOG $f_1 = 1$ and $f_\omega = 1$) is equal to $\binom{\omega-2}{g-2}$. Since f_1 can vary from 1 to $N-\omega$ (i.e., the fault pattern can occur anywhere in the array), the total number of such fault patterns is $(N-\omega)\binom{\omega-2}{g-2}$. Thus, the number of fault patterns of size g and width $\leq (\lceil \frac{g}{2} \rceil - 1)g + \lfloor \frac{g}{2} \rfloor + 1$ is

$$\sum_{\omega=g}^{(\lceil \frac{g}{2} \rceil - 1)g + \lfloor \frac{g}{2} \rfloor + 1} (N-\omega)\binom{\omega-2}{g-2}.$$

Therefore, P(occurrence of a FP of size g and width $\leq (\lceil\frac{g}{2}\rceil - 1)g + \lfloor\frac{g}{2}\rfloor + 1)$

$$= \sum_{\omega=g}^{(\lceil\frac{g}{2}\rceil-1)g+\lfloor\frac{g}{2}\rfloor+1} (N-\omega)\binom{\omega-2}{g-2}p^g(1-p)^{N-g}$$

Combining these two steps we get, P(sys. failure in the presence of g defectives)

$= P$(occurrence of a FP of size g and width $\leq (\lceil\frac{g}{2}\rceil - 1)g + \lfloor\frac{g}{2}\rfloor + 1) \cdot$

P(a FP of size g and width $\leq (\lceil\frac{g}{2}\rceil - 1)g + \lfloor\frac{g}{2}\rfloor + 1$ is catastrophic)

$$= \left[\sum_{\omega=g}^{(\lceil\frac{g}{2}\rceil-1)g+\lfloor\frac{g}{2}\rfloor+1} (N-\omega)\binom{\omega-2}{g-2}p^g(1-p)^{N-g}\right]\left[\frac{\sum_{n=0}^{\lfloor\frac{g-1}{2}\rfloor}\frac{1}{n+1}\binom{2n}{n}\binom{g-1}{2n}}{\binom{(\lceil\frac{g}{2}\rceil-1)g+\lfloor\frac{g}{2}\rfloor}{g-1}}\right]$$

in the case of bidirectional links, and

$$= \left[\sum_{\omega=g}^{(g-1)^2+1} (N-\omega)\binom{\omega-2}{g-2}p^g(1-p)^{N-g}\right]\left[\frac{\frac{1}{g}\binom{2g-2}{g-1}}{\binom{(g-1)^2}{g-1}}\right]$$

in the case of unidirectional links.

The system reliability is the probability of system being operational. Thus, we have the following theorem:

Theorem 3 *Given $G = \{g\}$, p and N, the reliability of VLSI linear array in the presence of g defective PEs is*

$= 1 - P$*(system failure in the presence of g defective PEs)*

$$= 1 - \left[\frac{\sum_{n=0}^{\lfloor\frac{g-1}{2}\rfloor}\frac{1}{n+1}\binom{2n}{n}\binom{g-1}{2n}}{\binom{(\lceil\frac{g}{2}\rceil-1)g+\lfloor\frac{g}{2}\rfloor}{g-1}}\right]\left[\sum_{\omega=g}^{(\lceil\frac{g}{2}\rceil-1)g+\lfloor\frac{g}{2}\rfloor+1} (N-\omega)\binom{\omega-2}{g-2}p^g(1-p)^{N-g}\right]$$

in the case of bidirectional links, and

$$= 1 - \left[\frac{\frac{1}{g}\binom{2g-2}{g-1}}{\binom{(g-1)^2}{g-1}}\right]\left[\sum_{\omega=g}^{(g-1)^2+1} (N-\omega)\binom{\omega-2}{g-2}p^g(1-p)^{N-g}\right]$$

in the case of unidirectional links.

However, the system may fail in the presence of more then g defective processors also. But no matter how hard one tries, one can not make the system unusable by removing less then g processors and their incident links. Thus,

$$P\text{(system failure)} = \sum_{n=g}^{N} P\text{(sys. failure in the presence of } n \text{ defectives)} \quad (3)$$

Thus, to compute the system reliability, we need to compute the probability of system failure in the presence of $n > g$ defective PEs, which is quite involved and will not be considered here. For this reason, we simply consider the problem of computing the system reliability in the presence of g defective processors in this paper.

4   Linear Array with Link Redundancy $G = \{2, 3, \ldots, k, g\}$

In general, we consider linear array with link redundancy $G = \{2, 3, \ldots, k, g\}$ for $k < g - 1$. The reliability of such system can be obtained by applying the same technique stated before for link redundancy $G = \{g\}$ in a straightforward way. Arguing as we did before, the total number of distinct fault patterns of size g and width less then or equal to ω in a linear array with link redundancy $G = \{2, 3, \ldots, k, g\}$ is equal to $\binom{\omega-1}{g-1}$. Note that this number does not depend on the link structure. We will use Theorem 2 for the number of distinct CFPs. Thus, we get P(a FP of size g and width $\leq (\lceil \frac{g}{2} \rceil - 1)g + \lfloor \frac{g}{2} \rfloor + 1$ is catastrophic)

$$= \frac{1 + \sum_{n=1}^{\lfloor \frac{g-k}{2} \rfloor} \sum_{r=2}^{n} \left[\binom{n-1}{r-1}^2 - \binom{n-1}{r-2}\binom{n-1}{r} \right] \left(\frac{g-k-2(n-r)(k-1)}{2n} \right)}{\binom{(\lceil \frac{g}{2} \rceil - 1)g + \lfloor \frac{g}{2} \rfloor}{g-1}} \tag{4}$$

for bidirectional links, and P(a fault pattern of size g and width $\leq (g-1)^2 + 1$ is catastrophic)

$$= \frac{1 + \sum_{n=1}^{\lfloor \frac{g-k}{2} \rfloor} \sum_{r=2}^{n} \left[\binom{n-1}{r-1}^2 - \binom{n-1}{r}\binom{n-1}{r-2} \right] \left(\frac{g-k-(n-r)(k-2)}{2n} \right)}{\binom{(g-1)^2}{g-1}} \tag{5}$$

for unidirectional links.

Note that the probability of occurrence of a fault pattern of size g and width $\leq (\lceil \frac{g}{2} \rceil - 1)g + \lfloor \frac{g}{2} \rfloor + 1$ for bidirectional links and width $\leq (g-1)^2 + 1$ for unidirectional links does not depend on the link structure. So, we have the following theorem for link redundancy $G = \{2, 3, \ldots, k, g\}$:

Theorem 4 *Given* $G = \{2, 3, \ldots, k, g\}$, $k < g - 1$, p *and* N, *the reliability of VLSI linear array in the presence of* g *defective PEs is*

$= 1 - P$*(system failure in the presence of* g *defective PEs)*

$$= 1 - \left[\frac{1 + \sum_{n=1}^{\lfloor \frac{g-k}{2} \rfloor} \sum_{r=2}^{n} \left[\binom{n-1}{r-1}^2 - \binom{n-1}{r-2}\binom{n-1}{r} \right] \left(\frac{g-k-2(n-r)(k-1)}{2n} \right)}{\binom{(\lceil \frac{g}{2} \rceil - 1)g + \lfloor \frac{g}{2} \rfloor}{g-1}} \right] \times$$

$$\left[\sum_{\omega=g}^{(\lceil \frac{g}{2} \rceil - 1)g + \lfloor \frac{g}{2} \rfloor + 1} (N-\omega) \binom{\omega - 2}{g - 2} p^g (1-p)^{N-g} \right]$$

in the case of bidirectional links, and

$$= 1 - \left[\frac{1 + \sum_{n=1}^{\lfloor \frac{g-k}{2} \rfloor} \sum_{r=2}^{n} \left[\binom{n-1}{r-1}^2 - \binom{n-1}{r}\binom{n-1}{r-2} \right] \left(\frac{g-k-(n-r)(k-2)}{2n} \right)}{\binom{(g-1)^2}{g-1}} \right] \times$$

$$\left[\sum_{\omega=g}^{(g-1)^2+1} (N-\omega) \binom{\omega - 2}{g - 2} p^g (1-p)^{N-g} \right]$$

in the case of unidirectional links.

5   Discussions and Conclusions

Assuming a fault pattern which may or may not be catastrophic and a set of redundant links, we used combinatorial modelling to evaluate the reliability of the linear VLSI arrays in cases where the links are unidirectional or bidirec-

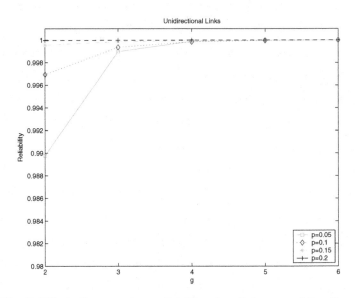

Fig. 7. Effect of g on system reliability when links are unidirectional

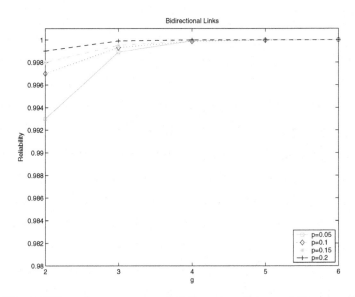

Fig. 8. Effect of g on system reliability when links are bidirectional

tional. Closed-form reliability expressions were obtained for link configurations with just one redundant link (see Theorem 3) and also for the general link configuration (see Theorem 4). In order to see the effect of redundant link on system reliability, we evaluated the expressions in Theorem 3 for various values of p and g, keeping N fixed. The results are shown in Figures 7 and 8. As expected, we found reliability improvement with larger g. More interestingly, when the probability of PE failure is small, the difference in reliability is more visible for smaller values of g. Therefore, when the probability of PE failure is high, it is better to go with redundant links of larger length. In other words, to get reliability very close to 1, we need to choose large g when the probability of PE failure is high.

References

1. Balasubramanian, V. and Banerjee, P., A fault tolerant massively parallel processing architecture. *J. of Parallel and Distributed Computing,* 4, 1987, 363-383.
2. Bruck, J., Cypher, R. and Ho, C. T., Fault-tolerant mesh with minimal number of spares. *Proc. of the 3rd IEEE Symp. on Parallel and Distributed Processing,* 1991, 288-295.
3. De Prisco R. , Monti, A. and Pagli, L., Testing and reconfiguration of VLSI linear arrays. *Theoretical Computer Science,* 197, 1998, 171-188.
4. De Prisco, R. and Santis, A. D., Catastrophic faults in reconfigurable systolic linear arrays. *Discrete Applied Math.,* 75(2), 1997, 105-123.
5. Kuo, S. and Fuchs, W. K., Efficient spare allocation for reconfigurable array. *IEEE Design and Test,* 1987, 24-31.
6. Maity, S., Roy, B. K. and Nayak, A., On enumeration of catastrophic fault patterns. *Information Processing Letters,* 81(4), 2002, 209-212.
7. Maity, S., Roy, B. K. and Nayak, A., Enumerating catastrophic fault patterns in VLSI linear arrays with both unidirectional and bidirectional links. *INTEGRATION, The VLSI Journal,* 30(2), 2001, 157-168.
8. Nayak, A., Pagli, L., and Santoro, N., Combinatorial and graph problems arising in the analysis of catastrophic fault patterns. *Congressus Numerantium,* 88, 1992, 7-20.
9. Nayak, A., Pagli, L., and Santoro, N., On testing for catastrophic faults in reconfigurable arrays with arbitrary link redundancy. *INTEGRATION, The VLSI Journal,* 20, 1996, 327-342.
10. Nayak, A., Santoro, N., and Tan, R., Fault-intolerance of reconfigurable systolic arrays. *Proc. FTCS-20,* 1990, 202-209.
11. Negrini, R., Sami, M. G., and Stefanelli, R., Fault-tolerance techniques for array structures used in supercomputing. *IEEE Computer,* 19(2), 1986, 78-87.
12. Pradhan, D. K., Fault-Tolerant Computer System Design. Computer Scince Press, United Kingdom, 2003.
13. Pagli, L. and Pucci, G., Counting the number of fault patterns in redundant VLSI arrays. *Information Processing Letters,* 50, 1994, 337-342.

A Technique to Ensure Reliability in a WDM Optical Backbone Network with Contemporary Link Failures

Swarup Mandal[1], Sougata Bera[2], and Debashis Saha[3]

[1] XLRI Jamshedpur, School of Management,
C. H. Road(East) Jamshedpur: 831001,
Tel.: 91 657 2225506, Fax: 91 657 2227814
swarup@xlri.ac.in

[2] Jadavpur University, Calcutta: 700 032, Tel.: 91 33 24146002

[3] Indian Institute of Management Calcutta, D.H. Road, Joka, Calcutta: 700104,
Tel.: 91 33 24678300, Fax: 91 33 24678307
ds@iimcal.ac.in

Abstract. Contemporary link failures in a WDM optical network results in a very high value of call drop probability (CDP). In a backbone network, a link usually carries a huge amount of data and a low CDP is desirable. To address this issue, in this work, we propose a "path-based backup multiplexed survivable strategy", namely "dynamic recursive assignment of backup lightpath" (DRABLP). To ensure optimality in backup lightpath assignment, we have used a novel search algorithm, a variant of best first search. This algorithm is triggered at the occurrence of each failure and subsequent repair of a link. We have studied the performance of DRABLP w.r.t. CDP and new call blocking probability for varying network load. A comparison with another "path-based backup multiplexed survivable strategy", namely "without recursive assignment of backup Lightpath" (WORABLP), shows that DRABLP has smaller CDP than WORABLP when there are consecutive link failures within short span of time.

Keywords: Optical Network, WDM lightpath, Reliability.

1 Introduction

With millions of wavelength-miles laid out in typical global and nation wide networks, fiber optics cable in a WDM optical network [1], [12] is the most failure prone component. Survivability in a WDM network usually refers to the ability of the network to reconfigure and reestablish communication upon failures. Here, higher survivability ensures higher reliability. It is very important for backbone network as each link carries a huge amount of data. Thus, failure to reestablish communication on a link failure may cause retransmission of large amount of data, thereby, causing a revenue loss for a network operator. Hence, low call drop probability (CDP) is a desirable feature of a WDM optical backbone network. To ensure low CDP, a network requires redundant capacity to survive a failure. The survivability strategies in WDM networks are broadly classified as *reactive* and *proactive* methods [2]. In a

A. Sen et al. (Eds.): IWDC 2004, LNCS 3326, pp. 338–346, 2004.
© Springer-Verlag Berlin Heidelberg 2004

reactive method, when an existing lightpath fails, a search is initiated to find a new lightpath, which does not use the failed component. This has an advantage of low overhead in the absence of failures [2]. However, this does not guarantee successful recovery always, because an attempt to establish a new lightpath may fail due to resource shortage at the time of failure recovery. To overcome the shortcomings of *reactive* methods, *proactive* methods can be employed. In a *proactive* method, backup lightpaths are identified a priori, and resources are reserved along the backup lightpaths at the time of establishing the primary lightpath [1] itself. Hence, the recovery time of a *proactive* method is much lower than that of a reactive method. Both *proactive* and *reactive* methods can be either *link-based* or *path-based* [3], [4]. The link-based method employs *local detouring*, while the path-based method employs *end-to-end detouring* [2]. For better resource utilization, multiplexing techniques are employed [2].

1.1 Previous Works and Motivation

In the related studies [3], [4], [5], [6], [7], [8], on backup multiplexing, authors assumed that mean time between failures (MTBF) are large enough to allow the failed link to be operational before the next failure occurs. In [13] authors have evaluated the protection reconfiguration for multiple failures in WDM mesh networks, whereas, in [14] authors have considered the pre-emptive reprovisioning in mesh optical networks, and in [15] authors have made a comprehensive study on backup reprovisioning to remedy the effect of multiple-link failures in WDM mesh networks. In this paper, we have considered a situation where MTBF is less than mean time to recover (MTTR) i.e, where there are multiple contemporary link failures. Let us explain the problem with an example.

For the network in Fig.1, when the link L_{34} fails, the primary lightpath 4-3(λ_0) through the link L_{34} is rerouted via the corresponding backup light path 4-1-3(λ_0) i.e. 4-1-3(λ_0) will be new primary lightpath for the call corresponding to the primary lightpath 4-3(λ_0) before link failure. As a consequence of this rerouting, the primary lightpath 1-2 (λ_0), whose backup lightpath was 1-3-2(λ_0) before failure, will no longer have a backup lightpath until L_{34} is restored. Also, the backup lightpath, 3-4-1(λ_1) for the primary lightpath 3-1(λ_2) will no longer be there. Thus, on failure of the link L_{34}, primary lightpaths, 3-1(λ_2), 1-2 (λ_0), and 4-1-3(λ_0) (newly rerouted) are affected and will not have backup lightpaths. In this situation, if link L_{13} fails too, then the calls corresponding to the lightpath 3-1(λ_2), and 4-1-3(λ_0) (newly rerouted) have to be dropped.

Thus, to protect the calls corresponding to the affected primary lightpaths, viz. 3-1(λ_2), 1-2 (λ_0), and 4-1-3(λ_0), even after the failure of the link L_{34}, new backup lightpaths need to be established preemptively. This motivates us to solve the problem by "*dynamic recursive assignment of backup lightpath*" (DRABLP) technique, which falls under the category of "*path-based backup multiplexed survivable strategy*" for WDM networks. In fact, every failure and repair will trigger our algorithm to result into assignment of new backup lightpaths. The problem of re-establishing backup lightpaths for the affected primary lightpaths can be viewed as a variant of *dynamic lightpath establishment problem* [9] which is known to be NP-hard in literature.

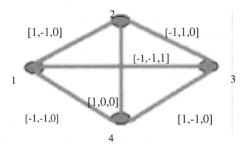

Fig. 1. WDM optical network with primary lightpaths PG={1-2 (λ_0), 4-2 (λ_0), 4-3 (λ_0), 3-2 (λ_1), 3-1 (λ_2)} and backup lightpaths, BG={1-3-2 (λ_0), 4-1-2 (λ_1) ,4-1-3(λ_0), 3-1-2(λ_1), 3-4-1(λ_1)}. The bit pattern of L_{23} , [-1,1,0], indicates that the wavelength λ_0 is used for a backup lightpath, λ_1 is used for a primary lightpath and λ_2 is not in use

1.2 Our Contribution

In this paper, the problem of re-establishing backup lightpaths for the affected primary lightpaths is formulated as a combinatorial optimization problem and a state space search technique is used to solve it. We have considered a WDM network without wavelength converter in the nodes. Upon failure of a link, a search is initiated to reassign all the affected backup lightpaths. A new call request will be blocked, if the network cannot allocate a pair of lightpaths, namely primary and backup lightpaths. An ongoing call will be dropped if a primary lightpath is affected on a link failure and does not have a backup lightpath prior to this link failure (i.e the call is affected by consecutive link failures). We have studied the performance of DRABLP with respect to CDP and new call blocking probability (NCBP). The results as obtained are compared with the performance of another *"path-based backup multiplexed survivable strategy"*, namely, *"without recursive assignment of backup lightpath"* (WORABLP). In WORABLP, if a primary lightpath is affected on a link failure, then it is reestablished through its backup lightpath, identified when the call is admitted (i.e the backup lightpath prior to this link failure will be new primary lightpath). Since there is no reassignment of back lightpath in WORABLP, this new primary lightpath will not have any backup lightpath.

1.3 Organization of Paper

This paper is organized in five sections. Following introduction in Section 1, a mathematical formulation of the problem is presented in Section 2. Section 3 is devoted to the description of the solution technique. Section 4 contains the experimental results and discussions, and Section 5 concludes the paper.

2 Mathematical Formulation

Let us assume a WDM optical network of N nodes. Now, a link, L_{mn}, connecting a nodes n and m fails. Here, our problem is to re-establish the backup lightpaths of the primary lightpaths affected due to this link failure. For mathematical formulation of this problem, let us also assume the followings notations:

P^{mn}
: set of primary lightpaths in the link L_{mn} before the failure, where P_i^{mn} represents i^{th} primary lightpath in the link L_{mn}

B^{mn}
: set of backup lightpaths in the link L_{mn} before the failure, where B_j^{mn}, represents j^{th} backup lightpath.

BP^{mn}
: set of backup lightpaths of the set of primary lightpaths P^{mn}, where, BP_i^{mn}, the ith element of BP^{mn}, the backup lightpath of the primary lightpath P_i^{mn}.

$P\_of\_B^{mn}$
: set of primary lightpaths corresponding to the set of backup lightpath B^{mn} where, $P\_of\_B_j^{mn}$, the jth element of $P\_of\_B^{mn}$, the primary lightpath of the backup lightpath B_j^{mn}.

$P\_backup\_shared^{mn}$
: set of primary lightpaths which shared one or more links of one or other element of the set of backup lightpaths, BP^{mn}

AP
: set of the primary lightpaths affected due to the link failure, where,

$$AP = P\_of\_B_j^{mn} \cup BP^{mn} \cup P\_backup\_shared^{mn}$$

PH
: set of sets of disjoint route paths of the route paths corresponding to each of the primary lightpath in AP where, PH_k is the set of disjoint route paths corresponding to the kth primary lightpath, AP_k.

BL
: set of backup lightpaths needed to be re-established corresponding to the set of primary lightpaths in AP.

PH_T
: be the set of route paths which contain at least one element from PH_k $\forall k$.

Let $F(PH\_T)$ represent the number of backup lightpaths which can not be successfully re-established through the set of route paths, PH_T (Here route path is the path between a source node to a destination node of a call in a WDM network and consists of a set of nodes and connecting links (fibers)). Let W represent the set of all such PH_Ts. So, our objective is to find out an optimal set of route paths, PH_T^* for which the number of backup lightpaths, which cannot be successfully re-established, is minimized. This can be mathematically represented as:

$$F(PH\_T^*) = \min_{\forall q}(F(W_q)) \tag{1}$$

3 Solution Technique

A combinatorial optimization problem can be formulated as a state space search problem to solve it by a search techniques. In this work, we have used a novel search technique, namely SMDS. This search technique is a variant of *best first* search technique. It terminates with an optimal reassignment of backup lightpaths (i.e. a goal having optimal value of objective function) [10].

3.1 State Space Formulation

Let BL: $\{BL_1, BL_2, ..., BL_T\}$ be the backup lightpaths need to be re-established. PH_k: $\{PH_{k1}, PH_{k2}, ..., PH_{kY}\}$ be the set of route paths through which BL_k may be re-established. A *state* in the state space consists of a set of backup lightpaths BL', yet to be considered for relocation and a set of physical route path, PH_T through which one or more backup lightpaths of the set BL are re-established. The *start node* of the search tree consists of BL' identical to BL and PH_T as set to *null*. In the search tree, each of the nodes in level k corresponds to a distinct option of the route path through which the backup lightpath BL_k , may be re-established. If the route path in an option doesn't have a light path (i.e. no common wavelength is available on all links in the route path) to re-establish backup lightpath BL_k then the cost of the node corresponding to the route path option will be obtained by incrementing the cost of its parent node by 1. On the other hand if there is a available lightpath in the route path for re-establishing BL_k, the cost of the node will be identical to its parent and the route path will be added to the set PH_T. Again in the search tree all nodes of a level r (r>k) will not have BL_K as a member of the set BL'. Thus the *leaf* nodes of the search tree will have BL' as set to *null* and represent the *goal* nodes. The cost of a leaf node (goal node) will indicate the number of backup lightpaths, which are not possible to be re-established. The search tree, as described above, can be represented as shown in Fig.2. From the above representation, it is clear that the depth of the tree is equal to the number of backup lightpaths needed to be re-established on a link failure.

Here, the proposed search algorithm is to find out a goal node from the above tree, which satisfies the objective function, defined in equation (1).

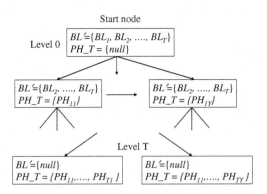

Fig. 2. State space tree

Theorem 1: *The worst-case space complexity of the state space tree a shown in the Fig. 2 is $O(Y^{(T+1)})$.*

Proof: Let Y be the maximum number of physical route paths for a backup lightpaths, i.e. $\| PH_k \| = Y$ and T be the number of backup lightpaths to be established i.e. $\| BL \| = T$. A backup lightpath can be routed through Y different ways. Thus, a state in the state space will have a maximum Y children. Again the number of levels in the tree is T as there are T backup lightpaths to be re-established. Hence, maximum number of states in the state space can be obtained by the following series.

$$1 + Y + Y^2 + Y^3 + \ldots\ldots\ldots + Y^T = \frac{Y^{T+1} - 1}{Y - 1} \qquad (2)$$

From the above we get the worst case space complexity as $O(Y^{(T+1)})$.

3.2 Search Algorithm

The search algorithm used is a variant of Best First Search [10] .It comprises two phases namely, forward phase and backtracking phase [11]. In *Forward phase*, the algorithm explores the search tree, level by level. All nodes generated are stored in a linear list. The *start* node is assigned as *level 0* and stored in the list. After this the algorithm runs iteratively, working on one level at each iteration. At any level k it orders nodes using the cost of the node and expand the first node (in a depth first manner) by generating all children at level $(k+1)$. Since in our state space representation of the problem every leaf node in the search tree represents a feasible solution, the forward phase is bound to terminate with a solution. The *backtracking phase* executes depth-first branch and bound (DFBB)[10] starting at each unexpanded node. DFBB is performed in the reverse order, i.e., from the last level generated down to level 1.After the completion of the forward phase, this phase is used to improve the solution. This phase continues until the list, generated in the forward phase, becomes empty to conclude that the found solution is optimal.

4 Results and Discussion

In order to study the performance of our technique, we have coded the algorithm in C language to run on a 1.7 GHz Pentium IV machine under Borland C++ environment. For carrying out experiments, we have taken a standard NSFNET networks having six wavelengths in each of its link with $\frac{MTTR}{MTTF}$ as 20. We have taken simulation run for 20,000 cumulative call requests. This cut-off is experimentally decided. As shown in the Fig. 3, the network stabilizes when the cumulative request of calls is 15,000 (this point is marked as *saturation point*). These 20,000 calls are generated following Poisson distribution with a mean arrival rate of λ. Duration of these calls are exponential distributed with a mean service rate of μ. Load ξ in the network is defined as Erlang following the equation (3). In simulation, problem instances are generated by varying the network loads. NCBP (as defined by the equation (4)) and CDP (as defined by the equation (5)) are calculated from the data noted for the calls requested after the *saturation point*.

$$\xi = \lambda \cdot \frac{l}{\mu} \tag{3}$$

where, μ is the mean call arrival rate and λ is call service rate

$$NCBP = \frac{Total \quad number \quad of \quad calls \quad requested \quad - Total \quad number \quad of \quad calls \quad admitted}{Total \quad no \quad of \quad call \quad requested} \tag{4}$$

$$CDP = \frac{Total \quad number \quad of \quad calls \quad dropped}{Total \quad no \quad of \quad call \quad admitted} \tag{5}$$

The variations of NCBP and CDP with network load are shown in the Fig. 4 and Fig. 5 respectively.

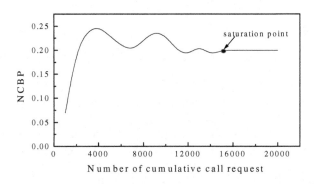

Fig. 3. New Call Blocking Probability (NCBP) over the Simulation Period

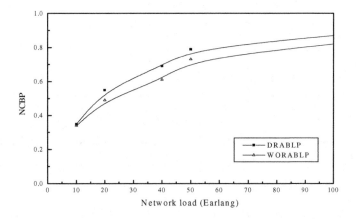

Fig. 4. NCBP versus Network load

Fig. 4 and Fig. 5 show that NCBP and CDP are increasing with the increase of network load. The reason behind it is, as load increases the amount of redundant resource decreases. Less amount of resource is available for new calls to be admitted and resulting in a higher NCBP. Again, when load increases, a link failure affects higher number of primary lightpaths leaving higher probability of CDP.

Fig. 4 shows that the NCBP is lesser for WORABLP than that for DRABLP. This result can be explained as follows. On link failures the CDP for DRABLP is lesser than that for WORABLP as shown in Fig. 5. Thus, for a load in the network, DRABLP will have higher realization of network resources leaving smaller portion of it for a new call admission. This is due to the fact that, once a call is admitted, the probability of it is being served is higher in case of DRABLP than that of WORABLP.

Fig. 5 also shows that the difference in CDP is increasing with the increase of network load. As the network load increases, failure of a link affects larger number of primary lightpaths. Since there is no reassignment of backup lightpaths for WORABLP, in higher load, consecutive link failure causes more calls to be dropped.

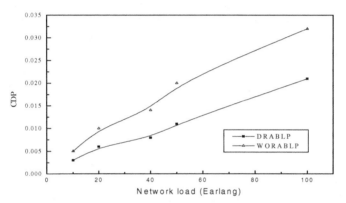

Fig. 5. CDP versus Network load

5 Conclusion

In this paper, we have formulated the novel problem of "ensuring reliability in WDM optical backbone network with *contemporary link failures*" as a state space search problem. We have suggested a strategy, namely DRABLP to handle the problem. An efficient algorithm for finding an optimal reassignment of backup lightpaths on link failures is also developed. The performance of DRABLP in terms of CDP and NCBP w.r.t network load shows that above strategy can be helpful to a backbone network operator to ensure high reliability in an efficient manner.

References

1. Ramaswami, R., Sivarajan, K. : Optical networks: A Practical Perspective. Morgan Kaufmann Publishers, 2nd Edition.
2. Mohan, G., Rammurthy, C. S.: Lightpath Restoration in WDM Optical Networks. IEEE Network, Nov./Dec. (2000).

3. Doshi, B.T., et al.: Optical Network Design and Restoration. Bell Labs Tech J., Jan-Mar. (1999) 58–84.
4. Rammamurthy, S., Mukherjee, B.: Survivable WDM Mesh Network.Part 1- Protection. proc. IEEE INFOCOM '99 (1999) 744–51.
5. Mohan, G., Murthy, C.S.R.: Routing and Wavelength Assignment for Establishing Dependable Connections in WDM Networks. Proc. IEEE Int'l Symp. Fault-Tolerant Comp. June (1999) 94–101.
6. Ramamurthy S., Mukherjee , B.: Survivable WDM Mesh Network s, Part-II – Restoration. Proc. ICC '99 (1999).
7. Mohan, G., Samani, A.K.: Routing Dependable Connections With Specified Failure Restoration Guarantees in WDM Networks. Proc. IEEE INFOCOM'00, Mar. (2000).
8. Hjalmtysson, G., Yates, J., Choudhury, S.: Restoration Services for the Optical Internet. Photonics East, November. (2000)
9. Mandal S., Jana S., and Saha, D.: A Heuristic Search for Dynamic Lightpath Establishment in WDM Optical Networks with Limited Wavelength Conversion Capability. IEEE ICCT' 03 April, (2003).
10. Nilsson, N. J.: Artificial Intelligence: A New Synthesis. Morgan Kaufmann Publisher, (1998).
11. Mandal, S., Saha, D.: Optimal Reassignment of Backup Lightpaths in WDM optical Networks. IIM Calcutta, WPS-474/2003 (2003).
12. Zhang, J., Mukherjee, B. : Review of Fault Management in WDM Mesh Networks: Basic Concepts and Research Challenges, IEEE Network, Special Issue on Protection, Restoration, and Disaster Recovery, vol. 18, no. 2, pp. 41–48, (2004)
13. Kim, S., Lumetta, S. :Evaluation of Protection Reconfiguration for Multiple Failures in WDM Mesh Networks, Proc., OFC'2003, pp. 785–787, (2003)
14. Ramamurthy, R., Akyamac, A.: Labourdette, J-F., Chaudhuri, S.: Pre-emptive Reprovisioning in Mesh Optical Networks, Proc., OFC'2003, pp. 785–787, (2003)
15. Zhang, J., Zhu, K., . Mukherjee, B. : A Comprehensive Study on Backup Reprovisioning to Remedy the Effect of Multiple-Link Failures in WDM Mesh Networks, Proc, IEEE International Conference on Communications (ICC-04), Paris, (2004).

Formal Proof of Impossibility of Reliability in Crashing Protocols

K. Gopinath, Anil K. Pugalia, and K.V.M. Naidu

Computer Science & Automation
Indian Institute of Science, Bangalore

Abstract. In a strictly asynchronous system with process failures, it has been known that distributed consensus is impossible[FLP85]. It also has been shown that without persistence, no data link layer can work correctly (this includes all the well known and widely used protocols such as HDLC, etc) [FLMS93]. This work has been extended recently to study the fault span of crash failures[JV00]. In this paper, we present a formal proof of the non-existence of correct crashing network protocols with either unreliable FIFO, reliable FIFO or reliable non-FIFO links using the Input/Output Automata formalism in PVS, a verification system based on higher-order logic.

1 Introduction

In a strictly asynchronous system with process failures, it has been known that consensus is impossible[FLP85]. It also has been shown that without persistence, no data link layer can work correctly (this includes all the well known and widely used protocols such as HDLC, etc.)[FLMS93]. This work has been extended recently to study the fault span of crash failures[JV00].

Higher-level protocols such as TCP that guarantee reliability do so by introducing time into the model[Kes97]. For example, a crucial assumption in TCP is that a system *should* not boot and accept packets after a crash before twice the mean life time of a packet.

A **crashing network protocol**[JV00] is an asynchronous protocol that has no non-volatile memory at nodes that can survive and restart. Thus after crash and restart, a node in such a protocol returns to a pre-specified start state. We consider crashing protocols that work with unreliable-FIFO links i.e. FIFO links that can drop packets (CAML - Crashing, Asynchronous, Memoryless, Lossy), with reliable-FIFO links i.e. FIFO links that never drop packets (CAM - Crashing, Asynchronous, Memoryless) and finally, with reliable non-FIFO links i.e. links that delivers packets out of order but never drop them (CAMO - Crashing, Asynchronous, Memoryless, Out of order).

For proving properties of these models, we need an abstraction that allows us to represent links (with arbitrary number of packets) and nodes. Finite state models cannot be used as crashes can populate the links with arbitrary sets of packets from various runs; hence approaches that use abstraction to map

A. Sen et al. (Eds.): IWDC 2004, LNCS 3326, pp. 347–352, 2004.
© Springer-Verlag Berlin Heidelberg 2004

infinite sets of states into finite ones are ruled out. Hence, an approach such as Input/Output Automata (IOA)[LT89] is useful. IOA differ from NDFA in that the set of states need not be finite. Second, more than one start state is permitted (this convention is appropriate for a nondeterministic machine). Third, the alphabet of actions is partitioned into three categories of input, output and internal actions, and a special enabling condition is imposed for input actions only. Fourth, no final states are specified.

From the verification point of view, the first difference plays a prominent role. CTL operators[McM92] are computed using iterative algorithms that have worst case complexity of the order of the number of states in the automaton. Hence, they are well suited for finite state automaton but simply fail in case of an infinite state IOA and hence we cannot use CTL and its operators to express the IOA. Hence, we have modeled IOA as a special theory using sequences in PVS, a verification system using higher-order logic.

In this paper, we present a proof of the non-existence of correct crashing network protocols with either unreliable FIFO (CAML) or reliable FIFO (CAM) or reliable non-FIFO (CAMO) links using IOA formalism in PVS. Our proofs also attempt reuse but a significant portion still remained to be done afresh.

It is a constructive proof rather than a deductive one and closely models the basic construction in [FLMS93] and more directly the one in [JV00]. The basic construction in [FLMS93] that proves the impossibility of a data link protocol without persistence is as follows. A series of alternating crashes are used to force a node R to send the first i packets of the sequence of normal crashless packets. This causes the other node S (after another crash) to send the packets needed to force node R to send the first $i + 1$ packets before crashing again. By continuing inductively, we force the receiver to emit the entire sequence of packets it would have emitted in an execution. At this point we stop the construction, and crash the sender and receiver. The result is that the link from the receiver to sender has the complete sequence of packets sent in an execution. This is sufficient to cause data link protocols to fail because the complete sequence could include the responses to any initial handshake packets, as well as all the data acks. Thus even if all the sender's initial packets are lost, including the first data item, the sender will be fooled into thinking all is well. The construction in [JV00] generalizes the above to initialize the link with a concatenation of two send sequences from possibly two different executions of the same crashing protocol.

The nodes and link are modelled in PVS as follows. As there is no persistence in the nodes, it suffices to indicate the node state just by a bit for either a unique start state or not. The state of a link is the packets on the link. As the link in CAM and CAML is a FIFO, the sequence of packets has been modeled by a queue where as a link in CAMO is non-FIFO i.e. packets are delivered in any order, we use finite sets. Hence we have two IOA corresponding to the node and link respectively. Due to lack of space, we omit discussion of the PVS model of IOA. They are available in a TR[IISc].

2   Non-existence of Correct Crashing Network Protocols

We discuss the three cases (CAML, CAM, CAMO) here. While CAM subsumes the CAML case (if CAM is incorrect, CAML also being incorrect follows), a separate proof is needed to handle the stronger statement of the CAML case.

The main theorem to be proved for the CAML model is as follows: CAML model protocols can be driven by a sequence of crashes to any global state where each node is in a state reached in some (possibly different) run, and each link has an arbitrary mixture of packets sent in (possibly different) runs. Here $\to$ means "possible to transit to".

Theorem: Unreliable FIFO (CAML) Any State: Let A be any arbitrary crashing protocol. Let $N[i]$ and $L[i]$ be the state of node i and link i respectively. Let $[N, L]$ be any possible state for a system with nodes connected to links with some arbitrary connectivity with $[N_0, L_0]$ being the initial state. Then $[N_0, L_0] \to [N, L]$

The main theorem to be proved for the CAM model is as follows: CAM model protocols can be driven by a sequence of crashes to any global state, where each node is in a state reached in some (possibly different) run, for some link states of the links. The the only difference between CAM and CAML models is that all possible combination link states of the links may not be possible in CAM.

Theorem: Reliable FIFO (CAM) Any Node state: Let N be any possible node state vector. Then there exists a state $[N, L]$ such that $[N_0, L_0] \to [N, L]$.

The main theorem to be proved for the CAMO model is as follows: CAMO model protocols can be driven by a sequence of crashes to any global state, where each node or link of an acyclic component of the network is in a state reached in some (possibly different) run, for some link states of the links. We do not bother about states of other nodes or links.

Theorem: Reliable non-FIFO (CAMO) Any Node state: Let $[N, L]$ be any possible state vector for some arbitrary acyclic component of the graph. Then there exists a state vector $[N1, L1]$ such that at the nodes and links of the acyclic component, $N(i)$ and $N1(i)$ ($L(i)$ and $L1(i)$ respectively) are same and $[N_0, L_0] \to [N1, L1]$.

Each action of a node or a link is a predicate over an ordered state pair depicting the transition from the first element of the pair to the next. **nreceive** is an input action performed on a node automaton to receive a packet. **nsend** is an output action performed by a node automaton to send a packet. **ncrash** is an input action performed on a node automaton depicting its crashing behaviour. **lreceive** is an output action performed by a link automaton to make some node receive the first packet[1] on it. **lsend** is an input action performed on a link automaton by sending a packet on it, from a node. **llose** is an internal action performed in a link automaton depicting its lossy behaviour.

---

[1] Here, we have the pre-condition that the packet being received must be the first one in case of FIFO links

Now, to model a crashing network protocol, these node and link I/O automata need to be composed. The composite state is the composition of the vector of node states and the vector of the link states. The resulting composite actions are: **receive(i,j,p)** is an action for node j receiving packet p from link (i,j), sent by node i. **send(i,j,p)** is an action for node i sending packet p to link (i,j), to be received by node j. **crash(i)** is an action corresponding to the crashing of node i. **lose(i,j,p)** is an action corresponding to the loss of packet p from the link (i,j).

2.1   Proof of Main Theorem for CAML

The outline of the proof is as follows. We have simplified the notation for easy accessibility; for a complete description see[JV00]. SND_j is a send sequence on the jth link whereas SND^j is a send sequence in the jth state. The intuition behind each of these lemmas and corollaries is also given (for a detailed explanation, refer to[JV00]).

Crash: $[N, L] \rightarrow [N', L]$ with $N'[i]$ the start state of node i: after a crash at node i, its state becomes the start state. This captures the effect of lack of persistence. This is proved in PVS through 2 lemmas.

FIFO loss: $[N, L] \rightarrow [N, L']$ with L' a subsequence of L: after a packet is dropped, the new link state is a "subsequence" of the old (in the way we have defined subsequence, not PVS library's notion). This captures the effect of allowing arbitrary packet loss on a link. This requires 6 proofs of lemmata in PVS.

Rotate Node j: $[N, RCV_j\ O] \rightarrow [N', O\ SND_j]$: $N'[j]$ is the state of jth node (starting from the start state) after receiving all its msgs on link and sending responses to the link. This captures the effect of asynchrony and locality. First, the jth node is crashed and then made to receive all its packets. It then sends all its outgoing packets to enter state $N'[j]$. *Rotate:* $[N, RCV\ O] \rightarrow [N', O\ SND]$: N' is the state of all nodes after processing all messages on the links. This follows by applying the previous transformation to each node in turn. 2 lemmata are required.

Send2RecvIncr: $[N, SND^k\ O] \rightarrow [N, RCV^{k+1}\ O]$: a receive sequence in the $k + 1$th state always is a subsequence of a send sequence in the kth state. All packets received in a link must be sent before the last receive. Reception of a packet moves the system from the kth state to the $k + 1$th state, hence the validity of *Send2RecvIncr*. Similarly, *Send2Recv:* $[N, SND^k\ O] \rightarrow [N, RCV^k\ O]$ as a receive sequence in the kth state is a subsequence in the $k + 1$th state. 2 lemmata are required.

RotateIncr: $[N, SND^k\ O] \rightarrow [N', O\ SND^{k+1}]$: using *Rotate* and *Send2RecvIncr*. *RotateWithoutIncr:* $[N, SND^k\ O] \rightarrow [N_0, O\ SND^k]$: follows from application of *Send2Recv*, *Rotate*, *Crash*. *Any Rotate:* $[N_0, O\ SND\ O'] \rightarrow [N_0, SND\ O'\ O]$, $O'O$ concat of send seqs: follows from repeated application of *RotateWithoutIncr*. 2 lemmata are required.

Increment: $[N_0, O\ SND^k\ O'] \rightarrow [N_0, O\ SND^{k+1}\ O']$ *Concat:* $[N_0, L_0] \rightarrow [N_0, L]$, L concat of send seqs. 2 lemmas are required for each.

NodeGen: $[N', GO] \rightarrow [N, O]$ states that there exists G a node state generator N' to N. This requires 6 lemmas to be proved.

LinkGen: $[N, G] \rightarrow [N, L]$ states that there exists G a link state generator for L. *Playout*: $[N_0, G_n G_l] \rightarrow [N, L]$ states that starting from the initial node states, there are link state generators G_n, G_l *Any State*: $[N_0, L_0] \rightarrow [N, L]$. These require 2 lemmas.

Discussion of the PVS Proof. The lossy links lead to the concept of subsequences of packets that are needed while proving the above corollaries and lemmas. These subsequences are different from what is provided in the PVS libraries. To model them was a tricky part. We used a predicate P to model the arbitrary dropping of link contents from a sequence to give our notion of subsequence. As the proof of the main theorem is an "existential" proof, it turned out to be a constructive proof rather than a deductive one. This results in fewer possibilities for automation, leading to high manual effort (over 1200 manual proof steps here). Often, the proof would split into sub-proofs with formulae containing existential quantifiers. A thorough study was needed to discover what particular instantiation would prove it.

Most of these "existential" proofs were approached using inductive proof techniques - in which case it resulted into 2 or 3 subproofs. The inductive step almost in all cases turned out to be a non-trivial "existential" proof. Even to prove the basis turned out to be non-trivial in many cases.

2.2   Reuse of Definitions and Proofs in CAM Model

Next we consider crashing protocols that work with reliable FIFO links (CAM - Crashing, Asynchronous, Memoryless). Because of the similarity of this theorem with that of CAML's, we were able to reuse many of the lemmas proved in the previous chapter. However, because of some of the differences, we had to prove few more new lemmas as well for the main theorem. Apart from the lemmas, the definitions of node, link and their composition were also reused to a large extent.

The definitions of the node were used exactly same as in the CAML model as in both the models, nodes crash. However, a link in this model does not have a lose action. Hence, their composition is also similar except for the composed action lose. Thus, the definitions for node, link and their composition for the CAM model are the same except for the extra **llose** and **lose** actions respectively.

Apart from the axioms, lemmas, corollaries and the main theorem in CAML model, everything else has been completely reused in the CAM model. The axioms used in CAM model are, however, different from those in CAML model. 6 lemmas were reused as is, 4 with minor changes, 3 were new and the rest (11) had to be proved from scratch. Though 600-700 steps of the previous proofs were reusable, over 500 proof steps had to be done from scratch, inspite of the full efforts at re-use. In the CAML case, the proofs were rather short using the generic strategies such as *skosimp* (skolemization followed by simplifying), *assert* (use std built-in decision procedures), *expand* (substitution), *apply-extensionality* and finally *grind* (a std strategy). However in the CAM case, there were quite a few more manual steps before *grind* could be finally applied. Also, in many cases, we had to apply *grind* carefully with particular exclude options to make progress in the proof.

2.3   Proof of Main Theorem for CAMO

Many basic definitions and lemmas for this case are similar except that we have to replace finite sets for queues and change the operations like concatenation appropriately; however, in many cases, the proofs have to be done from scratch due to fundamental differences between queues and sets.

To prove the theorem for the CAMO model, we need to drive the states of an acyclic component of the graph rathen than that of the whole graph. A *ACyclicComponent* data type has a set of links and vertices and a function that defines a linear ordering on it. Now, given a required state to which an acyclic component has to be taken on an execution sequence, we construct a sequence of states of the whole network such that if the network is at a certain state in the sequence then it can be forced to go to the next state of the sequence. Then we use induction to show that there is an execution sequence which takes a network in the first state of the sequence to the last state of the sequence. Then we show that the first state is the initial state of the network in which all nodes and links are in their initial states and last state is in the required state.

3   Conclusions

Given that there are some commonalities among the three models (for example, crashes), some reuse is possible but many proofs had to be redone from scratch, either because the underlying abstractions changed (sets vs queues) or the exact form of the theorem itself changed. Using the libraries provided in PVS has been very useful but sometimes the form required is not exactly what is desired.

References

[McM92]   K L McMillan. Symbolic Model Checking. *An approach to the state explosion problem, PhD Thesis, Carnegie Mellon University,* 1992

[LT89]   Nancy A Lynch, Mark R Tuttle. An Introduction to Input/Output Automata. *CWI Quarterly, 2(3):219-246,* September, 1989

[JV00]   Mahesh Jayaram, George Varghese. The Fault Span of Crash Failures. *JACM* 47(2): 244-293 (2000).

[FLMS93]   Alan Fekete, Nancy Lynch, Yishay Mansour, John Spinelli. The Impossibility of Implementing Reliable Communication in the Face of Crashes. *JACM, Vol 40, No 5, pp 1087-1107,* November 1993

[FLP85]   Fischer, Lynch, Patterson. Impossibility of distributed consensus with one faulty processor, JACM'85

[Kes97]   An Engineering Introduction to Networks, Addison-Wesley

[IISc]   IISc-CSA-TR-9 http://csa.iisc.ernet.in/TR/2004/9

Altera Max Plus II Development Environment in Fault Simulation and Test Implementation of Embedded Cores-Based Sequential Circuits

Sunil R. Das[1,2], Chuan Jin[1], Liwu Jin[1], Mansour H. Assaf [1],
Emil M. Petriu[1], and Mehmet Sahinoglu[2]

[1] School of Information Technology and Engineering, Faculty of Engineering,
University of Ottawa, Ottawa, Ontario K1N 6N5, Canada
[2] Department of Computer and Information Science,
Troy State University Montgomery, Montgomery, AL 36103, U.S.A

Abstract. A Verilog HDL-based fault simulator for testing embedded cores-based synchronous sequential circuits is proposed in the paper to detect single stuck-line faults The simulator emulates a typical BIST (built-in self-testing) environment with test pattern generator that sends its outputs to a CUT (circuit under test) and the output streams from the CUT are fed into a response data analyzer. The fault simulator is suitable for testing sequential circuits described in Verilog HDL. The subject paper describes in detail the architecture and applications of the fault simulator along with the models of sequential elements used. Results on some simulation experiments on ISCAS 89 full-scan sequential benchmark circuits are also provided.

1 Introduction

Large-scale integration has added enormous complexity to the process of testing. This complexity is due mainly to the reduction in the ratio of externally accessible points (primary inputs and outputs) to internal inaccessible points in the circuit. We can classify the integrated circuit testing techniques into three broad categories, viz. 1) testing of purely combinational circuits or synchronous sequential circuits (full-scan) using design for testability (DFT) techniques; 2) built-in self-testing techniques that generate their own test vectors for circuits using built-in hardware; and 3) testing of general digital (sequential) circuits with test vectors that are externally generated and applied. For purely combinational circuits, a number of methods are known that automatically generate tests with satisfactory fault coverage. For synchronous sequential circuits, scan design is often used to reduce the test generation problem to a combinational circuit testing problem that is considerably less difficult. In scan design, all memory elements of the circuit are chained into one or more shift registers such that a synchronous sequential circuit can be partitioned into a purely combinational circuit and a shift register that can be tested separately. While this technique has been successfully used in commercial systems, the percentage of logic added (10-20%) for testability has performance and cost penalties that are not always acceptable. Built-in self-testing (BIST) is a test methodology in which a circuit (chip, board, or system) can test itself; in other words, the testing (test generation, test application, and response verification) could be accomplished through built-in

A. Sen et al. (Eds.): IWDC 2004, LNCS 3326, pp. 353–360, 2004.
© Springer-Verlag Berlin Heidelberg 2004

hardware. Actually, BIST is a combination of two concepts: built-in test (BIT) and self-test (ST). This technique is intended to solve some of major testing problems like test time and volume, test cost and diagnosis [1] – [16].

The automatic test generator (ATG) produces the test vectors for application to the CUT and the response data from an entire test sequence are compressed into a single value called a signature, which is then compared to the signature of a fault-free circuit. A fault is detected if the test signature is different from the good signature. A typical BIST scheme is composed of an automatic test pattern generator, the CUT, and a test data analyzer. The test data analyzer consists of a response compaction unit, storage for the good signature, and a comparison unit. In the BIST approach, the circuit is designed to have a self-test mode in which it generates test vectors and analyzes the response. The objective is to apply all possible vectors to the combinational part of the circuit. In very large circuits, either the combinational portion is partitioned into independent sections, or the entire circuit has to be tested by random test vectors. However, the hardware overhead of BIST is even higher than that of the scan design; about 20-50% test logic may have to be added for BIST.

The test generation problem for general sequential circuits is recognized to be very difficult, tedious, and as yet, unsolved. The memory elements contribute to the poor controllability and observability of logic. Most test generators for sequential circuits can perform reasonably well only on circuits with up to 1,000 gates. Therefore, VLSI designers manually develop test vectors using the knowledge of the functional behavior of the circuit. These tests are generated to exercise critical paths and functions with selected data patterns. In spite of the enormous effort, the quality of manually generated test vectors, as often verified by fault simulation, appears questionable. There exists hence a critical need to develop an automatic sequential circuit test generator that can handle VLSI chips, specially today's embedded cores-based system-on-chip (SOC), and, at a reasonable computing cost, can achieve high fault coverage. This is the main objective of the present work. Equally important is the objective to combine the two processes of test generation and fault simulation.

2   Test Generation and Fault Simulation for Embedded Cores-Based Sequential Circuits Under Altera Max Plus II Design Environment

The response of a sequential circuit depends on its primary inputs and the stored internal states. The stored states can retain their values over time. Thus, combinational test generation methods can be applied to sequential circuits if the element of time is introduced. Many sequential circuit test generators have been devised on the basis of the fundamental combinational algorithms. There are available approaches like nine-value algorithm, SOFTG (a sequential version of PODEM), backtrace algorithms, verification-based techniques, SCIRTSS (Sequential CIRcuit Test Search System), functional and expert system methods to deal with the complex problem of sequential circuit testing, which could not be elaborated due to lack of available space.

The Verilog HDL is one most common hardware description languages (HDL) used by integrated circuit (IC) designers. It also allows for mixed-level designs, where users can describe a design at both high and low levels of logic simulation and synthesis. The designers are choosing top-down design and mixed-level design to contend with ever-increasing complexities and shrinking time-to-market cycles. The hardware description languages (HDLs) are languages used to design hardware with. As the name implies, an HDL can also be used to describe the functionality of hardware as well as its implementation. The HDLs allow designers to describe designs at higher levels of abstraction, such as architectural or behavioral, and provide a path to logic synthesis. They permit the design to be simulated earlier in the design cycle in order to correct errors or experiment with different architectures. The designs described in HDL are technology-independent, easy to design and debug, and are usually more readable than schematics, particularly for large circuits.

The first HDL was ISP, invented by Bell and Newell. This language was also the first to use the term *register transfer level*. This came from the use of ISP in describing the behavior of the PDP-8 computer as a set of registers and logical functions describing the transfer of data from source register to destination register. Subsequent HDLs included VHSIC, HDL (VHDL), UDLI (which was developed by NTT), HiLo, which was the predecessor to Verilog, and ISP', which was a successor to ISP (implemented by the N-dot simulator).

The principal feature of a hardware description language is that it contains the capability to describe the function of a piece of hardware independently of the implementation. The great advance with modern HDLs was the recognition that a single language could be used to describe the function of the design and also to describe the implementation. This allows the entire design process to take place in a single language, and thus with a single representation of the design. The Verilog Hardware Description Language, usually just called Verilog, was designed and first implemented by Moorby at Gateway Design Automation. The first major extension was Verilog-XL, which added a few features and implemented the famous "XL algorithm" which was a very efficient method for doing gate-level simulation. This marked the beginning of Verilog's growth period. Many leading-edge electronic designers began using Verilog at this time because it was fast at gate level simulation, and had the capabilities to model at higher levels of abstraction. These users began to do full system simulation of their designs, where the actual logic being designed was represented by a netlist and other parts of the system were modeled behaviorally.

Synopsys delivered the first logic synthesizer that used Verilog as an input language. This was a major event, as now the top-down design methodology could actually be used effectively. The design could be done at the *register transfer level*, and then Synopsys' *design compiler* could translate that into gates. With this event, the use of Verilog increased dramatically. The second major trend began to emerge, and that was the use of Verilog-XL for sign-off certification by ASIC vendors. As Verilog became popular with the semiconductor vendors and customers, they began to move away from their own proprietary simulators, and started allowing customers to simulate using Verilog-XL for timing certification. As more ASIC vendors certified Verilog-XL, they requested more features, especially related to timing checks, back annotation, and delay specification. In response, Gateway implemented many new features in the language and simulator to accommodate this need.

Cadence Design Systems acquired Gateway and continued to market Verilog as both a language and a simulator. In 1995, Verilog became an IEEE standard. Now, Verilog simulators are available for most computers at a variety of prices, having a variety of performance characteristics and features.

2.1 Digital Circuit Designing and Verilog HDL

The Verilog hardware description language is widely used in both industry and academia for describing digital systems. The language supports the early conceptual stages of design with its behavioral level of abstraction, and the later implementation stages with its structural level of abstraction. The language provides hierarchical constructs, allowing the designer to control the complexity of a description. Digital systems are highly complex. At their most detailed level, they may consist of millions of elements, as would be the case if we viewed a system as a collection of logic gates or pass transistors. From a more abstract viewpoint, these elements may be grouped into a handful of functional components such as cache memories, floating-point units, signal processors, or real-time controllers. Hardware description languages have evolved to aid in the design of systems with this large number of elements and wide range of electronic and logical abstractions.

The Verilog language describes a digital system as a set of modules. Each of these modules has an interface to other modules as well as a description of its contents. A module represents a logical unit that can be described either by specifying its internal logical structure – for instance, describing the actual logic gates it is comprised of, or by describing its behavior in a program-like manner – in this case, focusing on what the module does rather than on its logical implementation. These modules are then interconnected with nets, allowing them to communicate.

Verilog supports a design at many different levels of abstraction. Three of them are very important: behavioral level; register transfer level; and gate level. Behavioral level describes a system by concurrent algorithms (behavioral). Each algorithm in itself is sequential; viz. it consists of a set of instructions that are executed one after the other. *Functions, tasks,* and *always* blocks are the main elements. There is no regard to the structural realization of the design. Register transfer level designs specify the characteristics of a circuit by operations and the transfer of data between the registers. An explicit clock is used. RTL design contains exact timing possibility; operations are scheduled to occur at certain times. In gate level, within the logic level, the characteristics of a system are described by logical links and their timing properties. All signals are discrete signals. They can only have definite logical values (0, 1, X, Z). The usable operations are predefined logic primitives (AND, OR, NOT, etc. gates). Using gate level modeling might not be a good idea for complex logic. But if one requires high speed, low power, and least gates, then it is better to use gate level design so that one can use one's brain to optimize the design. Some designs do full custom design, where logic is optimized at transistor level, like processors.

Verilog can be used to describe designs at four levels of abstraction: 1) algorithmic level (much like C code with *if, case,* and *loop* statements); 2) register transfer level (RTL uses registers connected by Boolean equations); 3) gate level (interconnected AND, NOR, etc.); and 4) switch level (the switches are MOS transistors inside gates). The language also defines constructs that can be used to control the input and output of simulation. More recently, Verilog is used as an input for synthesis programs which will generate a gate-level description (netlist) for the circuit. Some Verilog constructs are not synthesizable. Most designers will want to synthesize their circuits, so nonsynthesizable constructs should be used only for test benches. These are program modules used to generate I/O needed to simulate the rest of the design. There are two types of codes in most HDLs. *Structural* is a verbal wiring diagram without storage.

```
assign a=b & c | d;  /* "|" is an OR */
assign d= e & (~c);
```

Here the order of the statements does not matter. Changing e will change a. *Procedural* that is used for circuits with storage, or as a convenient way to write conditional logic.

```
Always @ (posedge clk) // Execute the next statement on every rising clock edge.
Count <=count+1;
```

Procedural code is written like C code and assumes every assignment is stored in memory until overwritten. For synthesis with flip-flops generates too much storage. 27 is a basic sequential circuit in ISCAS 89 benchmark circuits, and there are different numbers of D flip-flops in every sequential circuit as memory units. Let us describe a D flip-flop by Verilog HDL as given below.

```
module ndff(q,d,rst,clk);
input clk,rst,d;
output q;
reg q;
always @(posedge clk or posedge rst)
if (rst==1) q<=0;
else q<=d;
endmodule
```

3 Simulation Under Max Plus II Version 10.1

Altera's Max Plus II development software is a fully integrated programmable logic design environment. This easy-to-use software supports the Altera *Acex, Flex, Max,* and *Classic* programmable device families, and works in both PC and Unix environments. Altera's Max Plus II development software offers flexibility and performance, and allows seamless integration with industry-standard design entry, synthesis, and verification tools. The software is a comprehensive tool for the design, compilation, and simulation of digital circuit designs. The software gives designers the flexibility to enter a design using all the major design entry methodologies, including: VHDL, Verilog HDL, schematic capture, design entry utilizing megafunctions and the library of parameterized modules (LPM), Altera hardware description language (AHDL), and waveform. By giving designers control over the entry format and the ability to mix and match design entry methodologies, Max Plus II development software minimizes development time. The software consists of 11 application programs and *manager*. The different design entry applications can be active simultaneously, allowing designers to switch between them with a click of the mouse or a menu command. At the same time, the user can run one of the background applications, i.e., the compiler, simulator, timing analyzer, or programmer.

4   General Structure of Sequential Circuit Test Method

At first, we introduce the general structure of the sequential circuit testing method. We implemented the fault simulation approach using C language on IBM-compliant PC (Pentium III – 1 GHz). In the program, we use system function of C to call Max Plus II for compiling and simulating a CUT. A CUT is represented by Verilog HDL gate-level description. The executable file and CUTs (ISCAS 89 sequential benchmark circuits) will be stored in the same file fold.

Initialization. The goal in the initialization phase is to generate random signal, create an input vector file for the CUT, and reset all flip-flops that are in the unknown state.

Hardware Implementation of Random Number Generator. In BIST techniques, deterministic exhaustive or compact, pseudoexhaustive, or pseudorandom test patterns are used. Using algorithms (such as PODEM), the reduced test sets can be generated on-chip at a low hardware cost with high fault coverage. The autonomous linear feedback shift register (ALFSR) can be used to generate pseudorandom test vectors. An ALFSR is a serial connection of D flip-flops with no external inputs and Exclusive-OR (XOR) gates providing the feedback.

Software Simulation of Random Number Generator. We focus in the paper on implementing the random signal generator through software simulation. Then, according to a specified sequential circuit, we will put the random number into a *.vec* file according to the format of Altera's Max Plus II development software. Finally, we will get the vector file and use the *vector* as inputs for the sequential circuit. We implement the random number generator (RNG) using C language. The *random_number() function* is a portable, fast and good pseudorandom number generator. When we need some random number, we simply call the random_number() functions. Initializing the function with a certain seed will produce exactly the same series of random numbers on all platforms. The *random_number() functions* will return high quality equally distributed random numbers.

Fault Injection and Fault Simulation. Next we implement one of the most important and complex parts in the problem – fault injection and simulation. *1) Hardware fault injection.* The hardware fault injection technique is imperative in order to iteratively inject faults to every mutually exclusive wire, and to test for both stuck-at-0 and stuck-at-1 logic faults. In fault injection scheme, every mutually exclusive wire has a multiplexer introduced within it, which allows us to either run the wire as such, or inject stuck-at-0 or stuck-at-1 faults. If the values of the select signals of any multiplexer are at "00", then we will run the wire as such, while if the values are at "01", then we will inject a stuck-at-1 fault indicated by the logical 1 value coming into the multiplexer, and if the values are at "10", then we will inject a stuck-at-0 fault indicated by the logical 0 value coming into the multiplexer. Finally, if the values are at "11", then we will again assume normal operation of the wire. *2)*

Software fault injection. In this paper, we focus on software fault injection, that is, we will simulate the above part – hardware fault injection scheme with entire software method.

Input Part, Inside Wire, and Output Part Fault Simulation. The pseudocode descriptions of the algorithms that perform the input part, inside wire part, and output part testing for a sequential circuit by compilation and simulation under Altera's Max Plus II development environment also could not be provided. However, Tables 1 and 2 furnish some insights into simulation experience on ISCAS 89 full-scan sequential benchmark circuits.

Table 1. Testing time, numbers of DFFs, gates, inverters, and internal wires of ISCAS 89 sequential benchmark circuits

CUT name	No. of DFFs in the CUT	No. of gates and inverters in the CUT	No. of wires of the CUT	No. of test vectors used for simulation	Testing time (sec)
s27	3	10	12	72	60
s298	14	119	127	72	660
s344	15	160	164	186	966
s382	21	158	173	184	1200
s444	21	181	196	207	1264
s526	21	193	208	219	1249
s641	19	379	374	435	3939
s820	5	289	275	314	1917
s832	5	287	273	312	1649
s953	29	395	401	442	4102
s1238	18	508	512	542	5481
s1423	74	657	726	750	12121

Table 2. Fault coverage, numbers of DFFs, internal wires, and detected faults of ISCAS 89 sequential benchmark circuits

CUT name	No. of DFFs in the CUT	No. of wires of the CUT	No. of detected faults	Fault coverage (%)
s27	3	12	34	100
s298	14	127	203	74.6
s344	15	164	343	93.2
s382	21	173	90	24.7
s444	21	196	86	21.0
s526	21	208	79	18.2
s641	19	374	758	87.5
s820	5	275	317	50.8
s832	5	273	345	55.6
s953	29	401	834	94.8
s1238	18	512	885	82.0
s1423	74	726	581	38.8

Acknowledgement

This research was supported in part by the Natural Sciences and Engineering Research Council of Canada under Grant A 4750.

References

1. Das, S. R., Ramamoorthy, C. V., Assaf, M. H., Petriu, E. M., Jone, W.-B.: Fault Tolerance in Systems Design in VLSI Using Data Compression Under Constraints of Failure Probabilities. IEEE Trans. Instrum. Meas. **50** (2001) 1725-1747
2. Bardell, P. H., McAnney, W. H., Savir, J.: Built-In Test for VLSI: Pseudorandom Techniques. Wiley Interscience, New York (1987)
3. Jone, W.-B., Das, S. R.: Space Compression Method for Built-In Self-Testing of VLSI Circuits. Int. J. Comput. Aided VLSI Des. **3** (1991) 309-322
4. Karpovsky, M., Nagvajara, P.: Optimal Robust Compression of Test Responses. IEEE Trans. Comput. **C-39** (1990) 138-141
5. Lee, H. K., Ha, D. S.: On the Generation of Test Patterns for Combinational Circuits. Tech. Rep. 12-93, Dept. Elec. Eng., Virginia Polytec. Inst. and State Univ., Blacksburg, VA (1993)
6. Li, Y. K., Robinson, J. P.: Space Compression Method with Output Data Modification, IEEE Trans. Comput. Aided Des. **6** (1987) 290-294
7. McCluskey, E. J.: Built-In Self-Test Techniques. IEEE Des. Test Comput. **2** (1985) 21-28
8. Pomeranz, I., Reddy, L. N., Reddy, S. M.: COMPACTEST: A Method to Generate Compact Test Sets for Combinational Circuits. Proc. Int. Test Conf. (1991) 194-203
9. Pradhan, D. K., Gupta, S. K.: A New Framework for Designing and Analyzing BIST Techniques and Zero Aliasing Compression. IEEE Trans. Comput. **C-40** (1991) 743-763
10. Reddy, S. M., Saluja, K., Karpovsky, M. G.: Data Compression Technique for Test Responses. IEEE Trans. Comput. **C-37** (1988) 1151-1156
11. Saluja, K. K., Karpovsky, M.: Testing Computer Hardware Through Compression in Space and Time. Proc. Int. Test Conf. (1983) 83-88
12. Savir, J.: Reducing the MISR Size. IEEE Trans. Comput. **C-45** (1996) 930-938
13. Chakrabarty, K.: Test Response Compaction for Built-In Self-Testing. Ph.D. Dissertation, Dept. Comp. Sc. Eng., Univ. Michigan, Ann Arbor, MI (1995)
14. Assaf, M. H.: Digital Core Output Test Data Compression Architecture Based on Switching Theory Concepts. Ph.D. Dissertation, Sch. Info. Tech. Eng., Univ. Ottawa, Ottawa, ON, Canada (2003)
15. Rajsuman, R.: System-on-a-Chip: Design and Test. Artech House, Boston, MA (2000)
16. Jin, C.: Test Implementation of Embedded Cores-Based Sequential Circuits Using Verilog HDL Under Altera Max Plus II Development Environment. M.A.Sc. Thesis, Dept. Sys. Sc., Univ. Ottawa, Ottawa, ON, Canada (2004)

A Distributed Contention Resolution Scheme to Reduce Blocking Probability in Optical Burst Switching Networks

Ashok K. Turuk and Rajeev Kumar

Department of Computer Science and Engineering
Indian Institute of Technology Kharagpur
Kharagpur, WB 721 302, India
{akturuk, rkumar}@cse.iitkgp.ernet.in

Abstract. In this paper, we propose a distributed contention resolution scheme to reduce blocking probability in optical burst-switching networks. The scheme takes priority, propagation delay from the ingress router, and the burst-size into account to resolve contention, and guarantees that at least one of the bursts succeeds when contention occurs. We use a control packet to delay transmission of the contending burst at ingress router. We compare the performance of our scheme, by simulation, and show that the proposed scheme outperforms the earlier scheme in reducing the blocking probability. For simulation, we generated bursty traffic using an M/Pareto distribution.

1   Introduction

Three switching techniques that are well studied to carry IP traffic over WDM networks are – optical circuit switching, packet switching and burst switching. Each switching paradigm has its own limitations when applied to optical Internet. Circuit switching also known as wavelength routing in WDM networks is not bandwidth-efficient unless the duration of transmission is much longer than the circuit establishment period. Setting up the circuits (lightpaths) takes considerable amount of time and it is shown that the lightpath establishment in optical networks is an NP-hard problem [1], though many heuristics and approximation algorithms exist, see [2] and the references therein. On the other hand, optical packet switching is flexible and bandwidth-efficient. However, the technology for optical buffers and processing in the optical domain is yet to mature for commercialization.

In this context, optical burst switching (OBS) [3] is emerging as a potential new switching paradigm which is expected to provide high-bandwidth transport services at optical layer for bursty traffic in a flexible, efficient and feasible way. OBS which is an hybrid of the circuit and packet switching paradigms, encapsulates the fine-granularity of packet-switching and the coarse-granularity of circuit switching, and thus it combines benefits of the both while overcoming some of their limitations. It requires lesser complex technology than the technology needed for packet switching.

Recently many studies have been done for OBS networks, e.g., [3,4,5,6]. On the basis of the signaling used, OBS may be broadly classified into two types: Just-Enough-

A. Sen et al. (Eds.): IWDC 2004, LNCS 3326, pp. 361–372, 2004.
© Springer-Verlag Berlin Heidelberg 2004

Time (JET) and Tell-n-Go (TAG) [3, 4]. OBS-JET uses an offset time (mostly called base-offset time) between each burst and its control packet. The base-offset time is the total time involved in processing the control packet from source to destination. In OBS-JET, a node sends out a control packet and transmits the burst after the base-offset time. If any of the intermediate node fails to reserve the required resources, the burst is dropped at that node. To efficiently utilize the resources, OBS-JET uses a delayed reservation (DR) technique where resources are reserved at the time that the burst is expected to arrive. In OBS-TAG, the burst is sent immediately after the control packet. In such OBS-TAG networks the intermediate node requires fiber-delay lines to buffer the bursts while the control packet is being processed at the node.

One of the key design issues in OBS is the reduction in blocking probability of the bursts arising due to resource contention at an intermediate router. Due to the non-availability of optical buffers contending bursts are simply dropped at the intermediate core router [7, 8]. Fiber-delay lines have been proposed as an alternate to buffers, e.g., [9], however they can handle delays only for a fixed duration. Therefore, such lines are not suitable in the context of bursts which are characterized by variable delays.

In such a technological scenario, for buffer-less burst-switching networks, the conventional priority schemes such as the fair-queuing strategy which requires the use of buffers, can no longer be applied. Therefore, one of the alternatives to support QoS in a buffer-less optical burst-switching network is to reduce the blocking probability of the bursts due to resource contention at intermediate nodes. To support the QoS requirements of different applications in optical burst-switching networks, QoS provisioning must be built into OBS. Additionally, any scheme to reduce the blocking of high priority traffic should not increase blocking of lower-priority traffic sensitively. Also, in prioritized traffic the delay experienced by high priority traffic should be lower.

Different mechanisms to resolve contention and to support QoS in optical burst-switching networks for prioritized traffic classes have been proposed in the literature. For example, Yoo and Qiao [7, 8] and Yoo et al. [9] proposed a scheme based on extra-offset time. They assigned an extra-offset time to each priority class in addition to the base-offset time. The highest priority class is assigned the maximum extra-offset time while no extra-offset time is assigned to the lowest priority class. In other words, in their scheme the traffic of the highest priority class has to wait for a maximum duration before it is transmitted while the lowest priority class traffic is transmitted immediately after the base-offset time and is delayed for a minimum duration. However, in prioritized classes of traffic, it is desirable that the traffic belonging to highest priority class should have a minimal waiting period at the source while the traffic of lower priority class may be delayed for a longer duration. Moreover, in [7, 8, 9] if more than one requests of the same priority arrive at an intermediate node and request for the same resources, all the requests are dropped.

There are many other studies done by other researchers too. Boudriga [10] assigned a different delay time to each class in order to isolate higher priority class from the lower priority class. Lee and Griffith [11] presented a traffic engineering technique to support QoS in optical Internet. The mechanism proposed by them tries to utilize the available wavelengths efficiently in order to provide lower delays. Kim et al. [12] proposed a deflection routing mechanism to reduce burst losses. They defined threshold functions to reroute the contending bursts. Deflected bursts may take a longer path to reach its destination. Yoo *et al.* [9] and Fan *et al.* [13] calculated the blocking probability of each class when fiber delay lines are deployed at the intermediate nodes. Most of the researchers have attempted to reduce the blocking probability of different classes of traffic in order to provide differentiated services.

In this paper, we present a scheme to reduce burst loss and to support QoS in optical burst-switching networks for prioritized classes of traffic. Our aim is to reduce the blocking probability of the bursts arising due to resource contention at intermediate nodes. Our proposed scheme inherits the delay-reservation technique of JET. However, it differs in the signaling protocol. When contention occurs at an intermediate node, the proposed scheme takes the following three parameters into account to allocate resources – (i) Priority of the request, (ii) propagation delay of the request from the ingress node, and (iii) burst-size of the request. Our scheme guarantees that at least one of the bursts succeeds when contention occurs due to arrival of the requests of the same priority; this is not the case with other OBS schemes where all the bursts get dropped. Thus, the proposed scheme reduces the overall burst-loss in networks due to contention and the decision to delay the transmission or drop the burst is taken on the basis of the propagation delay of the request from the ingress router.

The rest of the paper is organized as follows. Architecture and notations used are described in Section 2. In Section 3, the signaling protocol and the structure of the control packets are detailed. Simulation results are presented in Section 4 and compared with another OBS protocol. Finally, some conclusions are drawn in Section 5.

2   Architecture and Notations

We model an optical network by means of a directed graph $G(V, E)$ where V is the set of vertices (nodes) and E represents the set of links/edges in the network. Two types of nodes (here after, we use the terms node and router interchangeably) are identified: edge routers and core routers (Fig. 1). Dark circles indicate the edge routers (ingress and egress) and Squares indicate the core routers. Every edge router has $(n_e - 1) \times N_p$ electronic buffers where n_e is the number of edge routers, N_p is the number of priority classes supported in the network. Each buffer belongs to a specific pair of priority class and egress router. The core router has no buffer; this is a desirable feature of the

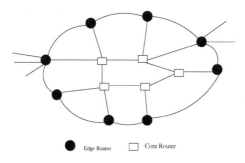

● Edge Router   □ Core Router

Fig. 1. A Burst-Switch Network

optical burst-switching network. Besides, processing and forwarding the control packet, core router has the capability of generating its own control packets depending on the conditions as will be mentioned in Section 3. A core router acts as a transit router for data-traffic. Thus, the data-traffic remains in the optical domain from ingress to egress router. Propagation delay between every pair of adjacent vertices in graph G is assumed to be t_p. Let D_N be the number of nodes along the diameter of graph G. Then, the maximum propagation delay of a control packet between any two edge routers in graph G is $T_p = (D_N - 1) \times (t_p + \tau_p)$. Here τ_p is the processing delay of a control packet at each router. We assume this maximum propagation delay, T_p, in graph G to be the base-offset time in the burst-switching network that we consider.

We define the following three situations that can occur when an intermediate router receives a reservation request:

- *No contention* (NC): When no contention for resources occurs at the intermediate core router.
- *Contention resolved* (CR): When contention occurs at an intermediate core router, and the propagation delay between the core router and the (contending) requesting ingress router is $\tau \leq T_p/2$. In this case if a request is sent from the core router to the ingress router to delay the transmission of the burst, the request can reach the ingress router before the expiry of the base-offset time (T_p). Hence, the transmission of the burst can be delayed and the burst will not be dropped at the core router.
- *Contention-not-resolved* (CNR): When contention occurs at an intermediate core router and the propagation delay between the core router and the requesting ingress router is $\tau > T_p/2$. In this case if a request sent from the core router to the ingress router to delay the transmission of the burst, cannot reach the ingress router before the expiry of base-offset time (T_p). Thus, the burst transmitted immediately after the base-offset time will be dropped at the core router.

3   Signaling Protocol and Control Packets

In most of the burst-switching networks, when resource contention occurs at an intermediate node the contending burst is dropped at that node. To reduce such a burst-drop, the burst-switching networks proposed by Yoo's research group [3, 4, 5, 6] assign an extra-offset time to each class of traffic in addition to the base-offset time. They attempted to reduce overlap of bursts in time. In such schemes, the traffic of the highest priority class is assigned the maximal extra-offset time whereas no offset time is assigned to the lowest class traffic. In other words, high priority traffic has to wait for a longer duration at the ingress router even if the required resources are available at the core routers. On the other hand, it is always expected, for a prioritized traffic, that the traffic of the high priority class should experience lower delay at the ingress router. Moreover, such schemes do not resolve resource contention if two requests have the same priority and arrive at an intermediate core router at the same time. In addition, the low priority requests in case of a contention are always dropped leading to starvation.

Unlike in other OBS schemes, where a contending request is always dropped, in our proposed scheme the decision to drop or delay the transmission is taken on the basis of the propagation delay of the request from the ingress router. Moreover in our scheme if contention arises due to the arrival of requests of the same priority at the same time, the contention is resolved on the basis of following three parameters: (i) priority of the request (ii) propagation delay of the request from the ingress node and (iii) burst-size of the request. Proposed scheme guarantees that at least one burst succeeds when a contention occurs. A burst whose request was not further delayed, is transmitted after the base-offset time. The decision to delay the transmission is taken at the intermediate core router where contention has occurred. Thus, the transmission of a burst is delayed on-demand in our scheme whereas in schemes based on extra-offset time, each priority class traffic is delayed by a pre-determined period of time in addition to the base offset-time.

We use two types of control packets: (i) *forward* (F) and (ii) *reverse* (R) control packets. The proposed scheme inherits all the other features of JET, e.g., the delayed reservation technique and the separation of data and control channels. The basis of our scheme is that the ingress router sends a F-control packet for requesting reservation. If resources have been reserved the burst is transmitted; this is a trivial case. If resource contention occurs at an intermediate core router, the F-control packet is either dropped or modified on the basis of the above mentioned three parameters, and a R-control packet is sent back to the ingress router. On receiving the R-control packet, a router either releases the reserved resources or updates the reservation request as specified in the R-control packet. In our scheme, a F-control packet is modified only once.

In the following subsections, we describe the F and R control packets and the signaling protocol used.

3.1   Control Packets

F-**Control Packet** : When a burst arrives at an ingress router, it sends out a F-control packet requesting for reservation. Resources are reserved using the delayed reservation technique, analogous to the one discussed in [3]. The structure of the F-control packet is shown in Fig. 2. It consists of the following fields:

- f-path is the explicit forward path that the F-control packet takes from the ingress to the egress router. The burst follows this path from the ingress to egress router,
- r-path is the reverse path of the forward f-path. For example, if f-path is $1 \to 4 \to 7 \to 9$, then r-path is $9 \to 7 \to 4 \to 1$,
- t is the propagation delay from the ingress router to the current core router. When a router receives the F-control packet, it updates the value of t to $t + t_p$,

Fig. 2. F-control packet

Fig. 3. R-control packet

- W is the wavelength requested for reservation by the ingress router,
- s is the source/ingress router,
- d is the destination/egress router,
- If F-control packet is modified, the value of T indicates the time at which the required resources are to be reserved by the current router (initially the value of T is set to *zero* by the ingress router),
- Value of m equal to *one* indicates that the F-control packet has been modified (initially the value of m is set to *zero* by the ingress router). An intermediate node modifies the F-control packet by setting the value of m to *one*.
- rid is the request identity, and
- p indicates the priority of the request.

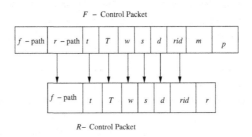

Fig. 4. Formation of a R-control packet from F-control packet

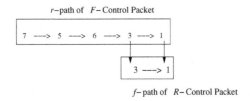

Fig. 5. Copying of a f-path to a r-path

When an intermediate core router receives the F-control packet, one of the following three possible situations arises : (i) NC, (ii) CR or (iii) CNR. The action taken by the core router depends on the value of m in the F-control packet and one of the above three situations. The intermediate core router updates the value of t in the F-control packet to $t + t_p$. The actions taken by the core router for both values of m and for all the three possible situations are discussed below.

Case I: *When the value of m in the F-control packet is equal to* zero. One of the following happens:

1. NC : Required resources can be reserved at the core router and the F-control packet is forwarded to the next node in the path.

2. CR : This is a situation in which $t \leq T_p/2$. The following actions are taken at the router: (i) the time at which the required resources are available, is found, and the resources are reserved from this time onwards, (ii) the value of T in F-control packet is set to this value, (iii) the value of m in the F-control packet is set to *one*, (iv) a R-control packet is formed (formation of R-control packet is explained below) is sent to the ingress router 's', and (v) the F-control packet is sent to the next node in the path.
3. CNR: This is a situation in which $t > T_p/2$. The following actions are taken at the core router: (i) a R-control packet is formed and sent to the ingress router 's', and (ii) the F-control packet (reservation request) is dropped.

Case II: *When the value of m in F-control packet is equal to* one. One of the following happens:

1. NC : Following actions are taken at the core router: (i) value of T in the F-control packet is updated to $T + t_p$, (ii) resources are reserved from the time, T and (iii) the F-control packet is sent to the next node in the path.
2. CR : Following actions are taken at the core router: (i) value of T in the F-control packet is updated to $T + t_p$, (ii) if the required resources are available from the time T onwards **then** (a) they are reserved from the time, T (b) the F-control packet is sent to the next node in the path. **else** (a) a R-control packet is formed and sent to the ingress router 's', and (b) the F-control packet is dropped.
3. CNR : The following actions are taken: (i) R-control packet is formed and the value of r-field is set to *one*, (ii) R-control packet is sent to the ingress router 's', and (iii) F-control packet is dropped.

R-Control Packet : A R-control packet is formed at an intermediate core router where the resource conflict has occurred. The structure of a R-control packet is shown in Fig. 3. Each of the fields of a R-control packet is described below:

f-path is the explicit path that the R-control packet takes from the core router to the ingress router 's'. The semantics of the t, T, w, s, d and rid fields of the R-control packet are identical to that of the F-control packet. A value of r equal to *zero* indicates that resources are to be reserved from the time specified in field T, and a value equal to *one* indicates the resources are to be released. A R-control packet is formed from the F-control packet and the formation is explained below:

The r-path of the F-control packet is copied into the f-path of the R-control packet and all the other fields of the F-control packet are copied to the corresponding fields of the R-control packet (Fig. 4). Copying the r-path of the F-control packet into the f-path of the R-control packet is illustrated in Fig. 5. In this illustration, we have assumed a resource conflict occurred at core router 6. Remaining elements of the r-path of the F-control packet excluding node 6 is copied into the f-path of the R-control packet. The R-control packet follows this f-path to reach the ingress router 1 for whose reservation request, the resource contention has occurred.

Processing of a R-Control Packet : On receiving a R-control packet, a node updates the values of t and T in the control packet to $t + t_p$ and $T - t_p$, respectively. If the value of $t < T_p$ and the value of r is *zero* **then** the reserved resources for request number

rid from the ingress router 's' to the egress router 'd' are updated and reserved from the time T onwards **else** resources are released. If the node is the ingress router 's', the R-control packet is dropped after processing. If the value of $t < T_p$ then R-control packet is forwarded to the next node in the f-path else the R-control packet is dropped at that node.

When a contention occurs at an intermediate core router the following rules are applied to modify the F-control packet and to form a R-control packet:

Rule 1: *An arriving request finds the required resources busy.*

For an m value equal to *zero* and $t \leq T_p/2$ do the following: modify the F-control packet by setting the value of m field to *one* and the value of the T field to the time at which required resources are available. Form R-control packet and set the value of r-field to *zero*. For value of m equal to *one* or $t > T_p/2$ do the following: form a R-control packet, set the value of r-field to *one*, and drop the F-control packet.

Rule 2: *Two requests of different priorities arrive at a core router at the same time.*

Reserve the resources for the high priority request and forward its F-control packet to the next node in its path. For *zero* value of m of the low priority request and $t \leq T_p/2$ do the following: modify its F-control packet and form a R-control packet as stated in Rule 1. For m value of low priority request equal to *one* or $t > T_p/2$ do the following: form a R-control packet, set value of r-field to *one*, and drop the F-control packet.

Rule 3: *Two requests of same priorities arrive at a core router at the same time.*

The following actions are taken: (i) If their t-values are different, find the request with maximal value of t, reserve the resources for this request and send its F-control packet to the next node in its path. The other request is processed as stated in Rule 2 for a low priority request. Here we admit the request which has the maximum propagation delay from the ingress router so that the resources reserved will be efficiently utilized. (ii) For the same values of t in both requests, find the request with maximal burst-size. Reserve the resources for this request and forward its F-control packet to the next node in its path. The other request is processed as stated in Rule 2 of low priority request. By choosing the larger burst-size, we aim to reduce the loss rate of the bursts in the whole network.

3.2   Signaling Protocol

1. On arrival of burst at the ingress router, send a F-control packet to the core router on the path requesting for reservation of resources.
2. Process the F-control packet at each of the intermediate core routers. One of the following action is taken depending on the status of the requested resource at the core router.
   (a) For NC situation: Reserve the requested resource and send the F-control packet to next router on path.
   (b) For CR situation: Modify F-control packet and send to the next router on the path after reserving the required resources. Form a R-control packet and send to the ingress router.

(c) For CNR situation: Drop the F-control packet. Form a R-control packet and send to the ingress router.

3. Process R-control packet at each router.

4   Simulation Results

We simulate a burst-switching network consisting of edge routers (ingress and egress) and core routers as shown in Fig. 1 through our own simulator written in C++ on linux platform. The propagation delay, t_p, between any two adjacent nodes in the burst-switching network is assumed to be 1 ms. The processing time of each control packet at the router is assumed to 0.25 ms. The maximum propagation delay, TP, between any two edge routers calculated as mentioned in Section 2 is 5 ms. We assume the maximum propagation delay to be the base-offset time of the burst-switching network. We take the number of wavelengths available on each link in the range of 6 to 8. We assume there is no wavelength conversion and there exist no optical buffers in the switches.

We consider bursty traffic in our simulation as the traffic in the Internet is reported to be bursty in nature [14]. For this, we assume exponential inter-arrival of bursts, and the burst size to be determined by an M/Pareto distribution. For simplicity and without loss of generality, we consider two classes of traffic: class 0 (low priority) and class 1 (high priority). We generate high priority traffic with a probability of 0.4 and consider the burst size of high priority traffic double the size of low priority traffic. We treat load as the number of requests made by the edge routers. Traffic is generated at the edge routers only.

We compare the simulation results of our scheme with that of Yoo and Qiao [8]. The extra-offset time for high-priority traffic in [8] is taken to be 1 ms, we use the same quanta of time in our simulation. In this paper, we include simulation results for burst blocking probability as the performance metric for comparison. The other performance metrics obtained by simulation will be presented during the conference.

First, we include the plots for overall blocking probability of bursts in Fig. 6. Number of wavelengths available in each link is assumed to be six. It is evident from Fig. 6 that

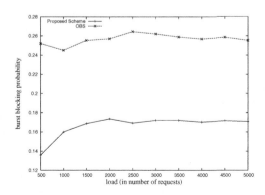

Fig. 6. Overall Blocking probability of bursts. (The number of wavelengths on each link is 6.)

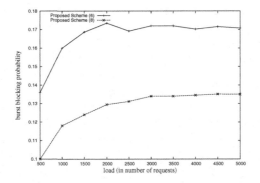

Fig. 7. The Blocking probability in the proposed scheme for different number of wavelengths

the blocking probability across the load in the proposed scheme is much lower than that in their OBS scheme [8]. The lower blocking probability in our scheme is attributed to the signaling mechanism that we adopt in resolving resource contention. This is already discussed and illustrated by an example in the previous section.

We observe from the simulation results that the blocking probability of high and low priority bursts in the proposed scheme is lower than those obtained in OBS [8]. This is due to the resource contention resolution technique that we adopt in our scheme. This can be trivially shown by suitable examples taking different priorities. To study the effect of number of wavelengths on the blocking probability, we varied the number of wavelengths available on each link form six to eight. The wavelength selection strategy that we adopted in our simulation for both OBS and the proposed scheme is to select the available wavelength with lowest index. We plotted the overall blocking probability of bursts by varying the number of wavelengths in Fig. 7 and 8 for the proposed scheme and OBS, respectively. From Fig. 7, it is observed that the blocking probability in our scheme decreases with increase in number of wavelengths while the blocking probability for OBS remains the same as shown in Fig. 8. Since the request pattern remains the same

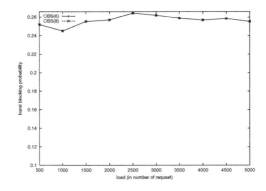

Fig. 8. The Blocking probability in other OBS [8] for different number of wavelengths

in our simulation, the contention among the requests also remains the same. As a result the increase in number of wavelengths in OBS [8] could not reduce the blocking probability. This is an interesting phenomenon that we can reduce the blocking probability by increasing the wavelengths in the proposed scheme though this is not the case with other OBS schemes. Nonetheless, in other OBS schemes too, we may reduce the blocking probability by adopting some other wavelength selection strategy at the ingress router. We envisage that the proposed scheme will still outperform the other OBS schemes employing any other wavelength selection mechanism.

From our simulation we, therefore, conclude that the proposed scheme, in general, outperforms OBS [8] in reducing the blocking probability. As expected with increase in wavelengths the blocking probability decreases in the proposed scheme, and thus, the scheme scales well with the wavelengths. Additionally, in the proposed scheme, if a request is blocked the reserved resources are partly released resulting in an efficient resource utilization; this is not the case with other OBS schemes.

The above observations are made based on comparing our scheme with one of the OBS schemes developed by Yoo's research group [8]. Main contribution in performance improvement of the proposed scheme is due to the reason that our scheme *too* drops or delays a burst under certain consideration, however, we *always* admit *at least* one of the bursts in case of a contention. We expect to get a performance improvement in terms of blocking probability over most of the other variants of OBS schemes, e.g., [10, 12, 13].

5   Conclusions

In this paper, we have proposed a scheme for QoS provisioning by reducing the blocking probability of the bursts in optical burst-switching networks. In our scheme, when resource contention occurs the decision to drop or delay a burst is decided on the basis of the following three parameters: Priority, propagation delay, and burst-size. The scheme guarantees that at least one of the bursts succeeds when contention occurs and thus reduces the overall blocking probability. We compared the blocking probabilities of the bursts in our scheme with another OBS scheme [8] by simulation. We found that our scheme outperforms the other OBS scheme in terms of the blocking probability. With increase in wavelengths on each link we found that the blocking probability decreases while in other OBSs it remains the same. This is because the burst contention is not resolved in other OBSs since there is no wavelength conversion in the burst-switching networks that we have considered. In absence of wavelength conversion, other schemes need an efficient wavelength selection strategy at the ingress router to reduce the blocking probability.

Future work may extend this work to multiple classes of services, propose an efficient wavelength selection strategy, study the delay experienced by the bursts at the ingress router, and study the effect of the proposed strategy on end-to-end delay and jitter of user applications.

References

1. Chlamtac, I., Ganz, A., Karmi, G.: Lightpath Communications: An Approach to High Bandwidth Optical WANs. IEEE Transactions on Communications **40** (1992) 1171 – 1182
2. Dutta, R., Rouskas, G.: A Survey of Virtual Topology Design Algorithm for Wavelength Routed Optical Netwroks. Optical Netwrok Magazine **1** (2000) 73–89
3. Yoo, M., Qiao, C.: Optical Burst Switching (OBS) - A New Paradigm for an Optical Internet. Journal of High Speed Networks **8** (1999) 69 – 84
4. Yoo, M., Qiao, C.: Just-enough-time(JET): A High Speed Protocol for for Bursty Traffic in Optical Networks. IEEE/LEOS Technologies for a Global Information Infrastructure (1997) 26 – 27
5. Yoo, M., Jeong, M., Qiao, C.: A High Speed Protocol for Bursty Traffic in Optical Networks. In: SPIE Proceedings All Optical Communication Systems: Architecture , Control and Network Issue. Volume 3230. (1997) 79 – 90
6. Qiao, C., Yoo, M.: Choices, Features and Issues in Optical Burst Switching. Optical Network Magazine **1** (2000) 36 – 44
7. Yoo, M., Qiao, C.: A New Optical Burst Switching (OBS) Protocol for Supporting Quality of Service. In: SPIE proceedings, All Optical Communication Systems: Architecture, Control and Network Issue. Volume 3531. (1998) 396 – 405
8. Yoo, M., Qiao, C.: Supporting Multiple Classes of Service in IP over WDM Networks. In: Proceedings of IEEE GLOBECOM 99, December 1999. (1999) 1023 – 1027
9. Yoo, M., Qiao, C., Dixit, S.: QoS Performance in IP over WDM Networks. IEEE Journal on Selected Areas in Communications, Special Issues on Protocols for Next Generation Optical Internet **18** (2000) 2062 – 2071
10. Boudriga, N.: Optical Burst Switching Protocol for Supporting QoS and Adaptive Routing. Computer Communications **26** (2003) 1804 – 1812
11. Lee, S., Griffith, D., Song, J.S.: Lambda GLSP setup with QoS requirement in optical Internet. Computer Communications **26(6)** (2003) 603 – 610
12. Kim, H., Lee, S., Song, J.: Optical Burst Switching with Limited Deflection Routing Rules. IEICE Trans. Commun. **E86-B** (2003)
13. Fan, P., Feng, C., Wang, Y., Ge, N.: Investigation of The Time-Offset-Based QoS Support with Optical Burst Switching in WDM Networks. In: IEEE International Conferences on Communications, 2002. Volume 5. (2002) 2682 – 2686
14. Paxson, V., Floyd, S.: Wide Area Traffic: The Failure of Poisson Modeling. IEEE/ACM Transaction on Networking **3** (1995) 226 – 244

Polynomial Interpolation on OTIS-Mesh Optoelectronic Computers

Prasanta K. Jana

Department of Computer Science and Engineering,
Indian School of Mines, Dhanbad-826004, India
prasantajana@yahoo.com

Abstract. Two Parallel algorithms for polynomial interpolation are presented on an $N \times N$ OTIS-Mesh. The algorithms are based on N-point Lagrange interpolation. The first algorithm is shown to run in $8\sqrt{N} - 6$ electronic moves and 3 OTIS moves. The second one has an improved time complexity of $6\sqrt{N}$ - 4 electronics moves and 2 OTIS moves. The scalability of the algorithms is also discussed.

1 Introduction

An OTIS-Mesh [3], [4], [5] is a model of optoelectronic parallel computers which is gaining much interest among researchers. An $N \times N$ OTIS-Mesh is built around N groups. Each group is basically an $\sqrt{N} \times \sqrt{N}$ two-dimensional mesh. The diameter of this network is $4\sqrt{N} - 3$. An OTIS-Mesh overcomes the drawbacks of a two-dimensional mesh, for example, large diameter or low bisection width; but retains the benefits of the mesh. It can simulate an $\sqrt{N} \times \sqrt{N} \times \sqrt{N} \times \sqrt{N}$ four-dimensional mesh [6]. Many parallel algorithms for various computation including image processing [7], matrix multiplication [8], basic operations such as data sum, consecutive sum, concentrate [9], BPC permutation [10] have been successfully mapped on this model.

Given a set of tabulated values $y_1, y_2, \ldots, y_N$ of the function $y = f(x)$ at some discrete points $x_1, x_2, \ldots, x_N$, the problem of polynomial interpolation is to find the value of the function at some intermediate point z, where $x_1 \leq z \leq x_N$. Polynomial interpolation has many applications, such as, in cardiology, petroleum exploration, geological mapping etc. Several parallel algorithms for polynomial interpolation based on Lagrange formula have been reported in [11], [12], [13], [14],[15], [16], [2] in the recent years.

In this paper, we propose two parallel algorithms for polynomial interpolation on an $N \times N$ OTIS-Mesh. The algorithms are based on N-point Lagrange's formula. The first algorithm requires $8\sqrt{N} - 6$ electronic moves plus 3 OTIS moves. The second parallel algorithm has an improved time complexity of $6\sqrt{N}$ - 4 electronics moves plus 2 OTIS moves.

A. Sen et al. (Eds.): IWDC 2004, LNCS 3326, pp. 373–378, 2004.
© Springer-Verlag Berlin Heidelberg 2004

2 Topology of OTIS-Mesh

In an $N \times N$ OTIS-Mesh (shown in Fig. 1 for $N = 4$), N^2 processors are organized into N groups in which each group is basically an $\sqrt{N} \times \sqrt{N}$ two-dimensional mesh. Each group G is indexed by a pair (g_x, g_y) where g_x and g_y are row and column indices of the group assuming the layout of an $\sqrt{N} \times \sqrt{N}$ lattice. Then the processor placed in the p_x row and p_y column within the group $G(g_x, g_y)$ is denoted by $P(g_x, g_y, p_x, p_y)$ for $1 \leq g_x, g_y, p_x, p_y \leq \sqrt{N}$. The links between the processors within a group are electronic and they will be called intragroup links. These links follow the two dimensional mesh topology, i.e., the processor $P(g_x, g_y, p_x, p_y)$ is connected with the processor $P(g_x, g_y, p'_x, p'_y)$ iff $\left| p_x - p'_x \right| + \left| p_y - p'_y \right| = 1$ for $1 \leq g_x, g_y, p_x, p_y, p'_x, p'_y \leq \sqrt{N}$. The processors of different groups are interconnected by optical links according to OTIS rule, i.e., the processor $P(g_x, g_y, p_x, p_y)$ is directly connected to the processor $P(p_x, p_y, g_x, g_y)$. These links will be referred as interblock links. In Fig. 1, electronic links and optical links are shown by solid and dashed arrows respectively. While analyzing of our proposed algorithms, we count the data moves along the electronic links (i.e., electronic moves) and that on optical links (i.e., optical moves) separately. We assume that all these links are bi-directional. Each processor has some local registers depending on the need of a parallel algorithm. We use a special symbol ' $*$ ' for four coordinates to denote the set of processors with all possible values.

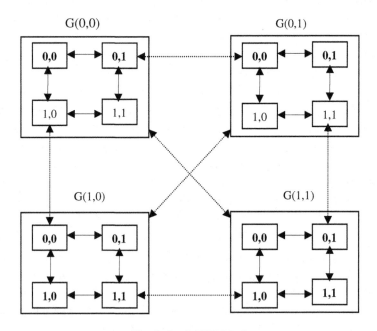

Fig. 1. 4×4 OTIS-Mesh

3 Proposed Algorithms

Given a set of tabulated values $\{(x_i, y_i)\}$, $i = 1, 2, \ldots N$, where $y = f(x)$, the N-point Lagrange formula [1] for polynomial interpolation is given by

$$P(x) = \pi(x) \sum_{i=1}^{N} \frac{y_i}{(x - x_i)\pi'(x_i)}$$

where $\pi(x) = \prod_{i=1}^{N} (x - x_i)$ and $\pi'(x_i) = \prod_{j=1, j \neq i}^{N} (x_i - x_j)$, $i = 1, 2, \cdots, N$

Algorithm 1

/*Steps 1 through 7 store the data points row wise and column wise */
Step 1. For all i, k, $1 \leq i$, $k \leq \sqrt{N}$ do in parallel

Input $x_{\sqrt{N}(k-1)+i}$ to $A(i, 1, k, 1)$

Input x to $C(i, 1, k, 1)$

Step 2. Broadcast locally the contents of A and C registers stored in step 1 to all processors along the same row of the group.

Step 3. For all j, l, $1 \leq j$, $l \leq \sqrt{N}$ do in parallel

Input $x_{\sqrt{N}(l-1)+j}$ to $B(1, j, 1, l)$

Step 4. Broadcast locally the contents of B register stored in step 3 to all processors along the same column of the group.

Step 5. Perform an OTIS move on A, B and C register contents stored in steps 2 and 4.

Step 6. Broadcast locally the contents of A and C registers stored in step 5 to all processors along the same row of the group.

Step 7. Broadcast locally the contents of B registers to all processors stored in step 5 along the same column of the group.

Step 8. For all i, j, k, l, $1 \leq i$, j, k, $l \leq \sqrt{N}$ do in parallel

If $A(i, j, k, l) \neq B(i, j, k, l)$ then

$$A(i, j, k, l) \leftarrow \frac{C(i, j, k, l) - B(i, j, k, l)}{A(i, j, k, l) - B(i, j, k, l)}$$

Else $A(i, j, k, l) \leftarrow 1$

Step 9. Form the local product with the contents of the A registers along the same row of each group and store it in $A(i, j, k, 1)$, $1 \leq i$, j, $k \leq \sqrt{N}$.

Step 10. Perform an OTIS move on the contents of the A registers stored in step 9.

Step 11. Form the local product with the contents of A registers stored in step 10 along the same row of each group $G(*, 1)$ and store it in $A(i, 1, k, 1)$, $1 \leq i$, $k \leq \sqrt{N}$.

Step 12. For all i, k, $1 \leq i$, $k \leq \sqrt{N}$ do in parallel.

$$B(i, 1, k, 1) \leftarrow y_{\sqrt{N}(k-1)+i}$$

Step 13. For all $i, k, 1 \le i, k \le \sqrt{N}$ do in parallel

$$A(i,1,k,1) \leftarrow A(i,1,k,1) * B(i,1,k,1)$$

Step 14. Form the local sum with the contents of the $A(i, 1, k, 1)$, $1 \le i, k \le \sqrt{N}$ along the same column of each group and store them in $A(i, 1, 1, 1)$, $1 \le i \le \sqrt{N}$.

Step 15. Perform an OTIS move on the contents of $A(i, 1\ 1,1)$, $1 \le i \le \sqrt{N}$.

Step 16. Form the final result by adding the contents of $A(1, 1, k, 1)$ column wise for $1 \le k \le \sqrt{N}$ and store it in $A(1, 1, 1, 1)$. ∎

Time Complexity: Since one piece of data can be moved at a time along an electronic link, the contents of the registers A and C in step 2 can be broadcast in pipelining (i.e., the content of C register trails by that of A register). This requires $\sqrt{N}$ electronic moves. Step 6 also requires $\sqrt{N}$ electronic moves by similar pipelining. Each of the steps 4, 7, 9, 11, 14 and 16 requires $\sqrt{N} - 1$ electronic moves. Steps 5, 10, 15 each requires a single OTIS move. Therefore the above algorithm requires $8\sqrt{N} - 6$ electronic moves and 3 OTIS moves.

We now outline how the above algorithm can be modified when p^2 (for $p < n$) processors will be available as follows. For the sake of simplicity, we assume that $N = kp$, where k is an integer. It can be noted that the algorithm first stores the input data points $x_1, x_2, ..., x_N$ row wise and column wise followed by sum of product computation. Now, suppose N input data points are grouped into $k = N / p$ sets: $\{x_1, x_2, ..., x_p\}$, $\{x_{p+1}, x_{p+2}, ..., x_{2p}\}$, ..., $\{x_{(k-1)+1}, x_{(k-1)+2}, ..., x_{kp}\}$. For a given input set to the p columns, the rows are successively fed with possible input sets and each time the required product terms are formed. Then the input sets to the columns are successively changed to update the partially computed results and the same procedure is repeated until the final interpolated value is generated in processor $P(1, 1, 1, 1)$. The time complexity of the modified algorithm will be $O(k\sqrt{N})$.

Algorithm 2

Step 1. For all $i, j, 1 \le i, j \le \sqrt{N}$ do in parallel

Input $x_{\sqrt{N}(i-1)+j}$ to $A(i, j, 1, 1)$

Input $y_{\sqrt{N}(i-1)+j}$ to $D(i, j, 1, 1)$

Input x to $B(i, j, 1, 1)$

Step 2. On each group, broadcast locally the contents of A and B registers stored in step 1 to all processors of the corresponding group.

Step 3. For all $i, j, k, l, 1 \le i, j, k, l \le \sqrt{N}$ do in parallel

$$C(i, j, k, l) \leftarrow A(i, j, k, l)$$

Step 4. Perform an OTIS move on the contents of A registers of all groups.

Step 5. For all $i, j, k, l, 1 \le i, j, k, l \le \sqrt{N}$ do in parallel

If $C(i, j, k, l) \ne A(i, j, k, l)$ then

$$A(i, j, k, l) \leftarrow \frac{B(i, j, k, l) - A(i, j, k, l)}{C(i, j, k, l) - A(i, j, k, l)}$$

Else $A(i, j, k, l) \leftarrow 1$

Step 6. Form the local product with the contents of the A registers on each group and store it in $A(i, j,1,1)$, $1 \leq i, j \leq \sqrt{N}$.

Step 7. For all $i, j = 1$ to $\sqrt{N}$ do in parallel

$$A(i, j,1,1) \leftarrow A(i, j,1,1) * D(i, j,1,1)$$

Step 8. Perform an OTIS move on the contents of the A registers stored in step 7.

Step 9. Add the contents of the A registers of the group $G(1, 1)$ to form the final result.   ■

Time Complexity: Step 1 requires constant time. Step 2 can be performed by first sending the contents of the A and B registers initially of a group down column one of that group in pipeline fashion (i.e., the content of the B register trails the content of the A register by one column processor). This requires $\sqrt{N}$ electronic moves. Next the contents of A and B registers are broadcast along rows in another $\sqrt{N}$ electronic moves using a similar pipelining. Thus step 2 requires $2\sqrt{N}$ electronic moves. Further, each of the steps 6 and 9 requires $2(\sqrt{N} - 1)$ electronics moves and steps 4 and 8 each requires a single OTIS move. Therefore, the above algorithm requires $6\sqrt{N} - 4$ electronics moves plus 2 OTIS moves.

4 Conclusion

In this paper, we have presented two parallel algorithms for polynomial interpolation. The algorithms are based on N-point Lagrange interpolation which are mapped on an $N \times N$ OTIS-Mesh. Our first algorithm (Algorithm 1) has been shown to run in $8\sqrt{N} - 6$ electronic moves and 3 OTIS moves. The second algorithm (Algorithm 2) has an improvement over Algorithm 1 that runs with $6\sqrt{N} - 4$ electronics moves and 2 OTIS moves. We have also shown how the algorithms can be modified when p^2 ($p < n$) processors will be available.

References

1. Hildebrand,F.B.: Introduction to Numerical Analysis. McGraw-Hill, New Work(1956).
2. Das, D., Dey, M., Sinha, B. P.: A new network topology with multiple meshes. IEEE Trans. Computers. 68 (1999) 536–551.
3. Marsden, G., Marchand, P., Harvey, P., Esener, S.: Optical transpose interconnection system architectures. Optics Letters.18 (1993) 1083–1085.
4. Sahni, S.: Models and Algorithms for Optical and Optoelectronic Parallel Computers. International Journal of Foundations of Computer Science. 12 (2001) 249–264.
5. Wang, C. F., Sahni, S.: OTIS Optoelectronic Computers. In Parallel computation using optical interconnection, K. Li, Y. Pan and S. Q. Zhang Eds. Kluwer Academic (1998).
6. Zane, F., Marchand, P., Paturi, R., Esener, S.: Scalable network architectures using the optical transpose interconnection system (OTIS). J. of Parallel and Distributed Computing. 60 (2000) 521–538.
7. Wang, C. F., Sahni, S.: Image processing on the OTIS-Mesh optoelectronic Computer. IEEE Transactions on parallel and Distributed Systems. 11(2000) 97–109.
8. Wang, C. F., Sahni, S.: Matrix Multiplication on the OTIS-Mesh Optoelectronic Computer. IEEE Transactions on Computers. 50 (2001) 635–645.

9. Wang, C. F., Sahni, S.: Basic Operation on the OTIS-Mesh Optoelectronic Computer.IEEE Transactions on Parallel and Distributed Systems. 9 (1998)1226-1236.
10. Wang, C. F., Sahni, S.: BPC permutations on the OTIS – Mesh optoelectronic computer. In Proceedings on the Fourth International conference on Massively Parallel Processing Using Optical Transpose Interconnection (1997) 130-135.
11. Goertzel, B. : Lagrange interpolation on a processor tree with ring connections. J.   of Parallel and Distributed Computing. 22 (1994) 321-323.
12. Sengupta, S., Das, D., Sinha, B. P., Ghosh, M.: A Fast parallel algorithm for   polynomial interpolation using Lagrange's formula. In Proceedings of Intl. Conference on High Performance Computing (HiPC) (1995) 701-706.
13. Jana, P. K., Sinha, B. P.: Fast parallel algorithm for polynomial interpolation,. Computers Math. Applic. 29 (1995) 85-92.
14. Joshep, Ja Ja.: An Introduction to Parallel Algorithms. Addison Wesley, Massachusetts (1992).
15. Jana, P. K., Sinha, B. P.: Efficient parallel algorithms for Lagrange and Hermite interpolation. International Journal of Applied Science and Computations. 4 (1997) 118-136.
16. Capello, P. R., Gallopoulos, E., Koc, C. K. : Systolic computation of interpolating polynomials. Computing. 45 (1990) 291 – 307.

A New Network Topology with Multiple Three-Dimensional Meshes

Nahid Afroz[1], Bhabani P. Sinha[2], Rabiul Islam[1], and Subir Bandyopadhyay[1]

[1] School of Computer Science, University of Windsor, Windsor, Ontario, Canada N9B 3P4
{afroz, islamh, subir}@uwindsor.ca
[2] Indian Statistical Institute, Calcutta, 700 108, India
bhabani@isical.ac.in

Abstract. A new network topology, called the 3D Multi-Mesh (3D MM) is presented here which is an extension of the Multi-Mesh architecture [2]. This network consists of three-dimensional meshes (termed as 3D blocks), each having n^3 processors, interconnected in a suitable manner so that the resulting topology is 6-regular with processors and a diameter of only $3n$. It is expected that this architecture will enable more efficient algorithm mapping compared to existing architectures.

1 Introduction

The interconnection network defines the connections between different processors in a multi-processor system [4]. The architecture of the interconnection network has a crucial role in the performance of the multiprocessor system - both in terms of the speed of communication and the time to run an application. Two-dimensional mesh [4], [6], [7] is one of the most popular architectures due to its inherent simplicity and ease of algorithm mapping. In a two-dimensional (2D) mesh, nodes are arranged in a grid pattern [8]. Except for the boundary processors, all other processors are connected to their respective neighbors to the left, right, above and below through bi-directional links [8]. Mesh networks represent a good compromise among the contradictory requirements of static network parameters and are easy to implement and extend. Variations of the mesh topology are possible, depending on whether there is any wrap-around or diagonal interconnections among the nodes, e.g., torus, Illiac IV [4], [7], multi-dimensional mesh [7]. Efficient mapping of many fundamental and most frequently used algorithms on variations of the mesh structure have been reported [2], [3], [4], [7].

The multi-mesh topology proposed in [2] uses the 2D mesh of processors with, say $n \times n$ processors, as its basic building block. The multi-mesh uses n^2 2D meshes. The multi-mesh has the advantage that, with the same number of processors and the same number of links, as in the case of other mesh-based architectures, it has a much lower diameter [2]. Many important algorithms can be mapped to the multi-mesh in an efficient manner [2], [3].

A. Sen et al. (Eds.): IWDC 2004, LNCS 3326, pp. 379–384, 2004.
© Springer-Verlag Berlin Heidelberg 2004

In this paper we have extended the idea of the multi-mesh to define a new topology called the *3-dimensional multi-mesh* (henceforth called the 3D MM). The basic building block of the proposed 3D MM is a three dimensional mesh of processors with, say $n \times n \times n$ processors, which we will call a *3D block*. We may visualize a 3D block of processors as consisting of n planes of two-dimensional meshes of processors. A 3D block with $n = 3$ is shown in Figure 1. The 3D MM consists of n^3 such 3D blocks arranged in a three-dimensional array, so that the resulting topology is 6-regular with $N = n^6$ processors, interconnected in a suitable manner. We will call such a network a 3D MM of order n. Figure 2 shows a 3D MM network of order 3.

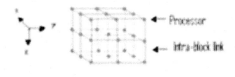

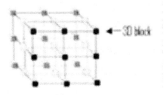

Fig. 1. A 3D building block   **Fig. 2.** A 3D MM network

2 The 3D Multi-mesh Topology

The basic building block of the 3D Multi-mesh network is a three dimensional mesh in which processors are arranged along three orthogonal dimensions, say x, y and z, so that a processor P(x, y, z) is connected to six other neighboring processors at P(x+1, y, z), P(x-1, y, z), P(x, y+1, y, z), P(x, y-1, z), P(x, y, z+1) and P(x, y, z-1), when they exist, for all x, y and z, $1 \leq$ x, y, z $\leq n$. A 3D block has $(n-2) \times (n-2) \times (n-2)$ processors, each having 6 intra-block links i.e., to other processors inside the same block. Each remaining processor lies on the six faces[1] of the cube and has 3, 4 or 5 intra-block links, depending on the position of the processor in the block. We now consider n^3 such 3D blocks, which we arrange along the three orthogonal dimensions (Figure 2). We designate with the symbols α, ß and γ respectively (to make them distinct from x, y and z) the coordinate values of a 3D block along the three orthogonal dimensions. Thus, we now have a total of n^6 processors where each processor can be uniquely identified by the six coordinate values α, ß, γ, x, y, z which we will denote by P(α, ß, γ, x, y, z). We will characterize any particular 3D block by a given set of values for α, ß and γ coordinates and we will denote a block by B (α, ß, γ). We connect all the processors on the six faces of each 3D block to the processors on the faces of other 3D blocks by one or more inter-block links so that each processor eventually has exactly six links to other processors (either in the same 3D block or in other 3D block(s)). The rules for inter-block connections are given below:

---

[1] A face of a cube represents the first or the last plane of 3D mesh. A processor P(x, y, z) on the face of a cube have the value of 1 or n for at least one of the coordinates x, y or z.

Inter-block Rule 1 (Links from y = 1 and y = n planes): The processor P (α, $\boldsymbol{\beta}$, γ, $\mathbf{x}$, 1, z) is connected to the processor P (α, $\mathbf{x}$, γ, $\boldsymbol{\beta}$, n, z) by a symmetric link for all α, γ, z where $1\leq \alpha$, β, γ, x, z $\leq n$. We denote this by $\forall\alpha$, γ, z, P (α, $\boldsymbol{\beta}$, γ, $\mathbf{x}$, 1, z) $\leftrightarrow$ P (α, $\mathbf{x}$, γ, $\boldsymbol{\beta}$, n, z). Such links allow us to interchange only the values of β and x and we will refer to these links using the notation $\forall\alpha$, γ, z ($\boldsymbol{\beta} \leftrightarrow \mathbf{x}$). We note that the value of z is not changed for the processors connected by these links.

Inter-block Rule 2 (Links from x = 1 and x = n planes): The processor, P ($\boldsymbol{\alpha}$, β, γ, 1, y, z) is connected to the processor P ($\mathbf{z}$, β, γ, n, y, $\boldsymbol{\alpha}$) by a symmetric link for all $\forall\beta$, γ, y where $1\leq \alpha$, β, γ, y, z $\leq n$. We denote this by $\forall\beta$, γ, y, P ($\boldsymbol{\alpha}$, β, γ, 1, y, z) $\leftrightarrow$ P ($\mathbf{z}$, β, γ, n, y, $\boldsymbol{\alpha}$). Such links allow us to interchange only the α and z values and we will refer to these links using the notation $\forall\beta$, γ, y ($\boldsymbol{\alpha} \leftrightarrow \mathbf{z}$). We note that the value of y is not changed for the processors connected by these links.

Inter-block Rule 3 (Links from z = 1 and z = n planes): The processor P (α, β, $\boldsymbol{\gamma}$, x, y, 1) is connected to the processor P (α, β, $\mathbf{y}$, x, $\boldsymbol{\gamma}$, n) by a symmetric link for all α, β, x where $1\leq \alpha$, β, γ, x, y $\leq n$. We denote this by $\forall\alpha$, β, x, P (α, β, $\boldsymbol{\gamma}$, x, $\mathbf{y}$, 1) $\leftrightarrow$ P (α, β, $\mathbf{y}$, x, $\boldsymbol{\gamma}$, n). Such links allow us to interchange only the γ and y values and we will refer to these links using the notation $\forall\alpha$, β, x ($\boldsymbol{\gamma} \leftrightarrow \mathbf{y}$). We note that the value of x is not changed for the processors connected by these links.

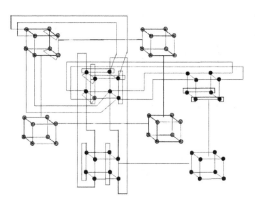

Fig. 3. A 3D MM with $n = 2$

From the above rules, we note the following important fact. Starting from a given 3D block, identified by coordinates ($\alpha1$, $\beta1$, $\gamma1$), we can always find a suitable processor on one of its surfaces, from which we can reach, using only one inter-block link, any other 3D block, identified by ($\alpha2$, $\beta2$, $\gamma2$), provided exactly 2 of the coordinates of ($\alpha1$, $\beta1$, $\gamma1$) are identical to the corresponding coordinates of ($\alpha2$, $\beta2$, $\gamma2$). A 3D MM with $n = 2$ is shown in Figure 3 where all the inter-block links for the processors of block B($\alpha1$, $\beta1$, $\gamma1$) are shown. Using the inter-block connection rules, we get a network where each processor is connected to exactly 6 other processors. The connections are somewhat complicated; to simplify the situation, in Figure 4, we are showing only the blocks having α = 1 and γ = 1 of a 3D MM of order 3. We show only the inter-block connections along the y-axis for the processors having z = 1.

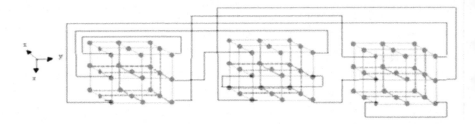

Fig. 4. Interconnections along the y-coordinate for some processors

3 Topological Properties of the 3D MM

The diameter and the connectivity are very important metrics for any interconnection network. An interconnection network with a higher connectivity is preferable since it implies better fault tolerance and higher capability for load balancing.

Theorem 1[2]: The diameter of this network is equal to 3n.

The diameter of the 3D MM is only O($N^{1/6}$) in contrast to O($N^{1/3}$) on a 3-dimensional torus with the same node degree of 6. We note that the Multi-Mesh has a diameter of O($N^{1/4}$) with a node degree of 4 that was shown to be attractive with respect to other topologies [2], [4],[5]. Table 1 shows a comparison between the diameter of a hypercube, Multi-Mesh and 3D MM network for different total number of nodes (N). Thus, for N = 4096, the diameter of both the 3D MM network and the binary hypercube is equal to 12, but the node degree of the corresponding hypercube is 12, while that of the 3D MM network is only 6. In other words, the diameter for networks with 4096 processors is less and the node degree is constant.

Table 1. Diameters of the hypercube, the Multi-Mesh and the 3D MM

# of nodes	Hypercube		Multi-Mesh		3D MM	
	Node degree	Dia-meter	Node degree	Dia-meter	Node degree	Dia-meter
64	6	6	4	6	6	6
4096	12	12	4	16	6	12
256K	18	18	4	44	6	24
16M	24	24	4	126	6	48

Theorem 2: The connectivity of a 3D MM network is 6.

---

[2] Proofs of all theorems are omitted due to lack of space.

4   Message Routing in the 3D Multi-mesh

The routing algorithm determines the path from source S = P(α1, β1, γ1, x1, y1, z1) to destination D = P(α2, β2, γ2, x2, y2, z2), $1 \leq \alpha$1, β1, γ1, x1, y1, z1, α2, β2, γ2, x2, y2, z2 $\leq n$ for point to point communication. The length of the path in the worst possible situation determines the performance of a routing algorithm. The 3D block corresponding to S (D) is B (α1, β1, γ1) (respectively B (α2, β2, γ2)). We will use the term *boundary processor* to denote a processor P (α, β, γ, x, y, z) such that exactly two of the coordinates x, y, z are either 1 or n. We have shown that, for a suitable choice of the exit point from the source block, we can choose a corresponding entry point for the destination block to define a path PT1. Keeping in mind the choices for the entry/exit points for PT1, we chose another set of entry/exit points to define a path PT2 so that one of these paths must be of length less than or equal to $3n$. The idea used in this algorithm is similar to that used in [2]. Due to lack of space, details of the algorithm are omitted.

5   Summation/Average/Minimum/Maximum in the 3D Multi-mesh

We may use the 3D MM to compute the sum of up to n^6 data values stored in the n^6 processors of a 3D MM of order n. The same idea may be used to compute the average, maximum or minimum of up to n^6 data values. The scheme we use is similar to that used in [2] for the multi-mesh. We assume that each processor has three registers X, Y and Z for data communication in the three axes and will use X(α, β, γ, x, y, z) (Y(α, β, γ, x, y, z) and Z(α, β, γ, x, y, z)) to denote the X(respectively Y and Z) register in processor P(α, β, γ, x, y, z). The data is initially in register Z of all n^6 processors in the 3D MM. The main idea of the algorithm, is to i) compute, in parallel, the sum of all numbers in each 3D block, ii) communicate the partial sums to blocks B(α, β, 1), $1 \leq \alpha$, $\beta \leq n$, iii) compute the sum of the partial sum of all numbers in B(α, β, 1), $1 \leq \alpha$, $\beta \leq n$ and communicate the partial sums to blocks B(α, 1, 1), $1 \leq \alpha \leq n$, iv) compute the sum of the partial sum of all numbers in B(α, 1, 1), $1 \leq \gamma \leq n$ and v) communicate the result to block B(1, 1, 1). Details are omitted due to lack of space.

6   Conclusions

In this paper we have presented a new architecture for interconnection networks. We have established that it has attractive diameter and constant node degree. Due to lack of space, we have not presented how the inter-block links may be realized using WDM wavelength routing technology and how such links may use schemes for fault tolerance. We are investigating a number of other algorithms on this architecture and will report our progress in the near future.

References

1. S. G. Akl, "The Design and Analysis of Parallel Algorithms", Prentice-Hall Inc.(1989)
2. D. Das, M. De and B. P. Sinha, "A new network topology with multiple meshes", IEEE Trans. on Comp., 48, (1999) 536-551
3. M. De, D. Das, M. Ghosh and B. P. Sinha, "An efficient sorting algorithm on the Multi-Mesh network," IEEE Trans. on Comp., 46, (1997) 1132-1137
4. K. Hwang and F. A. Briggs,Computer Architecture and Parallel Processing. New York: McGraw-Hill (1989)
5. F. T. Leighton, Introduction to Parallel Algorithms and Architectures. San Mateo, CA: Morgan Kaufmann (1992)
6. A. Sen, S. Bandyopadhyay and B. P. Sinha, " A new architecture and a new metric for lightwave networks," IEEE Journal of Lightwave Technology, 19, (2001) 913-925
7. Q. F. Stout, "Mesh connected computers with broadcasting," IEEE Trans. Computers, 32, (1983) (826-830)
8. S. Rajasekaran, "Randomized Algorithms for packet routing on the Mesh", Advances in Parallel Algorithms, (1992) 227-301

Adaptive Fault Tolerant Routing in Star Graph

Rajib K. Das

Tezpur University, Tezpur - 784028, Assam, India

Abstract. In this paper a fault tolerant routing algorithm on star graph
is proposed. Each node in an n-star is associated with a fault-vector
of $d = \lceil \frac{3(n-1)}{2} \rceil$ bits, which is an approximate measure of the number
and distribution of faults in the neighborhood. The routing algorithm
based on the fault-vector finds the shortest path between any source-
destination pair in presence of large number of faulty nodes or links.
Simulation results show that the % of cases where the algorithm fails to
find a shortest path even when a shortest path exists, is as low as 2.7
with 140 node or link faults in a 7-star.

1 Introduction

In [1] the star graph was proposed as an attractive alternative to the n-cube,
because of its many desirable features like node symmetry, edge symmetry, hierarchical structure, and sub-logarithmic diameter. The properties of star-graph
is well studied in literature, [2], [3].

The inter-processor communication problem in star graph has drawn considerable interest among the researchers [2]. In [2], an easy algorithm for routing for
point to point communication in star graphs has been developed. The diameter
of the n-star graph is also shown to be equal to $\lfloor \frac{3(n-1)}{2} \rfloor$.

A lot of research has been carried out on the fault tolerant properties and
fault tolerant routing on star graphs. In [4], a distributed routing algorithm is
presented. Because the algorithm uses backtracking technique the path length
may be more than the shortest path. In an n-star graph, if the number of faults
is at most $n-2$, the path length is increased by at most $2i+2$, where i is $O(\sqrt{n})$.
Also, an efficient broadcasting algorithm on the faulty star graphs is presented.

In this paper, we have presented a routing algorithm which does not involve
backtracking. The backtracking algorithm incurs some penalty on the length of
the path. Even with the number of faults $\leq n-2$ in an n-star, the penalty can
be as large as 12 in a 10-star.

In [5] a fault tolerant routing algorithm based on node-disjoint paths has
been proposed. There, if the total number of faulty nodes at any given time is
less than $n-1$ in an n-star, the messages are routed on a path of length $d+e$
where d is the minimum distance between the source and destination and e is
0, 2 or 4. We have introduced a concept of fault-vector which is similar to the
safety vector in Hypercube [6]. Like [6] our algorithm does not succeed all the
time but the simulation results show that the probability of failure is very low
even with large number of faults.

A. Sen et al. (Eds.): IWDC 2004, LNCS 3326, pp. 385–390, 2004.
© Springer-Verlag Berlin Heidelberg 2004

The organization of the paper is as follows. Section 2 describes some basic properties of star graph relevant to our routing algorithm. Section 3 introduces the fault vector and presents the fault tolerant routing algorithm. Section 4 presents some experimental results and Section 5 concludes the paper.

2   Preliminaries and Basic Properties

Definition 1. The n-star graph is the Cayley graph on the group G consisting of all permutations on n symbols, and the set of generators g defined as follows. The set g consists of $n-1$ generators $\{g_2, g_3, \cdots, g_n\}$ where g_i switches the ith symbol with the first and leaves the remaining symbols in their original positions.

2.1   Properties of Shortest Path

In this paper we focus on the communication problem which is called unicasting, i.e, sending a message from a particular source to a particular destination. The path from a node s to another node t can be identified as a sequence of generators $g_2, g_3, \ldots g_n$. For example in a 4-star, the path from 1234 to 4321 can be represented by the sequence $g_4 g_2 g_3 g_2$.

Any path from a node u to another node v can be represented by a generator sequence $S = g_{i_1} g_{i_2} \ldots g_{i_m}, g_{i_j} \in \{g_2, g_3, \ldots g_n\}$. In such case we write $S(u) = v$.

Definition 2. Two paths S^1 and S^2 are equivalent if $S^1(u) = S^2(u)$.

The following lemmas are taken from [3] with a little modification.

Lemma 1. Let $S = g_{i_1} g_{i_2} \ldots g_{i_n} g_{i_1}$, where $g_{i_1}, g_{i_2}, \ldots g_{i_n}$ are all distinct. Then S is equivalent to a set of $n-1$ node disjoint paths listed as follows :

$$g_{i_2} g_{i_3} \cdots g_{i_n} g_{i_1} g_{i_2}$$
$$g_{i_3} g_{i_4} \cdots g_{i_1} g_{i_2} g_{i_3}$$

$$\vdots$$

$$g_{i_n} g_{i_1} \cdots g_{i_{n-1}} g_{i_n}$$

Such a path is denoted by $C(g_{i_1} g_{i_2} \ldots g_{i_n})$ and is called a path of type C.

Definition 3. Let $S = g_{i_1} g_{i_2} \ldots g_{i_n}$ where all g_{i_j} are distinct. Such a path is called a path of type O.

Let $X(S)$ denote the set of generators any of which can be the first generator in the shortest path from u to $S(u)$.

Any path between two nodes u and v can be written as $S = A C_1 C_2 \ldots C_k$, where A is a path of type O and C_i, $1 \leq i \leq k$ are paths of type C. Paths of either type can be absent in S.

Lemma 2. [3] If $S = A C_1 C_2 \ldots C_k$ then $X(S) = \cup_{i=1}^{k} X(C_i) \cup X(A)$.

Definition 4. The neighbor of u along generator g_i is denoted by u^i.

Let S give a shortest path from u to $S(u)$ and $g_i \in X(S)$. Then the shortest path from u^i to $S(u)$ is denoted by $S - g_i$.

3   Fault Tolerant Routing

For a node u we define a fault-vector which is similar to the idea of safety vector in Hypercube [6]. The fault-vector for a node u is a d length vector $(u_1, u_2, \ldots u_d)$, where $d = \lfloor \frac{3(n-1)}{2} \rfloor$ for an n-star.

Definition 5. The function $f(k)$, where k is an integer, is defined as follows :

$$f(k) = \begin{cases} \frac{2k}{3}, & \text{if } k \bmod 3 = 0 \\ 2\lfloor \frac{k}{3} \rfloor + 1, & \text{otherwise} \end{cases}$$

The fault-vector is defined recursively as follows : If a node u is faulty then its fault-vector is $(0, 0, \cdots 0)$. If node u is an end node of a faulty link, the other end node will be considered as having a fault-vector of $(0, 0, \cdots 0)$ by node u. For a non-faulty node u,

$$u_1 = \begin{cases} 0, & \text{if } u \text{ is an end-node of a faulty link} \\ 1, & \text{otherwise} \end{cases}$$
for $k = 2, 3 \cdots d$,
$$u_k = \begin{cases} 0, & \text{if } \sum_i u_{k-1}^i < n - f(k) \\ 1, & \text{otherwise} \end{cases}$$

The heuristic for fault tolerant routing (named as FTR) takes help of the fault-vector which is computed at every node after $\lfloor \frac{3(n-1)}{2} \rfloor - 1$ rounds of communication among nodes of the n-star.

Routing Algorithm for the Source Node
Algorithm FTR(u, v, m) /* u: source, v : destination, m : message */
Step 1: Get the generator sequence S such that $S(u) = v$.
    $k \leftarrow |S|$
Step 2: Get $X(S)$
Step 3: If $(|X(S)| = 1)$ /* Unique path */
    Let $X(S) = \{g_i\}$.
    If u^i is fault-free and the link (u, u^i) is fault-free
        send $(m, S - g_i, v)$ to u^i; return;
        else return("no shortest path");
Step 4: If $(|X(S)| > 1)$ /* Not a unique path */
    if there exists $g_i \in X(S)$ such that $u_{k-1}^i = 1$
        send $(m, S - g_i, v)$ to u^i; return;
Step 5: If there exists $g_i \in X(S)$ such that $u_k^i = 1$
        send $(m, S - g_i, v)$ to u^i; return;
Step 6: /* routing using fault vector fails */
    If there exists $g_i \in X(S)$ such that
    u_i is fault-free and the link (u, u^i) is fault-free
        send $(m, S - g_i, v)$ to u^i; return;
    else return("no shortest path found ");

The above algorithm is for routing from the source node. For intermediate nodes the algorithm is almost the same except that intermediate nodes won't have to compute the generator sequence S, as it will receive it along with the message.

4   Experimental Results

We simulated our fault tolerant routing algorithm on 6-star and 7-star (the algorithm is applicable to star-graph of any size though) with number of faults ranging from 10 to 140.

For a fixed number of faults we have taken a random fault distribution and the routing algorithm is applied for different source destination pairs. For a given fault distribution we have taken 100,000 source destination pairs randomly and noted the % of cases where the routing algorithm is able to find the shortest path. We compare this value with the optimum value (% of cases where the shortest path exists). Finally, we found the average value over 25 different fault distributions with same number of node-faults or link-faults. The experimental results are shown in Table 1 to 6. The second column in each table corresponds to the case where shortest paths are found using fault-vector. Percentage of optimal

Table 1. In a 6-star and in an 8-cube, when all faults are node faults

6-star			8 -cube			
#of faults	Fault Vec.	Optimum	# of faults	Safety Vec.	Ext. Safety Vec.	Optimum
10	97.25	98.13	6	99.99	99.99	99.99
20	94.60	96.29	10	99.97	99.97	99.98
30	91.91	94.48	20	99.03	99.03	99.91
40	89.21	92.75	30	90.74	90.74	99.77

Table 2. In a 6-star and in an 8-cube, when half the faults are node faults

6-star			8 -cube			
#of faults	Fault Vec.	Optimum	# of faults	Safety Vec.	Ext. Safety Vec.	Optimum
10	97.96	98.59	6	99.97	99.98	99.99
20	95.88	97.16	10	99.82	99.95	99.98
30	93.66	95.74	20	95.81	99.70	99.93
40	91.49	94.43	30	72.49	98.45	99.85

Table 3. In a 6-star and in an 8-cube, when all faults are link faults

6-star			8 -cube			
#of faults	Fault Vec.	Optimum	# of faults	Safety Vec.	Ext. Safety Vec.	Optimum
10	98.62	99.02	6	99.90	99.96	99.98
20	97.20	98.03	10	99.50	99.91	99.97
30	95.63	97.05	20	88.30	99.70	99.92
40	94.04	96.10	30	52.79	99.35	99.87

Table 4. In a 7-star and in a 10-cube, when all faults are node faults

7-star			10 -cube			
#of faults	Fault Vec.	Optimum	# of faults	Safety Vec.	Ext. Safety Vec.	Optimum
10	99.50	99.69	8	99.99	99.99	99.99
30	98.53	99.07	30	99.98	99.98	99.99
50	97.58	98.46	50	99.55	99.55	99.99
70	96.64	97.85	60	98.22	98.22	99.99
90	95.67	97.23	70	93.83	93.83	99.97
120	94.16	96.33				
140	93.09	95.76				

Table 5. In a 7-star and in a 10-cube, when all the faults are link faults

7-star			10 -cube			
#of faults	Fault Vec.	Optimum	# of faults	Safety Vec.	Ext. Safety Vec.	Optimum
10	99.79	99.87	8	99.99	99.99	99.99
30	99.41	99.61	30	99.62	99.98	99.99
50	99.02	99.36	50	86.01	99.95	99.99
70	98.61	99.10	60	63.41	99.93	99.99
90	98.16	98.86	70	42.67	99.91	99.98
120	97.44	98.48				
140	96.96	98.23				

Table 6. In a 7-star and a 10-cube, when half the faults are link faults

7-star			10-cube			
#of faults	Fault Vec.	Optimum	# of faults	Safety Vec.	Ext. Safety Vec.	Optimum
10	99.65	99.79	8	99.99	99.99	99.99
30	98.97	99.34	30	99.98	99.98	99.99
50	98.29	98.91	50	96.91	99.94	99.99
70	97.60	98.47	60	88.34	99.88	99.99
90	96.87	98.04	70	71.86	99.74	99.98
120	95.72	97.41				
140	94.89	96.99				

outing is also reported (in the third column). In the absence of similar results on star graph we have put for comparison the simulation results in Hypercube using afety vector and extended safety vector [7]. The columns 5,6 and 7 correspond to he success percentages using safety vector, extended safety vector and optimal outing in hypercubes respectively.

From the tables it seems that the performance of routing using safety vector n Hypercube is superior than that of our proposed algorithm in star graph. or example, the success percentage of routing using extended safety vector is 0.74 with 30 node faults in an 8-cube, where as the corresponding value of our roposed algorithm is 89.21 with 40 node faults in a 6-star. But if we look at the differences with the corresponding optimum percentages, the performance of the proposed algorithm in the presence of node faults only is quite acceptable. When half or all the faults are link faults the performance of the routing algorithm in Star is better than that of routing algorithm using safety vector but worse than the routing algorithm using extended safety vector. Even then the difference between the values corresponding to the proposed algorithm and optimum is maximum 3.54 and 2.69 in 6 and 7-star respectively. Also, it should be noted that the percentage of cases where shortest path exists is more than 99 in Hypercube even with large number of faults and the corresponding figures in Star graph are considerably lower.

5   Conclusion

A fault-tolerant algorithm for routing in faulty star graph has been presented in this paper. First, each node computes its fault-vector after $O(n)$ rounds of information exchanges and then the routing algorithm uses these fault-vectors as navigation tool. The algorithm does not involve back-tracking and can tolerate large number of node as well as link faults. Also, the algorithm routes by the shortest path only and as such there are no penalty hops like in [4]. The % of cases where the routing algorithm fails but a shortest path exists are maximum 3.5 in a 6-star with 40 node faults and 2.7 in a 7-star with 140 node faults.

A we can see that moving from safety vector to extended safety vector leads to considerable improvement in performance at the cost of extra computation. Similar improvements can be tried on the fault vector of star graph. This paper concentrates on the shortest path. A natural extension of this work could be to find a sub-optimal path when no shortest path is found by the algorithm FTR.

References

1. Akers, S. B., Harel, D., Krishnamurthy B.: The star graph : An attractive alternative to the n-cube. In: Proc. of Int. Conf. on Parallel Processing. (1987) 393–400
2. Akers, S. B., Krishnamurthy, B.: A group theoretic model for symmetric Interconnection Networks. IEEE Transaction on Computers. **38** (1989) 555–566
3. Misic, J., Jovanovic, Z.: Routing function and deadlock avoidance in a star graph. Journal of Parallel and Distributed Computing. (1994) 216–228
4. Bagherzadeh, N., Nassif, N., Latifi, S.: "A routing and broadcasting scheme on faulty star graphs. IEEE Trans. on Computers, **42** (1993). 1398–1403
5. Day, K., Ayyoub, A. E. A. I.: Reliable Communication in faulty star. In: Proc. of International Parallel and Distributed Processing Symposium. (2002)
6. Wu, J.: Adaptive fault-tolerant routing in cube-based multicomputers using safety vectors. IEEE Transaction on Parallel and Distributed Systems. **9** (1998) 321–334
7. Wu, J., Gao, F., Li, Z., Min, Y.: Optimal and Reliable communication in Hypercubes Using Extended Safety Vectors. IEEE Transactions on Reliability (to appear)

Routing and Wavelength Assignment in Wavelength Division Multiplexing Networks

Ajit Pal and Umesh Patel

Department of Computer Science and Engineering,
IIT Kharagpur, Kharagpur-721 302, India
apal@cse.iitkgp.ernet.in

Abstract. The problem of wavelength routing and assignment (WRA) to ligh-paths in a multi-hop wavelength division multiplexed (WDM) optical network has been addressed in this paper. The wavelength assignment problem has been solved by mapping it to a heuristic based clique partitioning problem. For routing a connection, K-shortest paths are found out and a path having minimum link interference with other paths in the network is assigned. Physical hop (PH) balancing has also been done to balance physical hops and load. The efficacy of the algorithm has been tested on several networks for various lightpath demands through extensive simulation. The wavelength assignment and timing efficiencies are studied and compared with the existing best-known wavelength assignment algorithms. It has been observed that, for a wide range of light-path requests, the proposed algorithm performs favorably when compared with the existing ones.

1 Introduction

The enormous bandwidth of optical fiber medium has the potential to provide the bandwidth requirement of present-day emerging applications. It has also been established that WDM is the most viable technology that overcomes the opto-electronic bandwidth mismatch between the end-users electronic rate and the huge bandwidth of the optical fiber [1]. The WDM technology allows a number of non-overlapping wavelength bands, each providing a separate communication channel, to coexist on a single fiber. A WDM optical fiber network comprises optical wavelength switches/routers interconnected by point-to-point fiber links. End-users may communicate with each other through all-optical (WDM) channels known as *lightpaths*, which may span over more than one fiber links. However, the number of wavelengths available is limited by the technology. This has opened up the classical problem of wavelength routing and assignment (WRA) – *Given a constraint on the number of wavelengths, establish a required set of lightpaths for a given network, set up the routes for these lightpaths and assign wavelengths such that maximum number of lightpaths are established* [3]. The problem of establishing lightpaths, with the objective of minimization of the number of wavelengths needed, minimization of the lighpath blocking probability, for a fixed number of wavelengths, is also known as the lightpath establishment problem (LEP). LEP is of two types - one is static LEP

A. Sen et al. (Eds.): IWDC 2004, LNCS 3326, pp. 391–396, 2004.
© Springer-Verlag Berlin Heidelberg 2004

(SLEP), where a set of lightpaths and their wavelengths are identified in advance and the other one is dynamic LEP (DLEP), where lightpath management is on demand, i.e., they are established and terminated on the fly. SLEP can be formulated as a mixed-integer linear program, which is NP-complete [2], [3]. In order to make the problem more tractable, SLEP is normally partitioned into two sub-problems: routing, and wavelength assignment. Each sub-problem can be solved separately. On the other hand, the dynamic version considers random connection arrival time and departure times and assigns wavelengths on a per-connection basis. Among the various formulations, iterative approach by Zhang and Acompara [2], longest lightpath-first by Chlamtac et al. [6], TILDA (traffic Independent LDA), and RLDA (Random LDA) proposed by Ramaswami and Sivarajan [5], Simulated annealing by Mukherjee [4], and genetic algorithm approach of Saha et. al. [7] are worth mentioning. The focus of the works reported in [2], [4], [5], [6] and [11] is mainly on SLEP, whereas DLEP has been considered in [7], [8], [9] and [10].

Like the previous works, we have also considered RWA as two separate problems in this paper. The wavelength assignment problem is formulated as clique-partitioning problem and used heuristic to partition the graph. For routing, Dijkstra's shortest-path algorithm is used. As wavelength assignment efficiency depends on routing, we have utilized this dependency to avoid likely collision of paths while routing. We obtained K-shortest paths and assigned a path, which has minimum link interference with other paths in the network. We also ensured balance of physical hops and load on a path by PH balancing. We have compared wavelength assignment pattern and blocking probability with that of Zhang and Acompara [2] algorithm, subsequently referred to as Z-A algorithm.

The paper is organized as follows. The wavelength assignment problem modeled as clique partitioning problem is presented in section 2. Routing and wavelength assignment dependency and PH-balancing, which is an improvement of the basic algorithm is discussed in section 3. Section 4 presents simulation results for the parameter called blocking probability. Section 5 concludes the paper.

2 Clique-Partitioning

As we have mentioned above Dijkstra's algorithm is used for the routing connections. So, the shortest path is used to set up a connection from node i to node j, for all node pairs of i, j, ..., N. Once the routes for the connections are fixed, we need to assign wavelength to each of these connections optimally. For this purpose we have modeled it to the clique-partitioning problem. Each connection request from node i to node j has been represented as a node. So, the number of nodes in a graph is equal to number of connection requests. An edge is assigned between two nodes if they do not share a common link between them. This graph is called as *compatibility graph*. For the network topology shown in Fig. 1, the compatibility graph is given in Fig. 2. If two nodes are connected in the compatibility graph, we can assign same wavelength to these two connections, represented by these nodes in the network. In the same manner for three nodes, if all three are connected with each other, same wavelength can be assigned to the links corresponding to these nodes. This is basically a complete graph,

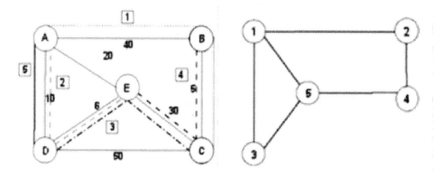

Fig. 1. Physical Topology and Connection Requests

Fig. 2. Compatibility Graph for Physical Topology in Figure 1

where each node is connected to all other nodes. This is known as a *clique* in graph theory. As each clique represents the group of nodes for which same wavelength can be assigned, number of cliques in a graph represents the total number of wavelengths required for the network. So, we would like to partition the graph in such a way that it forms minimum number of cliques. As this is a NP-complete problem, we used heuristic based algorithm to find near optimal solution.

2.1 Clique Partitioning Heuristic

In each iteration of the algorithm, a pair of nodes is picked up from the graph, and they are merged. The merged node is given a priority. A node with highest degree is selected as a first node of the pair, if no node has a priority; otherwise a node with a priority is selected. The degree of a node is indicative of the probability that the node will be in the largest possible clique of the graph. If multiple nodes with the highest degree exist, the node that has maximum sum of its neighbors is selected. Nodes x and y are then merged into z, and z is given a priority. Merging of two nodes x and y is done as follows. A node w is compatible with the merged node z, if w is compatible with both x and y. Once two nodes are merged, the algorithm starts a new iteration. During selection of y, if $|Y| = 0$, i.e. x is not compatible with any node, then it is removed from the graph, and the algorithm enters a new iteration. x represents a clique in the original graph. The algorithm terminates when the graph is left with no node.

2.2 Results

The algorithm has been tested in a simulated environment with the standard network topologies such as 24 node NSFNET using predicted traffic metrics and found that in most of the cases our algorithm performs similar to form a virtual topology. Graph in the Fig. 3 shows the wavelength assignment pattern of our algorithm compared to that of Z-A algorithm for the traffic metrics predicted for the year 2003 [2]. From the graph we can observe that initially our algorithm outperforms the other one, but it gradually ends up with taking the same number of wavelengths as that of Z-A algorithm. Towards the end it can assign wavelength to fewer connections as compared to initial part.

3   Routing and Wavelength Assignment Dependency

Although routing and wavelength assignments are commonly tackled separately, in practice they are interrelated. While working with examples we observed that most of the traffic are distributed around the edges. So, some of the resources are heavily loaded, while most of others remain unutilized. We have tried to add a dynamic parameter, which can take care of the number of wavelengths used on links. Hence, came the idea of *load distribution among the links*. To implement this, we found out K-shortest paths for each connection request. For routing a connection, we assign a path to the connection, which has minimum load out of these K-shortest paths. The maximum load of a link on a path is defined as the load on the path. Load on the link is the number of times it is used in the connections, which is actually the count of number of wavelengths used on this link. After exhaustive simulations on known networks and traffic, and also on known networks and random traffic we found that our algorithm saves 14 -34% wavelengths. The results are also comparable to the recently reported results by Mandal and Saha [11]. Wavelength assignment pattern based on our algorithm is shown in Fig. 4.

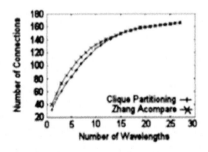

Fig. 3. Wavelengths VS Number of Connections for Clique-Partitioning Algorithm

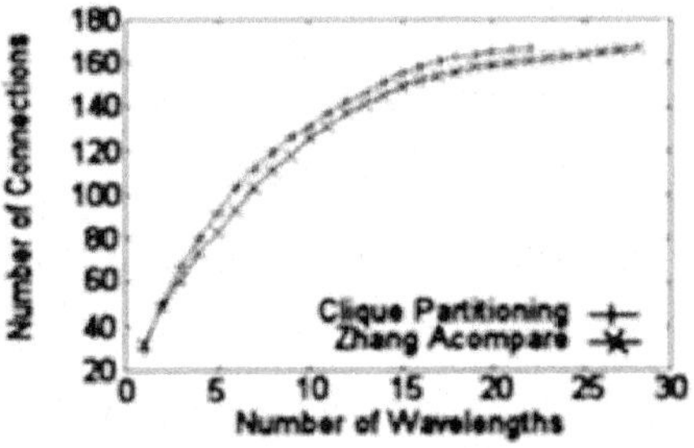

Fig. 4. Wavelengths VS Number of Connections using K-shortest paths

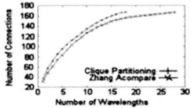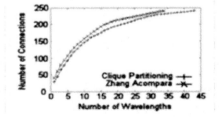

Fig. 5. Wavelengths VS Number of Connections with PH balancing

Fig. 6. Wavelengths VS Number of Connections for Random traffic matrix

3.1 PH Balancing

Due to the use of non-optimal paths for the connections, the number of physical hops is likely to increase. Since it increases equipment cost, we must keep a check on this important parameter. With minor modification in our algorithm we can achieve the *Load-Hop balancing*, which has been referred to as *PH balancing*. First we assign shortest path to as many connections as possible, and if shortest path increases load considerably, non-optimal paths are assigned. We have observed that this leads to a saving of 10-15 physical hops compared to our earlier algorithm. Figure 5 shows the wavelength assignment pattern of this updated algorithm. Simulation results on a large set of data have established that it not only decreases the number of physical hops, but it also saves wavelengths. Since it takes lesser physical hops, the interference of links decreases automatically and that results into saving of wavelengths. This could be the possible explanation of the simulation results.

3.2 Random Traffic Metrics

To compare the performance of our algorithm for a wide range of data set we generated random traffic metrics. We found out that the performance of the algorithm is consistent even for such heterogeneous dense traffic demands. The experimental results with random traffic pattern are shown in Fig. 6.

4 Blocking Probability

Since we used clique partitioning for wavelength assignment, it cannot account for quality factor of traffic, it considers each lightpath equally important. So in order to test the quality of the lightpaths set up by our algorithm, we have used blocking probability as a performance metric. Requests for connection from node i to node j are generated considering the probability of a connection request in traffic demand matrix t_{ij}. Since our algorithm sets up more connections compared to Z-A algorithm with the same number of wavelengths, for a network with enough number of wavelengths it performs better in terms of blocking probability as shown in Fig. 7.

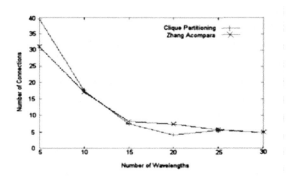

Fig. 7. Wavelengths VS Blocking Probability

5   Conclusion

An efficient algorithm for wavelength assignment in WDM networks has been proposed in this paper. The simulation results are very encouraging in terms of number of wavelengths taken and blocking probability. PH balancing is another important observation for the improvement of our results. By balancing between physical hops on a path and load on the path we ensure that the algorithm do not take more wavelengths by decreasing the actual physical hops taken. It leads not only to decrease in the number of physical hops, but also improves the performance of the algorithm in terms of the number of wavelengths.

References

1. B. Mukherjee: WDM Optical Communication Networks: Progress and Challenges. IEEE Journal of selected areas of communications, Vol. 18. No. 10, (2000) 1810-1824
2. Z. Zhang and A. S. Acampora: A Heuristic Wavelength Assignment Algorithm for Multihop WDM networks with Wavelength Routing and Wavelength Re-Use, IEEE/ACM Transactions on Networking, Vol. 3, No. 3 , (1995) 281-288
3. R.Ramaswami and K.N.Sivarajan: Routing and Wavelength Assignment in All-Optical Networks. IEEE/ACM Transactions on Networking, Vol. 3. No. 5, (1995) 489-500
4. B. Mukherjee, et. al.: Some Principles for Designing a Wide-Area Optical network, IEEE/ACM Trans. Networking, vol.4, No. 5, (1996) 684-695
5. R.Ramaswami and K.N.Sivarajan: Design of Logical Topologies for Wavelength-Routed Optical Networks, IEEE journal of selected areas of communications, Vol. 14. No. 5, (1996) pp. 840-851
6. I.Chlamtac, A.Ganz and G.Karmi: Lightpath Communication: Novel Approach to High Bandwidth Optical WANs, IEEE Transactions on communications, Vol. 40. (1992) 1171-1182
7. D.Saha et. al.: An Approach to Wide Area WDM Optical Network Design using Genetic Algorithm, Computer communication, vol.22, (1999) 156-172
8. G. Sen, S. K. Bose, T. H. Cheng, C.Lu and T.Y. Chai: Efficient Heuristic Algorithms for Light-path Routing and Wavelength Assignmeint in WDM Networks under Dynamically Varying Loads, Elsevier Computer Communications,Vol. 24, (2001) 364- 373
9. Jun Zhou and Xin Yuan: A study of Dynamic Routing and Wavelength Assignment with Imprecise Network State Information, Proceedings of the international conference on parallel processing Workshop, (2002) 207-216
10. Hui Zang, Jason P. Jue, Laxman Sahasrabuddhe, Ramu Ramamurthy and Biswanath Mukherjee: Dynamic Lightpath Establishment in Wavelength-Routed WDM Networks, IEEE Communication Magazine, Vol. 39, No. 9, (2001) 100-108
11. S. Mandal and D. Saha: An Efficient Heuristic Search for Optimal Wavelength Requirement in WDM Optical Networks, Proceedings of the International Conference on High Performance Computing (HiPC), LNCS 2913, Springer-Verlag, (2003) 323-332

Designing the MDVM-Stub and Memory Estimator

Susmit Bagchi and Mads Nygaard

Department of Computer and Information Science,
Norwegian University of Science and Technology,
Trondheim, Norway
susmit@idi.ntnu.no

Abstract. Although the high-end mobile applications, such as virtual organization (VO) and client-server applications of Singapore Software Support (SES), are becoming a reality, however, the general-purpose operating systems are not completely capable to handle the challenges of mobile computing paradigm. One of the main challenges of mobile computing system is the resource constraint of mobile devices. The mobile distributed virtual memory (MDVM) concept intends to overcome the resource constraints of mobile devices. This paper describes the architecture of MDVM-Stub component and a novel algorithm for memory estimation. The experimental results demonstrate that the algorithm utilizes free RAM as MDVM from 90% to 0% based on the instantaneous memory-load and 45% on the average.

1 Introduction

The availability of portable computing devices having access to WWW [9] has created a set of high-end mobile applications such as, m-commerce, SES [6] and virtual organization [7]. The mobile devices are limited in hardware resources [11], battery power and operate in doze mode to reduce power requirement [2][10]. The existing wireless communication technology is restricted in terms of bandwidth and reliability [10]. The existing operating systems offer very little support for managing and adapting to the mobile computation paradigm [1][3]. Researchers have proposed that the mobile applications can be supported utilizing remote server based resources [4][5]. An example is the use of remote memory on servers in mobile computing system [8]. As a novel approach, the concept of mobile distributed virtual memory (MDVM) is introduced to enable mobile clients exploiting server resources using mobile communication network [13]. The MDVM system allows mobile clients to utilize server CPU and memory for data cache and process execution purposes [13]. In this paper, we describe the design model of MDVM system and a novel algorithm for main memory estimation based on logistic equation. The algorithm is implemented in monolithic kernel of Linux 2.4.22. The experimental results demonstrate that the algorithms effectively track the memory-load variation of the system and the instantaneous utilization of free RAM as MDVM varies from 90% to 0% based on the instantaneous memory-load of server. However, on average the utilization is figured at about 45%. The paper is organized as followings. Section 2 describes the concept of MDVM system. Section 3 illustrates the architectural components of MDVM-Stub and the system model. Section 4 describes the memory

A. Sen et al. (Eds.): IWDC 2004, LNCS 3326, pp. 397–411, 2004.
© Springer-Verlag Berlin Heidelberg 2004

estimation function. Section 5 describes the algorithm based on the estimation function. Section 6 describes the implementation and experimental evaluations. Section 7 and 8 state the background work and conclusion respectively.

2 MDVM System Concept

The concept of mobile distributed virtual memory (MDVM) will allow the roaming employee of the virtual organization to utilize the resources of remote servers. The mobile clients can use server memory and CPU resources to achieve the functionalities such as, **memory space for large data cache, virtual memory space** and **CPU for processes execution** [13]. The conceptual view of the MDVM design architecture is illustrated in Figure 1. From the view of mobile client, MDVM is the remote virtual memory space accessible from anywhere in the mobile communication network and such memory can migrate from cell to cell in order to save communication bandwidth, time and cost. The W-CDMA [6] based mobile network can be used to connect to TCP/IP based corporate LAN, web servers and the MDVM servers.

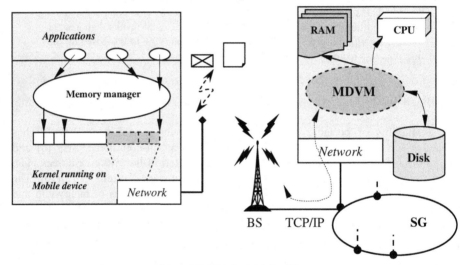

Fig. 1. MDVM for Mobile Clients

3 MDVM Architectural Components

3.1 The MDVM-Stub Component

The MDVM system architecture is comprised of the MDVM-Stub (MC) and MDVM-Server (MS). The jobs performed by MC subsystem include: 1. *Resource estimation and allocation,* 2. *Memory management* and 3. *Command processing and system services.* The components of MC subsystem are illustrated in Figure 2. The data cache allocation for mobile clients is done in the physical memory to improve the performance because the disk access latency is an order higher than the memory access latency. The MC subsystem locks the page frames in RAM while allocating the data cache for mobile clients in order to avoid cache page swap made by virtual memory manager of the kernel. The execution space is resident in the virtual address space of the system and is controlled by the virtual memory manager of the kernel. However, because of the page locking and mobility of the clients, the demand for MDVM in a cell may change in short time leading to the change in memory-pressure on the kernel of MDVM servers in the cell. The MC subsystem uses the resource estimator to estimate the total available memory resource in the system periodically to avoid steep increase of memory-load leading to thrashing. The resource estimator periodically estimates resources with the help of the kernel timer. The job of the command IO processor involves the processing of commands sent by MS subsystem and returning the results or sending commands to MS subsystem. The functions of the memory manager block of MC subsystem are to allocate/de-allocate/lock the page frames and to allow MS subsystem to utilize the allocated page frames for the data cache of mobile clients. The memory manager block uses the memory-load information supplied by resource estimator before performing frame allocation. The allocation/de-allocation of page frames uses the memory interface by the memory manager of MC. The memory manager uses the virtual memory manager of the kernel to manipulate the page frame table. The function of command IO processor is to process the commands sent by MS subsystem and to send a command to MS subsystem. The command-reply communication uses the packet based IO and uses IO interface between MS and MC subsystems. The scheduler and process manager interfaces and the kernel data structures are used by MC subsystem in order to collect process-wise resource consumption data, state of execution and to control the process execution by manipulating the scheduling parameters.

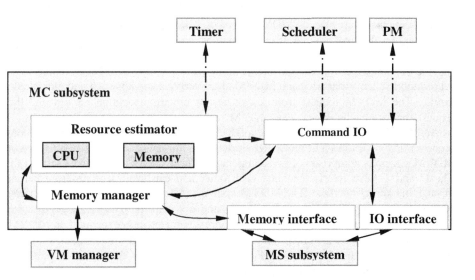

Fig. 2. Internal Components of MC Subsystem

3.2 MDVM System Model

The memory management system of the operating systems can be modelled with abstract and precise formalism in order to represent the design architecture. The abstract modeling of the system architecture and memory management mechanisms allow the generalization of the concept and the easiness of understanding without tying up to a particular kind of implementation. In this section, an abstract model of the MDVM system is formulated. One of the main components of the MDVM system architecture is the server group (SG). Each server in a SG offers a set of pages from its virtual address space to the mobile clients in order to fulfil the storage and execution space needs of the clients. Let, the set of server groups in a MDVM system architecture is represented by S_g such that, $S_g = \{g_1, g_2, ...g_b\}$. There is no constraint on the $|g_i|$ meaning that $\forall g_i, g_j \in S_g$, either $|g_i| = |g_j|$ or $|g_i| \neq |g_j|$. Let z be a MDVM server and $z \in g_j$. Let $V_z = \langle 0, 1, 2, ...,G-1 \rangle$ is the set of virtual addresses available at z. The virtual address spaces can be segmented or paged. The MDVM system design model considers the paged virtual memory management system. A page p_z is consisting of a set of addresses $E_z = \{e_j \mid 0 \leq j < |p_z|\}$ residing at z such that $p_z \subset V_z$. Let n_z represents the total number of virtual memory pages available at z. The page frames of a system are generally numbered and indexed in the page frame table. If all the page frames of z are numbed by f then, $\forall e_j \in E_z, e_j = f. |p_z| + q, 0 \leq q < |p_z|$ and $f = 0, 1, 2, ..., h$. Hence, a page p_z residing at z can be given by the ordered pair $\langle f, q \rangle$. The address map is the function to translate the virtual addresses into the physical memory addresses. Let β_t is such a function translating the memory addresses for the entire time space t. Then, β_t can be computed as, $\beta_t : v_z \rightarrow \langle f, q \rangle \cup \{\phi\}$ where $v_z \subseteq V_z$. The set of page frames residing at z can be given as, $P^z_M = \{p_w \mid 0 \leq w \leq m-1, m>0\}$. According to the definition of the virtual memory, the set of virtual address pages available at z can be computed as, $P^z_V = P^z_M \cup S_z$ and $|P^z_V| = n_z$. The set of pages $S_z = \{d_0, d_1, ...,d_{u-1}\}$ represents the swap space at MDVM server z, where $u = n_z - |P^z_M| + 1$. If the function $r(g_i)$ computes the total amount of virtual memory resource of the server group $g_i \in S_g$ then, $r(g_i) = \cup_{i=1, c} P^i_V$ such that $c = |g_i|$. A MDVM server of a SG residing in a cell is capable to handle multiple mobile clients in the corresponding cell. Let C_z represents a set of mobile clients that are using MDVM at the server z and k is such a mobile client, $k \in C_z$. The MDVM request from k consists of process execution request and the request for data cache pages. The MDVM request from k is composed of $\langle \alpha^r_k, v^c_k \rangle$, where α^r_k is the set of virtual address spaces of the requested execution of the remote process r and v^c_k is the set of requested virtual pages for data cache. The architecture of MDVM system is comprised of two components. These are a stub (D) and a server (T). The D and T have interface among each other and can avail services from kernel through the kernel interface. The MDVM system can be modelled as a list of mapping functions given by $\langle \delta_D, \{\delta^P_T, \delta^C_T\} \rangle$. The δ_D and δ^C_T map the data cache pages for a mobile client and the δ^P_T maps the virtual addresses for process execution on MDVM servers as requested by the client. The definitions of the δ_D and δ^P_T functions are given as, $\delta_D : P^z_V \rightarrow P^z_M$ and $\delta^P_T : P^z_V \rightarrow (\alpha^r_k \times P^z_V) \cup \{\phi\}$ such that, $\beta_t(\alpha \subseteq \alpha^r_k) \in p_z$ and $p_z \in P^z_M$. Let $B \in [0, 1]$ represents the state of the set of cache pages of k maintained at z. The values in B indicate whether the data cache pages are swappable or not. The values in B make it possible to either realize a binary logic or a multi-valued logic to recognize the state of the cache pages. Suppose, the function f^C_T is performed by T for the cache pages such that $f^C_T : v^c_k \rightarrow (\{\delta_D(v^c_k)\} \cup L) \times B$, where $L \subset P^z_M \cup \{\phi\}$. The symbol L signifies a set of page frames that are mapped by D but not used by T. Hence, L can be considered as a list of mapped free page frames. The list is maintained in order to enhance the memory utilization by keeping track of the previously mapped but unused page frames, if any. Suppose, at time instant t, $L \neq \phi$. This indicates that in the next time space t+, the memory map performed by δ_D and the residue in L cannot be overlapped, i.e. $\{\delta_D(v^c_k)\} \cap L = \phi$. Due to the mobility and limitation of battery power of clients or due to the change in the state of the wireless communication, a mobile client may go into doze mode or may get disconnected from the MDVM server z. Let H_z is the set of disk swap spaces at z maintained by T, $H_z \not\subset S_z$. Then, the function f^S_T is defined as, $f^S_T : P^z_M \times B \rightarrow H_z$. Thus, the cache page map of MDVM system, δ^C_T, can be realized as a composition of functions given by $(f^S_T \circ f^C_T)$. In the time space t, the virtual memory v^c_k may reside in page frames or in disk swap space depending on the state of the mobile client.

4 Memory Estimation in MDVM System

4.1 The Memory Estimation Function

The most of the modern operating systems manage main memory in pages where a page size may vary from one operating system to another. The memory allocation and release in operating system is mainly page based at the lower levels. In other view, the entire main memory available in a MDVM server can be considered as a population M indicating the maximum number of available page frames in the server. Let, m_o^t be the page population out of M those are allocated up until any time t. The MDVM requests coming from the mobile clients could be very randomly varying. It would be restrictive if we assume any particular probability density function while estimating the randomness in MDVM requests. On the other hand, the logistic equation could be more appropriate to estimate the page population dynamics periodically in MDVM system. The logistic equation is often used to measure chaos and has wide range of applications in physics, chemistry and economics to measure the dynamics of some chaotic phenomenon. In MDVM system, we do not assume any particular probability density model to estimate the memory utilization and demands from mobile clients. Rather, we employ logistic equation to estimate memory utilization periodically. The logistic equation of page population dynamics can be given by the differential equation $d/dt(m_o^t) = (r/M).m_o^t.(M-m_o^t)$ where r is called the bitonic potential and $r \geq 0$ in usual cases. The discrete from of the aforesaid differential equation can be given by a quadratic recurrence relation as $\omega_o^{t+1} = r.\omega_o^t.(1-\omega_o^t)$ where $\omega_o^t = m_o^t/M$. If m_f^t is the population of free pages at any time t and $\delta^t(\omega_f^t)$ is the memory estimation function for MDVM at any t, then in next instant t+1, $m_f^{t+1} = m_f^t - \delta^t(\omega_f^t)$ where ω_f^t is equal to m_f^t/M. The value of $\delta^t(\omega_f^t)$ can be derived as $M.(1 - \omega_f^t).(r.\omega_f^t - 1)$. The memory estimation function for MDVM system always keeps 10% of the main memory of MDVM servers free for the emergency situation. In any case, for all t, $m_f^t \leq M$. Hence $\omega_f^t \leq 1$ and $\delta^t(\omega_f^t) \geq 0$ for all t. This leads to the characteristic equation of memory estimation function for MDVM given by $(r/M)(m_f^t)^2 - r.m_f^t + 0.9M \geq 0$. Solving this characteristic equation one can get the possible value of $r \geq 3.6$. The resulting quadratic recurrence relation takes the form $\omega_o^{t+1} = 4.\omega_o^t.(1 - \omega_o^t)$ where r is chosen as an integer equal to 4. The graphical representation of the equation of ω_o^{t+1} is shown in Figure 3 where, x_o and x_n are ω_o^t and ω_o^n respectively and $n > t$.

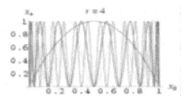

Fig. 3. Characteristics Map of ω_o^{t+1}

Hence, the memory estimation function for MDVM can be presented as $\delta^t(\omega_f^t) =$ M.$(1 - \omega_f^t).(4\omega_f^t - 1)$. It is evident from the equation of $\delta^t(\omega_f^t)$ that $(1 - \omega_f^t)$ is a monotonically decreasing function and $(4\omega_f^t - 1)$ is a monotonically increasing function of ω_f^t for monotonically increasing ω_f^t and vice versa. Hence, the $\delta^t(\omega_f^t)$ can be thought of as a balancing equation.

4.2 The Maxima-Minima of Estimator

In order to find the maxima of the estimator, the following differential equation has to be satisfied $\partial/\partial\omega_f^t (\delta^t(\omega_f^t)) \mid_t = 0$. Solving this equation one can get $\omega_f^t = 0.625$. Hence, the estimator approaches maximum limiting value as free memory ratio approaches 62.5%. However, when $\omega_f^t = 0.25$ the estimator approaches to zero value. This means, the estimator approaches to zero while free memory ratio approaches to 25%. Thus, the estimator is monotonically increasing in the range of free memory ratio of 25% and 62.5%. However, the estimator monotonically decreases for all $\omega_f^t > 0.625$. Hence, the memory estimator algorithm computes the allocable free memory for MDVM as $(1 - \delta^t(\omega_f^t))$ where $0.625 \leq \omega_f^t \leq 0.9$. The final form of the memory estimation function for MDVM, $e(m_f^t)$, can be given as: $e(m_f^t) = \delta^t(\omega_f^t)$, $\omega_f^t < 0.625$ and $e(m_f^t) = (1 - \delta^t(\omega_f^t))$, $0.625 \leq \omega_f^t \leq 0.9$. The characteristics map of $\delta^t(\omega_f^t)$ and $(1 - \delta^t(\omega_f^t))$ is illustrated in Figure 4, where Estimation function 1 represents $\delta^t(\omega_f^t)$ and Estimation function 2 represents $(1 - \delta^t(\omega_f^t))$. The characteristic map of $e(m_f^t)$ is depicted in Figure 5. In Figures 4 and 5, the vertical axis (Memory ratio) signifies the (estimated or free memory/M) values in the range [0,1].

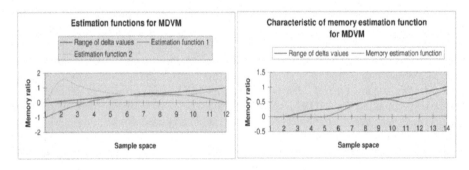

Fig. 4. Characteristics Map of $\delta^t(\omega_f^t),(1-\delta^t(\omega_f^t)),\omega_f^t$ **Fig. 5.** Characteristics Map of $e(m_f^t)$

5   The Estimation Algorithm

The estimation operation involves periodic estimation of the maximum allocable free memory as MDVM to the mobile clients and the estimation algorithm chooses the decision threshold regarding memory management of MDVM system. The MDVM management decision set is consisting of four logic values namely, ALLOCATE, RELEASE, WAIT and WATCH. These logic values control the allocation and estimation in four possible phases based on ω_f^t and ω_d^t, where $\omega_d^t = m_d^t/M$ and m_d^t is the total allocated MDVM amount at time t in a system. The possible range of ω_d^t is [0,1] and this range is divided into three segments such as [0,0.5), [0.5,0.7] and (0.7,1] indicating the low amount of allocated MDVM, the average amount of allocated MDVM and the high amount of allocated MDVM respectively. The ALLOCATE logic value indicates that the memory allocation decision has been made to allocate MDVM to mobile clients. The RELEASE logic indicates that the memory should be released in order to reduce the existing memory load in the system. The WAIT and WATCH logic values indicate that the allocator should temporarily stop allocating or releasing main memory any further. This is the delay period inserted by the memory estimator freezing any memory management actions in order to understand the dynamics of the memory load in the system. The WAIT logic indicates the delay of single time quanta and the WATCH decision logic freezes the operation of memory allocator for an integral multiple of single time quanta. The algorithm always ensures that at least 10% of main memory remains free even after allocation of $\delta^t(\omega_f^t)$ at time t. The pseudo code of memory estimation algorithm is given in Figure 6 in the C language syntax. The *command* variable indicates the memory management decision logic and the *mem_alloc_amount* variable indicates the maximum allocable main memory at any time t as MDVM. The MDVM allocator allocates free RAM of MDVM server to the mobile clients based on pages according to the memory management decision taken by MDVM estimation algorithm.

```
//TIME_OUT=wait time out value of kernel timer scheduling delay;
MDVM_Estimation_Algorithm
(M,ω_d^t,m_f^t,δ^t(ω_f^t),command,wait_time,mem_alloc_amount){
     if(command = = WATCH) wait_time = wait_time -1;
     else if(wait_time = = NULL) {
          switch(δ^t(ω_f^t)) {
          case δ^t(ω_f^t) ≤ NULL:
               if( ω_d^t > 0.7) command = RELEASE;
               else if (ω_d^t < 0.5) {
                    command = WAIT; wait_time = NULL;}
               else if(ω_d^t ≥ 0.5 && ω_d^t ≤ 0.7){
                    command = WATCH; wait_time = TIME_OUT;}
          case δ^t(ω_f^t) > NULL:
                    mem_alloc_amount = M.e(m_f^t);
     if(0.9m_f^t - M.e(m_f^t)< NULL) mem_alloc_amount = 0.9m_f^t;
                         command = ALLOCATE; }
          }
}
```

Fig. 6. Pseudo Code of MDVM Estimation Algorithm

6   Implementation

The memory estimation and allocation algorithms related to MDVM system are implemented in the Linux kernel as a dynamically loadable module. The LOC (lines of source code) is around 500. In the rest of this section, the brief description of the kernel implementation is presented.

6.1   Data Structures and Kernel Interfaces

The implementation of the MDVM estimation algorithm is done in Linux kernel version 2.4.22. The implementation of the algorithm is done as a software device driver dynamically loadable in the kernel as a module. The schematic diagram describing the implementation of the software architecture is given in Figure 7 where MA stands for memory allocator and E stands for memory estimator.

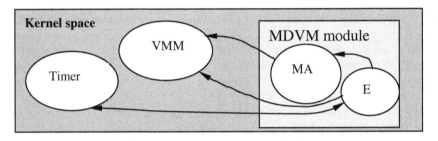

Fig. 7. Schematic Diagram of MDVM Estimator and Allocator in Linux Kernel

The MDVM module maintains a doubly linked circular list (*MDVM_Page_Frame_Desc*) containing the pointers to the kernel data structure (*struct page*) holding the page frame descriptors, the logical address of the page (*logical_address*), the status of the page (*status*), the size of the page frame pool (*size*) and a pointer to the next node of the list. In another structure (*Command*), the MDVM module maintains the total amount of the MDVM allocated (*total_mdvm*), the command proposed by the estimator algorithm (*command*) and the number of page frames (*frame_num*). In addition, the MDVM module constructs another data structure (*Timer_Irq_Pager*), which contains a kernel timer object (*Timer*), a variable indicating the locking mode of the structure (*lock*) to perform concurrent operations on the structure, a *wait_time_out* variable indicating the time out quanta of the timer and a pointer referencing to the command structure. These data structures are presented in Table 1.

Table 1. Data Structures Used in MDVM Module

MDVM_Page_Frame_Desc	Command	Timer_Irq_Pager
struct page *page_frame	CHAR command	struct timer_list Timer
ULONG logical_address	ULONG total_mdvm	INT lock
INT status	ULONG frame_num	UINT wait_time_out
ULONG size		pCommand pCmd
MDVM_Page_Frame_Desc *pNextNode		

The entry point for the kernel to the MDVM module is *MDVM_Entry()* function, which registers the module with the kernel by *register_chrdev()* with a device major number as 250. The device file entry structure, provided by the kernel while module registration, is updated as given in Table 2.

Table 2. The Device File Entry Data Structure of MDVM Module

Device file operations	Descriptions
open: MDVM_open	To open the MDVM module by kernel
read: MDVM_read	To read the MDVM software device
write: MDVM_write	To write to the MDVM software device
release: MDVM_close	To close and unload the MDVM module
mmap: MDVM_VMA_map	To handle the page faults occurred in mapped VMA

Table 3. The Kernel Functions Used by MDVM Module

Kernel functions	Descriptions
si_meminfo()	To get the main memory status of the system
__get_free_pages()	To allocate a set of page frames
virt_to_page()	To claim the page frame reference pointer which is used to lock the page frames in RAM (PG_locked)
free_pages()	To release the page frames to kernel

The main set of internal kernel calls related to the memory management operations used by the MDVM module is given in Table 3.

6.2 Estimator Scheduling and Kernel Timer

MDVM module accomplishes the periodic memory estimation using the timer interrupt vector. MDVM module uses the Linux kernel timer to schedule the execution of the memory estimation algorithm. The *init_timer()* and *add_timer()* kernel functions are used to initialize and schedule the execution of the estimation algorithm, and *mod_timer()* kernel function is used to modify the execution intervals dynamically by controlling the timer activation delay in terms of jiffies. The MDVM module inserts the estimator E in the timer queue only once and later E re-inserts itself in the timer queue for the deferred execution after completing the current execution sequence. The *del_timer()* kernel function is used to release the timer object finally before unloading the MDVM module from the kernel.

6.3 Experimental Environment

The test bed of the experiments conducted consists of a 2.5GHz Pentium IV based single processor PC running Slackware distribution of Linux kernel 2.4.22. The system resources and the peripherals are summarized in Table 4.

Table 4. Experimental Environment Specification

Resources	Descriptions	Resources	Descriptions
RAM, Swap space	452262 Kbytes, 1004052Kbytes	Secondary IDE master, slave	AOPEN DVD RW, CD RW
Primary IDE	WDC- 80GB	On board LAN	100Mbps Ethernet

6.4   Experiment Sets

The entire set of experiments is categorized into four classes as: **Experiment I:** In this set, the MDVM allocation (MA) is not activated and only the memory estimation algorithm (E) executes. The local processing load on the system is nil except the kernel daemons of the Linux 2.4.22. This experiment captures the response of the memory MDVM estimation algorithm E without any interference from the memory usage by local processes on servers and memory usage due to MDVM allocation. Hence, this experiment represents the response of MDVM estimation algorithm in a free running server system; **Experiment II:** In this experiment, the MDVM estimation algorithm executes under a set of local server process load. The set of server processes are given in Table 5. However, there is no MDVM allocation. This experiment illustrates the behaviour of the MDVM estimation algorithm under the memory demands from the local server processes without any allocation of MDVM to mobile clients; **Experiment III:** In this experiment, the MDVM estimator E and the memory allocator MA execute together but there are no local server processes. The aim of this experiment is to capture the response of the MDVM estimation algorithm under the memory load exerted by the MDVM allocation only; **Experiment IV:** This experiment aims at understanding the response of the MDVM estimation algorithm under the combined memory load exerted by the local server processes and by the MDVM allocation. In this experiment, the set of local processes executes on server is same as given in Table 5.

Table 5. Local Process Load on MDVM Server

Local server processes	Description
Real-Time video	This is a multimedia video streaming application
GNU C compiler	This is a C compiler that continuously compiles a set of files
GIMP IPS	This is a image processing application software package
Dictionary Search	This is a dictionary search application
Office Editor	This is an Editor application software package
Application Benchmark	Randomly allocate and release the memory chunks periodically

6.5   Implementation Results

For the set of four experiment classes, the time interval period for the execution of MDVM estimation algorithm is chosen moderately as 30sec in order to avoid too frequent as well as too delayed period of estimation. The delay period of execution due to WATCH logic employs 150sec delay. The measurements are taken in terms of instantaneous free main memory in the server, allocated MDVM to mobile clients, estimated MDVM upper limit of allocation in intervals and the dynamics of command phases created by MDVM estimator E while making the memory management decisions. The graphical representations of the free main memory dynamics, estimations made by MDVM estimation algorithm E, % utilization of free main memory as MDVM and the memory management decision phases governed by MDVM estimation algorithm are presented in Figures 8 to 20. The % utilization of MDVM is calculated as $100(m_d^t / m_f^t)$, where m_d^t is the estimated MDVM at time t. In the waveform representation of the response of MDVM estimation algorithm, the decision threshold logic level 1 on the vertical axis represents ALLOCATE decision, logic level 0.5 on the vertical axis represents WATCH command, logic level 0 on the vertical axis represents WAIT command and logic level -1 on the vertical axis represents RELEASE command. The average values of the % utilization of main memory as MDVM are presented in Table 6.

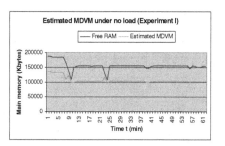

Fig. 8. MDVM Estimation in Exp. I

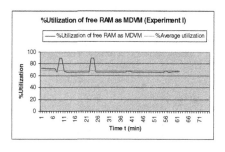

Fig. 9. %Utilization in Exp. I

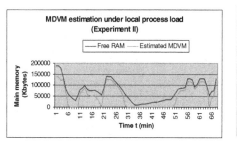

Fig. 10. MDVM Estimation in Exp. II

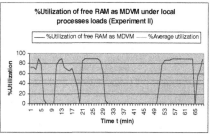

Fig. 11. %Utilization in Exp. II

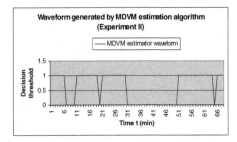

Fig. 12. Response Waveform in Exp. II

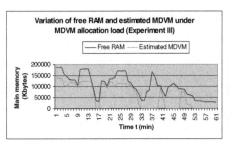

Fig. 13. MDVM Estimation in Exp. III

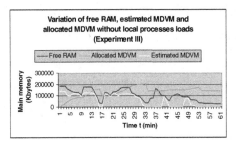

Fig. 14. MDVM Variation in Exp. III

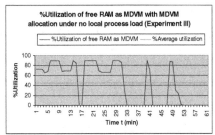

Fig. 15. %Utilization in Exp. III

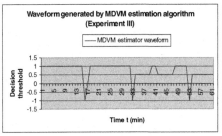

Fig. 16. Response Waveform in Exp. III

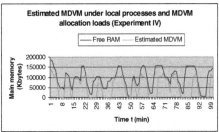

Fig. 17. MDVM Estimation in Exp. IV

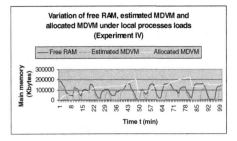

Fig. 18. MDVM Variation in Exp. IV

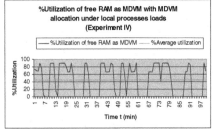

Fig. 19. %Utilization in Exp. IV

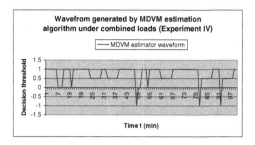

Fig. 20. Response Waveform in Exp. IV

Table 6. The %Average Utilization of Free RAM as MDVM

Experiment	%Average utilization	Experiment	%Average utilization
I	68.43%	II	46.77%
III	44.68%	IV	45.08%

The instantaneous utilization of main memory as MDVM can very from 90% to 0% depending on the instantaneous memory-load of the MDVM server. It is evident from Table 6 that the MDVM estimation algorithm is less sensitive to the abrupt variation of free memory over a period of time, and averages the overall utilization to 45% approximately. Hence, the MDVM estimation algorithm may not produce jitters in the response due to abrupt variation of memory load. However, as the graphical presentations illustrates, the algorithm is capable to closely follow the dynamic variation of the memory load on the system and act appropriately.

7 Related Work

Prior works have addressed the issues in operating system related to mobility in the area of file systems [16][17][18], data management [19][11][20][21] and network-layer routing protocols addressing schemes and packet filtering [22][23][24]. Other works include issues related to caching and file system [16][18][25][26] and mobile communication system [27][28][29]. The DVM system becomes non-scalable under the condition of mobility of clients [30][31]. The DVM system assumes that network bandwidth is high and network topology is static. The bandwidth of existing disk drives is lower than that of high-speed network [14]. The aim of existing DVM system is to investigate the performance gain through remote paging over high-speed network. The majority of the remote memory paging system and the DVM system ([30][31]) target to the stationary client-server architectures on wired LAN. However, the issues related to the location transparency of the remote memory under mobility, virtual memory management under dynamic memory-pressure and virtual memory migration among servers are not investigated.

8 Conclusion

The concept of MDVM is developed to support the high-end mobile applications in virtual organization architecture. This paper describes the design and implementation of MDVM-Stub component, MDVM system model and a novel memory estimation algorithm to realize MDVM system. The monolithic kernel architecture of Linux is chosen for experimental prototype design and implementation of the MDVM system. The designing of MDVM in monolithic kernel will provide user transparency, performance, greater control on system resources and required system services. The experimental evaluations of memory estimation and allocation algorithms demonstrate that the instantaneous utilization of main memory as MDVM may vary from 90% to 0% based on instantaneous memory-load of the MDVM server. However, the overall utilization of free RAM as MDVM is approximately 45% on average. In addition, the algorithms are efficient to keep track of the memory-load dynamics of the MDVM servers. The MDVM estimation algorithm always keeps 10% of instantaneous free RAM untouched and stops MDVM allocation when the free memory goes below 25% of total RAM.

References

[1] Black A., Inouye J., System Support for Mobility, ACM SIGOPS, Ireland, 1996.
[2] Duchamp D., Issues in Wireless Mobile Computing, 3rd Workshop on Workstation OS, 1992.
[3] Bolosky W. et. al., OS Direction for the Next Millennium, Microsoft Research, Redmond.
[4] Forman G., Zahorjan J., The Challenges of Mobile Computing, UW CSE TR#93-11-03, 1994.
[5] Marsh B. et. al., Systems Issues in Mobile Computing, MITL-TR-50-93, Princeton, 1993.
[6] Nadia M., Kin Y., Designing Wireless Enterprise Applications on Mobile Devices, ICITA 2002.
[7] MOWAHS, IDI, NTNU, 2003, www.mowahs.com.
[8] Shigemori Y. et. al., A proposal of a Memory Management Architecture for Mobile Computing Environment, IEEE DEXA, 2000.
[9] Weiser M., Some Computer Issues in Ubiquitous Computing, ACM Communications, 1993.
[10] Pitoura E. et. al., Dealing with Mobility: Issues and Research Challenges, TR-CSD-93-070, 1993.
[11] Badrinath R. et. al., Impact of Mobility on Distributed Computations, ACM OS Review, 1993.
[12] Bender M. et. al., Unix for Nomads: Making Unix Support Mobile Computing, USENIX, Mobile & Location-Independent Computing Symposium, 1993.
[13] Susmit B., Mads N., On the Concept of Mobile Distributed Virtual Memory System, IEEE DSN, International Conference on Dependable Systems and Networks, Italy, 2004.
[14] Schilit B., Duchamp D., Adaptive Remote Paging for Mobile Computers, TR-CUCS-004-91, Columbia University, February 1991.
[15] Chen B., The Impact of Software Structure and Policy on CPU and Memory System Performance, PhD Thesis, CMU-CS-94-145, 1994.

[16] Tait D. et. al., Detection and Exploitation of File Working Sets, TR-CUCS-050-90, Columbia, 1990.

[17] Kistler J., Satyanarayanan M., Disconnected Operation in the Coda File System, ACM Transactions on Computer Systems, February, 1992.

[18] Tait D., Duchamp D., Service Interface and Replica Management Algorithm for Mobile File System Clients, 1st International Conference on Parallel and Distributed Information Systems, 1991.

[19] Badrinath R., Tomasz I., Replication and Mobility, In Proc. Of 2nd IEEE Workshop on Management of Replicated Data, November 1992, pp. 9-12.

[20] Alonso R., Korth H., Database System Issues in Nomadic Computing, MITL, December 1992.

[21] Tomasz I., Badrinath R., Querying in Highly Mobile Distributed Environments, In 8th International Conference on Very Large Databases, 1992, pp. 41-52.

[22] Ioannidis J., Duchamp D., Maguire G., IP-Based Protocols for Mobile Internetworking, ACM SIGCOMM, September 1991, pp. 235-245.

[23] Wada H. et. al., Mobile Computing Environment Based on Internet Packet Forwarding, In Winter USENIX, January, 1993.

[24] Zenel B., Duchamp D., Intelligent Communication Filtering for Limited Bandwidth Environments, IEEE 5th Workshop on HotOS-V, May 1995.

[25] Mummert L. et. al., Variable Granularity Cache Coherence, Operating Systems Review, 28(1), 1994, pp. 55-60.

[26] Mummert L., Exploiting Weak Connectivity in a Distributed File System, PhD Thesis, CMU, 1996.

[27] Lin C., An Architecture for a Campus-Sized Wireless Mobile Network, PhD Thesis, Purdue, 1996.

[28] Lee J., Routing and Multicasting Strategies in Wireless Mobile Ad Hoc Network, PhD thesis, California, 2000.

[29] Akyol B., An Architecture for a Future Wireless ATM Network, PhD Thesis, Stanford, June 1997.

[30] Khalidi Y. et. al., The Spring Virtual Memory System, Sun Microsystem Lab., TR-SMLI-93-9, February 1993.

[31] Ballesteros F. et. al., Adaptable and Extensible Distributed Virtual Memory in the Off Microkernel, TR-UC3M-CS-1997-02, Madrid, January 1997.

Improved Algorithm for Minimum Cost Range Assignment Problem for Linear Radio Networks

Gautam K. Das, Sasthi C. Ghosh, and Subhas C. Nandy

Indian Statistical Institute, Kolkata - 700 108, India

Abstract. The unbounded version of the 1D range assignment problem for radio-stations is studied. Here a set of n radio stations are placed arbitrarily on a line. The objective is to assign ranges to these radio-stations such that the total power consumption is minimum. A simple incremental algorithm is proposed which produces optimum solution in $O(n^3)$ time and $O(n^2)$ space. This improves the running time of the best known existing algorithm by a factor of n.

1 Introduction

A multihop mobile radio network, is a self-organized and rapidly deployable network in which neither a wired backbone nor a centralized control exists. The network nodes communicate with one another over scarce wireless channels in a multi-hop fashion. Its importance has been increased due to the fact that, there exists situations where the installation of traditional wired network is impossible, and in some cases, even if it is possible, it involves very high cost in comparison to radio-networks. Several variations of routing, broadcasting and scheduling problems on radio-networks are discussed in [2, 4, 6, 11, 12].

A radio-network is a finite set of *radio-stations* S located on a geographical region which can communicate each other by transmitting and receiving radio signals. Each radio-station $s \in S$ is assigned a range $\rho(s)$ (a positive real number). A radio-station s can communicate (i.e., send a message) directly (i.e., in *1-hop*) to any other station t, if the Euclidean distance between s and t is less than or equal to $\rho(s)$. If s can not communicate directly with t due to its assigned range, then communication between them can be achieved using *multi-hop transmissions*. If the number of hops (h) is small, then communication between a pair of radio-stations happens very quickly, but the power consumption of the entire radio-network becomes high. On the other hand, if h is large, the power consumption decreases, but communication delay takes place. The power $power(s)$ required by a radio station s to tramsmit a message to another radio-station s' satisfies $\frac{power(s)}{d(s,s')^\beta} > \gamma$ [11], where $d(s, s')$ is the Euclidean distance between s and s', β is referred to as the distance-power gradient which may vary from 1 to 6 depending on various environmental factors, and $\gamma(\geq 1)$ is the transmission quality of the message. We assume the ideal case, i.e., $\beta = 2$ and $\gamma = 1$. The total cost of a range assignment $\mathcal{R} = \{\rho(s) \mid s \in S\}$ is written

A. Sen et al. (Eds.): IWDC 2004, LNCS 3326, pp. 412–423, 2004.
© Springer-Verlag Berlin Heidelberg 2004

as $cost(\mathcal{R}) = \sum_{s \in S} power(s) = \sum_{s \in S}(\rho(s))^2$. The tradeoffs between the power consumption of the radio-network and the maximum number of hops needed between a communicating pair of radio-stations are studied extensively in [9, 10]. In 1D variation of this problem, the set S of n radio stations are placed arbitrarily on a line. Several variations of *1D h-hop range assignment problem* are studied in [9]. For the uniform chain case, i.e., where each pair of consecutive points on the line is at distance δ, the tight upper bounds in the minimum cost of range assignment is shown to be $OPT_h = \Theta(\delta^2 n^{\frac{2^{h+1}-1}{2^h-1}})$ for any fixed h. In particular, if $h = \Omega(\log n)$ in the uniform chain case, then $OPT_h = \Theta(\delta^2 \frac{n^2}{h})$. For the general problem in 1D, i.e., where the points are arbitrarily placed on a line, a 2-approximation algorithm is proposed in [3] for h-hop range assignment. The worst case running time of this algorithm is $O(hn^3)$. For the unbounded case, i.e., where $h = n - 1$, a dynamic programming based $O(n^4)$ time algorithm is given in [9] which produces a range assignment achieving minimum cost. Efficient polynomial time algorithm for the optimal 1D range assignment for broadcasting from a single node is available in [5].

We propose a simple algorithm for the unbounded version of 1D range assignment problem. It runs in $O(n^3)$ time and $O(n^2)$ space. This improves the existing time complexity result on this problem by a factor of n keeping the space complexity invariant [9]. In spite of the fact that the model considered in this paper is very simple, it is useful in studying road traffic information system where the vehicles follow roads and messages are to be broadcasted along lanes. Typically, the curvature of the road is small in comparison to the transmission range so that one may consider that the vehicles are moving on a line [3]. Several other vehicular technology applications of this problem can be found in [1, 7, 8, 10].

2 Preliminaries

Let $S = \{s_1, s_2, \ldots, s_n\}$ be a set of n radio-stations placed on a line. Without loss of generality, we name the elements of S as $\{s_1, s_2, \ldots, s_n\}$, ordered from left to right.

Definition 1. *A range assignment for the set of radio-stations S is a vector $\mathcal{R} = \{\rho(s_1), \rho(s_2), \ldots, \rho(s_n)\}$, where $\rho(s_i)$ denotes the range assigned to radio-station $s_i \in S$.*

Definition 2. *Given a range assignment $\mathcal{R}$, the corresponding communication graph, denoted by $G_{\mathcal{R}} = (S, E_{\mathcal{R}})$ is a directed graph whose set of vertices correspond to the radio-stations in S, and the edge set $E_{\mathcal{R}} = \{(s_i, s_j) | d(s_i, s_j) \leq \rho(s_i)\}$.*

Definition 3. *A communication graph $G_{\mathcal{R}}$ corresponding to a range assignment $\mathcal{R}$ is said to be h-hop connected if from each vertex $s_i \in S$ there exists a directed path of length less than or equal to h to every other vertex $s_j \in S$.*

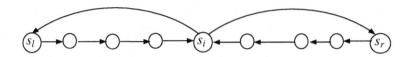

Fig. 1. Proof of Lemma 2

For each radio-station s_i, we maintain an array D_i which contains the set of distances $\{d(s_i, s_j), j = 1, \ldots, n, j \neq i\}$. Now we have the following lemma.

Lemma 1. *For any given* h, *if* $\mathcal{R} = \{\rho_1, \rho_2, \ldots, \rho_n\}$ *denotes the optimum range assignment of* $\{s_1, s_2, \ldots, s_n\}$ *then* $\rho_i \in D_i$ *for all* $i = 1, 2, \ldots, n$.

Proof. Let us assume that $\rho_i = r$ for some i, and $r \notin D_i$. Let $G_{\mathcal{R}}$ be the corresponding communication graph. Surely, $Min\{D_i\} \leq r \leq Max\{D_i\}$, since failing the left-hand terminal condition disables s_i to transmit its message to any member in $S \setminus \{s_i\}$, and the right-hand terminal condition ensures the 1-hop reachability of s_i to all other vertices in S. Assume that the elements in D_i are sorted in increasing order, and there exist a pair of consecutive elements $\alpha, \beta \in D_i$ such that $\alpha < r < \beta$.

Consider a different range assignment $\mathcal{R}' = \{\rho_1, \rho_2, \ldots, \rho_{i-1}, \alpha, \rho_{i+1}, \ldots, \rho_n\}$, and its corresponding communication graph $G_{\mathcal{R}'}$. It is easy to observe that $G_{\mathcal{R}} \equiv G_{\mathcal{R}'}$. Thus, the *h-hop* connectivity of each vertex in S to all other vertices is maintained for the range assignment $\mathcal{R}'$. Again, $cost(\mathcal{R}') = cost(\mathcal{R}) - r^2 + \alpha^2 < cost(\mathcal{R})$. Hence we have the contradiction that $\mathcal{R}$ is the optimum range assignment. $\square$

Note: The result stated in Lemma 1 is valid if the range assignment problem is considered in any arbitrary dimension.

From now onwards, we shall restrict ourselves to the unbounded version of the problem, i.e., $h = n - 1$. Here the optimal solution corresponds to a range assignment such that the communication graph $G_{\mathcal{R}}$ is strongly connected, and the sum of powers of all the stations is minimum. The following two lemmata indicates two important features of the optimum range assignment.

Lemma 2. *Let* ρ *be the range assigned to a vertex* s_i; s_r *and* s_ℓ *be respectively the rightmost and leftmost radio-stations such that* $d(s_i, s_r) \leq \rho$ *and* $d(s_i, s_\ell) \leq \rho$. *Now, if we consider the optimum range assignment of the radio stations* $\{s_\ell, s_{\ell+1}, \ldots, s_i, \ldots, s_{r-1}, s_r\}$ *only subject to the condition that* $\rho(s_i) = \rho$, *then*

- *the range assigned to the radio-station* $s_\alpha = d(s_\alpha, s_{\alpha+1})$ *for all* $\alpha = \ell, \ell + 1, \ldots, i - 1$, *and*
- *the range assigned to the radio-station* $s_\beta = d(s_\beta, s_{\beta-1})$ *for all* $\beta = i+1, i+2, \ldots, r$.

Proof. See Fig. 1. $\square$

Lemma 3. *In optimum range assignment* $\mathcal{R} = \{\rho_1, \rho_2, \ldots, \rho_n\}$, $\rho_1 = d(s_1, s_2)$ *and* $\rho_n = d(s_{n-1}, s_n)$.

Proof. On the contrary, let us assume that $\rho_1 = d(s_1, s_i)$, where $i > 2$. We now need to consider two cases: (i) $\rho_i < d(s_1, s_i)$, and (ii) $\rho_i \geq d(s_1, s_i)$. In Case (i), let us consider a modified assignment $\mathcal{R}'$ with $\rho'_i = d(s_1, s_i) = \rho_1$ and $\rho'_j = d(s_j, s_{j+1})$ for $j = 1, 2, \ldots, i - 1$. Note that, the communication graph of the modified range assignment $\mathcal{R}'$ is still strongly connected, and $cost(\mathcal{R}') \leq cost(\mathcal{R})$. The equality takes place if $d(s_i, s_{i-1}) > d(s_i, s_{i+1})$. In Case (ii), there is no need to assign $\rho_1 = d(s_1, s_i)$. Only the assignment of $\rho_j = d(s_j, s_{j+1})$ for all $j = 1, 2, \ldots, i - 1$ will make the communication graph strongly connected. The second part of the lemma can be proved in exactly similar manner.   □

Our proposed algorithm is an incremental one. We denote the optimal range assignment of a subset $S_k = \{s_1, s_2, \ldots, s_k\}$ by $\mathcal{R}_k = \{\rho_1^k, \rho_2^k, \ldots, \rho_k^k\}$. Here the problem is: given $\mathcal{R}_j$ for all $j = 2, 3, \ldots, k$, obtain $\mathcal{R}_{k+1}$ by considering the next radio station $s_{k+1} \in S$. An almost similar dynamic programming approach is used in [9] for solving the same problem in $O(n^4)$ time. Our approach is based on a detailed geometric analysis of the optimum solution, and it solves the problem in $O(n^3)$ time.

3   Method

We assume that for each $j = 2, 3, \ldots, k$, the optimal range assignment of $S_j = \{s_1, s_2, \ldots, s_j\}$ is stored in an array $\mathcal{R}_j$. The elements in $\mathcal{R}_j$ correspond to $\{\rho_1^j, \rho_2^j, \ldots, \rho_j^j\}$, and $cost(\mathcal{R}_j) = \sum_{\alpha=1}^{j}(\rho_\alpha^j)^2$. The radio-station s_{k+1} is the next element under consideration. An obvious choice of $\mathcal{R}_{k+1}$ for making the communication graph $G_{\mathcal{R}_{k+1}}$ strongly connected is $\rho_{k+1}^{k+1} = d(s_k, s_{k+1})$ and $\rho_k^{k+1} = max(d(s_k, s_{k+1}), \rho_k^k)$. Lemma 4 says that this may not lead to an optimum result.

Lemma 4. $cost(\mathcal{R}_k)+(d(s_k, s_{k+1}))^2 \leq cost(\mathcal{R}_{k+1}) \leq cost(\mathcal{R}_k)+(d(s_k, s_{k+1}))^2+ (max(d(s_k, s_{k+1}), \rho_k^k))^2$.

Proof. In $\mathcal{R}_{k+1}$, s_{k+1} will receive range equal to $d(s_k, s_{k+1})$ for connecting it with its closest member in S_k(see Lemma 3). Thus, the left hand side of the inequality follows. The equality takes place when s_{k+1} is reachable from some member in S_k with its existing range assignment in $\mathcal{R}_k$.

If the above situation does not take place, then one needs to extend the range of some member in S_k to reach s_{k+1}. The right hand side inequality follows from the obvious choice s_k for which the range is to be extended to $d(s_k, s_{k+1})$.   □

Illustrative examples are demonstrated in Fig. 2, where the distance between each two consecutive nodes is shown along that edge; the range assigned for each node before and after inserting radio-station s_5 are shown in paranthesis and square bracket respectively. From the lefthand inequality of Lemma 4, the range of s_{k+1} (i.e., ρ_{k+1}^{k+1}) needs to be assigned to $d(s_k, s_{k+1})$ (see the range assigned to s_5 in both the figures). Now we analyze the different cases that may

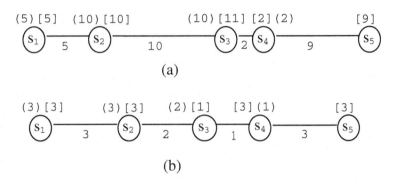

Fig. 2. Proof of Lemma 4

be observed in $\mathcal{R}_k$, and the actions necessary for all those cases such that at least one member of S_k can communicate with s_{k+1} in 1-hop, and the total cost becomes minimum.

The simplest situation occurs if $d(s_i, s_{k+1}) \leq \rho_i^k$ for at least one $i = 1, 2, \ldots, k$. In this case, $\rho_i^{k+1} = \rho_i^k$ for all $i = 1, \ldots, k$. If $d(s_i, s_{k+1}) > \rho_i^k$ for all $i = 1, \ldots, k$, then we need to increase the range of some member in S_k for the communication from S_k to s_{k+1}. This may sometime need changes in different elements of $\mathcal{R}_k$ to achieve $\mathcal{R}_{k+1}$. We have demonstrated two examples in Fig. 2, where the optimal range assignment of $\{s_1, s_2, s_3, s_4, s_5\}$ is obtained from that of $\{s_1, s_2, s_3, s_4\}$. In Fig. 2(a) the optimal range assignment is obtained by incrementing the range of s_3 only. But in Fig. 2(b), in addition to incrementing the range of s_4, the range of s_3 is needed to be decremented to get the optimal assignment.

We use $\mathcal{R}_{k+1}^i$ to denote the optimum range assignment of the members in S_{k+1} subject to the condition that $\rho_i^{k+1} = d(s_i, s_{k+1})$. Now, $\mathcal{R}_{k+1}$ can be obtained by identifying an i^* such that $cost(\mathcal{R}_{k+1}^{i^*}) = Min_{s_i \in S_k} cost(\mathcal{R}_{k+1}^i)$. Thus, while computing $\mathcal{R}_{k+1}$, we need to compute $\mathcal{R}_{k+1}^i$, for all $i = 1, 2, \ldots, k$.

3.1   Computation of R_{k+1}^i

As mentioned above, $\mathcal{R}_{k+1}^i = \{\rho_1, \rho_2, \ldots, \rho_{k+1} | \rho_i = d(s_i, s_{k+1})\}$. Let s_ℓ be the leftmost radio-station such that $d(s_i, s_\ell) \leq \rho_i$. This implies, s_i can communicate with all the radio-stations $\{s_\ell, s_{\ell+1}, \ldots, s_{i-1}, s_i, s_{i+1}, \ldots, s_{k+1}\} = SS^i$ (say) in 1-hop. We need to recall that $S_{k+1} = S_{\ell-1} \bigcup SS^i$. Let $SS^i = SS_L^i \cup SS_R^i$, where $SS_L^i = \{s_\ell, s_{\ell+1}, \ldots, s_{i-1}, s_i\}$, and $SS_R^i = \{s_{i+1}, s_{i+2}, \ldots, s_{k+1}\}$. We define the term *left-cover* of s_i to denote the node s_ℓ. In other words, in the revised assignment of s_i, s_ℓ (to the left of s_i) can be communicated from s_i in 1-hop but no member in $S_{\ell-1}$ can be communicated from s_i in 1-hop.

By applying Lemma 2, we assign $\rho_\alpha = d(s_\alpha, s_{\alpha-1})$ for all $s_\alpha \in SS_R^i$, and $\rho_\beta = d(s_\beta, s_{\beta+1})$ for all $s_\beta \in SS_L^i \setminus \{s_i\}$. Due to this *changed range assignment*, none of the nodes SS_R^i can communicate with a node to the left of s_i in 1-hop, but there may exist some member(s) in the set SS_L^i whose *left-cover* is in $S_{\ell-1}$. Let s_m be the node of minimum index such that $s_m = left\text{-}cover(s_j)$ for some

$s_j \in SS^i_L$. We now need to consider the following three cases depending on whether (i) $m < \ell$, (ii) $m = \ell = 1$, and (iii) $m = \ell \neq 1$.

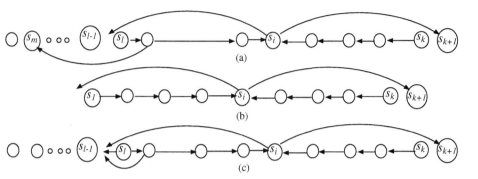

Fig. 3. Illustration of (a) Case (i), (b) Case (ii), and (c) Case (iii)

Case (i) $[m < \ell]$: Here we keep the range assignment of SS^i unchanged (with respect to new assignment). Using the same argument as stated in Lemma 2, we update the range of the radio-station s_γ to $\rho_\gamma = d(s_\gamma, s_{\gamma+1})$ for all $\gamma = m, m + 1, \ldots, \ell - 1$ (see Fig. 3(a)). Thus, the strong connectivity is maintained in the communication subgraph with radio-stations $\{s_m, s_{m+1}, \ldots, s_{\ell-1}, s_\ell, \ldots, s_i, \ldots, s_{k+1}\}$ since a member in SS^i_L communicates with s_m and $s_{\ell-1}$ communicates with s_ℓ. This new assignment of range may cause some one to the left of s_m to be reachable in 1-hop from $\{s_m, s_{m+1}, \ldots, s_{\ell-1}\}$. From now onwards, the left-most such node (if exists) will be considered as *left-cover* of s_i, and the set SS^i_L is updated as $SS^i_L \cup \{s_m, s_{m+1}, \ldots, s_{\ell-1}\}$. This indicates that SS^i is also updated accordingly, and m is considered to be as ℓ. Again, we need to consider one among the cases (i)-(iii). Note that, while calculating the *left-cover* of the updated set of nodes SS^i_L, we need to consider only the newly added nodes in SS^i_L.

Case (ii) $[m = \ell = 1]$: Here, the range assigned to all the nodes in S_{k+1} are done optimally, subject to $\rho_i = d(s_i, s_{k+1})$. Thus, this assignment corresponds to $\mathcal{R}^i_{k+1}$ (see Fig. 3(b)).

Case (iii) $[m = \ell \neq 1]$: Here several nodes in SS^i_L exist whose assigned range enables it to communicate with s_m in 1-hop but not with s_{m-1}. Thus, Case (i) fails to recur but the Case (ii) has not been satisfied (see Fig. 3(c)). At this stage, we have an important Observation.

Observation 1. *If Case (iii) happens while computing $\mathcal{R}^i_{k+1}$ then assuming $\rho(s_i) = d(s_i, s_{k+1})$, the optimum range assignment for $S_{k+1} \setminus S_{m-1} = \{s_m, s_{m+1}, \ldots, s_i, \ldots, s_k, s_{k+1}\}$ is as follows:*

- $\rho(s_i) = d(s_i, s_{k+1})$ *(as assumed)*,
- $\rho(s_j) = d(s_{j-1}, s_j)$ *for all $j = i+1, i+2, \ldots, k+1$, and*

- $\rho(s_j) = d(s_j, s_{j+1})$ *for all* $j = m, m+1, \ldots i-1$.

This leads to define a new notion, called *covering index*, as stated below.

Definition 4. *The covering index m in $\mathcal{R}^i_{k+1}$, corresponds to a node s_m (to the left of s_i including itself) such that in the optimum range assignment of the set of radio-stations $\{s_m, s_{m+1}, \ldots, s_i, \ldots, s_k, s_{k+1} | \rho(s_i) = d(s_i, s_{k+1})\}$ no radio-station in the above set can reach a radio-station in S_{m-1} in 1-hop.*

After defining the covering index m (> 1) for $\mathcal{R}^i_{k+1}$, we have $SS^i = \{s_m, s_{m+1}, \ldots, s_i, \ldots, s_k, s_{k+1}\}$. Note that, none of the members in SS^i can communicate with $S_{k+1} \setminus SS^i$, and hence the communication graph does not remain strongly connected (with respect to the new assignment). But, as we have not changed the range assignment of $S_{m-1} = \{s_1, s_2, \ldots, s_{m-1}\}$, at least one of them communicates with SS^i (as it was in $\mathcal{R}_k$). We now need to increase the range of any one member in SS^i_L to restore the strong connectivity of the communication graph of S_{k+1}. Lemma 5, stated below helps in handling this situation.

Definition 5. *Let $\{s_\alpha, s_{\alpha+1}, \ldots, s_\beta\}$ be a sequence of consecutive radio-stations with assigned ranges $\{r_\alpha, r_{\alpha+1}, \ldots, r_\beta\}$ such that $r_\alpha \geq d(s_\alpha, s_\beta)$, and $r_j = d(s_j, s_{j+1})$ for all $j = \alpha+1, \alpha+2, \ldots, \beta-1$. The critical-range in $\{r_{\alpha+1}, \ldots, r_{\beta-1}\}$ is $r_\delta = Max_{j=\alpha+1}^{\beta-1} r_j$. A revised assignment for the critical-range r_δ is obtained by changing the assignment of s_j to $r_j^* = d(s_j, s_{j-1})$ for all $j = \alpha+1, \alpha+1, \ldots, \delta$. The ranges assigned to s_α and $s_{\delta+1}, \ldots, s_{\beta-1}$ remains unchanged. In Fig. 4(a), observe the radio-stations $\{s_\alpha, \ldots, s_\beta\}$. The critical range is marked, and the revised assignment is shown in Fig. 4(b).*

Lemma 5. *If in a strong connected communication graph among a set of radio-stations $\{s_1, s_2, \ldots, s_n\}$ with range assignment $\mathcal{R} = \{r_1, r_2, \ldots, r_n\}$ and total cost C, there exists a pair of radio-stations (s_m, s_j) $(j > m+1)$ such that s_j can communicate with s_m in 1-hop, and there exists another pair of radio-stations (s_α, s_β) with $\alpha < \beta - 1 < j$ where s_α can communicate with s_β in 1-hop, then the revised assignment corresponding to critical-range in $\{r_\alpha, r_{\alpha+1}, \ldots, r_{\beta-1}\}$ maintains the strong connectivity in the communication graph, and the total cost in the revised assignment is less than C.*

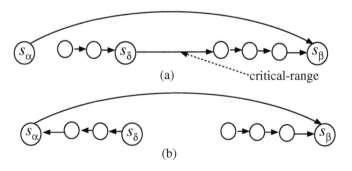

Fig. 4. Illustration of (a) *critical-range* and (b) revised assignment

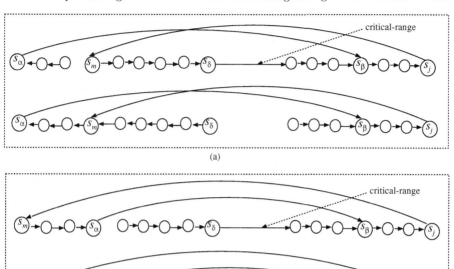

Fig. 5. Proof of Lemma 5

Proof. Two different instances of critical range and their corresponding revised assignments have been demonstrated in Fig. 5(a) and 5(b). The strong connectivity in the revised assignment is maintained due to the fact that s_j can communicate with all the radio-stations from s_{j-1} to s_m (in 1-hop), and s_α can communicate with all radio-stations from $s_{\alpha+1}$ to s_β in 1-hop, and all other nodes can mutually communicate (using ≥ 1 hop(s)) via s_α and/or s_j. The communication path of the other nodes is clear from Fig. 5(b).   □

After identifying the covering index s_m ($m > 1$), we have $SS^i = \{s_m, s_{m+1}, \ldots, s_i, \ldots, s_k, s_{k+1}\}$. Note that, as we have not yet changed the range assignments of $S_{m-1} = \{s_1, s_2, \ldots, s_{m-1}\}$, at least one member of them can communicate with a member in SS^i. We choose the rightmost one, say s_ν ($\nu \leq m - 1$); let it be communicating with s_μ ($\mu \geq m$). If $\mu > m$, then a critical range (as illustrated in Fig. 5(a)) is observed within $s_m, s_{m+1}, \ldots, s_\mu$. We name it as *type-1* critical range. Note that, if $\mu = m$, *type-1* critical range is not observed.

Next, we consider each member $s_\alpha \in SS^i_L$ whose assigned range ρ_α satisfies $\rho_\alpha < d(s_\alpha, s_{m-1})$, and increase its range to $\rho'_\alpha = d(s_\alpha, s_{m-1})$. This establishes a connection between SS^i_L and S_{m-1}. But, this may create a *critical range* if there exists a 1-hop connection from some s_j to s_m with $j - m \geq 2$ (see Fig. 5(b)). We refer this as *type-2* critical range. We consider the larger one among *type-1* and *type-2* critical ranges, and apply Lemma 5 to reduce the total cost. In order to retain the connectivity from S_{m-1} to SS^i_L with minimum cost, we use $\mathcal{R}_{m-1}$ or $\mathcal{R}_m$ as stated below.

- If one of the radio-stations in S_{m-1} can communicate with a member of SS_L^i in 1-hop due to its assigned range in $\mathcal{R}_{m-1}$, then the strong connectivity in the communication graph of all the nodes in S_{k+1} is already maintained. As the range assignment of $\mathcal{R}_{m-1}$ is optimum, the optimality of $\mathcal{R}_{k+1}^i$ can be achieved by choosing a radio-station s_α such that the change in ρ_α to ρ'_α and elimination of critical range produces maximum gain in the total cost. Here, the total cost of range assignment is equal to $cost(\mathcal{R}_{m-1}) + \sum_{\gamma=m}^{k+1} \rho'_\gamma$, where ρ'_γ is the final range assigned to s_γ after this operation.

- If $\mathcal{R}_{m-1}$ is such that none of the radio-stations in S_{m-1} can communicate with a member in SS_L^i in 1-hop, then the strong connectivity in the communication graph of the nodes in S_{k+1} can not be asured using $\mathcal{R}_{m-1}$. Here, we need to consider the situation when s_m was inserted in $\mathcal{R}_{m-1}$ to compute $\mathcal{R}_m$. At that time, we obtained the optimal assignment $\mathcal{R}_m$ by (i) assigning the range of s_m to $d(s_{m-1}, s_m)$, and (ii) changing $\mathcal{R}_{m-1}$ in an optimal manner so that the $cost(\mathcal{R}_m)$ is minimum. Here, we need not have to perform step (i), but step (ii) is necessary. Thus, here the optimal cost is $cost(\mathcal{R}_m) - (d(s_{m-1}, s_m))^2 + \sum_{\gamma=m}^{k+1} \rho'_\gamma$, where ρ'_γ is same as mentioned in the earlier paragraph.

3.2   Algorithm

Our incremental algorithm considers the radio-stations $s_k \in S$, placed on a line, from left to right. For each s_{k+1}, we compute R_{k+1} by identifying an s_{i*} whose range is to be revised (to $\rho_{i*} = d(s_{i*}, s_{k+1})$) for communicating from S_k to s_{k+1}. This needs computation of R_{k+1}^i for different $s_i \in S_k$ using the method described in the earlier subsection. But, we can accelerate our algorithm by ignoring the computation of R_{k+1}^i for some values of i as stated in the following results.

Lemma 6. *Let m and m' be the covering indices for computing $\mathcal{R}_{k+1}^i$ and $\mathcal{R}_{k+1}^j$ respectively, where $s_i, s_j \in S_k$. Now, if $j < i$ then $m' \leq m$. Furthermore, if s_ℓ is left-most element which is 1-hop reachable from s_j then $m' = m$ if and only if $\ell \geq m$.*

Proof. The first part of the lemma trivially follows from the fact that if s_j is to the left of s_i and $d(s_j, s_{k+1}) > d(s_i, s_{k+1})$, then $SS^i \subseteq SS^j$. The second part follows from the following two arguments:

- In $\mathcal{R}_{k+1}^i$ the ranges assigned to each node $s_\alpha \in SS_L^i (= \{s_m, s_{m+1}, \ldots, s_i\})$ is $d(s_\alpha, s_{\alpha+1})$.
- While computing $\mathcal{R}_{k+1}^j$, we assign range of each node $s_\beta \in \{s_\ell, s_{\ell+1}, \ldots, s_j\}$ equal to $d(s_\beta, s_{\beta+1})$.

Since no node to the right of s_m (including itself) can reach s_{m-1}, the claim in this case follows. $\square$

Lemma 7. *Let m be observed as the covering index while computing $\mathcal{R}_{k+1}^i$ for a radio-station $s_i \in S_k$. During the computation of $\mathcal{R}_{k+1}^j$ for $s_j \in S_k$ with $j < i$, if s_ℓ is 1-hop reachable from s_j and $\ell \geq m$ then $cost(\mathcal{R}_{k+1}^j) > cost(\mathcal{R}_{k+1}^i)$.*

Proof. As $j < i$, $d(s_j, s_{k+1}) > d(s_i, s_{k+1})$. Next, we need to consider the reduction due to *critical range* for computing $cost(\mathcal{R}_{k+1}^i)$ and $cost(\mathcal{R}_{k+1}^j)$.

The critical range for $\mathcal{R}_{k+1}^i$ is $Max(d(s_{m+1}, s_{m+2}), d(s_{m+2}, s_{m+3}), \ldots, d(s_{i-2}, s_{i-1}))$. By Lemma 6, $m = m'$. So, the critical range for $\mathcal{R}_{k+1}^j$ is $Max(d(s_{m+1}, s_{m+2}), d(s_{m+2}, s_{m+3}), \ldots, d(s_{j-2}, s_{j-1}))$. As the latter set of distances is a subset of the former set of distances, the critical range of $\mathcal{R}_{k+1}^j \leq$ critical range of $\mathcal{R}_{k+1}^i$. Thus, the lemma follows. □

In our modified algorithm, we start with $\mathcal{R}_k = \{\rho^k(s_1), \rho^k(s_2), \ldots, \rho^k(s_m)\}$, and the set of radio stations S_k whose assigned range is beyond s_k. We consider each member in $s_j \in S_k$ from right to left, and test it by extending its range for 1-hop connection with s_{k+1}. We use four temporary scalar locations, namely i^*, opt, m and cr. Initially, $i^* = k$; opt contains the optimum cost of $\mathcal{R}_{k+1}^{i^*}$; m and cr contain respectively the *covering index* and *critical range* for s_{i^*}. While considering $s_j \in S_k$, $j < i^*$, if $d(s_j, s_{k+1}) \leq d(s_m, s_j)$, then extending range of s_j is not cost-effective (by Lemma 7); so, we would not compute $\mathcal{R}_{k+1}^j$. If $d(s_j, s_{k+1}) > d(s_m, s_j)$, we start scanning from s_m towards left to find the *covering index* (say m') for s_j. But, after identifying the covering index m', we need to consider every element in $S_{m'}$ for its 1-hop connection with $s_{m'-1}$ to restore the strong connectivity of the communication graph. At each step, the critical range cr' is identified as described in the earlier subsection, and the optimal cost for $\mathcal{R}_{k+1}^j$ is computed as follows:

$$opt' = opt - ((d(s_{i^*}, s_{k+1}))^2 - (\rho(s_{i^*}))^2) + ((d(s_j, s_{k+1}))^2 - (\rho(s_j))^2)$$
$$+ ((d(s_{cr}, s_{cr+1}))^2 - (d(s_{cr'}, s_{cr'+1}))^2)$$

If $opt' < opt$, then all the temporary fields need to be updated appropriately. The process continues until S_k is empty or $m = 1$. Finally, another pass is required to compute $\mathcal{R}_{k+1}^{i^*} = \{\rho^{k+1}(s_1), \rho^{k+1}(s_2), \ldots, \rho^{k+1}(s_{k+1})\}$, which will be stored in $\mathcal{R}_{k+1}$ for further use.

3.3 Complexity

In order to obtain the time complexity of computing $\mathcal{R}_{k+1}$, we need to assume the worst case situation where no element $s_\alpha \in S_k$ exists with $\rho_\alpha^k \geq d(s_\alpha, s_{k+1})$. Here, the range of one member, say $s_i \in S_k$, needs to be increased (i.e. ρ_i^k is to be increased to $\rho_i^{k+1} = d(s_i, s_{k+1})$ to communicate from S_k to s_{k+1}. If T_i denote the time needed to compute $\mathcal{R}_{k+1}^i$, then the total time complexity of computing $\mathcal{R}_{k+1}$ is $\sum_{s_i \in S_k} T_i$. We now calculate the worst case value of T_i.

As we have mentioned in Section 3.1, we compute *covering-index* m (see Definition 4) by repeatedly applying Case (i). Each iteration of Case (i) resets the ranges of the newly discovered elements in SS^i, and identifies the *left-cover* m. Thus, the total time for all the iterations of Case (i) is $O(k + 1 - m)$, where m is the *covering-index* for s_i.

Finally, if Case (ii) is reached (i.e., $m = \ell = 1$), the process terminates. If Case (iii) takes place then exactly one element in $s_j \in SS_L^i$ needs to be increased to $d(s_j, s_{m-1})$. This may give birth to a *critical range* as mentioned in Definition

5 and Lemma 5. Finally, computing the revised costs need another $(i-m)$ time. Thus, we have the following theorem stating the worst case time complexity of the algorithm.

Theorem 1. *The time complexity of our proposed algorithm for the optimal range asignment of the 1D unbounded range assignment problem is $O(n^3)$ in the worst case. The space complexity is $O(n^2)$.*

Proof. As discussed earlier, the computation of R_{k+1} needs $\sum_{s_i \in S_k} T_i$ time where T_i is the time for computing R^i_{k+1}.

The total time for all the iterations of Case (i) for arriving either Case (ii) or Case (iii) needs $O(k)$ time in the worst case. Finally, if Case (ii) happens, the time for the necessary update the ranges is $O(k+1)$. If Case (iii) takes place with several node reaching s_m but not s_{m-1} then for each of them the *critical index* is to be searched. But the total time required remains $O(k-m+1)$ since the search for *critical index* proceeds from right to left in sequential manner. Thus computation of R^i_{k+1} needs $O(k)$ time in the worst case. As $|S_k| = k$ in the worst case, the time required for computing R_{k+1} is $O(k^2)$. The lemma follows from the fact that the process needs n iterations for considering all the elements in S_n in order. □

4   Conclusion

The time complexity of the proposed algorithm is $O(n^3)$ which is an improvement by a factor n for the unbounded version of 1D range assignment problem over its existing result [9]. We mentioned Lemmata 6 and 7 for further accelarating the algorithm, but could not use it to improve the time complexity result. We hope, a careful analysis may improve both time and space complexity of the problem.

References

1. M. A. Bassiouni and C. Fang, *Dynamic channel allocation for linear macrocellular topology*, Proc. ACM Symp. on Applied Computing (SAC), pp. 382-388, 1998.
2. I. Chlamtac and A. Farago, *Making transmission schedules immune to topology changes in multihop packet radio networks*, IEEE/ACM Trans. on Networking, vol. 2, pp. 23-29, 1994.
3. A. E. F. Clementi, A. Ferreira, P. Penna, S. Perennes, R. Silvestri, *The minimum range assignment problem on linear radio networks*, Algorithmica, vol. 35, pp. 95-110, 2003.
4. B. S. Chlebus, L. Gasieniec, A. Gibbons, A. Pelc, and W. Rytter, *Deterministic broadcasting in unknown radio networks*, Proc. 11th Annual ACM-SIAM Symp. on Discrete Algorithms (SODA), pp. 861-870, 2000.
5. A. E. F. Clementi, M. Di Ianni and R. Silvestri, *The minimum broadcast range assignment problem on linear multi-hop wireless networks*, Theoretical Computer Science, vol. 299, pp. 751-761, 2003.

6. A. E. F. Clementi, P. Penna, R. Silvestri, *The power range assignment problem in radio networks on the plane*, Proc. Symp. on Theoretical Aspects of Computer Science (STACS-00), pp. 651-660, 2000.
7. K. Diks, E. Kranakis, D. Krizanc and A. Pelc, *The impact of knowledge on broadcasting time in radio networks*, Proc. Annual European Symposium on Algorithms (ESA), LNCS 1643, pp. 41-52, 1999.
8. E. Kranakis, D. Krizanc and A. Pelc, *Fault-tolerant broadcasting in radio networks*, Proc. Annual European Symposium on Algorithms (ESA), LNCS 1461, pp. 283-294, 1998.
9. L. Kirousis, E. Kranakis, D. Krizanc and A. Pelc, *Power consumption in packet radio networks*, Theoretical Computer Science, vol. 243, pp. 289-305, 2000.
10. R. Mathar and J. Mattfeldt, *Optimal transmission ranges for mobile communication in linear multihop packet radio networks*, Wireless Networks, vol. 2, pp. 329-342, 1996.
11. K. Pahlavan, A. Levesque, *Wireless Information Networks*, John Wiley, New York, 1995.
12. S. Ulukus and R. D. Yates, *Stochastic power control for cellular radio systems*, IEEE Trans. Communications, vol. 46, pp. 784-798, 1998.

Optimal Schemes for Channel Assignment Problem in Wireless Networks Modeled as 2-Dimensional Square Grids

B.S. Panda[1], Mahesh Kumar[1], and Sajal K. Das[2]

[1] Department of Mathematics,
Indian Institute of Technology, Delhi,
Hauz Khas, New Delhi, 110 016, India
bspanda@maths.iitd.ernet.in
jca030024@ccsun50.iitd.ac.in
[2] Department of Computer Science and Engineering,
The University of Texas at Arlington,
Arlington, TX 76019, USA
das@cse.uta.edu

Abstract. This paper presents optimal schemes for channel assignment problem in wireless networks modeled as 2-dimensional square grids. Given the reuse distance σ (an integer ≥ 5), using minimum number of colors, our algorithm assigns colors(channels) to the vertices (radio stations) in such a way that the color difference between the adjacent vertices is at least 2, and two vertices x and y receive the same color only when the distance between x and y is at least σ.

1   Introduction

Technology advances and rapid development of hand-held wireless systems has facilitated the rapid growth of wireless communication and mobile computing. The enormous growth of wireless networks has made the efficient use of the scarce radio spectrum important (see [1],[5]). The **Channel Assignment Problem (CAP)** is the task of assigning channels (frequencies) from a radio spectrum to a set of radio stations, satisfying certain constraints. The main difficulty in efficient use of the radio spectrum is the **interference** caused by unconstrained simultaneous transmissions. Interference can be eliminated (or at least reduced) by means of suitable channel assignment techniques, which partition the given radio spectrum into a set of disjoint channels that can be used simultaneously by the stations which maintain acceptable radio signals. Since radio signals get attenuated over distance, two stations in a network can use the same channel without interferences provided the stations are spaced sufficiently apart. Stations that use the same channels are called **co-channel stations**. The minimum distance at which a channel can be reused with no interference is called the **co-channel reuse distance** (or simply **reuse distance**) and is denoted by σ .

A. Sen et al. (Eds.): IWDC 2004, LNCS 3326, pp. 424–434, 2004.
© Springer-Verlag Berlin Heidelberg 2004

In a **dense** network (i.e., a network where there are a large number of transmitters and receivers in a small area), interference is more likely. Thus, reuse distance needs to be high in such networks. Moreover, channels assigned to nearby stations must be separated in value by at least a gap which is inversely proportional to the distance between the two stations. A minimum **channel separation** δ_i is required between channel assigned to stations at distance i where $i < \sigma$, such that δ_i decreases when i increases. The purpose of channel assignment algorithm is to assign channels to transmitters in such a way that

1. The co-channel reuse distance and the channel separation constraints are satisfied, and
2. The span of the assignment, defined to be the difference between the highest and the lowest channels assigned, is as small as possible.

The Channel Assignment Problem with Separation (CAPS) is known to be NP-Hard [4],[8] and remains so for planar graphs, bipartite graphs, chordal graphs, and split graphs (see [8]).

In this paper, we investigate the channel assignment problem for wireless networks modelled as 2-dimensional square grids. We consider the case where the channel separation is 1 for all but adjacent stations and 2 for adjacent stations.The motivations for the study of CAPS on 2-dimensional square grid are as follows.

(i) The channel assignment problem for the d-dimensional square grid places an upper bound on solution for the problem for a suitable d'-dimensional cellular grid (see [2]), and the cellular grid are used in practice for wireless network, and
(ii) It was left as an open problem in [2].

In this paper, we present optimal schemes for channel assignment modelled as 2-dimensional square grids for $\sigma \geq 5$ with a channel separation of 2 for adjacent stations. Optimal solution for the channel assignment problem in 2-dimensional square grid for $\sigma = 3$ and 4 is presented in [2] and the problem was left open for $\sigma \geq 5$.

The rest of the paper is organized as follows. In section 2, we formally define CAPS and discuss it on grids. Section 3 presents optimal schemes for channel assignment in 2-dimensional square grid. We prove the correctness of schemes and prove that it is optimal. Section 4 concludes the paper.

2   Channel Assignment Problem with Separation

The **channel assignment problem with separation** (CAPS) can be modelled as an appropriate coloring problem on an undirected graph $G = (V, E)$ representing the network topology, whose vertices in V correspond to radio stations, and edges in E correspond to pair of stations that can hear each other's transmission. Let $d(x, y)$ denote the distance between the vertices x and y in G. A k-coloring of a graph G=(V,E) is a function $f : V \rightarrow \{0, 1, \ldots, k\}$, such that for all $u, v \in V$, $f(u) \neq f(v)$ if $uv \in E$. The k-coloring problem of a graph is to find a minimum integer k such that G has a k-coloring. **CAPS**, which can be seen as a variant of k-coloring problem, is defined as follows:

CAPS (G, σ, δ)

Given an undirected graph G, an integer $\sigma > 1$, and a vector of positive integers $\delta = (\delta_1, \delta_2, \ldots, \delta_{\sigma-1})$, find an integer, $g > 0$, so that there is a function $f : V \rightarrow \{0, 1, \ldots, g\}$, such that for all $u, v \in V$ and for each i, $1 \leq i \leq \sigma - 1$, if $d(u, v) = i$, then $|f(u) - f(v)| \geq \delta_i$.

This assignment is referred to as a $g - L(\delta_1, \delta_2, \ldots, \delta_{\sigma-1})$ coloring of the graph G, and **CAPS**(G, σ, δ) is sometime referred to as the $L(\delta)$ coloring problem for G. Note that, this coloring uses only $(g+1)$ colors in the set $\{0, 1, \ldots, g\}$, but does not necessarily use all the $(g + 1)$ colors. A $g - L(\delta_1, \delta_2, \ldots, \delta_{\sigma-1})$ coloring of G is **optimal** iff g is the smallest number witnessing a solution for CAPS(G, σ, δ).

2.1   Grids

For any d-dimensional lattice[1], $\mathcal{L}$, the minimal distance in the lattice is denoted by $\mu(\mathcal{L})$, (See [3],[6]). The infinite graph, denoted as $\mathcal{G}(\mathcal{L})$, corresponding to the lattice $\mathcal{L}$ consists of the set of lattice points as vertices; each pair of lattice points that are at a distance $\mu(\mathcal{L})$ constitute the edges of $\mathcal{G}(\mathcal{L})$. Henceforth, we will not make a distinction between the lattice points in $\mathcal{L}$ and the corresponding vertices in $\mathcal{G}(\mathcal{L})$. Given a lattice $\mathcal{L}$, for any two points u and $v \in \mathcal{L}$, let $d_{\mathcal{G}(\mathcal{L})}(u, v)$ denote the distance between vertices u and v in $\mathcal{G}(\mathcal{L})$.

The lattice $\mathbf{Z}^d$ is the set of ordered d-tuples of integers. The graph, $\mathcal{G}(\mathbf{Z}^2)$ is the 2-dimensional square grid. Now, $V(\mathcal{G}(\mathbf{Z}^2)) = \{(x, y)|x, y \in Z\}$, and $E(\mathcal{G}(\mathbf{Z}^2)) = \{(x_1, y_1)(x_2, y_2)| |x_1 - x_2| + |y_1 - y_2| = 1\}$.

3   Coloring for $\mathcal{G}(\mathbf{Z}^2)$

We first find a lower bounds on the coloring of $\mathcal{G}(\mathbf{Z}^2)$. We then present optimal coloring schemes for $\mathcal{G}(\mathbf{Z}^2)$ for different σ with a separation constraint of 2 for adjacent vertices.

3.1   Coloring Strategy

Before presenting the actual coloring scheme, we present an intuitive discussion of the strategy that we will use to color $\mathcal{G}(\mathbf{Z}^2)$.

First we will provide a lower bound on the number of colors used to color $\mathcal{G}(\mathbf{Z}^2)$ that is $n(\sigma, 2)$. We will use the notation (x, y) to denote a vertex in $\mathcal{G}(\mathbf{Z}^2)$.

---

[1] A lattice is a partially ordered set in which the least upper bound and greatest lower bound exist for every pair of elements.

The strategy used to color $\mathcal{G}(\mathbf{Z}^2)$ is to convert the coloring problem of the infinite graph $\mathcal{G}(\mathbf{Z}^2)$ into coloring problem of some finite graph and by showing that the solution for the infinite graph can be obtained by translating these vertices of the finite graph, suitably. In this finite graph we identify the base segment on a base line. The base line is the set of vertices $\{(x_0, 0)|x_0 \text{ is an integer}\}$. The base-segment is the set of vertices $(x_0, 0)$ with $0 \le x_0 < n_\sigma$, where n_σ is the number of colors used to color $\mathcal{G}(\mathbf{Z}^2)$ optimally, with a reuse distance of σ. Note that $n_\sigma \ge n(\sigma, 2)$ as $n(\sigma, 2)$ is the lower bound on the coloring. This base-segment is translated to fill up the finite graph.

Let n_σ be the total number of colors used to color the infinite graph $\mathcal{G}(\mathbf{Z}^2)$ optimally with reuse distance σ. If we can give a coloring scheme for a finite graph containing the points $0 \le x < n_\sigma$ and $0 \le y < n_\sigma$ which satisfies both reuse and separation constraints, then the finite graph can be translated to color the infinite graph $\mathcal{G}(\mathbf{Z}^2)$ optimally.

3.2   Lower Bound

Let $n(\sigma, d)$ denote the minimum number of colors used to color $\mathcal{G}(\mathbf{Z}^d)$ with reuse distance σ. The following lemma presents a lower bound on $n(\sigma, d)$.

Lemma 3.2.1 [2]: $n(\sigma, d) = n(\sigma, d-1) + 2\sum_{i=1}^{\lfloor \frac{\sigma}{2} \rfloor} n(\sigma - 2i, d-1)$.

For $d = 2$, we have the following:

Lemma 3.2.2: $n(\sigma, 2) = \begin{cases} \frac{\sigma^2}{2} & \text{if } \sigma \text{ is even} \\ \frac{\sigma^2+1}{2} & \text{if } \sigma \text{ is odd} \end{cases}$.

Proof: Let $\{ \ldots, v_{-n}, v_{-(n-1)}, \ldots, v_1, v_2, \ldots, v_n, \ldots \}$ be the vertices in $\mathbf{Z}$ such that v_i is joined to v_{i-1} and v_{i+1}. Now $d(v_i, v_{i+j}) \le \sigma - 1$, for $1 \le j \le \sigma - 1$. So the vertices $v_i, v_i + 1, \ldots, v_{i+\sigma-1}$ will receive different colors. The vertex $v_{i+\sigma}$ can get the same color as the vertex v_σ and this coloring scheme can be repeated at v_σ. Therefore $n(\sigma, 1) = \sigma$. Now,

$$n(\sigma, 2) = n(\sigma, 1) + 2\sum_{i=1}^{\lfloor \frac{\sigma}{2} \rfloor} n(\sigma - 2i, 1), \text{ by Lemma 3.2.1}$$

$$= \sigma + 2\sum_{i=1}^{\lfloor \frac{\sigma}{2} \rfloor}(\sigma - 2i) = \sigma + 2\left[\sigma \cdot \left\lfloor \frac{\sigma}{2} \right\rfloor - \left\lfloor \frac{\sigma}{2} \right\rfloor \left(\left\lfloor \frac{\sigma}{2} \right\rfloor + 1\right)\right].$$

If σ is even , then $\left\lfloor \frac{\sigma}{2} \right\rfloor = \frac{\sigma}{2}$. $n(\sigma, 2) = \frac{\sigma^2}{2}$. If σ is odd, then $\left\lfloor \frac{\sigma}{2} \right\rfloor = \left(\frac{\sigma-1}{2}\right)$ and hence $n(\sigma, 2) = \frac{\sigma^2+1}{2}$. Hence the proof.   □

3.3   Optimal Coloring for $\sigma \ge 5$

We would be dealing with odd σ and even σ separately. Let us denote by n_σ the lower bound on the coloring to color $\mathcal{G}(\mathbf{Z}^2)$ and let K be the shift in the color of the vertices. First we shall color the baseline segment, that is the set of vertices $\{(x_0, 0) \mid 0 \leq x_0 < n_\sigma\}$. Below we present our coloring scheme for $\sigma \geq 5$.

Grid Coloring Schemes

Scheme-I: σ even and ≥ 5 {

- For this scheme
  - ⋆ $K = \sigma - 1$.
  - ⋆ Define the coloring for the vertex $(x_0, 0)$ as
  $$f(x_0) = \begin{cases} n_\sigma - 2x_0 - 1 & \text{if } x_0 \bmod n_\sigma \leq \frac{n_\sigma}{2} - 1 \\ 2n_\sigma - 2 - 2x_0 & \text{if } \frac{n_\sigma}{2} \leq x_0 \bmod n_\sigma \leq n_\sigma - 1 \end{cases}$$
- For any arbitrary vertex (x, y) the coloring is
  - ⋆ $C(x, y) = f(x_0)$, where,
  $$x_0 = \begin{cases} x - (Ky \bmod n_\sigma) & \text{if } x - (Ky \bmod n_\sigma) \geq 0 \\ n_\sigma + (x - (Ky \bmod n_\sigma)) & \text{if } x - (Ky \bmod n_\sigma) < 0 \end{cases}$$

}

Scheme-II: σ odd and ≥ 5 {

- For this scheme
  - ⋆ $K = n_\sigma - 1$.
  - ⋆ Define the coloring for the vertex $(x_0, 0)$ as
  $$f(x_0) = \begin{cases} n_\sigma - 2 - 2x_0 & \text{if } x_0 \bmod n_\sigma \leq \frac{n_\sigma - 3}{2} \\ 2(n_\sigma - 1 - x_0) & \text{if } \frac{n_\sigma - 1}{2} \leq x_0 \bmod n_\sigma \leq n_\sigma - 1 \end{cases}$$

- For any arbitrary vertex (x, y) the coloring is
  - ⋆ $C(x, y) = f(x_0)$, where,

  $$x_0 = \begin{cases} x - (Ky \bmod n_\sigma) & \text{if } x - (Ky \bmod n_\sigma) \geq 0 \\ n_\sigma + (x - (Ky \bmod n_\sigma)) & \text{if } x - (Ky \bmod n_\sigma) < 0 \end{cases}$$

}

In the "Grid coloring schemes" the point on the base line, i.e., $(x_0, 0)$, and the vertex in the line L just above the base line which will have the same color as $(x_0, 0)$ is $(x_0 + K, 1)$. Also the point on the line just above the line L which will have same color will be $(x_0 + 2K, 2)$ and proceeding so on we get, the vertices having same color as $(x_0, 0)$ in the finite graph forms the set

$$\left\{ \left([x_0 + rK] \bmod n_\sigma, r \right) \quad r = 0, 1, \ldots, n_\sigma - 1 \right\}.$$

Theorem 3.3.1. The **Grid Coloring schemes** satisfy the channel reuse constraints.

Proof: Consider two distinct vertices having the same color, i.e.
$a = (x_0 + r_1K, r_1)$; $b = (x_0 + r_2K, r_2)$, where $r_1 \neq r_2$. then the distance.
$d(a, b) = |r_1K - r_2K| + |r_1 - r_2| = |r_1 - r_2| (K + 1)$
As the two vertices are distinct, we have $|r_1 - r_2| \geq 1$.
Hence, $d(a, b) \geq K + 1$,

Case(i): σ is even
Then, $K = \sigma - 1$. So,
$$d(a, b) \geq (\sigma - 1) + 1 = \sigma.$$
Thus, $d(a, b) \geq \sigma$. Thus the channel reuse constraint is satisfied for this scheme..

Case(ii): σ is odd
Then, $K = n_\sigma - \sigma$. So,
$$d(a, b) \geq n_\sigma - \sigma + 1,$$
$$= \frac{\sigma^2 + 1}{2} - \sigma + 1 = \sigma + \frac{(\sigma - 1)(\sigma - 3)}{2}$$
$$\geq \sigma \ [\text{Because } \sigma \geq 5 \,].$$
$$\text{Thus, } d(a, b) \geq \sigma.$$

Hence, the channel reuse constraint is satisfied for the "Grid coloring schemes". $\boxed{\cdot}$

Lemma 3.3.2. Let d be the distance between the vertices having consecutive colors . Then for even σ, $d \in \{\frac{1}{2}, \frac{n_\sigma}{2}, \frac{n_\sigma - 2}{2}\}$ and for odd σ, $d \in \{\frac{1}{2}, \frac{n_\sigma + 1}{2}, \frac{n_\sigma - 1}{2}\}$.

Proof: Let $(x_0, 0)$, $(y_0, 0)$ be the vertices such that,
$$|f(x_0) - f(y_0)| = 1$$

Now $d\Big((x_0, 0), (y_0, 0)\Big) = |x_0 - y_0|$.

Case (i): σ is even
Then,
$$f(x_0) = \begin{cases} n_\sigma - 2x_0 - 1 & \text{if } x_0 \bmod n_\sigma \leq \frac{n_\sigma}{2} - 1 \\ 2n_\sigma - 2 - 2x_0 & \text{if } \frac{n_\sigma}{2} \leq x_0 \bmod n_\sigma \leq n_\sigma - 1 \end{cases}$$
Subcase(i) $x_0, y_0 \leq \frac{n_\sigma}{2} - 1$
Then,
$$|f(x_0) - f(y_0)| = |(n_\sigma - 2x_0 - 1) - (n_\sigma - 2y_0 - 1)|,$$
$$= 2|x_0 - y_0|.$$

Since $|f(x_0) - f(y_0)| = 1$, we get

$$|x_0 - y_0| = \frac{1}{2}.$$

Subcase(ii) $\frac{n_\sigma}{2} \leq x_0, y_0 \leq n_\sigma - 1$
Then,

$$|f(x_0) - f(y_0)| = |(2n_\sigma - 2 - 2x_0) - (2n_\sigma - 2 - 2y_0)|$$
$$= 2|x_0 - y_0|$$
$$\text{Again} |x_0 - y_0| = \frac{1}{2}$$

Subcase(iii) $x_0 \leq \frac{n_\sigma}{2} - 1$ and $\frac{n_\sigma}{2} \leq y_0 \leq n_\sigma - 1$

Then, $|f(x_0) - f(y_0)| = |(n_\sigma - 2x_0 - 1) - (2n_\sigma - 2 - 2y_0)|$
$$= |2(y_0 - x_0) - n_\sigma + 1|$$
Since $|f(x_0) - f(y_0)| = 1$,
we have $|2(y_0 - x_0) - n_\sigma + 1| = 1.$
Then either $2(y_0 - x_0) - n_\sigma + 1 = 1$
$$\Rightarrow |x_0 - y_0| = \frac{n_\sigma}{2}.$$
or $2(y_0 - x_0) - n_\sigma + 1 = -1,$
$$\Rightarrow |x_0 - y_0| = \left| \frac{n_\sigma - 2}{2} \right|,$$
$$= \frac{n_\sigma - 2}{2}.$$

Subcase(iv) $y_0 \leq \frac{n_\sigma}{2} - 1$ and $\frac{n_\sigma}{2} \leq x_0 \leq n_\sigma - 1$

Then, $|f(x_0) - f(y_0)| = |(2n_\sigma - 2 - 2x_0) - (n_\sigma - 2y_0 - 1)|$
$$= |2(y_0 - x_0) + n_\sigma - 1|$$
Since, $|f(x_0) - f(y_0)| = 1$,
we have $|2(y_0 - x_0) + n_\sigma - 1| = 1.$
Then, either $2(y_0 - x_0) + n_\sigma - 1 = 1$
$$\Rightarrow |x_0 - y_0| = \left| \frac{2 - n_\sigma}{2} \right|$$
$$= \frac{n_\sigma - 2}{2}$$
or, $2(y_0 - x_0) + n_\sigma - 1 = -1$
$$\Rightarrow |x_0 - y_0| = \left| \frac{-n_\sigma}{2} \right|$$
$$= \frac{n_\sigma}{2}.$$

Therefore, the distance between vertices having consecutive colors is either $\frac{1}{2}$ or $\frac{n_\sigma}{2}$ or $\frac{n_\sigma-2}{2}$.

Case(ii) σ is odd

Using the similar analysis as in Case (i) and applying the definition for $f(x_0)$ for this case, it is easy to show that the distance between vertices having consecutive colors for the odd scheme is either $\frac{1}{2}$ or $\frac{n_\sigma+1}{2}$ or $\frac{n_\sigma-1}{2}$. $\boxdot$

However, note that the distance $\frac{1}{2}$ between consecutive colors is not possible as the distance between two vertices in $\mathcal{G}(\mathbf{Z}^2)$ is always an integer. Thus the distance between consecutive color vertices is $\frac{n_\sigma}{2}$ or $\frac{n_\sigma-2}{2}$ for even σ; and it is $\frac{n_\sigma+1}{2}$ or $\frac{n_\sigma-1}{2}$ for odd σ.

Theorem 3.3.3. The "Grid coloring schemes" satisfies channel separation constraint .

Proof: Let (x,y) be a vertex. The adjacent vertices of (x,y) are $(x+1,y),(x-1,y),(x,y+1)$ and $(x,y-1)$. In order to show that the channel separation constraint is satisfied it is enough to show that the vertices (x,y) and $(x,y+1)$ do not have consecutive colors, as the other cases are easy. Now $(x,y+1)$ has the same color as the vertex

$$\left((x+(y+1)(n_\sigma-K))mod\ n_\sigma,y\right).$$

So, we have to show that (x,y) and $\left((x+(y+1)(n_\sigma-K))mod\ n_\sigma,y\right)$ do not have consecutive colors. It is sufficient to show this for the base line for which $y=0$. Therefore, the two vertices are $(x,0)$ and $\left((x+n_\sigma-K)mod\ n_\sigma,0\right)$.

Case(i): $x+n_\sigma-K < n_\sigma$

Then the two vertices become $(x,0)$ and $(x+n_\sigma-K,0)$. Hence,

$$d\left((x,0),(x+n_\sigma-K,0)\right)=n_\sigma-K.$$

Subcase(i): σ is odd Then the distance between vertices having consecutive colors is $\frac{n_\sigma+1}{2}$ or $\frac{n_\sigma-1}{2}$. Also $K=n_\sigma-\sigma$ for odd σ, therefore $n_\sigma-K=\sigma$.
Claim: $n_\sigma-K \neq \frac{n_\sigma+1}{2}$ and $n_\sigma-K \neq \frac{n_\sigma-1}{2}$,

$$i.e.,\quad \sigma \neq \frac{n_\sigma+1}{2}\quad \text{and}\quad \sigma \neq \frac{n_\sigma-1}{2}.$$

Proof: If possible, suppose $\sigma=\frac{n_\sigma-1}{2}$
$\Rightarrow 2\sigma=\frac{\sigma^2+1}{2}-1$ [since $n_\sigma=\frac{\sigma^2+1}{2}$ for σ odd]

$\Rightarrow \sigma^2 - 4\sigma - 1 = 0$, $i.e.$ $\sigma = 4.23$ or -0.47.
These values of σ are not possible because $\sigma \geq 5$.

Now If possible, suppose $\sigma = \frac{n_\sigma + 1}{2}$,
$\Rightarrow 2\sigma = \frac{\sigma^2 + 1}{2} + 1$[by definition of n_σ]
$\Rightarrow \sigma^2 - 4\sigma + 3 = 0$, $\sigma = 1$ or 3.
These values of σ are not possible because $\sigma \geq 5$
Thus in the case of odd "σ" the **channel separation constraint** is satisfied.

Subcase(ii): σ is even. Then the distance between vertices having consecutive colors is $\frac{n_\sigma}{2}$ or $\frac{n_\sigma - 2}{2}$.
Also $K = \sigma - 1$, therefore $n_\sigma - K = n_\sigma - \sigma + 1$.
Claim: $n_\sigma - \sigma + 1 \neq \frac{n_\sigma}{2}$ and $n_\sigma - \sigma + 1 \neq \frac{n_\sigma - 2}{2}$.
Proof: If possible, suppose $n_\sigma - \sigma + 1 = \frac{n_\sigma}{2}$
$\Rightarrow \frac{n_\sigma}{2} - \sigma + 1 = 0$
$\Rightarrow \frac{\sigma^2}{4} - \sigma + 1 = 0$ [since $n_\sigma = \frac{\sigma^2}{2}$ for σ even]
$\Rightarrow \sigma^2 - 4\sigma + 4 = 0$, $i.e.$ $\sigma = 2$.
This values of σ is not possible as $\sigma \geq 5$.

Now If possible, suppose $n_\sigma - \sigma + 1 = \frac{n_\sigma - 2}{2}$
$\Rightarrow \frac{n_\sigma}{2} - \sigma + 2 = 0$
$\Rightarrow \frac{\sigma^2}{4} - \sigma + 2 = 0$, $i.e.\sigma^2 - 4\sigma + 8 = 0$.
This quadratic equation in σ has no real root implying these values of σ are not possible because σ is real and takes integer values. Thus, for **even** σ also, the **channel separation constraint** is satisfied.

Case(ii): $n_\sigma \leq x + n_\sigma - K \leq 2n_\sigma$

Then $(x + n_\sigma - K) \bmod n_\sigma = (x + n_\sigma - K) - n_\sigma = x - K$.
Thus, the vertex $(x, 1)$ will have the same color as $(x - K, 0)$ and
the distance $d\Big((x,0),(x - K,0)\Big) = x - x + K = K$.

Subcase(i): σ even In this case $K = \sigma - 1$.

Claim: $\sigma - 1 \neq \frac{n_\sigma}{2}$ and $\sigma - 1 \neq \frac{n_\sigma - 2}{2}$.
Proof: If possible, suppose $\sigma - 1 = \frac{n_\sigma}{2}$
$\Rightarrow \sigma - 1 = \frac{\sigma^2}{4}$
$\Rightarrow \sigma^2 - 4\sigma + 4 = 0$, $i.e.$ $\sigma = 2$.
These values of σ are not possible as we are taking $\sigma \geq 5$.
Now if possible suppose, $\sigma - 1 = \frac{n_\sigma - 2}{2}$
$\Rightarrow \sigma = \frac{\sigma^2}{4}$
$\Rightarrow \sigma^2 - 4\sigma = 0.$, $i.e.$ $\sigma = 0$ or 4.

These values of σ are also not possible as $\sigma \geq 5$.

Thus **Channel Separation Constraint** is thus satisfied for even σ.

Subcase(ii): σ is odd Claim: $n_\sigma - \sigma \neq \frac{n_\sigma + 1}{2}$ and $n_\sigma - \sigma \neq \frac{n_\sigma - 1}{2}$.
Proof: If possible, suppose $n_\sigma - \sigma = \frac{n_\sigma + 1}{2}$
$\Rightarrow \frac{n_\sigma}{2} - \sigma - \frac{1}{2} = 0$
$\Rightarrow \frac{\sigma^2}{4} - \sigma - \frac{1}{2} = 0$ [by definition of n_σ]
$\Rightarrow \sigma^2 - 4\sigma - 2 = 0$,   *i.e.* $\sigma = 4.45$ or -0.45.
These values of σ are not possible as we are taking $\sigma \geq 5$.

Finally, if possible, suppose $n_\sigma - \sigma = \frac{n_\sigma - 1}{2} \Rightarrow \frac{n_\sigma}{2} - \sigma + \frac{1}{2} = 0$
$\Rightarrow \sigma^2 - 4\sigma + 2 = 0$,   *i.e.* $\sigma = 3.415$ or 0.585.
These values of σ are not possible as we are taking $\sigma \geq 5$. Thus the channel separation constraint is satisfied for odd σ. $\boxed{\cdot}$

Thus our Grid coloring schemes satisfy both the **channel separation** and **channel reuse constraints**. Since the number of colors used matches to the lower bound, our coloring is **optimal**.
We have considered infinite $2 - D$ square grid. However, for a finite $2 - D$ grid our Grid coloring scheme optimally colors the grids in linear time.

4   Conclusion

In this paper, we have presented an optimal scheme for channel assignment problem in wireless Networks modeled as 2-dimensional square grids for reuse distance $\sigma \geq 5$. It would be interesting to solve the Channel Assignment Problem with Separation for higher dimensional grids.

References

1. A. A. Bertossi, C. M. Pinotti, and R. B. Tan. *Efficient Use of Radio Spectrum in Wireless Networks with Channel Separation between Close Stations.* In Proceedings of the DIAL M Workshop: pp. 18-27, 2000.
2. A. Dubhashi, M.V.S. Shashanka, A. Patil, R. Shanshank,and A. M. Shende. *Channel Assignment for Wireless Networks Modelling as d-Dimensional Square Grids.* Lecture Notes in Computer Science (LNCS-**2571**), Springer Verlag, pp. 130-141, 2002.
3. D. S. Rajan and A. M. Shende. *A Characterization of Root Lattices.* Discrete Mathematics,**161**, pp. 309-314, 1996.
4. H. L. Boedlander, T. Kloks, R. B. Tan, and J. van Leeuwen. *λ-Colouring of Graphs.* In Proceedings of STACS, pp. 395-406, 2000.
5. I. Katzela and M. Naghshineh. *Channel Assignment Schemes for Cellular Mobile Telecommunication Systems: A Comprehensive Survey.* IEEE Personal Communications. pp. 10-31, June 1996.

6. J. Conway and N. Sloane. *Sphere Packing, Lattices and Groups*. Springer Verlag, second edition, 1993.
7. M. C. Goloumbic. *Algorithmic Graph Theory and Perfect Graphs* Academic Press, 1980.
8. T. Calamoneri and R. Petreschi. *On the Radiocolouring Problem*, Lecture Notes in Computer Science (LNCS-**2571**), Springer Verlag, pp. 118-127, 2002.

Mobility Tolerant Broadcast in Mobile Ad Hoc Networks

Pradip K Srimani[1] and Bhabani P Sinha[2]

[1] Department of Computer Science, Clemson University, Clemson, SC 29634–0974
[2] Advanced Computing & Microelectronics Unit, Indian Statistical Institute,
Calcutta 700108, India

Abstract. A new deterministic broadcast protocol for an ad hoc network is proposed in this paper which avoids re-computation of the transmission schedule, even when the topology of the network changes due to the mobility of the nodes. The basic idea is to use a successive partitioning scheme by representing the identifier of each node (an integer) in an arbitrarily chosen radix system; the protocol then computes the specific time slots in which a particular node should transmit its message. The proposed protocol is simple, easy to implement and needs lesser broadcast time than that in [BBC99].

1   Introduction

Mobile ad hoc networks are being increasingly used for military operations, law enforcement, rescue missions, virtual class rooms, and local area networks. A mobile multi-hop network consists of n identical mobile hosts (nodes) with unique identifiers $0, \ldots, n-1$. These mobile hosts communicate among each other via a packet radio network. When a node transmits (broadcasts) a message, the nodes in the *coverage area* of the sender can simultaneously receive the message. A node i is called a *neighbor* of node j in the network if node j is in the *coverage area* of node i. This relationship is time varying since the nodes can and do move.

In this paper we consider the important problem of broadcasting in an ad hoc network; braodcast is defined to be a process where a source node transmits a message to be received by every node in the network (this is different from broadcast at the MAC layer wherein we are just trying to reach all of our one-hop neighbors). In our model [BP97, BBC99], the system consists of multi-hop time-slotted radio networks without collision detection mechanism (although collision detection protocols have been proposed and used in radio networks [LM87, BYGI92]). An important characteristic of this model is that the nodes share the same transmission channel; thus, collision is possible when more than one neighbor transmit at the same time slot (round)[1] and correct message reception is prevented since there is no collision detection mechanism; the broadcast protocol itself should guarantee the reception of messages in presence of possible collisions. The model assumes the ad hoc network to be composed of a set of processors which may be stationary or mobile and they communicate in synchronous time slots or *rounds*. At any given time a node i can correctly receive a message from one of its neighbors,

---

[1] we use slot and round interchangeably to mean the same thing.

A. Sen et al. (Eds.): IWDC 2004, LNCS 3326, pp. 435–446, 2004.
© Springer-Verlag Berlin Heidelberg 2004

say j, iff j is the *only* neighbor of i transmitting at that time. The broadcast problem in multi-hop networks have been extensively studied; various centralized, distributed, deterministic and randomized algorithms have been proposed [BYGI92, LBA93, CK87, Bas98, PR97]; excellent comparisons of these techniques are given in [BP97, BBC99]. Most of these algorithms do not consider the mobility of the nodes in the sense that they do not account for the dynamic topology of the networks in any cost effective way. The authors in [BBC99] first formulated the requirements of efficient broadcast protocols in presence of node mobility. A broadcast protocol must be: (1) *Mobility Independent* (the broadcast must be correctly completed independent of the knowledge of the identities of the neighbors of a node and the mobility of the nodes), (2) *Deterministic* (an a priori upper bound on the broadcast completion time can be ascertained), (3) *Distributed* (the nodes execute the protocol without the knowledge of the topology of the entire network), (4) *Simple* (computational overhead at each node is minimized). The authors in [BBC99] then proposed a general algorithmic scheme to design broadcast protocol where each node can compute its transmission schedule depending only on global network parameters like n, the number of nodes in the network, $\mathcal{D}$, the diameter of the network, and Δ, the degree of the network. They also showed that their protocols are optimal in light of the lower bounds established in [BP97].

In this paper, we propose a new deterministic distributed broadcast protocol that completes the broadcast in less time. In section 2, we introduce the system model [BBC99] and describe the new protocol in section 3 using the successive partitioning scheme. Section 4 compares the new protocol with those in [BBC99] while section 5 concludes the paper.

2   System Model and Previous Work

A multi-hop ad hoc radio network is modeled by an undirected graph $G = (V, E)$ where $V = \{0, 1, \cdots, n - 1\}$ is the set of computing nodes and E is the set of bidirectional edges (an edge exists between two nodes iff they are in the hearing range of each other). The set of neighbors of node i is denoted by $N(i)$ and Δ, the degree of the network is defined as $\Delta = \max_{i \in V} |N(i)|$. The diameter of the network $\mathcal{D}$ is defined to be $\mathcal{D} = \max_{i,j \in V} d(i, j)$ where $d(i, j)$ is defined to be the number of hops between the two nodes i and j. There is one distinguished node in the network, called the source s (which is the initiator of the broadcast message); any node i, $0 \le d(s, i) = \ell \le \mathcal{D}$ is said to belong to the *layer* ℓ of the network. A distributed deterministic broadcast protocol is executed at each node and it should have the following characteristics:

- Execution time is discrete; the time axis is divided into *frames*, each frame being made up of τ *rounds* (numbered 0 through $\tau - 1$, where τ is the frame length. The source node s transmits a message m before the start of any frame.
- In each round, any node is either a transmitter or a receiver. A node cannot transmit a message unless it has received it. Before receiving the message, every node is set to *receive mode*, and after receiving the message, every node is set always to the *transmit mode*. A node can receive the message m iff at any round the node acts as a receiver and exactly one of its neighbors transmits the message.

- The transmission schedule of any node i is a priori computed deterministically by using n, the identifier (ID) of the node i, and Δ of the network. For this, every node executes the following general protocol, where my_id is the identifier of the node.

Protocol at node i:
find_my_slots (my_id, n, Δ)

- The broadcast is complete at round t of a frame f, iff all the nodes have been informed of the message m by round t of frame f.

We make the following assumptions about the system of nodes in the ad hoc network [BBC99].

1. Nodes are synchronized on a slot or round basis – each node has a counter which is set to 0 at the beginning of each frame and is incremented by 1 at each subsequent round.
2. When a node receives a message m, it waits for the beginning of a new frame. At that time, the counter is incremented at each time slot or round and the node transmits according to its pre-determined transmitting slots in the frame.
3. The nodes which have received the message during the broadcast process are said to be *covered* by the broadcast, and those which have not yet received the message are called *uncovered*. At any phase of the broadcast, the sets of covered and uncovered neighbors of a given node id will be denoted by $N_c(id)$ and $N_u(id)$, respectively. *A set C of covered nodes is termed as a **conflicting set** if there is at least one neighbor common to all the nodes in C that has not yet received the message.* It is assumed that at least one node from a conflicting set remains in the hearing range of any neighboring uncovered node. Also, the network never gets disconnected.

Remark 1.

1. The above scheme does the broadcast in a layer by layer fashion, i.e., all nodes at layer ℓ, $1 \leq \ell \leq \mathcal{D} - 1$, become informed of the message m before any node at layer $\ell + 1$.
2. The broadcast is complete in at most $\mathcal{D} \times \tau$ rounds.
3. The procedure to compute the transmission slots for each of the nodes should be independent of the identity of the current neighbors of the node.

3 Proposed Approach

Each node transmits (broadcasts) messages only in some specific time slots. We need to specify these time slots for each node so as to guarantee that no matter what the network topology is, eventually every node would receive the broadcast message from only one single node during at least one such time slot. Every node identifies these transmission time slots by executing the protocol find_my_slots (my_id, n, Δ) which is done in the following way. The set of nodes V is partitioned in some disjoint blocks following some rule so that any given pair of nodes will be partitioned in two different blocks (call this as *level 1 partitioning* of V). If Δ, the maximum number of neighbors of a node is 2, then we associate a time slot (round) to each of these partition blocks, meaning thereby that every node in a block will transmit its message during its assigned time slot or round. This guarantees that a given pair of neighbors of a node will transmit at two different rounds, and thus, we are done for $\Delta = 2$. If, however, $\Delta \geq 2$, then each of the above partition blocks (having size smaller than n) is further partitioned in disjoint blocks following the same rule (call this as *level 2* partitioning of V). If $\Delta \leq 7$, then we would show that associating a unique time slot to each of these partition blocks generated after level 2 partitioning of V would guarantee that there will be at least one time slot during which only one of the neighbors of a given node will be transmitting. In general, if $\lfloor \log_2 \Delta \rfloor = h$, then we successively generate level i ($2 \leq i \leq h$) partitions of V from the blocks of level $i - 1$ partition, assign a unique time slot to each of the generated blocks after level h partition. We would show, in what follows, that this guarantees at least one round in each frame during which every node would have only one of its Δ neighbors transmitting the message.

3.1   Successive Partitioning Scheme

The successive partitioning scheme is based on radix encoding of the node IDs in the set V (integers 0 through $n-1$). We assume a radix $r, r \geq 2$ and we assume that $n = r^m$, for some integer m, to simplify the discussions. Each node $id \in V = \{0, 1, 2, \cdots, n-1\}$, is converted into an m-digit code in radix r number system as $id = d_{m-1} d_{m-2} \cdots d_0$, where $0 \leq d_i \leq r - 1$, for all i, $0 \leq i \leq m - 1$. Consider the d_i values of each node for a specific i; the set V is partitioned into r disjoint blocks $B_i(j), 0 \leq j \leq r - 1$, i.e., $d_i(id) = j \Rightarrow id \in B_i(j)$. Since there are m different digits (m different values of i), we get m different partitions of V, each into r different blocks. Based on the value of i-th digit in each $id \in V$, we partition V in r different disjoint blocks. Thus, if $d_i(id) = j, j = 0, 1, \cdots, r - 1$, then we place id in the block $B_i(j)$ of the partition. Note that V can be partitioned in m such ways, each induced by one digit position $i, 0 \leq i \leq m - 1$. The total number of blocks generated by these partitions is rm. A given id value is a member of exactly m of these blocks.

Definition 1. *The blocks $B_i(j), 0 \leq i \leq m - 1, 0 \leq j \leq r - 1$ will be called the* **blocks of level-1 partitioning**, *and are denoted by $P(1, k), k = 0, 1, \cdots, rm - 1$, where $P(1, k) = B_i(j)$ if $k = ri + j$. Each block $P(1, k), 0 \leq k \leq rm - 1$, has exactly n/r elements (nodes). Henceforth, we use only the P notation to denote the partition blocks; the B notation was introduced to show the intuitive physical significance of the partitioning blocks.*

Example 1. Let $n = 64$ and $r = 4$ (See Figure 1). Hence, m = 3, i.e., each of the 64 id values will be encoded in a 3-digit code in radix 4 system. The 0-th digit position (least significant digit) induces the partition of V in four blocks, e.g., $B_0(0), B_0(1), B_0(2)$ and $B_0(3)$, where $B_0(0) = (0, 4, 8, 12, 16, 20, 24, 28, 32, 36, 40, 44, 48, 52, 56, 60)$, $B_0(1) = (1, 5, 9, 13, 17, 21, 25, 29, 33, 37, 41, 45, 49, 53, 57, 61), B_0(2) = (2, 6, 10, 14, 18, 22, 26, 30, 34, 38, 42, 46, 50, 54, 58, 62)$, and $B_0(3) = (3, 7, 11, 15, 19, 23, 27, 31, 35, 39, 43, 47, 51, 55, 59, 63)$. Similarly, blocks $B_1(0), B_1(1), B_1(2)$ and $B_1(3)$ (induced by the next significant digit position) are given by $B_1(0) = (0, 1, 2, 3, 16, 17, 18, 19, 32,$ $33, 34, 35, 48, 49, 50, 51)$, $B_1(1) = (4, 5, 6, 7, 20, 21, 22, 23, 36, 37, 38, 39, 52, 53, 54,$ $55)$, $B_1(2) = (8, 9, 10, 11, 24, 25, 26, 27, 40, 41, 42, 43, 56, 57, 58, 59)$, and $B_1(3) =$ $(12, 13, 14, 15, 28, 29, 30, 31, 44, 45, 46, 47, 60, 61, 62, 63)$. Similarly, $B_2(0) = (0, 1, 2,$ $\cdots, 15)$, $B_2(1) = (16, 17, 18, \cdots, 31)$, $B_2(2) = (32, 33, 34, \cdots, 47)$, and $B_2(3) =$ $(48, 49, 50, \cdots, 63)$. Thus, the level-1 partitioning is computed as $P(1, 0) = B_0(0)$, $P(1, 1) = B_0(1), P(1, 2) = B_0(2), P(1, 3) = B_0(3)$, $P(1, 4) = B_1(0), P(1, 5) =$ $B_1(1)$, $P(1, 6) = B_1(2), P(1, 7) = B_1(3)$, $P(1, 8) = B_2(0), P(1, 9) = B_2(1)$, $P(1, 10) = B_2(2), P(1, 11) = B_2(3)$. $\qquad\square$

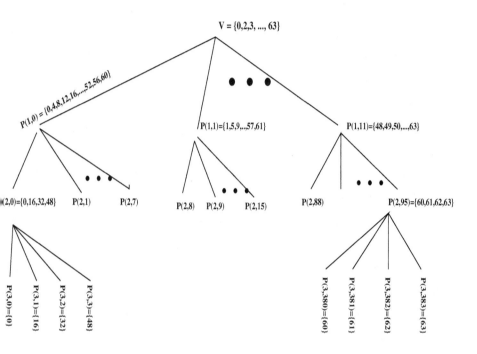

Fig. 1. Partition Tree for $n = 64$ and $r = 4$

Lemma 1. *For an arbitrary subset R of the set V, there exists at least one $P(1, k), 0 \leq k \leq rm - 1$, which contains at most $\lfloor |R|/2 \rfloor$ elements of R.*

Proof. Consider the m-digit radix r codes of the elements in R. Since all these codes are distinct, there exists at least one digit position which consists of at least two different values v_1 and v_2, $0 \leq v_1, v_2 \leq r - 1$ in all these codes. This means that the elements of R will be placed in at least two different blocks of the partitions at level 1. One of these blocks must contain at most $\lfloor |R|/2 \rfloor$ elements.

Lemma 2. *Each element in any arbitrary block $P(1, k), 0 \leq k \leq rm - 1$ of level-1 partition can be uniquely re-coded by using only $m - 1$ digits in radix r number system.*

Proof. Let $j = \lfloor k/r \rfloor$. It follows from the definition that the block $P(1, k)$ is induced by j-th digit, d_j, $(0 \le j \le m-1)$ of the radix-r codes for the elements in V. Consider an element $id \in P(1, k)$. Let the m-digit code for id be $d_{m-1}d_{m-2} \cdots d_{j+1}d_j d_{j-1} \cdots d_0$. Since $\forall\, id \in P(1, k)$, the value of d_j is same, it does not play any role in distinguishing the elements in $P(1, k)$. Thus, if we have a new $(m-1)$-digit code for each id in $P(1, k)$ given by $d_{m-1}d_{m-2} \cdots d_{j+1}d_{j-1} \cdots d_0$, by removing the j-th digit in each code, then these $m-1$-digit codes are sufficient to uniquely identify the elements in $P(1, k)$. It follows from this process of re-coding that each element $id \in P(1, k)$ is mapped to a unique element $id' \in V_1 = \{0, 1, 2, \cdots, n/r - 1\}$ by the following one-to-one and onto mapping: $id' = (\lfloor \alpha/r^{j+1} \rfloor) \times r^j + \alpha \ MOD \ r^j$, where $\alpha = id - d_j \times r^j$.

Example 2. In Example 1 ($n = 64$ and $r = 4$), consider $P(1, 7) = (12, 13, 14, 15, 28, 29, 30, 31, 44, 45, 46, 47, 60, 61, 62, 63)$. We have $j = \lfloor 7/4 \rfloor = 1$. Considering the m-digit radix-r codes of each of these ids in $P(1, 7)$, we see that $d_1 = 3$ for all these ids. Hence the set of α values for these elements are $\{0, 1, 2, 3, 16, 17, 18, 19, 32, 33, 34, 35, 48, 49, 50, 51\}$. The set of id' values for these elements is $\{0, 1, 2, 3, 4, 5, 6, 7, 8, 9, 10, 11, 12, 13, 14, 15\}$, which can be uniquely identified by 2-digit radix-4 codes as follows: 12: (0 0), 13: (0 1), 14: (0 2), 15: (0 3), 28: (1 0), 29: (1 1), 30: (1 2), 31: (1 3), 44: (2 0), 45: (2 1), 46: (2 2), 47: (2 3), 60: (3 0), 61: (3 1), 62: (3 2), 63: (3 3).   □

Consider any one of the blocks $P(1, k), 0 \le k \le rm - 1$, where each element (integer) has a unique r-radix code using $(m-1)$ digits, $d_{m-2}d_{m-3} \cdots d_1 d_0$. We apply the partitioning process on each of these blocks using the digits similar to the level-1 partitioning we applied to the entire set V. We call this level-2 partitioning.

Definition 2. *If we partition the elements of $P(1, i), 0 \le i \le rm - 1$, into r blocks in $(m-1)$ different ways, each induced by a digit of the new $(m-1)$-digit code, the new blocks are called the blocks of level 2 partitioning. If a level-2 block is obtained from $P(1, k)$ induced by its j-th digit code d_j, $0 \le j \le m-2$, such that $d_j = \beta$, $0 \le \beta \le r-1$, we denote this block by $P(2, k)$, where $k = r \times (m-1) \times i + r \times j + \beta$.*

Example 3. Consider the previous example again. We have $r(m-1) = 8$. Hence the blocks from level-2 partitioning are given as $P(2, 56) = (12, 28, 44, 60)$; $P(2, 57) = (13, 29, 45, 61)$; $P(2, 58) = (14, 30, 46, 62)$; $P(2, 59) = (15, 31, 47, 63)$; $P(2, 60) = (12, 13, 14, 15)$; $P(2, 61) = (28, 29, 30, 31)$; $P(2, 62) = (44, 45, 46, 47)$; $P(2, 63) = (60, 61, 62, 63)$.   □

Remark 2.

1. Each block $P(1, k)$ of level-1 partition generates $r(m-1)$ blocks of level-2 partition. The total number of blocks in level-2 partition is given by $r^2 m(m-1)$.
2. Each level-2 block, $P(2, k), 0 \le k \le r^2 m(m-1) - 1$ is of size n/r^2.
3. An arbitrary node $id \in V$ will belong to exactly $m(m-1)$ blocks of level-2 partition.

Lemma 3. *Given any subset R of V such that $|R| \le 2n/r$, there exists a block $P(2, k), 0 \le k \le r^2 m(m-1) - 1$ which contains at most $\lfloor |R|/4 \rfloor$ elements of R.*

Proof. By Lemma 1, there exists a partition $P(1,k), 0 \leq k \leq rm - 1$ which contains at most $\lfloor |R|/2 \rfloor \leq n/r$ elements of R. This level-1 block $P(1,k)$ is now subjected to level-2 partitioning and by similar arguments as in the proof of Lemma 1, we get a level-2 block of size $\lfloor |R|/4 \rfloor$.

The partitioning process can now be generalized. We generate blocks of level-$(i+1)$ partition from the blocks of level-i partition, $i \geq 1$, as follows. For each element $id \in P(i,k)$, we compute $j = \lfloor k/r \rfloor$ and $\alpha = id - d_j \times r^j$, where $d_{m-i-1} \cdots d_0$ is the $(m-i)$-digit radix-r code of the element id. We then map id to $id' = (\lfloor \alpha/r^{j+1} \rfloor) \times r^j + \alpha \; MOD \; r^j$, so that all the elements in $P(i,k)$ are now mapped to a set of integers $\{0, 1, ..., r^{m-i} - 1\}$ via a one-to-one and onto mapping. These id' values, corresponding to the elements of $P(i,k)$, are used to re-code the elements of $P(i,k)$ into $(m-i-1)$-digit radix-r numbers to generate the blocks of level-$(i+1)$ partition. This successive partitioning scheme is illustrated by a *partition tree* in which V is the root with blocks $P(1,k)$ as its children, and at every successive level i, $P(i,k')$ is a child of $P(i-1,k), 1 < i \leq m$, iff $P(i,k')$ is obtained from the block $P(i-1,k)$. An example partition tree for $r = 4$ and $n = 64$ is shown in Figure 1. Note that at level i (root considered to be at level $i = 0$), we get the blocks $P(i,k), 0 \leq k \leq r^i \times m \times (m-1) \times \cdots \times (m-i+1) - 1$ corresponding to level-i partitioning. As before, blocks $P(i+1,k')$ obtained from $P(i,k), i \geq 1$, are numbered with k' from $r(m-i)k$ to $r(m-i)(k+1) - 1$. The partitioning process is formalized as shown in Figure 2; note that we assume the availability of a simple primitive (procedure) $radix\_code(value, q, r, D)$ where $value, q$ and r, are integer inputs, and D is a q-dimensional output array of integers; it converts the integer *"value"* ($0 \leq value \leq r^q - 1$) to a q-digit radix-r number and stores the digits in locations $D(0)$ through $D(q)$ (from least significant digit to most significant digit).

Lemma 4. *Given an arbitrary subset R of V such that $|R| \leq n \times (\frac{2}{r})^i$ for some $i, i \geq 0$, there exists a block $P(i+1,k)$, at level-$(i+1)$ partitioning, that contains at most $\lfloor |R|/2^{i+1} \rfloor$ elements of R.*

Proof. Since $|R| \leq n/(r/2)^i, \forall i \geq 0$, we can apply level-1 partitioning on elements of R to get at least one block, say R_s, of size at most $(n/2)/(r/2)^i$. If $i \geq 1$, then $(n/2)/(r/2)^i \leq n/r$, (for $r \geq 2$) and hence we can apply level-2 partitioning on block R_s. We use induction on $j, 1 \leq j \leq i+1$ to show that it is possible to successively apply level-1 through level-$(i+1)$ partitioning on the smallest block at each step. The induction hypothesis is true for $j = 1$ and $j = 2$. Assume it holds up to level-j partitioning. Hence, after level j partitions ($j < i+1$), we get at least one block, say R'_s, which contains at most $|R|/2^j$ elements of R. Now $|R'_s| \leq 2^{i-j}n/r^i \leq n/r^j$, since $2^{i-j} \leq r^{i-j}$. It is now possible to apply level $(j+1)$ partitions on R'_s. Thus, the induction hypothesis is verified to be true for all values of j up to $i+1$.

Theorem 1. *Given any arbitrary subset R of V, $2^h \leq |R| \leq 2^{h+1} - 1$, $h \geq 0$ and $n \geq r^h(2^{h+1} - 1)/2^h$, there exists at least one block of level-j partitioning, $j \leq h$, which contains only one element of R.*

Proof. It follows from the previous discussions that every time we apply the partitioning scheme corresponding to a specific level on a given set of elements, there will be at least one block with no more than half the number of elements in the given set. Given that $2^h \leq |R| \leq 2^{h+1} - 1$, it follows that h many levels of partitioning are sufficient. From Lemma 4, we see that for h successive levels of partitioning to be applied to the smallest block derived from the previous partitioning step, $|R| \leq 2^h n/r^h$, i.e., $2^{h+1} - 1 \leq 2^h n/r^h$. Hence the theorem.

Example 4. Let $n = 64$, $r = 4$ and $R = \{0, 1, 2, 4, 5, 6, 16, 17, 18, 20, 22, 32, 33, 34, 36\}$. Since there are 15 elements in R, $h = 3$ for this example. Applying level-1 partitioning, the partition blocks derived from R are : (0, 4, 16, 20, 32, 36), (1, 5, 17, 33), (2, 6, 18, 22, 34); (0, 1, 2, 16, 17, 18, 32, 33, 34), (4, 5, 6, 20, 22, 36); (0, 1, 2, 4, 5, 6), (16, 17, 18, 20, 22), (32, 33, 34, 36). The smallest cardinality of all these blocks is 4. Consider a smallest block, say (32, 33, 34, 36). The elements in this block will first be mapped as $32 \rightarrow 0$, $33 \rightarrow 1$, $34 \rightarrow 2$, and $36 \rightarrow 4$. Then these will be recoded in radix 4 system as follows: 32: (0 0), 33: (0 1), 34: (0 2), 36: (1 0). Level-2 partitioning then generates the following blocks from (32, 33, 34, 36): (32, 36), (33), (34); (32, 33, 34), (36). Thus, another level of partitioning is not even necessary to generate a singleton block from R.   □

3.2   Transmission Schedule

We use the successive partitioning scheme, developed in the previous section, to design the transmission schedule of an arbitrary node in an ad hoc network. Consider a given node with identification number my_id; the node knows only its own identification

Procedure $find\_partition$ $(value, i, h, offset, Flag)$;
    begin
        $radix\_code(value, m - i + 1, r, D)$;
        for $j := 0$ **to** $m - i$ **do**
            begin
                $temp \leftarrow r \times (j - 1) + D(j)$;
                set $Flag(i, offset + temp) \leftarrow 1$;
                if $i \leq h - 1$ **then**
                    begin
                        $value \leftarrow value - D(j) \times r^j$;
                        $value \leftarrow (value\ DIV\ r^{j+1}) \times r^j + value\ MOD\ r^j$;
                        $offset \leftarrow r \times (m - i) \times temp$;
                        $find\_partition(value, i + 1, h, offset, Flag)$;
                    end;
            end
    end
    end procedure;

Fig. 2. Partitioning Algorithm

number and n, total number of nodes in the network and Δ, the degree of the network. Given Δ, we compute h such that $2^h \leq \Delta < 2^{h+1}$. The node then computes the blocks of the level-h partitioning, $P(h, k)$, $0 \leq k \leq r^h \frac{m!}{(m-h)!} - 1$. In each frame, the node with identification number my_id will transmit during a time slot or round k iff $my\_id \in P(h, k)$. The details of the pseudo-code for the protocol to be used at each node to compute its own transmission slot or round is given in Figure 3. Note that $Flag[]$ is a two dimensional array and $T[]$ is a one-dimensional array; $Flag(i, j)$ is set to 1 iff my_id value of a node belongs to the block $P(i, j)$, and $T(k)$ is set to 1 iff $Flag(h, k)$ is set to 1. $Flag$ and T are both initialized to all zero values. The variable $offset$ is used for properly numbering the partition blocks at any level.

```
procedure compute_slot (Flag, h, T);
    begin
        for k := 0 to [r^h × m × (m − 1) × · · · × (m − h + 1) − 1] do
            if Flag(h, k) = 1 then T(k) ← 1;
    end
end procedure;
procedure find_my_slots(my_id, n, Δ);
    begin
        h = ⌊log₂ Δ⌋;
        offset ← 0;
        Flag ← 0;     /*initializes the two-dimensional array Flag(i, k) */
        T ← 0;        /*initializes the one-dimensional array T(i) to all zero values */
        find_partition (my_id, 1, h, offset, Flag);
        compute_slot(Flag, h, T);
end procedure
```

```
/* code to be exceuted by each node having my_id as its identifier */

begin
    h = ⌊log₂ Δ⌋;
    max_slot_number ← r^h × m × (m − 1) × · · · × (m − h + 1) − 1
    find_my_slots(my_id, n, Δ);
    for frame_number := 1 to D − 1 do
        for i := 0 to max_slot_number do
            if T(i) = 1 then transmit the message;
end.
```

Fig. 3. Transmission protocol at each node

Theorem 2. *Consider a node x which has not received the message at the beginning of a frame and there is at least one node y, that has the message, among the set R of neighbors of node x. During this frame, there exists at least one time slot $T(k)$, $0 \leq k \leq r^h \frac{m!}{(m-h)!} - 1$, when exactly one of the informed neighbors of node x will transmit the message and node x will receive it correctly (without collision).*

Proof. Let R be the set of neighbors of node x that are informed (i.e., already have the message to transmit) at the beginning of the frame. Clearly, $|R| \leq \Delta$. Consider the blocks $P(h,k)$, $0 \leq k \leq r^h \frac{m!}{(m-h)!} - 1$, generated by level-$h$ partitioning of the vertex set V; by Theorem 1, there exists at least one k such that block $P(h,k)$ contains only one element of the set R. So, during time slot $T(k)$, exactly one node from the set R will transmit and node x will correctly receive the message.

Consider the entire broadcast process. The source node s transmits the message. All its neighbors, set to *receive mode*, receive the message from s. Suppose the frames start after this. That means, all nodes of layer 1 have the message received at the beginning of frame 1. These nodes will then be set to *transmit mode* so that they would now transmit the message in their respective time slots of frame 1 as specified above. Since any node in layer 2 will have at most Δ neighbors in layer 1, it follows that after the completion of frame 1 transmissions, all nodes in layer 2 will receive the message. This process continues for the successive layers so that at the beginning of frame i, $i \geq 2$, all nodes in layer i have received the message successfully and they are ready to transmit the message during frame i at their respective time slots. By theorem 2, it follows that all nodes in layer $i + 1$ will receive the message at the end of frame i. Thus, at the end of frame $\mathcal{D} - 1$, all nodes of the layer $\mathcal{D}$ of the network will receive the message, and the broadcast is complete. Hence, we have the following result.

Theorem 3. *The broadcast process completes in* $(\mathcal{D} - 1)$ *frames consisting of a total of* $(\mathcal{D} - 1) \times \tau$ *rounds (where* $\tau = r^h \frac{m!}{(m-h)!}$*), or in* $\mathcal{O}(\mathcal{D} r^h \log_r^h n)$ *time.*

Remark 3. In light of the $\Omega(\mathcal{D} \log n)$ lower bound [BP97] for deterministic distributed broadcast protocol in mobile multi-hop networks, our bound as given in Theorem 3 is tight when $h = 1$, i.e., for networks with $\Delta = 3$.

Remark 4. It is to be noted that for radix $r = 2$ the frame length needed by our protocol (Theorem 3) is exactly the same as that needed by the protocol *Division* of [BBC99].

Theorem 4. *Our protocol is resilient to node mobility as long as mobility assumption (section 2, assumption 3) is valid.*

Proof. By assumption, when the nodes are mobile, the network never gets disconnected, and at least one node from a conflicting set always remains in the hearing range of any neighboring uncovered node. Now, consider the situation after frame i, $i \geq 1$. At this stage, because of the layer by layer fashion of broadcast, the nodes in the conflicting sets constitute the last layer of nodes which have so far received the message. The neighboring uncovered nodes of each conflicting set would be a member of the next layer of nodes.

4   Comparison with Protocols in [BBC99]

Authors in [BBC99] have proposed two protocols for deterministic distributed broadcast in multi-hop mobile ad hoc networks. Our purpose in this section is to demonstrate the

Table 1. Number of Rounds τ in a Frame for Different $n,.r$, Δ

n	r	$\lceil \log_r n \rceil$	values of τ for				n	r	$\lceil \log_r n \rceil$	values of τ for			
			Δ=3	Δ=7	Δ=15	Δ=31				Δ=3	Δ=7	Δ=15	Δ=31
256	2	8	16	224	2688	26880	16384	2	14	28	728	17472	384384
256	3	6	18	270	3240	29160	16384	3	9	27	648	13608	244944
256	4	4	16	192	1536	6144	16384	4	7	28	672	13440	215040
256	5	4	20	300	3000	15000	16384	5	7	35	1050	26250	525000
256	6	4	24	432	5184	31104	16384	6	6	36	1080	25920	466560
256	7	3	21	294	2058	--	16384	7	5	35	980	20580	288120
256	8	3	24	384	3072	--	16384	8	5	40	1280	30720	491520
512	2	9	18	288	4032	48384	65536	2	16	32	960	26880	698880
512	3	6	18	270	3240	29160	65536	3	11	33	990	26730	641520
512	4	5	20	320	3840	30720	65536	4	8	32	896	21504	430080
512	5	4	20	300	3000	15000	65536	5	7	35	1050	26250	525000
512	6	4	24	432	5184	31104	65536	6	7	42	1512	45260	10888640
512	7	4	28	588	8232	57624	65536	7	6	42	1470	41160	864360
512	8	3	24	384	3072	--	65536	8	6	48	1920	61440	1474560
1024	2	10	20	360	5760	80640	4194304	2	22	44	1848	73920	2808960
1024	3	7	21	378	5670	68040	4194304	3	14	42	1638	58968	1945944
1024	4	5	20	320	3840	30720	4194304	4	11	44	1760	63360	2027520
1024	5	5	25	500	7500	75000	4194304	5	10	50	2250	90000	3150000
1024	6	4	24	432	5184	31104	4194304	6	9	54	2592	108864	3919104
1024	7	4	28	588	8232	57624	4194304	7	8	56	2744	115248	4033680
1024	8	4	32	768	12288	98304	4194304	8	8	64	3584	172032	6881280

relative superiority of our proposed protocol over these two existing protocols. Note that all three protocols operate under exactly the same system model; specifically each of these protocols executes the broadcast in a layer by layer fashion using the same frame length at each layer; thus the frame length τ is used as the performance metric for the protocols. The first protocol of [BBC99], called *Simple* does not use Δ, the degree of the network; thus the frame length does not depend on Δ; the frame length is always n. The protocol *Division* of [BBC99] does use Δ as does our proposed protocol; the frame length required by *Division* is same as that needed by our protocol when we choose $r = 2$ (Remark 4). Our proposed protocol has the added advantage of tuning the value of r to suit a particular value of given Δ in order to reduce the frame length. Table 1 shows the required number of rounds (τ) per frame by the proposed scheme for different values of n, r and Δ (the values of τ shown for $r = 2$ are also equal to the number of rounds per frame needed by the Division protocol of [BBC99]). The minimum value of τ for a given value of n and Δ (over possible choices of r) is shown by bold entries in the table. Out of these minimum values, those which are smaller than the corresponding values of n, are also boxed by rectangles. We make the following observations:

- As noted in [BBC99], the *Division* protocol remains better than the *Simple* protocol as long as $h < \log_2 n/(\log_2 \log_2 n + 1)$ (since for larger h values the frame length, τ, exceeds n); note that this bound on h is approximate and not exact. Our protocol remains better than the *Simple* protocol as long as $h < \log_r n/(\log_r \log_r n + 1)$ (the bound is approximate, not exact) by suitably choosing r. For higher values of n, the range of h and hence that of Δ over which the protocol remains better than *Simple* is larger in our protocol. For example, for $n = 16384$, and $\Delta = 15$ (corresponding to $h = 4$), frame length τ for our protocol is 13440 ($< n$) (by choosing $r = 4$) compared to 17472 for the Division protocol ($r = 2$ in our protocol).

- For lower values of Δ (corresponding to when $h < \log_r n / (\log_r \log_r n + 1)$ after proper choice of r), frame length τ in our protocol is always less than or equal to that in the *Division* protocol and in most cases substantially less. For example, for $n = 256$ and $\Delta = 7$, the minimum τ is 192 (for $r = 4$) which is smaller than the corresponding value of 224 for the *Division* protocol. This improvement is more prominent for larger values of n and Δ. For example, for $n = 4194304$ and $\Delta = 31$, the minimum value of τ in our method is 1945944 ($r = 3$), while the number of rounds needed in the *Division* is 2808960.

Acknowledgement

Srimani's work was supported by an NSF Award # ANI-0219485.

References

[Bas98]   S. Basagni. *On the Broadcast and Clustering Problems in Peer-to-Peer Networks.* PhD thesis, University degli Studi di Milano, Milano, Italy, May 1998.

[BBC99]   S. Basagni, D. Bruschi, and I. Chlamtac. A mobility-transparent deterministic broadcast mechanism for ad hoc networks. *IEEE Transactions on Networking*, 7(6):799–807, December 1999.

[BP97]   D. Bruschi and M. D. Pinto. Lower bounds for the broadcast problem in mobile radio networks. *Distributed Computing*, 10:129–135, 1997.

[BYGI92]   R. Bar-Yehuda, O. Goldreich, and A. Itai. On the time complexity of broadcast in multi-hop radio networks. *Journal of Computer and Systems Science*, 45:104–125, August 1992.

[CK87]   I. Chlamtac and S. Kutten. Tree based broadcasting in multihop radio networks. *IEEE Transactions on Computers*, C-36(10), October 1987.

[LBA93]   C. Lee, J. E. Burns, and M. H. Ammar. Improved randomized broadcast protocols in multi-hop radio networks. In *Proceedings of International Conference on network Protocols*, pages 234–241, San Francisco, CA, 1993.

[LM87]   W. F. Lo and H. T. Mouftah. Collision detection and multitone tree search for multiple access protocols on radio channels. *IEEE Journal on Selected Areas Communication*, SAC-5:1035–1040, July 1987.

[PR97]   E. Pagani and G. P. Rossi. Reliable broadcast in mobile multihop packet networks. In *Proceedings of MOBICOM 97*, pages 34–42, Budapest, Hungary, 1997.

Distributed Mobility Tracking for Ad Hoc Networks Based on an Autoregressive Model*

Zainab R. Zaidi and Brian L. Mark

Dept. of Electrical and Computer Eng.,
George Mason University,
Fairfax, VA 22030, U.S.A.
{zzaidi, bmark}@gmu.edu

Abstract. In ad hoc networks, node mobility causes the network topology to change dynamically over time, which complicates important tasks such as routing and flow control. We propose a distributed scheme for accurately and efficiently tracking the mobility of nodes in ad hoc networks. A first-order autoregressive model is used to represent the evolution of the mobility state of each node, which consists of position, velocity, and acceleration. Each node uses an extended Kalman filter to estimate its mobility state by incorporating network-based signal measurements and the position estimates of the neighbor nodes. Neighbor nodes exchange their position estimates periodically by means of HELLO packets. Each node re-estimates its mobility model parameters, allowing the scheme to adapt to changing mobility characteristics. In practice, a small number of reference nodes with known coordinates is required for accurate mobility tracking. Simulation results validate the accuracy of the proposed tracking scheme.

1   Introduction

The absence of a fixed infrastructure in mobile ad hoc networks makes them suitable for applications such as military battlefields, disaster relief, emergency situations, and low cost commercial communication systems. However, the flexibility of a highly dynamic ad hoc network complicates important network control and management tasks such as routing, flow control, and power management. The mobility of nodes leads to dynamic changes in link availability, resulting in frequent route failures. This can adversely affect network performance in terms of increased packet loss or delay. If the dynamics of the network topology could be predicted in advance, a route discovery mechanism could select paths that were more stable or long-lived in order to avoid or reduce route failures. In ad hoc networks, the network topology dynamics can be inferred from the mobility of

---

* This work was supported by the U.S. National Science Foundation under Grant No. ACI-0133390 and Grant No. CCR-0209049, as well as by a grant from the Cleveland Foundation.

A. Sen et al. (Eds.): IWDC 2004, LNCS 3326, pp. 447–458, 2004.
© Springer-Verlag Berlin Heidelberg 2004

the nodes. Therefore, a mechanism to track node mobility could be of significant benefit to resource management in ad hoc networks.

We present a distributed scheme to accurately track real-time node mobility in an ad hoc network in terms of an autoregressive model (AR-1) of mobility [1]. The AR-1 model is sufficiently simple to enable real-time mobility tracking, but general enough to accurately capture the characteristics of realistic mobility patterns in wireless networks. Some of the more prominent mobility models (cf. [2]) that have been proposed in the literature include random walk models, the random waypoint model, Gauss-Markov models, and linear system models. The random walk and random waypoint models have the important feature of simplicity, making them amenable for use in simulations and in some cases analytical modeling of wireless network behavior. However, recent work has shown that such models do not accurately represent actual user trajectories in real wireless networks [3]. Consequently, such models may result in misleading characterizations of network performance. Moreover, such models are not sufficiently rich to enable accurate and precise real-time mobility tracking.

A linear system model of mobility can capture the characteristics of realistic mobile trajectories and has been applied to real-time mobility tracking for cellular and ad hoc networks [4, 5]. However, the specification of an optimal set of linear system model parameters is not straightforward. Mobility tracking schemes derived from the linear dynamic system model perform well as long as the model parameters match the mobility characteristics of the user. However, they cannot adapt to significant changes in the model parameters over time. The AR-1 model has a similar structure to the linear system model. An important feature of the AR-1 model is that optimal parameter estimates for the model can be determined efficiently via the Yule-Walker equations [6].

Our proposed mobility estimation scheme integrates optimal parameter estimation via the Yule-Walker equations with mobility state estimation using Kalman filtering. The mobility state estimation scheme utilizes network-based signal measurements, such as received signal strength indicators (RSSI) or time-of-arrival of signals (TOA), to infer relative distances between neighbor nodes. A key feature of the proposed tracking scheme is that it provides estimates of position, velocity, and acceleration for each node. The algorithm is distributed and computationally feasible for real-time tracking applications, as it requires that each node performs a constant number of Kalman filtering and Yule-Walker steps at each estimation instant. Further, the mobility information generated by the tracking scheme can be used to predict future mobility behavior and hence future link availability in an ad hoc network.

The integrated mobility estimation scheme can adapt to changes in the mobility characteristics over time, since the model parameters are continuously re-estimated using new observation data. Moreover, the tracking scheme incurs relatively low communication overhead, which consists of periodic broadcasts of short HELLO messages containing mobility state information. Each node executes a Kalman filter to track its mobility state based on the observation data received from neighbor nodes. The accuracy of the tracking scheme improves as the nodal density increases. The presence of a small number of reference nodes with known coordinates in the network is needed to maintain accurate mobility tracking performance.

Several location estimation algorithms have been proposed in the literature for ad hoc wireless networks. The global positioning system (GPS) has been applied to location-aided services in ad hoc networks [7, 8, 9]. This technology has some limitations, as GPS receivers require a clear view of the sky in the line-of-sight of the satellites, which precludes their use in indoor or RF-shadowed environments. Moreover, the size, energy consumption, and cost of GPS receivers can make them impractical for some types of ad hoc networks or for certain types of nodes in an ad hoc network. In [10], position estimates of the network nodes or terminodes (terminals plus nodes) are obtained by triangulating TOA signals. However, the implementation of this scheme has significant overhead and delay problems due to the need to coordinate network topology information among the mobile nodes.

Other approaches to location tracking using network-based signal measurements require a relatively large number of reference nodes with known coordinates placed throughout the network [11, 12]. The location tracking scheme proposed in [11] uses angle-of-arrival (AOA) measurements to triangulate the position of nodes in the network. The mobility tracking scheme proposed in [12] is closest in spirit to the scheme proposed in the present paper in that it employs Kalman-filtering based on a dynamic system model of mobility. However, the scheme of [12] relies on the presence of at least three special references nodes with known coordinates for each mobile node. In contrast, our proposed tracking scheme requires the presence of a small number of reference nodes, i.e., at least two reference nodes, in the network. Moreover, the scheme of [12] assumes that the model parameters are known, whereas our scheme re-estimates the model parameters at each estimation cycle.

The work described in the present paper extends the AR-1 model-based mobility tracking scheme developed for cellular networks in [1] and the linear system model-based tracking scheme for ad hoc networks in [5]. Unlike cellular networks, ad hoc networks do not have fixed base stations with known coordinates which the mobile units can use as reference points. The relay points in an ad hoc network are generally themselves mobile and their coordinates must also be estimated. Thus, the problem of accurate mobility estimation is more challenging in an ad hoc network. The mobility tracking scheme presented here effectively deals with the constraints imposed by the ad hoc networking environment. The algorithm proposed in the present paper differs from the one presented in our earlier paper [5] in the following aspects: 1) the mobility model used is the AR-1 model, which supports adaptive re-estimation of model parameters, rather than the linear system model; 2) the Kalman filter-based state estimation is distributed among the nodes.

The remainder of the paper is organized as follows. Section 2 reviews the linear system model of mobility as well as the AR-1 mobility model of [1]. Section 3 presents our distributed mobility tracking algorithm. Some representative numerical results are discussed in section 4. Finally, section 5 concludes the paper.

2   Mobility Models

In this section, we briefly describe two mobility models: the linear system model (cf. [4]) and the AR-1 mobility model introduced in [1]. The AR-1 model provides the basis for our proposed mobility tracking scheme as discussed in section 3. The linear system model is used to generate mobility patterns for our simulation experiments presented in section 4.

2.1   Linear System Mobility Model

The linear system model has been applied to tracking dynamic targets in [13, 14] and location tracking in cellular networks [4, 15, 16]. The mobile unit's state at time n is defined by a (column) vector[1]

$$s_{n,i} = [x_{n,i}, \dot{x}_{n,i}, \ddot{x}_{n,i}, y_{n,i}, \dot{y}_{n,i}, \ddot{y}_{n,i}]', \tag{1}$$

where $x_{n,i}$ and $y_{n,i}$ specify the position, $\dot{x}_{n,i}$ and $\dot{y}_{n,i}$ specify the velocity, and $\ddot{x}_{n,i}$ and $\ddot{y}_{n,i}$ specify the acceleration of the mobile node N_i at time n in the x and y directions in a two-dimensional grid. The discrete-time state equation of the linear dynamic system is given by

$$s_{n+1,i} = As_{n,i} + Bu_n + w_n, \tag{2}$$

where $u_n = [u_{x,n}, u_{y,n}]'$ is a vector of two independent semi-Markov processes and the process w_n is a 6×1 discrete-time zero mean, stationary Gaussian vector with autocorrelation function $R_w(k) = \delta_k Q$, where $\delta_0 = 1$ and $\delta_k = 0$ when $k \neq 0$, and Q is the covariance matrix of w_n. The matrices A, B, and Q depend on the sampling time interval T and another parameter α, which is defined as the reciprocal of the acceleration time constant (see [15]).

The specification of an optimal set of linear system model parameters, i.e., α and the semi-Markov processes $u_{x,n}$ and $u_{y,n}$ is not straightforward in general. Mobility tracking schemes derived from the linear dynamic system model are accurate as long as the model parameters match the mobility characteristics of the user. However, they cannot adapt to significant changes in the model parameters over time.

2.2   AR-1 Mobility Model

The AR-1 mobility model differs from the linear system model in that the semi-Markov processes, i.e., $u_{x,n}$ and $u_{y,n}$, are not incorporated in state evolution. In the AR-1 mobility model [1], the mobility state of node N_i at time n is also defined by (1). The AR-1 model for the mobility state $s_{n,i}$ of node N_i is given as follows:

$$s_{n+1,i} = A_i s_{n,i} + w_{n,i}, \tag{3}$$

---

[1] The notation $'$ indicates the matrix transpose operator.

where A_i is a 6×6 transformation matrix, the vector $w_{n,i}$ is a 6×1 discrete-time zero mean, white Gaussian process with auto-covariance matrix Q_i. Numerical experiments with the real mobility data of mobile stations (cf. [1]) indicate that the AR-1 model is sufficient to describe the movement dynamics of nodes in a mobile networking environment. In the AR-1 model, the matrix A_i and the covariance matrix Q_i are completely general and can be estimated based on training data using the Yule-Walker equations [6]. This allows the model to accurately characterize a wide class of mobility patterns. Using the Yule-Walker equations (see [1]), a MMSE (Minimum Mean Squared Error) estimate of A_i, denoted by $\hat{A}_i^{(n)}$, where n specifies the amount of training data available, can be obtained from the mobility state data $s_{1,i}, \cdots, s_{n,i}$. Similarly, an estimate, $\hat{Q}_i^{(n)}$, of the noise covariance matrix can be obtained.

3 Mobility Tracking Algorithm

In our proposed distributed mobility tracking scheme, each node tracks its own mobility state using the signal strengths derived from packets received from neighbor nodes. Fig. 1 shows a block diagram of the main components of the mobility tracking algorithm to be executed at each node, in this case node N_1. The given node N_1 requires partial knowledge of $\hat{s}_{n|n-1,j}$ and $M_{n|n-1,j}$ from its neighbor nodes N_j, $j = 0, 2, 3$, in addition to the RSSI or TOA signal measurements. We remark that not all elements of $\hat{s}_{n|n-1,j}$ and $M_{n|n-1,j}$ are used in the mobility state estimation. The HELLO packets, transmitted once every estimation cycle, contain the position estimates of N_j, i.e., the first and fourth elements of the estimated mobility state vector ($\hat{s}_{n|n-1,j}(1)$ and $\hat{s}_{n|n-1,j}(4)$) and their associated variances, i.e., $M_{n|n-1,j}(1,1)$ and $M_{n|n-1,j}(4,4)$, where the numbers in parentheses indicate indices of the matrix. This position information can also be piggybacked onto data packets if the data communication is already in process. Thus, the communication overhead incurred by the distributed scheme is relatively small and the computational overhead of the state estimation process is distributed among the individual nodes.

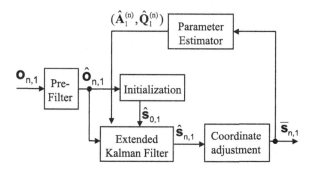

Fig. 1. Block diagram of mobility tracking algorithm

The observation vector $o_{n,1}$ is provided as input to a pre-filter module in Fig. 1. Pre-filtering is done to reduce the noise in the observation data provided as input to the estimation scheme. The pre-filter consists of an averaging filter and outputs a vector of reduced-noise observations $\hat{o}_{n,1}$ (cf. [16]). The output of the pre-filter, $\hat{o}_{n,1}$ is provided as input to both the initialization module and the Kalman filter. The initialization module initializes the node's positions in a local coordinate system as described in [10]. The initial mobility state, i.e., $\hat{s}_{0,1}$, consists of the initial position coordinates with the velocity and acceleration components set to zero. The output $\hat{s}_{n,1}$ of the Kalman filter is the estimate of the mobility state in the local coordinate system. Finally, the coordinate adjustment module transforms the local state vector $\hat{s}_{n,1}$ into a global state vector $\bar{s}_{n,1}$. Coordinate adjustment can be done using the scheme of [10], which uses standard techniques of rotation and translation of cartesian coordinate systems. The state estimates $\hat{s}_{n,i}$ are used to re-estimate the AR-1 model parameters $\hat{A}_i^{(n)}$ and $\hat{Q}_i^{(n)}$ at time n. A recursive model parameter estimator for the AR-1 model is given in [1].

3.1   Observation Vector

We assume that a given node N_1 receives RSSI or TOA signals from three or more neighboring mobile nodes. Observability arguments (cf. [16]) show that Kalman filter-based estimation can yield meaningful state estimates with fewer than three observations from fixed base stations with known locations, but tracking accuracy improves with the number of independent observations. For node N_1, an observation vector is constructed consisting of the three signal measurements from neighbor nodes, i.e.,

$$o_{n,1} = \begin{cases} (p_{n,10}, p_{n,12}, p_{n,13})', & \text{for RSSI,} \\ (\tau_{n,10}, \tau_{n,12}, \tau_{n,13})', & \text{for TOA,} \end{cases} \tag{4}$$

where $p_{n,ij}$ denotes the RSSI received at node N_i from node N_j and $\tau_{n,ij}$ denotes the TOA measured at N_i from N_j. The general observation or measurement equation in a wireless environment is written as follows:

$$o_{n,ij} = h(\Delta s_{n,ij}) + \rho_{n,ij}, \tag{5}$$

where $h(\cdot)$ is a nonlinear function that relates the state $s_{n,ij}$ to the observation data (either RSSI or TOA) and $\rho_{n,ij}$ is a zero mean, stationary Gaussian process(cf. [1]).

To apply the extended Kalman filter for estimating the state vector, the observation $o_{n,ij}$ can be linearized about the estimated state vectors[2] $\hat{s}_{n|n-1,i}$ and $\hat{s}_{n|n-1,j}$ (cf. [1]):

$$o_{n,ij} \approx h(\Delta s_{n,ij}^*) + H_{n,ij}\left(\Delta s_{n,ij} - \Delta s_{n,ij}^*\right) + \rho_{n,ij}, \tag{6}$$

---

[2] We use the Kalman filter notation $\hat{s}_{n|n,i}$ and $\hat{s}_{n|n-1,i}$ to denote the state estimates for N_i at time n given the observations vectors up to times n and $n-1$, respectively.

where $\Delta s_{n,ij}^* = \hat{s}_{n|n-1,i} - \hat{s}_{n|n-1,j}$ and the vector $H_{n,ij}$ is given by (cf. [1])

$$H_{n,ij} = \frac{\partial h}{\partial \Delta s} \Big|_{\Delta s = \Delta s_{n,ij}^*} . \tag{7}$$

Define $\zeta_{n,ij} = H_{n,ij}(s_{n,j} - \hat{s}_{n|n-1,j})$. The conditional density of $\zeta_{n,ij}$ given the previous observations can be approximated by a Gaussian density as follows:

$$f(\zeta_{n,ij}|O_{n,j}) \sim N(0, H_{n,ij} M_{n|n-1,j} H_{n,ij}'), \tag{8}$$

where $M_{n|n-1,j} = \mathrm{Cov}[s_{n,j}|O_{n-1,j}]$. The above expression uses the fact that the conditional density of a mobility state given the observations can be approximated by a Gaussian density (cf. [17]), i.e., $f(s_{n,j}|O_{n,j}) \sim N(\hat{s}_{n|n,j}, M_{n|n,j})$. The expression for the conditional density can be verified easily using (3) and (6). The linearized observation vector for node N_1 is then given as

$$o_{n,1} \approx h(\Delta s_{n,1}^*) + H_{n,1}(s_{n,1} - \hat{s}_{n|n-1,1}) + \zeta_{n,1} + \rho_{n,1}, \tag{9}$$

where

$h(\hat{s}_{n,1}) = [h(\Delta \hat{s}_{n,10}), h(\Delta \hat{s}_{n,12}), h(\Delta \hat{s}_{n,13})]', \quad H_{n,1} = [H_{n,10}', H_{n,12}', H_{n,13}']',$
$\zeta_{n,1} = [\zeta_{n,10}, \zeta_{n,12}, \zeta_{n,13}]', \qquad\qquad\qquad \rho_{n,1} = [\rho_{n,10}, \rho_{n,12}, \rho_{n,13}]'.$

The noise terms $\zeta_{n,1j}$ and $\rho_{n,1j}$ are zero-mean independent Gaussian distributed variables with variances $\sigma_{\zeta,1j}^2$ and σ_ρ^2, respectively.

3.2   Extended Kalman Filter

The steps in the extended Kalman filter are given as follows (cf. [18]). The algorithm is executed on node N_1 and N_0, N_2, and N_3 are the neighbor nodes.

Initialization:

1. $\hat{s}_{0|-1,1}$ is initialized as discussed in section 3.3
2. $M_{0|-1,1} = I_6$

Recursive estimation (time n, $n = 1, 2, \cdots$):

1. $H_{n,1j} = \frac{\partial h}{\partial \Delta s} \Big|_{\Delta s = \hat{s}_{n|n-1,1} - \hat{s}_{n|n-1,j}}$; $j = 0, 2, 3$
2. $\sigma_{\zeta,1j}^2 = H_{n,1j} M_{n|n-1,j} H_{n,1j}'$; $j = 0, 2, 3$
3. $R_1 = \mathrm{diag}[\sigma_{\zeta,10}^2, \sigma_{\zeta,12}^2, \sigma_{\zeta,13}^2] + \sigma_\rho^2 * I_3$
4. $K_{n,1} = M_{n|n-1,1} H_{n,1}' (H_{n,1} M_{n|n-1,1} H_{n,1}' + R_1)^{-1}$
5. $\hat{s}_{n|n,1} = \hat{s}_{n|n-1,1} + K_{n,1}(\hat{o}_{n,1} - h(\hat{s}_{n|n-1,1}))$ [Correction step]
6. $\hat{s}_{n+1|n,1} = A_1 \hat{s}_{n|n,1}$ [Prediction step]
7. $M_{n|n,1} = (I - K_{n,1} H_{n,1}) M_{n|n-1,1} (I - K_{n,1} H_{n,1})' - K_{n,1} R_1 K_{n,1}'$
8. $M_{n+1|n,1} = A_1 M_{n|n,1} A_1' + Q_1$

where $M_{l|k,1} = \mathrm{Cov}(s_{l|k,1})$, $l = n, k \in \{n, n-1\}$, $K_{n,1}$ is the Kalman gain matrix, and R_1 is the covariance matrix of the noise in measurements.

3.3   Initialization Module

To create a coordinate system in the network, one of the nodes, say N_0, assumes the role of the origin. The origin node could be determined by a simple election protocol. The origin node N_0 then sets its position coordinates as $(x_0, y_0) = (0, 0)$ and chooses two of its neighbors, say nodes N_1 and N_2, respectively, to determine the x and y axes of the local coordinate system. More precisely, N_1 is chosen to lie on the positive x axis and the coordinates of node N_2 are chosen to have a positive y-component. The coordinates of N_1 and N_2 are initialized as follows (cf. [10]):

$$(x_1, y_1) = (\hat{d}_{01}, 0), \quad (x_2, y_2) = (\hat{d}_{02} \cos \theta_{12}, \hat{d}_{1,02} \sin \theta_{12}),$$

where $\hat{d}_{ij} = e^{(\kappa_j - \hat{o}_{n,ij})/10\gamma}$ denotes the initial distance estimate between nodes N_i and N_j, and $\theta_{12} = \arccos\left((\hat{d}_{01}^2 + \hat{d}_{02}^2 - \hat{d}_{12}^2)/2\hat{d}_{01}\hat{d}_{02}\right)$ denotes the angle from the position vector corresponding to node N_1 to that corresponding to N_2, with $0 \leq \theta_{12} \leq \pi$. The coordinates (x_1, y_1) and (x_2, y_2) could be computed by the origin node N_0 and transmitted to nodes N_1 and N_2, respectively. After this is done, the nodes N_0, N_1, and N_2, completely determine a local coordinate system. Once the coordinates of a given node have been initialized, the node broadcasts its coordinates within its neighborhood. If a given node N_k has at least three neighbors, N_i, N_j, N_l, with their coordinates already defined in the local coordinate system (e.g., N_0, N_1, and N_2), the node can initialize its position coordinates via triangulation as follows:

$$\begin{bmatrix} x_k \\ y_k \end{bmatrix} = 0.5 \begin{bmatrix} x_i - x_j \ y_i - y_j \\ x_i - x_l \ y_i - y_l \end{bmatrix}^{-1} \begin{bmatrix} -\hat{d}_{ik}^2 + \hat{d}_{jk}^2 + x_i^2 - x_j^2 + y_i^2 - y_j^2 \\ -\hat{d}_{ik}^2 + \hat{d}_{lk}^2 + x_i^2 - x_l^2 + y_i^2 - y_l^2 \end{bmatrix}.$$

The initialization process starts at N_0, i.e., the origin of the local coordinate system and propagates outward until a maximal set of nodes in the network is initialized within the coordinate system.

4   Numerical Results

In this section, we present some representative simulation results to demonstrate the operation and performance of the proposed mobility tracking scheme.

4.1   Simulation Setup and Assumptions

The results presented here were obtained using a Matlab-based simulation model of an ad hoc network comprised of 30 nodes. Random mobile trajectories for each of the nodes were generated using the linear system model discussed in section 2.1. The first 50 position coordinates of each node are used to initialize the AR-1 model parameters as described in section 2.2. An appropriate training data set is required for proper initialization of the AR-1 model parameters. In our simulation experiments, each mobile trajectory contains almost 350 sample points and the transmission range of all the nodes is assumed to be 400 m. Each node uses signal measurements from all neighbor nodes to estimate its mobility state.

RSSI measurements at time n were generated using the lognormal shadowing fading model [19]:

$$p_{n,ij} = \kappa_j - 10\gamma \log(d_{n,ij}) + \psi_{n,ij}, \tag{10}$$

where $p_{n,ij}$ is the RSSI received at node N_i from node N_j, $d_{n,ij}$ is the distance between the nodes, and $\psi_{n,ij}$ is a zero mean, stationary Gaussian process with a standard deviation of 4 dB. The parameter κ_j is assumed to be zero and γ is set to 8. TOA measurements yield similar results to RSSI measurements (cf. [1]). The difference in performance in real scenarios depends on the accuracy with which the signal measurements are collected, especially in the case of TOA, and on the accuracy of the assumed lognormal signal propagation model in the case of RSSI.

The initial positions of these nodes are assumed to be uniformly distributed in a square 600 m × 600 m area, but they are subsequently allowed to move outside this area. The initial speed and acceleration, in each dimension, are assumed to be zero for all nodes. The discrete-time interval is set as $T = 0.1$ s. The dynamic system model parameters are set as follows: $\alpha = 1$ s^{-1} and $\sigma_1 = 1$ dB (cf. section 2.1). The discrete command processes $u_x(t)$ and $u_y(t)$ for the three mobile nodes are independent semi-Markov processes, each taking on five possible levels of acceleration comprising the set $\mathcal{L} = \{-1, -0.5, 0, 0.5, 1\}$ in units of m/s^2. This set of acceleration levels is capable of generating a wide range of dynamic motion. The initial probability vector π for the semi-Markov model (SMM) governing $u_x(t)$ and $u_y(t)$ is initialized to a uniform distribution. The elements of the transition probability matrix for the SMM are initialized to a common value of $1/5$. We assume that the dwell times in each state are uniformly distributed with a common mean value of $2T$ s, where T is the sampling interval.

4.2   Mobility Estimation

A sample simulation result showing the tracking of 30 mobile nodes is illustrated in Fig. 2, where the coordinates are represented in meters. The initial coordinates of each node are marked with ∗, as shown in Fig. 2. The first 50 position coordinates of each node are used to initialize the AR-1 model parameters A_i and Q_i for each node N_i. Fig. 2 shows mobility tracking results when two additional stationary reference nodes are located at $(0, -300)$ and $(0, 300)$ (not shown in Fig. 2). One node is selected to serve as the origin of the local coordinate system and the two nodes closest to the origin are chosen to determine the x and y axes of the local system. We note that the estimation error is larger for the nodes moving further away from the rest of the nodes than the nodes which stay closer to the other nodes. As nodes move further apart, there are fewer neighbor nodes to provide independent observations. We also remark that tracking accuracy gen-

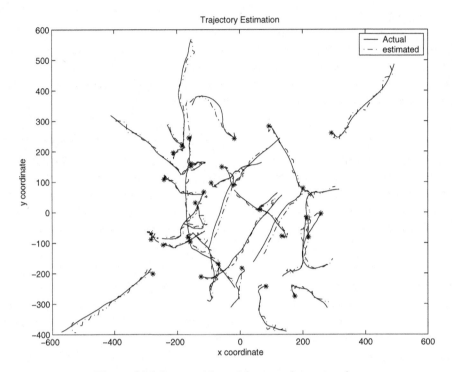

Fig. 2. Mobility tracking with two reference nodes

erally improves with increasing nodal density, again since the presence of more neighbors provides more observation data for the state estimation process.

We compared the performance of the proposed tracking scheme with a similar tracking scheme based on the linear system model, in which the model parameters are assumed to be known. Mobility tracking performance can be quantified in terms of root mean square estimation error (RMSE). We use root mean squared error (RMSE) as a figure of merit to compare a given trajectory $\{x_n, y_n\}$ and its estimated trajectory $\{\hat{x}_n, \hat{y}_n\}$:

$$\text{RMSE} = \sqrt{\frac{1}{N} \sum_{n=1}^{N} [(\hat{x}_n - x_n)^2 + (\hat{y}_n - y_n)^2]} \tag{11}$$

Table 1 shows RMSE results for various scenarios in terms of the sample mean, μ_{RMSE}, and standard deviation, σ_{RMSE}, of the RMSE statistic, which are computed using 500 independently generated sample experiments. The first column in the table indicates the estimation scheme and the second column shows the availability of model parameters. The third column indicates the standard deviation, σ_ψ, of the shadowing noise in the RSSI measurements. The table shows that the integrated AR-1 estimator has a slightly larger mean RMSE compared to the state estimator with complete knowledge of the linear system model parameters. Interestingly, the standard deviation of the RMSE is smaller for the AR-1 based estimator. From Table 1, we also observe that increasing the shadowing nodes tends to degrade tracking performance, but tracking performance remains fairly stable even for a standard deviation of $\sigma_\psi = 8$ dB. Moreover, the presence of three reference nodes in the network improves the accuracy of the estimator when compared against the case of two reference nodes.

Table 1. RMSE of mobility tracking over 500 sample experiments

Estimation Scheme	Model Parameters	σ_ψ (dB)	μ_{RMSE} (m)	σ_{RMSE} (m)
Linear System	known	4	4.39	8.4
Integrated AR-1 with 2 references	unknown	4	8.78	3.99
Integrated AR-1 with 3 references	unknown	4	7.38	1.46
Linear System	known	8	7.45	12.6
Integrated AR-1 with 2 references	unknown	8	13.62	5.66
Integrated AR-1 with 3 references	unknown	8	10.96	2.91

5 Conclusion

We have proposed a distributed scheme for tracking node mobility in ad hoc networks based on an autoregressive model of mobility. The tracking scheme estimates both the current mobility state and re-estimates the mobility model parameters in an integrated fashion. Thus, the scheme does not require prior knowledge of mobility model parameters and can adapt to wireless networking scenarios where the mobility model parameters are not known or may change with time. Simulation results show that the proposed tracking scheme performs accurately under a variety of wireless networking scenarios with a small number of reference nodes. The mobility tracking scheme can be applied in a variety of scenarios to enhance the performance of routing, mobility management, and resource allocation in mobile ad hoc networks. In ongoing work, we are investigating the application of the mobility tracking scheme to predict future link availability in order to enable more efficient routing and improved quality-of-service provisioning in ad hoc networks.

References

1. Zaidi, Z.R., Mark, B.L.: Mobility Estimation for Wireless Networks Based on an Autoregressive Model. In: Proc. of IEEE Globecom, Dallas, TX (2004 (to appear))
2. Bettstetter, C.: Smooth is better than sharp: A random mobility model for simulation of wireless networks. In: Proc. of ACM MSWiM. (2001) 19–27
3. Camp, T., Boleng, J., Davies, V.: Survey of mobility models for ad hoc network research. Wireless Communication and Mobile Computing (WCMC), Special issue on Mobile Ad Hoc Networking **2** (2002) 483–502
4. Liu, T., Bahl, P., Chlamtac, I.: Mobility modeling, location tracking, and trajectory prediction in wireless ATM networks. IEEE J. Selected Areas in Comm. **16** (1998) 922–936

5. Zaidi, Z.R., Mark, B.L.: A mobility tracking model for wireless ad hoc networks. In: Proc. of IEEE WCNC. Volume 3., New Orleans, LA (2003) 1790–1795
6. Lim, J.S., Oppenheim, A.V.: Advanced Topics in Signal Processing. Prentice Hall, Englewood Cliffs, NJ 07632 (1987)
7. Basagni, S., Chlamtac, I., Syrotiuk, V.R., Woodward, B.A.: A Distance Routing Effect Algorithm for Mobility (DREAM). In: Proc. of ACM MobiCom. (1998) 76–84
8. Basu, P., Khan, N., Little, T.D.C.: A mobility-based metric for clustering in mobile ad hoc networks. In: Proc. of Distributed Computing System Workshop. (2001) 413–418
9. Blazevic, L., Buttyan, L., Capkun, S., Giordano, S., Hubaux, J., Boudec, J.: Self-Organization in Mobile Ad-hoc Networks: The Approach of Terminodes. IEEE Communication Magazine 39 (2001) 166–174
10. Capkun, S., Hamdi, M., Hubaux, J.: GPS-free positioning in mobile ad-hoc networks. In: Proc. of 34th HICSS. (2001) 3481–3490
11. Niculescu, D., Nath, B.: Ad hoc positioning system (APS) using AOA. In: Proc. of IEEE Infocom. (2003) 1734–1743
12. Pathirana, P.N., Savkin, A.V., Jha, S.: Mobility modeling and trajectory prediction for cellular networks with mobile base stations. In: Proc. of ACM MobiHoc 2003. (2003) 213–221
13. Singer, R.A.: Estimating optimal tracking filter performance for manned maneuvering targets. IEEE Trans. Aerosp. Elect. Syst. 6 (1970) 473–483
14. Moose, R.L., Vanlandingham, H.F., McCabe, D.H.: Modeling and estimation for tracking maneuvering targets. IEEE Trans. Aerosp. Elect. Syst. 15 (1979) 448–456
15. Mark, B.L., Zaidi, Z.R.: Robust mobility tracking for cellular networks. In: Proc. of IEEE ICC. Volume 1., New York, NY (2002) 445–449
16. Zaidi, Z.R., Mark, B.L.: Real-time Mobility Tracking Algorithms for Cellular Networks based on Kalman Filtering. IEEE Trans. on Mobile Computing (to appear) (2005)
17. H. Vincent Poor: An Introduction to Signal Detection and Estimation. Springer-Verlag, New York (1988)
18. Brown, R.G., Hwang, P.Y.: Introduction to Random Signals and Applied Kalman Filtering. 3rd edn. John Wiley & Sons, New York (1997)
19. Gudmundson, M.: Correlation model for shadowing fading in mobile radio systems. Electronic Letters 27 (1991) 2145–2146

Broadcast and Gossiping Algorithms for Mobile Ad Hoc Networks Based on Breadth-First Traversal

Koushik Sinha[1] and Pradip K. Srimani[2]

[1] Department of Computer Science, University of Arizona, Tucson, AZ 85719
sinha_kou@yahoo.com
[2] Department of Computer Science, Clemson University, Clemson, SC 29634
srimani@cs.clemson.edu

Abstract. We present a deterministic broadcast algorithm for the class of mobile ad hoc networks where the mobile nodes possess collision detection capabilities. The algorithm is based on a breadth-first traversal of the network, allows multiple transmissions in the same time slot and completes broadcast in $O(n \log n)$ time in the worst case. It is mobility resilient even for networks where topology changes are very frequent. The idea of this broadcast algorithm is then extended to develop a gossiping algorithm having $O((n + D)D \log n)$ worst case run time, where D is the diameter of the network graph, which is an improvement over the existing algorithms.

Keywords: mobile computing, ad hoc networks, deterministic broadcast, breadth-first broadcast, gossiping.

1 Introduction

In a single channel ad hoc network, all the nodes communicate over a unique common radio frequency, and a message transmitted by a node reaches all its neighbors (within its hearing zone) in the same time step. However, more than one node may also start to transmit in the same time slot, and that would result in the messages being garbled beyond recognition, which we term as a *collision*. A node is said to have a *collision detection capability* if it can detect such garbled messages. The nodes may or may not possess such collision detection capability. Depending on this, there are two different models of message communication protocols in ad hoc networks [17].

Important message communication problems involved in an ad hoc network include broadcasting, multicasting and gossiping. The simplest broadcast algorithm in an ad hoc network is round-robin, which works in $O(nD)$ time steps, where n is the total number of nodes in the network and D represents the diameter of the network [4]. In [8], an $O(n \log^2 n)$ time deterministic algorithm for broadcasting was presented. $O(D\Delta \log^2 n)$-time broadcast algorithms were given in [10], [11], where Δ represents the maximum node degree. For networks

A. Sen et al. (Eds.): IWDC 2004, LNCS 3326, pp. 459–470, 2004.
© Springer-Verlag Berlin Heidelberg 2004

with large diameters, [13] presents a deterministic broadcast algorithm that requires $O(D + \log^5 n)$ time, with $D = \Omega(\log^5 n)$. The protocol in [5] completes the broadcast in $O(D \log^2 n)$ steps. [4] talks of another deterministic broadcast protocol requiring $O(D 2^h \log^h n)$ steps, where h is the minimum integer in the range $1 \leq h < \log n$, satisfying the inequality $\Delta \leq 2^{h+1} - 1$.

In [3], a randomized broadcast protocol working in $O(D \log n + \log^2 n)$ time was given which is optimal [16] for $D \leq n^{1-\epsilon}$, where ϵ is any constant > 0.

Several results on deterministic and randomized gossiping algorithms are available in the literature [7], [8], [9], [10], [11], [12], [14], [15]. In [8], the authors showed the existence of an $O(n^{3/2} \log^2 n)$ - time deterministic algorithm (without any actual construction of the algorithm) for gossiping in ad hoc networks. In [9], a randomized distributed algorithm was presented that performs radio gossiping in an expected time of $O(n \log^4 n)$. Authors in [10], [11] presented a deterministic gossiping algorithm for unknown ad hoc radio networks working in time $O(D \Delta^2 \log^3 n)$.

Most of the research works on designing protocols for broadcast in ad hoc networks focus on the scenario where the nodes do not possess collision detection capabilities. With the rapid advances in technology, mobile terminals with collision detection capabilities may soon become common in the future. Some results on this are already reported in the literature [6], [1], [2]. In [1], [2], deterministic broadcast algorithms based on depth-first broadcast in ad hoc networks with collision detection capabilities of the mobile terminals have been presented. For highly mobile networks, however, an execution time proportional to the number of bits in the message is required for mobility resilience in [1], [2].

In this paper, we first present a deterministic algorithm for broadcast in ad hoc networks with collision detection capabilities present at the mobile terminals. The algorithm is based on breadth-first traversal of the nodes, which allows simultaneous transmission by multiple nodes as opposed to the depth-first broadcast in [2]. Although this may result in collisions at the receiving nodes, the proposed algorithm can detect and take corrective measures to eventually avoid collisions. This algorithm is mobility resilient and takes $O(n \log n)$ time in the worst case. Compared to the algorithm in [4], the worst-case performance of our proposed algorithm is better for high values of node degree Δ and diameter D.

We then propose a gossiping algorithm, extending the above idea of breadth-first broadcast technique. The proposed gossiping algorithm completes in $O(Dn \log n + D^2 \log n)$ time, which is better than the $O(n^{3/2} \log^2 n)$ time needed by the algorithm in [8]. For large values of Δ, the time complexity of this proposed algorithm is comparable to the $O(D \Delta^2 \log^3 n)$ time algorithm in [11].

2 System Model

A radio network is defined as a directed graph with n vertices that represent mobile terminals or processors. Each node is assigned a unique identifier from the set $\{1, 2, \ldots, n\}$. If the exact value of n is not known, then we can apply the technique described in [8] to find an upper bound on the node id within a factor of 2. Initially the nodes do not possess any information about the network topology. All communication links are assumed to be bi-directional. We say a node v is *neighbor* of u, if they are within each other's hearing zone. We assume that the network is connected at all times. In the broadcast problem, one node is distinguished as the *source node* (also termed as the *root*), which has a message M to be broadcast.

There is a single channel over which all the nodes in the system transmit. Time is assumed to be slotted and all transmissions are edge-triggered, that is, they take place at time slot boundaries. In a particular time slot, a station can transmit and/or listen to the channel.

It is assumed that the mobile terminals possess *collision detection capabilities*. We introduce the concept of *layers* to help understand how the broadcast message propagates in the network and how collisions are resolved. The source node is the only node in layer 0, all nodes within the hearing zone of the source node forming layer 1, and in general, all nodes within the hearing zone of the nodes in layer i and which are not in layer $i-1$, form the layer $i+1$, for $i \geq 1$.

3   Breadth-First Broadcast

3.1   Preliminaries and the Basic Idea

A transmission of M by the source node will be received by all nodes in layer 1. The nodes in layer 1 would then transmit the message to the nodes in layer 2. However, at this point, a node in layer 2 may receive a collided message due to simultaneous transmission from more than one node in layer 1. In general, such a situation can also arise from simultaneous transmissions by nodes in different layers in the same time slot. Our proposed protocol first identifies such a collision at the receiving node through some appropriate acknowledgement signals from the receiving node and then selectively drops out one or more of the transmitting neighboring nodes (dropped out nodes do not transmit the message) at each of the succeeding stages (what we term as *rounds*), so that eventually collision is avoided at each of the receiving nodes.

At any instant of time, a node may be in any one of the four states described below.

– **receive** : node is ready to receive data transmitted by any other node
– **collision** : node has received a collided message
– **active** : node has received the message correctly, but not transmitting it
– **transmit** : node will transmit the message

A *round* of transmission normally consists of (1) one or more slots for transmitting the actual message, depending on the length of the message and (2) three slots for receiving acknowledgement(s) from the neighboring nodes. However, as explained below, some more control signal slots are used in a round at regular intervals of time, in order to guarantee collision-free reception of the message by all receiving nodes. The *acknowledgement slots* are :

– slot S for receiving an acknowledgement from the nodes which received the message correctly without any collision.

- slot C for receiving an acknowledgement from the receiving node(s), if the corresponding receiving node(s) detected a *collision*.
- Slot N can be used to indicate either of the two situations : (i) for receiving an acknowledgement which would indicate that it did not receive any message (clean or collided) in this round although it received a collided message in the previous round(s), or (ii) it is yet to receive anything (clean or collided) in the message slot.

Every transmitting node takes decision depending only on the type of acknowledgements received by it in the three slots S, C and N respectively, associated with the previous message transmission slot. If a transmitting node receives an acknowledgement (which may come from a number of nodes in *receive* state) in slot S, it implies that the corresponding nodes in *receive* state have received the message correctly without any collision. These receiving nodes would become *active* in the successive rounds. If an acknowledgement is received by the transmitting node in the C slot, it implies one or more of the receiving nodes have experienced a collision during the previous message slot. Collision is resolved by preventing some of the nodes from transmitting in the subsequent rounds. However, such an action may cause some of the receiving nodes which suffered collision, in not receiving the message in the immediate next round (this may happen if all the neighboring transmitting nodes of a receiving node are dropped out). At this point, the corresponding receiving node sends an acknowledgement in N slot. The transmitting node(s) receiving an N ack, tries to transmit again in the succeeding rounds so that eventually all neighboring nodes receive the message correctly.

In general, it is possible that after a particular round, some nodes in a given layer, say j, will receive the message correctly and hence, will become *active*, while others in the same layer have experienced collision and so they are in *collision* state. Two possible scenarios may arise :

1. While these *active* nodes in layer j start transmitting the message, their messages can also reach some of the nodes of the same layer j which are still in *collision* state. This would cause further problems in resolving collision due to messages coming from the transmitting nodes of layer $j-1$. To avoid such a situation and to simplify the collision resolution algorithm, an active node in layer j would first test through some additional control signals (described below), if it is a neighbor of any node of the same layer j in *collision* state. If so, then this active node does not immediately move to the *transmit* state.

2. Consider the scenario consisting of 4 nodes, 3 in layer j (some of the nodes in this layer are yet to receive the message correctly), and one in layer $j+1$ (Fig. 1). Out of the 3 nodes in layer j, node v is *active*, and the other two are in *collision* state. One of these nodes, x is adjacent to node v as well, while the other node u is adjacent to the node w in layer $j+1$ which is still in *receive* state. Suppose v starts transmitting the message to w even when u is in the collision state. It may happen that w receives a collided message (due to transmission from some other active node(s) like v in layer j), and so some of these nodes in layer j will be dropped from transmitting, depending

on the bit pattern of their id's. Essentially, we drop out all but the node with the maximum *id* value, and this is done by successively scanning the bit pattern of the node *id* from the most significant bit. It is to be noted that the decision to drop out or move to *transmit* state is done in a completely distributed fashion - each of the *active* nodes scan their id bits and take the decision independent of other nodes. During this dropping out process, node *u* may become *active*. Node *u* (because of its independent decision to transmit) may now cause collision at *w*. The solution is to keep the node *v* in *active* state until no node like *w* exists (which has some parent in *collision* state in layer *j*).

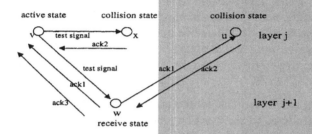

Fig. 1. Role of the Control Signals

To handle the above mentioned two scenarios, we introduce additional control signals in a *round* to test if an *active* node *v* in layer *j* can move to *transmit* state while satisfying the following two conditions,

1. without causing a collision to any node in the same receiving layer *j*, or
2. if its message is received by a node *w* (in *receive* state) at layer *j* + 1, then whether *w* can also be in the hearing zone of some node, say *u* (in *collision* state) at layer *j*.

We augment a round with four additional control slots as follows :

− *test* : 1-bit test signal sent by an *active* node only
− *ack1* : 1-bit acknowledgement signal sent by a node in *receive* state which received the test signal above
− *ack2* : 1-bit acknowledgement signal sent by a node in *collision* state which received either the *test* signal or *ack1* signal
− *ack3* : 1-bit signal sent by a node in *receive* state which got the *test* and *ack2* signals

The overall structure of a round with the control signals is shown in Fig. 2. The four control signals and the three acknowledgement signals S, C and N are each 1-bit long. To minimize overhead, these control signals are included in a round only every log n rounds.

Additionally, for mobility resilience, the source node will repeat transmitting the message every log n rounds. The complete stepwise broadcast algorithm is described below. For details, the reader is referred to [1].

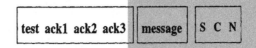

Fig. 2. Structure of a round

3.2   Algorithm bf_broadcast

We use a local variable *round_count*, initialized to 0, at each node to keep track of the round number in which a node received M. The source node transmits its *round_count* variable along with the message. Subsequently, the source node and all such nodes which have received the message correctly (i.e., the nodes in *active* or *transmit* state), would increment their respective *round_count* variables at the start of successive rounds. Whenever a node transmits the message, the current value of the $round_count$ at that node is appended with this transmitted message. The following steps are executed by all nodes in parallel for broadcasting a message.

Step 1 : (initialization) The source node sets its state to *transmit*. All other nodes set their states to *receive*. The following steps are executed in each of the successive rounds.

Step 2 : (actions taken by the source node) If *round_count* MOD log $n = 0$, then transmit M.

Step 3 : .(test for eligibility of an *active* node to move to *transmit* state). If the state is *active* and *round_count* MOD log $n = 0$, then execute the steps 3.1, 3.2 and 3.3.

> **Step 3.1 :** Send a *test* signal (one of the four control signals) and wait for *ack2* or *ack3* signals.
>
> **Step 3.2 :** If neither *ack2* or *ack3* signals received in respective slots, then node state changed to *transmit*, set *transmission_count* $= 0$ and set *scanned_bit_position* $=$ log $n - 1$.
>
> **Step 3.3 :** Increment *round_count* by 1 and go back to Step 2 for next round.

Step 4 : .(*transmit* state actions) : If node state is *transmit*, then execute steps 4.1 to 4.5.

> **Step 4.1:** If *transmission_count* $= 0$, then transmit the message, increment *transmission_count* by 1, and wait for acknowledgement signals in the S, C and N slots.
>
> **Step 4.2 :** If an ack was received in the C slot of the preceding round, then
>
> > **Step 4.2.1 :** if the *id* bit value at the current *scanned_bit_position* is 1 and the node transmitted the message in the immediate previous round, then retransmit M, increment *transmission_count* by 1, decrement *scanned_bit_position* by 1, and look for S, C and N signals again.
>
> **Step 4.3 :** If an ack received in the N slot but not in C, then
> /* there is some node in *receive* state having *only* the dropped out nodes (including this node) from which it received the message; hence we need to restart transmission from this node */

Step 4.3.1 : if the node's *id* bit at the *scanned_bit_position* is 0, then transmit the message, increment *transmission_count* by 1, decrement *scanned_bit_position* by 1, and look for S, C and N signals.

Step 4.4 : If an ack was received only in the slot S but not in C and N, then the state of the node is changed back to *active*.   /* successful transmission to some node */

Step 4.5 : Increment *round_count* by 1 and goto Step 2 for execution in the next round.

Step 5 : (*receive* state actions) : If node state is *receive*, then execute steps 5.1 to 5.4.

Step 5.1 : If a signal is received in *test* slot, then send *ack1*. If signal received in *ack2* slot, then send *ack3* signal.

Step 5.2 : If received clean M, then send an ack in S slot and change state to *active*.

Step 5.3 : If collision heard in *message* slot, then send ack in C slot and change state to *collision*.

Step 5.4 : Go back to Step 2 for execution in the next round.

Step 6 : .(*collision* state actions) : If node state is *collision*, then execute steps 6.1 to 6.5.

Step 6.1 : If a signal received in either *test* slot or *ack1* slot, then send the *ack2* signal.

Step 6.2 : If clean signal received in the *message slot*, then send an ack in S slot and change state to *active*.

Step 6.3 : If collision in the *message* slot, then send an ack in C slot.

Step 6.4 : If no signal is received in the message slot, but a collided message was received in the previous round, then send an acknowledgement signal in the N slot.

Step 6.5 : Go back to Step 2 for execution in the next round.

To illustrate the basic ideas of the above algorithm, we consider the following two examples.

Example 1. Consider the network in Fig. 3, where the nodes 111111, 111110, 110110, 110010 and 110001 are the sender nodes at some stage (round), and the nodes a, b, c, d and e are the receiving nodes. Node d receives the clean message from the node 110110, but each of nodes a, b, c and e detects a collision. Following the steps of the algorithm, nodes 110110 and 110001 are dropped out as sender nodes, after the testing of the third bit from the most significant bit side. c then receives the clean message from the node 111110 in the next round. Subsequently, node 111110 is dropped out after the sixth bit so that nodes a and b get clean message from 111111 in the next round. Node 110010 receives special ack signal from node e corresponding to the third bit position so that node 110010 transmits in the next round. Thus, node e would receive the message from node 110010.

Example 2. Consider the network in Fig. 4, where the nodes 000011, 000010 and 000001 are the transmitting nodes, and nodes a, b and c are the receiving nodes.

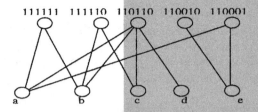

Fig. 3. An Example for Collision Resolution by the Broadcast Algorithm

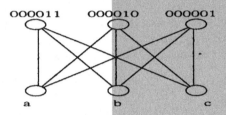

Fig. 4. Another Example for Collision Resolution by the Broadcast Algorithm

Following the steps of the algorithm, none of the sender nodes transmits the message in the first round. Nodes 000011, 000010 and 000001 begin transmission from round 2. Node 000001 is dropped out after the fifth bit (from the msb side) testing, and node 000010 is dropped out after the sixth bit. Finally, nodes a, b and c receive the clean message from node 000011.

3.3   Mobility Resilience

The layer-by-layer transmission of the message as in [4] and periodic retransmission of the message by the source node after every log n rounds ensures that even if a node moves from a layer j to a layer i before it has received the message M and after all nodes in layer i have finished transmitting M, where $i > j$ (i.e., it is now at a smaller distance from the source node s), it will still be able to receive the broadcast message correctly at some point of time. Thus, the algorithm *bf_broadcast* works correctly even when the network topology changes very frequently.

3.4   Complexity

Lemma 1. *At least one node is guaranteed to have received the message correctly, after every $2 \log n$ rounds of transmission.*

Proof : Because of the typical nature of dropping out successive transmitting nodes causing a collision, it is guaranteed that every $2 \log n$ rounds, at least one node of the receiving layer j (assuming that transmitting layer is $j - 1$) gets the message correctly. The factor of 2 is included to take care of the fact that if a bit tested for 1 causes a *no signal* to the receiving nodes, this bit is flipped to 0. Since there are a maximum of log n such flipping, the claim is justified.

Theorem 1. *The algorithm bf_broadcast takes $O(n \log n)$ rounds to complete the broadcast in the worst case.*

Proof : Since an active node will be tested for eligibility for transmission every $\log n$ rounds, the maximum waiting time to start transmission to the next layer, after all nodes in a layer have correctly got the message, is $\log n$. That is, effectively we may assume that each layer j completes its broadcast in $(2p_j + 1) \cdot \log n$ rounds, (where p_j is the number of nodes in layer j), after which the next layer starts transmitting the message even when there is no overlap in the broadcast from different layers. Hence, the worst case time for broadcast is $\sum (2p_j + 1) \log n = 2n \log n + D \log n$, where D is the diameter of the graph.

However, after every $\log n$ rounds, we add the initial four 1-bit control slots at the beginning of the transmission round. Hence, the total number of slots (irrespective of 1-bit or multiple bits) is $4(2n + D) \log n + 4(2n + D) = 4(2n + D)(\log n + 1)$.

3.5   Performance Comparison

To compare the performance of the breadth-first broadcast algorithm with the exisiting algorithms, we consider the following example.

Example 3. Let $n = 1024$, $\Delta = 15$, $h = 3$ and $D = 60$.

The algorithm in [4] would need $D.2h. \log n(\log n1) \cdots (\log nh + 1)$ slots $= 60 * 8 * 10 * 9 * 8 = 3,45,600$ time slots. On the other hand, the proposed breadth-first broadcast algorithm needs $4(2n + D).(\log n + 1)$ slots $= 4(2 * 1024 + 60)(10 + 1) = 92,752$ time slots.

4   Gossiping

Under the collision detection model, we now extend our idea of breadth-first broadcast to devise an algorithm for gossiping among the nodes of the ad hoc mobile network so that every node u has some message m_u to be broadcast to all other nodes of the network.

4.1   Basic Idea

In the algorithm *bf_broadcast* of the previous chapter, some of the nodes in *transmit* state at say, layer $j - 1$, are selectively dropped out so that eventually a receiving node in the layer j would have exactly one transmitting node as its neighbor. A node in layer j receiving the message without any collision sends an *ack* signal in the S slot.

Specifically, consider the situation in which the nodes $u_1, u_2, \cdots, u_k$ all receive the message m_r (originating from the root node r) without any collision from only one single transmitting parent node u, as shown in Figure 5.

Subsequently u receives an *ack* signal in the S slot. Now, the node u, instead of immediately changing its state to *active* as in the *bf_broadcast* algorithm, would first execute a procedure *gather_messages* to collect the messages to be broadcasted from each of the nodes $u_1, u_2, \cdots, u_k$, and then will change its state

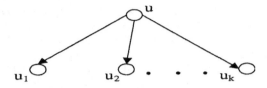

Fig. 5. Collision-free message transmission from node u to its neighbors

to *active*. Also, each of the nodes $u_1, u_2, \ldots, u_k$ receiving a clean message will change its state to a new state *back transmit*, in which it would respond to all control signals generated by u for message gathering, instead of immediately going to *active* state as in the *bf_broadcast* algorithm. Executing this modified algorithm (call it algorithm *gossip*), the messages of $u_1, u_2, \ldots, u_k$ in layer j move one layer up, i.e., to the node u in layer $j - 1$. Hence, D (D being the diameter of the network) such calls to algorithm *gossip*, would cause the messages of all nodes to reach the root node r. One more call to the algorithm *bf_broadcast* would complete the required message transfers for gossiping.

The procedure *gather_messages* called by a node u will successively select the neighboring node with the maximum *id*, that is yet to transmit its message m_{u_i} to u, from the nodes $u_1, u_2, \cdots, u_k$, by using the procedure *find_next_max_id* in [1]. u collects all such messages. Note that when u will send a control message for this purpose, only those of its neighbors in *back transmit* state would respond. After a node u_i sends its message to u, it changes its state to *active*. Finally, on return from the procedure *gather_messages*, node u changes its state to *active*.

To implement the above idea, we introduce a fifth possible state of a node, called *back transmit*, in addition to the four states *receive, collision, active* and *transmit* as mentioned in the previous section.

4.2   Algorithm Gossip

We make the following changes in the algorithm *bf_broadcast* of the previous section to convert it to the algorithm *gossip*. First, we define a new procedure called *gather_messages* as follows :

Procedure gather_messages
    send a query signal and look for an acknowledgement;
    /* acknowledgement will be sent only by its children in *back transmit* state */
    while (acknowledgement received)
    begin
        find_next_max_id (i);   /* i is the current node executing this step */
        send a command to this node for transmitting its message;
        receive the message from the child node;
        send a query signal and look for acknowledgement;
    endwhile;
end procedure.

Next, if the state of a node is *transmit*, then in the *bf_broadcast* algorithm, Step 4.3 is modified as follows :

Step 4.3 : If an acknowledgement was received only in the slot S but not in C and N, then execute procedure *gather_messages* and the state of the node is changed back to *active*.

Also, if the state of a node is *receive*, then step 5.2 for the case when clean signal is received in the *message* slot, will now be as follows :

Step 5.2 : If a clean signal is received in *message slot*, then send an acknowledgement in S slot, and change the state of the node to *back transmit*.

Finally, we add the following actions corresponding to the *back transmit* state :

```
if (state = back transmit) then
begin
  repeat
    respond to control signals from the parent for finding the
    next maximum id among all of its children who are still in back transmit state;
    if (command received from the parent to transmit its message) then
    begin
      transmit the message; /* message is sent to the parent */
      state = active;
    endif;
  until state = active;    /* end repeat loop */
endif;    /* end of state = back transmit */
```

4.3   Complexity

It follows from the above discussions that the procedure *gather_messages* will need at the most $(2\lceil \log n \rceil + 1)\Delta$ slots, where Δ is the maximum degree of a node; the term '1' being added to account for the message communication slot from u_i to u, $1 \le i \le k$. However, when we sum over all such nodes u during one complete pass of the algorithm *gossip*, the actual time needed to execute all the calls to procedure *gather_messages* will be limited to $(2\lceil \log n \rceil + 1)(n-1)$ slots.

Hence, the overall worst-case time complexity of the algorithm for gossiping is equal to $[8(2n+D)\log n + (2\lceil \log n \rceil + 1)(n-1)](D+1) = O(Dn \log n + D^2 \log n)$, which is better than the $O(n^{3/2} \log^2 n)$ time in [8]. For large values of Δ, the time complexity of our proposed algorithm is comparable to the $O(D\Delta^2 \log^3 n)$ - time algorithm in [11].

5   Conclusions

We have presented deterministic mobility-resilient algorithms for broadcast and gossiping in ad hoc networks with collision detection capabilities of the mobile terminals, which are based on the breadth-first traversal of the nodes in the network. The broadcast algorithm takes $O(n \log n)$ time in the worst case and works better than that in [4], for high values of node degree Δ and diameter D. The proposed gossiping algorithm completes in $O(Dn \log n + D^2 \log n)$ time, which is better than the $O(n^{3/2} \log^2 n)$ time needed by the algorithm in [8], and comparable to the $O(D\Delta^2 \log^3 n)$ - time algorithm in [11] for large values of Δ.

References

1. K. Sinha, "Deterministic Broadcast and Gossiping in Ad hoc Networks", *MS Thesis, Clemson University, South Carolina, USA*, August 2003.
2. K. Sinha and P. K. Srimani, "Broadcast algorithms for mobile ad hoc networks based on depth-first traversal", Proc. Third International Workshop on Wireless Information Systems (WIS), April 13-14, 2004, Porto. Portugal, pp. 170-177.
3. R. Bar-Yehuda, O. Goldreich and A. Itai, "On the time-complexity of broadcast in multi-hop radio networks : an exponential gap between determinism and randomization", *J. computer and System Sci.*, Vol. 45, pp. 104-126, Aug. 1992.
4. S. Basagni, D. Bruschi and I. Chlamtac, "A mobility transparent deterministic broadcast mechanism for ad hoc networks", *IEEE Trans. Networking*, Vol. 7, pp. 799-807, Dec. 1999.
5. I. Chlamtac and O. Weinstein, "The wave expansion approach to broadcasting in multihop radio networks", *IEEE Trans. Communications*, Vol. 39, pp. 426-433, March 1999.
6. B. Chlebus, L. Gasieniec, A. Gibbons, A. Pelc and W. Rytter, "Deterministic broadcasting in unknown radio networks", *Proc. of SODA 2000*, pp. 861-870, 2000.
7. B. Chlebus, L. Gasieniec, A. Lingas and A. Pagourtzis, "Oblivious gossiping in ad hoc radio networks", Proc. 5th International Workshop on Discrete Algorithms and Methods for Mobile Computing and Communications (DIALM 2001), 2001, pp. 44-51.
8. M. Chrobak, L. Gasieniec and W. Rytter, "Fast broadcasting and gossiping in radio networks", *Proc. 41st IEEE Symp. Found. of Computer Science (FOCS'2000)*, pp. 575-581, 2000
9. M. Chrobak, L. Gasieniec and W. Rytter, "A randomized algorithm for gossiping in radio networks", Proc. 7th Annual International Computing and Combinatorics Conference (COCOON 2001), 2001, Vol. 11, pp. 483-492.
10. A. E. F. Clementi, A. Monti and R. Silvestri, "Distributed multi-broadcast in unknown radio networks", *Proc. 20th ACM Symp. on Principles of Distributed Computing (PODC'2001)*, pp. 255-263, 2001.
11. A. E. F. Clementi, A. Monti and R. Silvestri, "Round robin is optimal for fault-tolerant broadcasting on wireless networks", Proc. 9th Annual European Symp. on Algorithms (ESA 2001), 2001, pp. 452-463.
12. A. E. F. Clementi, A. Monti and R. Silvestri, "Selective families, superimposed codes, and broadcasting in unknown radio networks", *Proc. 12th ACM-SIAM Symp. on Discrete Algorithms (SODA'2001)*, pp. 709-718, 2001.
13. I. Gaber and Y. Mansour, "Broadcast in radio networks", *Proc. 6th Annual ACM-SIAM Symp. Discrete Algorithms*, pp. 577-585, 1995.
14. L. Gasieniec and A. Lingas, "On adaptive deterministic gossiping in ad hoc radio networks", Information Processing Letters, Vol. 83, pp. 89-93, 2002.
15. P. Indyk, "Explicit constructions of selectors and related combinatorial structures, with applications", Proc. 13th ACM-SIAM Symp. on Discrete Algorithms (SODA 2002), 2002, pp. 697-704.
16. E. Kushilevitz and Y. Mansour, "An $\Omega(D \log n/D)$ lower bound for broadcast in radio networks", *SIAM J. Computing*, Vol. 27, pp. 707-712, June 1998.
17. K. Nakano and S. Olariu, "Randomized initialization protocols for ad-hoc networks", *IEEE Trans. Parallel and Distributed Systems*, Vol. 11, pp. 749-759, 2000.

RINGS: Lookup Service for Peer-to-Peer Systems in Mobile Ad-Hoc Networks

Kalpesh Patel, Sridhar Iyer, and Krishna Paul

Kanwal Rekhi School of Information Technology, IIT Mumbai, India
{kalpesh, sri, krishna}@it.iitb.ac.in

Abstract. A Peer-to-Peer (P2P) system consists of a set of nodes in which every node shares its own resources and services among other nodes in the system. These peer-to-peer systems are basically overlay networks, work on top of fixed network infrastructure. With the increasing popularity of mobile ad-hoc networks, it becomes necessary to think of P2P systems that can efficiently work in mobile environments.

Putting current P2P applications into mobile environments, results in multiple layer flooding because these applications will maintain different peer routes than that of by network layer. Also, routes at the application layer may not be necessarily optimal at the network layer. Here, we address this problem and propose a novel, controlled-flooding based protocol named *RINGS* which works at network layer and helps P2P systems to work in mobile environment efficiently. *RINGS* reduces query lookup cost by evenly distributing data indices throughout the network, thus reducing network layer routing overhead.

1   Motivation

As of today, a lot of work has been done in the area of P2P and MANET independently. P2P protocols and applications are widely available in distributed computing field. All those P2P protocols work as virtual overlay networks on top of fixed network infrastructure. Deploying current P2P protocols on ad-hoc network induces multiple layer redundancy and duplication in terms of messages and communication between nodes. As for example, *Chord*[3] working as overlay network, forms a cluster of nodes on top of TCP/IP layer. The fact is that a pair of nodes, which are neighbors at overlay network, might be far away from each other at network layer as shown in Fig. 1. For example, query lookup cost for *Chord* is $log(N)$ at the application layer but due to this fact, the overall cost will be increased.

This problem brings the idea of having an efficient network layer routing protocol. If application layer tasks can be assigned to network layer, routing redundancy can be avoided. Thus, we propose a protocol, named *RINGS*, to optimize overall query lookup cost. *RINGS* provides query lookup service at network layer rather than at application layer and thus eliminates application layer routing overhead. Further, *RINGS* follows *controlled-flooding* approach at the network layer, so query does not flood the whole network.

A. Sen et al. (Eds.): IWDC 2004, LNCS 3326, pp. 471–476, 2004.
© Springer-Verlag Berlin Heidelberg 2004

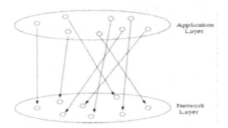

Fig. 1. Positions of application layer nodes from network layer perspective

Rest of the paper is organized as follows. Section 2 gives an overview of current P2P protocols. Section 3 contains the detailed *RINGS* protocol. Analysis and comparisons are made in section 4. Section 5 shows simulation results. Section 6 concludes the work.

2   Related Work

A handful of P2P protocols and architectures have been proposed so far. Nearly all of them fail to match with mobile environments.

Napster[1] has been among the first protocols, which introduced P2P concepts in computer networks. Although it follows some of P2P paradigms, it fails to be characterized as a complete P2P network as it relies on centralized servers. While *Gnutella 0.4* [2] follows simple broadcast based technique to communicate with peer node in the network. Gnutella, if deployed in ad-hoc networks, results in *multiple layer flooding* as ad-hoc network layer protocols also are based on flooding. *Gnutella 0.6*, an enhanced version is available which decreases the flooding overhead significantly, but still overall flooding is high.

Chord[3] is a scalable, distributed look-up protocol, which efficiently locates the node that stores a particular data item or service. Our analysis and simulation results show that in fact, performance of *Chord* degrades in mobile ad-hoc networks. *CAN* [4] essentially offers the same functionality as a hash table. i.e. it maps 'keys' to 'values'. Functionally, it is very much similar to *Chord*.

A protocol named *MPP* in [5] emphasizes on communication between application layer and network layer to deploy Peer-to-Peer systems in mobile environments. The problem is, *MPP* broadcasts the query throughout the network and gets the result. There is a need of network layer protocol, which can reduce this flooding.

3   Protocol in Detail

RINGS provides lookup service, which operates at the network layer. It assumes that all lookup queries are forwarded from application layer to network layer to enable RINGS lookup service. RINGS is basically a *proactive* protocol, which spreads data index into the network beforehand. Data indices are stored in the network such a way that lookup cost reduces to a constant factor. Thus, it avoids query lookup flooding as it generally happens with current P2P protocols.

3.1   Architecture

RINGS, being a network layer protocol, has to communicate with application layer to facilitate data query and results. So, we assume that communication is happening between application layer and network layer. [5] has already suggested a protocol, which establishes this communication.

Whenever a node joins the network, it originates a request packet and sends it down to network layer. Request packet can be either of two types: *Advertisement Packet* or *Lookup Packet*. For the *Advertisement Packet*, node generates index of its own data internally and tags it with the packet. *Lookup Packet* is used while data query processing. Depending upon the packet type, network layer forms either QUERY_PACKET or ADV_PACKET and forwards it to neighbors.

3.2   Data Advertisement

RINGS is basically a proactive protocol. After getting *Advertisement Packet*, node needs to spread index into the network. Further sequence of events can be described as:

1. Network layer forms a packet called ADV_PACKET and forwards it to neighbors. The fields of ADV_PACKET include *source_ID, sender_ID, seq_number, index_size, route_to_source,* and *hop_count*. Here, *sender_ID* is the identifier of the node, which forwards the packet whereas *route_to_source* is a complete route from the current node to source. To identify unique packet, ADV_PACKET includes sequence number. Sequence number along with source_ID uniquely identifies the packet.
2. *RINGS* Protocol selects a number called *Index-Hop K* at the start of the network. This number remains same for all nodes throughout the network. Nodes, lying on $(n * K)^{th}$-hop circle stores the index and forward the packet further, where $n = 1, 2, 3...$ Other nodes simply forward the packet. At this point of time, we assume that network nodes have sufficient storage space to store remote indices. The above process forms a set of imaginary circles of nodes with the center indicates the source of the data. See Fig. 2

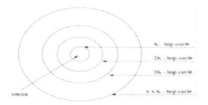

Fig. 2. A set of imaginary circles for a node

For example, if the value of *Index-Hop* is kept 2, all nodes on the circle of $n * K$ hops will store the index where $n = 1, 2, 3, ...$

3. Above procedure is followed by each node in the network.

3.3   Routing Table

Every node maintains a routing table. The routing table entry contains source_ID, sender_ID, sequence number, TTL(Time-To-Live), hop-count.

The main purpose of routing table is to avoid receiving duplicate packets. If node receives packet with same *source_ID* and same *sequence number* again within *TTL* time, node drops the packet. Each time node receives an ADV_PACKET, it updates routing table entry depending on the *Advertisement packet* fields.

3.4   Query Lookup

Whenever a node wants a particular data, it forwards the QUERY_PACKET to its neighbors. In any case, the query gets the results within maximum of $K/2$ hops. Thus, query does not flood throughout the network. As for example, if the value of K is kept 4, it means $n*4$ hops away nodes has stored the index. Thus the upper limit on the *lookup cost* for any node in the network reduces to 2 hops.

3.5   Mobility

Until now, we have assumed that all nodes in the network are static. If nodes move frequently in the network, it is difficult to trace them. The advantage of *RINGS* protocol is, mobility have none or little impact on performance of the protocol. It has been shown that, in order to achieve maximum *throughput* and *connectivity*, number of neighbors per node in mobile network can be taken as $log(N)$, where N is the number of nodes in the network. Given that, if the value of *Index-Hop K* is kept to 2, a node can get the query results from maximum of $log(N)$ as average number of neighbors is taken as $log(N)$. Out of that, if as much as $log(N) - 1$ nodes leave from or move in the network, a node can get results from at least one node. Extending this equation, we can conclude that, in general, a node gets at least one node inside the nearest circle which can satisfy its query, even if L number of nodes from nearest circle move away from the network where L is,

$$L = (log(N) - 1)^{K/2} \tag{1}$$

where $K = 2, 4, 6, ...$

4   Analysis and Comparison

As mentioned earlier, current P2P protocols are application layer protocols. If these protocols are put in mobile ad-hoc environments, the overhead of network layer should also be counted in overall routing overhead. Now from network layer perspective, neighbors at the application layer may not be neighbors at network layer. In worse case, they could be at the different edges of the network.

Application layer has different routes than that of network layer. So, the effective lookup cost between source and destination is the sum of application layer lookup cost and network layer routing cost, which indeed is larger. For example, lookup cost for *Chord* protocol is $log(N)$ at the application layer(please refer [3] for more details) but the overall lookup cost is larger.

In order to count network layer hops, we need to find out the average distance between any two nodes at the network layer. According to [6], the average distance d between any two nodes at the network layer can be taken as,

$$d = 2\alpha \left(\sqrt{N/\pi} \right)$$

where α is a constant and N is total number of nodes in the network. So, effective lookup cost L_{chord} for *Chord* protocol is,

$$L_{chord} = d * log(N) \tag{2}$$

In *RINGS*, any node has to contact nearest *Index-Hop* circle to get the data index, which is maximum of $K/2$ hops away. Taking average number of neighbors per node as $log(N)$, we can say that node forwards query to $log(N)$ nodes. In turn, each of $log(N)$ nodes forwards query to its neighbors. Continuing this way, query will be forwarded to L_{RINGS} number of nodes before reaching to nearest *Index-Hop* circle, where L_{RINGS} is,

$$L_{RINGS} = log(N) * (1 + (log(N) - 1) + (log(N) - 1)^2 +$$

$$... + (log(N) - 1)^{K/2-1}) \tag{3}$$

Comparison of both costs is shown graphically in Fig. 3 in next section.

5   Simulation Results

5.1   Simulation Setup

RINGS protocol has been simulated independently of any existing network simulators like NS2 etc. Various scenarios has been taken to check the efficiency of RINGS in terms of, number of nodes store indices for a node in the network, total remote indices per node etc. Nodes are distributed in the network randomly and RINGS protocol is performed on them. Each node in the network was assigned index value from random distribution. All these experiments were run for different values of *Index-Hop* K starting from $K = 1$ to $K = 5$. The results from initial simulation indicate that performance can be improved by using RINGS.

5.2   Results

As indicated earlier, each node stores indices of some other nodes. We want to measure how the value of these average remote indices per node varies over the value of *Index-Hop*. First graph of Fig. 3 shows different measures of average remote indices per node for the different value of *Index-Hop*. It can be observed that the value $K = 4$ balances between the *lookup cost* and *per node storage requirement*. Second graph of Fig. 3 shows the comparison between Eq. (2) and (3). It indicates that *lookup cost* decreases significantly in RINGS if the value of *Index-Hop* is kept 4 while *Chord* performs better than *RINGS with Index-Hop = 6*, if number of network nodes is kept low. If number of nodes increases, performance of RINGS increases as compare to *Chord*.

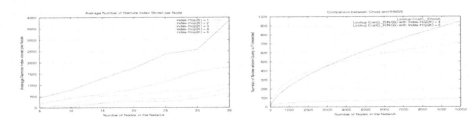

Fig. 3. Simulation Results

6 Conclusion

We observed that current P2P protocols fail to perform well in mobile ad-hoc networks. So, we suggest a simple but effective protocol *RINGS*, which optimizes network layer query routing. *RINGS* reduces query lookup cost by evenly distributing data indices throughout the network. Our initial simulation results show the improvement from the suggested protocol.

References

1. Napster Protocol Specification. June 2000.
2. Gnutella protocol specification v0.4. 2002.
3. Ion Stoica, Robert Morris, David Karger, M. Frans Kaashoek, and Hari Balakrishnan. Chord: A scalable peer-to-peer lookup service for Internet applications. In Proceedings of ACM SIGCOMM, pages 149-160. ACM Press, 2001.
4. Sylvia Ratnasamy, Paul Francis, Mark Handley, Richard Karp, and Scott Shenker. A scalable content addressable network. In Proceedings of ACM SIGCOMM 2001.
5. Florian Niethammer Rudiger Schollmeier, Ingo Gruber. Protocol for peer-to- peer networking in mobile environments. In Proceedings of IEEE International Conference on Computer Communications and Networks (ICCCN'03), October 2003.
6. Sverrir Olafsson. Scalability, capacity and local connectivity in ad hoc networks. Mobile and Wireless Communications: Key Technologies and Future Applications(P. Smyth (Ed.)), IEE-BT Exact Communication Technology.

Performance Analysis of Location Caching with Fixed Local Anchor in Wireless Networks*

Ki-Sik Kong and Chong-Sun Hwang

Dept. of Computer Science and Engineering, Korea Univ.,
1, 5-Ga, Anam-Dong, Sungbuk-Gu, Seoul 136-701, Korea
{kskong, hwang}@disys.korea.ac.kr

Abstract. In this paper, we propose an efficient combined location management scheme using the concepts of the two existing location management schemes: the FLA scheme [1] and the Caching scheme [2]. The motivation behind the proposed scheme is to exploit the advantages of the two existing schemes. That is, the FLA scheme exploits locality in a user's mobility pattern, and the Caching scheme exploits locality in a user's calling pattern. By combining the advantages of both the FLA scheme and Caching scheme, the proposed scheme can reduce the frequent access to the HLR, and thus effectively results in significant reduction of the total location management cost. The analytical results indicate that the proposed scheme significantly outperforms the other existing schemes regardless of the mobile user's call-to-mobility ratio in terms of the total location management cost.

1 Introduction

Personal Communications Service (PCS) networks provide wireless services to subscribers that are free to travel, and the network access point of a mobile terminal (MT) changes as it moves around the network coverage area. A location management scheme, therefore, is necessary to effectively keep track of the MTs and locate a called MT when a call is initiated [3]. There are two commonly used standards for location management: IS-41 and GSM [4]. Both are based on a two-level database hierarchy, which consists of Home Location Register (HLR) and Visitor Location Registers (VLRs). The whole network coverage area is divided into cells. There is a Base Station (BS) installed in each cell and these cells are grouped together to form a larger area called a Registration Area (RA). All BSs belonging to one RA are wired to a Mobile Switching Center (MSC). The MSC/VLR is connected to the Local Signal Transfer Point (LSTP) through the local A-link, while the LSTP is connected to the Regional Signal Transfer Point (RSTP) through the D-link. The RSTP is, in turn, connected to the HLR through the remote A-link [5]. Location management is one of the most

---

* This work was supported by the Korea Research Foundation Grant (KRF-2003-041-D00403).

A. Sen et al. (Eds.): IWDC 2004, LNCS 3326, pp. 477–488, 2004.
© Springer-Verlag Berlin Heidelberg 2004

important issues in PCS networks. As the number of MTs increases, location management scheme under the IS-41 has gone through many problems such as increasing traffic in network, bottleneck to the HLR, and so on. To overcome these problems under the IS-41, a number of works have been reported. In [1], a local anchor scheme was proposed to reduce the signaling traffic due to location registration by eliminating the need to report location changes to the HLR. A VLR close to the MT, which could be designated as a fixed local anchor in advance or not, is selected as a local anchor. Instead of transmitting registration message to the HLR, location change is reported to the local anchor. Since the local anchor is close to the MT, the signaling traffic incurred by location registration is reduced. A caching scheme [2] was proposed to reduce the signaling cost for call delivery by reusing the cached information about the called MT's location from the previous call. When a call arrives, the location of the called MT is first identified in the cache instead of sending query messages to the VLR. When a cache hit occurs, the caching scheme can save one query to the HLR and traffic along some of the signaling links as compared to the IS-41. This is especially significant when the call-to-mobility ratio (CMR) of the MT is high. However, a penalty has to be paid when there is "location miss" since the cache information is not always up-to-date. Most existing researches on location management in wireless networks [1, 2, 6, 7, 8] have been proposed to alleviate the burden on the HLR. However, compared to the IS-41 standard, most of these schemes can achieve cost reduction only for a certain class of mobile users with a specific range of CMR. On the contrary, the proposed scheme can achieve cost reduction almost regardless of an MT's CMR by effectively combining the advantages of both the caching scheme and the fixed local anchor scheme. The motivation behind this scheme is to exploit a user's movement locality as well as call locality.

This paper is organized as follows. Section 2 introduces a proposed scheme. In Sect.3, a user mobility model for performance analysis is described. In Sect.4, we derive the location management costs under the several schemes to investigate the performance of the proposed scheme. Numerical results are given in Sect.5. Finally, conclusions are given in Sect.6.

2   The FLA-Caching (Location Caching with Fixed Local Anchor) Scheme

In this section, we introduce the proposed scheme called a FLA-Caching scheme. Under this scheme, the MSC of the newly entered RA registers the MT's location at a fixed local anchor (FLA), which is a specific VLR designated per each LSTP area. The FLA has a table indicating the current serving MSC/VLR for the MTs in its LSTP area. Also, the HLR of the MTs will then be informed of the ID of the new FLA. Note that the FLA may also be the current serving VLR of the MTs or not. Figure 1 and 2 shows the signaling diagram for location registration and call delivery under the FLA-Caching scheme. In Fig.1 and 2, the "( )" indicates the message number, the "[ ]" indicates the cost for the particular

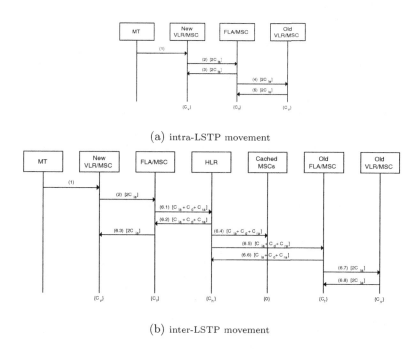

(a) intra-LSTP movement

(b) inter-LSTP movement

Fig. 1. Location Registration

signaling exchange, and the "{ }" at the bottom of the figure indicates the cost
for accessing the particular database. These signaling and database access costs
will be discussed in more detail in Sect.4 and 5.

2.1 Location Registration

The location registration procedure under the FLA-Caching scheme is described
as follows (see Fig.1).

1) An MT moves into a new RA and sends a location update message to the
   new MSC through the nearby BS.
2) The new MSC sends a location registration message to its designated FLA
   in its LSTP area.
3) The FLA checks for the MT's profile. If there is not an MT's record in the
   FLA, which means that the MT has just moved into a new LSTP area,
   then go to step 6). Otherwise, it updates the MT's record to indicate the
   associated new VLR, and sends a registration acknowledgment message to
   the new MSC together with a copy of the MT's profile.
4) The FLA sends a registration cancellation message to the old MSC.
5) The old MSC removes the record for an MT at its associated VLR and sends
   a registration cancellation acknowledgment message to the FLA (Location
   registration is complete. Do not continue to the next step.).
6) If there is not an MT's record in the FLA, we have the following.

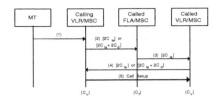

(a) When the calling MSC has location cache for the called FLA

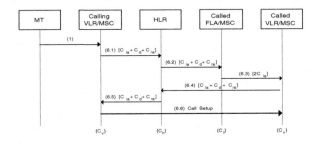

(b) When the calling MSC does not have location cache for the called FLA

Fig. 2. Call Delivery

6.1) The MSC associated with the MT's new FLA sends a location registration message to the HLR.

6.2) The HLR updates the MT's record to indicate the MT's new FLA and sends a copy of the MT's profile to the new FLA.

6.3) The FLA updates the MT's record to indicate the associated new VLR, and sends a registration acknowledgment message to the new MSC/VLR together with a copy of the MT's profile.

6.4) The HLR sends a location update message to all the MSCs which have location cache for that MT, which updates the MT's location cache to indicate the MT's new FLA.

6.5) The HLR sends a registration cancellation message to the MT's old FLA, which removes the MT's record.

6.6) The old FLA sends a registration cancellation acknowledgment message back to the HLR.

6.7) The old FLA sends a registration cancellation message to the MT's old MSC, which removes the MT's record.

6.8) The MT's old MSC sends a registration cancellation acknowledgment message back to the old FLA (Location registration is complete).

2.2   Call Delivery

The call delivery procedure under the FLA-Caching scheme is described as follows (see Fig.2). For more details, see Sect.4.1.

1) The calling MT sends a call initiation signal to its serving MSC through the nearby BS.
2) The calling MSC checks if it has location cache which indicates the FLA of the called MT. If yes, it sends a location request message to the called FLA. Otherwise, go to the step 6).
3) The FLA forwards the location request message to the called MSC.
4) The called MSC allocates a temporary location directory number (TLDN) to the MT and sends it to the calling MSC.
5) The calling MSC now sets up a connection to the called MSC using this TLDN (Call delivery is complete. Do not continue to the next step.).
6) If the calling MSC does not have location cache for the called FLA, we have the following.
   6.1) The calling MSC sends a location request message to the HLR of the MT.
   6.2) The HLR sends a location request message to the called FLA.
   6.3) The called FLA forwards a location request message to called MSC.
   6.4) The called MSC allocates a TLDN to the MT and sends it to the HLR.
   6.5) The HLR forwards the TLDN to the calling MSC.
   6.6) The calling MSC now sets up a connection to the called MSC using TLDN (Call delivery is complete).

3   User Mobility Model

For the analysis of an MT's movement behavior, we assume a fluid flow mobility model. The model assumes that MTs are moving at an average speed of v, and their movement direction is uniformly distributed over $[0, 2\pi]$, and that all the RA area are of the same rectangular shape and size, and form together a contiguous area. The parameters used in this model are summarized as follows.

- γ : the border crossing rate for an MT out of an RA
- λ : the border crossing rate for which an MT still stays in the same LSTP area
- μ : the border crossing rate for an MT out of an LSTP area

From [9], the border crossing rate γ for an MT out of an RA is derived as

$$\gamma = \frac{4v}{\pi\sqrt{S}} \tag{1}$$

where S is the RA area size. We assume an LSTP area is composed of N RAs. Therefore, the border crossing rate μ for an MT out of an LSTP area is

$$\mu = \frac{4v}{\pi\sqrt{NS}} \tag{2}$$

Note that an MT that crosses an LSTP area will also cross an RA. So, the border crossing rate λ for which the MT still stays in the same LSTP area is obtained from Eq.(1) and (2):

$$\lambda = \gamma - \mu = (1 - \frac{1}{\sqrt{N}})\gamma \tag{3}$$

Figure 3 shows a continuous-time Markov chain model, which describes the location registration of an MT, where $a_{i,i+1} = \lambda$ and $b_{i,0} = \mu$. The state of a continuous-time Markov chain, i $(i \geq 0)$, is defined as the number of RAs that an MT has passed by. The state transition $a_{i,i+1}(i \geq 0)$ represents the MT's movement rate to an adjacent RA under the same LSTP area, and the state transition $b_{i,0}(i \geq 1)$ represents the MT's movement rate to another RA out of the LSTP area. We assume π_i to be the equilibrium state probability of state i. Thus, we can obtain

$$\lambda \pi_i = (\lambda + \mu)\pi_{i+1} \tag{4}$$

$$\lambda \pi_0 = \mu \sum_{k=1}^{\infty} \pi_k \tag{5}$$

Using the Eq.(4) and (5), π_i can be expressed in terms of the equilibrium state probability π_0 as

$$\pi_i = (\frac{\lambda}{\lambda + \mu})^i \pi_0 = (1 - \pi_0)^i \pi_0 \tag{6}$$

where π_0 is the equilibrium state probability of state 0. By using the law of total probability, π_0 can be obtained as

$$\pi_0 = \frac{\mu}{\lambda + \mu} = 1 - \frac{\lambda}{\lambda + \mu} = 1 - \theta, \quad where \ \theta = \frac{\lambda}{\lambda + \mu} \tag{7}$$

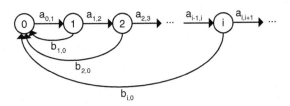

Fig. 3. State transition diagram of a continuous-time Markov chain

4 Cost Analysis

In this section, based on the user mobility model given in the previous section, we derive the location registration costs, the database access costs, and the total costs for the FLA-Caching scheme, the FLA scheme, Caching scheme, and the IS-41, respectively. Table 1 shows the costs and parameters used for the cost analysis.

Table 1. Costs and parameters

Parameter	Description
C_{la}	Cost for sending a signaling message through the local A-link
C_d	Cost for sending a signaling message through the D-link
C_{ra}	Cost for sending a signaling message through the remote A-link
C_v	Cost for a query or an update of the VLR
C_f	Cost for a query or an update of the FLA
C_h	Cost for a query or an update of the HLR
ϕ	Probability (Caller and callee are located within the same LSTP area)
δ	Probability (Callee are located in the FLA area)
p	Probability (Calling MSC has location cache for the called MT under the FLA-Caching scheme)
q	The MT's CMR (Call-to-Mobility Ratio)
k	The number of the MSCs which have location cache for the called MT
τ	Cache hit ratio under the Caching scheme

4.1   FLA-Caching Scheme

According to the user mobility model given in the previous section, the average location registration cost under the FLA-Caching scheme ($U_{FLA-Caching}$) is

$$U_{FLA-Caching} = \pi_0 C_{inter}^{FLA-Caching} + C_{intra}^{FLA-Caching} \sum_{i=1}^{\infty} i\pi_i$$

$$= (1 - \theta)C_{inter}^{FLA-Caching} + \frac{\theta}{1 - \theta}C_{intra}^{FLA-Caching} \qquad (8)$$

where $C_{intra}^{FLA-Caching}$ and $C_{inter}^{FLA-Caching}$ represent the location registration costs under the FLA-Caching scheme when the intra-LSTP movement and the inter-LSTP movement of an MT occur, respectively (refer to Fig.1(a) and (b)).

$$C_{intra}^{FLA-Caching} = 4 \times 2C_{la} + (2C_v + C_f) = 8C_{la} + (2C_v + C_f) \qquad (9)$$

$$C_{inter}^{FLA-Caching} = 4 \times (C_{la} + C_d + C_{ra}) + 4 \times 2C_{la} + k \times (C_{la} + C_d + C_{ra})$$
$$+ (2C_v + 2C_f + C_h) \qquad (10)$$

Note that when the inter-LSTP movement of the MT occurs, the HLR should update all the location caches for that MT in the networks. On the other hand, the average call delivery cost under the FLA-Caching scheme ($S_{FLA-Caching}$) is

$$S_{FLA-Caching} = pC_{cache}^{FLA-Caching} + (1 - p)C_{nocache}^{FLA-Caching} \qquad (11)$$

where $C_{cache}^{FLA-Caching}$ and $C_{nocache}^{FLA-Caching}$ represent the call delivery costs under the FLA-Caching scheme when the calling MSC has location cache for the called MT, and when the calling MSC does not have location cache for the called MT.

$$C_{cache}^{FLA-Caching} = \phi(\delta C_1 + (1 - \delta)C_2) + (1 - \phi)(\delta C_3 + (1 - \delta)C_4) \qquad (12)$$

$$C_{nocache}^{FLA-Caching} = \delta C_5 + (1 - \delta)C_6 \qquad (13)$$

$$C_1 = (2C_{la} + C_v + C_f) + 2C_{la} \qquad (14)$$
$$C_2 = (2C_{la} + C_v + C_f) + (2C_{la} + C_v) + 2C_{la} \qquad (15)$$
$$C_3 = (2C_{la} + 2C_d + C_f + C_v) + (2C_{la} + 2C_d) \qquad (16)$$
$$C_4 = (2C_{la} + 2C_d + C_f + C_v) + (2C_{la} + C_v) + (2C_{la} + 2C_d)(17)$$
$$C_5 = 4(C_{la} + C_d + C_{ra}) + (C_v + C_f + C_h) \qquad (18)$$
$$C_6 = 4(C_{la} + C_d + C_{ra}) + (C_v + C_f + C_h) + (2C_{la} + C_v) \qquad (19)$$

Depending on whether the caller and the called MT are located within the same LSTP area or not, or whether the called MT is located in the FLA area or not, four different possible costs for the call delivery can generate when the calling MSC has location cache for the called MT. Also, the costs from C_1 through C_4 represents such costs for the call delivery under the FLA-Caching scheme, respectively.

Here, C_1 means the call delivery cost when the caller and called MT are located within the same LSTP area, and the called MT is found in the FLA area. C_2 means the call delivery cost when the caller and the called MT are located within the same LSTP area, and the called MT is found in the other VLR area, not the FLA area. Similarly, C_3 means the call delivery cost when the caller and the called MT are located in the different LSTP areas, and the called MT is found in the FLA area. C_4 means the call delivery cost when the caller and the called MT are located in the different LSTP areas, and the called MT is found in the other VLR area, not the FLA area. On the other hand, C_5 and C_6 represent the call delivery costs when the called MT is found in its FLA area, and when the called MT is found in the other VLR area, not the FLA area, respectively. Finally, the total cost under the FLA-Caching scheme ($T_{FLA-Caching}$) can be expressed as

$$T_{FLA-Caching} = U_{FLA-Caching} + qS_{FLA-Caching} \qquad (20)$$

4.2   FLA (Fixed Local Anchor) Scheme

The average location registration cost under the FLA scheme (U_{FLA}) is

$$U_{FLA} = \pi_0 C_{inter}^{FLA} + C_{intra}^{FLA} \sum_{i=1}^{\infty} i\pi_i = (1 - \theta)C_{inter}^{FLA} + \frac{\theta}{1 - \theta}C_{intra}^{FLA} \qquad (21)$$

where C_{intra}^{FLA} and C_{inter}^{FLA} represent the location registration costs under the FLA scheme when the intra-LSTP movement and the inter-LSTP movement of an MT occur, respectively. These costs are as follows.

$$C_{intra}^{FLA} = C_{intra}^{FLA-Caching} = 4 \times 2C_{la} + (2C_v + C_f) = 8C_{la} + (2C_v + C_f)(22)$$
$$C_{inter}^{FLA} = 4 \times (C_{la} + C_d + C_{ra}) + 4 \times 2C_{la} + (2C_v + 2C_f + C_h) \qquad (23)$$

In the same way as shown in the previous subsection, we can derive the average call delivery cost under the FLA scheme (S_{FLA}) as follows.

$$S_{FLA} = C_{nocache}^{FLA-Caching} = \delta C_5 + (1 - \delta)C_6 \qquad (24)$$

Finally, the total cost under the FLA scheme (T_{FLA}) can be expressed as

$$T_{FLA} = U_{FLA} + qS_{FLA} \tag{25}$$

4.3   Caching Scheme

The average location registration cost ($U_{Caching}$) and the average call delivery cost ($S_{Caching}$) under the Caching scheme are expressed as

$$U_{Caching} = U_{IS-41} = \{(1 - \theta) + \frac{\theta}{1 - \theta}\}\{4(C_{la} + C_d + C_{ra}) + (2C_v + C_h)\} \tag{26}$$

$$S_{Caching} = \tau C_{hit}^{Caching} + (1 - \tau)C_{miss}^{Caching} \tag{27}$$

where $C_{hit}^{Caching}$ and $C_{miss}^{Caching}$ represent the call delivery costs under the Caching scheme when the location cache information for the MT is correct, and when the location cache information for the MT is obsolete, respectively.

$$C_{hit}^{Caching} = \phi(4C_{la} + 2C_v) + (1 - \phi)(4C_{la} + 4C_d + 2C_v)$$

$$C_{miss}^{Caching} = \phi(4C_{la} + 2C_v) + (1 - \phi)(4C_{la} + 4C_d + 2C_v) + S_{IS-41}$$

$$= \phi(4C_{la} + 2C_v) + (1 - \phi)(4C_{la} + 4C_d + 2C_v)$$

$$+ 4(C_{la} + C_d + C_{ra}) + (2C_v + C_h) \tag{28}$$

Finally, the total cost under the Caching scheme ($T_{Caching}$) can be expressed as

$$T_{Caching} = U_{Caching} + qS_{Caching} \tag{29}$$

4.4   IS-41

The average location registration cost (U_{IS-41}) and the average call delivery cost (S_{IS-41}) under the IS-41 are expressed as

$$U_{IS-41} = \{(1 - \theta) + \frac{\theta}{1 - \theta}\}\{4(C_{la} + C_d + C_{ra}) + (2C_v + C_h)\} \tag{30}$$

$$S_{IS-41} = 4(C_{la} + C_d + C_{ra}) + (2C_v + C_h) \tag{31}$$

Finally, the total cost under the IS-41 (T_{IS-41}) can be expressed as

$$T_{IS-41} = U_{IS-41} + qS_{IS-41} \tag{32}$$

5   Numerical Results

In this section, we evaluate the performance of the FLA-Caching scheme by comparing with the IS-41, the Caching scheme, and the FLA scheme. We define the relative cost of each scheme as the ratio of the total cost for each scheme to that for the IS-41. A relative cost of 1 means that the costs under both schemes

Table 2. Cost analysis

set	C_{la}	C_d	C_{ra}
1	1	3	3
2	1	3	5
3	1	5	7
4	1	5	10

(a) Signaling cost

set	C_v	C_f	C_h
5	1	2	3
6	1	2	5
7	1	3	3
8	1	3	5

(b) Database access cost

are exactly the same. For the analysis, we set N, δ, v, S, ϕ, and k to be 64, 1/64, 5.6 km/h, 5 km^2, 0.2, and 3. Most parameters used in this analysis are set to typical values found in [6, 7, 8, 9]. For τ, $\tau = \frac{q}{1+q}$ is used [6]. On the other hand, we set p to be 0.7 . These are based on the collected actual data that more than 70 % of the calls made by callers in a week are to their top 5 callees [8]. This means that if we choose to cache top 5 callee's location information at the caller's MSC, then nearly 70 % of the calls made in a week are serviced by location caching. Based on these facts, we assume that these information are obtained from each MT's calling and mobility profile maintained at the HLR.

5.1   Signaling Cost

We first evaluate the case when the signaling cost dominates by setting the database access cost parameters, C_v, C_f and C_h to 0. Parameter sets 1 and 2 show the cases when the cost for sending a message to the HLR is relatively low. Parameter sets 3 and 4 show the cases when the cost for sending a message to the HLR is relatively high. Figure 4 shows the relative signaling costs for the Caching scheme, the FLA scheme, and the FLA-Caching scheme when the parameter sets 1 and 4, as given in Table 2(a), are used. We can see that the FLA-Caching scheme results in the lowest relative signaling cost as compared with other schemes. On the other hand, in Fig.4, as q increases, the signaling cost of the Caching scheme is getting lower, and that of the FLA scheme is getting higher. This is due to the fact that as q increases, the call delivery procedure becomes dominated, and thus the cost of the Caching scheme decreases. On the contrary, the relative cost of the FLA scheme increases. Note, however, that the relative signaling cost of the FLA-Caching scheme is almost constant regardless of the change of q.

5.2   Database Access Cost

In the following, we evaluate the case when the database access cost dominates by setting the signaling cost parameters, C_{la}, C_d, and C_{ra} to 0. Figure 5 shows the relative database access costs for the Caching scheme, the FLA scheme, and the FLA-Caching scheme when the parameter sets 5 and 8, as given in Table 2(b), are used. As mentioned above, as q increases, the database access cost of the Caching scheme decreases because less database query is required. On the contrary, the relative cost of the FLA scheme increases because more database query is necessary. Similar to Fig.4, the database access cost of the FLA-Caching scheme shown in Fig.5 is also almost constant regardless of the change of q.

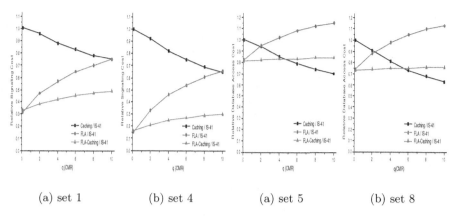

(a) set 1   (b) set 4   (a) set 5   (b) set 8

Fig. 4. Relative signaling cost   **Fig. 5.** Relative database access cost

5.3   Total Cost

We compare the relative total cost of the FLA-Caching scheme with that of the IS-41, the Caching scheme, and the FLA scheme. Figure 6 demonstrates the relative total costs for each scheme when the parameter sets 1 and 5, and the parameter sets 4 and 8 are used. The results shown in Fig.6 indicate that the

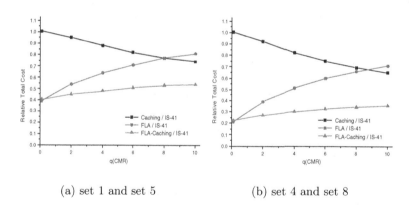

(a) set 1 and set 5   (b) set 4 and set 8

Fig. 6. Relative total cost

FLA-Caching scheme results in the lowest relative total cost when compared with other schemes regardless of the change of q. The basic ides of the FLA-Caching scheme is to exploit the each advantage of the two schemes. That is, the Caching scheme exploits locality in the user's calling pattern, and the FLA scheme exploits locality in a mobile user's mobility pattern. By combining these two characteristics in both schemes, the FLA-Caching scheme can decrease the frequent access to the HLR, and thus effectively results in significant reduction of the total cost. In the FLA-Caching scheme, when the inter-LSTP movement of the MT occurs, the HLR should update all the location caches for that MT throughout the networks. Note, however, that as the probability of the inter-LSTP movement of the MT is relatively small, the cost of updating the location caches is not significant. Due to the space limitation, even if we only show the relative total costs for the two combination of the parameter sets in Fig.6, all other combination of the parameter sets also indicate almost the same tendency as shown in Fig.6.

6 Conclusions

In this paper, in order to overcome many problems such as increasing traffic in network, bottleneck to the HLR, and so on, a location management scheme called the FLA-Caching scheme was proposed. The motivation behind the FLA-Caching scheme is to exploit the each advantage of the two existing schemes, i.e., the Caching scheme and the FLA scheme. In short, the primary idea of the FLA-Caching scheme is to exploit a user's movement locality as well as a user's call locality at the same time. By combining these two characteristics in both schemes, the FLA-Caching scheme can decrease the frequent access to the HLR, and thus effectively results in significant reduction of the total location management cost. The analytical results indicate that the FLA-Caching scheme significantly outperforms the other existing schemes regardless of the user's CMR.

References

1. J. Ho, F. Akyildiz., "Local anchor scheme for reducing signaling costs in personal communications networks," *IEEE/ACM Trans. Networking.*, vol.4, no.5, Oct. 1996.
2. R. Jain, Y. B. Lin, and S. Mohan, "A caching strategy to reduce network impacts of PCS," *IEEE J. Sel. Areas Comm.*, vol.12, no.8, pp. 1434-1444, Oct. 1994.
3. F. Akyildiz et al., "Mobility Management in Next-Generation Wireless Systems," *Proc. IEEE*, vol. 87, no. 8, pp. 1347-84, Aug. 1999.
4. S. Mohan and R. Jain, "Two user location strategies for personal communications services," *IEEE Personal Commun.*, pp. 42-50, First Quarter 1994.
5. D. R. Wilson, "Signaling system no.7, IS-41 and cellular telephony networking," *Proc. IEEE*, vol. 80, pp. 664-652, Apr. 1992.
6. K. Kong, J. Gil, Y. Han, U. Song, and C. Hwang, "A forwarding pointer-based cache scheme for reducing location management cost in PCS networks," *Journal of Information Science and Engineering*, vol.18, no.6, pp.1011-1025, Nov. 2002.
7. R. Jain and Y. B. Lin, "An auxiliary user location strategy employing forwarding pointers to reduce network impacts of PCS," *ACM-Baltzer J. Wireless Networks*, vol.1, no.2, pp. 197-210, Jul. 1995.
8. N. Shivakumar and J. Widom, "User profile replication for faster location lookup in mobile environments," *Proc. ACM/IEEE MOBICOM '95*, pp. 161-169.
9. F. Baumann and I. Niemegeers, "An evaluation of location management procedures," *Proc. UPC '94*, pp.359-364, Sep. 1994.

On the Optimization Trade-Offs of Expanding Ring Search

Jahan Hassan[*,1] and Sanjay Jha[2]

[1] School of Information Technologies, The University of Sydney
Sydney, NSW 2006, Australia
jahan@it.usyd.edu.au

[2] School of Computer Science and Engineering, The University of New South Wales
Sydney, NSW 2052, Australia
National ICT Australia Ltd., Bay 15, ATP, Eveleigh, NSW1430, Australia
sjha@cse.unsw.edu.au

Abstract. In decentralized and unstructured networks, such as peer-to-peer and Ad-hoc wireless networks, broadcasting of queries is frequently used for obtaining required information. However, because of the inherent overhead of broadcasting in terms of bandwidth, energy, and processing power consumption, various techniques are used to minimize those overhead. Expanding Ring Search (ERS) is one such technique. Although ERS helps to reduce the overhead of broadcasting, it does not reduce the expected locating time. In this paper, we analyze the locating time and overhead that are two contradicting metrics of ERS performance.

1 Introduction

In unstructured and decentralized networks, or in networks where there is no prior knowledge of the location of the target information, broadcast of query packets is commonly used. While broadcasting finds the target information in the lowest possible time, it incurs heavy overhead in terms of bandwidth, energy, and processing power consumption at the network nodes. Therefore, mechanisms are often used as an optimization strategy. Expanding Ring Search (ERS) is one such technique. ERS is used over the plain broadcast in Peer-to-Peer (P2P) networks, multicasting, ad-hoc wireless networks, Mesh networks, etc. [1, 2, 4, 6, 5]. Current use of ERS found in literature emphasizes on reducing the effects of flooding; its optimization and adverse effect on the locating time is not considered however. With incremental search of ERS, the locating time increases. We have studied the optimization of broadcast overhead using ERS in [3], and have shown that there exists a search threshold (L) for which ERS can be minimized for any *random* topology. We assumed a start and increment TTL of 1 in that work. We also showed that a badly selected L *can* lead to more cost than that of network-wide broadcasting. In this paper, we generalize the broadcast cost model of ERS

---

[*] Part of the work was done when the author was at the University of New South Wales.

A. Sen et al. (Eds.): IWDC 2004, LNCS 3326, pp. 489–494, 2004.
© Springer-Verlag Berlin Heidelberg 2004

for any given start and increment TTL, and also provide a generic model of the expected locating time. With the aid of the developed modes, we study the impact of different start and increment TTL values on ERS performance.

The rest of the paper is organized as follows. In section 2, we provide analytical models of ERS followed by section 3 where we provide our experimental results for our proposed models using two types of network topologies: power-law topology and random topology. We conclude our paper in section 4.

2   Performance Model of ERS

2.1   System Description and Probabilities

The system we model has N network nodes that are arranged in rings. All nodes that are one hop away from the source of broadcast form Ring 1, nodes that are two hop away form Ring 2 etc., where Ring i has n_i $(0 < n_i < N)$ nodes. There are a total of M rings in the network. Node distribution on the rings depend on the network's topology. More on this can be found in [3].

Costs at network nodes due to forwarding of query packets will be referred to as bandwidth cost[1]. Bandwidth cost for a given query is defined by the number of nodes that have to broadcast the query. The cost for a network-wide broadcast is simply N (all nodes will broadcast). However, when a *limited radius search* is initiated with a radius of k (TTL is set to k), the broadcast cost for the search, B_k, is basically the number of nodes contained in all the rings up to $(k-1)$ which is given by:$B_k = 1 + \sum_{i=1}^{k-1} n_i$. When the source node initiates a search, the information may reside in any of the remaining node in the network with uniform probability. With n_i nodes in Ring i, the probability that the information can be found in Ring i is $\frac{n_i}{N-1}$. For modeling tractability, we assume a perfect communications system without any packet loss due to bit error or collision at the MAC layer.

2.2   The Search Expansion Function (SEF)

Let the "Search Expansion Function" (SEF) define how the TTL will be incremented, and the resultant TTL for the next ERS attempt, when the previous search fails. In ERS studies reported so far, the TTL is incremented linearly with a fixed value. For example, work presented in [8,6] incremented TTL with the fixed value of 2, while Royer et. al. [9] used a fixed increment of 1. In this section, we define the linear SEF for ERS as this is the SEF currently used by ERS applications. However, exploration of other types of SEFs, such as exponential, certainly makes an interesting future study.

Let a denote the start TTL, and b denote the fixed increment value for the next TTL if the previous search fails. If x denotes the ERS attempt number,

---

[1] Forwarding cost of ERS query packets can also include other cost at the nodes, such as processing cost, energy consumption, etc. However, models presented in this paper remains valid.

then the linear SEF can be defined as $f(x) = a + (x - 1) \times b$, where $f(x)$ denotes the TTL value for attempt number x. If ω_L is an integer number that denotes the maximum possible retry (search threshold) in the linear SEF for a given network topology, we can define it in terms of a, b and M. The preference that the maximum number of retries should be less than the total rings in the network (with respect to the source) gives us the following condition from the expression of $f(x)$: $\omega_L < \frac{M-a}{b} + 1$.

2.3   Expected Bandwidth Cost

Given the described system, we now proceed to describe our model that computes the expected broadcast cost as a function of L, a, and b ($\beta(L)_{ab}$). ERS starts with a TTL of a, and each time it fails, the TTL is incremented by b. Therefore, in the 1st attempt (L=1), the TTL is set to a, and it is set to $a + b$ only if the first search fails (L=2). There are two main components of $\beta(L)_{ab}$, details of which can be found in [3]. The first component is the expected cost if the information is located in any of the attempts starting from 1 up to L. The second component of $\beta(L)_{ab}$ is the cost incurred if the information is located outside search threshold L. Note that the value of L can only be whole integers (discrete values). Therefore, we have:

$$\beta(L)_{ab} = \sum_{i=1}^{L} \left(P(i) \sum_{k=1}^{i} B(k) \right) + \left(1 - \sum_{i=1}^{L} P(i) \right) \left(\sum_{k=1}^{L} B(k) + N - 1 \right) \quad (1)$$

Let us refer to the expressions of probability and broadcast costs, i.e., $P(i)$s and $B(i)$s, in the above equation as *logical* expressions. In order to calculate the expected cost, we need a mapping between the logical and physical (or actual) values. The actual expressions relate to the physical rings in the topology. The mapping has been shown in section 2.5.

2.4   Expected Locating Time

Let T denote the timeout after which the next incremented search is initiated, if no reply is received within this time. The T value can either be a dynamic value and vary as the search diameter varies, or can be a fixed value regardless of the search diameter. For example, in AODV draft version 10, the T value was dependent on the TTL value and changed as the TTL changed. In AODV version 11 however, a fixed value for T was used regardless of the TTL value. We use the fixed T value approach here. Locating time for each try will vary from 0 to T. We use the average from this range ($= T/2$) in our expression for expected locating time, denoted by $E[t]$, as given below:

$$E[t] = P(1) \times T/2 + P(2) \times (T + T/2) + \cdots +$$
$$P(L) \times \{(L - 1)T + T/2\} + P(G) \times (LT + T/2)$$
$$= T \sum_{i=1}^{L} (i - 1) \times P(i) - LT \sum_{i=1}^{L} P(i) + LT + 0.5T \quad (2)$$

The logical representation of probability, such as $P(1), P(2)$, etc. in Equation 2 are can be mapped to the physical representation in the way shown in section 2.5.

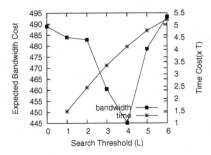 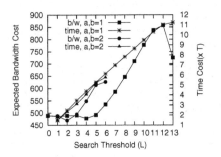

Fig. 1. Power-Law Topology1:N=490, M=7 **Fig. 2.** Power-Law Topology2:N=490,M=14

2.5   Mapping of Logical and Physical Expressions

In order to see the relationship of logical $P(i)$s and their corresponding physical probabilities $P^{ph}(i)$s, let us assume that ERS starts with the TTL of a and each time a search fails, it increments the TTL by b, until the search threshold exceeds the search threshold value of L (TTL of $a + (L-1) \times b$). We can derive the following relationship between the logical and physical location probability values in terms of a and b:

$$P(i) = \begin{cases} \sum_{j=1}^{b} P^{ph}(a + (i-2)b + j) & \text{if } (i-2) \geq 0, \\ \sum_{j=1}^{a} P^{ph}(j) & \text{otherwise.} \end{cases} \quad (3)$$

For the logical representation of bandwidth cost $(B(i))$, we get the general expression for the logical bandwidth cost in terms of a and b as: $B(j) = B_{a+(j-1)b}$.

3   Numerical Experiments and Results

For our experimental study, the random topologies were generated using our random topology generator [3], and the power-law topologies were generated using the PLOD power-law topology generator [7]. Eq. 1 and 2 were used to produce results for the generated topologies. We have experimented with a large number of network topologies for both random and power-law categories, and obtained similar results. Therefore, we discuss our findings in terms of a few representative graphs presented here.

Figures 1 and 2 show representative graphs for power-law topology. In each of these figures, expected bandwidth cost plotted against $L = 0$ denotes the broadcast cost if no ERS was used (network-wide flooding), while other bandwidth cost values on the graphs are for ERS search. We also plot the expected locating time, labelled as "Time Cost" (in units of T), to show how it grows as L grows.

In [3], we demonstrated that there exists an optimum search threshold (L') for which the broadcast cost is minimum using ERS, for any *random* topology. We also showed that L' lies within the small range of $[2, 4]$. Figures 1 and 2, as well as the random topology presented in Tables 1 & 2 substantiate the same finding. We also have experimented with some regular topologies (hexagonal, and circular), and found similar results.

While for most applications of ERS, the evidence of having an optimum threshold is of great utility, for some it may not be enough. Applications with a tight delay-budget need to consider how the selection of L impacts the locating time. As can be expected, as well as evidenced by the expected locating time graphs, expected locating time increases with each repeated ERS attempt. For example, Figure 1 shows that locating time increases from about 1.5 to 4 units, when L is increased from 1 to 4.

Let's now investigate the effect of selecting a and b values that are greater than 1. While Figure 1 plots results for $a, b = 1$ only, Figure 2 plots the bandwidth and time graphs for two sets of a, b values. From Figure 2, it is evident that the use of $a, b = 2$ resulted in a *lower* L' ($= 2$) than when $a, b = 1$ was used ($= 4$). Also, the optimum cost and expected locating time (at L') in the case of $a, b = 2$ is *lower* than that of $a, b = 1$.

Table 1. Different a values for a Random Topology $(b = 1)[N = 194, M = 19]$

a Value	Lowest B/W Cost	Related Time Cost
$a = 2$	$186.533676(L' = 2)$	2.323834
$a = 3$	$183.00(L' = 1)$	1.396373
$a = 4$	$177.00(L' = 1)$	1.308290
$a = 5$	$179.00(L' = 1)$	1.230570
$a = 6$	$183.00(L' = 1)$	1.173575
$a = 7$	$183.00(L' = 1)$	1.116580

Table 2. Different b values for a Random Topology $(a = 1)[N = 194, M = 19]$

b Value	Lowest B/W Cost	Related Time Cost
$b = 2$	$183.844559(L' = 2)$	2.323834
$b = 3$	$177.673569(L' = 2)$	2.147668
$b = 4$	$179.409332(L' = 2)$	1.992228
$b = 5$	$183.176178(L' = 2)$	1.878238
$b = 6$	$183.005173(L' = 2)$	1.764249

We have experimented how the selection of a, b values *individually* impact the expected bandwidth cost and locating time, and whether there can be *optimum* values for a and b. Results for a random topology network are summarized in Tables 1 and 2. We can see that a and b also have optimum values producing lowest bandwidth cost. For the random topology, we have $a = 4$ as the optimum a value (b kept constant), and $b = 3$ as the optimum b value (a kept constant). For any given topology, bigger the individual values for a and b, smaller the expected locating time. This is because bigger a, b values will incur less number of ERS attempts thus involving less waiting time. By properly tuning the a or b values, further reduction in bandwidth cost and time can be achieved when compared to the common values of $a, b = 1$. We have also experimented with the optimum a, b values as a combination. We had kept the a value at the optimum (4), then varied the b value. We had then kept the b value at the optimum (3), then varied the a value. We found that keeping the a at its optimum gives results in the lowest bandwidth cost (177.00) at $L = 1$, no matter what the b value is.

4   Conclusion

ERS is a well-known technique which minimizes the overhead of broadcast in decentralized and unstructured networks. In this paper, we have provided performance analysis of ERS in terms of *any* start and increment TTL. We have studied two conflicting performance metrics: the expected cost, and expected locating time. Designing an ERS such that the search cost (in terms of bandwidth, processing etc.) is minimized, increases the expected locating time, and vice versa. We derived important results that can be summarized as following: (1) for any given network topology, there is an optimal search threshold (L') minimizing the expected broadcast cost. The L' is a small value and lies withing the small range of $[2 - 4]$. This result is significant because they are topology independent and hence can be useful for a network node even if it cannot obtain the topology of the entire network., (2) use of the start and increment TTL values that are greater than 1 results in lower bandwidth cost & locating time, and (3) further tuning of ERS is possible; there is an optimum value for the start and increment TTL (individually). This tuning may need topology information.

References

1. *The gnutella protocol specification v0.4* http://www9.limewire.com/developer/gnutella_protocol_0.4.pdf, 2000
2. K. Carlberg and J. Crowcroft: Building shared trees using a one-to-many joining mechanism, ACM Computer Communication Review, pp.5-11, 1997.
3. Jahan Hassan and Sanjay Jha: Optimising Expanding Ring Search for Multi-Hop Wireless Networks, In proceedings of IEEE GLBECOM, 2004.
4. David B Johnson and David A Maltz: Dynamic Source Routing in Ad Hoc Wireless Networks, Mobile Computing, Vol. 353, Kluwer Academic Publishers, 1996.
5. B. Schrick and M. Riezenman: Wireless broadband in a box, IEEE Spectrum, No.6, pp.34-43, June 2002.
6. C. E. Perkins and E. Royer and S. Das: Ad hoc On-Demand Distance Vector (AODV) Routing, www.ietf.org/rfc/rfc3561.txt, IETF Request For Comment, July 2003.
7. Christopher R. Palmer and J. Gregory Steffan: Generating network topologies that obey power laws, In proceedings of IEEE GLOBECOM, November, 2000.
8. Q. Lv , P. Cao, E. Cohen, K. Li, and S. Shenker: Search and Replication in Unstructured Peer-to-Peer Networks, In proceedings of the International Conference on Supercomputing, June 2002.
9. Elizabeth Royer: Routing in Ad-hoc Mobile Networks: On-Demand and Hierarchical Strategies,Ph.D Thesis, University of California at Santa Barbara, December 2000.

Dynamic Location Management with Personalized Location Area for Future PCS Networks

Jun Zheng[1], Emma Regentova[1], and Pradip K. Srimani[2]

[1] Deaprtment of Electrical and Computer Engineering,
University of Nevada, Las Vegas
4505 Maryland Parkway, Las Vegas, NV 89154, USA
{jzheng, regent}@egr.unlv.edu
[2] Department of Computer Science, Clemson University
Clemson, SC 29634, USA
srimani@cs.clemson.edu

Abstract. Effective location management is critical for future personal communication service (PCS) networks, which envision smaller cells comprising a vast number of mobile terminals. In this paper we present a dynamic location management scheme with personalized location areas. The proposed technology takes into account the mobility patterns of the individual users in the system. The continuous time Markov chain is employed to model the system and analyze the location management cost. The personalized location areas are dynamically defined for each mobile terminal using a heuristic algorithm. Simulation results show that the proposed scheme offers a lower signaling cost than that achieved by some known methods.

1 Introduction

In *personal communication service* (PCS) networks, the location of each mobile terminal (MT) has to be tracked consistently to guarantee successful call delivery [1]. This process of tracking locations of mobile users at any given time is called *location management*. Location management implies two basic logical procedures, namely *location update* and *paging*; each in turn contributes to the total location management cost.

In current PCS networks, such as the Global System for Mobile Communications (GSM), the entire service area is divided into several *location areas* (LAs) and each LA is composed of one or more cells. The location update takes place when the MT moves between LAs. When an incoming call arrives for the MT, the system performs paging by sending polling messages to all the cells in the MT's last reported LA. This always-update location tracking strategy works well for a relatively small number of mobile users. For future PCS networks, such as Universal Mobile Telecommunication System (UMTS), the population

A. Sen et al. (Eds.): IWDC 2004, LNCS 3326, pp. 495–501, 2004.
© Springer-Verlag Berlin Heidelberg 2004

of MTs will increase dramatically. Also, many new services like multimedia over telephony are provided. In order to meet the quality of service requirements, the cell size is reduced that allows for saving the power of transmission and greater frequency reuse [1]. However, smaller cells adversely cause more frequent cell crossing by MTs. The latter circumstance in turn leads to higher cost of location management.

Various LA-based schemes have been proposed to reduce the signaling cost for location management, which can be divided into two major categories: static and dynamic [1]. In the former group, the whole system is partitioned into number of LAs, which are fixed and same for all users. The partitioning is done for obtaining an optimal total management cost for all MTs [2]. In contrast, dynamic LA is based on the mobility behavior and call patterns (call arrival rate) of individual MT. Some important dynamic LA schemes are time-based LA, movement-based LA and distanced-based LA [1]. In [3], several strategies are proposed to group cells into location areas by considering movement behavior of individual MT's. The LAs are fixed for each MT but could be different for different MTs. The authors of [4] consider MT's mobility pattern to create a personalized LA for each. Once a MT leaves its current LA, a new LA will be defined based on the probabilities of crossing the boundaries of cells, or so-called transition probabilities. The new LA might have overlaps with the old one. The problem with these schemes is that they group cells only based on the transition probabilities between cells. The grouping is bounded by the LA size, which is computed as the number of cells in the area. When performing the grouping, there is no way to learn about the changes in the location management cost.

In this paper, we develop a dynamic location management scheme with a personalized location area (PLA) for each MT and evaluate its performance. We use continuous time Markov chain (CTMC) to analyze the location management cost; and then describe a heuristic algorithm to determine the personalized location area of a minimum cost.

2   Dynamic Location Management with Personalized Location Area

The essence of the proposed dynamic location management scheme lies in designing LAs for each MT individually and providing this information to them. Once the MT enters the PCS system, a personalized LA is found by minimizing the total location management cost based on the movement behavior of the MT in the system. The system then sends the IDs of all cells in the designed LA to the MT and the latter stores them in the local memory. If the MT moves into a new cell, it checks if the new cell's ID is in the list. If it is not found, then MT sends a location update message to the system and a new personalized LA is created. When there is an incoming call, the system will page all the cells in the LA to identify the cell of MT's current location and to deliver the call. Fig. 1 shows an example of the proposed location management scheme. The system has 16 cells indicated on the right hand diagram by circles. Initially the MT

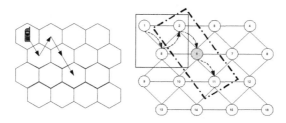

Fig. 1. Example of Dynamic Location Management Scheme; Left: MT roaming. Right: Forming location areas

resides in cell 1 and the designed personalized LA for the MT includes cells 1, 2 and 5 (bounded by the solid rectangle). When the MT moves into either cell 5 or cell 2, there is no location update performed. If a call arrives when the MT is in cell 2, the system will page all three cells to find the MT and deliver the call. The location update is performed when the MT moves for example from cell 2 to cell 6 (see, shaded circle). A new LA will be formed with cells 2, 6 and 11 (see, dashed rectangle). Note that the new LA overlays the previous one.

3   Personalized Location Area Design

We assume the network has an arbitrary topology. The PCS network can be represented as a bounded-degree, directed graph $G = (V, E)$, where V is the set of nodes representing the cells and E is a set of edges representing the interconnections between the cells. $|V|$ is denoted as the number of nodes in G. Two adjacent cells i and j relate by two directed edges (i, j) and (j, i) in the graph. The MT's movement in the network is modeled as a random walk. Under the random walk model, for each MT, there is a predefined probability p_{ij} of moving from cell i to cell j with $\sum_j p_{ij} = 1$. The residence time of the MT in cell i is assumed to be exponentially distributed with the mean $1/\lambda_{mi}$.

The behavior of the MT in a predefined LA is modeled after a continuous time Markov chain (CTMC) with absorbing states. The absorbing state denotes the state of MT of moving out of the current LA. The state space of the CTMC is $S = \{1, \ldots, k, k + 1\}$ where states 1 to k are transient states that represent the cells in the LA and state $k + 1$ is the absorbing state that represents the neighboring cells of the LA (cells $k + 1$ to n). The generation matrix of the CTMC can be written as

$$
\mathbf{Q} = \begin{pmatrix} \mathbf{A} & \mathbf{B} \\ \mathbf{O} & 0 \end{pmatrix} = \begin{pmatrix} -\lambda_{m1}\sum_{j\neq 1} p_{1j} & \lambda_{m1}p_{12} & \cdots & \lambda_{m1}p_{1k} & \lambda_{m1}\sum_{j=k+1}^{n} p_{1j} \\ \vdots & \vdots & \vdots & \vdots & \vdots \\ \lambda_{mk}p_{k1} & \lambda_{mk}p_{k2} & \cdots & -\lambda_{mk}\sum_{j\neq k} p_{kj} & \lambda_{mk}\sum_{j=k+1}^{n} p_{kj} \\ 0 & 0 & \cdots & 0 & 0 \end{pmatrix}
$$

$$(1)$$

where $\mathbf{A}$ is an $k \times k$ matrix with grouping the transition rates in the transient states, $\mathbf{B}$ is column vector with $\mathbf{B} = -\mathbf{A}\mathbf{e}^T$ and $\mathbf{e} = [1\ 1\ \ldots\ 1]$, $\mathbf{O}$ is a $1 \times k$

zero matrix. Without loss of generality, we assume the first cell that the MT enters in the LA is cell 1. Thus, the initial probability vector for this CMTC is $\mathbf{p}_0 = [1 \; 0 \; \dots \; 0]$.

Given τ_a is the time to reach the absorbing state from $t = 0$, the probability distribution of the time until absorption can be written as

$$F_a(t) = Pr\{\tau_a \leq t\} = 1 - \mathbf{p}_0 e^{\mathbf{B}t} \mathbf{e}^T, t \geq 0 \tag{2}$$

The average residence time of the MT in the LA $\bar{t}$ which equals to the mean time to absorption $E(\tau_a)$ is then given by

$$\bar{t} = E(\tau_a) = -\mathbf{p}_0 \mathbf{B}^{-1} \mathbf{e}^T \tag{3}$$

The total location management cost for MT in a specific LA K is defined as

$$C(K) = c_p \lambda_c N + c_u \Phi_u \tag{4}$$

where N is the number of cells in the LA, λ_c is the call arrival rate for the MT, Φ_u is the location update rate of the MT for the LA K which equals to $1/\bar{t}$, c_p and c_u are the per-cell paging cost and the unit location update cost, respectively. The first component of the right side of Equation 4 corresponds to the paging cost and the addend is the location update cost.

A personalized LA is formed such that the total location management cost is minimized. Because of the complexity of the optimization problem is high, an iterative greedy heuristic algorithm that yields a sub-optimal result is proposed as a rational alternative. The heuristic algorithm performs as follows.

Define:
LA: set of cells in the designed LA
TLA: set of cells in the temporary LA to be checked
$\Gamma(A)$: the set of neighboring cells of LA A
v: LU cell of the MT
C_{min}: minimum signaling cost corresponding to the designed LA
C^*: minimum signaling cost corresponding to TLA palatino

1. Initialize LA = $\{v\}$, TLA = LA and Γ(TLA), C_{min} = C(LA) = $c_p \lambda_c$
   + $c_u \lambda_{mv}$
2. Include a new cell into the LA
   $C^* = \infty$
   For cell i in the Γ(LA)
      Let TLA' = TLA $\cup$ $\{i\}$
      Calculate $\bar{t}$(TLA') and C(TLA')
      If C(TLA') < C^*
         C^* = C(TLA'), TLA = TLA'
      End
   End
   If C^* < C_{min}
      C_{min} = C^*, LA = TLA

```
    End
3.  If  C_min  <  c_p λ_c(|TLA|+1)
        Stop
    Else
        Find Γ(TLA)
        Goto Step 2
    End
```

Note that in step 1, $C_{min} = C(\text{LA}) = c_p \lambda_c + c_u \lambda_{mv}$ is the total signaling cost of the LA only including the LU cell v. In Step 3, the algorithm will terminate if C_{min} is less than $c_p \lambda_c(|\text{TLA}|+1)$ which is the paging cost of grouping when one more cell is added to the temporary LA. If the condition is met, there is no need in further check because trivially C_{min} will be less than the total cost incurred by adding any single cell.

4   Simulation

In this section we present results of simulations performed to evaluate the performance of the proposed dynamic location management scheme. We assume the incoming call follows a Poisson process with mean λ_c. The residence time of the MT in each cell is exponentially distributed with mean $1/\lambda_{mi}(i = 1, 2, \ldots, |V|)$.

In the first study, we use a network with 25 cells. The system is organized in a hexagonal grid structure for the simulation purpose, although arbitrary cell topology can be used. The transition probabilities between cells are randomly generated. We compare the proposed PLA scheme with the always-update (AU) and the distance-based location area (DBLA) schemes. The distance threshold of DBLA is set to $D = 1$. The incoming call rate (number of calls per hour) is $\lambda_c = 2$. The average mean residence time of MT in the system is taken as $1/\lambda_m = 180, 360, 540, 720$ or 900s which corresponds to the call-to-mobility ratio (CMR) 0.1, 0.2, 0.3, 0.4 and 0.5, respectively. The per-cell paging cost c_p is 1 and the unit location update cost c_u is 10. The simulation is conducted for all the schemes using the same trace. The total number of calls generated for

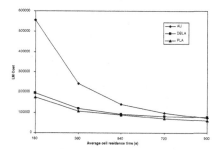

Fig. 2. Performance comparison of location management schemes

each simulation run is 10,000. 20 simulation runs are performed for each CMR instance. The result is obtained mean value of the 20 runs.

The results are shown in Fig. 2. For low CMR region (CMR = 0.1 to 0.4), DBLA performs better than AU. When the CMR becomes larger (CMR = 0.5), AU is better than DBLA. As we know, DBLA employs a larger location area than that of AU to reduce the location update rate, and consequently the location update cost. That in turn releases the paging cost. When the CMR is low, the location update rate is high and the location update cost dominates the total signaling cost. When the CMR increases, the location update rate decreases and the paging cost contributes the total signaling cost. The proposed PLA scheme defines the personalized LA by minimizing the location management cost according to the MT's movement behavior in the system and the system parameters, which makes it better candidates compared to the counterparts such as AU and DBLA.

Next, we compare the performance of the proposed scheme with the static LA (SLA) scheme [3] with the same structure and the parameters. The network has 20 cells as shown in Figure 3 of [3]. To make the CMR to 0.2 as in [3], we set the mean residence time for each cell is set to 360s and the call arrival rate is 2 calls per hour. We compare the proposed PLA scheme with the SLA scheme using the Strategy_Max_Gain partition method that gives the best result among the four strategies proposed in [3]. The location management costs for PLA and SLA obtained from simulation are 61,008 and 65,299, respectively. The results demonstrate that the proposed dynamic scheme outperforms the SLA scheme.

5   Conclusion

We have proposed the dynamic location management scheme designed for future PCS networks. In essence, a personalized location area is formed for each MT based on MT's mobility pattern in the system and with the location management cost as the objective function to be minimized. A heuristic algorithm assists in finding an optimal solution. Based on the simulation results, it can be concluded that the developed scheme significantly reduces the location management cost compared to some known schemes such as AU, DBLA and static LA, thus it can be considered as a viable candidate for future PCS networks.

Acknowledgement

Srimani's work was supported by an NSF Award # ANI-0219485.

References

1. Wong, V., Leung, V. C. M.: Location Management for Next-Generation Personal Communication Networks. IEEE Network, Sept./Oct. (2001) 18-24.

2. Demestichas, P., Georgantas, N., Tzifa, E. et al.: Computationally Efficient Algorithms for Location Area Planning in Future Cellular Systems, Computer Communications, 23(2000) 1263-1280.
3. Lee, G., Chen, A. L. P.: The Design of Location Regions Using User Movement Behaviors in PCS Systems, Multimedia Tools and Applications, 15(2001) 187-202.
4. Subrata,, R., Zomaya, A. Y.: Dynamic Location Management for Mobile Computing, Telecommunication Systems, 22(2003) 169-187.

Improvement of Paging Cost by Updating Using Paging Delay Divergence

Daisuke Senzaki, Goutam Chakraborty, M. Matsuhara, and H. Mabuchi

Department of Software & Information Sc.,
Iwate Prefectural University
g231b014@edu.soft.iwate-pu.ac.jp
goutam/masafumi/mabu@soft.iwate-pu.ac.jp

Abstract. Distance-based approach is most efficient among the three strategies, namely time-based, zone-based, and distance based, used for location management of mobile hosts (MHs) in a cellular PCN. In this work, we made one important observation about the optimum distance and then proposed a new updating strategy. When the MHs are static, depending on where they had last updated, the paging cost and delay could be high for the incoming calls during the static period. To avoid this situation we use the variance of paging delay as a measure of the mobility of the host. We have shown that using this parameter as an indicator for updating, we can reduce the paging cost to a great extent. The improvement is shown by simulation.

1   Introduction

Public communication service (PCS) networks employ a cellular architecture. Communications to or from all the mobile hosts within a cell are via the base station by radio channels.

The signal, sent to find the called person, is the *paging* signal. If all the cells are *paged* simultaneously, then the user could be located with probability 1 and in the first trial, without any delay. This is called a pure or *blanket paging*. When the number of cells is large, as with present day PCS systems, pure paging would generate enormous signaling traffic. In order to avoid such a costly *paging*, the mobile user has to report its location time to time to the system. This process of reporting is called *location update*. For the system to be always aware of the present location of the mobile host, this update should be done every time the MH crosses the boundary of a cell. But, that again is very inefficient.

Presently, location updates are triggered after some certain threshold condition is satisfied, as follows (1) *Time based* [1], where the mobile user updates at constant intervals;(2)*Movement based* [2], where, every time the mobile user crosses a boundary, a counter is increased by 1, and when the count reaches a threshold, the user updates; (3)*Distance based* [3], where the user updates when he moves certain threshold distance from the last updated location.

In general, distance based approach is efficient for most of the users [4]. In [5] we have shown that for a fast moving mobile host with a definite direction

A. Sen et al. (Eds.): IWDC 2004, LNCS 3326, pp. 502–507, 2004.
© Springer-Verlag Berlin Heidelberg 2004

of movement, longer distance leads to overall cost reduction compared to MH moving slow within a few cells. For an individual user, the mobility varies within the day, during different hours of the day. Yet, it is impossible to adaptively change the distance. We propose that paging delay divergence would be a suitable parameter to determine the mobility. When this parameter is zero i.e., the MH is static, it should update, so that during that period the paging cost and delay would be minimum, if selective paging is used. This updating strategy is the main contribution.

The details of the mobility models are described in section 2. In section 3 the idea of the proposed updating strategy is explained. In section 4, the simulation set-up is explained. Section 5 contains the experimental results, and section 6 is the conclusion.

2   Mobility Model

The mobility model is the description of the day to day movements of the mobile users. The random walk model no longer describes the pattern of movement of the present day mobile users. In fact, most of the mobile users travel with some purpose. Many of them repeats a certain route on every working days. On weekends, at some certain time of the day, most of the movements are from residential area towards shopping malls.

A mobile user can either stay in its present cell or move to enter any one of its six neighboring cells. The probability of crossing any of the six adjacent cells are p_{NE}, p_N, p_{NW}, p_{SW}, p_S, and p_{SE} respectively. Here, N stands for North, E for East, S for South, and W for West. The probability to remain in the same cell is $1 - (p_{NE} + p_N + p_{NW} + p_{SW} + p_S + p_{SE})$. This is in addition to a default stay time in a cell, which has a fixed and a stochastic part. By changing the values of the six directional movement probabilities, and manipulating their values depending on movement history and model type at every cell crossing step, we could simulate various movement behaviour. We have shown in [5] that optimum distance for MH with different movement patterns differs.

3   Trigger Update - When the MH Is Static

For all the MHs there are periods of movements and static states. For most of the present day mobile users, the routine movement is from home to office and back. There are long static periods at home, and in the office. The idea of using different distances during movement and static state is impractical and too costly to implement. But, at least when the MH is static we can reduce the paging cost by updating it's location from the static cell and using selective paging. By that, though the same threshold distance is used, the overall cost will be much lower.

This is further explained with Fig. 1. Here the MH last updated in cell •, and then reach his office in cell ×. Let us suppose that the threshold distance is 4. As the MH has not crossed the threshold distance, it will not update after reaching cell ×. Now, whatever call the MH receives during his whole stay in the office, the paging delay will be 3, and every time 37 cells has to be paged to reach him and incurring a delay of 4. Though the threshold distance is not crossed, and the value of threshold distance is not changed, if the MH updates once after reaching office, this delay and paging cost would be minimized for the whole period of stay in the office.

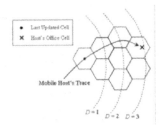

Fig. 1. Paging cost during static state

Now the question is how to know whether the MH is now static or still on move? When the mobile host is moving, the paging delay varies stochastically. As shown in Fig. 1, the paging delay is same for all incoming calls when the mobile host is static, i.e., the divergence of paging delay is zero. Thus, when the divergence of paging delay is zero, but paging delay is not, one can conclude that the MH has moved from the last updated location, not crossed the distance threshold, and is now static. Under such condition, we need to trigger a fresh update to improve the paging cost and delay. Below we propose a simple algorithm to trigger this update.

At the MSC the information of paging delay is available. We need to store that for last ν calls. Suppose paging delay for the ν successive calls are say, $\delta_1, \delta_2, \ldots \delta_\nu$, and their variance is σ. Then, in addition to usual updates, an extra update is triggered using the following simple algorithm:

Algorithm *TriggerUpdate:*
01   **if** ($(\sigma == 0) \wedge (\delta_\nu > 0)$)
02   **then** trigger update

Storing ν number of paging delays and running the above algorithm hardly involve any extra cost. In section 4 we will show by simulation that a big cost saving could be achieved by introducing this extra update.

4   The Simulation Set-Up

We assumed hexagonal cells. In the simulation, a network of 100×100 cells in mesh structure was considered. The algorithm to simulate the movement of mobile hosts were done in such a manner that crossing the edge of the network did not occur, and the travel routes are confined within the region of the whole network.

How different movement models are implemented, is roughly described in Section 3. The time is slotted, and a MH can cross a cell boundary only once in a single time slot. A mobile host is allowed to travel for 1440 time slots. Assuming 1 time-slot is equal to 1 min. this period covers a whole day. The movement consists of fast directed movement (e.g. from home to office), static periods (at home or at office), slow localized movements etc.

The call arrival is according to Poisson distribution. The probability of one call coming in a single time-slot is ϵ, which is set at 3 different values within the day, the highest value being 0.08. According to Poisson distribution, the probability of k calls arriving in a single time-slot is

$$p(k) = \frac{e^{-\epsilon} \epsilon^k}{k!}$$

that is, the probability of at least one call arriving in a single time-slot is, $1 - e^{-\epsilon}$. Maximum one incoming call is allowed in a time-slot.

We used selective paging [6]. While paging, the cell from which last updation was done, is paged first. If not found, all cells which could be accessed by one cell-crossing, i.e., six surrounding cells are paged. This continues until the MH is successfully located. For $D = 4$, in the worst case this could result in $1+6+12+18$ cell paging and a delay of 4.

5   Results with Triggered Updates

Basically the location management cost consists of three factors, the location update cost, paging cost, and the paging delay. In distance based strategy with selective paging, the paging delay is restricted to a maximum, depending on the threshold distance D. In this study, we consider the delay cost to be zero [3], assuming it to be always tolerable. The total location management cost, with this assumption, can be expressed as $C = \alpha \times N_{lu} + N_{pg}$. α is the weightage of update cost with respect to paging cost, whose value is set at 50 [5].

We know that with the present cell size, a threshold distance of 3 or 4 is optimum. This is also true for an individual MH, when his mobility varies over the day. But the situation is different when the MH is static at a single cell for a long period of time. As explained in section 3, a MH may suffer long delay and paging cost if the location of last update is different from the cell where he is static. Here we trigger an update as described in section 3. We will show by experiments the improvement of cost due to this additional updating.

We did simulations with 1000 MHs over a period of 100 days, where a single day consists of 1440 time-slots. The incoming call rate varies over the hours of the day, almost zero from midnight till early morning and high during business hours. All the results are an average over the whole set of 1000×100 data.

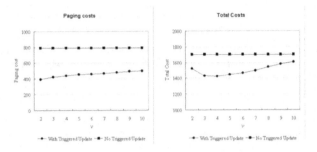

Fig. 2. On the left the change in paging cost with respect to ν is shown. On the right the change in total cost with respect to ν is shown

We assume that the cost of the triggered update is same as the update done while crossing the distance threshold, though in reality the triggered update does not involve any wireless band.

In the first set of experiments we showed how the paging and the total cost depends on ν - the number of previous paging delay data used. Please see Fig. 2. When ν is low, it is possible that even when the MH is not really static, a triggered update is done. This leads to unnecessary updates, and the total cost is high. So when we see the total cost, it is minimized at $\nu = 4$. This depends on the incoming call rate too. But the overall effect is invariant. When the incoming

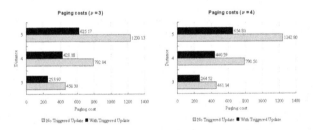

Fig. 3. On the left the change in paging cost for different distances when $\nu = 3$. On the right the change in paging cost for different distances when $\nu = 4$

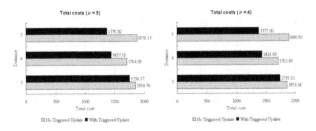

Fig. 4. On the left the change in total cost for different distances is shown when $\nu = 3$. On the right the change in total cost for different distances is shown when $\nu = 4$

call rate is very high, a triggered update even when the MH is static for a brief period of time would lead to cost saving, in which case again the value $\nu \approx 3$ or 4 is optimum.

In Fig. 3 and Fig. 4, we have shown how much paging cost and total cost are saved by introducing the extra triggered updates. Obviously, when we see the paging cost only, lower the distance lesser is the cost, though we need more updates. When we see the total cost, the threshold distance of 4 with $\nu = 4$ gives the minimum total cost and a 20% cost decrease is achieved. Though this is dependent on the parameter values used in our experiments, we can always find optimum values corresponding to any cellular network using similar experiments.

6   Conclusion and Discussion

We have proposed a triggered update strategy, when the MH is static at a station for long time to reduce the paging cost and delay. A simple algorithm is given, and the improvement in paging and total cost is shown by experiments. Of course, the exact amount of improvement may vary depending on the parameter values of the network.

We have not given any analytical model and theoretical analysis to support our experimental results. An analytical case for the proposed results might provide a better insight into the performance. We also like to add other types of mobility models like activity-based mobility, and check the validity of our conclusions.

References

1. C. Rose and R. Yates, "Minimizing the average cost of paging under delay constraints," Wireless Networks, 1(2):211-219, July 1995.
2. A. Bar-Noy, I. Kessler and M. Sidi, "Mobile users: To update or not to update?" Wireless Networks, 1(2):175-185, July 1995.
3. J. S. M. Ho and 1. F. Akyildiz, "Mobile user location update and paging under delay constraints," Wireless Networks, 1(4):413-425, December 1995.
4. A. Bera, and N. Das, "Performance analysis of dynamic location updation strategies for mobile users," Proceedings of the International Conference on Distributed Computing Systems, pp.428-435, April 2000.
5. D. Senzaki, Goutam Chakraborty, M. Matsuhara, H. Mabuchi, "Distance based location management in cellular PCS network - a critical study," 18th. IEEE International Conference on Advanced Information Networking and Applications (AINA 2004), Vol.2, pp. 95-98, 29-31 March, 2004, Fukuoka, Japan.
6. I. F. Akyildiz and J. S. M. Ho, Y. B. Lin, "Movement-based location update and selective paging for PCS networks," IEEE/ACM Transactions on Networking, 4(4):629-638, August 1996.

Distributed Power Control in Sensor Networks: A Game Theoretic Approach

Shamik Sengupta and Mainak Chatterjee

Department of Electrical and Computer Engineering
University of Central Florida
Orlando, FL 32816-2450
{shamik, mainak}@cpe.ucf.edu

Abstract. In wireless sensor networks, where energy of the sensor nodes are finite, power control is an important issue to consider. In this paper, we present a game-theoretic approach to solve the power control problem in CDMA based distributed sensor networks. A non-cooperative game is formulated and the existence of Nash equilibrium is studied for the sensor nodes operating under incomplete information. With the help of this equilibrium, we devise a distributed algorithm for optimal power control and prove that the system is power stable if the nodes comply with certain transmission thresholds. We show that even in the distributed non-cooperative scenario, it is in the best interest of the nodes to remain within these thresholds. The power level at which a node should transmit, to maximize its utility, is also evaluated. Numerical results prove that with the proposed algorithm, the sensor nodes are able to achieve best possible payoff by consuming less power, resulting in extended network lifetime.

1 Introduction

The advancement of wireless communication technologies coupled with the techniques for miniaturization of electronic devices have enabled the development of low-cost, low-power, multi-functional sensor networks. The tiny sensor nodes in these networks consist of sensing mechanisms, information gathering and data processing capabilities, and are capable of communicating untethered in short distances [1]. With emerging technologies, these sensor nodes will decrease in size, weight and cost by orders of magnitude. Also, the spatial and temporal resolution will increase and the accuracy will improve. Some sensor networking applications do not allow the possibility of human intervention due to difficulty in accessing such areas. As a result, in most cases sensor networks are deployed for only once with finite amount of energy available with the sensor nodes, which makes the power control a major concern for these networks. As the amount of energy available with the sensor nodes decreases with any kind of information transfer, efficient power control for information transfer is a requirement for these systems. Moreover, efficient power control can reduce the unnecessary interference and extend the lifetime of the sensor networks.

A. Sen et al. (Eds.): IWDC 2004, LNCS 3326, pp. 508–519, 2004.
© Springer-Verlag Berlin Heidelberg 2004

The power control algorithms available for cellular CDMA systems [2, 3, 4] cannot be directly applied to current distributed sensor networks. Such centralized algorithms require extensive control signalling and are not applicable in truly distributed scenario - where there is no central authority and each node has the knowledge of local information only. The natural question is then, who or what will control the power of the nodes. In such cases, where control theoretic approaches fail, we apply a game theoretic approach to regulate the power levels of the nodes and investigate whether any optimality is achievable. A game is played by all the players/nodes in the system simultaneously picking their individual strategies. This set of choices results in some strategy profile s ∈ S, which we call the outcome of the game. We typically assume all the players are rational and pick their strategy in such a way so as to maximize their utility. For every action of a node in response to the system's action, the node has a *payoff*. If there is a set of strategies with the property that no player can benefit by changing his strategy unilaterally while the other players keep their strategies unchanged, then that set of strategies and the corresponding payoffs constitute the *Nash equilibrium*. Though the existence of Nash equilibrium is not guaranteed in a game, the closer the system is to this equilibrium, the closer the system is to performance optimality. A game can be played in two modes. Either the players have complete information about the system in which case the game is a *complete information game* or the players have no or partial knowledge of the system in which case the game is an *incomplete information game*. Due to the distributiveness of sensor networks, the nodes do not have information about the strategies taken by other nodes and thus we have to devise games with incomplete information.

In this paper, we devise a distributed algorithm for power control, which helps the sensor nodes in minimizing power consumption and maximizing payoff and utility. The algorithm is based on a non-cooperative game of incomplete information, where sensor nodes only have information about their own power levels, signal to interference ratio (SINR) perceived from the system and its own channel condition. A node might choose not to cooperate and act in a "selfish" manner to obtain better utility from the system and transmit at a high power level. This kind of non-cooperation will eventually increase the interference level and thus might prove harmful to the system. We prove that it is in the best interest of the nodes that they cooperate and comply with the transmit power levels. As no information about the strategies taken by other nodes are needed in this game, control signals are rarely needed helping nodes in conserving energy.

The rest of the paper is organized as follows. In section 2, we formulate the non-cooperative game under incomplete information and establish the utility functions. Net utility equations are formed and Nash equilibrium is studied in 3. We calculate the thresholds for transmission power and channel conditions based on the equilibrium obtained. In section 4, we detect the desired power level for transmission under all possible conditions to obtain best payoff. Numerical results are presented in section 5. Conclusions are drawn in the last section.

2   Non-cooperative Game Under Incomplete Information

Before we devise the game strategies, let us first study the distribution of the nodes and calculate the expected number of nodes that contributes towards the interference and noise of a node.

2.1   Node Distribution

Let us assume that the interference range of a node is r_I. Thus, the area of the interference region is $a_I = \pi r_I^2$. We consider that there are M homogeneous nodes that are uniformly random distributed over a region of area A. The probability that a node has m neighbors within the interference range is binomially distributed [5]

$$\Pr[m \text{ neighbors}] = \binom{M-1}{m} \left(\frac{a_I}{A}\right)^m \left(1 - \frac{a_I}{A}\right)^{M-m-1}. \tag{1}$$

For $M \gg 1$ and $a_I \ll A$, the above binomial distribution is well approximated by the Poisson distribution:

$$\Pr[m \text{ neighbors}] \approx \frac{(\rho a_I)^m}{m!} e^{-\rho a_I} \tag{2}$$

where $\rho = \frac{M}{A}$ is the node density. Under the Poisson approximation, the expected number of nodes within the interference range of the receiver is $\sum_{m=0}^{M-1} m \frac{(\rho a_I)^m}{m!} e^{-\rho a_I}$. Theoretically, for randomly scattered nodes, the maximum number of interferers can extend upto infinity. For all practical purposes, we can consider the maximum number of interferers to be the expected value plus three times the standard deviation, σ [6]. Thus, the maximum number of interferers is

$$N = \sum_{m=0}^{M-1} m \frac{(\rho a_I)^m}{m!} e^{-\rho a_I} + 3\sigma \tag{3}$$

2.2   Game Formulation

We consider a time-slotted CDMA based sensor network and focus our attention on a particular node with its expected N neighbors within the interference range. Due to homogeneity of the nodes, we assume that all the nodes transmit with a power chosen from a set S, where S consists of all permissible power levels ranging from the minimum transmit power P_{min} to maximum transmit power P_{max}. Then, if node 1 chooses its power level $s_1 \in S$, node 2 chooses its power level $s_2 \in S$ and so on, we can describe such a set of strategies chosen by all $N + 1$ (a node with its N neighbors) nodes as one ordered $N+1$-tuple,

$$\mathbf{s} = \{s_1, s_2, \cdots, s_{N+1}\} \tag{4}$$

This vector of individual strategies is called a strategy profile (or sometimes a strategy combination). For every different combination of individual choices of strategies, we would get a different strategy profile **s**. A node will choose its strategy (to transmit or not to transmit, or to increase or decrease its power), and correspondingly, will choose a power level if it decides to transmit. Rationally, a node should choose its own power level depending on the power levels chosen by all other nodes, but in a distributed sensor network like the one under consideration, it is not possible for a node to know about the strategies of the rest of the nodes.

Based on such a situation, measure of satisfaction becomes one of the most important concern for the nodes. Depending only on the information available to a node i.e., its power level, channel condition and SINR, it calculates its utility gained from the system and correspondingly chooses its transmission power level. We call this utility value obtained by ith node as u_i. Basically, this utility depends on the strategy taken by the ith node, (i.e., s_i) and the strategies of all its neighboring nodes denoted by the vector $\mathbf{s_{-i}}$ which are not known to node i. To emphasize that the ith node has control over its own power level s_i only, we modify the utility notation and call it $u_i(s_i, \mathbf{s_{-i}})$. Thus utility value of node i can be expressed from [7] as,

$$u_i(s_i, \mathbf{s_{-i}}) = \frac{Lb}{Fs_i} f(\gamma_i) \tag{5}$$

where, L is the number of information bits in a packet of size F bits. b is the transmission rate in bits/sec using strategy s_i. $f(\gamma)$ is the efficiency function which increases with SINR. It measures the frame success rate and is defined as, $f(\gamma) = (1 - 2P_e)^F$, where P_e is the bit error rate (BER). For example, with non-coherent FSK modulation scheme, $P_e = 0.5e^{-\frac{\gamma}{2}}$. γ_i denotes the SINR of node i (assuming, node i is also transmitting at the same time slot), and is given from [7] as,

$$\gamma_i = \frac{W}{b} \frac{g_i s_i}{\sum_{k \neq i} g_k s_k + \chi} \tag{6}$$

where, W is the available spread-spectrum bandwidth, χ is the additive white Gaussian noise (AWGN) at the receiver, and g_k is the set of path gains. Thus, the utility achieved by node i can be defined as,

$$u_i(s_i, \mathbf{s_{-i}}) = \frac{Lb}{Fs_i} f\left(\frac{W}{b} \frac{g_i s_i}{\sum_{k=0, k \neq i}^{l} g_k s_k + \chi} \right) \tag{7}$$

where, l denotes the subset of neighbors that are active and influence the ith node. Note, l can take values from 0 to N as obtained from equation (3). It can be easily seen that with increase of other active nodes in the network, utility obtained by ith node decreases. Another significant aspect of our formulation is that the utility obtained by a node when it decides not to transmit is 0.

3   Net Utility

Now let us consider the cost/penalty incurred by a node when it decides to transmit. In a non-cooperative game of incomplete information, the cost to a node must be considered, otherwise each node will try to transmit at the highest possible power in order to achieve the best utility. The tradeoff here is the energy consumption which is proportional to the transmit power. A node transmitting at high power will decrease the SINR of other nodes and reduce their utility and the nodes will react by increasing their power levels. This feedback will result in all the nodes increasing their transmit power levels and faster consumption of the battery. To combat this situation, we define *net utility* as the utility achieved minus the cost incurred.

We consider two cases for finding the net utility. First, we assume that the channel conditions are fixed. Under such a scenario, we inspect if there should be any power threshold level for the nodes to obtain best utility. In subsection 3.2, we assume varying channel conditions and inspect the strategy that should be followed by the nodes to maximize their utility.

3.1   Net Utility with Fixed Channel Condition

Under fixed channel condition, to gain better utility, nodes try to transmit at a high power which eventually drains their battery quickly. If the strategy of a node is to transmit at power $P \in S$, the cost is a function of P which we denote by $A(P)$. P is a random variable denoting transmitting power of a node. It can be noted that $A(P)$ is an increasing function of P. Thus, the net utility of ith node can be written as

$$\text{net utility}_i = \begin{cases} u_i(s_i, \mathbf{s_{-i}}) - A(P) & \text{if node is transmitting} \\ 0 & \text{if node is silent.} \end{cases} \qquad (8)$$

Attaining Nash Equilibrium. Let us now analyze the existence of Nash equilibrium. If a node is allowed to transmit at any calculated power, then it is obvious that

$$\int_0^\infty f_P(x)dx = 1 \qquad (9)$$

i.e., the node transmits with probability 1. However, for all practical purposes, a node cannot transmit at arbitrarily high power and must decide on a maximum threshold power P_t. The imposition of the threshold implies that the node will not transmit at all if its calculated transmit power is above the threshold P_t. In other words, exceeding this threshold will introduce non-beneficial net utility for the node. Due to this restriction, the probability that a node transmits (or does not transmit) will be dependent on the threshold P_t; smaller the threshold, smaller the probability of transmission. Thus a node transmits at a power level not exceeding P_t, i.e., $0 < P \le P_t$. Then the probability that a node is transmitting can be given by,

$$\int_0^{P_t} f_P(x)dx = p(P_t) \tag{10}$$

where, $f_P(x)$ is the probability density function of P. If all nodes obey the threshold and transmit at a power not exceeding P_t, then the expected net utility of ith node (if the node is active) can be given by,

$$E[\text{net utility}_i] = \sum_{l=0}^{N} (u_i(s_i, \mathbf{s_{-i}}) - A(P))C_l^N(p(P_t))^l(1 - p(P_t))^{N-l} \tag{11}$$

As $\sum_{l=0}^{N} C_l^N(p(P_t))^l(1 - p(T))^{N-l} = 1$, equation (11) can be rewritten as

$$E[\text{net utility}_i] = \sum_{l=0}^{N} u_i(s_i, \mathbf{s_{-i}})C_l^N(p(P_t))^l(1 - p(P_t))^{N-l} - A(P) \tag{12}$$

If we define $U_i(P_t)$ as,

$$U_i(P_t) = \sum_{l=0}^{N} u_i(s_i, \mathbf{s_{-i}})C_l^N(p(P_t))^l(1 - p(P_t))^{N-l} \tag{13}$$

then the expected net utility obtained by ith node is given by,

$$E[\text{net utility}_i] = U_i(P_t) - A(P) \tag{14}$$

A node can be in two modes; either it is active and transmitting or it is silent. If the node is transmitting, then the expected net utility is given by equation (14). If the node is silent then by definition the expected net utility is 0. Thus, the *achievable gain* (net utility considering both modes) obtained by node i is

$$G_i(P_t) = \int_0^{P_t} [U_i(P_t) - A(x)]f_P(x)dx$$

$$= U_i(P_t)p(P_t) - \int_0^{P_t} A(x)f_P(x)dx \tag{15}$$

For the sake of convenience, let us denote

$$\int_0^{P_t} A(x)f_P(x)dx = B(P_t)$$

Then, equation (15) can be written as

$$G_i(P_t) = U_i(P_t)p(P_t) - B(P_t) \tag{16}$$

Next, we show, if nodes follow the threshold P_t, then even without the knowledge of other node's power levels, the system can attain Nash equilibrium, i.e., they will reach a stable state where the *gain* of an individual node cannot be increased further by unilaterally changing the strategy of that node. For a node, the expected net utility for transmission and for being silent should be equal at the threshold, i.e., when $P = P_t$. Therefore, the solution to the equation,

$$U_i(P_t) - A(P_t) = 0 \tag{17}$$

will be the required threshold for the power level. We will now show why maintaining this threshold will help reach the Nash equilibrium.

Let us assume T_1 be the solution to the equation (17). Then the average achievable gain of ith node obtained from the system is given by,

$$G_i(T_1) = \int_0^{T_1} [U_i(T_1) - A(x)] f_P(x) dx$$
$$= U_i(T_1)p(T_1) - B(T_1) \tag{18}$$

But suppose, a node unilaterally changes its strategy and changes the threshold value to T_2. Then the average achievable gain obtained by this particular node is given by

$$G_i(T_2) = \int_0^{T_2} [U_i(T_1) - A(x)] f_P(x) dx$$
$$= U_i(T_1)p(T_2) - B(T_2) \tag{19}$$

The difference between $G_i(T_1)$ and $G_i(T_2)$ is given by,

$$G_i(T_1) - G_i(T_2) = [U_i(T_1)p(T_1) - B(T_1)] - [U_i(T_1)p(T_2) - B(T_2)] \tag{20}$$

where, we use equation (17) to find the value of $U_i(T_1)$. Substituting the value of $U_i(T_1)$ in the above equation, we get,

$$G_i(T_1) - G_i(T_2) = A(T_1)[p(T_1) - p(T_2)] - [B(T_1) - B(T_2)] \tag{21}$$

Two cases might arise depending on the relative values of T_1 and T_2.

• **Case 1:** $T_1 > T_2$

In this case, equation (21) can be written as

$$G_i(T_1) - G_i(T_2) = \int_{T_2}^{T_1} [A(T_1) - A(x)] f_P(x) dx \tag{22}$$

Since $A(P)$ is an increasing function of power level P, $A(T_1) - A(x) > 0$ for $x < T_1$. Therefore for $T_1 > T_2$,

$$G_i(T_1) - G_i(T_2) > 0. \tag{23}$$

- **Case 2:** $T_1 < T_2$

In this case, equation (21) can be written as

$$G_i(T_1) - G_i(T_2) = -\left[\int_{T_1}^{T_2}[A(T_1) - A(x)]f_P(x)dx\right] \tag{24}$$

Applying the same logic, we find $A(T_1) - A(x) < 0$ for $T_1 < x \leq T_2$ which gives

$$G_i(T_1) - G_i(T_2) > 0 \tag{25}$$

Thus, for both the cases we find $G_i(T_1) > G_i(T_2)$. This shows that a node's average achievable gain cannot be increased further by changing its strategy unilaterally. Therefore T_1 is the power threshold for attaining the Nash equilibrium in the non-cooperative, incomplete information game.

3.2   Net Utility with Varying Channel Conditions

In this section, we show existence of a threshold for channel condition necessary for attaining Nash Equilibrium. We observe that the cost/penalty of the nodes will now depend on the channel conditions; better the channel conditions, lower is the cost. Thus, we define the cost as inversely proportional to the continuously varying channel condition C. Let this cost be $\xi(\frac{1}{C})$ which is a decreasing function with C. Then, the net utility of ith node can be written as,

$$\text{net utility}_i = \begin{cases} u_i(s_i, \mathbf{s_{-i}}) - \xi(\frac{1}{C}) & \text{if node is transmitting} \\ 0 & \text{if node is silent.} \end{cases} \tag{26}$$

Attaining Nash Equilibrium. We hypothesize that a node should transmit, only if its channel condition is better than a given threshold. Let this threshold be C_t. Therefore, the probability of a node transmitting is

$$\int_{C_t}^{\infty} f_C(x)dx = p'(C_t) \tag{27}$$

where, $f_C(x)$ is the probability density function of C. Then, similar to the equations presented in subsection 3.1, the expected net utility of ith node (if the node is active) can be given by,

$$E[\text{net utility}_i] = \sum_{l=0}^{N}(u_i(s_i, \mathbf{s_{-i}}) - \xi(\frac{1}{C}))C_l^N(p'(C_t))^l(1 - p'(C_t))^{N-l}$$

$$= \sum_{l=0}^{N} u_i(s_i, \mathbf{s_{-i}})C_l^N(p'(C_t))^l(1 - p'(C_t))^{N-l} - \xi(\frac{1}{C})$$

Next, defining $U_i'(C_t)$ as $\sum_{l=0}^{N} u_i(s_i, \mathbf{s_{-i}})C_l^N(p'(C_t))^l(1 - p'(C_t))^{N-l}$, the expected net utility of node i can be given by,

$$E[\text{net utility}_i] = U_i'(C_t) - \xi(\frac{1}{C}) \tag{28}$$

The gain obtained by the node i is

$$G_i'(C_t) = \int_{C_t}^{\infty} [U_i'(C_t) - \xi(\frac{1}{x})] f_C(x) dx$$
$$= U_i'(C_t) p'(C_t) - B'(C_t) \qquad (29)$$

where $B'(C_t) = \int_{C_t}^{\infty} \xi(\frac{1}{x}) f_C(x) dx$.

Now we will show that if the nodes act rationally and transmit only when the channel condition is better than C_t, then Nash equilibrium can be reached. As before, the solution to $U_i'(C_t) - \xi(\frac{1}{C_t}) = 0$ gives the value of the threshold.

Let C_1 be the solution. Then, the average achievable gain of ith node is given by,

$$G_i'(C_1) = \int_{C_1}^{\infty} [U_i'(C_1) - \xi(\frac{1}{x})] f_C(x) dx = U_i'(C_1) p'(C_1) - B'(C_1) \qquad (30)$$

Suppose, a node unilaterally changes its strategy and decides the threshold be C_2. Then the average achievable gain for that node will be

$$G_i'(C_2) = \int_{C_2}^{\infty} [U_i'(C_1) - \xi(\frac{1}{x})] f_C(x) dx = U_i'(C_1) p'(C_2) - B'(C_2) \qquad (31)$$

The difference in the gain is given by

$$G_i'(C_1) - G_i'(C_2) = [U_i'(C_1) p'(C_1) - B'(C_1)] - [U_i'(C_1) p'(C_2) - B'(C_2)]$$
$$= U_i'(C_1)[p'(C_1) - p'(C_2)] - [B'(C_1) - B'(C_2)]$$
$$= \xi(\frac{1}{C_1})[p'(C_1) - p'(C_2)] - [B'(C_1) - B'(C_2)] \qquad (32)$$

Again, two cases might arise depending on the relative values of C_1 and C_2.

- **Case 1:** $C_1 > C_2$

$$G_i'(C_1) - G_i'(C_2) = -\left[\int_{C_2}^{C_1} [\xi(\frac{1}{C_1}) - \xi(\frac{1}{x})] f_C(x) dx \right] > 0 \qquad (33)$$

- **Case 2:** $C_1 < C_2$

$$G_i'(C_1) - G_i'(C_2) = \left[\int_{C_1}^{C_2} [\xi(\frac{1}{C_1}) - \xi(\frac{1}{x})] f_C(x) dx \right] > 0 \qquad (34)$$

which shows, a node cannot increase its gain by unilaterally changing its strategy.

4   Detecting Transmission Power to Maximize Payoff

So far, we have evaluated the maximum power level and minimum channel condition, that a node must comply with. However, in most cases the nodes will use power levels that are below the maximum allowed. Thus the right transmit power needs to be evaluated which will depend on the SINR, which again depends on the strategies adopted by the other nodes. Due to the unreliability of the wireless channels, the successful transmission of a packet is probabilistic. We first find this probability of successful transmission. Let C, P and R be the random variables denoting channel condition, transmitting power and received power respectively, where received power consists of received desired signal power and received undesired signal power from other active nodes in the network and noise from the surroundings. We assume that these random variables are uniformly distributed between $\{C_{min}, C_{max}\}$, $\{P_{min}, P_{max}\}$ and $\{R_{min}, R_{max}\}$ respectively. Then, we define the probability of successful packet transmission as

$$p_s = \frac{P}{P+R} \times \frac{C - C_{min}}{C_{max} - C_{min}} \tag{35}$$

This definition of p_s is compatible with the axioms of probability in the sense that $0 \le p_s \le 1$. When a node transmits with the best possible power, under best possible channel condition and very low received power, the probability of successful transmission tends to 1. In contrast, when a node transmits at low power, under worst channel condition and high received power, the probability of successful transmission tends to 0.

Now, once the probability of successful transmission is defined, it is time to find the desired power level, at which the packets should be sent. In doing so, our main objective is to maximize the payoff of the transmitting sensor node. We consider the scenario, where the transmitter node continues to retransmit until the transmission is successful. Let, the power level chosen by the transmitter node be P, and there are $(n-1)$ unsuccessful transmission followed by successful transmission. Then the expected power consumption by the transmitter node can be given by,

$$E[\text{Power Consumption}]_P = \sum_{n=1}^{\infty} n(1 - p_s)^{n-1} \times p_s \times P = \frac{P}{p_s} \tag{36}$$

Now, we have the expected power efficiency for a power level P, which we can simply define as the inverse of the expected power consumption, where the probability of successful transmission is given by p_s. We combine these two factors to find the payoffs for a certain power level P which we define as

$$(payoff)_P = p_s \times E[\text{Power Efficiency}]_P = \frac{p_s}{E[\text{Power Consumption}]_P} \tag{37}$$

where, $(payoff)_P$ is the payoff and $E[\text{Power Consumption}]_P$ is the expected power consumption of the node for transmitting at power level P. A node can thus choose the power level which would maximize its payoff.

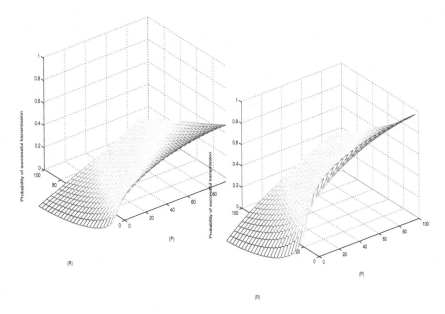

Fig. 1. Probability of successful transmissions for $\mathcal{C} = 0.5$ and $\mathcal{C} = 1.0$

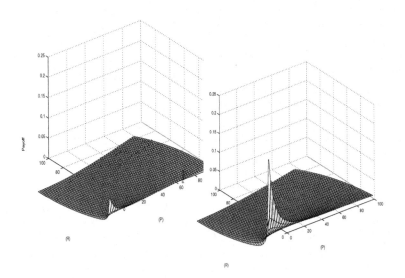

Fig. 2. Payoffs for $\mathcal{C} = 0.5$ and $\mathcal{C} = 1.0$

5   Numerical Results

We consider a network with homogeneous sensor nodes which can transmit uniformly in the range $\{P_{min}, P_{max}\}$. We assume the channel condition experienced
by the nodes as a quantitative factor, which can take values uniformly in the
range $\{C_{min}, C_{max}\}$ such that, $\mathcal{C} = \frac{C - C_{min}}{C_{max} - C_{min}}$ takes values in the range $(0-1)$.
$\mathcal{C}$ can be thought as a normalized measure of the channel condition. We consider
P_{min} as 1mW and P_{max} as 100mW. We show our results considering maximum
received power as 100mW.

In figure 1, we show the probability of successful transmissions for different
values of transmitting power and received power. The values of $\mathcal{C}$ were considered

as 0.5 and 1.0 respectively. As expected, with improvement in channel condition, the probability of successful transmissions increases. Moreover, we find that, the probability of successful transmission is more when the received power is less. This clearly indicates that with more number of active nodes, the probability of successful transmission decreases.

In figure 2, we present the payoffs obtained by a node for $C = 0.5$ and 1.0 respectively. These plots serve as a guideline for calculating the desired transmitting power for various received power and channel conditions. More precisely, if R is low, and P is high, then the payoff is not maximized. To obtain the best payoff at low received power, the transmitting power must also be low. The plots also reveal the existence of an upper bound in transmit power as was obtained in section 3.1; a condition to reach Nash equilibrium.

6 Conclusions

In this paper, we presented a game-theoretic approach to solve the power control problem encountered in sensor networks. We used non-cooperative game of incomplete information and studied the behavior of Nash equilibrium. We found the existence of Nash equilibrium assuming that there exist minimum and maximum threshold for channel condition and power level respectively. We suggest that a node should only transmit when its channel condition is better than the minimum threshold and its transmission power level is below the threshold power level. We also evaluated the desired power level at which the nodes should transmit to maximize their payoffs under any given condition.

References

1. I.F. Akyildiz, W. Su, Y. Sankarasubramaniam and E. Cayirci, "A Survey on Sensor Networks", *IEEE Communications Magazine*, Vol. 40, No. 8, August 2002, pp. 102-114.
2. A. El-Osery and C.T. Abdallah, "Distributed Power Control in CDMA Cellular System", *IEEE Antennas and Propagation Magazine*, Aug 2000, Vol. 42, No. 4, pp. 152-169.
3. S.A. Grandhi, R. Vijayan,D.J. Goodman, J. Zander, "Centralized power control in cellular radio systems", *IEEE Transactions on Vehicular Technology*, Volume: 42, Issue: 4, Nov. 1993, pp. 466-468.
4. J. Zander, "Performance of optimum transmitter power control in cellular radio systems", *IEEE Transactions on Vehicular Technology*, Volume: 41, Issue: 1, Feb. 1992, pp. 57-62.
5. S. De, D. Pados, C. Qiao and M. Chatterjee "Topological and MAI Constraints on the Performance of Wireless CDMA Sensor Networks", Proc. of *IEEE INFOCOM*, Hong Kong, 2004.
6. A.L. Garcia, Probabilty and random processes for electrical engineering, Addison-Wesley, 1989.
7. Y. Xing and R. Chandramouli "Distributed discrete power control for bursty transmissions over wireless data networks", *IEEE International Conference on Communications* (ICC), 2004.

A K-Connected Energy-Saving Topology Control Algorithm for Wireless Sensor Networks

Lei Zhang[1], Xuehui Wang[2], and Wenhua Dou[1]

[1]School of Computer,
[2]School of Mechatronics Engineering and Automation,
National University of Defense Technology, Changsha 410073, China
findzhanglei@hotmail.com

Abstract. We propose a distributed k-connected (KC) energy saving topology control algorithm for wireless sensor networks. Each node constructs a local k-connected sub-network independently based on the neighbor topology information, and adjusts its transmission power using a Max-Min method to save energy. We prove KC algorithm preserves the network connectivity (even k-connectivity if the neighbor topology is k-connected). Performance simulation shows the effectiveness of our proposed algorithm.

1 Introduction

Wireless sensor networks have been the focus of many recent research for its applications in military and environment surveillance. Since sensors are typically powered by batteries, energy-saving is a prime consideration in these networks. Topology control via per-node transmission power adjustment has been shown to be effective in extending network lifetime and increasing network capacity.

Several energy-saving topology control algorithms [1]-[5] have been proposed to create a power-efficient network topology in wireless sensor networks with limited mobility. Ramanathan et al. [1] proposed the CONNECT and BICONN-AUGMENT algorithms to solve the 1-connected and 2-connected energy-saving topology control problems, but both CONNECT and BICONN-AUGMENT are centralized algorithms with poor scalability. Roger Wattenhofer al. [2] introduced a cone-based distributed topology control algorithm (CBTC) with the support of directional antenna, but directional antenna is usually unusable for sensor networks. Ning Li [5] devised the LMST algorithm basing on the local minimum spanning tree theory, LMST only maintains 1-connectivity of the network and need the position system to identify the mutual distance between neighbor nodes, which may be inapplicable.

Compared with CBTC and LMST, our proposed k-connected (KC) energy saving topology control algorithm need not directional antenna or position system support. We prove KC algorithm preserves the network connectivity (even k-connectivity if the neighbor topology is k-connected) and dramatically reduces the node power consumption. Performance simulation shows the effectiveness of our proposed algorithm.

A. Sen et al. (Eds.): IWDC 2004, LNCS 3326, pp. 520–525, 2004.
© Springer-Verlag Berlin Heidelberg 2004

2   The K-Connected (KC) Energy-Saving Topology Control Algorithm

Suppose n sensor nodes are arbitrarily deployed in a two-dimensional plane. Each node is equipped with an omni-directional antenna with adjustable transmission power in the range of 0 to $P_{s\,max}$. V denotes the sensor node set in the network, $\forall u \in V$, if node u can communicate with node $v(v \in V)$ using the maximum transmission power, node v is called a neighbor of node u, all the neighbors of node u constitute its neighbor set V_N^u (including node u). network connectivity can be measured by k-edge connectivity or k-vertex connectivity, the latter is stronger than the former. Since node failure is more common than link failure in wireless sensor networks, we use k-vertex connectivity in this paper. The KC algorithm is composed of the following four phases: topology information collection, local topology construction, transmission power adjustment and mobility manipulation.

2.1   Topology Information Collection

Each node broadcasts a HELLO message using the maximum transmission power $P_{s\,max}$ to its neighbors, by measuring the receiving power of HELLO messages, node u can determine the minimum power $P_{s\,min}^{(u,v)}$ required to reach its neighbor node v as in [5]. Assume the remaining battery energy of node u is W_u, we define the lifetime of link (u,v) as

$$T_{max}^{(u,v)} = \frac{W_u}{P_{s\,min}^{(u,v)}} \qquad (1)$$

so link (u,v) can be regarded as a directed edge between node u and v with two weight values: $P_{s\,min}^{(u,v)}$ and $T_{max}^{(u,v)}$, all these directed edges construct edge set E, thus $G = (V,E)$ is a directed graph representing the global network topology. Each node can obtain the link information to its neighbors by receiving HELLO messages, it broadcasts these information in a Neighbor Link Information Message (NLI) using the maximum transmission power. After receiving the NLI messages from all the neighbors, node u can build its neighbor topology information graph $G_N^u = (V_N^u, E_N^u)$, where E_N^u is the edge set among all the nodes in V_N^u.

2.2   Local Topology Construction

On obtaining the neighbor topology information graph, each node builds a k-connected subgraph $G_N^{u\prime} = (V_N^u, E_N^{u\prime})$ using the following local k-connected energy-saving topology control(LKC) algorithm.

Step 1. Construct a subgraph $G_N^{u\prime} = (V_N^u, E_N^{u\prime})$ without any edges , i.e. $E_N^{u\prime} = \phi$. $\forall x \in V_N^u$, set its minimum transmission power P_{min}^x to 0, $P_{min}^x = 0$.

Step 2. $\forall x,y \in V_N^u$, merge the two directed edges $e_{P,T}^{(y,x)}$ and $e_{P,T}^{(x,y)}$ between them into a undirected edge $e_{P,T}^{xy}$, the weight values of the new undirected edge are:

$$P_{s\,\min}^{xy} = \max(P_{s\,\min}^{(x,y)}, P_{s\,\min}^{(y,x)}) \quad T_{\max}^{xy} = \min(T_{\max}^{(x,y)}, T_{\max}^{(y,x)})$$

The purpose of this step is to avoid the unidirectional link in the network, because MAC protocols usually require bidirectional links for proper operation.

Step 3. Sort the edges in $G_N^u = (V_N^u, E_N^u)$ according to its lifetime $T_{\max}^{xy}$ in a non-increasing order, the sort result is denoted as S.

Step 4. If S is empty, terminate the algorithm, else retrieve the first edge $e_{P,T}^{xy}$ from S.

Step 5. If node x and y are in the same k-connected subgraph of $G_N^{u\,'} = (V_N^u, E_N^{u\,'})$, go to step 4; else add edge $e_{P,T}^{xy}$ to $E_N^{u\,'}$ and update the transmission power by performing the following two steps.

$$if \quad P_{\min}^x < P_{s\,\min}^{xy}, \quad set \quad P_{\min}^x = P_{s\,\min}^{xy}$$

$$if \quad P_{\min}^y < P_{s\,\min}^{xy}, \quad set \quad P_{\min}^y = P_{s\,\min}^{xy}$$

Step 6. If $G_N^{u\,'}$ is k-connected, terminate the algorithm, else go to step 4.

2.3   Transmission Power Adjustment

On termination of the LKC algorithm, node u obtains the transmission power $P_{\min}^x$ for each node in V_N^u, it broadcasts these information to its neighbors in a Transmission Power Control(TPC) message and adjusts its transmission power using a Max-Min method. Assume P_{TPCx}^u is transmission power of node u in the received TPC message from neighbor x, node u compares P_{TPCx}^u with $P_{\min}^u$ and records the the less one:

$$P_{ux} = \min(P_{\min}^u, P_{TPCx}^u)$$

After receiving the TPC messages from all neighbors, node u set its transmission power P_u to the maximum of P_{ux}:

$$P_u = \max\left(P_{ux}, \forall x \in V_N^u \, and \neq u\right)$$

The final network topology after transmission power adjustment is denoted as $G_0 = (V, E_0)$. The Max-Min transmission power adjustment further removes some redundant paths while preserving the network connectivity, which is proved in Lemma 1.

Lemma 1. $\forall u \in V$, if $G_N^{u\,'} = (G_N^u, E_N^{u\,'})$ obtained by LKC algorithm is k-connected, after the Max-Min transmission power adjustment, $\forall v \in V_N^u$ and $v \neq u$, there are at least k disjoint paths between node u and v in $G_0 = (V, E_0)$.

Proof. $\forall u \in V$, $v \in V_N^u$, $v \neq u$, because $G_N^{u\,'} = (G_N^u, E_N^{u\,'})$ and $G_N^{v\,'} = (G_N^v, E_N^{v\,'})$ are k-connected graph, we denote the k disjoint paths between u and v in $G_N^{u\,'} = (G_N^u, E_N^{u\,'})$ as $p_u^1, p_u^2, ...p_u^k$, and those in $G_N^{v\,'} = (G_N^v, E_N^{v\,'})$ as $p_v^1, p_v^2, ...p_v^k$. After the Max-Min transmission power adjustment, the transmission power of node u is:

$$P_u = \max\left(\min(P_{\min}^u, P_{TPCv}^u), \forall v \in V_N^u \, and \, v \neq u\right)$$

which implies $P_u \geq \min(P^u_{\min}, P^u_{TPCv})$, if $P^u_{\min} > P^u_{TPCv}$, the k disjoint paths between node u and v are $p^1_v, p^2_v, ...p^k_v$, else they would be $p^1_u, p^2_u, ...p^k_u$. Therefore after the Max-Min transmission power adjustment, there are at least k disjoint paths between node u and v in $G_0 = (V, E_0)$.

2.4   Mobility Manipulation

To manipulate the mobility of sensor nodes, each node should broadcast HELLO message periodically, the interval between two broadcasts is determined by the mobility speed. When any node finds the neighbor topology is changed, it will rebroadcast the Neighbor Link Information message to notify its neighbors to update the neighbor topology information graph and readjust the transmission power from scratch.

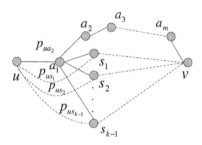

Fig. 1. The topology derived by KC algorithm is k-connected

Theorem 1. *$\forall u \in V$, if the neighbor topology $G^u_N = (V^u_N, E^u_N)$ is k-connected, the final topology $G_0 = (V, E_0)$ obtained by KC algorithm is also k-connected.*

Proof. Let $n(u, v)$ represents the number of edges along a path p_{uv} between node u and v in $G_0 = (V, E_0)$, $n(u, v)=1$ means u and v are directly connected, $n(u, v)=2$ means there is an intermediate node between u and v along path p_{uv}. $\forall u \in V, v \in V$,if $n(u, v)=1$, node v is node u's neighbor, by Lemma 1, there are k disjoint paths between u and v in $G_0 = (V, E_0)$. Assume when $n(u, v) = m$ ($m \geq 1$), there are k disjoint paths between node u and v in $G_0 = (V, E_0)$, now we prove the assumption is still held for $n(u, v) = m+1$.

When $n(u, v) = m+1$, we denote the m intermediate nodes along path p_{uv} as $a_1, a_2...a_m$, so there exists a path $p_{a_1v} = (a_1, a_2...a_m, v)$ between node a_1 and v, $n(a_1, v) = m$, according to our assumption, there exist k disjoint paths between node a_1 and v in $G_0 = (V, E_0)$ (including path p_{a_1v}). Consider the k nodes that are directly connected with a_1 on the k disjoint paths, denote them as $a_2, s_1, s_2...s_{k-1}$, if we can find k disjoint paths from u to these k nodes: $p_{ua_2}, p_{us_1}, p_{us_2}\cdots p_{us_{k-1}}$, then there must exist k disjoint paths between node u and v, as illustrated in Fig. 1.

Because node u and $a_2...a_m$ are a_1's neighbors, they are in the same neighbor set, by Lemma 1, there exist k disjoint paths between each pair of these nodes in $G_0 = (V, E_0)$. Now we will show how to find the k disjoint paths from u to $a_2, s_1, s_2...s_{k-1}$. For node a_2, obviously a path $p_{ua_2} = (u, a_1, a_2)$ exists between node u and a_2 in $G_0 = (V, E_0)$. For node s_1, because there are k disjoint paths between node u and s_1 in $G_0 = (V, E_0)$, at most one of them will intersect with p_{ua_2}, we can find a disjoint path p_{us_1} from the remaining k-1 ones. Similarly, for node s_{k-1}, among its k disjoint paths to node u at most k-1 of them will intersect with path $p_{ua_2}, p_{us_1}, p_{us_2} \cdots p_{us_{k-2}}$, the last disjoint one is $p_{us_{k-1}}$. So we can find k disjoint paths $p_{ua_2}, p_{us_1}, p_{us_2} \cdots p_{us_{k-2}}, p_{us_{k-1}}$ from node u to $a_2, s_1, s_2 \ldots s_{k-1}$ respectively, which implies there also exist k disjoint paths between node u and v, thus when $n(u, v) = m+1$, there are still k disjoint paths between node u and v in $G_0 = (V, E_0)$. Therefore the final topology $G_0 = (V, E_0)$ obtained by KC algorithm is k-connected.

3   Performance Evaluation

We evaluate the performance of KC algorithm through simulations. Assume n nodes are uniformly distributed in a $l \times l$ square area, two-ray ground propagation model is used for the wireless channel, the maximum transmission power is 0.2818w, the receiving threshold is 3.652E-10w and the corresponding maximum transmission range is 250m.

In the first simulation, we set n=100 and l =1000m, Fig. 2 shows four sample topologies derived using the maximum transmission power, CBTC, LMST, and KC (k=1) algorithm, from which we can see CBTC, LMST and KC all dramatically reduce the average node degree while maintaining network connectivity, a smaller average node degree usually implies less contention/interference and better spatial reuse. Moreover, KC outperforms both LMST and CBTC.

In the second simulation, we fix the distribution area l=1000m and vary the number of nodes from 50 to 300, Fig. 3 shows the average transmission power under different topology control algorithms , we can see the transmission power

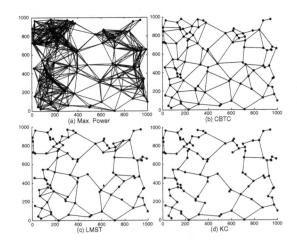

Fig. 2. Sample topologies derived under different topology control algorithms

under KC algorithm is the minimum. With the node density increasing, the average distance between each pair of neighbor nodes becomes closer. Hence, the nodes need lower transmission power to ensure the network connectivity.

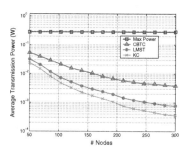

Fig. 3. Average transmission power under different topology control algorithms

References

1. R. Ramanathan and R. Rosales-Hain, "Topology control of multihop wireless networks using transmit power adjustment," in Proc. IEEE INFOCOM 2000, Tel Aviv, Israel, Mar. 2000, pp. 404–413.
2. L. Li, J. Y. Halpern, P. Bahl, Y.-M. Wang, and R. Wattenhofer, "Analysis of a cone-based distributed topology control algorithm for wireless multi-hop networks," in Proc. ACM Symposium on Principles of Distributed Computing, Newport, Rhode Island, United States, Aug. 2001, pp. 264–273.
3. R. Wattenhofer, P. Bahl L. Li, and Y. M. Wang, "Distributed Topology Control for Power Efficient Operation in Multihop Wireless Ad Hoc Networks," in Proceedings of INFOCOM, April 2001.
4. Y.-C. Tseng, Y.-N. Chang, and B.-H. Tzeng, "Energy-efficient topology control for wireless ad hoc sensor networks," In Proc. Int. Conf. Parallel and Distributed Systems (ICPADS 2002).
5. N. Li, J. C. Hou, and L. Sha, "Design and analysis of an MSTbased topology control algorithm," in *Proc. IEEE INFOCOM 2003*, San Francisco, CA, USA, Apr. 2003.

Locating Objects in a Sensor Grid

Buddhadeb Sau[1] and Krishnendu Mukhopadhyaya[2]

[1] Department of Mathematics,
Jadavpur University,
Kolkata - 700032, India
buddhadebsau@indiatimes.com
[2] Advanced Computing and Microelectronics Unit,
Indian Statistical Institute,
203, B. T. Road, Kolkata - 700108, India
krishnendu@isical.ac.in

Abstract. Finding the location of an *object*, other than the sensor in a sensor network is an important problem. There is no good technique available in the literature to find the location of objects. We propose a technique to find the location of objects in a sensor grid. The locations of the sensors are assumed to be known. A sensor can only sense the number of objects present in its neighborhood. This small information injects low traffic in the network. The computations are carried out completely in the base station.

1   Introduction

Micro-sensor is a small sized and low powered electronic device with limited computational and communicational capability. A *Sensor Network* [1] is a network containing some ten to millions of such micro-sensors (or simply sensors). Location finding is an important issue [4, 5, 6, 7] in a sensor network. It usually involves transmission of huge information and a lot of complex computations. Heavy transmission load drains the energy and shortens the life of the network [4]. An efficient location finding technique is required that involves little information passing, like only the counts, angles or distances of objects. Counting of objects needs simpler mechanism and hardware than those for angles or distances etc.

Several techniques are available for finding the location of a sensor with unknown position [2, 8, 10, 11]. But finding the location of objects has not received much attention. We propose a technique for finding locations of objects based only on the counts of objects sensed by different sensors. We formulate a system of linear equations for this purpose. The variables in the system are binary in nature. Standard techniques for solving a system of linear equations takes polynomial time whenever the system has a unique solution. Otherwise, the system gives an infinite number of solutions. But in our case, usually the system of equations does not possess a unique solution. But the number of solutions should be finite, as the variables are binary in nature. One can determine the positions of

A. Sen et al. (Eds.): IWDC 2004, LNCS 3326, pp. 526–531, 2004.
© Springer-Verlag Berlin Heidelberg 2004

the objects in exponential time on the number of cells in a grid. Our algorithm finds the locations of objects with much better complexity.

Section 2 describes the model and problem. In Section 3 we propose the algorithm to find locations of objects. Section 4 deals with the analysis of the algorithm. In Section 5 simulation results are presented. Finally, we present our conclusion in Section 6.

2   The Model and Problem Statement

We assume that the geographical area under consideration is divided into a two dimensional grid[3] with the following assumptions:

– The sensors are static and their positions are known.
– The objects to be sensed are indistinguishable to the sensors.
– The field is split into equal sized and small rectangular regions. Each of the smallest regions is termed as a *cell*.
– Each cell has unique spatial co-ordinate in two dimensions.
– A cell can contain at most one sensor and at most one object.
– A sensor can sense only 9 cells (the cell in which it resides and the eight neighboring cells).
– A sensor is capable of counting the number of objects in its neighborhood.
– A sensor node communicates its location and the count of the objects sensed, to the base station.

The sensors may be placed in any manner, either by some design or through random placements. After placing the sensors, the positions of these sensors are determined with some localization technique. In this work, we assume that once the placement is complete, the sensors remain static. We consider a two dimensional field. The field is divided into $m \times n$ identical cells. A cell can be uniquely identified by a pair of integers (i, j) when the cell lies in ith row and jth column in the field. We assume that a sensor or an object of our interest is small enough to fit inside a cell.

A sensor detects an object by optical, ultrasound or radio energy reflection or by any other mean. Intensity of energy decreases with the increase in distance. Therefore, a sensor can not sense objects placed beyond a finite region around it. This region is termed as the *locality* or *sensing region* of the sensor. We assume that the locality consists of 9 cells. The locality of a sensor at (u, v) consists of the cells (u, v), $(u, v \pm 1)$, $(u \pm 1, v)$ and $(u \pm 1, v \pm 1)$. We introduce a binary variable x_{uv} corresponding to the cell (u, v). The value of 1 is assigned to a variable, x_{uv}, if and only if the cell (u, v) contains an object and value 0 for no object. x_{uv} indicates the number of objects in the cell (u, v). If c is the count of the objects recorded by the sensor at (u, v) then,

$$
\begin{aligned}
&x_{u-1\,v-1} + x_{u-1\,v} + x_{u-1\,v+1} + x_{u\,v-1} \\
&+ x_{u\,v} + x_{u\,v+1} + x_{u+1\,v-1} + x_{u+1\,v} + x_{u+1\,v+1} = c
\end{aligned}
\tag{1}
$$

The equation (1) contains 9 variables. This equation alone is not enough for finding the location of objects. A sensor sends own position and the count of objects in its locality to the base station. The base station generates many equations with information from different sensors. Even then, the base station may not find the exact locations of all objects. Our proposed algorithm calculates the probabilities, p_{uv}, that the cell (u, v) contains an object.

The problem to the base station may be stated formally as:

Problem 1. Suppose, the field is equipped with p sensors, s_1, s_2, $\cdots$, s_p placed in a two dimensional grid field of size $m \times n$. Let (u_i, v_i) be the location of the sensor s_i in the grid. c_i denotes the number of objects observed by s_i. Note that a sensor at the border of the grid does not have 9 neighbors. Using equation (1) we obtain a system of linear equations as:

$$x_{u_i-1\ v_i-1} + x_{u_i-1\ v_i} + x_{u_i-1\ v_i+1} + x_{u_i\ v_i-1}$$
$$+x_{u_i\ v_i} + x_{u_i\ v_i+1} + x_{u_i+1\ v_i-1} + x_{u_i+1\ v_i} + x_{u_i+1\ v_i+1} = c_i \qquad (2)$$

for $i = 1, 2, \ldots, p$ where $x_{uv} \in \{0, 1\}$ and $x_{uv} = 0$ for the cell (u, v) beyond the grid. Find the *complete set of probabilities, p_{uv}, $u = 1, 2, \cdots m$, $v = 1, 2, \cdots n$.*

Fig. 1 shows a scenario of a 4×5 sensor grid. A bullet in a cell indicates that the cell contains an object. The grid contains 6 sensors s_1, s_3, s_4, s_5 and s_6 at locations $(1, 2)$, $(2, 3)$, $(2, 4)$, $(3, 4)$, $(4, 2)$ and $(4, 5)$. They found 0, 3, 2, 2, 2 and 0 objects respectively.

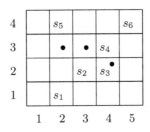

Fig. 1. An example showing sensors marked by s_i's and objects denoted by •

The system of equations corresponding to the scenario in Fig. 1 is:

$$
\begin{aligned}
x_{11} + x_{12} + x_{13} + x_{21} + x_{22} + x_{23} &= 0 \\
x_{12} + x_{13} + x_{14} + x_{22} + x_{23} + x_{24} + x_{32} + x_{33} + x_{34} &= 3 \\
x_{13} + x_{14} + x_{15} + x_{23} + x_{24} + x_{25} + x_{33} + x_{34} + x_{35} &= 2 \\
x_{23} + x_{24} + x_{25} + x_{33} + x_{34} + x_{35} + x_{43} + x_{44} + x_{45} &= 2 \\
x_{31} + x_{32} + x_{33} + x_{41} + x_{42} + x_{43} &= 2 \\
x_{34} + x_{35} + x_{44} + x_{45} &= 0
\end{aligned}
$$

The system of equations will be solved to find the probabilities, p_{uv}.

3   The Algorithm

While solving the system of equations (2) we take the advantage of the binary nature of the variables. The set of all possible solutions to the system is termed as the *solution set* and denoted by S.

Three markers A, B and C are used against each variable, x_{uv}. A indicates x_{uv} takes any value irrespective of the values of other variables in the solution set. B denotes x_{uv} may take 0 or 1 depending on the values of other variables in the solution set. C indicates that x_{uv} may take only one of 0 and 1 whatever may be the value of the other variables in the solution set. Our algorithm counts the number of solutions rather than finding the solution set to the system.

Algorithm 1 (ObjectLocation:)

Step-1: Initially, each variable is marked A and $S = \emptyset$.

Step-2: For $i = 1$ to p perform Step-3 through Step-5.

Step-3: Let S_i be the set of the variables in the in the i-th equation. Let B_i be the set of those variables in S_i which are marked B.

Step-4: For each of solution $s \in S$ do
From the solution s, take out the portion corresponding to the variables in B_i, say s'.
If (the number of 1's in this portion exceeds c_i)
Remove s from S.
Else   / this portion satisfies the i-th equation */*
Find all possible combinations of 0s and 1s for the variables in S_i satisfying the i-th equation. Insert the combinations into S by replicating the combination for the variables marked B.
End if

Step-5: In the i-th equation the variables marked A are changed to B. If any variable marked B has only one value (0 or 1), use the mark C for it and rewrite the system accordingly.

Step-6: Let b be the size of the solution set. For each cell (u, v)

$$Compute : \quad P_{uv} = \begin{cases} x_{uv} & when\ x_{uv}\ is\ marked\ C \\ \frac{c_{uv}}{b} & when\ x_{uv}\ is\ marked\ B \end{cases}$$

/ Note that no variable remains marked A at the end of computation as each variable is seen by at least one sensor. */*

Step-7: End.

4   Analysis of the Algorithm

The first step in the algorithm take $O(mn)$ time. Steps 2, 3 and 5 take $O(1)$ time. Step 4 is repeated for each solution. Therefore, Step 4 has the time complexity of

O (the number of solutions in the solution set). Step 2 through Step 5 will be repeated p times (where p is the number of sensors). Step 6 takes another $O(mn)$ time. The time complexity of the algorithm is

$$O(mn + p \times \{the\ number\ of\ solutions\ in\ the\ solution\ set\}).$$

If $p = O(mn)$ the time complexity of the algorithm becomes

$$O(mn \times \{the\ number\ of\ solutions\ in\ the\ solution\ set\}).$$

Traditional methods solve the system in $O(mnp)$ time when the number of solution is unique. In case of unique solution, the time complexity of our algorithm becomes $O(mn)$.

5   Simulation Results

We simulated our algorithm on a computer and counted the number of operations. The results are shown in Tables 1. For convenience, we use the following symbols in the tables: m, n and p denote the numbers of rows, columns and sensors in the grid field respectively. For an $m \times n$ grid, $AvgSol$ and $MaxSol$ denote the *expected* and *maximum* number of solutions to the system. $OpCount$ and $MaxOp$ indicate the *expected* and *maximum* number of operations (comparison operations to check the validity as mentioned in the step 4 in the algorithm) to solve the system.

We note that the simulation results are consistent with our analysis. Though there can be a large number of operations in the worst case ($MaxOp$), the average operation count ($OpCount$) is far lower than that. The number of operations increases as the density of sensors goes down. That can be attributed to the fact that lower sensor density leads to higher number of cells on which we cannot make a definite conclusion.

Table 1. Results for $p = 70\%$ of mn

m	n	p	AvgSol	$mn \times$ AvgSol	$mnp \times$ AvgSol	OpCount	MaxSol	$mn \times$ MaxSol	$mnp \times$ MaxSol	MaxOp
3	2	6	3	20	124	81	8	48	288	174
4	4	13	1	21	280	288	4	64	832	814
7	6	31	2	117	3645	1952	16	672	20832	6508
8	8	46	2	166	7654	4728	16	1024	47104	27203
10	9	65	1	175	11407	4845	8	720	46800	34673
11	10	79	4	522	41277	24573	24	2640	208560	273293
12	11	94	4	561	52734	13933	36	4752	446688	177720
12	12	102	9	1418	144676	78822	128	18432	1880064	696576
13	12	111	27	4227	469263	73315	456	71136	7896096	914846
14	13	129	4	846	109172	28901	48	8736	1126944	185601
15	15	159	5	1248	198551	114626	48	10800	1717200	903595
16	15	170	12	2880	489600	45547	128	30720	5222400	254950

6   Conclusion

The technique, proposed in this paper, considers only the location of a sensor the number of objects in its locality. The required hardware for this would be far simpler than those for distance or angle estimation. The proposed algorithm takes time of the order of the number of cells in the grid times the number of different solutions to the system. A careful selection of data structure can achieve better time complexity.

A sensor may consult with neighboring nodes to reduce the data for communication over the network. Our Algorithm is devised for a Sensor Grid and in future we plan to devise techniques for object location in an arbitrary sensor field. One can also address the problem of object location when the cells can contain multiple objects or the sensors or objects are mobile.

References

1. Akyldiz, I.F., Su, W., Sankarasubramaniam, Y., Cayh'ci, E.: Wh'eless Sensor Networks: A Survey. Computer Networks, Vol. 38, No. 4. **March** (2002) 393–422
2. Bulusu, N., Heidemann, J., Estrin, D.: GPS-less Low Cost Outdoor Localization For Very Small Devices. IEEE Personal Communications Magazine, Vol. 7, No. 5. **October** (2000) 28–34
3. Chakrabarty, K.,Iyenger, S.S., Qi, H., Cho, E.: Grid Coverage for Surveillance and Target Location in Distributed Sensor Networks. IEEE Transactions on Computers, vol. 51, No. 12. **October** (2002) 1448–1453
4. Dasgupta, K., Kalpakis, K., and Namjoshi, P.: Improving the Lifetime of Sensor Networks via Intelligent Selection of Data Aggregation Trees. Proc. of the SCS Comm. Networks and Distributed Systems Modelling and Simulation Conf. (CNDS 03). Orlando, Florida **January** (2003) 19–23,
5. Heinzelman, W., Chandrakasan, A., and Balakrishnan, H.: Energy-Efficient Communication Protocol for Wireless Microsensor Networks. Proc. of the Hawaii International Conference on Systems Sciences. Maui, Hawaii **January** (2000) 4–7
6. Li, X.Y., Wan, P.J., Frieder, O.: Coverage in Wireless Ad-hoc Sensor Networks. ICC (2002)
7. Meguerdichian, S., Koushanfar, F., Qu, G., Potkonjak, M.: Exposure In Wireless Ad-Hoc Sensor Networks. Proc. 7th Int. Conf. on Mobile Computing and Networking (MobiCom'01). Rome, Italy **July** (2001) 139–150
8. Priyantha, N., Chakraborty, A., Balakrishnan, H.: The Cricket Location-Support System. Int. Proc. of ACM MobiCom. ACM, Boston, MA (2000) 32–43.
9. Raghunathan, V., Schurgers, C., Park, S., Srivastava, M.B.: Energy-aware wireless microsensor networks. IEEE Signal Processing Magazine, vol. 19, No. 2. IEEE **March** (2002) 40–50
10. Savvides, A., Han, C. M., Srivastava, B.: Dynamic Fine-Grained Localization in Ah-Hoc Networks of Sensors. Int. Proc. of ACM MOBICOM. ACM, Rome, Italy (2001)
11. Thrun, S., Fox, D., Burgard, W., Dellaert, F.: Robust Monte Carlo Localization for Mobile Robots. Artificial Intelligence (2001)

A Novel Remote User Authentication Scheme Through Dynamic Login Identity

Manik Lal Das, Ashutosh Saxena, and V. P. Gulati

Institute for Development and Research in Banking Technology,
Castle Hills, Road No.1, Masab Tank, Hyderabad-500057, India
{mldas, asaxena, vpgulati}@idrbt.ac.in

Abstract. Password authentication is a technique to verify the legality of a user to prevent any kind of possible malicious depredations. The technique is regarded as one of the most convenient methods for remote user authentication. In 1981, Lamport introduced the first well-known password-based remote user authentication scheme. Since then many static login-ID based remote user authentication schemes have been proposed. The problem of static login-ID based remote user authentication technique is that it cannot restrict the registered users from distribution of their login-IDs to unregistered users. Additionally, the adversary can impersonate a valid login on intercepting the static login-ID and other login request's parameters. In this paper, we present a dynamic login-ID based remote user authentication scheme using smart cards. In our scheme, the remote system receives a dynamic login-ID for every login request and decides whether the login request is valid or not. On employing dynamic login-ID in each login session, the scheme prevents the adversary from forged login-ID attacks. The use of smart card restricts the registered users from distribution of their login-IDs and avoids the scenario of **many** logged in users with the **same** login-ID. One of the prominent applications of the scheme is digital library. The scheme uses RSA and one-way hash function for secure login request generation and verification. The remote system of the scheme does not maintain any passwords or verifier table for validation of the login request. Moreover, the scheme provides a flexible password change option, where users can change their passwords at any time without any assistance from the remote system.

References

1. L. Lamport. Password authentication with insecure communication. Communications of the ACM, Vol. 24, No. 11, pp. 770–772, 1981.
2. Manik Lal Das, Ashutosh Saxena and Ved P. Gulati. A Dynamic Remote User Authentication Scheme Using Smart Cards. IEEE Trans. on Consumer Electron., Vol. 50, No.2, pp. 629-631, 2004.
3. R. L. Rivest, A. Shamir and L. Adleman. A method for obtaining digital signatures and public-key cryptosystems. Communications of the ACM, Vol. 21, No. 2, pp. 120–126, 1978.

A. Sen et al. (Eds.): IWDC 2004, LNCS 3326, p. 532, 2004.
© Springer-Verlag Berlin Heidelberg 2004

A Probabilistic Admission Control Algorithm in Wireless/Mobile Cellular Networks[*]

Monir Hossain[1] and Mahbub Hassan[1,2]

[1] School of Computer Science & Engg.,
The University of New South Wales NSW 2052, Australia
{monirh, mahbub}@cse.unsw.edu.au
[2] National ICT Australia Ltd.,
Locked bag 9013 Alexandra, NSW 1435, Australia
mahbub.hassan@nicta.com.au

Abstract. Due to huge popularity of wireless service, *public transport vehicles* (PTV) might provide wireless Internet service through *Mobile Local Area Network* (MLAN) where *mobile router* (MR) is the main controlling element. MR can ask necessary resources to cellular base stations so that it can provide the guaranteed service of on-board users. The other users, non-PTV users, might observe variations of available resource in the cellular networks. If the admission control is performed by using the current available resource information then the network might see huge *call interruption ratio* (CIR) whenever the available resource for non-PTV users decrease. Therefore, it is necessary to propose an efficient admission control algorithm for these networks. In this paper, we propose a *probabilistic admission control* (PAC) algorithm for providing guaranteed service to PTV calls and reducing fluctuation in the wireless networks. Admission control is applied only for non-PTV calls not PTV calls. The admission decision of non-PTV calls depends not only current traffic conditions such as available resource but also admission probability. We have proposed two call interruption thresholds: *max* and *min*. If the observed CIR is less than *min* then admission probability is 1. On the other hand, if the observed CIR is greater than *max* then admission probability is 0. If the CIR is between *min* and *max* then admission probability will be in between 0 and 1. The relationship between CIR and admission probability is linear. Our scheme tries to serve PTV calls even by interrupting one or more non-PTV calls. The performance of this algorithm is evaluated through discrete event simulation. The arrival process of non-PTV and PTV calls is Poisson. Each non-PTV call needs one *Bandwidth Unit* (BU), and the PTV calls need different number of BUs at different time. The performance metrics of our scheme are CBP of PTV, CBP of non-PTV, CIR, and fluctuation in terms of total serving calls. Simulation results show that CIR can be maintained precisely between *min* and *max*. Moreover, the proposed algorithm can provide the guaranteed service to PTV calls, minimize CBP of non-PTV calls, and minimize fluctuation. Results also show that there is a trade off between CIR and CBP of non-PTV calls.

---

[*] This research was partially funded by the Australian Research Council (ARC) Discovery Grant DP0452942.

A. Sen et al. (Eds.): IWDC 2004, LNCS 3326, p. 533, 2004.
© Springer-Verlag Berlin Heidelberg 2004

A Rough Neuro Data Mining Approach for Network Intrusion Detection

Tarun Bhaskar and B. Narasimha Kamath

Indian Institute of Management Calcutta,
D H Road, Kolkata, India 700104
{tarun, nkamath}@email.iimcal.ac.in

Abstract. Network security is one of the major concerns of modern organizations. Precise and accurate detection of attacks need modern tools which utilize past data and current trends to evaluate the situation under consideration. Data mining techniques like rule induction, neural networks, genetic algorithm, fuzzy logic and rough sets have been used for classification and pattern recognition of attacks. Zhu *et al.*[*] have compared the different data mining methods in the context of intrusion detection and have shown that rough sets holds an edge over the neural network. In this paper we have shown that genetic algorithm based learning mechanism can improve the performance of neural network. The comparison shows that this method performs as efficiently as the rough set method if not better. But the variance in both these methods is significantly high, which is an undesirable system characteristic. To gain accuracy and precision we propose rough-neuro approach, a robust hybrid technique for intrusion detection. The worst case scenario analysis demonstrates the supremacy of the hybrid approach. Statistical analysis confirms the precision of the hybrid rough-neuro over rough sets and genetic algorithm based neural networks. We have evaluated by comparing against the current best known methods of intrusion detection. The paper goes on to statistically show that there is no significant difference in the average efficiency of these methods. However, the variation of rough-neuro method is significantly less than that of the other two methods at 99% confidence level. The rough neuro method outperforms the other methods with respect to the worst case efficiency and standard deviation and hence should be the chosen one in intrusion detection systems.

---

[*] D. Zhu, G. Premkumar, X. Zhang, and C.H.Chu, Data mining for intrusion detection: A comparison of alternative methods, *Decision Sciences*, 32(4): 635-660, 2001.

A. Sen et al. (Eds.): IWDC 2004, LNCS 3326, p. 534, 2004.
© Springer-Verlag Berlin Heidelberg 2004

An Efficient Implementation of Distance-Based Update Scheme Using Directional Cell Identification Codes

Subrata Nandi[1] and Manish K. Raushan[2]

[1, 2] Department of Computer Science and Engineering, National Institute of Technology, Durgapur (DU) PIN-713209 ,WB, India
sn_nitdgp@yahoo.co.in; sn_comp@nitdgp.ac.in;
manish_raushan@indiatimes.com

Abstract. Distance computation is the key to the design of several adaptive location management schemes (distance-based, speed-based etc.) for cellular mobile networks. Distance can be measured in terms of number of cells Mobile Unit (MU) is far from the last updated cell (LUC). Distance computation is a real challenge as updates are triggered by the mobile unit (MU), which does not have knowledge of the service area layout. A novel technique using Cell Identification Code (CIC-DIS) exists in literature, which encodes each cell with a 4-bit locally unique code. Considering hexagonal cells arranged in a 2-D rectangular grid, the cell in the ith row and j^{th} column would have the code [$i\%3$ $j\%3$] in binary. CIC-DIS coding works only for uniform 2-D grid of hexagonal cells. We propose an efficient direction based cell identification coding (CIC-DIR) technique, which an enhancement of the CIC-DIS. In CIC-DIR each BS continuously broadcast through the downlink control channel in GSM a sequence of 4-bit codes according to the following rule:1st code contains the CIC of the cell to which the BS belongs. Next six codes contain CIC of its six neighbors in a certain order that is to be followed by all BSs. The 8th code in the sequence is a special code 1111, used only to delimit the sequence (should not be used as CIC). Each MU is required to store only the current cell CIC (c_cic) in memory. Whenever the MU moves to a new cell it first synchronizes with respect to the new sequence by identifying the delimiter code 1111, then checks the relative position of c_cic within the new sequence, say x. This x is identified as the side or direction with respect the last cell through which it moves. To compute distance, the cells surrounding the LUC are considered to be organized in several concentric rings with the LUC at the center. Therefore, it is obvious that the displacement value will be same as the ring number to which the new cell belongs. It is observed that the total set of cells C_{tot} in each ring can be divided in two subsets C_{222} and C_{321}. The six sides in each cell can be divided in three subsets S^{+}, S^{-} and S^{0} transition through which causes distance value to be incremented by one, decremented by one and remain unchanged respectively. Cells belonging to subset C_{222} will have two side members each in S^{+}, S^{-} and S^{0}, whereas cells belonging to subset C_{321} will have three side members in S^{+}, one in S^{-} and two in S^{0}. It is observed that the Nth cell in R^{th} ring belongs to C_{321} if ($(N\%R)==0$). After each move the new ring number R'(distance value) will be equal to R+1, R-1or R depending on whether side x through which it moved belongs to S^{+}, S^{-} and S^{0} respectively, conditions for which are derived. The new cell number N' can also be calculated from N and R easily after each move. The MU requires storing values of c_cic, N and R only. Thus the distance computation is simple and can be implemented with little additional overhead.

A. Sen et al. (Eds.): IWDC 2004, LNCS 3326, p. 535, 2004.
© Springer-Verlag Berlin Heidelberg 2004

Application of Formal Methods for Analysis of Authentication Protocols

Ritesh Kumar Tiwari

Center for Data Engineering, International Institute of Information Technology,
Gachibowli, Hyderabad, India-500019
ritesh@students.iiit.net

Abstract. Authentication is a process by which communicating entities prove their identity. As per *BAN* logic[1], an important but not the only goal of authentication between two entities A and B is to establish *First Level Belief* and *Second Level Belief*.

$$A \mid\equiv \ A \xleftrightarrow{K_{ab}} B \ , \ B \mid\equiv \ B \xleftrightarrow{K_{ab}} A \quad and$$

$$A \mid\equiv \ B \mid\equiv \ B \xleftrightarrow{K_{ab}} A \ , \ B \mid\equiv \ A \mid\equiv \ A \xleftrightarrow{K_{ab}} B$$

Though *BAN* logic has been very successful in finding security flaws in many protocols, it still has got inherent weakness in *protocol idealization* and *logical postulates*. This paper proposes some additional constructs to enhance *belief representation* of logical postulates. The enhanced model is used to formally analyze *Neuman-Stubblebine* protocol[2]. Formal analysis using enhanced postulates brought a design vulnerability in classical protocol into light. In Neuman-Stubblebine protocol, entities pass the nonces unencrypted to server. If an eavesdropper can modify these nonces, then it can force the entities not to accept the genuine key which is distributed by server as session key.

This paper propose to symmetrically encrypt nonces along with other session message constituents so as to thwart the attack that might be launched against them. The enhanced logical postulates are used to prove resistance of modified protocol against detected attack.

References

[1] Burrows, M., Abadi, M., Needham, R.: A Logic of Authentication. ACM Transactions on Computer Systems, Vol. 8(1) (1990) 18–36
[2] Neuman, B.C., Stubblebine, S.: A Note on use of Timestamps as Nonces. ACM Operating Systems Review, Vol. 26(4) (1992) 82–89
[3] Paulson, L.C.: Mechanized proofs for a recursive authentication protocol. Computer Security Foundations Workshop (1997) 84–95
[4] Backes, M., Schunter, M.: From Absence of Certain Vulnerabilities towards Security Proofs. New Security Paradigms Workshop,(2003) 67–74
[5] Herzog, Jonathan: Computational Soundness for Standard Assumptions of Formal Cryptography. Ph.D. thesis, MIT (2004)

A. Sen et al. (Eds.): IWDC 2004, LNCS 3326, p. 536, 2004.
© Springer-Verlag Berlin Heidelberg 2004

BUSTRAP - An Efficient Travel Planner for Metropolitans

Sandeep Gupta[1,*] and M M Gore[2,**]

[1] Alcatel Development Center, Udyog Vihar, Gurgaon-122015, India
sandeep@cbsbit.com
[2] Department of Computer Science and Engineering,
Motilal Nehru National Institute of Technology, Allahabad-211004, India
mmgore@ieee.org

Abstract. In this paper, we are providing a solution for an efficient and up-to-date commuting planner for a public transport system used by masses. Here, we present design and implementation features of a proposed system to be used for planning a bus travel. This problem is relevant to a large metropolitan city, like New Delhi, where local bus service forms the life-line of the city. There are about 10,000 city buses running on 814 routes on Delhi's roads. Often, there are many ways to reach a destination and often, commuters, even locals, do not possess knowledge about most of these alternate routes. Also, buses do not adhere to their schedules due to heavy traffic. Thus it becomes very difficult to remember every possible way to reach a destination (considering that one may have to break one's journey and take another route to reach the destination).

Proposed BUSTRAP [1] solution aims at providing fairly accurate information about optimal way to reach a particular destination. Though we have implemented BUSTRAP as an SMS service, it can easily be adapted for other services like IVRS, WAP etc. stating one's current location and desired destination. The system will provide optimal ways to reach that place by bus - telling exact bus routes and numbers to board/ change according to the bus movement on the city roads at that time. We record location of buses at a few instances on the roads through sensors. Our system finds their current location and speculates future locations based on these real time records. We identify changeover points on a route according to which a route plan would be formed.

References

1. Sandeep Gupta: BUSTRAP: a metropolitan BUS TRAvel Planner (with special focus on New Delhi's public transport system) Master's thesis, Indian Institute of Information Technology, Allahabad, India, June 2004
   http : //wcc.iiita.ac.in/thesis2004/sandeep_wc02.pdf.zip

---

* Work completed during authors' association with IIIT Allahabad, India.
** Partially supported by Ministry of Human Resource Development Government of India sponsored project on Extended Transaction Processing.

A. Sen et al. (Eds.): IWDC 2004, LNCS 3326, p. 537, 2004.
© Springer-Verlag Berlin Heidelberg 2004

Distributed Evolutionary Algorithm Search for Multiobjective Spanning Tree Problem

Rajeev Kumar, P. K. Singh, and P. P. Chakrabarti

Department of Computer Science and Engineering
Indian Institute of Technology Kharagpur
Kharagpur, WB 721 302, India
{rkumar, pksingh, ppchak}@cse.iitkgp.ernet.in

Abstract. The problem of computing spanning trees along with specific constraints is mostly NP-hard. Many approximation and stochastic algorithms which yield a single solution, have been proposed. Essentially, the problem is multi-objective in nature, and a major challenge to solve the problem is to capture possibly all the (representative) equivalent and diverse solutions at convergence. In this paper, we formulate the generic multi-objective spanning tree (MOST) problem, and attempt to solve, in a novel way, with evolutionary algorithm (EA). We consider, without loss of generality, edge-cost and diameter as the two objectives. Since the problem is hard, and the Pareto-front is unknown, the main issue in such problem-instances is how to assess the convergence. We use a multiobjective evolutionary algorithm (MOEA) that produces diverse solutions without needing a priori knowledge of the solution space. We employ a distributed version of the algorithm and generate solutions from multiple tribes in order to have some approximation of the movement of the solution front. Since no experimental results are available for MOST, we consider two well known diameter-constrained spanning tree algorithms and modify them, for fair comparison, to yield a near-optimal solution-front. We observe that EA could provide superior solutions in the entire-range of the Pareto-front, which none of the existing algorithms could do.

MSIP: A Protocol for Efficient Handoffs of Real Time Multimedia Sessions in Mobile Wireless Scenarios

A. Ranjeeth Kumar and Sridhar Iyer

Kanwal Rekhi School of Information Technology,
IIT Bombay, Powai, Mumbai 400076, India
{ranjeeth, sri}@it.iitb.ac.in

Abstract. The support for IP mobility has become very important with the increasing growth of mobile applications. One of the key challenges for the deployment of such wireless Internet infrastructure is to efficiently manage user mobility. Mobility is handled by Mobile IP at the network layer and Session Initiation Protocol at the application layer. The main aim of these schemes is to provide seamless connectivity for ongoing communications and to keep the handoff latency delay as less as possible. The delay constraint becomes even more crucial for real-time application. These schemes have various drawbacks associated with them. The Mobile IP scheme has drawbacks like triangular routing, longer delays and the need for tunneling management. SIP solves the problems of triangular routing and tunneling, but it involves the time consuming process of obtaining a new IP address from the DHCP server after the handoff.

In this paper, we propose a hybrid scheme, MSIP, the integration of Mobile IP and SIP extracting the desirable features from these two schemes. MSIP reduces the handoff delay and results in better performance for real time applications. MSIP uses the call establishment of SIP. During the session, if the node roams into a new subnet, instead of the connection getting hung up till the node obtains a new IP address from a DHCP server, as it normally happens with SIP, the node uses Mobile IP 's tunneling scheme for transmission of packets. In MSIP we overcome the disadvantages of Mobile IP and SIP. As in Mobile IP, we are not tunneling the packets for the entire handoff session, but instead only till the node obtains a new IP address from the DHCP server. As in SIP, the communication is not hung up till the node obtains a new IP but instead for that period of time, Mobile IP's tunneling is used.

The Experimental results have shown a 0.3 sec reduction in handoff latency disruption time (i.e., the time taken to receive the first packet after the handoff occurs in the new subnet) than SIP.

A. Sen et al. (Eds.): IWDC 2004, LNCS 3326, p. 539, 2004.
© Springer-Verlag Berlin Heidelberg 2004

Network Management System Using
Web Server Controlled Mobile Agents

Ashutosh Upadhaya[1], Saurabh Vashishtha[1], Raman Grover[2], and A.K. Sarje[3]

[1] Trilogy E-Business Software India Pvt. Ltd.,
No.5, Salarpuria Infinity, Bannerghatta Road, Bangalore 560 029, India
[2] BayPackets Technologies, C-42,Sector –58, Noida,
(U.P)-201303, India
{letstalk2saurabh, groverraman}@yahoo.com
[3] Professor and Head of Department, Department of Electronics & Computer Engg.,
IIT Roorkee, Roorkee-247667, Uttaranchal, India
{aucstuec, sarjefec}@iitr.ernet.in

Abstract. Large, heterogeneous computer networks with ever changing topology and size are typical environments today which network management systems struggle to control. Unexpected events occur frequently in these networks resulting in failure situation. In this paper we have developed a real implementation of web based network management tool named as ManageNet. It uses the mobile agent technology. The agents as well as the additional resources that they require reside on a web server. These agents decentralize processing thus distributing processing load and reducing the traffic around the management station. ManageNet provides for remote agent creation whereby network management tasks can be initiated by logging on to the web server from any node in the network. It is equipped with daemon services that allow initiation of network management task in absence of administrator. We suggested and examined the ways of improving dependability and flexibility of network management systems using ManageNet.

A. Sen et al. (Eds.): IWDC 2004, LNCS 3326, p. 540, 2004.
© Springer-Verlag Berlin Heidelberg 2004

Security Scheme for Malicious Node Detection in Mobile Ad Hoc Networks

Punit Rathod[1], Nirali Mody[1], Dhaval Gada[1], Rajat Gogri[1], Zalak Dedhia[1], Sugata Sanyal[2], and Ajith Abraham[3]

[1] Mumbai University, India
{punit_r,nirali_mody, dhavalgada, rajatgogri, zalakdedhia}@rediffmail.com
[2] School of Technology and Computer Science,
Tata Institute of Fundamental Research, India
sanyal@tifr.res.in
[3] School of Computer Science and Engineering, Chung-Ang University, Korea
ajith.abraham@ieee.org

In Ad hoc On Demand Vector (AODV) routing protocol for Mobile Ad hoc Networks (MANET), malicious nodes can easily disrupt the communication. A malicious node that is not part of any route may launch Denial of Service (DoS) Attack. Also once a route is formed, any node in the route may turn malicious and may refrain from forwarding packets, modify them before forwarding or may even forward to an incorrect intermediate node. Such malicious activities by a misbehaving node cannot be checked for in pure AODV protocol. In this paper, a proactive scheme is proposed to detect the above-mentioned malicious activities.

A malicious node flooding the network with fake control packets, such as RREQs (Route Requests) causes congestion in the network. The processing of RREQ by the nodes in the network leads to further degradation in performance of the network. This abnormal behaviour is handled in our scheme by ensuring a fair distribution of resources among all contending neighbours. Incoming RREQs are processed only if number of RREQs from the said neighbour are below RREQ_ACCEPT_LIMIT. This parameter specifies a value that ensures uniform usage of a node's resources by its neighbors. Another threshold RREQ_BLACKLIST_LIMIT determines whether a node is acting malicious or not. If the number of RREQs go beyond RREQ_BLACKLIST_LIMIT then the node is blacklisted and all requests from it are blocked temporarily. Thus, isolating the malicious node.

Tampering of packets by a Malicious node in the route can be detected by promiscuous listening by the other nodes that are part of the route. This type of moral policing, done by the nodes, ensures detection of any mailcious activity taking place. To faciliItate detection, extra information regarding route is exchanged while route formation. This information contains the next-to-next-hop (NTNH) information in addition to the usual next-hop information. This information is used by a node to verify whether the next-hop node is forwarding the packets to the correct NTNH. This NTNH exchange is critical. To

A. Sen et al. (Eds.): IWDC 2004, LNCS 3326, pp. 541–542, 2004.
© Springer-Verlag Berlin Heidelberg 2004

provide security to it, promiscuous listening is proposed during the route formation also.

The series of simulations reveal that the proposed scheme provides a secured AODV routing protocol with minimal extra overhead as compared to pure AODV protocol.

High-Level Grid Execution Patterns

Kaizar Amin,[1,2] and Gregor von Laszewski[1]

[1] Argonne National Laboratory, Argonne, IL, U.S.A.
[2] University of North Texas, Denton, TX, U.S.A.

The Grid community under the auspices of the Global Grid Forum is moving in the direction towards standardizing the Grid architecture. However, the Grid standardization is an incremental process subject to continuous refactoring. Although such enhancements in the Grid architecture will ultimately prove beneficial for the entire Grid community, it imposes an undue overhead on the application developers to continuously keep abreast with these changes. Motivated by the need to provide an application development framework that shields the Grid users and application developers from the technological complexities of the Grid implementation, we present a suite of abstraction-based Grid execution patterns. Applications using our framework can concentrate on their objectives while being compatible with the latest Grid technologies.

The basic elements in our abstraction model are tasks and task graphs. A Grid task represents a unit of work in our framework such as jobexecution, filetransfer, or authentication. Hence, our model can support execution flows ordered as a directed acyclic graphs (task graphs). The task graph is a checkpointable entity facilitating fault-tolerance and mobility in execution flows. Three execution patterns are supported, namely, Handler-Execution, Resource-Execution, and Broker-Execution. The Handler-Execution pattern is centered around the capability provider attribute in a task. For every provider, there exists a handler that performs the abstract-to-protocol mapping of the Grid tasks. The Handler-Execution pattern forms the base pattern in our framework and is internally utilized by other patterns. The Resource-Execution pattern aggregates several Grid services into a single abstract Grid resource with a distinct scheduling policy for servicing its execution requests. Finally, the Broker-Execution pattern combines several execution resources to form an abstraction of a Grid context. It assigns a scheduling and brokering policy to the resource broker that behaves as a match-maker mapping the submitted tasks to an appropriate execution resource. ·

A prototype implementation of the abstraction model presented in this poster is available as a part of the Java CoG Kit v4. In the current distribution, we have implemented the Handler-Execution and Resource-Execution patterns. Ongoing efforts are concentrating towards the implementation of the Broker-Execution pattern. Our current implementation supports handlers for Globus Toolkit v2.4, Globus Toolkit v3.0.2, v3.2.0, v3.2.1, and secure shell (SSH). Additonally, the community has already shown that OGSI-based quality of service (QoS) aware execution architecture, and Unicore are possible. The next step will include developing support for GT4.

More Information: http://www.cogkit.org.

A. Sen et al. (Eds.): IWDC 2004, LNCS 3326, p. 543, 2004.
© Springer-Verlag Berlin Heidelberg 2004

Author Index

Lecture Notes in Computer Science

For information about Vols. 1–3247

please contact your bookseller or Springer